P.S.87
15th additional
congress

Life and Work
of
Susan B. Anthony

Life and Work
of
Susan B. Anthony

Volume 2

By
IDA HUSTED HARPER

ARNO & THE NEW YORK TIMES
New York · 1969

SUSAN B. ANTHONY,

IN THE CALIFORNIA CAMPAIGN, 1896.

THE LIFE AND WORK

OF

SUSAN B. ANTHONY

INCLUDING PUBLIC ADDRESSES, HER OWN LETTERS
AND MANY FROM HER CONTEMPORARIES
DURING FIFTY YEARS

BY

IDA HUSTED HARPER

A Story of the Evolution of the Status of Woman

IN TWO VOLUMES

VOLUME II

ILLUSTRATED WITH PORTRAITS, PICTURES OF HOMES, ETC.

INDIANAPOLIS
THE HOLLENBECK PRESS

TO WOMAN, FOR WHOSE FREEDOM
SUSAN B. ANTHONY
HAS GIVEN FIFTY YEARS OF NOBLE ENDEAVOR
THIS BOOK IS DEDICATED

TABLE OF CONTENTS.

VOL. II.

CHAPTER XXX.

CHAPTER XXXI.

P. 544
" Dead Issue "
1882

(iii)

CHAPTER XLI.

CHAPTER XLII.

p. 759
"lofty patriotism"

p. 769
suffragists "insignificant minority"

CHAPTER XLV.

CHAPTER XLVI.

CHAPTER XLVII.

CHAPTER L.

LIST OF ILLUSTRATIONS.

VOL. II.

CHAPTER XXX.

POLITICAL CANDIDATES—WRITING THE HISTORY.

1880—1881.

URING her May lecture trip Miss Anthony was formulating a scheme for a series of conventions, opening and closing with a great mass meeting, which should influence the national political conventions to recognize in their platforms the rights of woman. As usual most of the women opposed this plan and as usual Miss Anthony carried the day. The following letters to Mrs. Spencer, national secretary, will serve as specimens of hundreds which she wrote with her own hand, before every similar occasion:

I want the rousingest rallying cry ever put on paper—first, to call women by the thousand to Chicago; and second, to get every one who can not go there to send a postal card to the mass convention, saying she wants the Republicans to put a Sixteenth Amendment pledge in their platform. Don't you see that if we could have a mass meeting of 2,000 or 3,000 earnest women, June 2, and then receive 10,000 postals from women all over the country, what a tremendous influence we could bring to bear on the Republican convention, June 3? We can get Farwell Hall for $40 a day, and I think would do well to engage it for the 2d and 3d, then we could make it our headquarters—sleep in it even, if we couldn't get any other places.

Besides this, I want to make the best possible use of all our speakers between June 3 and 21, when we shall have a mass meeting in Cincinnati, the day before the Democratic convention. My proposition is that I, as vice-president-at-large, call conventions of two days each at a number of cities. We could divide our speakers and thus fill in the entire two weeks between Chicago and Cincinnati with capital good work. How does the plan strike you? Can we summon the women from the vasty deeps—or distances? Can we get 5,000 or 10,000 to send on their postals? Do the petitions still come in? How many thousands of appeals and documents have you had printed and how many have you sent out?

(515)

After the ball was set rolling she wrote :

A letter from Mrs. Stanton tells of her being on the verge of pneumonia, and rushing home to rest and recruit. She is better and, since she has been to the dinner-table, I infer she is well enough to begin to work up the thunder and lightning for Indianapolis and Chicago. Now won't you at once scratch down the points with which you want to fire her soul and brain, and get her at work on the resolutions, platform and address? She won't go out to lecture any more this spring, and if you will only put her en rapport with your thought she will do splendid work in the herculean task awaiting us.

It is simply impossible for me to go to her at present, and we must all give her our ideas in the rough, from time to time, and let her weld them together as best she can; and then, as she says, when we meet in Indianapolis we all will put in our happiest ideas, metaphysical, political, logical and all other "cals," and make these the strongest and grandest documents ever issued from any organization of women. It does seem to me that if we can succeed in grinding out just the right appeal, demand, or whatever it may be called, the Republican convention must heed us. At any rate, we will do our level best at a strong pull, a long pull and a pull all together to compel them to surrender.

I enclose my list of May lecture engagements. I shall be able to help in money from them soon, and better than I could in any other way. I watch both Congress and our State legislatures, but the "scamps" are vastly better at promising than fulfilling. The politicians, of course, expect all this flutter and buncombe about doing something for women in New York—in California—in Iowa—is going to spike our guns and make us help the Republican party to carry all before it; but we must not be thus fooled by them.

After a lecture at Waynesburg, Penn., when she had gone to her train at 4 A. M. to find it an hour late, she wrote on the ticket-office shelf, by the light of a smoky lamp, this letter to her sister :

Just three years ago this day was our dear Hannah's last on earth, and I can see her now sitting by the window and can hear her say, "Talk, Susan." I knew she wanted me to talk of the future meetings in the great beyond, all of them, as she often said, so certain and so beautiful to her ; but they were not to me, and I could not dash her faith with my doubts, nor could I pretend a faith I had not ; so I was silent in the dread presence of death. Three years—and yet what a living presence has she been in my thoughts all the days! There has been scarcely one waking hour that I have not felt the loss of her. We can not help trying to peer through the veil to find the certainty of things over there, but nothing comes to our eyes unless we accept the Spiritualistic testimony, which we can not wholly do.

Well, only you and I are left of mother's four girls, and when and how we also shall pass on is among the unknown problems of the future. Of course

I feel and know that your loss is far beyond mine ; for never was there a child who so faithfully devoted herself to a mother, and made all other interests subserve that mother's happiness as did you, and I feel, too, that but for you I never could have done my public work.

The great series of conventions began with the May Anniversary, which was held at Indianapolis, the 25th and 26th, in the Park Theater, Miss Anthony presiding. All arrangements had been made and all expenses assumed by the local suffrage society under the leadership of Mrs. Sewall. The Sentinel, edited at that time by Colonel J. B. Maynard, welcomed the convention in a strong editorial declaring for woman suffrage in unmistakable terms. The very successful meetings closed with a handsome reception tendered by Mrs. John C. New.

The mass meeting opened in Farwell Hall, Chicago, June 1, the day before the Republican convention, with delegates from twenty-six States, and continued in session three days. The welcoming address was made by Elizabeth Boynton Harbert, the speakers comprised the most prominent women of the nation, the audience numbered 3,000 and the enthusiasm was unprecedented in all the records of this movement.[1] The History of Woman Suffrage says :

The mass convention had been called for June 2, but the crowds in the city gave promise of such extended interest that Farwell Hall was engaged for June 1, and before the second day's proceedings closed, funds were voluntarily raised by the audience to continue the meeting the third day. So vast was the number of letters and postals from women who desired to vote, that the whole time of each session could have been spent in reading them—one day's mail alone bringing them from twenty-three States and three Territories. Some contained hundreds of names, others represented town, county and State societies. Many were addressed to the different nominating conventions, Republican, Greenback, Democratic, while the reasons given for desiring to vote ranged from the simple demand, through all the scale of

[1] The Chicago press gave very satisfactory reports of this meeting, but the Springfield Republic was vulgar and abusive, called the ladies "withered beldames," "cats on the back roof," and advised them to "go home and attend to their children, if they had any, and if not, to engage in that same occupation as soon as they could regularly do so."
The charge being so often made that the leaders of the suffrage movement were a lot of old maids and childless wives, Miss Anthony prepared a list showing that sixteen of the most prominent were the mothers of sixty-six children. Of the pioneers she herself was the only one who never married. Of the younger speakers Phœbe Couzins was the only one who remained single.

those connected with good government and morality. So highly important a contribution to history did the Chicago Historical Society deem these expressions that it made a formal request to be put in possession of all letters and postals, with a promise that they should be carefully guarded in a fire-proof safe.

A large parlor in the Palmer House was tendered to the ladies by the proprietor for business meetings and for a reception room.   They were visited by a number of Republican delegates, many of whom were thoroughly in favor of a suffrage plank in the platform and of giving the ladies seats in the convention.   A letter was sent to the chairman of the Republican national committee, Don Cameron, signed by one hundred and eighteen United States senators and representatives, asking that seventy-six seats on the floor of the convention be given to as many accredited delegates from the National Suffrage Association.   Although the veteran soldiers and sailors were liberally provided for, Mr. Cameron granted only ten seats to the women, and those not to the association in its official capacity but as "guest" tickets for seats on the platform.   Miss Anthony was allowed *ten* minutes before a *sub*-committee to present the argument for a suffrage plank.   It was favorably regarded by scattered members of various delegations, but the platform was silent on the subject.

The Republican convention of 1880 did not even adopt the "recognition" planks of 1872 and 1876, and all the demonstrations of this great mass meeting of women had not the slightest influence, because made by a disfranchised class. Before closing they adopted a resolution that they would support no party which did not endorse the political equality of woman; but all the "support" which they could give or withhold was not likely to be considered of much value by political leaders.

Miss Anthony and four others attended the Greenback-Labor Convention, a few days later, in the same city.   They were well received. Mrs. Gage read the suffrage memorial in open session and Miss Anthony was permitted to address the convention.   This privilege was violently opposed by Dennis Kearney, who said that "his wife instructed him before he left California not to mix up with woman suffragists, and if he did she would meet him at the door with a flat-iron when he came home." Failing to frighten the convention with Mrs. Kearney's flat-iron, he declined to hear Miss Anthony's speech and left the hall in disgust. The committee refused to incorporate a suffrage plank in its platform, but the next day in convention, after the nominations were concluded, a delegate introduced an equal suffrage resolution which passed by a large majority.

The delegates and speakers of the National Association then held meetings at Milwaukee, Wis., Bloomington, Ill., Grand Rapids, Mich., Lafayette and Terre Haute, Ind., and reached Cincinnati in time for the Democratic National Convention, June 22. They were received here with unexpected courtesy. Mayor Prince, of Boston, and Mr. Eaton, of Kansas, presented their request for seats, and sixteen were granted them on the floor of the house, just behind the delegates. A committee room was placed at their disposal and their notices and placards were printed by the convention. A hearing was given before the platform committee, with no limit as to time, and after several had spoken the others were invited to do so. The chairman, Henry Watterson, declared himself in favor of the plank desired. The delegations from Maine, New York and Kansas also were favorable. Miss Anthony was escorted to the platform upon the arm of Carter Harrison, amid wild applause, given a seat beside the presiding officer, Wade Hampton, and the clerk was ordered to read the address which she presented.[1] After all this parade, however, the platform contained not the slightest reference to the claims of women or, in fact, to their existence. The results of the appeal to the Republican and Democratic conventions were precisely the same, except that the latter administered the dose with chivalry.

[1] The Cincinnati Commercial said at this time: "Miss Anthony is the same clear, calm reasoner—a woman of the same firm convictions and with the same forcible, dignified and essentially womanly manner of expressing them—that she has always been. While in Cincinnati she is the guest of her cousin, Mrs. A. B. Merriam, of Walnut Hills, where many call upon her and find a talk with a woman so earnest and fine in intellectual power to be a genuine satisfaction. On the 'woman question,' she is hopeful but not a hopeless enthusiast. She is too clear-headed for that, and has overcome too many obstacles not to appreciate the requisite momentum and the force necessary to produce it. Her life is great in that it has made a larger life and higher work possible to other women, who share her aspirations without her invincible strength to carve their way."

The National Prohibition Convention at Bloomington, Ill., officially invited the suffrage advocates to meet with them and participate in their proceedings. Phœbe Couzins was sent as a delegate, and the convention adopted the following plank: "We also demand that women having privileges as citizens in other respects, shall be clothed with the ballot for their own protection, and as a rightful means for the proper settlement of the liquor question." This body, it will be noticed, not only demanded the ballot for woman but told her what she would be expected to do with it.

While not at all surprised, Miss Anthony was greatly disgusted with the action of the Republican and Democratic conventions, but, determined to leave nothing undone, she soon afterwards called upon General Garfield at Mentor. He was cordial and expressed himself in favor of equality for woman in matters of education, work, wages and civil rights, but was not ready to declare himself in favor of the suffrage and, as was always the case, urged that the issue be not pressed during *that* campaign. Mrs. Blake and others visited General Hancock, the Democratic candidate, and the New York Sun reports the interview in part:

Mrs. Blake said the delegation had come to ask the general what hope the woman suffrage party might entertain in case any measure came before him, as President, which bore upon granting women the ballot. The general replied that the movement was a growing one, and that everything which tended toward the amelioration of woman's condition had his sympathy. In the course of conversation he said that women should be paid equally with men for the same work equally well performed.

Mrs. Slocum said that the delegation desired a decided expression from him as to whether he would or would not veto any measure favorable to woman suffrage that might come before him as President. The general replied that if such a measure were voted upon by Congress as a constitutional amendment, it would not come before the President. If, however, Congress accorded women the right to vote in the District of Columbia, he certainly would offer no obstruction.

Mrs. Blake asked if he considered women as "people."

"Undoubtedly," replied the general. "He would be a bold man who would undertake to say they were not."

"Then, general," said Mrs. Blake, "we ask nothing more than what you say in your letter of acceptance: ‘ It is only by a full vote, a free ballot and a fair count that the people can rule in fact, as required by the theory of our government.’ ”

“ I am perfectly willing,” said General Hancock, “ that you should say I take my stand on that paragraph in my letter of acceptance.”

In order to exhaust every resource, Miss Anthony, on August 17, addressed this letter to each of the presidential candidates :

As vice-president-at-large of the National Woman Suffrage Association, I am instructed to ask you if, in the event of your election, you, as President of the United States, would recommend to Congress the submission to the several legislatures of a Sixteenth Amendment to the National Constitution, prohibiting the disfranchisement of United States citizens on account of sex. What we wish to ascertain is whether you, as President, would use your *official influence* to secure to the women of the several States a *national guarantee* of their right to a voice in the government on the same terms with men. Neither platform makes any pledge to secure political equality to women— hence we are waiting and hoping that one candidate or the other, or both, will declare favorably, and thereby make it possible for women, with self-respect, to work for the success of one or the other or both nominees. Hoping for a prompt and explicit statement, I am, sir, very respectfully yours.

General Hancock did not so much as acknowledge the receipt of this, but General Garfield answered promptly, writing with his own hand :

Your letter of the 17th inst. was duly received. I take the liberty of asking your personal advice before I answer your official letter. I assume that all the traditions and impulses of your life lead you to believe that the Republican party has been and is more nearly in the line of liberty than its antagonist, the Democratic party; and I know you desire to advance the cause of woman. Now, in view of the fact that the Republican convention has not discussed your question, do you not think it would be a violation of the trust they have reposed in me, to speak “ as their nominee ”—and add to the present contest an issue which they have not authorized ?

Again, if I answer your question on the ground of my own private opinion, I shall be compelled to say that, while I am open to the freest discussion and fairest consideration of your question, I have not yet reached the conclusion that it would be best for woman and for the country that she should have the suffrage. I may reach it; but whatever time may do to me, that fruit is not yet ripe on my tree. I ask you, therefore, for the sake of your own question, do you think it wise to pick my apples now ? Please answer me in the frankness of personal friendship.

With kind regards, I am, very truly yours.

Under date of September 9 Miss Anthony sent a spirited reply :

Yours of the 25th ult. has waited all these days that I might carefully consider it.

First.—The Republican party did run well for a season in the "line of liberty," but since 1870, its congressional enactments, majority reports, Supreme Court decisions, and now its presidential platform, show a retrograde movement—not only for women but for colored men—limiting the power of the national government in the protection of United States citizens against the injustice of the States, until what we gained by the sword is lost by political surrenders. We need nothing but a Democratic administration to demonstrate to all Israel and the sun the fact, the sad fact, that all is lost by the Republican party. I mean, of course, the one vital point of national supremacy in the protection of United States citizens in the enjoyment of their right to vote, and the punishment of States or individuals thereof, for depriving citizens of the exercise of that right. The first and fatal mistake was in ceding to Rhode Island the right to "abridge" the suffrage to foreign born men ; and to all the States to "deny" it to women, in direct violation of the principle of *national supremacy*. From that time, inch by inch, point by point has been surrendered, until it is only in name that the Republican party is the party of national supremacy. Grant did not protect the negro's ballot in the presidential election of 1876—Hayes can not in 1880—nor will Garfield be able to do so in 1884—for the "scepter has departed from Judah."

Second.—For the candidate of a party to add to the discussions of the contest an issue unauthorized or unnoted in its platform, when that issue is one vital to its very life, it seems to me would be the grandest act imaginable. For doing that very thing, with regard to the protection of the negroes of the South, you are today receiving more praise from the best men of the party than for any and all of your utterances inside the line of the platform. I know, if you had in your letter of acceptance, or in your New York speech, declared yourself in favor of "perfect equality of rights for women, civil and political," you would have touched an electric spark which would have fired the hearts of the women of the entire nation, and made the triumph of the Republican party more grand and glorious than any it ever has seen.

Third.—As to picking fruit before it is ripe ! Allow me to remind you that very much fruit is never picked; some is nipped in the bud; some is worm-eaten and falls to the ground; some rots on the trees before it ripens; some, too slow in ripening, is bitten by the early frosts of autumn; while some rare, ripe apples hang until frozen and worthless on the leafless boughs ! Really, Mr. Garfield, if after passing through the war of the rebellion and sixteen years in Congress; if after seeing and hearing and repeating that *no class* ever got justice and equality of chances from any government except it had the power—the ballot—to clutch them for itself; if after all your opportunities for growth and development, you can not yet see the truth of the great principle of individual self-government; if you have reached only the idea of class-government, and that, too, of the most hateful and cruel form—bounded by sex —there must be some radical defect in the ethics of the party of which you are the chosen leader.

No matter which party administers the government, women will continue to get only subordinate positions and half pay, not because of the party's or the President's lack of chivalric regard, but because, in the nature of things, it is impossible for any government to protect a disfranchised class in equality of chances. Women, to get justice, must have political freedom. But pardon this long trespass upon your time and patience, and please bear in mind that it is not for the many good things the Republican party and its nominee have done in extending the area of liberty that I criticise them, but because they have failed to place the women of the nation on the plane of political equality with men. I do not ask you to go beyond your convictions, but I do most earnestly beg you to look at this question from the standpoint of the woman—alone, without father, brother, husband, son—battling for bread. It is to help the millions of these unfortunate ones that I plead for the ballot in the hands of all women.

With great respect for your frank and candid talk with one of the disfranchised, I am, very sincerely yours.

On the strength of Hancock's perfectly non-committal interview and Garfield's frank letter, several of the prominent Democratic women rushed into a campaign for that party, whereupon Miss Anthony called them down in vigorous language. After expressing her indignation at the many false newspaper reports of her correspondence and interview with General Garfield, she said :

He has always stood ready to aid us in getting our demand before Congress, and was one of the three who reported in favor of a special woman suffrage committee in the House the last session. He has actually done a thousand things a thousand times more friendly to woman suffrage than Hancock now *talks* of doing. Then, again, Hancock has given us no public statement that, if elected, he will recommend a Sixteenth Amendment in his inaugural;

and in his letter of acceptance he said nothing more that can be twisted into suffrage for women than Garfield did in his, and there is no more in the Democratic platform that can be thus construed than there is in the Republican.

I never intended that the National Association should accept any sort of "under the ink or between the lines" as favorable pledges; and before *I* shall consent to put my name to any document favoring either candidate, I must see in black and white, in the candidate's own pen tracks, something to warrant such favoring. Mere gallantry will not do.

During the campaign which followed, neither she nor the other leading women of the country did any public work, and both parties lost the splendid services which would have been gladly rendered had they recognized the simple principle of justice. When the success of Garfield was practically assured, Miss Anthony wrote to a friend on the evening of election day : "I am fairly holding my breath tonight, waiting for the morning reports, as I feel it will be an overwhelming triumph for the Republican party. If their majority should be immense, perhaps it will give them courage and strength to speak for woman—and so let us hope and hope on."

As Mrs. Stanton's health forbade her going on the lecture platform in the autumn of 1880, and as Miss Anthony had now enough money ahead to dare claim a little leisure from public work, they decided to settle down to the serious business of writing the History of Woman Suffrage. For this purpose Miss Anthony went to Tenafly in October and ensconced herself in Mrs. Stanton's cosy home among the "blue hills of Jersey." The work already was advanced far enough to show that it could not possibly be restricted to the one volume into which it had enlarged from the 500-page pamphlet at first intended, and the task loomed up in an appalling manner. Mrs. Elizabeth Thompson, the generous patron of so many progressive movements, gave Miss Anthony $1,000 for immediate expenses and so they went on with the work, delving among old papers and letters, compiling, cutting, pasting, writing and re-writing, sending over and over to the women of different States for local history, going into New York again and again to see the publishers, and performing all the drudgery demanded by such an undertaking, which can be appreciated only by the few who have experienced it.

Miss Anthony hated this kind of work and it was torture for her to give up her active life and sit poring over the musty records of the past. Her diary contains the usual impatient expressions of this feeling, and in her letters to friends she says: "O, how tired and sick I am of boning down to facts and figures perpetually, and how I long to be set free from what to me has been a perfect prison for the last six months!" She stuck to it with Spartan heroism, however, knowing that otherwise it never would be done, but she was not unwilling occasionally to sally forth and fill a lecture engagement or attend a convention. At the Rhode Island annual meeting she made the principal address, and the next day went, with Mrs. J. Ellen Foster, to Danbury, Mass., to call on John G. Whittier. Almost his first words were, "And so our dear Lucretia Mott is gone!" She had died the evening before, November 11, aged nearly eighty-eight.

Miss Anthony had expected her death, but was inexpressibly grieved to lose from out her life that sweet presence which had been an inspiration for thirty years, whose staunch support had never failed, even when friends were fewest and fortune at its lowest ebb. In times of greatest perplexity she could slip down to the Philadelphia home for sympathy and encouragement, and there was always a corner in the pocketbook from which a contribution came when it was most needed. If ever any human character was without a flaw it was that of Lucretia Mott. Her motto was "Truth for authority, not authority for truth." She faded away like a spirit and her dying words, whispered many times during the last day or two, were, "O, let me go, let this little standard bearer go!" For freedom, for peace, for temperance, for equality, she was indeed the standard bearer through all her long and beautiful life.

On election day, prompted no doubt by the unconquered and unconquerable Miss Anthony, Mrs. Stanton made an effort to vote. This act created much excitement and called forth columns of comment in the newspapers, to the great amusement of the two conspirators in their quiet retreat.

Toward the end of 1880, Miss Anthony wrote to the treasurer, Mrs. Spofford, asking if she did not think it would be best to omit the National Convention of 1881, giving as reasons that there had been such a surfeit of conventions during the past year and that she was very busy with the History. Mrs. Spofford was much surprised, for Miss Anthony never had been known to yield in the matter of holding this annual meeting, even when all others were opposed, but she advised against postponement and by the next mail received this reply:

I feel exactly as you do about having the convention. I have never for a moment felt ready *not* to hold it. I wrote you under Mrs. Stanton's orders not to tell you how I felt, as that would be sure to influence you. Now I have read her your letter and told her my determination was to go ahead. She won't promise to attend, she never does, but I never fail to take her with me when I am on the spot, as I shall be when the time comes next January. So you may save us each a bedroom away up, no matter how lofty—you know I love the fresh air of the high heavens. Don't give yourself one moment's uneasiness in regard to the convention. I am going to set about it and am bound to make it one of the best, if not the best ever held in Washington, and you shall have Mrs. Stanton too, unless I miss my guess.

At the same time came the following from Mrs. Stanton: "Your kind invitation I fully appreciate, and feel that the pleasure of seeing you is one of the compensations of these conventions, which I dread more than I can tell. But Susan says truly that when she is at hand, she always dragoons me into what she considers my duty, so I never venture to say what I will or will not do. Although I have solemnly vowed I will go nowhere this winter, I should not be surprised if I found myself in Lincoln Hall the middle of January."

The Thirteenth Annual Convention of the National Association opened January 18, 1881, Elizabeth Cady Stanton in the chair. The first session was devoted to a memorial service for Lucretia Mott. The stage was decorated with draperies and flowers and a large portrait of Mrs. Mott stood on an easel. An exquisite floral harp was presented by the colored citizens of the District. In the audience were many distinguished people, including Mrs. Hayes and her guests from the White House, members of the Supreme Court and of Congress, and other noted personages. The music was rendered by the

Harriet Purvis.

colored choir of St. Augustine's Church.   Miss Anthony said in part :   " The highest tribute she could pay was that during the past thirty years she had always felt sure she was right when she had the sanction of Lucretia Mott.   Next to that of her own conscience she most valued the approval of her sainted friend ; and it was now a great satisfaction that in all the differences of opinion as to principles and methods in their movement, Mrs. Mott had stood firmly with the National Association, of which she was, to the day of her death, the honored and revered vice-president."   Short and touching addresses were made by Mrs. Sewall, Miss Couzins, Frederick Douglass and Robert Purvis, and the eulogy was delivered by Mrs. Stanton.

There was an effort during this convention to secure in Congress a " standing committee on the rights of women."   It was ably advocated by Senator McDonald and defeated largely through the smooth manipulation of Roscoe Conkling.   The convention closed with a reception and supper for the delegates, given by Mrs. Spofford at the Riggs House.

Miss Anthony and Mrs. Stanton went from Washington to the home of Mrs. Mott, where they were welcomed by her daughters, who sent for Sarah Pugh, and the old friends had a lovely day, made sacred by reminiscences of the dear one gone forever.   For more than a quarter of a century this had been Miss Anthony's stopping-place when in Philadelphia,[1] but she was welcomed at once into another beautiful home, that of the wife and daughters of J. Heron Foster, founder of the Pittsburg Dispatch.   All were deeply interested in the great question, and Julia and Rachel henceforth were ranked among the most earnest and valued workers.

It was soon afterwards that a reporter of the Chicago News started the following paragraph :

Susan B. Anthony has never condescended to love a man but she lavishes a heap of affection on a little gray Skye terrier which she takes around with her wherever she goes.   This dog was given her by Elizabeth Cady Stanton, and having recently lost a favorite Newfoundland pet, she accepted the frolic-

[1]This and the hospitable homes of Robert and Harriet Purvis, Sarah Pugh, and Adeline and Annie Thomson, sisters of J. Edgar Thomson.

some Skye with hearty gratitude. She has taught the apt brute every variety of trick and its intelligence seems to be unlimited. The little creature sleeps on her bed, eats from her hand, has blankets, gold and silver collars and every kind of ornament and comfort. Miss Anthony is accompanied by this accomplished canine everywhere, and during the recent convention in Washington " Birdie," as the dog is called, occupied a prominent place on the platform, either cuddled up in her voluminous lap or coiled in a frowsy heap at her feet.

This was copied into many newspapers throughout the country, often accompanied by editorial comment, facetious, disapproving, and sometimes deducing from this text the solemn fact that every woman's nature must have something to love, or that while women were so frivolous they had no right to ask for the ballot. This extract from a half-column editorial in the New York Graphic will serve as an example :

There is something wrong here. If Miss Anthony were to carry around with her a Newfoundland or a good bloodhound the spectacle would have nothing incongruous in it. If she would make a pet of a six-barrelled revolver and another of a large club that would be appropriate. But a Skye terrier, a miserable, little, whining pup, a coached, coddled and coaxed dog making repeated journeys in a basket and fed on crackers and milk—what sort of a thing is this for a person of reformative powers to be associated with? It is an argument in favor of woman's rights that women are capable of all the masculinity necessary to voting and the making of laws; but who ever heard of a President, a senator, a member of the House of Representatives, a legislator of any kind, going about with a sick dog in his arms, soothing the little wretch into its proper sleep, providing it with its regular nourishment and superintending its morning awakenings and the accompanying ablutions?

Women can never come to the head of the government, can never assist to a large extent in its management, until they reform these weaknesses. It isn't necessary that they should chew tobacco and swear, and perhaps they needn't smoke cigars and drive fast horses; but their leaders must abandon the pet dog, the favorite kitten, the especial hen and the abominable bird. They may still sew and still wear the petticoat; but if they enter politics they must submit to the hard raps that men expect, without putting their hands to their eyes and sobbing that their feelings have been hurt. There must be reform, and Miss Anthony and Mrs. Stanton must set about it in earnest and at once.

A Skye terrier for Miss Anthony! Merciful heavens! after all these years has it come to this? Catnip for Julius Cæsar! Boneset tea and black stockings with garters for Alexander the Great! A locket with hair in it on the bosom of the first Napoleon! A Skye terrier! We have fallen upon evil days.

Under this in her scrap-book Miss Anthony wrote, " Doesn't

this cap the climax ?'' Of course, there was not the slightest foundation for the paragraph. Miss Anthony never owned a dog or any pet animal, not from dislike but because she felt that humanity needed all her time and affection.

Work on the History was at once resumed, as its editors were now convinced that it never could be finished except by the hardest kind of labor without cessation. Of the able assistance rendered by many women throughout the country, perhaps that of Clarina Howard Nichols was the most valuable. She possessed not only great literary ability but also the true editorial instinct and was one of the few left of the ''old guard.'' Out of her fine memory she wove a number of delightful chapters, all written while lying on her back an almost helpless invalid and over seventy years old. She had long ago gone to California to be with her children, and Miss Anthony's weekly letters to her were of the most loving character and answered in the same affectionate strain. Mrs. Nichols hesitated to use the names of those who had been most violent in their opposition to the rights of women, because she disliked to make their children blush for them, but Miss Anthony wrote :

History ought to be true, and the men and women who at the time enjoyed the glory of opposing us ought to be known to posterity even if it is to their children's sorrow; just as those who suffered the torments of ridicule and hatred then, now enjoy the rewards, and their children and grandchildren glory in their ancestors. Robert Dale Owen's daughter, in writing up the Indiana Constitutional Convention and her father's opponents, withheld their names from sympathy for their children. I have told her, that as she now rejoices in what was then considered her father's reproach, so she should let the children of those men hang their heads now for what then was their father's pride. Isn't that fair? Garrison used to say, '' Where there is a sin, there must be a sinner.'' When people understand that their descendants and all Israel will know of their deeds, a hundred years hence, maybe they will learn to be and do better.

I am a genuine believer in the doctrine of letting the seed bear its fruit on the sower's own ground. For us not to give the names of our opponents, but only of those who were wise and good, not only would not be true history, but would rob the book of one-half its interest. If all persons felt that their children must suffer for their wrong-doings, they would be more cautious, but the belief that all their ill record is to be hidden out of sight helps them to go

ANT.—34

on reckless of truth and justice. It is not in malice or with a desire to make any one suffer, but to be true to history that every name should stand and be judged as the facts merit.

Miss Anthony in reality seldom carried out this theory, but usually desired that personal failings should not be recorded and handed down to posterity. She scarcely could be persuaded to allow the bare facts in many instances to be stated lest surviving relatives should be hurt thereby.

Without knowing where the money was to be obtained for publishing the History but determined that it should be done, Miss Anthony pushed on the work. The steel engravings cost $126 apiece and where women were unable or unwilling to pay for their own, she herself assumed the responsibility. To Mrs. Nichols she wrote: "I shall have your picture and that of Ernestine L. Rose if it takes the last drop in the bucket."[1] Because of the unpopularity of the subject the large firms would not consider the publication of this work, which it was now found would fill two huge volumes, but arrangements were concluded finally with Fowler & Wells. In their great anxiety to get their work before the public while they yet lived to see it properly done, each chapter was hurried to the publishers the moment it was completed and immediately stereotyped and printed, which made revising, condensing and re-arranging impossible.

The first volume was issued in May, 1881, a royal octavo of 900 pages, bringing the record down to the beginning of the Civil War. It is not an exaggeration to say that no history during the century had been more favorably received by the press. The New York dailies contained from one to two or more columns of most complimentary reviews. The National Citizen and Ballot-Box gave up almost an entire edition to notices of the History taken from New York, Boston, Philadelphia, Chicago and other papers, with not a disparaging criticism. Most of them echoed the sentiment of the New York Sun: "We have long needed an authentic and exhaustive

---

[1] The women of Kansas contributed $75 toward Mrs. Nichols' picture as a testimonial to her suffrage work in that State.

account of the movement for the enfranchisement of women ; "
and of the Chicago News : "The appearance of this book,
long expected by the friends, is not only an important literary
occurrence, but it is a remarkable event in the history of civilization."   The personal commendations from such men as
President Andrew D. White, of Cornell University, Hon. C.
B. Waite, of Chicago, Rev. William Henry Channing, and
from scores of eminent women, would in themselves require
several chapters.

Nobody realized so well as the authors the imperfections of
the work, but when one considered that it had to be gathered
piecemeal from old letters, personal recollections, imperfect
newspaper reports, mere scraps of material which never had
been put into shape as to time and place, the result was remarkable.   They were indeed correct in their assertion that no
one but the actual participants ever could have described the
early history of this movement to secure equal rights for
women.   "We have furnished the bricks and mortar," they
said, "for some future architect to rear a beautiful edifice."
These "bricks and mortar" were supplied almost wholly by
Miss Anthony, who, from the beginning, had carefully preserved every letter, newspaper clipping and report, and whose
persistent and endless labor in collecting facts, dates, etc.,
never can be estimated or sufficiently appreciated ; and it is
not probable that any more forcible or graceful pens than those
of Mrs. Stanton and Mrs. Gage ever will be found to enhance
their splendid work.

Truly yours as ever

Matilda Joslyn Gage

So unanimous and hearty was the reception of this book, to which they had devoted every moment of spare time for five years, that they felt encouraged to spend the next five, if necessary, upon the other volume, which the mass of material now demanded ; but if all the criticism had been unfavorable and everybody had declared the work not needed, they still would have gone straight on to the finish, because they realized so strongly the value of putting into permanent form the story of the struggle for the emancipation of woman.   Many letters were received urging that it was too soon to write this history, to which Mrs. Stanton invariably responded in her humorous way : ''Well, we old workers might perhaps have 'reminisced' after death, but I doubt if the writing mediums could do as well as we have done with our pens.   You say the history of woman suffrage can not be written until it is accomplished.   Why not describe its initiative steps ?   The United States has not completed its grand experiment of equality, universal suffrage, etc., and yet Bancroft has been writing our history for forty years.   If no one writes up his own times, where are the materials for the history of the future ? ''

Before the task should be resumed, however, there must be a little rest and a great deal of work of another kind.   The diary says :   '' Had a man today and toted all my documents out to the barn, storing them in big boxes, then packed my winter clothes away in the attic, so that my room might be renovated for Theodore Stanton and his bride from Paris.''   Miss Anthony then returned home, filled several lecture engagements and in May started for Massachusetts, stopping at Tenafly to take Mrs. Stanton with her in order that she might not escape.

CHAPTER XXXI.

IT had been decided this year of 1881 to take the anniversary meeting into the very heart of New England, and for the first time the National Association went to Boston, opening in Tremont Temple, May 26. The address of welcome was made by Harriet H. Robinson, wife of "Warrington," the well-known newspaper correspondent, and there were several new speakers in the convention, including A. Bronson Alcott, Mary F. Eastman, Anna Garlin Spencer, Frank Sanborn, ex-Governor Lee, of Wyoming, the noted politician, Francis W. Bird, Harriette Robinson Shattuck and Rev. Ada C. Bowles. The ladies had no cause to complain of the hospitality of this conservative New England center. The Boston Traveller expressed the general sentiment in saying:

The National Suffrage Association has reason to congratulate itself on one of the most notable and successful conventions ever held. Boston's attitude to her distinguished guests has been uniformly hospitable, the audiences have been large and enthusiastic, the press co-operative in every sense. The eminent women who are its leaders are ladies whose acquaintance is an unmixed pleasure, and not least in importance have been the friendships formed and renewed at this meeting. The business management of the convention has been superb; the sympathy between audience and speakers reciprocal.

The guests received an invitation from Governor John D. Long to visit the State House and were received by him in person. In his remarks he said he believed women should vote, not because they are women but because they are a part of the people and government should be of the people

(533)

regardless of sex; he thought the extension of suffrage to women could not fail to give stability to the government. Mrs. Hooker thanked him for coming to their support and in her letter describing the occurrence she says: "Miss Anthony standing close to the governor said in low, pathetic tones, 'Yes, we are tired, we are weary with our work. For thirty years some of us have carried this burden, and now if we might put it in the hands of honorable men, such as you, how happy we would be.'" The ladies also accepted an invitation from Mayor Prince to visit the city hall and were cordially received by him. They were invited to inspect the great dry goods store of Jordan, Marsh & Co. and see the arrangements for the comfort and pleasure of the employes, many of whom were women. Miss Anthony, Mrs. Stanton and Mrs. Robinson were entertained at the Parker House by the famous Bird Club.

Miss Anthony received several beautiful floral offerings during the convention, and also a handsome pin in the shape of a Greek cross. The golden bar from which it was suspended bore the letters S. B. A., on the points were the initials N. W. S. A., and on the reverse was engraved, "Presented by the Citizens' Suffrage Association of Philadelphia as a token of gratitude for her life-long devotion to the interests of woman." The little presentation speech was made in a most tender and graceful manner by May Wright Sewall. The Boston Globe in describing the scene pays this compliment:

Miss Anthony was as deeply touched as she was surprised. Recovering herself, she responded eloquently and in her usual interesting and magnetic manner. Of all the eminent women who are here, no one is such a favorite with a Boston audience as Susan B. Anthony. Her courage and strength and the patient devotion of a life consecrated to the advancement and the elevation of womanhood, her invincible honor, her logic and her power to touch and sway all hearts, are felt and reverently recognized. The young women of the day may well feel that it is she who *has made life possible* to them; who has trodden the thorny paths and, by her unwearied devotion, has opened to them the professions and higher applied industries; nor is this detracting from those who now share with her the labor and the glory. Each and all recognize the individual devotion, the purity and singleness of purpose that so eminently distinguish Miss Anthony.

The convention closed with a reception at the elegant home of Mrs. Fenno Tudor, on Beacon Hill.

After leaving Boston, this distinguished body of women made the sweep of New England, holding conventions in Providence, R. I.; Portland, Me.; Dover, Concord and Keene, N. H.; Hartford and New Haven, Conn. The national board of officers received an infusion of new blood this year through the election of May Wright Sewall, chairman executive committee, and Rachel Foster, corresponding secretary. Miss Anthony writes, "It is such a relief to roll off part of the burden on stronger, younger shoulders." This entire round of conventions was arranged by Miss Foster, a remarkable work for an inexperienced girl.

At Concord Miss Anthony was entertained in the family of her old friend and co-laborer, Parker Pillsbury, and after her departure Mrs. Pillsbury wrote: "I am so very happy to know you personally, and I thank you for the compliment you bestow in asking me to enroll my name among the most grand and noble women of our land. I shall enjoy being counted worthy to place it in company with dear Miss Anthony. Mr. Cogswell says many men (some members of the Legislature among them) in talking with him have expressed unexpected satisfaction in the speeches of the convention just holden—especially in yours, and he says, 'She is a host in herself, I like her practical common sense.'"

There was comfort in a letter received at this time from Elizabeth Boynton Harbert, president of the Illinois Suffrage Association and one of the Inter-Ocean staff:

Before entering upon our usual business talk, I want to wish you all beautiful and peaceful things this summer morning, and tell you of a rare and genuine tribute to yourself which brought tears of gladness to my own eyes when I heard it. In talking to some of the old workers, I referred to your life-long sacrifice and wondered how we could develop a similar spirit in our younger women, when Mrs. Zerelda Wallace said with great impressiveness: "My dear sisters, I want to say this, and to say it with a profound realization of all that it means, that to me, the person who, next to Jesus Christ himself, has shown to the world a life of perfect unselfishness, is Susan B. Anthony." I tell you this, my dear friend, because I believe such a tribute from such a woman will lighten some of the burdens.

Many similar letters were now received every year, and were as sweet and fragrant flowers in a pathway which had contained more thorns than roses.

In the hot summer of 1881 Miss Anthony went again to Albany to spend the last weeks with another friend, Phebe Hoag Jones, who passed away July 27. She was the intimate associate of Lydia Mott and the last of that little band of Abolitionists so conspicuous in the Democratic stronghold of Albany for many years preceding the war. At her death Miss Anthony felt that she had no longer an abiding place in the State capital, and expressed this feeling in a letter to Mrs. Spofford, who replied: " You speak of no longer having a home in Albany. Why, the best homes in that city should be gladly opened to you, and some day those people will wake up and wonder why they did not take you in their arms and hearts and help you in your work."[1]

All the letters during this summer are filled with sorrow over the assassination, long suffering and death of President Garfield. After all was ended Miss Anthony wrote to a friend :

In the reported death-bed utterances of our President, the only one which has grated on my ears was that in answer to the query whether he had made a will: " No, and he did not wish one, as he could trust the courts to do justice to his wife and children." How little even the best of men see and feel the dire humiliation and suffering to the wife, the widow, who is left to the justice of the courts! My heart aches because of man's insensibility to the cruelty of thus leaving woman. How can we teach them the lesson that the wife suffers all the torment under the law's assuming her rights to her property and her children, which the husband would, should it assume similar ownership and control over him, his property and children after his wife's death.

What a twelve weeks these have been, and what a funeral pall has rested upon us the past week. Every nook and corner, every mountaintop and valley is shrouded in sorrow for this crime against the nation. Today the ministers are preaching their sermons on the life and character of Garfield. Our Unitarian, Mr. Mann, made his special point on the fact that all the people of every sect had united in endorsement of Garfield's religion, which was most emphatically one of life and action, natural, without cant or observance of the outward rites and ceremonies. There is no report of even a minister's being asked to pray with him. When the bells told of the people's day of spe-

[1] This comment applies with equal force to Albany today. It is the only city in the United States where Miss Anthony has not a standing invitation to a number of hospitable homes.

cial prayer for his life, he exclaimed, "God bless the people," but covered his face, as much as to say, "Nothing but science can determine this case."

In the late summer and fall Mrs. Stanton had a tedious and alarming attack of malarial fever, and Miss Anthony was greatly distressed because some of her family insisted that it was produced by the long, hard strain of the work on the History. She writes: "It is so easy to charge every ill to her labors for suffrage, while she knows and I know that it is her work for woman which has kept her young and fresh and happy all these years. Mrs. Stanton has written me that during her illness ' she suffered more from her fear that she never should finish the History than from the thought of parting with all her friends.' "

The National Prohibition Alliance, which met in New York, October 18, invited her to take an official part in its proceedings. She declined to do so but attended the meeting and, after a visit to Mrs. Stanton, went to Washington to the national convention of the W. C. T. U. She had three reasons for this : 1st, she understood there was to be an attempt to supersede Miss Willard, to whom she had become very much attached ; 2d, an effort was to be made to commit the association to woman suffrage ; and 3d, she had made up her mind to see President Arthur on business connected with her own organization. She sat in the convention through all the three days' sessions and, on motion of Mrs. J. Ellen Foster, was invited to address it and was introduced by Miss Willard in words of strong approval. A prominent woman who was opposed to Miss Willard's re-election went among the delegates, assuring them in the most solemn manner that Miss Willard had insulted every one of them by introducing Miss Anthony on the platform, as she did not recognize God. "Well," replied one of them, an Indianapolis woman, "I don't know about that, but I do know that God has recognized her and her work for the last thirty years."

She had the pleasure of seeing Miss Willard triumphantly re-elected, an equal suffrage resolution adopted and a department of franchise established. "So the Christian craft of that

great organization has set sail on the wide sea of woman's enfranchisement," she comments. At the close of the convention this amusing card was sent to the press : "All presidents
of State delegations represented in the National W. C. T. U.
desire to explain, in refutation of a statement in the Post of
October 31, that, so far from 'capturing the convention,' Miss
Susan B. Anthony made no effort to influence their delegations
in public or in private, and is not, nor ever has been, a member of the W. C. T. U., either local, State or national, hence
has had no part in its deliberations."

The President, who was an old schoolmate of her brother
Daniel R., granted her a pleasant interview, arranged by Senator Jones, of Nevada, in which she urged him to recommend
in his message to Congress a standing committee on the rights
of women and also a Sixteenth Amendment which should enfranchise them. The reporters learned of this interview and,
as a result, newspapers throughout the country used a portion
of their valuable space in describing " how President Arthur
squeezed Susan B. Anthony's hand !"

On the way home she stopped in Philadelphia and, with
Rachel Foster and Adeline Thomson, called on George W.
Childs, who gave to her $50 for " the cause," and to each of
them one of his rare china cups and saucers. On November 7
work on the History was again resumed. The 29th was Wendell Phillips' seventieth birthday and Miss Anthony wrote
him a letter of congratulation, telling him that she always had
found comfort in the thought that, when there were differences
between them, she had had his respect if not his approval.
He replied with the following affectionate note: " Hearty
thanks for your congratulations. The band grows smaller
month by month. We ought to stand closer together. You
and I have differed as all earnest souls must. I trust each
always believed the other to be true in spirit. I know I always
did, touching yourself. You are good to assure me you have had
the same faith in me, and I hope when you reach threescore
and ten, some kind friend will cheer you with equally generous and welcome words."

The last entry in the diary for 1881 says: "The year closes down on a wilderness of work, a swamp of letters and papers almost hopeless." She attacked it, however, with that sublime courage which was ever her strongest characteristic, and at the end of the first week of the new year the heaviest part of the burden was lifted from her shoulders by the receipt of this letter from Mr. Phillips:

DEAR SUSAN: Our friend Mrs. Eliza Eddy, Francis Jackson's daughter, died a week ago Thursday. At her request, I made her will some weeks before. Her man of business, devoted to her for twenty-five years, Mr. C. R. Ransom (ex-president of one of our banks) is the executor. He and I were present and consulted, and we know all her intentions and wishes from long talks with her in years gone by. After making various bequests, she ordered the remainder divided equally between you and Lucy Stone. There is no question whatever that your portion will be $25,000 or $28,000. I advised her, in order to avoid all lawyers, to give this sum to you outright, with no responsibility to any one or any court, only "requesting you to use it for the advancement of the woman's cause."

After all the years of toil without financial recompense, of struggling to accomplish her work with wholly insufficient means, of depending from month to month on the few dollars which could be gathered in, Miss Anthony's joy and gratitude scarcely could find expression in words. She answered at once:

Your most surprising letter reached me last evening. How worthy the daughter of Francis Jackson! How it carries me back to his generous gift of $5,000; to that noble, fatherly man and that quiet, lovely daughter in his home. Never going to Boston during the past fifteen years, I had lost sight of her, though I had not forgotten her by any means. How little thought have I had all these years that she cherished this marvellous trust in me, and now I recognize in her munificent legacy your own faith in me, for such was her confidence in you that I feel sure she would not have thus willed, if you had not fully endorsed her wish. So to you, my dear friend, as to her, my unspeakable gratitude goes out. May I prove worthy the care and disposal of whatever shall come into my hands. Will you, as my friend and Mrs. Eddy's, ever feel free to suggest and advise me as to a wise use thereof? I am very glad it was your privilege to be with her through these years of her loneliness. I am pleased that you and Mr. Ransom propose to appropriate something to her faithful brother James, and most cheerfully do I put my name to the paper you enclose, with the fullest confidence that you would ask of me nothing but right and justice to all parties.

A few days afterwards she received another letter from Mr. Phillips:

You remember Mrs. Bacon (Mrs. Eddy's daughter) died about a week after she did. Her husband (who Mrs. Eddy knew would disturb her will if he could) is trying ostensibly to break it, really to force you and Lucy Stone to buy him off. The grounds on which he objects to the will are "that she was of unsound mind; that I and her executor exercised over her an undue influence in urging her to leave her money as she did; and that she did not know how much she was willing away." The truth is, we never said one word to her. It was her own plan entirely to leave it to woman's rights. Mr. Bacon knows there is not a ghost of a chance of his succeeding. The executor and I have retained Benjamin F. Butler and mean to fight to have Mrs. Eddy's will executed as she wished. The Misses Eddy sustain the will and wish it carried out to the letter, and say if it is broken they shall give their portion to the woman's rights cause, to you and Lucy. I'll tell you when any news is to be had. We are doing our best to protect your interests.

This was the beginning of litigation which continued for three years, and was a source of annoyance to Miss Anthony in other respects besides being deprived of the money. The fact of the bequest naturally being heralded far and wide by the newspapers, appeals and demands for a share of it poured in from all quarters, and she had much difficulty in persuading people that she had not the money already in her hands to be divided.

In company with Mrs. Stanton, Miss Anthony arrived in Washington January 16, 1882, to attend the Fourteenth Annual Convention. The effort to secure a special committee on woman suffrage which had failed in the Forty-sixth Congress was successful in the Forty-seventh, through the championship of Senators Hoar and John A. Logan, Representatives John D. White, of Kentucky, Thomas B. Reed and others. There was bitter opposition by Senator Vest, of Missouri, who declared it to be "a step toward the recognition of woman suffrage, which has nothing in it but mischief to the institutions and to the society of the whole country." In his zeal he dropped into poetry, saying,

"A woman's noblest station is retreat,
    Her fairest virtues fly from public sight,"

and so, of course, she had no need of a special committee. It was vigorously opposed also by Senator Beck, of Kentucky, who said "the colored women's votes could be bought for fifty cents apiece;" and by Senator Morgan, of Alabama, who made a stump speech on "dissevered homes, disbanded families, pot-house politicians seated at the fireside with another man's wife, women fighting their way to the polls through crowds of negroes and ruffians," etc.[1] It was carried in the Senate by a vote of 35 to 23; in the House, a month later, by a vote of 115 to 84. Miss Anthony says of this in her diary: "If the best of worldly good had come to me personally, I could not feel more joyous and blest."

In addition to the usual distinguished array of speakers were Rev. Frederick Hinckley, Representative G. S. Orth, of Indiana, Senator Saunders, of Nebraska, Clara B. Colby, Harriette R. Shattuck and Helen M. Gougar, all new on the National platform. The Senate committee on woman suffrage just appointed, granted a hearing January 20, and at its close expressed a desire to hear other speakers among the ladies on the following day. Miss Anthony and Mrs. Stanton presented each of the members of the committee with the first volume of the History of Woman Suffrage.

The convention closed with the usual handsome reception at the Riggs House and immediately afterwards most of the speakers went to Philadelphia, where Rachel Foster had arranged for another convention.[2] This was held at St. George's Hall, January 23, 24, 25, welcomed by Rev. Charles G. Ames, and was highly successful. A pleasant feature of this occasion was a luncheon given by that revered Quaker and temperance worker, Mrs. Hannah Whitall Smith, of Germantown, to twelve of the prominent speakers.

The two historians hastened back to their work, which was interrupted only by Miss Anthony's going to the New York State Suffrage Convention held in Chickering Hall, February 1.

[1] For full report of debate see History of Woman Suffrage, Vol. III, p. 198.

[2] Miss Anthony, Mrs. Sewall and Mrs. Jane Graham Jones remained over one day to appear before the House committee, presenting arguments in favor of abolishing the word "male" from the Constitution of Dakota before admitting it as a State.

Calls for her presence and help came from many parts of the country. "O, how I long to be in the midst of the fray," she writes, "and here I am bound hand and foot. I shall feel like an uncaged lion when this book is off my hands." On February 15, her birthday was celebrated by suffrage clubs in many places,[1] but she refused to be drawn out of her retreat, where she was remembered with telegrams, newspaper notices and gifts. In quoting a complimentary reference from the Rochester Herald, the Elmira Free Press commented :

The Herald says too little. Miss Anthony has labored for the most part without money, and from pure love of the principle to which she has devoted her life. She is as good a knight as has enlisted in any crusade, and has sacrificed as much and been as faithful and true. She has been thrice true, indeed, because of the ridicule showered on her as a woman trying to do a man's work. No man ever had the courage of his convictions as much as she. It takes a bold spirit to stand up against the dangers of gunpowder in the old-time, legitimate way; but it is a braver one that withstands ridicule and that mean cunning which makes wit of every act looking toward the advancement of women. The Free Press has perhaps had as many of the frowns of this "good gray poet" of the woman's cause as anybody. It has seen enough of them to know, however, that behind that somewhat frigid exterior is a sensitiveness which would well become a girl of sixteen rather than a lady of sixty-two and which shows that the woman is always the woman; and it wants to present its compliments to the bravest and grandest old lady within the circle of its acquaintance.

The Washington Republic furnished another example of the pleasant things said :

Miss Anthony, whom we know well and of whom we can speak from personal experience, is so broad in her charity, so cosmopolitan in her sympathies, that she will stand, without fearing speck or soil, beside any publican or sinner whose eyes have been opened to see the good in woman's rights, and who is willing to help on the work in his own way. For herself she never deviates from the principles she espoused when, stepping upon the rostrum to plead for disfranchised women, she determined that her life work should be endeavoring to procure for her sex all the rights and privileges of which exclusively male legislation had for ages defrauded them. With eyes steadily fixed upon the goal she has in view, neither the jeers nor ridicule of the crowds without, nor the jealous asides of those claiming to be workers in the same cause, have had power to distract her attention or make her turn from her labor to answer or rebuke.

[1] This national celebration of Miss Anthony's birthday by suffrage clubs was first suggested by Elizabeth Boynton Harbert, in her department, "Woman's Kingdom," in the Chicago Inter-Ocean.

The last of April the second volume of the History was completed and its editors found to their dismay that they still had enough material on hand for a third huge volume. Mrs. Stanton sailed for Europe with her daughter Harriot, and after Miss Anthony had read the last bit of proof and seen all safe at the publishers, she obeyed an urgent call from the women at Washington and hastened thither to look after the congressional committees on woman suffrage.

She was fortunate in her friends at court at this time, having two cousins, Elbridge G. Lapham and Henry B. Anthony, in the United States Senate, and her lawyer, John Van Voorhis, of Rochester, in the House of Representatives, all in favor of woman suffrage, and the two cousins on the "select committee" of the Senate. On June 5, 1882, this committee made a report in favor of a Sixteenth Amendment to the Constitution of the United States, signed by the Republican senators, E. G. Lapham, T. W. Ferry, H. W. Blair and H. B. Anthony. The minority report took the ground that suffrage was a matter which should be regulated solely by the States, not by Congress, and was signed by J. Z. George and Howell E. Jackson (Dems.), and James G. Fair (Rep.).

The following year, March 1, 1883, the House committee, John D. White, chairman, presented a favorable report. This was the first time woman suffrage had received a majority report from a Senate or House committee.[1]

Very sincerely,

John D. White

When Miss Anthony returned home she found this bright note from Harriot Stanton, dated Paris: " . . . Dear Susan,

[1] For full text of reports see History of Woman Suffrage, Vol. III., p. 263.

you often seem to me like a superb warhorse. You are completely swallowed up in an idea, and it's a glorious thing to be. Carlyle says, 'The end of man is an Action, not a Thought,' and what a realization of that truth has your life been. You have never stopped for idle culture or happy recreations. You are possessed by a moral force, and you act. You are a Deed, not a Thinking. . . . I should love to be your biographer. You are to other women of your time just what Greek architecture is to Gothic. I long to carve your literary image, and know I could.''

If Miss Anthony had any hope of rest it was soon dispelled. The legislature of Nebraska had submitted a woman suffrage amendment, and the women of that State called upon the National Association for assistance. After a vast amount of preliminary correspondence she left Rochester September 2, and travelled westward, leaving a trail of newspaper interviews in her wake, as she was intercepted by reporters at every city. En route she wrote to her friend Mrs. Nichols : '' Only think, I shall not have a white-haired woman on the platform with me, and shall be alone there of all the pioneer workers. Always with the 'old guard' I had perfect confidence that the wise and right thing would be said. What a platform ours then was of self-reliant, strong women! I felt sure of you all, and since you earliest ones have not been with us, Mrs. Stanton's presence has ever made me feel that we should get the true and brave word spoken. Now that she is not to be there, I can not quite feel certain that our younger sisters will be equal to the emergency, yet they are each and all valiant, earnest and talented, and will soon be left to manage the ship without even me.''

The opening convention was held in Boyd's Opera House, Omaha, September 26, 27, 28. The Bee was ironical and contemptuous in its treatment, heading its report '' Mad Anthony's Raid.'' The Herald, under control of a young son of U. S. Senator Hitchcock, was vulgar and abusive, referring to the question as a '' dead issue.'' The Republican, edited by D. C. Brooks, replied :

PRETTY LIVELY "DEAD ISSUE."—During the three days' sessions of the woman suffrage convention, we estimate that 7,000 people were in attendance. The Republican, in its three daily issues, and its coming weekly issue, will have laid the proceedings in full before about 75,000 readers, and the Bee and Herald will have given them nearly as many more. For a "dead issue" we submit this is a pretty respectable showing. Considered as a series of political meetings, the suffrage convention had more hearers than all the Democratic meetings and conventions held in Omaha during the last five years. The audiences were truly representative, embracing the business, professional and working interests of our city, and composed very largely of voters and citizens influential in politics.

The next convention was held in Lincoln with the same crowded houses. The newspapers were fair in their reports. The National Association raised $5,000 by contributions, mostly from outside the State. Miss Anthony gave her time and services and over $1,000 in money besides all she collected. Mrs. Foster and daughters contributed $500. Eleven speakers were kept in the field,[1] and all the complicated series of meetings was arranged and managed by Rachel Foster, assisted by Mrs. Colby. Miss Anthony herself spoke in forty counties, free transportation being given her by all the railroads in the State. On October 13, she held the famous debate at Omaha with Edward Rosewater, editor of the Bee, in the presence of an immense audience. Everywhere her meetings were perfect ovations, people coming in from a radius of twenty-five miles; and outside of Lincoln and Omaha, there was no audience-room large enough to hold the crowds.

A splendid force of Nebraska women conducted the campaign in behalf of the State. Every effort possible was made in the brief space of six weeks, but the masses of voters were not prepared for the question, most of the leading newspapers opposed it, and the women had no help from either of the political parties. In spite of these fatal drawbacks, the suffrage amendment received about one-third of the total vote.[2]

---

[1] Mrs. Sewall, Mrs. Gougar, Miss Couzins, Mrs. Minor, Mrs. Saxon, Miss Hindman, Mrs. Shattuck, Mrs. Mason, Madame Neymann, Mrs. Blake and Miss Anthony.

[2] After the election some of the students of the State University placed an effigy of Miss Anthony in a coffin and with torches and pallbearers started in a funeral procession. They were met by another crowd of students who, to preserve the honor of the university, overpowered them and took the effigy away.

ANT.—35

Miss Anthony returned home by way of St. Louis, where Mrs. Minor gave a large reception in her honor. When she reached Rochester she was invited by the Lincoln Club, one of the leading political organizations of the city, to give her address, "Woman Wants Bread, not the Ballot." The Democrat and Chronicle said in its report: "The large audience-room of the city hall was completely filled, and many extra seats were brought in. A number of prominent ladies and gentlemen occupied seats upon the platform. W. E. Werner, president of the club, in introducing the speaker, said it was fitting the hall should be full to overflowing with an audience anxious to hear the greatest advocate of one of the greatest questions of the day."

Miss Anthony had made a short trip to Washington immediately upon her return from Nebraska, to confer with the select committees on woman suffrage and also to make final arrangements for the approaching National Convention. It met in Lincoln Hall, January 23, 24 and 25, 1883, and she presided over its deliberations.

In response to many urgent letters written by Mrs. Stanton from England, and encouraged by friends at home who felt that she needed a long rest after more than thirty years of uninterrupted public work, Miss Anthony decided to make a trip abroad. As Rachel Foster contemplated a few years' study in Europe, the pleasant arrangement was made that she should undertake the financial management of the journey, act as interpreter and give Miss Anthony the care and attention her loving heart would suggest.[1] Miss Anthony's sixty-third birthday being near at hand, the friends in Philadelphia, led by the Citizens' Suffrage Association, Edward M. Davis, president, tendered her a reception, which circumstances rendered it necessary to hold on the 19th instead of the 15th of February. The Philadelphia Times gave this account:

[1] It was on this trip that, as "Miss Anthony" seemed too formal and "Susan" too familiar, Miss Foster adopted the endearing title "Aunt Susan." After they returned and a few of the younger workers most closely associated with her began to use this name, Miss Anthony did not object; but when it came into general use and not only older women and comparative strangers, but men also, and the newspapers, fell into the habit of calling her "Aunt Susan," she was very much annoyed and never heard or saw the name without an inward protest.

The parlor of the Unitarian church was filled to overflowing on the occasion of the farewell reception to Miss Susan B. Anthony. After prayer by Rev. Charles G. Ames, Robert Purvis, who presided, said in a brief and earnest address: " I have the honor, on behalf of the National Suffrage Association, to present to you these resolutions testifyiug to their high regard, confidence, and affection." After the applause which the resolutions evoked, Mr. Purvis continued: " I present these with feelings which I can not express in words, for my thoughts take me back in vivid recollection to those stormy periods of persecution and outrage when you, Miss Anthony, with the foremost in the ranks of the Abolitionists, battled for the freedom and rights of the enslaved race. You have lived, with many compeers, to see the glorious result of your labors in redeeming from the infamy and degradation of chattelism 4,000,000 slaves. That done, your attention was turned to the greater question—in view of numbers—of woman's emancipation from civil and political debasement."

Upon rising to reply Miss Anthony received an ovation. She said: " I feel that I must speak, because if I should hear all these words of praise and remain silent, I should seem to assent to tributes which I do not wholly deserve. My kind friends have spoken almost as if I had done the work, or the greater part of it, alone, whereas I have been only one of many men and women who have labored side by side in this cause. Philadelphia has had the honor of giving to the world a woman who led the way in this noble effort. Lucretia Mott and Elizabeth Cady Stanton were active in the good work ere my attention had been called to it. It was through their influence that I was led to consider and accept the then new doctrine. Alone I should have been as a mere straw in the wind. . . . I have known nothing the last thirty years save the struggle for human rights on this continent. If it had been a class of men who were disfranchised and denied their legal rights, I believe I should have devoted my life precisely as I have done in behalf of my own sex. I hope while abroad that I shall do something to recommend our work here, so as to make them respect American women and their demand for political equality. . . . ."

Letters, telegrams, flowers and gifts were received in great numbers.[1]

May Wright Sewall had this graphic description in the Indianapolis Times, owned and edited by Col. Wm. R. Holloway, an earnest advocate of woman suffrage :

The few days spent in Philadelphia by Miss Anthony prior to sailing were a series of fêtes. She spoke to over one thousand girls of the Normal School on the public duties of women; was officially invited to visit the Woman's

[1]Among the letters was the following from Senator John J. Ingalls: "I see by the papers that you are about to depart for Europe. Though I do not sympathize with the opinions whose advocacy has made you famous, yet I am not insensible to the great value of the example of your courageous and self-denying labors to the cause of American womanhood. I hope that none but prosperous gales may follow your ship, tnat your visit may be happy, and that your life may be spared till your aspirations are realized."

Medical College; was given a reception by the New Century Club; was tendered a complimentary dinner by Mrs. Emma J. Bartol, in her own elegant home, where ten courses were served and toasts were drunk to the guest of honor. . . . Letters of introduction, quite unsolicited, poured in from friends and countrymen personally unknown to her, who thus showed their desire to facilitate her meeting with the stars of various desirable circles abroad. At the public reception, Robert Purvis presented the following testimonial, beautifully engrossed on vellum, and encased in garnet velvet with gold borders:

"*Resolved,* That the National Woman Suffrage Association of the United States does hereby testify its appreciation of the life-long devotion of Susan B. Anthony to the cause of woman; that it acknowledges her as the chief inspirer of women in their struggle for personal liberty, for civil equity, and for political equality; that as one of the foremost of American women it commends her to the women of foreign lands.

"*Resolved,* That the members of the association rejoice in the approaching holiday of their beloved leader; that they will follow her wanderings with affection and sympathy; that during her absence they will steadfastly uphold the principles to which her life has been devoted; that on her return they will welcome her to a resumption of her labors and hold themselves ready to work under her able and devoted leadership."

Among the numerous letters and telegrams were messages from Wendell Phillips, Harriet Beecher Stowe, Frederick Douglass, Mary Clemmer, Helen Potter, Emma C. Bascom and Dr. Alida C. Avery. . . . Probably no testimony was more enjoyed than the following:

"ROCHESTER, N. Y., THE HOME OF SUSAN B. ANTHONY: In this open letter old friends and neighbors unite with all who honor the birthday of its true citizen, and express the sincere wish that Miss Anthony in her sojourn in strange lands may find what she has in full measure here at home—a genuine appreciation of her true womanliness, her sturdy adherence to honest conviction and her heroic stand, against all opposition, for the higher education and enfranchisement of women. Wishing her Godspeed and a safe return, we, the undersigned, do not need to assure her that neither the triumphs nor the defeats of her future public life will change our estimation of her, for to us she will ever remain what her life among us has proved her to be—a good, true woman, self-consecrated to the cause of woman in every land."

The signatures include the names of eighty of the leading men and women of Rochester; among them editors of the papers of both parties, pastors of the prominent churches, university professors, bankers, politicians, etc. Honor, if tardy, surely comes at last to the prophet in her own country. A song written for the occasion and inscribed to Miss Anthony, by Annie E. McDowell, one of the first editors of a woman's paper, was splendidly sung by Mr. Ford, the composer, who had set it to music.

Among the telegrams was this from her brother, D. R. Anthony: "Sixty-three years have crowned you with the honor and respect of the people of America, and with the love of your brothers and sisters." From the friends in Washington, D. C., came a plush case, on whose satin lining rested an exquisite point lace fichu and sleeve ruffles. A New York gentleman sent $100 to be used toward the purchase of an India shawl, writing: "I don't believe in woman suffrage, but I do believe in Susan B. Anthony." The Cheney Brothers sent a handsome black silk dress pattern; Helen Potter, a steamer rug; the Fosters, a travelling bag; Adeline and Annie Thomson, a silver cup; Robert Purvis, a gold-handled umbrella, and there were various other tokens of remembrance. Many of the leading papers contained an editorial farewell, with a hearty compliment and Godspeed. The Chicago Tribune, edited by Joseph Medill, offered this tribute:

The best known and most popular woman in the United States, engaged in public work, is Susan B. Anthony, the co-worker of Wm. Lloyd Garrison, Lydia Maria Child, Wendell Phillips, Lucretia Mott and others in the anti-slavery movement, and the fellow-laborer of Elizabeth Cady Stanton in the woman's rights movement. She ranks first among the warriors in this latter contest, because she has lived her life in its service and there has been no side issue to it. Neither father nor mother, husband nor children, have diverted her mind from her hobby, or led her to cease for a day from the prosecution of the task she set out to accomplish. . . . Miss Anthony is an American woman whom the better class of English people particularly, and of foreigners generally, will delight to honor, and one that her country-women are pleased to have represent them. She is, in point of character and ability, one of the few of her sex who have made themselves a name and a place in the history of her time. . . .

She has had occasion to speak sharply, to lecture women severely, when in her heart she would have preferred to praise; but women love her dearly all the same, and trust her implicitly. In integrity, stainless honor and generosity of sentiment and of deed she has no peer. She has stood the storm of raillery and abuse she aroused, as the leader of the "shrieking sisterhood," with perfect equanimity, and while others were cowed by the ridicule which was hardest of all to bear, Miss Anthony busied herself using this opportunity to show to women the real opinion of them entertained by the stronger sex.

Only those who are aware of the great and beneficent changes made in the laws relating to the rights of property, for instance, can at all estimate the good accomplished by these brave women. Almost all the leaders in the movement are gone. Mrs. Stanton and Miss Anthony, both elderly women, now remain in the work, and Miss Anthony alone still labors with the old-time zeal and freedom. She is at her best mentally and physically, and is likely to live many years to follow up the work she is now doing. The best lesson that women can learn from her life is that success in any one thing is secured only by the sacrifice of many others, and that for a woman to reach the highest place in her chosen pursuit is for her to work with an eye single to it, counting it a privilege to forego pleasures and affections which tend to distract and divide attention. Miss Anthony knew this secret of success, as she has proven.

When the history of the reform work done in this country in this century is written, no individual laborer will have higher praise than that which belongs to Miss Anthony. Honest, sincere, tolerant and kind, she has won the homage of her adversaries; for while there is but a small minority of men and women who believe in woman suffrage, there are none who fail to pay tribute to the sterling qualities of this representative woman.

The Kansas City Journal said good-by in these graceful words: "Susan B. Anthony will celebrate her sixty-third birthday tomorrow, and in a few days will sail for England. . . . . She goes abroad a republican queen—uncrowned to be sure, but none the less of the blood royal, and we have faith that the noblest men and women of Europe will at once recognize and welcome her as their equal. Fair winds waft her over the sea and home again!"

The two ladies sailed from Philadelphia on the morning of February 23, and a special dispatch to the New York Times thus announced their departure:

Miss Susan B. Anthony, accompanied by Miss Rachel Foster, embarked on the British Prince, of the American Steamship Line, at 9 o'clock this morning, for Liverpool. Notwithstanding the cold and cheerless weather, quite a number of persons stood patiently on the wharf, facing the raw and snow-laden air which blew from the river, waiting to see the steamer get under way and to catch a glimpse of the celebrated champion of woman's rights. A little before 10 o'clock Miss Anthony came out of her stateroom with several friends and, bidding them a final farewell, watched with sober countenance as they passed down the gang-plank. Among those present were Miss Mary Anthony, of Rochester, Miss Julia Foster, Miss Thomson, a sister of the first president of the Pennsylvania R. R.; Rev. Dr. Soule, formerly of Scotland; Mrs. M. Louise Thomas and Edward M. Davis. . . . .

Miss Anthony was attired in a black silk dress and wore a black velvet bonnet. A beaver-lined satin circular was drawn tightly about her form. She retired immediately to her stateroom, where a pleasant surprise awaited her in the shape of a handsome silk flag, the gift of a friend, which was suspended in a corner of the room. Her eyes rested upon the tasty and comfortable apartment, bearing numerous evidences of the kindly feeling and good wishes of her friends, with visible enjoyment and emotion.

CHAPTER XXXII.

1883.

O pen so well as Miss Anthony's own, can describe her delightful tour abroad, and although her letters were dashed off while travelling from point to point, or at the close of a hard day's sightseeing, and the entries in the diary are a mere word, they tell in a unique way her personal impressions. Because of limited space descriptions of scenery will be omitted in order to leave room for opinions of people and events.

ON BOARD THE BRITISH PRINCE, February 24.

MY DEAR MRS. SPOFFORD: Here we are at noon, Friday, steaming down Delaware Bay. We got along nicely until 3 P. M. yesterday, when we came to a standstill. "Stuck in the mud," was the report. There we lay until eight, when with the incoming tide we made a fruitless attempt to get over the bar; then had to steam back up the river to anchor, and lie there until nine this morning—twenty-four hours almost in sight of the loved ones! It is a break from all fastenings to friends to be thus cut loose from the wharf and wafted out into the waters. These long hours of delay have given me time to think of those left behind, and how very far short I have come of doing and saying all I should have done and said. . . .

From the diary:

Feb. 24.—The weather lovely; saloon cozy and pleasant with piano, flowers and canaries. There are only seven passengers, among them a Catholic priest, a dear little three-year-old child and a baby. We sent twenty letters on shore, written during the day we have been detained.

Feb. 25.—Today dawns with no possibility of communicating with a soul outside the ship, a lonely feeling indeed; but I am determined to get all the good I can to mind and body out of this trip, and as little harm as possible.

Feb. 26.—I sit at the captain's right hand at table. The sea is perfectly smooth; I wonder if this broad expanse can be rolled up into mountains.

4 P. M.—The wind and waves are beginning to roar. The priest shows signs of surrender.

Mar. 2.—Sea calm and dishes no longer have to be fastened to table. It seems like freedom again. I can think of nothing beyond shipboard, can see no moves to be made when we reach Liverpool.

Mar. 4.—Winds fair, sea smooth, whole company at breakfast. Captaiu Burton read the church service. Rachel played the piano and led the singing.

ON BOARD THE BRITISH PRINCE, March 5.

MY DEAR SISTER MARY: At lunch the captain said, " I'll soon show you land! It will be Mizzenhead, the farthest southwest point of Ireland." This is the first pen put to paper since I wrote you at the Delaware breakwater, eleven days ago. Think of it, oh, ye scribbling fairies, almost two weeks and not a letter written by S. B. A.!

Well, we are thus far and have had no more than what the sailors call a " stiff breeze" and only two whiffs of that sort. Since Thursday the weather has been lovely—bright sun and crisp air. Rachel succumbed one night when the " stiff breeze" first opened upon us, and I felt a little squalmy. The next morning a sudden lurch of the ship took both feet from under me and I was flat on my back. The following day while I was lying on a seat, reading and half-dozing, the first I knew I was in a heap on the floor. Then I learned it wasn't safe to lie down without a board fence in front. Again, in the evening I had taken the one loose chair in the saloon, drawn it under a lamp and seated myself very complacently to read, when lo, I was pitched over as if propelled from a ten-pounder! Three times and out—all in rapid succession—taught me to trust not to myself at all, but always to something fast to the ship. I haven't lost a meal during the whole trip. Another time I should take a larger stock of oranges, lemons and other fruit.

3 P. M.—We have just been up on the bridge for a first sight of the Emerald Isle. So long as there was no immediate prospect of setting foot on land, I could get up no spirit to write or think. I have worn the old velvet-trimmed black silk dress right through, and it is pretty well salted. I should love to have Lucy and Louise and Maud along on this trip, with sister Mary, too. What a jolly lot of tramps we would make! Well, their one ray of hope is to " pull through" the free academy and get on their own feet. There is plenty of good in store for all who can bring themselves in line to get it. Holding a dish right side up to catch the shower is the work for each one of us. How much I do think and hope for the three nieces now entering womanhood. For Susie B. Jr., and little Anna O. and Gula, I shall think and hope by and by. As for the nephews, I do not forget them, but they'll fight their way through somehow, as have all boys before them. . . .

Dinner is over and an hour's talk at table after it. The Englishman, Mr. Mullinor, summed up: "Your country will come to ruin from such doctrines as you woman's rights folks advocate;" and I have put the case to him to the best of my sea-brain's ability. This is the very first time I have let my tongue loose. We expect to be in Liverpool tomorrow early, and then I will write you. Just take it for granted all is well with me, and I will try to do the same with you.

Miss Anthony found at Liverpool a cordial letter from Mrs. A. A. Sargent, whose husband was now United States Minister to Germany. She welcomed her to Europe, saying: "You always have the entree to our home and hearts. Come and stay as long as you will." A note from Mrs. Stanton to her "beloved Susan" said: "I came up to London the moment I heard of the arrival of the British Prince. To think of your choosing a 'Prince' when a 'Queen' was coming! I am on the tiptoe of expectation to meet you. . . . I write in the suffrage rooms surrounded with ladies."

A week later the diary records: "Left London at 10 A. M. for Rome, Rachel and self, also Hattie Daniels, Alice Blatch and Mrs. Fanny Keartland, five in all, three of the Eagle and two of the Lion, each glorying in her own nationality!"

ROME, No. 75 VIA NAZIONALE, March 22.

MY DEAR SISTER : Here it is a whole month tomorrow since we took a last glimpse of each other and scarce a decent letter have I written you; but it is fearfully hard work to find the minutes. There is so much to tell, and the spelling and pronunciation of the names are so perfectly awful. . . . At Liverpool we drove two hours in the Princess and Sefton parks and then went to the city museum, where the most interesting things to us were the portraits of all the Bonapartes—men and women, old and young—Josephine's very lovely ; and to the city library, which is free. There is also an immense free lecture hall, which was built for an aquarium but found impracticable, so it is an enormous circle, seated from the circumference down to the center, with a large platform at one side and every step and seat cut out of solid stone. Here the most learned men of the English colleges give free lectures, the city fund being ample to meet all expenses. The librarian, on hearing we were Americans, took great pains to show us everything. Of course when he said, "We have over 80,000 volumes," I asked, "Have you among them the History of Woman Suffrage, by Mesdames Stanton, etc., of America?" And lo, he had never heard of it !

Thursday morning we took train—second-class carriage—for London. Mrs. Stanton was at the station, her face beaming and her white curls as lovely as ever, and we were soon landed at our boarding-house. Lydia Becker came to dinner by Mrs. Stanton's invitation, so she was the first of England's suffrage women for us to meet. Friday afternoon we glanced into the House of Commons and happened to see Gladstone presenting some motion. Spent the evening chatting with Mrs. Stanton—a world of things to talk over. . . .

Saturday we went again to Bayswater to see Mrs. Rose—found her very lonely because of the death of her devoted husband a year ago. She threw her arms around my neck and her first words were: "O, that my heart would break now and you might close my eyes, dear Susan!" She is vastly more isolated in England because of her non-Christian views than she ever was in America. Sectarianism sways everything here more now than fifty years ago with us.

That afternoon I left for Basingstoke, the new home of darling Harriot Stanton, now with Blatch suffixed. Her husband is a fine specimen of a young Englishman of thirty. Sunday morning he took me in a dog-cart through two gentlemen's parks, a pleasant drive through pasture and woodland, thousands of acres enclosed by a stone wall. When I said, "What a shame that all these acres should thus lie waste, while myriads of poor people are without an inch of ground whereon to set foot," he replied: "They would be no better off if all should be cut up into forty-acre farms and divided among the poor, for no man could possibly support a family upon one. The owners of these parks are actually reduced to poverty trying to keep them up." So you see it is of no use to talk of giving every Englishman a farm, when the land is so poor no one can make a living off of it. Of course this is not true of all England, but evidently its inhabitants must be fed from other countries. On our return I was conducted through the garden and greenhouse of Mr. Blatch's father, where I saw peach trees in blossom and grape vines budding. The tree-trunks were not larger than my arm and I exclaimed, "How many peaches can you get off these little trees?" "Why, last year, we had 250," said he. How is that by the side of our old farm harvest of 1,000 trees? And yet these English people talk as if they raised fruit! . . . .

The next day I returned to London and Mrs. Stanton and I called on Rev. William Henry Channing at the West End, and had a two hours' chat with him. . . . He was very cordial and on our leaving said, "I can't tell you how grateful I am for this interview. You have my blessing and benediction;" so we were glad at heart. Mr. Channing loves America above all other countries and feels it was a mistake for him to have left it. His elder daughter is the wife of Edwin Arnold. March 12 we dined with the son-in-law of William Ashurst, the friend of Wm. Lloyd Garrison—Mr. Biggs, and his four daughters. Caroline Ashurst Biggs, the second, is the editor of the Englishwoman's Review and one of the leading suffrage women of England.

Very sincerely yours

Caroline A. Biggs.

After dinner some twenty ladies and gentlemen came in and we had a delightful evening, but such a continual serving of refreshments!

Tuesday morning I went again to Mrs. Rose's and finding her bonneted and cloaked for a chair ride, I walked beside her, holding her hand, through Kensington Park. I hope and almost believe she will go back to America with me. I feel sure that we, who have not forgotten her early and won-

Yours very sincerely
Mentia Taylor

derful work for woman and for freedom of thought, will do all in our power to smooth her last days. . . . That evening Rachel and I went to see Irving and Ellen Terry in Much Ado About Nothing. The painting and the lights and shadows of the scenery were lovely, and I suppose the acting was good, but I can not enjoy love and flirtation exhibited on the stage any more than off. All passional demonstrations seem to belong to the two concerned, not to other persons. The lovemaking, however, was cooler, more distant and more piquant than usual.

Wednesday afternoon Mrs. Rebecca Moore, our old Revolution correspondent, took me to a meeting at Mrs. Müller's, about the Contagious Diseases Acts —fifty or sixty ladies present—was introduced, and several invited me to speak for them when I returned to London. Miss Rye, who has made between thirty and forty trips across the Atlantic with little girls, taking over more than 10,000 and placing them in good homes in Canada, was there and spoke. She said all her efforts could accomplish nothing in thinning out the more than 1,000,000 surplus women of the island. Not one seemed to dare speak out the whole of the facts and philosophy. Each premised, " I will not shock you by calling the names," etc. Mrs. Peter Taylor's reception that evening was an unusually brilliant affair. She is looked upon as the mother of the English movement, as Mrs. Stanton is of the American. She is a magnificent woman and acted the part of hostess most gracefully. Her husband is a member of Parliament. At eleven we went home and packed our trunks to be off for Rome on the morrow, half-regretting that we had planned to leave London. . . .

ROME, March 23.

MY DEAR SISTER: It is noon—Good Friday—and just set in for a steady rain, so I will give you the goings, seeings and sayings of our company since leaving London. . . . We started from Victoria Station—second-class carriage, no sleeper—for a three days' and two nights' journey to Rome. It looked appalling, even to so old a traveller as myself, but I inwardly said, " I can stand it if the younger ones can." The crossing of the straits of Dover was rough, the sea dashing over the sides of the boat, but Rachel and I went through the two hours without a quaver. At Calais we had the same good luck as at London—a compartment of the car all to ourselves. Here we were to be settled without change for that night and the next day, so with bags and shawl-straps, bundles, lunch-baskets and a peck of oranges, we adjusted ourselves. We breakfasted at Basle, after having pillowed on each other for the night as best we could. Now we were in the midst of the Jura mountains, and all day long we wound up and down their snowy sides and around the beautiful lakes nestling at their feet—through innumerable tunnels, one of them, the St. Gothard, taking twenty-three minutes—over splendid bridges and along lovely brooks and rivers.

We arrived at Milan at 7 :50 P. M., when even the bravest of our party voted to stop over twenty-four hours and try the virtues of a Christian bed. Rachel and I shared a large old-fashioned room with a soap-stone stove, where we had a wood-fire built at once. (Remember that all the houses have marble floors and stairs, and are plastered on the stone walls, so they seem like perfect cellars.) We had two single bedsteads (I haven't seen any other sort on the continent) with the same bedclothes covering both. Our big room was lighted with just two candles ! We "slept solid" till 8 A. M., when Rachel got out her Italian phrase-book, rang the bell and ordered a fire and hot water.

After fairly good steak and coffee, we five began a day of steady sight-seeing. . . . In the evening we went to the station, and here found a wood-fire in a fireplace and monstrous paintings of Christ and the saints on the walls. All who had trunks had now to pay for every pound's weight. I had brought only my big satchel and shawl-strap. We were not so fortunate as to find a compartment to ourselves but had two ladies added to our number, while four or five men in the next one smoked perpetually and the fumes came over into ours. We growled but that availed nothing, as men here have the right of way. At Genoa the ladies left us—midnight—and two men took their places. These proved to be seafarers and could talk English, so we learned quite a bit from them. At ten we were halted and rushed in to breakfast. Sunday afternoon we reached the Eternal City and came direct to the Pension Chapman, tired and hungry, but later went to St. John's Cathedral to vespers. . . . After dinner we were glad to lay ourselves away. We have a pleasant room, with windows opening upon a broad court and lovely garden and fountain. Monday we drove around the city for bird's-eye views from famous points. Such wonders of ruins upon ruins!

Sunday Evening.—It is of no avail that I try and try to write—when the sight-seeing is done for the day I am too tired. . . . Last evening the Coliseum was illuminated—a weird, wonderful sight. Today, Easter Sunday, I have seen crowds of people reverently kissing St. Peter's big toe. To-morrow we go to Naples for a week and then return and finish Rome.

NAPLES, March 27.

Here we are, Rachel and I, at the Pension Brittanique, far up a high hill, in a room overlooking the beautiful bay of Naples. It is lovely, lovely! The little island of Capri, the city, the bold shores and mountain setting—a perfect gem. . . . We have a little bit of wood-fire with the smallest sticks—twigs we should call them—two sperm candles to light our bedroom and no matches except what we furnish. But 8 o'clock is here and we are all to meet for breakfast. . . .

Yesterday was a lovely *May* day, and our party drove to the village of Resina, which is built forty feet above the ruins of Herculaneum. There, with a guide, we descended a hundred steps and walked through the old theater, over the same stone stairs and seats which two thousand years ago were occupied by the gayest of mortals. Then we went to the ruins of Pompeii and ate our lunch under large old trees growing upon the debris left by the great eruption. We passed through the narrow streets, over stone pavements worn by the tread of long-buried feet, through palaces, public gardens and baths, temples, the merchants' exchange, customhouse and magnificent theater. . . .

I have just received John Bright's splendid address before the 2,000 students of Glasgow University on being made Lord Rector. It fired my soul beyond all the ruins and all the arts in Rome or Naples. It is grand indeed, and reminds one of our own Wendell Phillips' address to the Harvard students two years ago.[1]

ROME, March 29.

To Madam Susan B. Anthony, of New York, U. S. A.:

MADAM: We had the honor to announce your coming to Rome some three weeks ago in the Italian Times. While we ourselves have an impressive appreciation of your distinguished mental acquirements, yet we would wish to carry to our numerous English-speaking subscribers on this continent some testimony of your presence in our midst. Therefore we place our columns at your disposal, and will esteem the privilege of presenting to the public any topic your facile pen may write. To this end we will wait upon you or be pleased to see you at our sanctum. With much respect, we are, Madam, your obedient servants,   THE PROPRIETORS OF THE ITALIAN TIMES.

[Only English newspaper published in Italy.]

ROME, April 1.

DEAR BROTHER D. R.: We have climbed Vesuvius. One feels richly paid when the puffing and exploding and ascending of the red-hot lava meet the ears and eyes. The mountains, the Bay of Naples, the sail to Capri and the Blue Grotto are fully equal to my expectations. . . . The squalid-looking people, however, and their hopeless fate make one's stay at any of these Italian resorts most depressing. Troops of beggars beset one all along the streets and roads, and with tradesmen there is no honesty. For instance, a man charged some twenty francs for a shell comb, then came down to seven, six, five, and finally asked, "What will you give?" I, never dreaming he would take it, said, "two francs," and he threw the comb into the carriage. . . . Saturday we took the cars from Naples to Palermo. Every mountainside having a few seven-by-nine patches of soil in a place, is terraced and covered with grape vines and lemon trees, the latter now yellow with fruit. On many I counted twenty and thirty terraces, each with a solid stone wall to hold the earth in place. It is wonderful what an amount of labor it costs to earn even the little the natives seem to care for. Our hotel here is an old monastery, and on one side of the court is the cathedral with its grotesque paintings. One becomes fairly sickened with the ghastly spectacle of the dead Christ. It is amazing how little they make of the living Christ.

On Monday morning we drove back over that magnificent road, and took the train to Naples. In the afternoon we went to Lake Avernus and into the grotto of the sibyls, the entrance to Dante's Inferno. It was a dark, cavernous passage and with the flaring candles making the darkness only more visible, we could not but feel there was reason for the old superstition. The narrowness of the streets of Naples—and they are without the pretense of a sidewalk—leave the men, women and children, horses and carriages, funny little donkeys with their big loads, the cows and goats (which are each night and morning driven along and halted at the doors while the pint cupful, more

[1]The many inquiries and directions in regard to the suffrage work, and the loving messages to friends and relatives at home, are omitted in the extracts made from Miss Anthony's letters; but they are of constant occurrence, and show that these were never absent from her thoughts.

or less, is milked to supply the people within) all marching along together in the filthy road, jostling each other at every step.

But we are back in Rome now and this forenoon we spent in the galleries of the Vatican. One is simply dazed with the wealth of marble—not only statuary, but stairs, pillars and massive buildings. We stop here till the 9th, then go to Florence.[1]

It is good for our young civilization to see and study that of the old world, and observe the hopelessness of lifting the masses into freedom and freedom's industry, honesty and integrity. How any American, any lover of our free institutions based on equality of rights for all, can settle down and live here is more than I can comprehend. It will be only by overturning the powers that education and equal chances ever can come to the rank and file. The hope of the world is indeed in our republic; so let us work to make it a *genuine* democracy, where every citizen—woman as well as man—shall be crowned with the one symbol of equality—the ballot. . . .

ROME, April 5.

MY DEAR SISTER: How these anniversary days of our dear mother's illness and death bring back to me everything, even at this distance and amid these strange surroundings. How she would have enjoyed these sights because of her knowledge and love of history. She could have told the Bible story of every one of these great frescoes. What a woman she would have been, could she have had the opportunities of education and culture which her granddaughters are having. . . .

Tell Mrs. Lewia Smith her lovely piece of lace has been honored with the wearing in London and Rome several times and has been pronounced beautiful; but I prize it most of all for the giver's sake. No one but she would have trudged through the slush and rain to get those splendid names to that testimonial. Nothing which came to me gave so much pleasure as those signatures of my own townsmen and women, from President Anderson all the way to the end of the list. . . . This evening Rachel has gone to a friend's to study German so as to make our way with that nationality. What a jumble, that by just crossing an imaginary line one finds people who can't understand a word one says!

Last evening we heard the grand Ristori render a part of Dante's Inferno and a selection from Joan of Arc. Of course I couldn't understand a word she said, but her voice, her gestures, her expression told the whole story. Then the music, vocal and instrumental, was the softest and sweetest. . . .

ZURICH, April 23.

MY DEAR SISTER: We spent Friday night at Milan—there took our last look at Italian cathedrals, as we did our first, and its own still holds highest place as to beauty. We left early next morning and very soon were among the Alps. . . . The eleven hours' stretch was tiresome and disgusting inside our compartment, with from three to five stalwart men puffing away at their pipes all day long, and at every station rushing out for a drink of wine or

---

[1] While in Florence, Miss Anthony was entertained by the Countess de Resse, daughter of Elizabeth B. Phelps, of New York, and by the Princess Koltzoff-Massalsky, the distinguished author and artist, known through Europe by her pen-name of Dora d'Istria.

beer. Our only chance of a free breath was to open the window, and then all the natives were in consternation!

We reached Zurich at six and, after a splendid dinner of roast chicken, green peas and lettuce, took a cab and called on Elizabeth Sargent, who is studying medicine at the university, and found her very happy and glad to see us. In the afternoon we took a delightful drive, as it was too cold and misty for the lake excursion we had intended. The highest Alps are still lost to us by fog and clouds. After supper we called at the American consulate. Think of our government supporting a consul in most of the twenty-two cantons of Switzerland!

Tuesday.—At Munich. We saw princes and princesses galore out driving this afternoon, but not the king. We leave tomorrow morning for Nuremberg, and reach Berlin Saturday, and there I hope to rest at least a week— but then the Emperor William must be seen, and lots of other curiosities. . . . If I could command the money, as soon as each of our girls graduated, I would take her first on a tour of her own continent and then through the old world, before she settled down to the hard work of life either in a profession or in marriage. Thus she would have much to think of and live over, no matter how heavy might be the burdens and sorrows of her after life. . . .

COLOGNE, May 8.

MY DEAR SISTER: We left Berlin yesterday morning after a delightful week with the Sargents. I do not believe our nation ever has been represented at any foreign court by such genuine republican women, in the truest and broadest sense, as are Mrs. Sargent and her daughters. Mr. Sargent, too, touches the very height of democratic principle. Their association with monarchial governments and subjects but makes them love our free institutions the more.[1]

Our last evening was spent with the Frau Dr. Liburtius—formerly Henriette Hirschfeldt—a practicing dentist in Berlin since 1869, who studied at the Philadelphia Dental College. No college in Germany will admit women. Frau Libertius is dentist for various members of the royal family as well as for the Sisters of Charity. She says there are no dental colleges in the world equal to those of America. . . .

May 10.—At Worms—where Martin Luther made his glorious declaration for the right of private judgment. There is a magnificent monument in a beautiful square; Luther's is the central statue—a standing one; below, at the corners, are sitting Huss, Savonarola, Wycliffe and Peter Waldo, and on a still lower pedestal are four more worthies—one of them Melancthon. . . . We spent Tuesday at Cologne—visited the splendid cathedral and the church of St. Ursula. The latter contains the bones of 11,000 virgins martyred at Cologne in the fifth century. Whole broadsides of chapels are lined with

---

[1] Miss Anthony occupied some rainy days, while here, in wrapping up papers and writing letters which she put in her official envelopes, bearing the revolutionary mottoes, "No just government can be formed without the consent of the governed," "Taxation without representation is tyranny." After a few days a dignified official appeared at the American legation with a large package of mail bearing the proscribed mottoes, and said, "Such sentiments can not pass through the post-office in Germany." So in modest, uncomplaining wraps the letters and papers started again for the land of the free.—E. C. S.

shelves of skulls, which the noble ladies of the twelfth century partly covered with embroidery. Wednesday we took steamer up the Rhine at six in the morning and landed at Mayence at eight. It was a beautiful panorama, but not surpassing all others I have seen. The vine-clad hillsides, the ruins of the old castles (nothing like as many of them as I had thought) and the winding of the river were all very lovely. We visited the cathedral, the monuments of Gutenberg and Schiller, and then the fortress and the remains of a Roman monument erected nine years before Christ. . . .

HEIDELBERG, May 11.

DEAR BROTHER D. R.: As I clambered among the ruins of Heidelberg Castle today, I wished for each of my loved ones to come across old ocean and look upon the remains of ancient civilization—of art and architecture, bigotry and barbarism. I am enjoying my "flying," though I would not again make such a rush, but I am getting a good relish for a more deliberate tour at some later day. All of life should not be given to one's work at home, whether that be woman suffrage, journalism or government affairs.

After being perpetually among people whose language I could not understand, it was doubly grateful to be in the midst of not only my countrymen but my dearest friends, and I enjoyed their society so much that I almost forgot there were any wonders to be seen in Berlin. But we did make an excursion to Potsdam—a jolly company of us, Mr. and Mrs. Sargent and their gifted daughter Ella, also the professor of Greek in your Kansas State University, Miss Kate Stephens. She interpreted the utterances of the ever-present guides, whose jabber was worse than Greek.

At Potsdam we were shown the very rooms in which Frederick the Great lived and moved and had his being, plotted and planned to conquer his neighbors. In the little church are myriads of tattered flags, taken in their many wars, and two great stone caskets in which repose the bodies of Frederick the Great and his father, Frederick William, peaceful in death, however warlike in life. We also visited the new palace where the present Emperor spends the summer. We saw parlors, dining-rooms, bedrooms, the plain, narrow bedstead the Emperor sleeps upon, the great workshop, in which are maps and all sorts of material for studying and planning how to hold and gain empires. I even peered into the kitchen and saw the pitchers, plates, coffee-pots and stew-pans. It was my first chance of a real mortal living look of things, so I enjoyed it hugely. There are rooms enough in these palaces for an army of people. All of these magnificent displays of wealth in churches, palaces and castles, citadels, fortifications and glittering military shows of monarchial governments, only make more conspicuous the poverty, ignorance and degradation of the masses; and all pleasure in seeing them is tinged with sadness.

From the diary for May :

12.—Showering, but I walked up the mountain to pay a last visit to Heidelberg Castle, the most magnificent ruin in Germany. Its ivy-covered towers always will be pictured in my memory.

13.—At Strasburg. We have driven over the city, looked at the wonderful fortifications and explored the great cathedral with its famous clock. We heard the grand organ and saw 250 priests conduct the services before an audience of 2,000 people, nine-tenths women. Then to St. Thomas' church and the monument to Marshal Saxe.

14.—Left for Paris and had a beautiful ride through Alsace and Lorraine, the lost kingdoms of France. It made me sad all day; I wanted them returned to their own mother country. Theodore Stanton and his wife Marguerite met us at the station.

15.—Madam de Barron has invited me to be her guest while here. Such a delightful home and intelligent hostess! I have a charming room, and this morning the sun is shining bright and warm and the robins are singing in the trees. My continental breakfast—rolls, butter and coffee—was sent to my room and, for the first time in my life, I ate it in bed. What would my mother have said?

16.—Went to grand opera last night; magnificent house, scenery, toilets, equipages; but with my three " lacks," a musical ear, a knowledge of French and good eyesight, I could not properly appreciate the performance.

17.—Theodore took me to the Chamber of Deputies to see how Frenchmen look in legislative assembly—very like Americans. Then we called on friends at the American Exchange and the Hotel Normandie, and I was too tired to go to U. S. Minister Morton's reception at night.

22.—Called and had a good chat with Charlotte B. Wilbour, of New York; called also on Grace Greenwood; visited the Hotel des Invalides and walked in the gardens.

23.—Theodore and Marguerite took me to St. Cloud by boat and back on top of tram-car. Delightful!

27.—Today, Sunday, we went to Père la Chaise and saw great crowds of Communists hanging wreaths on the wall where hundreds of their friends were shot down in 1871—a sorrowful sight.

28.—At noon we went to the College of France to witness the last honors to Laboulaye, the scholar and Liberal. Saw his little study and sadly watched the priests perform the services over his coffin.

29.—Left Paris at 9 A. M., Theodore and his little Elizabeth Cady going with me to the station. The parks and forests are green and lovely, the homes cozy and pretty, France is a beautiful country. I have enjoyed the last three months exceedingly, but I am very, very tired; and yet it is a new set of faculties which are weary, and the old ones, so long harped upon, are really resting.

To Miss Susan B. Anthony, PARIS.

MADAM: Having been informed of your arrival in Paris, I take the liberty of writing to ask from your courtesy the favor of a short interview. I have since several years heard of all the work you have done in behalf of womankind, and I need not say how happy I would be to meet a person who has so often been praised in my presence. Hoping you will forgive my intrusion, and have the great kindness to let me know when I may have the honor to call, I am, madam, very respectfully, your obedient servant,

[Of Le Soir.] A. SALVADOR.

ANT.—36

PARIS, May 20.

MY DEAR MRS. SPOFFORD: I have just come from a call on Mademoiselle Hubertine Auclert, editor of La Citoyenne. I can not tell you how I constantly long to be able to speak and understand French. I lose nearly all the pleasure of meeting distinguished people, because they are as powerless with my language as I with theirs. We called also on Leon Richer, editor of La Femme. He thinks it inopportune to demand suffrage for women in France now, when they are yet without their civil rights. I wanted so much to tell him that political power was the greater right which included the less. . . .

Miss Foster has gone to London for presentation at Court. She had the "regulation" dress made in Berlin—cream-white satin, low neck, *no sleeves at all*, and a four-yard train! . . . I have not decided when I shall go home, but before many months, for I long to be about the work that remains undone. The fact is, I am weary of mere sight-seeing. Amidst it all my head and heart turn to our battle for women at home. Here in the old world, with its despotic governments, its utter blotting out of woman as an equal, there is no hope, no possibility of changing her condition, so I look to our own land of equality for men, and partial equality for women, as the only one for hope or work.

PARIS, May 24.

MY DEAR RACHEL: I am glad to hear that you were not cheated out of teetering through the palace halls in front of the princess, and that you are not utterly prostrated by it. . . . I attended the suffrage meeting last evening, and heard and saw several men speak—*well*, I inferred from the cheering and shouting of "bravo!"

This afternoon I visited the tomb of Napoleon. It surpasses every mausoleum I have ever seen, not excepting that of Frederick the Third and Queen Louise in Berlin. It is well that his memory should be thus honored, for had he been born a hundred years later, when the march of civilization had pointed to some other goal to gratify his great nature than that of bloody conquest of empire, I believe he would have stood at the head of those who strive to make free and independent sovereigns of all men and all women. Everywhere here are reminders of the ravages of war, the madness of ignorance and unreason. I want to get away from them and their saddening associations. You will think I am blue. So I am, from having lived a purposeless life these three months. I don't know but the women of America, myself in particular, will be the greater and grander for it, but I can not yet see how this is to be. . . .

LONDON, June 7.

MY DEAR SISTER: For the hundredth time I am going to beg you to shut up the house and come over here. It does seem as if now we two sisters, left so alone, ought to be able to travel and enjoy together. You can not know how I long to have you with me; it hurts every minute to think of you treading round and round, with never a moment of leisure or enjoyment. Surely you have given a mother's love and care to our nieces for eight years, and now you can let them go out from under your eye. . . .

Rachel and I came up from Basingstoke on Sunday to attend a small recep-

tion at Mrs. Jacob Bright's. Her husband has championed woman suffrage
in Parliament for years, and she has led the few who have dared say, "And
married women, too, should have the franchise." When the powers that be
forbade her to include married women in the Parliamentary Suffrage Bill
now pending, Mrs. Bright withdrew and started a bill for their property
rights, which was passed last session and is now in force.

With kindest regards
from Mr. Bright & myself
Yours very truly
Ursula M. Bright

Monday morning we went to Bedford Park and spent two hours at Moncure
D. Conway's. His charming wife read us what a delegate here from the
American Unitarians says of Emerson, Alcott, Frothingham and George Rip-
ley—that all are wearying of their early theories and theologies and returning
to the old faith. Today I had an hour with William Henry Channing, and he
virtually told me this was true of himself! I exclaimed: "Do you mean to
say that you have returned to the belief in the immaculate conception of
Jesus and in the miracles—that you no longer explain all these things as you
used to do in your Bible readings at Rochester?" He replied: "I never
disbelieved in miracles. Man's levelling and tunnelling the mountains is a
miracle." Well, I was stunned and left. Even if all these grand men, in old
age, or when broken in body, decide that the conclusions of their early and
vigorous manhood were false, which shall we accept as most likely to be true
—the strong or the weakened thought? It is very disheartening if we are so
constituted that with our deepest, sincerest study we grope and dwell in error
through our threescore and ten, and after those allotted years find all we believed fact to be mere hallucination. It is—it must be—simply the waning
intellect returning to childish teachings.

That evening we visited the House of Commons and heard several members
speak as we peeped through the wire latticework of the ladies' cage. The
next afternoon we attended a large reception at Mrs. J. P. Thomasson's,
daughter of Margaret Bright Lucas and wife of a member of Parliament.
There we met the leading suffrage women. Wednesday morning I went to
Tunbridge Wells—thirty miles—to see Mrs. Rose, who is trying the waters

there in hope of relief. . . . I should have told you that I dined on Sunday with Margaret Lucas—John Bright's sister—and lunched today with Mrs. Mellen, mother-in-law of General Palmer, of Colorado, president of the Rio Grande R. R.—an elegant and wealthy woman.

LONDON, June 22.

MY DEAR SISTER: . . . Sunday morning we went to hear Stopford Brooke, a seceder from the established church. I could see no diminution in the poppings up and down, nor in the intonings and singsongs, but when, after a full hour of the incantations, he came to his sermon on the Christian duty of total abstinence, he gave us a splendid one. Before commencing he said that, from his request the previous Sunday, twenty members out of his congregation of 600 came to the meeting to form a Church Total Abstinence Society, and ten of those made special and earnest protest against the forma- tion of such a society! Can you imagine the chilliness of the spiritual air in that church as he laid down the Christian's duty of denying himself that he might save his fellow who had not the power to drink moderately?

Afterwards, we called on Hon. William D. Kelley, wife and daughter Florence, of Philadelphia. We also attended a reception at Emily Faithfull's and met a number of nice people; then took underground railway for Bedford Park and had tea with Eliza Orme, England's first and only woman lawyer— or as nearly one as she can be and not have passed the Queen's Bench. Her mother was lovely and so proud of her daughter and glad to see me. Miss Orme has a partner, Miss Richardson, who is a member of the London school board and has visited our schools in America. She says London has none public or private, to compare with those of the United States.

The next morning we went to hear Laura Curtis Bullard read her sketch of Mrs. Stanton, which is to go into Famous Women, the same book for which Mrs. Stanton is writing me up. In the afternoon we called on Miss Müller, who purchased a house and lives in it that she may be a householder, as is necessary to hold office. She too is a member of the school board. Miss Müller insisted that I should talk to the ladies there, about thirty of them, and so I did, sitting under the trees in her garden, where we had our tea. Thence we went to the women's suffrage parlors and met some fifty or sixty, and then to the Albemarle Club of both ladies and gentlemen, the only one of the kind in London. Then came a meeting at the Somerville Club—all ladies. A paper was read on the topic, "Sentiment is not founded on reason and is a hindrance to progress," and followed by a bright discussion, in which both Rachel and I were invited to take part. A pretty full afternoon and evening!

Wednesday morning I studied on my speech for the 25th under the auspices of the National Women's Suffrage Society. Harriot has so divided the subject, that Mrs. Stanton is to take the educational, social and religious departments, and S. B. A. the industrial, legal and political. That evening we went to the Court Theater with Mrs. Florence Fenwick Miller, another member of the London school board. The nights are all days here now--daylight till after 9 o'clock and again at 3. Rachel and I lunched with Mr. and Mrs. Jacob Bright, and had a splendid visit; then went to the school board meet-

Your loving friend
Priscilla Bright McLaren

ing. Saw there five of the seven women members, among them Miss Helen Taylor, stepdaughter of John Stuart Mill, and the senior woman member of the board. Today I spent an hour with Mrs. Lucas,

Cordially yours

Helen Taylor

sister of John and Jacob Bright, and this afternoon Rachel and I are going to a Women's Poor Law Guardian meeting, at which Mrs. Lucas is to preside and other ladies to speak. . . .

Just back from the meeting. In all England there are thirty-one women poor law guardians. There are 19,000 of the guardians elected and 1,000, mainly clergymen, are honorary. They have over 1,000,000 paupers to look after. The secretary, Mrs. Chamberlain, stated that in her section of London there were 16,000. The guardians overlook everything about the workhouses and asylums, get no pay, and yet the public hesitates to put women on the board. One man stirred up the handful present by saying, "suffrage not only for widows and spinsters, but for married women."

June 26.—Well, the ordeal is over and everybody is delighted. Moncure D. Conway said: "I have learned more of American history from your speech than I ever dreamed had been made during the past thirty years." Even the timid ones expressed great satisfaction. Mrs. Stanton gave them the rankest radical sentiments, but all so cushioned they didn't hurt. Mrs. Duncan McLaren came down from Edinburgh and Mrs. Margaret Parker from Dundee. Rachel said I made a good statement of the industrial, legal and political status of women in America. We went to tea with Mrs. Jacob Bright; then I took dinner with Mrs. Stanton at Mrs. Mellen's, getting up from table at 9:15 P. M.

Saturday Rachel and I drove four hours in Miss Müller's carriage and called on Lady Wilde, a bright, quaint woman. Sunday morning I went to Friends' meeting and had a look at John Bright, though I was not sure it was he until after the meeting was over; then he was gone, and I not introduced to him! In the afternoon I called on Miss Jane Cobden, daughter of Richard Cobden, a charming woman. Yesterday I presented her with a set of our History in memory of her noble father,

Most sincerely yours

Jane Cobden

and for her own sake also. I will not foreshadow the coming days but they are busy indeed. You will see that the Central Committee have put both my name and Mrs. Stanton's on the card for the meeting of July 5. . . .

LONDON, June 28.

MY DEAR SISTER: It is now just after luncheon and at 4 o'clock we are to be at Mrs. Jacob Bright's reception, tomorrow evening at one at Mrs. Thomasson's, which she gives to friends for the special purpose of meeting Stanton and Anthony, and Saturday at Frances Power Cobbe's—and so we go. Yesterday morning Miss Frances Lord—a poor law guardian—escorted us through Lambeth workhouse. It has 1,000 inmates and 700 more in the infirmary, and gives out-door relief to 2,000 besides.

[Jacob Bright presided over the Prince's Hall meeting, and William Woodall over that at St. James' Hall.[1] All of the prominent newspapers in Great Britain contained editorials on the meetings, and noted especially the addresses of Miss Anthony and Mrs. Stanton, speaking of them in a dignified and respectful manner.]

LONDON, July 13.

MY DEAR SISTER: My last letter was mailed the 3d. That afternoon I was at Rebecca Moore's reception. We dined at Miss Müller's and afterwards went to Horn's assembly rooms to a suffrage meeting. Her sister Eva, wife of Walter McLaren, M. P., was one of the speakers. . . . At 9 P. M., we went to a Fourth of July reception at Mrs. Mellen's, given in honor of Mrs. Stanton and Miss Anthony, and a brilliant affair it was. About 150 were there; she had elegant refreshments; and the young American girls gave songs, recitations, violin music, etc. Grace Greenwood recited her "Mistress O'Rafferty"—a woman's rights poem in Irish brogue—very rich and racy; her daughter Annie sang, also Mrs. Carpenter, of Chicago; Kate Hillard, of Brooklyn, Adelaide Detchon, the actress, and Mildred Conway recited; Frank Lincoln impersonated; Nathaniel Mellen sang a negro jubilee melody; Maude Powell played the violin. She is not fifteen yet and is a charming player. The company did not disperse until after one.

July 5, drove to Mrs. Mellen's to a 10 o'clock breakfast, and worked on Rachel's report of my Prince's Hall speech—you'll find it in full in the

---

[1] WOMEN'S SUFFRAGE.

A Public Meeting will be held in
ST. JAMES' HALL, PICCADILLY,
Thursday, July 5th, 1883,

In Support of the Resolution to be moved by Mr. Mason in the House of Commons, on July 6th, for extending the Parliamentary Franchise to Women who possess the qualifications which entitle men to Vote.

Doors open at 7.   Organ Recital 7 to 8.   The Chair will be taken at 8 o'clock by
WILLIAM WOODALL, ESQ., M. P.

Mrs. Fawcett.	W. S. Caine, Esq., M. P.	Mrs. Oliver Scatcherd.
Dr. Cameron, M. P.	Mrs. Fenwick Miller.	R.P.Blennerhassett,Esq.,M.P.
Miss Tod.	Arthur Arnold, Esq., M. P.	Miss Eliza Sturge.
J. P. Thomasson, Esq., M. P.	Miss Becker.	Thos. Roe, Esq., M. P.
Mrs. Beddoe.	A. Illingworth, Esq., M. P.	J. A. Blake, Esq., M. P.
Mrs. E. Cady Stanton.	Miss Müller.	W. Summers, Esq., M. P.
Miss Susan B. Anthony.	C. H. Hopwood, Esq., M. P.	Thos. Burt, Esq., M. P.

Mrs. Ashford, Miss Bewicke, Miss C. A. Biggs, Miss Cobden, Mrs. Cowen, Mrs. Ormiston Chant, Mrs. J. R. Ford, Mrs. Hoggan, M. D., Mrs. Lucas, Miss Frances Lord, Miss Lupton. Mrs. McLaren, Mrs. Paterson, Miss E. Smith, Miss Stacpoole, Mrs. J. P. Thomasson, Miss Laura Waittle, and other Ladies and Gentlemen are expected to be present.

Numbered Sofa Stalls, 2s. 6d.   Balcony and Reserved Seats, 1s.   Body of the Hall and Gallery Free.

Englishwoman's Review. In the evening Mrs. Thomasson gave a splendid dinner-party, and afterwards took us all in carriages to the St. James' Hall suffrage demonstration, where there was a fine audience of about 2,000. . . . Next morning I went to a meeting of the suffrage friends from various towns who had come up for the demonstration. At 8 P. M. Mrs. McLaren took me to the House of Commons, to witness Mr. Hugh Mason present the Women's Suffrage Bill; so I heard all the speeches pro and con, up to 1:30 A. M., and how tired I was! Mr. Jacob Bright's was the strongest and most earnest.

The morning of July 7, at the suffrage rooms, I heard strong protests against the way Mr. Mason disclaimed all intention of enfranchising married women. He carried the matter too far even for the most timid. In the afternoon, we went to the Somerville Club, and Rachel spoke beautifully on the need of union and co-operation among women. I followed her, and Mrs. McLaren moved a vote of thanks. . . . Rachel left for Antwerp this evening, to meet her mother and sister, and I returned to my room, lonesome enough. Sunday I lunched with Mrs. Lucas and Mrs. McLaren. I had calls from three factory-women, who told a sad story of the impossibility of getting even a dollar ahead by the most frugal and temperate habits.

Have I told you that I have a new dark garnet velvet? I wore it with my point lace at Mrs. Mellen's reception on the Fourth, and the India shawl I have worn today for the first time. . . . Tuesday I went with Mrs. Lucas to the Crystal Palace at Sydenham to a great national temperance demonstration. More than 50,000 people passed the gates at a shilling apiece, and we saw a solid mass of 5,000 boys and girls from all parts of the kingdom seated in a huge amphitheater, singing temperance songs—a beautiful sight. Then in another part of the palace was an audience of 2,000 listening to speeches. Among the speakers was Canon Wilberforce, a grandson of the great Abolitionist but a degenerate one. He said the reason the temperance movement was now progressing so rapidly was because the persons who led it were praying people, and that the Lord had willed it, and all depended on whether it was kept in the Lord's hands—if not, then it would fall back like the old Washingtonian movement in America. Mrs. Lucas was very wroth, and so was I. He never spoke of woman except as "maiden aunt" or "old grandmother," and advised the boys to take a little wine for the stomach's sake.

At 6 o'clock we went to Miss Müller's where I remained until today. She took me to the Gaiety Theater to see Sarah Bernhardt. What a magnificent actor! I never saw any man or woman who so absolutely buried self out of sight and became the very being personated. Though I couldn't understand a single word, I enjoyed it all until the curtain fell at half-past eleven. I was tired beyond telling, but felt richly repaid by the seeing. She must be master of her divine art thus to impress one by action alone. Today Mrs. McLaren invites me to dine at her son's, Charles McLaren, M. P. All this is written in a hurry but is perhaps better than nothing. It is so difficult to clutch a moment to write.

LONDON, July 19.

MY DEAR RACHEL: . . . I am to attend a suffrage meeting at the Westminster Palace Hotel Hall this afternoon, and tomorrow at 10:25 A. M. I start for Edinburgh with Mrs. Moore. I am bound to suck all the honey possible out of everybody and everything as they come to me or I go to them. It is such unwisdom, such unhappiness, not to look for and think and talk of the best in all things and all people; so you see at threescore and three I am still trying always to keep the bright and right side up. I am expecting a great ferment at the meeting today, for those who agree with Mrs. Jacob Bright have asked Mrs. Stanton to confer with them about what they shall do now. She advises them to demand suffrage for all women, married and single; but I contend that it is not in good taste for either of us to counsel public opposition to the bill before Parliament. . . . .

I wrote you about Miss ———. She is settled in the conviction that she never will marry any man—not even the one with whom she has had so close a friendship for the past ten years. She feels that to do the work for the world which she has mapped out she must eschew marriage, accepting platonic friendship but no more. I tell her she is giving her nature a severe trial by allowing herself this one particular friend, that if he does not in the end succeed in getting her to marry him, it will be the first escape I ever have heard of. She is a charming, earnest, conscientious woman, and I feel deeply interested in her experiment.

[After being royally entertained in London and making many little trips into the beautiful country around, Miss Anthony left for Edinburgh July 20, carrying with her many pleasant remembrances of friends.]

EDINBURGH, July 22.

MY DEAR SISTER: Here I am in Huntley Lodge, the delightful home of Mrs. Elizabeth Pease Nichol, whose name we so often used to see in the Liberator and the Anti-Slavery Standard, and of whom we used to hear from Mr. Phillips and others who had visited England. We had a most cordial welcome from Mrs. Nichol—a queenly woman. She is now seventy-seven, and lives in this handsome house, two miles from the center of the city, with only her servants. . . .

Mrs. Nichol has gone to her room to rest and Mrs. Moore and I are writing in the little, sunny southeast parlor. I have an elegant suite of three rooms, the same Mr. Garrison occupied when he visited here in 1867 and in 1877. Mrs. Nichol is one of the few left of that historic World's Anti-Slavery Convention of 1840. We are going to a "substantial tea" with Dr. Agnes McLaren, daughter of Duncan McLaren. She is very bright—spent four years in France studying her profession—has a good practice, takes a house by herself, and invites to it her friends. So many young Englishwomen are doing this, and indeed it is a good thing for single women to do.

The suffrage society—Eliza Wigham, president, Jessie M. Wellstood, secretary—has invited a hundred or more of the friends to an afternoon tea on Tuesday next in honor of my visit, and I am to make a brief speech, so what to say and how to say it come uppermost with me again. . . .

Elizabeth Pease Nichol

THE RAVEN HOTEL, DROITWICH, August 5.

MY DEAR FRIEND SUSAN B. ANTHONY: I have often wished to write thee since we parted in London, my heart has been so full of loving thought. It has been a greater trial than I can describe that I have been denied the pleasure of receiving thee in my home in Edinburgh. If it had been only for an hour, I should have looked back on that hour as one of great privilege. But even if we should not meet again, I have had a pleasure which seems almost like a dream to me, in having made the personal acquaintance of thyself and dear Mrs. Stanton. . . .

That thou shouldst have been on the 1st of August with the Elizabeth Pease of those grand anti-slavery times, revived in me the thought I expressed in moving a vote of thanks to thee and Mrs. Cady Stanton for the noble addresses you gave at the Prince's Hall Meeting in London; . . . that you had been brought here to give us the hand of rejoicing fellowship; and that it gave me great faith to believe the God of Justice was leading us on, and had brought England and America together by your presence amongst us at this most critical and hopeful time of our agitation. . . .

I have addressed thee in the dear singular person, because it seemed to me in harmony with the noble simplicity of thy character, and also more affectionate—just as I feel toward thee. Believe me, dear friend—I love so to call thee—thine very affectionately, PRISCILLA BRIGHT MCLAREN.

[The diary notes many teas and luncheons in Edinburgh, drives to Melrose Abbey, Holyrood Palace, Roslyn Castle, to the celebrated monuments, the old cathedrals and the university ; calls from distinguished professors and those interested in philanthropic movements, visits to public institutions, and lovely gifts from the new friends. Every day of the month was filled with pleasant incidents. The scenery through the lake and mountain regions Miss Anthony found so beautiful that, although there was a steady downpour of rain for days, she sat on the outside of boat or stage in order not to miss a moment of it. She hunted up the old home of Thomas Clarkson but could not find there a person who ever had heard of him. She went also to the Friends' meeting house at Ulverston, presented to the Society by George Fox and completed in 1688. To her such spots as these were more interesting and hallowed than towering castles and vine-clad abbeys.]

BALLACHULISH HOTEL, August 13.

MY DEAR SISTER: Miss Julia Osgood and I are here, waiting for sunshine. . . . . While in Edinburgh Mrs. Nichol drove us out to Craigmillar Castle, where I saw the very rooms in which Queen Mary lived. We bought for a shilling a basket of strawberries plucked—no, " pulled "—the old man who sold them said, from the very garden in which berries and vegetables were "pulled" for Queen Mary three hundred years ago. One evening Professor Blackie, of the Edinburgh University, dined with Mrs. Nichol. At my reception he had said he did not want to "see refined, delicate women going down into the muddy pool of politics," and I asked him if he had ever thought that, since the only places which were too filthy for women were those where men alone went, perhaps they might be so from lack of women. At dinner Mrs. Nichol rallied him on the report that he had been converted, and he admitted that it was true; so as he was leaving I said, "Then I am to reckon an Edinboro' professor among my converts?" He seized my hand and kissed it, saying, "I'll seal it with a kiss." Don't be alarmed—he is fully eighty years of age but blithe and frolicsome—sang and acted out a Scotch war-song in the real Gaelic.

On August 1 we saw 200 medical students capped—and not a woman among them, because the powers ruled that none should be admitted. That afternoon we called on Professor Masson, a great champion of co-education. We took tea with Mrs. Jane and Miss Eliza Wigham. The stepmother, now eighty-two, was Jane Smeale in 1840. In their house have visited Henry C. Wright, Parker Pillsbury, and of course Mr. Garrison. Mrs. Nichol went with us to Melrose by rail, from which we drove to Abbotsford. . . .

Tuesday at 2 o'clock Miss Osgood and I landed at Stirling. At 4:30 we reached Callander, where I found no trunk, and not a man of them could give a guess as to its whereabouts. They give you no check here, but just stick a patch on your trunk. I had expected not to find it at every stop, and now it was gone for sure; but the station-master was certain he could find it and forward it to me, so he wrote out its description and telegraphed in every direction. Meanwhile we went to a hotel for luncheon and there in the hall was my trunk! Nobody knew why or how it got there and all acknowledged our American check system superior. I was raging at their stupidity, and no system at all, but laughingly said, "You ought to send this trunk free a thousand miles to pay for my big scold at you." The man good-naturedly replied, "Where will you have it sent?" I answered "Oban," and he booked it.

At 6 o'clock we took the front seat with the driver on a great high stage which we mounted by a ladder—they call the stage the "machine"—and drove a few miles to the Trossachs Hotel, past Loch Achray and Loch Vennachar. . . . While the rain rested this noon I took a walk up the ravine and it seemed very like going up the mountain at Grandfather Anthony's. Indeed, there is nothing here more beautiful than we have in America, only everything has some historic or poetic association. . . .

BRUNTSFIELD LODGE, WHITEHOUSE LOAN, EDINBURGH, August 23.

MY DEAR SISTER: Here am I, back in Edinboro' again, at Dr. Jex-Blake's delightful home—at least one hundred and fifty years old, with an acre or more of garden all enclosed with a six-foot wall. Lodge means a walled-in house; loan means lane, and the street took its name from a white house which two hundred and fifty years ago stood in this road. Every day the doctor has taken me a long and beautiful ride in her basket-carriage, driving her own little pony, White Angel, or her bay horse, while her boy-groom rides in his perch behind. Today she drove me through Lord Rosebery's park of thousands of acres. It is lovely as a native forest—the roads macad-amized all through—and a palace-like residence set deep within. . . .

AMBLESIDE, August 27.

MY DEAR SISTER: Last Thursday I left Edinburgh for Penrith, which has a fine view of the lake and the hills beyond. Next morning I took steamer at Pooley Bridge. The trip the whole length of the lake was beautiful, but can not compare with Lake George—indeed, nothing I have seen equals that—but the hills (mountains, they call them here), the water and the sky all were lovely. At Patterdale I had a cup of tea, with bread and butter and the veri-table orange marmalade manufactured at Dundee. Thence I took a stage over Kirkstone Pass, and walked two miles up the hills to a small hotel with a signboard saying it is the highest inhabited house in England, 1,114 feet above the sea—not very much beside Denver's 6,000 and others in Colorado 10,000 or 12,000. Arrived at Ambleside to find the hotel overflowing, so they sent me to a farmer's house where I had a good bed, splendid milk and sweet butter. Saturday morning I went by coach to Coniston, then railway to Fur-ness Abbey, a seven-hundred-year-old ruin of magnificent proportions. After four hours there, I took a train to Lakeside and then steamer up Lake Win-dermere back to Ambleside. The hotel still being full, "the Boots," as they call the porter or runner, found me lodgings at a private house, where I am now. It is the tiniest little stone cottage, but they have a cow, so I am in clover. My breakfasts consist of a bit of ham, cured by the hostess, a boiled egg, white and graham bread with butter and currant jam, and a cup of tea.

Saturday evening I strolled out and entered the gate of Harriet Martineau's home. On the terrace I met the present occupants, Mr. and Mrs. William Henry Hills. They invited me to call in the morning, when they would be happy to show me over the house. In naming the hour they said: "We never go to church—we are Liberal Friends—real Friends." At that I immediately felt at home with them. I called and spent two hours sitting and chatting in the drawing-room where Harriet Martineau received her many distinguished guests, and in the kitchen saw the very same table, chairs and range which were there when she died, and sitting on the doorsill was the same black-and-yellow cat, said to be fourteen years old now. The Hills invited me to 5 o'clock tea, which we took in the library, where Miss Martineau used to sit and study as well as entertain her guests at dinner. It seemed impossible to realize that I was actually in her house. It is not large and is covered with ivy, which grows most luxuriantly everywhere. It fronts on a large field, much lower than the knoll on which it stands, and fine hills stretch off beyond. The old gardener, who has been here more than thirty years, still lives in a little stone cottage just under the terrace.

Yours affectionately,

H. Martineau

Mr. Hills is a great lover of America and its institutions. He is one of the very few I have met here who really love republicanism. Nearly every one clings to the caste and class principle, thinks the world can not exist if a portion of the people are not doomed to be servants, and that for the poor to have an ambition to rise and become something more than their parents makes them discontented. " Yes," I answer, " and that is just what I want them to be, because it is only through a wholesome discontent with things as they are, that we ever try to make them any better." . . .

DUBLIN, September 10.

MY DEAR SISTER: . . . I stayed in Belfast some days, and visited the Giant's Causeway with Miss Isabella Tod, amidst sunshine and drenching showers; still it was a splendid sight, fully equal to Fingal's Cave. The day before, we went nearly one hundred miles into the country to a village where she spoke at a temperance meeting. Here we were guests of the Presbyterian minister—a cousin of Joseph Medill, of the Chicago Tribune—and a cordial greeting he and his bright wife gave me. They have three Presbyterian churches in that one little village. All welcomed the woman speaker most kindly, but not a person could be urged to vote down the whiskey shops, as these are licensed by a justice of the peace, appointed by the Lord Chancellor of Ireland, who receives his appointment from the Queen of England!

Yours most truly

Isabella M. S. Tod

So all she could ask was that every one should become a total abstainer. I do not see how they can submit to be thus voiceless as to their own home regulations.

Saturday I took tea with Mrs. Haslam, a bright, lovely " come-outer" from the Friends. She had invited some twenty or thirty to be present at eight, and I spoke, they asking questions and I answering. Among them were a son of the Abolitionist Richard D. Webb, and ever so many nephews and nieces. Eliza Wigham's brother Henry and his wife had come ten miles to be there. . . . This afternoon I am going to the common council meeting with Alfred Webb, who is a member and a strong Home Ruler. The question of electing their own tax collector is to be discussed.

CORK, September 16.

MY DEAR SISTER: . . . Your heart would break if you were here to see the poverty and rags, and yet the people seem cheerful under it all. Something surely must be wrong at the root to bear such fruit. I have had an awfully " hard side of a board time " of ten hours in a third-class car, paying therefor just as much as I would on the N. Y. Central for a first-class ticket. I not only saved $4.25 by going third-class, but I saw the natives. Men, women, boys and girls who had been to the market towns with their produce were on the train, and to see them as they tumbled in toward evening, at town after town, one would think that whiskey and tobacco were the main articles they bought. Any number of men and boys, and at least four women, were drunk enough, and they brought bottles with them and added to their puling idiocy as they went on. Nothing short of a pig-sty could match the filth, but it is only in that class of cars that you see anything of the vast number of poor farmers and laborers. If they can not pay exorbitant rates, refined, educated men and women are thrust into pens and seated face to face with the smoking, drinking, carousing rabble. I have everywhere protested against this outrage and urged the women to demand that the railway companies should give them separate cars, with no smoking allowed. . . .

LEAMINGTON, October 1.

MY DEAR RACHEL: . . . I must have told you of my good times at Belfast with Miss Tod, who gave a reception for me and I had a welcome all round.

Miss Osgood met me at Cork, and we went by rail to Macroom. Tuesday morning we visited the convent, nuns' schools, and the poorhouse with 400 helpless mortals, old and young; then took an Irish jaunting-car, and were driven some forty miles through "the Gap" to Glengariff. It rained almost all the way, much to our disgust. Next morning we packed into two great stages with thirty or more others, and started for the lakes of Killarney; but soon the rain poured again, and as we were losing so much of the scenery we stopped half-way at Kenmare. We visited the convent and the Mother Abbess showed us every cranny. Thirty girls were at work on beautiful Irish point and Limerick lace. These nuns have 400 pupils, and give 200 of the poorest their breakfast and lunch—porridge and a bit of bread. At two we took stage again, the sky looked promising, but alas! for half an hour it fairly poured. Then it grew lighter, and we got very fine views of hills and dales. Killarney *is* lovely. . . .

Saturday I sauntered along the streets of Killarney, passed the market, and saw all sorts of poor humanity coming in with their cattle to sell or to buy. Many rode in two-wheeled carts without seat or spring, drawn by little donkeys, and nearly all the women and girls were bareheaded and barefooted. On the bridge I saw some boys looking down. I looked too and there was a spectacle—a ragged, bareheaded, barefooted woman tossing a wee baby over her shoulders and trying to get her apron switched around to hold it fast on her back. I heard her say to herself, "I'll niver do it," so I said, " Boys, one of you run down there and help her." At that instant she succeeded in getting the baby adjusted, and to my horror took up a bundle from the grass and disclosed a second baby! Then *I* went down. I learned that she had just come from the poorhouse, where she had spent six weeks, and before going further had laid her two three-weeks-old boys on the cold, wet grass, while she washed out their clothes in the stream. The clothing was the merest rags, all scrambled up in a damp bundle. She had heard her old mother was ill in Milltown and had "fretted" about her till she could bear it no longer, so had started to walk ten miles to her. I hailed a boy with a jaunting-car—told her to wait and I would take her home—got my luncheon—fed the boy's horse, bought lunch for boy and woman—and off we went, she sitting on one side of the car with her two babies, wet bundle, two milk bottles and rubber appendages, bare feet and flying hair, and I on the other, with the boy in front.

For a long way both babies cried; they were blue as pigeons, and had on nothing but little calico slips, no socks even. She had four children older than these—a husband who went to fairs selling papers and anything he could to support them all—and an aged father and mother who lived with them. She said if God had given her only one child, she could still help earn something to live on, but now He had given her two, she couldn't. When we reached Milltown I followed her home. It was in a long row of one-room things with a door—but no window. Some peat was smouldering under a hole in the roof called a chimney, and the place was thick with smoke. On the floor in one corner was some straw with a blanket on it, which she said was her bed; in another were some boards fastened into bed-shape, with straw packed in, and this belonged to her father and mother. Where the four other children, with the chickens and the pig, found their places to sleep, I couldn't see. I went to the home of another tenant, and there again was one room, and sitting around a pile of smoking-hot potatoes on the cold, wet ground—not a board or even a flag-stone for a floor—were six ragged, dirty children. Not a knife, fork, spoon or platter was to be seen. The man was out working for a farmer, his wife said, and the evidences were that "God" was about to add a No. 7 to her flock. What a dreadful creature their God must be to keep sending hungry mouths while he withholds the bread to fill them! . . .

I went back to Killarney heart-sick; wrote letters Sunday, and Monday took train for Limerick, where I rushed round for an hour or two. . . . Then went on to Galway. Tuesday morning took the mail-car to Connemara, and had company all the way—a judge, an Irish M. P., and two Dublin drummers—with whom I talked over the Irish problem. I had meant to make the tour of the western coast up to Londonderry, but my courage failed. It was to be the same soul-sickening sight all the way—only, I was assured, worse than anything yet seen. I took the stage back to Galway, every one saying it was sure to be a fine day, but it proved to be terrific wind and rain, and before I had gone ten miles my seat was a pool of water and it took all my skill to keep my umbrella right side out. . . . Once while the driver changed horses I stood in front of a big fire on the hearth of the best farmer's house I have seen here. Everything was clean and cheerful—two rooms—a bed made up with a spotless white spread—the old father smoking and the wife cooking dinner. She lifted a wooden cover from a jar and proudly showed me her butter—patted down with her hands, I could see—and near by was another jar with milk. Think of butter being made in a room full of tobacco-smoke! Then I went my last ten out of the fifty miles, having been soaking wet for eight hours. At my hotel I had room and fire on a "double-quick," bath-tub and hot water, and put myself through a regular grooming. In the morning I rode around Galway, saw Queen's College and the bay, and then took train for Belfast.

From the diary :

Sept. 11.—In Dublin. The Professor of Arabic took me through Trinity College, with its library of 200,000 volumes. Thence to the old Parliament House, now the Bank of Ireland. In the afternoon Alfred Webb went with me to the National League rooms and from there to Thomas Webb's for tea, where I saw the names of Garrison and N. P. Rogers written in 1840. We called on Michael Davitt, the leader of the Irish Land League, who impressed me as an earnest, honest man, deeply-rooted in the principles of freedom and equality, and claiming all for woman that he does for man.

Sept. 16.—At Youghal. Visited the home of Sir Walter Raleigh, Lady Hennessy, eighty years old, showing me around. Found in a library Children of the Abbey, and read again the story of Lord Mortimer and Amanda. Once it thrilled my young soul, but now it seems inexpressibly thin.

Sept. 20.—While I was talking in the car today with an Irishwoman about the poverty here, another behind me shouted: "It is very ill manners for an American to come over here and abuse the English government."

Sept. 29.—In Belfast. O, how I would like to purchase all the linen I want for myself and my friends! Have bought as much as I dared and after all perhaps I'm cheated—but it's done, so I won't worry.

Sept. 30.—Landed at Fleetwood and went direct to Rugby. Walked all around the famous school, but had not courage to go in and introduce myself to Doctor Jex-Blake, whose sister's guest I had so recently been.

Oct. 1.—At Leamington. Went direct to Kenilworth Castle, a grand old ruin; the home of Leicester, where Queen Elizabeth visited him in the olden days.

Oct. 2.—Mrs. Mullinor called at our hotel and accompanied us to Warwick Castle, a splendid pile. We lunched with her, and when Mr. M. put fork into the roast he remarked: "Wife asked me what she should order for dinner and I said, 'a leg of mutton, for Americans never see such a thing at home.'" We smiled and ate it with a relish.

Oct. 3.—At Stratford on Avon, and we have visited every spot sacred to the memory of Shakespeare, and walked through the meadows and down by the riverside. . . .

Oct. 4.—In Oxford. I have visited many of the colleges, and as I saw where all the millions of dollars had been expended for the education of boys alone, I groaned in spirit and betook me to Somerville and St. Margaret's Halls, where at least there is a shelter for girls, and a beginning.

Oct. 5.—In London; and how almost like getting home it seems to come back here.

LONDON, October 7.

MY DEAR SISTER: Mrs. Stanton feels that she must stay with Hattie till the baby is a month old, and then have a week for farewell visits in London. Cousins Fannie and Charles Dickinson are here. Today I learned that I should have a chance to see and hear John Bright at a convention of the Liberal Party at Leeds, October 17; all these together have made me put off leaving a little longer. Since yesterday we have been in the midst of a genuine London fog. It is now 10 A. M. and even darker than it was two hours ago, when we dressed and breakfasted by gaslight.   I saw smoky, foggy days here last March but they could not compare with this, and yet the people say, "O, this is nothing to what November will bring."   . . .

LONDON, October 27.

MY DEAR SISTER: Since I last wrote you I have visited Leeds where I was the guest of Mrs. Hannah Ford, who has an elegant home—Adel Grange. There were several other guests who had come to attend the great Liberal demonstration, among them Mrs. Margaret Priestman Tanner, a sister-in-law of John Bright, and his son Albert.   Mrs. Alice Scatcherd, of Leeds, was the person who had the sagacity to get women sent as delegates and secure them admission on terms of perfect equality.   The amendment was a great triumph. She invited the friends to meet next day at her house, where I saw John Bright's daughter, Mrs. Helen Clark, and Richard Cobden's, Miss Jane Cobden.   Both made speeches at the convention, and most fitting it was they should—the daughters of the two leading Radicals of a half century ago.

On Saturday, Mrs. Ford took me to Haworth, the home of the Brontë sisters. It is a bleak enough place now, and must have been even more so forty or fifty years ago when those sensitive plants lived there.   A most sad day it was to me, as I looked into the little parlor where the sisters walked up and down with their arms around each other and planned their novels, or sat before the fireplace and built air-castles.   Then there were the mouldering tombstones of the graveyard which lies in front and at one side of the house, and the old church-pew directly over the vault where lay their loved mother and two sisters.   And later, when Emily and Anne and the erring brother Branwell had joined the others, poor Charlotte sat there alone.   The pew had to be removed every time the vault was opened to receive another occupant.   Think of those delicate women sitting in that fireless, mouldy church, listening to their old father's dry, hard theology, with their feet on the cold, carpetless stones which covered their loved dead.   It was too horrible !   Then I walked over the single stone pathway through the fields toward the moor, opened the same wooden gates, and was, and still continue to be, dipped into the depths of their utter loneliness and sadness, born so out of time and place.   How much the world of literature has lost because of their short and ill-environed lives, we can guess only from its increased wealth in spite of all their adverse conditions.

From Leeds I went to Birmingham to attend an Anti-Contagious Diseases Acts conference, and there heard the serene, lovely Josephine E. Butler.

Josephine E Butler

Miss Müller has invited Mrs. Stanton and me to spend the rest of our time with her.   Mrs. Lucas and some others are going to Liverpool to say good-by to us.   The cordiality, instead of decreasing, grows greater and greater as the day of departure draws near. . . .   I dread stepping on shipboard, but long to set foot upon my native soil again.   Only think, I shall have been gone over nine months when I land in New York!

From the diary:

Oct. 13.—Last evening at Mrs. Rose's I met the daughter of Charles Brad·laugh, a talented young woman, whom the college refused to admit to botany lectures because of her father's atheism.

Oct. 18.—At Leeds. Liberal party convention; went this evening to hear John Bright remember to forget to mention the extension of suffrage to women in 1869 and 1870, and the property law for married women in 1882. He did not meet my expectations as a speaker, but far surpasses any other Englishman I have heard. None of them can touch Wendell Phillips.

Oct. 28.—Had a four hours' row on the Thames today with some friends. This evening went to hear Mrs. Annie Besant.

Nov. 2.—Have been out to Basingstoke to see the new baby. Mrs. Mona Caird lunched with us. Have heard Michael Davitt, Mr. Fawcett and Helen Taylor, all masterly speakers.

Lovingly yours

Frances Power Cobbe

LONDON, November 6.

MY DEAR SISTER: . . . . As soon as I finish this scribble I am to have 5 o'clock tea with Frances Power Cobbe. Tomorrow I go shopping, Thursday Millicent Garrett Fawcett is to dine with us, and Mrs. Peter Taylor is to call here, and all are to take "substantial tea" with dear, noble Mrs. Lucas, and then go to hear Henry Fawcett on the political issues. Friday afternoon we receive at Miss Müller's. Saturday morning I leave for Bristol to visit Miss Mary Estlin, Mrs. Tanner and the Misses Priestman, three sisters-in-law of John Bright, who give a reception in my honor. The 12th I visit Margaret E. Parker, at Warrington, and the next afternoon Mrs. Stanton and I both go to Alderley Edge, near Manchester, to the home of Mr. and Mrs. Jacob Bright.[1] On the 14th we attend the annual meeting of the Manchester

[1] A pleasant letter was received afterwards from Mrs. Bright, in which she made this playful reference to Miss Anthony's always depreciating herself in favor of Mrs. Stanton:

"We have thought of you often and hoped that the wind, which has been rough here, has been tempered on the Atlantic for your sakes. Apropos of the very beautiful allusion you made to Mrs. Cady Stanton's popularity and the effect produced by her personal appearance, I must tell you of a remark made by my little son John immediately after your departure. I found him sitting on the sofa in my bedroom, thinking deeply. 'Mamma,' he said, 'I wish you could get me a photograph of Miss Anthony. I think she has such a fine face. There is something about it so firm and yet so kind.' I said, 'Do you like her better than Mrs. Stanton?' 'Oh dear, yes, much better,' replied Johnnie. So you see she does not monopolize all the admiration!"

ANT.—37

Women's Suffrage Association, and on the 16th go to Liverpool where a reception will be given us in the afternoon. That evening we shall spend at our

Believe me, yours very truly

M.G. Fawcett.

hotel with the friends who go to see us off, and on the 17th we give ourselves to old ocean's care in the Cunarder Servia.

Don't worry now if you do not hear from me again until I touch Yankee soil; and don't worry if the wind blows or if you learn the vessel is late or lost. If the Servia fail to land me safe and sound, don't repine or stop because I am not, but buckle on a new and stronger harness and do double work for the good cause of woman. You have the best of judgment in our work and are capable of doing much if only you had confidence in yourself, so whatever comes to me, do you be all the more for the less that *I* am.

Half of Miss Anthony's nine-months' trip abroad had been spent in Great Britain. To her all the other attractions of the old world were as nothing compared with its living, breathing humanity. On the continent she was deprived of any exchange of thought with its people because she spoke no language but her own, and this made her prefer England; but there was another and a stronger interest—the great progressive movement which was going forward in regard to woman. Here she found women of fine intellect and high social position engaged in the same work to which she had given more than thirty years of her own life; and here she met sympathy and recognition which would have been impossible in any other country in Europe. Her central thought in going to Great Britain had been to secure the co-operation of Englishwomen in holding an international suffrage convention. At first her proposition met with no response. The most radical of English women were conservative compared to those of

Yours affectionately
Margaret Bright Lucas

America, but after they had become thoroughly acquainted with Mrs. Stanton and herself and prejudice had been supplanted by confidence, the idea began to be more favorably regarded. One serious difficulty in the way of the proposed convention lay in the fact that the suffrage women of England and Scotland were not themselves in thorough unison as to plans and purposes. No definite action was taken until the last afternoon of their stay, when, at the reception given in their honor by Dr. Ewing Whittle, in Liverpool, with the hearty concurrence of Mrs. McLaren, Mrs. Lucas, Mrs. Scatcherd and Mrs. Parker, who had accompanied Miss Anthony and Mrs. Stanton to see them safely on board their vessel, a strong committee was formed to promote international organization.

They sailed from Liverpool on the Servia, November 17, 1883. Among their fellow voyagers were Mrs. Cornelia C. Hussey, of Orange, N. J., to whom the cause of woman suffrage and Miss Anthony personally are deeply indebted; and Mrs. Margaret B. Sullivan, of Chicago, the distinguished editorial writer. There was some lovely weather, which was greatly enjoyed, but heavy fogs impeded the ship and it was just ten days from the time of starting when, on November 27, they steamed into New York harbor and stepped again on the shores of loved America.

CHAPTER XXXIII.

CONGRESSIONAL HEARINGS—VISIT TO NEW ORLEANS.

1884–1885.

MOST of the newspapers had a welcome for Miss Anthony. In a two-column report in the Rochester Democrat and Chronicle she is quoted as saying:

"I can scarcely tell you of the hospitality extended, the dinners, teas and receptions given in our honor. I had no idea we were so well-known in Great Britain or that there was such cordial feeling toward us. Of course, I met chiefly those known as Liberals and the sympathizers with our cause. Public sentiment there is rapidly growing in our favor. In the discussion I heard in Parliament not a Conservative uttered a word against the suffrage already possessed by women but relied upon the hackneyed argument that when married women were included there would be trouble."

"You saw the Queen, I suppose?"

"No; I thought more of seeing the Bright family than the Queen and I never happened to be near where she was. I really had very little leisure to look around. I am ashamed to say I did not visit Westminster until the morning before I came away, but it was simply for lack of time. The social idea was of more importance to me."

The New York Evening Telegram said editorially: "The statement of Miss Susan B. Anthony, in another column, illustrates the superb determination of that champion of woman's political rights. In the struggle which has constituted her life-work she has the rare advantage of not being able to comprehend defeat. Battling under the inspiration of an enthusiast—of a fanatic, some may be disposed to say—she knows no such word as fail. The most disheartening reverses appear to her inspired imagination but steps in an undeviating march of progress. It was enthusiasm such as this that made the career

(581)

of Joan of Arc. Without it, not even the broad intellect and strong soul of Miss Anthony could sustain the burden of the struggle which she is called upon to lead.'' The Washington correspondent of the Cleveland Leader thus began a long interview :

Susan B. Anthony is back from Europe, and is here for the winter's fight in behalf of woman suffrage. She seems remarkably well, and has gained fifteen pounds since she left last spring. She is sixty-three, but looks just the same as twenty years ago. There is perhaps an extra wrinkle in her face, a little more silver in her hair, but her blue eyes are just as bright, her mouth as serious and her step as active as when she was forty. She would attract attention in any crowd. She is of medium height and medium form but her face is wonderfully intellectual, and she moves about like the woman of a purpose that she is. She says she experiences far different treatment by public men now from what she did years ago. The statesman of the past always came to her with a smirk on his face as though he considered woman's rights nonsensical and thought himself wonderfully condescending to take notice of her at all. "Now," says she, "public men look upon our mission as a matter of business, and we are considered from that standpoint."

The interview closed :

"One question more, Miss Anthony. Will you please tell me what is your highest ideal of the woman of the future ?"
"It is hard to say," was the reply. "The woman of the future will far surpass the one of the present, even as the man of the future will surpass the one of today. The ages are progressive, and I look for a far higher manhood and womanhood than we now have. I think this will come through making the sexes co-equal. When women associate with men in serious matters, as they do now in frivolous, both will grow stronger and the world's work will be better done. I look for the day when the woman who has a political or judicial brain will have as much right to sit in the Senate or on the Supreme Bench as men have; when women will have equal property, business and political rights with men; when the only criterion of excellence or position shall be the ability and character of the individual; and this time will come. All of the Western colleges are now open to women, and send forth more than 2,000 women graduates every year. Think of the effect upon the race to come! The woman of the future will be a better wife, mother and citizen than the woman of today."

There were, however, some discordant notes in the symphony of pleasant things which by 1883 had become customary in the newspapers. For instance, the Cincinnati Times-Star headed its interview : "Susan Speaks—Miss Anthony Cor-

ralled by a Times-Star Correspondent—The Old Lady Wears
Good Clothes and Stops at First-class Hotels—Bubbling about
the Ballot.'' The smart reporter described the size of her foot,
devoted a paragraph to the question whether her teeth were
natural or artificial, and said : '' There must be money in being a
reformer, for Miss Anthony lives at the Riggs House in good
style, and expects to be there all winter, and this, after a summer in Europe, would be a pretty severe drain on any but a
long purse.'' When one thinks of Miss Anthony's uniform
kindness and courtesy to reporters, always granting an interview no matter how tired or how busy she might be, and assisting them in every possible way with information and suggestions, it is astonishing that any one of them could indulge
in petty, personal criticism and innuendoes.

Miss Anthony had now another friend at court, Col. Halbert
S. Greenleaf, of Rochester, having been elected to Congress.
Both he and his wife were strong and influential advocates of
suffrage, and her warm personal friends. The diary shows
that every day of December she was conferring with officials
and their wives who were friendly to the cause, making converts wherever possible and co-operating actively with the
District committee in all the drudgery of detail necessary to a
successful convention. It is only by reading her diary that
one can understand what a mental agony it was for Miss
Anthony to press this matter upon congressmen, year after
year, to be repulsed by those who were opposed and only tolerated by those in favor, who had many other matters on hand
which to them seemed of much greater importance. '' Oh, if
men only could know how hard it is for women to be forever
snubbed when they attempt to plead for their rights ! It is
perfectly disheartening that no member feels any especial interest or earnest determination in pushing this question of
woman suffrage, to all men only a side issue,'' she writes in
this little confidant ; but not even in her letters is there ever a
note of discouragement. To the world at large and to those
who were associated with her, she was always brave, bright
and hopeful. It causes a keen heartache to reflect upon how

she crucified herself for fifty years, unfaltering and uncomplaining, in order to make conditions better for womankind.

To Hon. William D. Kelley, of Pennsylvania, who believed in woman suffrage and voted for it, but did not feel enough interest to push the matter in Congress, she wrote, January 6, 1884:

No one shrinks more from making herself obnoxious than I do, and but for the sake of all women, your darling Florence included, I should never again say a word to you on the subject of using your influence to secure the passage of a Sixteenth Amendment proposition. Last winter you put off my appeal for help with, "This is the short session and the tariff question is of momentous importance." Now, since this is the "long session," will you not take hold of this work, and with the same earnestness that you do other questions?

It is cruel for you to leave your daughter, so full of hope and resolve, to suffer the humiliations of disfranchisement she already feels so keenly, and which she will find more and more galling as she grows into the stronger and grander woman she is sure to be. If it were your son who for any cause was denied his right to have his opinion counted, you would compass sea and land to lift the ban from him. And yet the crime of denial in his case would be no greater than in that of your daughter. It is only because men are so accustomed to the ignoring of woman's opinions, that they do not believe women suffer from the injustice as would men; precisely as people used to scout the idea that negroes, whose parents before them always had been enslaved, suffered from that cruel bondage as white men would.

Now, will you not set about in good earnest to secure the enfranchisement of woman? Why do not the Republicans push this question? The vote on Keifer's resolution showed almost a party line. Of the 124 nays, only 4 were Republicans; while of the 85 yeas, only 13 were Democrats. Even should you fail to get another committee, the discussion and the vote would array the members and set each man and party in their true places to be seen of all men, and all women too.

The term of the select committee on woman suffrage having expired with the close of the Forty-seventh Congress, a new one was appointed by the Senate of the Forty-eighth. The House committee on rules refused to report such a committee but placed the question in the hands of Representative Warren Keifer, of Ohio, who made a gallant fight for it on the floor, during which he said: "Is not the right of petition a constitutional right? Has not woman, in this country at least, risen above the rim and horizon of servitude, discredit and disgrace, and has she not a right, representing as she does in many instances great questions of property, to present her appeals to this national council and have them wisely and judiciously considered?   I think it is due to our wives, daughters, mothers and sisters to afford them an avenue through which they can legitimately and judicially reach the ear of this great nation.''

He was ably assisted by Mr. Belford, of Colorado.   The measure to appoint this committee was bitterly opposed by Mr. Reagan, of Texas, who said in a long speech : ''When woman so far misunderstands her duty as to want to go to working on the roads and making rails and serving in the militia and going into the army, I want to protect her against it.''   The vote resulted—yeas, 85, nays, 124; absent or not voting, 112.

Immediately after the return of members from the holiday recess, Miss Anthony wrote to each of the 112 asking how he would vote if the question came up again.   To these letters 52 replies were received, 26 from Republicans, all of whom would vote yes; 26 from Democrats, 10 of whom would vote yes, 10, no; while 6 did not know how they would vote.   As these 36 affirmative votes added to the 85 yeas would so nearly have overcome the adverse majority, John D. White, of Kentucky, at the solicitation of Miss Anthony, made another earnest effort in February to secure the desired committee, but the Democrats refused to allow the question to come to a vote.   She was greatly disappointed at the failure to get the select committee, but afterwards became of the opinion that it was more advantageous to return to the old plan of working through the judiciary committee.

Miss Anthony had to be continually on the alert to head off zealous but injudicious women who were determined to commit the suffrage movement to the various ologies and isms of the day, and especially to personal matters.   Even a woman so intellectually great as Mrs. Stanton could not be relied upon always to make her individual opinions subserve what was demanded of her position as president of the National Association.   In January Miss Anthony received a document which Mrs. Stanton had prepared as an '' open letter,'' to be signed by both of them officially and given to the press, congratulating Frederick Douglass upon his marriage to a white woman and sympathizing with him because of the adverse criticism it had called out! She especially urged that he be given a prominent place on the program at the approaching convention. Miss Anthony replied at once:

I do hope you won't put your foot into the question of intermarriage of the races. It has no place on our platform, any more than the question of no marriage at all, or of polygamy, and, so far as I can prevent it, shall not be brought there. I beg you therefore not to congratulate him publicly. Were there a proposition to punish the woman and leave the man to go scot free, then we should have a protest to make against the invidious discrimination.

The question of the amalgamation of the different races is a scientific one, affecting women and men alike. I do not propose to have it discussed on our platform. Our intention at this convention is to make every one who hears or reads believe in the grand principle of equality of rights and chances for women, and if they see on our program the name of Douglass every thought will be turned toward the subject of amalgamation and away from that of woman and her disfranchised. Neither you nor I have the right thus to complicate or compromise our question, and if we take the bits in our teeth in one direction we must expect our compeers to do the same in others. You very well know that if you plunge in, as your letter proposes, your endorsement will be charged upon me and the whole association. Do not throw around that marriage the halo of a pure and lofty duty to break down race lines. Your sympathy has run away with your judgment. Lovingly and fearfully yours.

It is hardly necessary to say that the "open letter" was not published.

Everybody's burdens were laid upon Miss Anthony's shoulders. In looking over the mass of correspondence it seems as if each writer wanted something and looked to her to supply it. All expected her to take the lead, to do the planning, to bear the responsibility, and usually she was equal to the demand, but even her brave spirit could not resist an occasional groan on the pages of the diary. When a new accession to the ranks, from whom she expected great assistance, wrote, "I do not know how to plan but tell me what to do and I will obey," she says, "My heart sinks within me; so few seem to use their brain-power on ways and means." And again:

"This drain of helpless women, able and willing to work but utterly ignorant of how to do it, wears me out body and soul." She was greatly distressed because so many of the younger women were frequently incapacitated by illness, and writes : "O, the weak-bodied girls of the present generation, they make me heart-sick ! "

But never did the women themselves know of these feelings. To the younger ones she wrote : " Don't give up ' beat ' at any of those places till I have dropped my plummet into them. . . . Your young shoulders will have to learn to bear the crotchets of all sorts of people and not bend or break under them. . . . Put all the blame on me ; they may abuse me but not you. . . . . It makes my heart ache every minute to see you so tired. . . . Vent all your ill-feelings on me but keep sweet as June roses to everybody else. It does not pay to lose your temper. . . . You will have to learn to let people pile injustice on you and then trust to time to right it all."   If on rare occasions she spoke a word of censure, it was followed by a letter in the next mail, full of sorrow and repentance. She always signed herself, even in the darkest hours, " Yours with love and hope." Beautiful optimism, sublime courage !

Sunday, February 3, 1884, Miss Anthony read in the morning papers of the sudden death of Wendell Phillips. He had been to her always the one being without a peer, the purest, sweetest, best of men. The news overwhelmed her with grief and she wrote at once to Robert Purvis :

How cut down I am at the telegram, "Wendell Phillips is dead," and I know you are equally so. I hope you can go on to Boston to the funeral, and help tenderly to lay away that most precious human clay. Who shall say the fitting word for Wendell Phillips at this last hour as lovingly and beautifully as he has done so many, many times for the grand men and women who have gone before him ? There seem none left but you and Parker Pillsbury to pour out your souls' dearest love in his memory. Would that I had the tongue of an angel and could go and bear my testimony to the grandeur of that noblest of God's works ! I can think of no one who can rightly and fully estimate that glorious character. What a sad hour for his beloved wife ! He said to me on my last visit: " My one wish has come to be that I may live to bury Ann." He doubtless knew of his impending disease of the heart. On whose shoulders will fall the mantle of Wendell Phillips ? When will the children of men ever listen to such a matchless voice ?   How poor t he world seems! In sorrow I am with you.

She could not stay away and, inclement as was the weather, went to Boston three days later to look for the last time upon the loved face.

At the request of many ladies in Washington the National Convention was held in March, instead of earlier in the winter, to avoid the social distractions which always precede the Lenten season.   The ladies were pleasantly received by President Arthur.[1]   This was an exceptionally brilliant convention, a noteworthy feature being the large number of letters containing the greetings of the distinguished men and women of Great Britain, whom Miss Anthony and Mrs. Stanton had met and interested during their trip abroad.   The following was read from Matthew Simpson, senior bishop in the Methodist church, among his last public utterances, as he died a few months later :

For more than thirty years I have been in favor of suffrage for woman.   I was led to this position, not by the consideration of the question of natural rights or of alleged injustice or of inequality before the law, but by what I believed would be her influence on the great moral questions of the day.   Were the ballot in the hands of women, I am satisfied that the evils of intemperance would be greatly lessened; and I fear, without that ballot, we shall not succeed against the saloons and kindred evils in large cities.   You will doubtless have many obstacles placed in your way; there will be many conflicts to sustain; but I have no doubt that the coming years will see the triumph of your cause, and that our higher civilization and morality will rejoice in the work which enlightened women will ac-   *M. Simpson* complish.[2]

Both Senate and House committees granted hearings, and eloquent addresses were made by delegates from many States. Miss Anthony said in part :

This is the fifteenth year we have appeared before Congress in person, and the nineteenth by petitions, asking national protection for women in the ex-

[1] An official request was sent to the heads of the departments to permit the women employes to attend one session of this convention but it was refused.   A few days later permission was given them to go to Mrs. McElroy's reception at the White House, and the male employes were given a half-holiday to attend the exercises on St. Patrick's Day.

[2] The Methodist bishops Bowman, Warren, Newman, Haven, Turner and Walters have favored woman suffrage.

ercise of their right to vote. In the winter of 1865 and 1866 we sent your honorable body a ten-thousand prayer, asking you not to put "male" in the second section of the proposed Fourteenth Amendment; and again we appealed to you by thousands of petitions that you would add "sex" after "race or color" in the Fifteenth, but all to no avail. Then by an eighty-thousand petition in 1871 we demanded the enactment of a declaratory law that women had the right to vote under the first section of the Fourteenth Amendment. This, too, was denied us, not only by Congress but by the Supreme Court, which held that the framers of the amendment had only "colored men" in their thought, therefore none others could come within its purview. From 1876 to the present we have from year to year poured into Congress hundreds of thousands of petitions asking you to take the initiative step for another amendment which shall specifically prohibit the disfranchisement of women.

But, you say, why do you not go to your several States to secure this right? I answer, because we have neither the women nor the money to make the canvasses of the thirty-eight States, school district by school district, to educate each individual man out of the old belief that woman was created to be his subject. Four State legislatures submitted the question of striking "male" from their constitutions—Kansas, Michigan, Colorado and Nebraska—and we made the best canvass of each which was possible for a disfranchised class outside of all political help. Negro suffrage was again and again overwhelmingly voted down in various States; and you know, gentlemen, that if the negro had never had the ballot until the majority of white men, particularly the foreign born, had voted "yes," he would have gone without it until the crack of doom. It was because of this prejudice of the unthinking majority that Congress submitted the question of the negro's enfranchisement to the legislatures of the several States, to be adjudicated by the educated, broadened representatives of the people. We now appeal to you to lift the decision of *our* question from the vote of the populace to that of the legislatures, that thereby you may be as considerate and just to the women of this nation as you were to the freedmen.

Every new privilege granted to woman has been by the legislatures. The liberal laws for married women, the right of the wife to own and control her inherited property and separate earnings, the right of women to vote at school elections in a dozen States, full suffrage in two Territories, all have been gained through the legislatures. Had any one of these beneficent propositions been submitted to the vote of the rank and file do you believe a majority would have placed their sanction upon it? I do not; and I beg you, Mr. Chairman and gentlemen of the committee, that you will at once recommend to the House the submission of the proposition now before you, and thus place the decision of this great constitutional question of the right of one-half the people of this republic to a voice in the government, with the legislatures of the several States. You need not fear that our enfranchisement will come too suddenly or too soon by this method. After the proposition shall have passed Congress by the requisite two-thirds vote, it may require five, ten or twenty years to secure its ratification by the necessary three-fourths of the State legislatures; but, *once submitted by Congress, it always will stand until ratified by the States.*

It takes all too many of us women from our homes and from the works of charity and education in our respective localities, even to come to Washington, session after session, until Congress shall have submitted the proposition, and then to go from legislature to legislature, urging its adoption. But when you insist that we shall beg at the feet of each individual voter of every one of the States, native and foreign, black and white, learned and ignorant, you doom us to incalculable hardships and sacrifices, and to most exasperating insults and humiliations. I pray you to save us from the fate of waiting and working for our freedom until we shall have educated the ignorant masses of men to consent to give their wives and sisters equality of rights with themselves. You surely will not compel us to await the enlightenment of all the freedmen of this nation and the newly-made voters from the monarchial governments of the old world!

Liberty for one's self is a natural instinct possessed alike by all men, but to be willing to accord liberty to another is the result of education, of self-discipline, of the practice of the golden rule. Therefore we ask that the question of equality of rights to women shall be decided by the picked men of the nation in Congress, and the picked men of the several States in their respective legislatures.

The Senate committee again submitted a majority report in favor of a Sixteenth Amendment enfranchising women, signed by T. W. Palmer, Blair, Lapham and Anthony. The minority report, by Joseph E. Brown, Cockrell and Fair, began: "The undersigned believe that the Creator intended that the sphere of the males and females of our race should be different," etc.

The House Judiciary Committee gave a majority report in the negative.[1] The minority report in favor was signed by Thomas B. Reed, Maine; Ezra B. Taylor, Ohio; Thomas M. Browne, Indiana; Moses A. McCoid, Iowa. It is one of the keenest, clearest expositions of the absurdity of the objections against woman suffrage that ever has been made, and ends with this trenchant paragraph:

It is sometimes asserted that women now have a great influence in politics through their husbands and brothers. That is undoubtedly true. But this is just the kind of influence which is not wholesome for the community, for it is influence unaccompanied by responsibility. People are always ready to

[1] Signed by Maybury, Michigan; Poland, Vermont; Tucker, Virginia; Hammond, Georgia; Culbertson, Texas; Moulton, Illinois; Broadhead, Missouri; Dorsheimer, New York; Collins, Massachusetts; Seney, Ohio; Bisbee, Florida.

recommend to others what they would not do themselves. If it be true that women can not be prevented from exercising political influence, is not that only another reason why they should be steadied in their political action by that proper sense of responsibility which comes from acting themselves? We conclude then, that every reason which in this country bestows the ballot upon man is equally applicable to the proposition to bestow the ballot upon woman, and in our judgment there is no foundation for the fear that woman will thereby become unfitted for all the duties she has hitherto performed.

Miss Anthony mailed 500 packages of copies of this report to different points for distribution. Upon the urgent invitation of the suffrage association of Connecticut she went there for a few days to assist at their State convention, but in a letter to Mrs. Spofford she said: "I shall return tomorrow night, if possible. I keep thinking of those men at the Capitol not doing what I want them to." She afterwards wrote to May Wright Sewall:

My plan is to get away from here the minute I can do so without letting our work suffer in Congress. A week ago the House Judiciary Committee voted down a motion to print our "hearing" speeches. Yesterday I went up and called out a Democrat who I knew had voted "no," and hence could move to reconsider, and he promised to go back and thus move, and did so, and Mr. Browne, of Indiana, asked leave of the House to print them. I wish you would write to Mr. Browne that he is splendid and our main help now in the committee. Cockrell has been trying to prevent printing the Senate "hearing," but Blair, Lapham, Palmer and Anthony are bound it shall be printed. Still, all would fall flat and dead if some one were not here to keep them in mind of their duty to us.

Yours &c

Thomas M. Browne

M C

Miss Anthony remained in Washington till April 14, managing her forces like an experienced general until the last gun had been fired. When she returned home ready to begin work on the History, she found to her amazement that the officer who had been charged with preparing the report of the Sixteenth National Suffrage Convention, a woman of great literary ability, had given it up in despair, declaring that it would be utterly impossible to make anything creditable out of such a mass of unsatisfactory material, most of which would have to be entirely re-written. Miss Anthony did not stop to sit down and weep, but wrote her at once to send to Rochester every document she had in her possession. Then, taking all of them to Mrs. Stanton, who had gone to her old paternal home at Johnstown, they arranged, edited, re-wrote and put into shape the conglomerate of letters, speeches, etc., and in less than two weeks prepared and sent to the printer the most complete report ever made of a National convention.[1]

The middle of May, after two years' interruption, Miss Anthony and Mrs. Stanton set themselves diligently to finish the third volume of the History of Woman Suffrage, all the boxes and trunks of material having been shipped from Tenafly. Although submerged in the avalanche of old documents, Miss Anthony's mind was full of current events. She writes in her journal June 2 : " I wait with bated breath the news from Oregon, where today the men are voting on the question of woman's enfranchisement. My heart almost stands stills. I hope against hope, but still I hope." When the news of the defeat comes, she says : " Dear Mrs. Duniway, with all that debt left on her shoulders, which she assumed to carry on the campaign ! I felt so agonized for her that on the very day of election I rushed to the bank and sent her $100. We must not leave her to carry it alone, after all her brave work. I have written a dozen letters to friends asking them to give her assistance. I feel like a lion champing the bars of his cage, shut up here digging and delving among the records of the past when I long to be out doing the

---

[1] Miss Anthony's letters show how desirous she was that everybody who assisted at these conventions should have full measure of credit: "They are earnest and anxious to do for woman's cause and I want them treated fairly and leniently as to all mistakes." Again she writes: "Since Oregon was never before represented in our conventions, her speakers must have more room in the report than we old stagers."

work of the present." In a letter received from Senator Palmer at this time he says :

I fully sympathize with your regret and chagrin over the reverse in Oregon but hardly with your conclusion, viz., that "the women should stop asking legislatures to submit this question to the electors, to have it killed by the majority, made up of ignorance and whiskey, native and foreign, and all go to Congress for success," etc. It seems to me that nothing is to be lost and much to be gained by local discussions and temporary defeats. You know in 1850 Webster, in his unfortunate Revere House speech, stigmatized the anti-slavery movement as "a rub-a-dub agitation," and Wendell Phillips closed his masterly philippic thereon with what was accepted as a motto: Agitate! Agitate!! Agitate!!! Another decade of that rub-a-dub agitation sufficed to divide the continent in a political earthquake and from out the chasm the negro emerged to citizenship. It may still require years to educate a majority of our women to demand the franchise and a majority of our men or their representatives in Congress and the legislatures, to proclaim it, but that the way leads through constant agitation I make no doubt. The still pool casts nothing to shore.

She watches events across the water and writes on July 7 : "Well, the House of Lords is today discussing whether 2,000,000 farm laborers shall have the ballot placed in their hands, while the half-million, more or less, women who employ them are left without it. What an outrage that Mr. Gladstone refused to allow Mr. Woodall's amendment to his bill to be at least voted upon! He applied the party whip and made voting for the woman suffrage amendment disloyalty to the government, and over one hundred Liberals, who had previously declared themselves in favor of women's sharing in this new extension of the franchise, voted against allowing them to do so. I do not believe a more humiliating abnegation of principle at the behest of a party leader ever was witnessed in our Congress."

The national political conventions in the summer of 1884 received the usual appeal to recognize the claims of women. The Republican, Democratic, Anti-Monopoly and Greenback parties equivocated, although the last two nominated Benjamin F. Butler, an avowed advocate of woman suffrage ; the Prohibition convention relegated the question to the States.[1] The American party put in a plank and nominated S. C. Pomeroy, a champion of woman suffrage, but it had too small a following to offer any hope of success. Blaine was not a friend, Logan was an earnest one ; Cleveland was not acceptable to many women, Hendricks had never shown himself favorable. In the midst of such a conglomeration the wise thing for all women would have been to remain non-partisan and take no share in the campaign. Miss Anthony and Mrs. Stanton, however, watching events from their secluded nook, issued a manifesto urging women to stand by the Republican party. They were led to take this action by the tendency of large numbers to rush to the support of the Prohibitionists, because of their suffrage plank ; and they believed that if women were determined to work for some political party, the Republican at that time held out most hope. This aroused the antagonism of the Prohibitionists and Democrats, both men and women, and afforded the strongest possible object lesson to Miss Anthony of the wisdom of henceforth adhering to her policy of non-partisanship until one of the *dominant* parties should declare unmistakably for woman suffrage and advocate it by means of press and platform.

[1] When Miss Anthony learned that this action had been taken with the sanction of Frances E. Willard, she pointed out to her in vigorous language how the Prohibition-Republicans had left that party this year because a temperance resolution had failed in the platform committee and had gone over to the Prohibition party, charging that the Republicans were cowardly. Yet the very first act of this Prohibition convention, to which Miss Willard was a delegate, was to abandon the idea of National Supremacy and accept that of State Rights in order to conciliate the southern members. She further said: "When the time comes in which it will be political expediency for the Prohibition party to throw woman suffrage overboard altogether, over it will go." Miss Willard lived to see this prophecy fulfilled at the National Prohibition Convention of 1896.

In August occurred the death of Sarah Pugh, the gentle Quaker and staunch Abolitionist, her old and faithful friend. It was followed by that of Frances D. Gage a few months later; and in December passed away the true and helpful ally, William Henry Channing. Each left a void in her heart, and yet the memory of these great souls impelled to renewed effort. There was no cessation of the work on the History, which was slowly evolved through the heat of summer and the beautiful days of early autumn, but by the end of October the funds were exhausted, the money left by Mrs. Eddy was still in litigation, and Miss Anthony again went on the lecture platform, speaking almost every night through November and December.

She did not fail, however, to look carefully after the interests of the Seventeenth National Convention which met as usual in Washington, January 20, 1885. A letter from Clarina Howard Nichols was sent to be read at this meeting, but the hand which penned it was stilled in death before it was received. Of all the pioneer workers with whom Miss Anthony had been associated in the early days so full of scorn, ridicule and abuse, Mrs. Nichols was among the nearest and dearest, a forceful speaker and writer, a tender, loving woman. It was in this convention that the resolution denouncing dogmas and creeds was introduced by Mrs. Stanton, and caused much commotion and heated argument. Miss Anthony opposed it, saying:

I object to the words "derived from Judaism." It does not matter where the dogma came from. I was on the old Garrison platform, and found long ago that the settling of any question of human rights by people's interpretation of the Bible is utterly impossible. I hope we shall not go back to that war. We all know what we want, and that is the recognition of woman's perfect equality. We all admit that such recognition never has been granted in the centuries of the past; but for us to begin a discussion here as to who established this injustice would be anything but profitable. Let those who wish go back into their history, but I beg it shall not be done on our platform.[1]

[1] Apropos of this discussion, an amusing anecdote is related of Miss Anthony. When confronted, in an argument, with the passage of scripture, "Wives, submit yourselves unto your own husbands," etc., she replied: "Gentlemen, no one objects to the husband being the head of the wife as Christ was the head of the church—to crucify himself; what we object to is his crucifying his wife."

The public, which always longed for a sensation at these suffrage conventions and was disappointed if it did not come, seized upon this resolution, and press and pulpit made it a text.   The following Sunday W. W. Patton, D. D., president of Howard University, preached in the Congregational church of Washington a sermon entitled, "Woman and Skepticism." He took the ground that as soon as women depart from their natural sphere they become skeptical if not immoral.   He gave as examples Hypatia, Madame Roland, Harriet Martineau, Frances Power Cobbe and George Eliot!   Then turning his attention to America he said that "the recent convention of woman suffragists gave evidence of atheism and immorality," and that "Victoria Woodhull was the representative of the movement in this country."[1]   And this when Mrs. Woodhull had not been on the suffrage platform for thirteen years!   Miss Anthony and Mrs. Stanton occupied front seats and at the close of the sermon went forward, shook hands with the preacher and Miss Anthony remarked earnestly :   "Doctor, your mother, if you have one, should lay you across her knee and give you a good spanking for that sermon."   "O, no," said Mrs. Stanton quickly, "allow me to congratulate you.   I have been trying for years to make women understand that the worst enemy they have is in the pulpit, and you have illustrated the truth of it."   Then, while the great divine was trying to recover his breath, they walked out of the church.   The nine days' commotion which this produced can be imagined better than described.   After some reflection Miss Anthony regretted that she should have been provoked into her remark, but Mrs. Stanton wrote :   "Don't worry a moment.   The more I think about it, the better I like it, because it was the most contemptuous thing which could have been said.   Like that shot at Lexington, it will go round the world."

On February 6, Thomas W. Palmer called up in the Senate the resolution for a Sixteenth Amendment and supported it by that masterly speech which ever since has been one of the

---

[1] This account of the sermon is taken from the reports of half a dozen reputable newspapers.

strongest suffrage campaign documents. At the request of Miss Anthony thousands of copies were sent out under his frank. She went from Washington to Boston to attend a meeting of the National branch of the Massachusetts association, and soon afterwards, on March 2, started for the New Orleans Exposition. She was warmly welcomed by Mrs. Caroline E. Merrick, wife of Judge E. T. Merrick, at whose lovely home she was entertained during part of her stay. It was her first visit to the Crescent City and she was soon deluged with invitations to speak and received many charming tokens of the justly-famed southern hospitality.

She spoke before the Woman's Club in the hall of the Continental Guards, with May Wright Sewall, representative from Indiana; gave seven addresses, in as many days, before schools and colleges and, by invitation of the Press Association, spoke in Agricultural Hall at the exposition and visited the headquarters of the different papers. The next day, by request of Commissioner Truman, she gave an address and held a reception at the New York headquarters. Her last appearance was at Tulane Hall under the auspices of the teachers of the city schools. She was everywhere beautifully received, although her doctrines were new and unpopular, and at the close of each meeting her audience crowded about her with words of appreciation and cordiality. Miss Anthony here met for the first time "Catherine Cole," of the editorial staff, and Mrs. Eliza J. Nicholson, owner and manager of the Picayune. The latter presented her with an Indian basket filled to overflowing with orange blossoms, and this tribute was paid in her paper:

THE APOSTLE OF WOMAN'S RIGHTS.—Miss Susan B. Anthony has made a most favorable impression upon the New Orleans public, and has by her gentleness and courtesy won many friends for herself and her cause. She came here a total stranger, and recognized the fact that there were many who did not approve of her or her doctrines. She has been sincere, truly polite and simply womanly in all her dealings with the southern people, and by these very qualities has commanded the respectful esteem of all. Miss Anthony has not striven to make herself "solid" with the people who give the best dinners. . . . The workingwoman, the unfashionable woman, have been made as heartily welcome as the leader of society; and for their appreciation they have been repaid by the friendship and esteem of one of the grandest old maids that ever lived.

The Times-Democrat and Daily States also gave full and favorable reports of her visit and lectures. The two weeks allowed for this holiday sped quickly away and Miss Anthony left for the North on March 20, laden with luncheon, flowers and many tokens of affection from the women of New Orleans. At Marshall, Tex., she dined with President and Mrs. Culver, of Bishops' University, and reached St. Louis Sunday evening, where she was the guest of her nephew, Arthur A. Mosher, and his wife. The next four or five weeks were spent in the lecture field at hard work, under the management of the Slayton Bureau. In answer to her letter of regret at not meeting Mrs. J. Ellen Foster at an Iowa convention, as she had requested, Mrs. Foster wrote: "I was sorry enough not to see you but I gave the people your message in the evening. Dear soul, how long you have stood for the truth delivered unto you! God bless your words and works. I do not see creeds and dogmas just as you see them, I do not believe in all that you do, but I believe in you!"

The last of April came the long-expected summons to Boston to receive the legacy of Mrs. Eddy, the courts having sustained the will. While eastward bound, crossing the State of Illinois, newspapers were brought on the train announcing the death of Grant, and she writes: "The weather is lovely and springlike today, but how still and solemn it seems out here on these broad prairies with that great general gone forever!" The case had been in litigation three years, Benjamin F. Butler appearing for Miss Anthony and Lucy Stone. His fees were very reasonable but several thousand dollars were swallowed up in the suit. The legacy, in first-class securities, stocks, bonds, etc., was paid April 27, each receiving $24,125.[1] Miss Anthony gives an amusing account, in one of her letters, of the awful nightmare she had on board the sleeper

---

[1] This is the only instance where a woman has bequeathed a large amount of money to the cause of equal rights, although a number of small bequests have been made. Women have given millions of dollars to churches, charities, and colleges for men but comparatively nothing to secure freedom for those of their own sex.

going home, when she dreamed that a woman was at the head of her berth stifling her while a man knelt in front, his hand cautiously creeping toward the inside pocket where she had sewed the money and bonds. She awoke with a scream and did not go to sleep again.

If this bequest had been left to Miss Anthony for her own personal use, she could not have felt one-half the joy she now experienced in having the means to carry on the work which always had been so seriously impeded for lack of funds. Of course its receipt was heralded far and wide by the papers, and appeals began to pour in from all sides, nor were they always appeals, but often demands. Scores of women considered themselves entitled to a share because the money had been left to further the cause of woman. One wanted it to help lift a mortgage on her home, others to educate their children, to pay a debt, to reward them for the valuable services they had given to woman suffrage, to start a paper, to carry one already started, and so on without end. The men also were willing to relieve her of a portion. "I am terribly oppressed by it all," Miss Anthony writes, "and nothing would make me happier than to respond to every one, but my money would melt away in a month." It was ludicrous and yet pitiful to see certain persons who had repudiated her in days gone by because she was too radical and too aggressive, discovering all at once how much they always had valued her and how anxious they had been for a long time to renew the old friendship—the common story, ancient as the world.

The one thing she was determined to do first of all was to complete the History of Woman Suffrage, upon which she and Mrs. Stanton had spent all the days that could be spared for nearly ten years. The work had been delayed by the many other demands upon their time, by their trips abroad, but more than all else by lack of money. The authors were to pay for composition, stereotyping, the making of the plates for the engravings and the printing of the same; Fowler & Wells for the paper, press-work, binding and advertising. Miss Anthony and her co-workers were to receive only 12½ per cent. commission on the sales. It readily may be seen that she did not go into this as a money-making scheme. Her only thought, her only desire, was to collect the facts in connection with the movement to secure the rights of women, before they should be scattered and lost, and to preserve and put them into shape for reference.

In preparing the first two volumes she had used every dollar she had been able to earn and all she could obtain from generous friends, and there were still large unpaid bills. Now, with plenty of money at her command, she bought out the rights of Fowler & Wells, and engaged Charles Mann, of Rochester, to print the third volume. Mrs. Stanton had returned to Tenafly, and there Miss Anthony again sent all the trunks and boxes of precious documents. She completed her lecture engagements and the first of June, 1885, found the two women once more hard at work.

"I really think of you with pity these hot midsummer days," wrote Mrs. Sewall to Mrs. Stanton, "under the lash of blessed Susan's relentless energy; but the reflection that she applies it with the most vigor to her own back enables one to regard that instrument, after all, with more admiration than terror." It was indeed true that Mrs. Stanton's luxury and ease-loving nature required much urging,[1] and while Miss Anthony took upon herself all the drudgery possible and all the financial anxiety and burden, she was compelled to keep Mrs. Stanton keyed up to do a great portion of the literary work. "It is the one drawback at every turn," she writes, "that I have not the faculty to frame easy, polished sentences. If I could but do this, I would finish up the History without asking aid of any one." And again: "It has been the bane of my life that I am powerless to put on paper the glimpses of thoughts which come and go like flashes of lightning." As has been said before in these pages, she is a perfect critic and delightful letter-writer, but finds difficulty in doing what is called "literary work." Practice undoubtedly would have enabled her to

---

[1] In one of Miss Anthony's letters she relates with amusement that Mr. Stanton had just come in and, seeing his wife lying on the couch, remarked, "Ah, resting, I see." "No," she replied, "I am exercising by lying down."

MISS ANTHONY AND MRS. STANTON.

WRITING THE HISTORY OF WOMAN SUFFRAGE.

overcome this, but she felt always that her chief strength lay in executive ability.

Early in June Miss Anthony slipped away from the work long enough to go to the Progressive Friends' meeting at Kennett Square, Penn., where she was the guest of Deborah Pennock and met, for the first time, Sarah J. Eddy. In her diary she says: "Last evening as I sat on the sofa Miss Eddy put her arms around me and said, 'I am so glad I love you; I should have felt very sorry if I had not.' And so should I, for the sake of her dear mother and grandfather, who had so much confidence in me." The two went on to New York together and then over to Mrs. Stanton's for a little visit, and the friendship formed at that time has been maintained ever since. Later when Miss Eddy was going to Rochester to a convention, Miss Anthony wrote Mrs. Hallowell: "I am sure you would be glad to entertain her; she is a sweet, lovely little woman; thoroughly sympathizing with everything and everybody that suffers injustice. I am very sorry that sister Mary and I must be away and can not have the dear girl with us."

Miss Anthony experienced a great disadvantage in being so far away from her publisher, the more especially as she had to send a chapter at a time, read proofs of each as soon as it was set up, send back corrected proof, get the revises, etc., and she soon found it necessary to spend about half her time in Rochester. The women who were preparing the chapters for their respective States delayed the work, neglecting to send them when promised; many occupied twice as much space as had been assigned them and were highly indignant when Mrs. Stanton used the blue pencil unsparingly on their productions. They vented their feelings on Miss Anthony, knowing that nothing they could say would ruffle Mrs. Stanton's equipoise, and she writes in her diary: "To decide between the two has almost torn me in twain. People who can write are so tenacious, each thinking her own style better than any other, while poor I don't know which is the best."

Every few weeks she was obliged to rush over to Fayetteville to confer with Mrs. Gage, who was industriously preparing her part of the work. Urgent appeals came from women in Michigan, Minnesota, Wisconsin, Kansas and Indiana that they could not possibly make a success of their State conventions unless she came to their assistance, but she steeled her heart against them and stuck closely to her task. From the lecture bureau came a list of ten engagments at $50 a night, but she refused them. Some of the expressions in her letters of those busy days show the state of her mind better than could volumes of description :

All the work of today put aside to grope into the old past. I feel like rushing to you this very minute, but here Mrs. Stanton and I are, scratching, scratching every hour, not each other's eyes but the History papers. I am a fish out of water. . . . It makes me feel growly all the time. . . . I can not get away from my ball and chain. . . . I think we'll make things snap and crackle a little. . . . This is the biggest swamp I ever tried to wriggle through. . . . We'll both put on our thinking caps and I guess get quite a lot of funnies in the reminiscences. . . . Now here is the publisher's screech for money. . . . O, to get out of this History prison! . . . . I am too tired to write—I mean too lazy. . . No warhorse ever panted for the rush of battle more than I for outside work. I love to make history but hate to write it.

On November 12 Mrs. Stanton's seventieth birthday was celebrated by a large reception held in the parlors of Dr. Lozier in New York, where Mrs. Stanton read a charming paper on "The Pleasures of Old Age." Her daughter, Harriot Stanton Blatch, sent the following bright and breezy message :

. . . How I wish I could give my congratulations in the flesh! Distance is the foe of love. Kiss dear Susan and let her kiss you for me. On November 12 I shall think of you both, for you two are not easily separated in my mind, and there will be a tenderness in my thoughts and a thankfulness that you both have lived. In your worries over the History, remember that at least one woman appreciates the fact that her life has been made easier because of your combined public work. You ought to be overflowing with gratitude for each other's existence, for neither without the other would have achieved the work you have accomplished. Every day of your lives let your hearts praise the good fortune that brought you together. Friendship is the grandest relation in the world, and I feel infinitely blessed in having two such women as friends. You and dear Susan are not yet to be sainted; you have no end of work in you still, and must labor on for many a long year, and gain many a triumphant victory. I throw up my cap and cry hurrah for you two grand old warriors! The curl is from Nora's little head. She shall be taught to reverence her Queen Mother and Maid of Honor Susan. Now farewell, dear ladies; I am wishing you on birthdays and every day a long and happy life.

The next morning came the cablegram announcing the sudden death in Switzerland of the mother of Julia and Rachel Foster. Miss Anthony dropped all work when the sisters arrived at New York, went with them to Philadelphia and rendered every possible consolation and assistance. But not even to go to Washington to push the work in Congress and arrange for the National Convention would she delay the task she was so anxious to finish. She wrote scores of letters, however, in regard to both, and the congressmen particularly had reason to feel that she had not forgotten their promises. Her long and persistent labors were rewarded, for the close of 1885 found the whole third volume of the History in the hands of the printers.

CHAPTER XXXIV.

1886—1887.

MISS ANTHONY started for Washington toward the last of January, 1886, with a lighter heart than she had possessed for many years. The dreadful burden of the labor on the History was lifted, all the bills were paid, she had given a helping hand to several of the old workers, which made her very happy, and she had one or two good dresses in her trunk. There was nothing which the paragrapher who hated what Miss Anthony represented, liked so well as to make disagreeable flings at her clothes, and yet it is an indisputable fact of history that she was one of the most perfectly dressed women on the platform, although her tastes were very plain and simple. A lady once wrote her asking if it would not be possible to make the suffrage conventions a little more æsthetic, they were so painfully practical. She sent the letter to Mrs. Stanton, who commented : "Well now, perhaps if we could paint injustice in delicate tints set in a framework of poetical argument, we might more easily entrap the Senator Edmunds and Oscar Wilde types of Adam's sons. Suppose at our next convention all of us dress in pale green, have a faint and subdued gaslight with pink shades, write our speeches in verse and chant them to a guitar accompaniment. Ah me! alas! how can we reform the world æsthetically ?"

The members of Congress always knew when Miss Anthony had arrived in Washington. Other women accepted their word that they were going to do something, and waited patiently at home. Miss Anthony followed them up and saw that they

(605)

did it. If she could not find them at the Capitol, she went to their homes. If they promised to introduce a certain measure on a certain day, she was in the gallery looking them squarely in the face. If they failed to do it, they found her waiting for them at the close of the session. Senator Blair wrote this humorous note January 15: "I thought just as likely as not you would come fussing round before I got your amendment reported to the Senate. I wish you would go home. Cockrell has agreed to let me know soon whether he won't allow the report to be made right off without any bother, and I have been to him several times before. I don't see what you want to meddle for, anyway. Go off and get married!"

I hope you will live always in this world, Heaven has got more than it's hare of good people already.

Sincerly & Respectfully
Henry W. Blair.

Miss Anthony has been directly connected with every action taken by Congress or by any congressional committee on the question of woman suffrage. There are on file among her papers hundreds of letters from members during the past thirty years, showing her energy and persistence in compelling attention to this subject, in learning who were its friends, in attempting to convert the doubters and in spurring the believers to effort. This is something for the women of the future to remember.

The Eighteenth Annual Convention opened February 17. Prominent features were a fine address by Rev. Rush R. Shippen, of All Souls church, and the first appearance on the platform of Mary F. Eastman, Ada C. Sweet, the pension agent, the eloquent southern speakers, Mrs. Elizabeth A. Meriwether and Mrs. Sallie Clay Bennett, and the talented German, Madame Clara Neymann. Among many letters was one from George W. Childs to Miss Anthony, saying: "I am always glad to hear from you and I keep track of your continued good work. Do not be discouraged. I take pleasure in sending the enclosed check ($100) with my sincere regards and very best wishes."

The crowds were so great that policemen had to be stationed at the door to prevent late comers from trying to enter during the evening sessions. The resolutions scored the bill before Congress proposing to disfranchise all Utah women, both Gentile and Mormon, to punish the crime of polygamy. The usual hearing was granted before the congressional committees. The fight for woman suffrage in the Forty-ninth Congress was conducted by Ezra B. Taylor, of Ohio, who prepared the favorable minority report of the House Judiciary Committee. The adverse majority report was signed by John Randolph Tucker, of Virginia.

On March 25 "the general" slipped up to New York City, to assist her forces at the State convention, and then hastened back to Washington to direct the main line of attack. The diary says:

March 30.—Went to House of Representatives, saw Messrs. Tucker and Taylor of judiciary committee; both promised to report soon. Then went to Senate, saw Messrs. Blair, Stanford and Bowen; all agreed to work to bring up our bill by May 1. In the evening took a cab and went in a pouring rain to Senator Stanford's, where I spent an hour. How keen and true are his perceptions in regard to public questions!

March 31.—Pouring rain, dark and muggy. I went to the Senate; sat with Mrs. Dolph and Mrs. Stanford; heard Senator Dolph's fine speech on the admission of Washington Territory as a State and his splendid word for woman suffrage. Mrs. Dolph took me home in her carriage.

April 1.—Went to the Senate again to secure pledges for votes and speeches for the Sixteenth Amendment Bill. Got Senator Dolph's strongest paragraphs, and at 8 P. M. went to the top floor of the Associated Press rooms and gave them to Mr. Boynton, who sent them over the wires.

April 9.—The United States Senate today voted down Eustis' motion to refuse to admit Washington Territory unless the woman suffrage clause were eliminated from its constitution, 25 to 12. Senator Ingalls was the only Republican who voted with the enemy.

A few days later Miss Anthony received the following from Mrs. Caroline E. Merrick, of New Orleans: ". . . I feel defrauded that I never knew you until last year. Judge Merrick says you are the most sensible person he ever met (without any sex qualifications, of course). Like you, I was indignant at Mr. Eustis in regard to his course toward Washington Territory. I was ashamed and blushed for my Louisiana senator that time. Thanks for your sympathy in my illness. When my head lies low I pray that you may find another and even better friend in my State, who will come to the front in the cause of equal rights for women." An extract from a letter of Rev. Olympia Brown to Mrs. Stanton shows how much the old workers as well as the young depended upon Miss Anthony: "I wish to inquire what has become of Susan? You know she is my North Star. I take all my bearings from her, and when I lose sight of her I wander helplessly, uncertain of my course."

The diary of April 30 says: "Heard Phœbe Couzins had been taken to Hot Springs, terribly crippled with rheumatism. Wrote her at once and enclosed $100, telling her I wanted it used to provide delicacies and make her comfortable. I have thought it would be Phœbe whom I should take with me on my southern tour next year, but I fear her work is done."

By the middle of May, 1886, the last bit of History proof was read, and unlimited leave of absence was granted Miss Anthony by her publisher, while the indexer and binder completed the work which was begun in 1876. On the 19th she started for Kansas, stopping for the usual visit in Chicago with her cousins. In Kansas she visited her brothers at Leavenworth and Fort Scott for nearly two months, making an oc-

*I am thine
ever faithfully and affectionately
Caroline E. Merrick*

casional speech. On the morning of July 4, under the auspices of the W. C. T. U., she addressed a large audience at Salina on, "The powerlessness of woman so long as she is dependent on man for bread." In the hot afternoon, as she was about to enjoy a nap, word came that a hundred people had united in a request that she should speak again, as they had come from ten to twenty miles on purpose to hear her; so she returned to the grove, and Mrs. Griffith, State evangelist, kindly yielded her hour. On July 11 Miss Anthony went again to Chicago, and on the 14th spoke at Lake Bluff Camp Meeting, which was under the management of Frances E. Willard. She then visited the summer homes of her cousins and of Elizabeth Boynton Harbert, at Lake Geneva. On this trip she was accompanied by her dearly-loved niece, Susie B., who went with her to Rochester and spent the summer. The diary briefly records:

September 28.—Left Chicago at noon and lunched with Miss Willard at Rest Cottage, Evanston. Her mother bright and charming at eighty-two, and Anna Gordon sweet as ever. It was very good to see Miss Willard under her own roof. Reached Racine in time for the State convention, was met by a delegation of ladies and taken to the home of Martha Parker Dingee, niece of the great Theodore Parker, a lovely woman. Fine audiences.

October 2.—Reached St. Louis at 8 A. M. As I was looking for my trunk I heard some one cry out, "Is that you, Susan?" and there were Phœbe Couzins and her father. I had made my trip that way for the special purpose of seeing her, expecting to find her confined to the house; so I went home and breakfasted with them.

October 4.—Reached Leavenworth and found Mrs. Colby and Mrs. Saxon ready to begin the campaign for arousing public sentiment to demand a bill from the next legislature to secure Municipal suffrage for women. Dr. Ruth M. Wood is the mainspring of the movement here.

This series of conventions was held in the congressional districts from October 5 to November 3, Mrs. Laura M. Johns, manager, assisted by Mrs. Anna C. Wait, president of the State Association, and by a number of capable and energetic Kansas women at each place visited. Under date of October 11, Miss Anthony wrote to eastern friends: "We are having the loveliest weather you ever dreamed of and the most mag-

ANT.—39

nificent audiences—no church or hall holding them. If our legislators, State or national, could only see these gatherings and look into the earnest faces of these people, coming so many miles in wagons to see and hear and get fresh courage, they would surely answer our demands by something else than silence.'' The press corroborated this description and the following special dispatch may be taken as a fair specimen :

The seventh district convention, the third of the series, has just closed in Lincoln, and was a beautiful ovation to Miss Anthony. Crowded houses greeted her—every available foot of space filled with chairs, window-sills utilized for seats, and conveyances drawn up outside of windows and filled with listeners. People came thirty, forty and fifty miles in buggies and wagons to shake hands with the pioneer suffragist. Grizzly-headed opposers succumbed to Miss Anthony's logic and came up to grasp her hand and say God bless her, and proved the depth of their fervor by generous financial aid to the cause she so ably represents. It is seldom that the beginner of a great reform lives to see such fruitage of her labors as does she. People often descant upon the indifference of women to the question of their own enfranchisement and to political matters generally; but there is serious doubt of greater interest ever having been shown by men in political meetings than women exhibit in these conventions. . . .

On the evening of the second day the house was so densely packed that a messenger for a glass of water had to go out through a window. But in spite of all discomfort and the many standing, the audience maintained perfect order and gave the utmost attention throughout Miss Anthony's speech of two hours. Learning that she would remain in Lincoln over Sunday the people importuned her to speak that afternoon in the Presbyterian church, which she did to a large audience.

The diary relates: ''A mother brought her four-weeks-old girl baby twenty-five miles in a carriage, so she might tell it, when grown, that Susan B. Anthony had taken it in her arms. 'And the trip has not hurt baby a particle,' she said brightly.'' And again it tells, with a good deal of gusto, that one Baptist minister was determined the suffrage speakers should not have his church and only yielded after several of the richest pew-holders declared they never would pay another dollar towards his salary if he did not. He then made his appearance at the meeting, opened it with his blessing and closed it with his benediction! Miss Anthony was not always able to speak to her own satisfaction. At Salina she lectured for the Y. M. C. A. and writes : "I went to the opera house and found a fine audience. Tried to give 'Moral Influence vs. Political Power,' but the spirit wouldn't soar; its wings flapped on the earth perpetually for the whole hour. I took my $25 from the treasurer and went home with a heavy heart. It is beyond my knowledge why, after speaking every day for a whole week, freely and decently, my wits should desert me and my tongue be tied just at the time when I am most anxious to do my best."

Two days' meetings were held at Abilene, Florence, Hutchinson, Wichita, Anthony, Winfield, Independence, Lawrence and Fort Scott. The speakers were entertained by prominent families, suffrage societies were formed at each place, the vast majority of public sentiment seemed favorable, and the collections paid all the expenses of the conventions.

In November and December a number of other speakers made a canvass of the State, and the following winter the legislature passed a bill conferring Municipal suffrage upon the women of Kansas. The bill was introduced in the Senate by R. W. Blue (Rep.) of Linn county; and in the House by T. T. Taylor (Rep.) of Reno county. It passed the Senate, 25 ayes, all Republicans; 13 noes, 10 Republicans and 3 Democrats; in the House 90 ayes, 84 Republicans and 6 Democrats; 21 noes, 5 Republicans and 16 Democrats. The bill was signed by Governor John A. Martin, February 15, 1887; and under its provisions women in that State have voted ever since at Municipal elections.[1]

Without a day's rest, Miss Anthony went direct from Kansas to Sandwich, Ill., to attend the State convention. After three days there and a Sunday in Chicago, Monday, November 8, found her at Racine, Wis., ready to begin a tour of conventions in every congressional district. That evening a reception was given her by Hon. and Mrs. M. B. Erskine, and the hospitality of their handsome home was offered for every day which she could spend in the city.

[1] Miss Anthony notes in her diary that she made her first Kansas campaign in '67 and the suffrage bill was signed on her sixty-seventh birthday. She received a letter of congratulation on the signing of the bill from Chief-Justice Horton, of Kansas.

With Mrs. Colby and Rev. Olympia Brown, assisted by local speakers, meetings were held at Waukesha, Ripon, Oshkosh, Green Bay, Grand Rapids, Eau Claire, LaCrosse, Evansville, Milwaukee and Madison.   At the last place the ladies spoke in the Senate chamber of the State House to an audience containing a number of dignitaries, among them President Bascom, of the State University, and his wife, who from this time were Miss Anthony's steadfast friends.   Mrs. Colby gives a graphic description of Miss Anthony's sudden outburst here, when several members had exasperated her by their remarks, which closes :   " I was writing at the secretary's desk and as I looked up I realized the full grandeur of the scene.   It was woman standing at the bar of the nation, pleading for the recognition of her citizenship.   Miss Anthony seemed positively Titanic as she leaned far over from the speaker's desk.   Her tone and manner were superb, and the vast and sympathetic audience caught the electric thrill. . . ."   In this city she was the guest of an old schoolmate, Elizabeth Ford Proudfit.   The meetings closed December 3, and Miss Anthony wrote Mrs. Spofford :

I intend now to make straight for Washington without a stop. I shall come both ragged and dirty. Think of two solid months of conventions, speaking every night! Don't worry about me. I was never better or more full of hope and good work. Though the apparel will be tattered and torn, the mind, the essence of me, is sound to the core. Please tell the little milliner to have a bonnet picked out for me, and get a dressmaker who will patch me together so I shall be presentable. Now for the Washington convention: Before settling upon the Universalist church, you would better pocket the insults and refusals of the Congregational church powers that be and send your most lovely and winning girls to ask for that. If you can't get it or the Metropolitan or the Foundry or the New York Avenue or any large and popular church, why take the Universalist, and then tell the saints of the fashionable churches that we dwell there because they refused us admission to their holy sanctuaries. Don't let us go into the heterodox houses, much as I love them, except because we are driven away from the orthodox.

In December the third volume of the History of Woman Suffrage at last was ready for the public, another book of nearly 1,000 pages.   It completed the story up to 1884, and like its predecessors was cordially received by the press.   The money swallowed up by this work hardly will be credited. Mrs. Stanton not being able or willing to revise the last volume until it was put into proof slips, and then making extensive changes, the cost for re-setting type was over $900. The fifty fine steel engravings and the prints made from them cost over $6,000. For proof reading $500 was paid, and for indexing, $250. Mrs. Stanton and Mrs. Gage, seeing that there never would be any profits from the books and that Miss Anthony proposed to give most of them away, sold out their rights to her, the former for $2,000 and the latter for $1,000. She also, as has been stated, bought out the interest of Fowler & Wells. When the first edition of the three mammoth volumes finally came into her sole possession, they represented an outlay on her part of $20,000.

While there were many criticisms from certain quarters as to various errors and so-called misstatements, and many threats to write a history which should be free from all imperfections, the fact remains that, although fifty years have passed since the inception of the great movement to secure equal rights for women, there never has been another attempt to preserve the story. But for Miss Anthony's careful collecting and saving of newspaper accounts, manuscripts of speeches, published reports and the correspondence of half a century, her persistent and determined effort for ten years to have them put into readable shape, and Mrs. Stanton's fine ability to do it, the student never would have been able to trace the evolution of woman from a chattel in the eye of the law to a citizen with legal and social rights very nearly equal to those of man. While there is necessarily some repetition, so long a time elapsing between the writing of the different volumes, and perhaps a little prolixity, there is not a dull page in the whole work and the reader will find it difficult to reach a place where she is willing to stop. It contains a resumé of early conditions; the persecutions endured by the pioneers in the struggle for freedom; the progress in each separate State, and in foreign countries; the action taken by different legislatures and congresses; the grand arguments made for equal rights; the position of woman in church and State.   Into whatever library the student may go seeking information upon this question, it is to these volumes he must look to find it in collected and connected form. If Miss Anthony had done no other work but to produce this History, she would deserve a prominent place on the list of immortal names.

It was necessary to put so high a price upon it, $15 a set in cloth and $19.50 in leather binding, as to make a large sale impossible.   Miss Anthony did not undertake it as a money-making scheme, and when the receipt of Mrs. Eddy's bequest enabled her to discharge all indebtedness connected with it, she felt herself at liberty to use it as a most valuable means of educating the people into an understanding of the broad principle of equality of rights.   At her own expense she placed the History in over 1,000 of the libraries of Europe and America, including the British Museum, the university libraries of Oxford, Edinburgh, Dublin, Paris, Berlin, Finland, Melbourne, Toronto, and many of the university and public libraries of the United States.   The members of the Senate and House Judiciary Committees in several Congresses were presented with sets, and there are hundreds of letters on file from prominent persons in England and this country acknowledging the receipt of the books.

Chapters might be made of commendatory letters received from officials, writers, public workers and friends in private life. A few specimens must suffice.   A letter from Senator H. B. Anthony to his "dear cousin," closed by saying: "The three volumes form a valuable history of the important enterprise in which you have borne so conspicuous and honorable a part, and you have added to the reputation of the name that we both bear."

Mary L. Booth, the gifted editor of Harper's Bazar, thus expressed her opinion of the work :

You and your colleagues have industriously placed on record a copious mass of documentary evidence which will be of the utmost value when the time arrives to sum up the final results. When this era comes, you will be foremost among the band of heroic pioneers who have endured discomfort, obloquy and privation of much that is dear to women for the sake of those who will profit by your labors while failing to recognize them. Posterity will do you this justice, whether your contemporaries do or not; but indeed, it is universally known to those with any knowledge of the facts, that among all the champions of women, none has been more distinguished for utter self-abnegation, single-heartedness and devotion to her life-work than Susan B. Anthony.

As you know, I have always felt the deepest interest in the elevation of women, which is synonymous with that of humanity, for man must be always on the plane of his wife, sister and mother. . . . The antagonism to political equality is rapidly disappearing, as it is beginning to be recognized that in politics, as in everything else, woman's help is needed, and the republic can not afford to have her stand aloof. But this phase of the subject has been so much misunderstood, both by men and women, that time is needed to clear away the mists of misconception which envelop it; and to prove that the co-operation of women in political life is not only just and expedient, but absolutely indispensable to the public weal.

I am now and always,

Yours faithfully,

Mary L. Booth.

No family in Rochester stood more steadfastly by Miss Anthony during all her long and eventful life than the Wilders—Carter, Samuel, Mrs. Maria Wilder Depuy and D. Webster. The last, in acknowledging the receipt of the books, wrote: "How much you have contributed to history in this grand publication! With woman as a part of humanity, what a revolution will be wrought! Changes everywhere—in social life, in morals, politics, business—and all for the better. In this world-revolution you have done a great work. My children are proud of the fact that you are my personal friend. I fully appreciate your gift. It will be a Bible in my home." From the philanthropist, Sarah B. Cooper, revered for her work in the kindergartens on the Pacific coast, came this tribute:

This book is the fruitage of all the years of your faith and work. It tells of the long preparation—the opening up of the forest; the blazing of the trail; the clearing of the underbrush; the deep sub-soiling; the lying fallow; the ploughing, sowing, harrowing, the patient tillage—and now comes the harvest. What courage, endurance, fidelity and faith! The pioneers of new thoughts and principles are the loneliest of mortals. Those who live ahead of their time must wait for the honors and plaudits of posterity to get their full meed of appreciation and reward. But after all, dear, honored friend, the richest reward of such a life as yours is *to have lived it.*

The History also was given to the libraries of those towns whose women would raise a certain amount towards various State suffrage campaigns, and in every possible way it always has been used for missionary work.[1]

The first week in 1887, in most inclement weather and against the protest of friends, Miss Anthony went all the way to Nebraska, to keep a promise to Mrs. Colby and other women of that State to attend their annual convention, January 7. She found a pleasant letter awaiting her at Lincoln, from her old friend, Mary Rogers Kimball, daughter of the noted Abolitionist, Nathaniel P. Rogers, and wife of the General Passenger Agent of the Union Pacific R. R., now living at Omaha, which closed: "How I wish you could come to us and rest a few days. Mr. Kimball would welcome you, as would every one of this household. You ought to make our home happy by coming once in a while. . . . Mother, who is able to walk a little and is interested in all you do and say,

---

[1] The total amount received from sales has been only $7,000. Now, however, in order to give the History the widest possible circulation, the price has been so reduced as to enable it to be placed in the hands of the reading public. It is the hope of Miss Anthony to publish the fourth volume in the year 1900, bringing the History up to that date.

sends her love and hopes to see you." She spoke at Chicago, January 13, in the First Methodist church, where she was introduced by the well-known Rev. H. W. Thomas.[1] She went from there to the Michigan convention at Lansing, January 14, and here was presented to the audience by Governor Cyrus G. Luce.

She reached Washington January 17, 1887, and rushed the preparations for the Nineteenth National Convention, which opened on the 25th at the Metropolitan M. E. church. Zerelda G. Wallace gave a noteworthy address; Senator Carey, of Wyoming, made an able speech and Mrs. Carey sat by Miss Anthony during the proceedings. The second day of the convention, January 26, marked a great epoch, the first vote ever taken in Congress on a Sixteenth Amendment. The previous month, December 8, 1886, Henry W. Blair had asked the Senate to consider the following joint resolution : "The rights of citizens of the United States to vote shall not be denied or abridged by the United States or by any State on account of sex." He supported this in a long and comprehensive speech covering the whole ground on which the demand is based, quoting from the favorable reports of the judiciary committees, exposing the weakness and fallacy of the objections, and making an unanswerable argument on the justice of granting political liberty to women.

At the urgent request of opposing senators the matter had been postponed until January 25, when it was again called up by Mr. Blair. The opposition was led by Joseph A. Brown, of Georgia, who described in detail the intentions of the Creator when he made woman, and declared that females had not the physical strength to perform military duty, build railroads, raise crops, sit on juries or attend night caucuses, but that

---

[1] At this meeting a yellow dog came on the platform and Miss Anthony is quoted as afterwards making this apt comment: "She says that, at least where women are concerned, the reporters are sure to seize upon some triviality and ring its changes to the exclusion of serious matters. She mentioned that when she spoke in Chicago last a dog ran across the stage and, springing up, laid his nose on her shoulder. 'I prophesied to the audience then,' she continued, 'that the dog would figure in the press reports more conspicuously than anything that was said or done, and so he did. He occupied half of the space in nearly every paper.'"

God had endowed men with strength and faculties for all these things. He stated that it was a grave mistake to say that woman is taxed without being represented, and added, "It is very doubtful whether the male or the female sex has more influence in the administration of the affairs of government and the enactment of laws!" He asserted that "the baser class of females would rush to the polls, and this would compel the intelligent, virtuous and refined females, including wives and mothers, to relinquish for a time their God-given trust and go, contrary to their wishes, to the polls and vote to counteract the other class;" and followed this by saying that "the ignorant female voters would be at the polls en masse, while the refined and educated, shrinking from public contact, would remain at home." He continued: "The ballot will not protect females against the tyranny of bad husbands, as the latter will compel them to vote as they dictate;" then in the next breath he declared: "Wives will form political alliances antagonistic to the husbands, and the result will be discord and divorce." In his entire speech Senator Brown ignored the existence of unmarried women and widows. He closed with copious extracts from "Letters from a Chimney Corner," written by some Chicago woman.

Senator Dolph, of Oregon, followed in a clear, concise argument, brushing away these sophistries by showing that such evils did not exist where women were enfranchised and voted at every election. He was interrupted by Senator Eustis, of Louisiana, who inquired whether he thought "it would be a decent spectacle to take a mother away from her nursing infant and lock her up all night with a jury?" Senator Dolph replied that there was not a judge in the world who would not excuse a woman under such circumstances, just as there were many causes which exempted men. He continued:

Government is but organized society. . . . It can only derive its just powers from the consent of the governed, and can be established only under a fundamental law which is self-imposed. Every citizen of suitable age and discretion has, in my judgment, a natural right to participate in its formation. The fathers of the republic enunciated the doctrine "that all men are created

equal; that they are endowed by their Creator with certain inalienable rights."
It is strange that any one in this enlightened age should be found to contend
that this is true only of men, and that a man is endowed by his Creator with
inalienable rights not possessed by a woman. The lamented Lincoln immor-
talized the expression that ours is a government "of the people, by the people, and for the people," and yet in reality it is far from that. There can be no
government by the people where half of them are allowed no voice in its
organization and control. . . . God speed the day when not only in all
the States of the Union and in all the Territories, but everywhere, woman
shall stand before the law freed from the last shackle which has been riveted
upon her by tyranny, and the last disability which has been imposed upon her
by ignorance; not only in respect to the right of suffrage, but in every other
respect the peer and equal of her brother, man.

Senator Vest, of Missouri, came to the rescue of Senator
Brown and in the course of his speech said :

I pity the man who can consider any question affecting the influence of
woman, with the cold, dry logic of business. What man can, without aversion, turn from the blessed memory of that dear old grandmother, or the
gentle words and caressing hand of that blessed mother gone to the unknown
world, to face in its stead the idea of a female justice of the peace or township constable ? For my part, I want when I go to my home—when I turn
from the arena where man contends with man for what we call the prizes of
this paltry world—I want to go back, not to be received in the masculine em-
brace of some female ward politician, but to the earnest, loving look and
touch of a true woman. I want to go back to the jurisdiction of the wife, the
mother; and instead of a lecture upon finance or the tariff, or upon the construction of the Constitution, I want those blessed, loving details of domestic
life and domestic love.

I have said I would not speak of the inconveniences to arise from woman
suffrage. I care not whether the mother is called upon to decide as a jury-
man, or a jurywoman, rights of property or rights of life, whilst her baby is
"mewling and puking" in solitary confinement at home. There are other
considerations more important, and one of them to my mind is insuperable.
I speak now respecting women as a sex. I believe that they are better than
men, but I do not believe they are adapted to the political work of this world.
I do not believe that the Great Intelligence ever intended them to invade the
sphere of work given to men, tearing down and destroying all the best influences for which God has intended them. The great evil in this country today
is emotional suffrage. Women are essentially emotional. What we want in

this country is to avoid emotional suffrage, and what we need is to put more logic into public affairs and less feeling.[1]

He presented a remonstrance against giving the ballot to women, signed by nearly 200 New England men, headed by President Eliot, of Harvard University, and including nearly fifty names prefixed by "Rev." He next drew from his budget a letter from Clara T. Leonard, of Boston, praying that the suffrage should not be granted to women, and Mr. Hoar remarked that the lady herself had been holding public office for a number of years.

Continuing Senator Vest said: "If we are to tear down all the blessed traditions, if we are to desolate our homes and firesides, if we are to unsex our mothers, wives and sisters, and turn our blessed temples of domestic peace into ward political assembly rooms, pass this joint resolution!" He now produced a document, entitled "The Law of Woman Life," and said: "This is signed Adeline D. T. Whitney— I can not say whether she be wife or mother. It contains not one impure or unintellectual aspiration. Would to God that I knew her so I could thank her in behalf of the society and politics of the United States. I shall ask that it be printed, as my strength does not suffice for me to read it."[2] It proved to be a long and involved essay begging that the ballot should not be given to women, and saying: "Are the daughters and granddaughters about to leap the fence, leave their own realm little cared for, undertake the whole scheme of outside creation, or contest it with the men? Then God help the men! God save the commonwealth!" Mr. Vest concluded with a blood-curdling picture of the French Revolution which would be repeated in this country if women were enfranchised.

Senator Blair then offered the appeal of the W. C. T. U. for the ballot, representing over 200,000 women, presented by Zerelda G. Wallace, who had reared thirteen children and grand-

---

[1] Both Senator Vest and Senator Brown had appealed wholly to the emotions in their speeches upon this question, which were overflowing with sentiment and "gush."

[2] This hardly corresponds with Senator Brown's glowing description of the physical strength conferred by the Creator on man so that he could do the voting for the family.

children, among them the author of Ben Hur. He submitted also the matchless arguments which had been made by the most intellectual women of the nation before the congressional committees from year to year, including that of Miss Anthony in 1880, and urged that the question should be submitted to the legislatures of the various States for settlement.

The vote was taken on the question of submitting a Sixteenth Amendment to the Constitution to the State legislatures for ratification, and resulted in 16 yeas and 34 nays, 26 absent.[1] Of the affirmative votes, all were Republican ; of the negative, 24 Democratic and 10 Republican. Senator Farwell, of Illinois, was roundly denounced by the Chicago Tribune for his affirmative vote. Senators Chace, Dawes and Stanford, who were paired, and Plumb, who was absent, announced publicly that they would have voted "aye."

Over fifty of the distinguished women in attendance at the convention were in the Senate gallery during this debate. The most sanguine of them had not expected the necessary two-thirds, but had worked to obtain a vote simply for the prestige of a discussion in the Senate, the printing of the speeches in the Congressional Record and the wide agitation of the question through the medium of press and platform which was sure to follow. They felt especially incensed at Senator Ingalls, as the sentiment of his State had just shown itself to be overwhelmingly in favor of woman suffrage, and they did not hesitate to score him in public and in private. As soon as the news of the vote reached the convention Miss Anthony roundly denounced him from the platform. In the evening she received a note from him saying : "Will you do me the favor to designate an hour at which it would be convenient for you to give me a brief interview ? " She did not answer, and on the

[1] *Yeas:* Blair, Bowen, Cheney, Conger, Cullom, Dolph, Farwell, Hoar, Manderson, Mitchell of Oregon, Mitchell of Pennsylvania, Palmer, Platt, Sherman, Teller, Wilson of Iowa. *Nays:* Beck, Berry, Blackburn, Brown, Call, Cockrell, Coke, Colquitt, Eustis, Evarts, George, Gray, Hampton, Harris, Hawley, Ingalls, Jones of Nevada, McMillan, McPherson, Mahone, Morgan, Morrill, Payne, Pugh, Saulsbury, Sawyer, Sewell, Spooner, Vance, Vest, Walthall, Whitthorne, Williams, Wilson of Maryland. *Absent:* Aldrich, Allison, Butler, Frye, Gibson, Gorman, Miller, Plumb, Ransom, Camden, Cameron, Chace, Dawes, Edmunds, Fair, Hale, Harrison, Jones of Arkansas, Jones of Florida, Kenna, Maxey, Riddleberger, Sabin, Stanford, Van Wyck, Voorhees.

31st she received another : " I called Thursday and Friday mornings, but was not able to reach you with my card. My errand was personal and I hope I may be more fortunate when you are again in the city." When she did see him she found his purpose was to declare a truce, which she declined, as he already had done the cause all the harm possible for him.

From Washington Miss Anthony went to assist at a convention in Philadelphia, and " felt guilty for days," she says in her diary, because she refused to go on to Connecticut. She enjoyed a brief visit with Professor Maria Mitchell at Vassar College ; and hastened to Albany to address the legislature in regard to the Constitutional Convention, " just as I did twenty years ago in the old Capitol," she writes. Then back to Washington to look after matters there, and thus on and on, never allowing herself to be delayed by weather, fatigue or social demands, month after month, year after year, with but one object in view, never losing sight of it for a moment, and making all else subservient to this single purpose.

In April she was terribly distressed at the malicious falsehoods which were sent out from Leavenworth in regard to the first voting of the women in Kansas, and says, " It will take oceans of breath and ink to counteract the baneful effects." On May 11, 1887, Frances E. Willard wrote her : " Will you please send me the form of resolution which would be the least that would satisfy you as a plank in the platform of the Prohibition party, or as a resolution to be adopted by the W. C. T. U.? I write this without authorization from any quarter, simply because I would like to find out what is the angle of vision along which you are looking." To this Miss Anthony replied :

What is the full significance of " would satisfy you ? " Do you mean so satisfy me that I would work, and recommend all women to work, for the success of the Third party ticket? Or do you mean the least that I think it should say for its own sake? If the first, I am not sure that the fullest endorsement would cause me to throw all my sympathies and efforts into line with the Prohibition party, any more than if the same full suffrage plank snould be put into the platform of the great Labor or Fourth party, which is pretty sure to take part in the presidential contest of 1888.

I can not answer for others, but I shall not pray or speak or work for the defeat of the nominees of the party of which every United States Senator who voted for us last winter is a leading member, and to which belongs every man but six in the Kansas Legislature who made the overwhelming vote giving municipal suffrage to the women of that State.   Not until a third party gets into power or is likely to do so, which promises a larger per cent. of representatives on the floor of Congress and in the several State legislatures who will speak and vote for woman's enfranchisement, than does the Republican, shall I work for it.   You see, as yet there is not a single Prohibitionist in Congress, while there are at least twenty Republicans on the floor of the United States Senate, besides fully one-half of the members of the House of Representatives, who are in favor of woman suffrage.   For the women of Kansas or Iowa to work for any third party would be ungrateful and suicidal.

Since I hope to live to see a Sixteenth Amendment Bill through Congress and three-fourths of the State legislatures, I do not propose to work for the defeat of the party which thus far has furnished nearly every vote in that direction.   If you will pardon me, I think it will be quite as suicidal a policy for the temperance women of the nation to work to defeat the party which contains so nearly all of their best friends and helpers.   What it seems to me should be done by all women who want reforms in legislation, is to appoint committees to confer with leading Republicans asking them to make pledges in the direction of suffrage and temperance, with the assurance of our support in case of the insertion of the planks we ask in their platform.   I fear, however, you are already pledged to the Third party, come what may, and if so it is of no use for me to advise.[1]

In May Miss Anthony again journeyed westward, though she says in her diary :   "It never was harder for me to start. A heavy nothingness is upon head and heart." She went first to the State Suffrage Convention at Indianapolis, where as usual she was a guest in the beautiful home of Mr. and Mrs. Sewall. A reception was given her at the Bates House and she was cordially greeted by several hundred ladies.   She went to meetings at Evansville, Richmond and Lafayette, and then to the Ohio convention at Cleveland ; here, as always, the guest of her loved friend, Louisa Southworth.

She writes May 26 : " Arrived home at 8 P. M. and found all well—the all consisting of sister Mary, the only one left." She was invited to meet with a large and conservative society of women who did not believe in equal suffrage.   All made nice little addresses and when Miss Anthony was called on she said :   " Ladies, you have been doing here today what I and a

[1] The skeptical can not but wonder whether the Republican party ever will have the grace and wisdom to justify the confidence which Miss Anthony has steadfastly placed in it, as regards this question, from the day of its birth.

few other women were denounced as 'unsexed' for doing thirty years ago—speaking in public;" and then proceeded to point the moral. She attended the commencement exercises of a young ladies' seminary, whose principal would not acknowledge a handsome gift from her pupils by a few remarks because she "considered it would look too strong-minded." Miss Anthony comments on the graduates' essays: "They had as much originality as Baedecker's Guide-book."

In July she went as the guest of her friend Adeline Thomson, of Philadelphia, for two weeks at Cape May and here had her first experience in sea-bathing, although she always had lived within a short distance of the ocean. She says: "This is my first seaside dissipation. It seems very odd to be one of the giddy summer resort people!" She took Miss Thomson with her up into the Berkshire hills of northwestern Massachusetts to Adams, her birthplace, and visited the home of her grandfather. In the early days of her peregrinations she used to come often to this picturesque spot, but it now had been twenty years since her last visit. Time does not bring many changes to the New England nooks or the people who live in them, and she greatly enjoyed the nine days spent with uncles, aunts and cousins, exploring the well-remembered spots. They went from here to Magnolia for a two weeks' visit at the seaside cottage of Mr. and Mrs. James Purinton, of Lynn, Mass. At this time, in answer to a request for advice, Miss Anthony wrote to Olympia Brown and Mrs. Almedia Gray, of Wisconsin:

I have your letters relative to bringing suits under the school suffrage law, and hasten to say to you that Mrs. Minor's and my own experience in both suing and being sued on the Fourteenth Amendment claim leads me to beseech you not to make a test case unless you *know* you will get the broadest decision upon it. If you get the narrow one restricting the present law simply to school-district voting, there it will rest and no judge or inspector will transcend the limit of the decision. My judgment would be to say and do nothing about the law, but through the year keep up the educational work, showing that such and such cities allowed women to vote for mayor, common council, etc., and by the next election many others will let women vote; and so in a few years all will follow suit. Let what you have alone and try for more; for all your legislature has power to give. It will be vastly more likely to grant municipal suffrage than your supreme court will be to give a decision that the school law already allows women to vote for mayor, council, governor, etc.

They thought best, however, to bring the suits ; the exact results which were predicted followed, and the school suffrage even was restricted until it was practically worthless.

During this summer Miss Anthony undertook to arrange her many years' accumulation of letters, clippings, etc., and knowing her reluctance ever to destroy a single scrap, Mrs. Stanton wrote from Paris : " I am glad to hear that you have at last settled down to look over those awful papers. It is well I am not with you. I fear we should fight every blessed minute over the destruction of Tom, Dick and Harry's epistles. Unless Mary, on the sly, sticks them in the stove when your back is turned, you will never diminish the pile during your mortal life. (Make the most of my hint, dear Mary.)" It is safe to say it was just as large at the end of the examination as at the beginning.

In September, 1887, Miss Anthony again made a circuit of conventions in every congressional district in Wisconsin and then turned her attention to Kansas. The officers of the State association had arranged a series of conventions for the purpose of demanding a constitutional amendment conferring *full* suffrage on women. Miss Anthony, with Mrs. Johns, Mrs. Letitia V. Watkins, State organizer, Rev. Anna Shaw and Rachel Foster, gave the month of October to this canvass. Senator Ingalls, in a speech at Abilene, had attempted to defend his vote in the Senate against the Sixteenth Amendment, and Miss Anthony took this as a text for the campaign. She had ample material for the excoriating which she gave him in every district in Kansas, as the Senator had declared : 1st, that suffrage was neither a natural nor a constitutional right, but a privilege conferred by the State; 2d, that no citizens should be allowed to participate in the formation of legislatures or the enactment of laws, who could not enforce their action at the point of a bayonet; 3d, that no immigrants should be allowed to enter the United States from any country on earth for the next twenty-five years ; 4th, that negro suf-

ANT.—40

frage had been an absolute and unqualified failure ; 5th, that while there were thousands of women vastly more competent than men to vote upon questions of morality, they never should be allowed to do so—simply because they were women.

It hardly need be said that Miss Anthony found little difficulty in reducing to tatters these so-called arguments, and that her audiences were in hearty sympathy. To borrow her own expression, she "tried to use him up so there was not an inch of ground under his feet." When the convention was held at Atchison Mrs. Ingalls invited sixteen of the ladies to a handsome luncheon, where the senator placed Miss Anthony at his right hand and made her the guest of honor. She proposed that he debate the question of woman suffrage with her but he refused on the ground that he could not attack a woman, so she served up this objection in her speech that evening. To a reporter he is said to have given the reason that he "would not stoop to the intellectual level of a woman."

The month of November was given to holding a two days' convention in each of the thirteen congressional districts of Indiana. These meetings were arranged by the State secretary, Mrs. Ida H. Harper, and the strong force of speakers, Miss Anthony, Mrs. Wallace, Mrs. Sewall and Mrs. Gougar, aroused great enthusiasm and made many converts.[1] This ended three months of constant travelling and speaking almost every day and evening. On the first of December Miss Anthony writes : "I have laid me down to sleep in a new bed nearly every night of this entire time."

But the 10th found her in Washington fresh and vigorous for the work of the coming winter. She was anxious to know whether the reports of the Senate debate had been franked and sent out as promised and, to her inquiry, Senator Blair answered with his usual little joke : "I have had the speeches, etc., attended to and trust that the mails will do you justice if the males do not. But remember that men naturally fight for their lives, and on the same principle, you shall for yours !"

[1] Conventions were held at Evansville, Vincennes, Bloomington, Kokomo, Logansport, Wabash, Lafayette, South Bend, Fort Wayne, Muncie, Anderson, Madison and New Albany. The largest of the series was at Terre Haute, where the opera house, donated by the citizens, was crowded both evenings with an audience representing the culture and intelligence of the city, and the convention was welcomed by the mayor, Jacob C. Kolsom.

CHAPTER XXXV.

UNION OF ASSOCIATIONS—INTERNATIONAL COUNCIL.

1888.

A PRECEDING chapter described the forming in 1869 of the American Woman Suffrage Association at Cleveland, O., the overtures for union by the National Association the next year, and their rejection. No further efforts were made and each body continued to work in its own way. At the annual meeting of the American Association in Philadelphia, October 31, 1887, the following resolution from the business committee was unanimously adopted :

WHEREAS, The woman suffragists of the United States were all united until 1868 in the American Equal Rights Association; and *whereas*, The causes of the subsequent separation into the National and American Woman Suffrage Societies have since been largely removed by the adoption of common principles and methods; therefore

Resolved, That Mrs. Lucy Stone be appointed a committee of one from the American Woman Suffrage Association to confer with Miss Susan B. Anthony of the National and, if on conference it seems desirable, that she be authorized and empowered to appoint a committee of this association to meet a similar committee appointed by the National to consider a satisfactory basis of union, and refer it back to the executive committee of both associations for final action. HENRY B. BLACKWELL,
Corresponding Secretary, A. W. S. A.

After conferring with the officers of the National Association, Miss Anthony informed Mrs. Stone that she would meet her in Philadelphia any time until December 9, and after that in Washington. She replied that she was not able to travel even so far as Philadelphia and, after some correspondence, Miss Anthony agreed to go to Boston. On the afternoon of

(627)

December 21, 1887, accompanied by Rachel Foster, corresponding secretary of the National, she met Mrs. Stone and Alice Stone Blackwell, at No. 3 Park street, Boston, and held an extended conference in regard to the proposed union. Two days later Mrs. Stone sent to Miss Anthony, who was still in that city, the following :

In thinking over the points raised at our informal conference, it seems to me that the substantial outcome is this: The committees appointed by us respectively, if we conclude to appoint them, must each agree upon a common name, a common constitution and a common list of officers for the first year. A subsequent acceptance of these by each association will thereafter constitute the two societies one society. If you think there is a fair probability of coming to an agreement I will proceed to appoint my committee.

As the formal overtures for union have come from the American Association, it will be appropriate that our committee should draw up the plan for union which appears to them the most feasible, and forward it to Miss Foster, to be submitted to yours. Then your committee will suggest such modifications as they may think needful; and, if a mutually satisfactory result can be reached, the name, constitution and list of officers will go to the executive committee of each association for final action.

Christmas Day Miss Blackwell sent to Miss Foster a comprehensive plan for a union of the two societies, closing as follows : '' Since many members of the National society regard Mrs. Stone as the cause of the division, and many members of the American regard Mrs. Stanton and Miss Anthony as the cause of it, Mrs. Stone suggested that it would greatly promote a harmonious union, for those three ladies to agree in advance that none of them would take the presidency of the united association.'' Early in January this formal announcement and letter were sent to Miss Foster :

The committee of the National to sit in counsel with that of the seven appointed by Lucy Stone, of the American, shall be: May Wright Sewall, *Chairman*, Harriette R. Shattuck, Olympia Brown, Helen M. Gougar, Laura M. Johns, Clara B. Colby, Rachel G. Foster, *Secretary*.[1]

I hope all will sink personalities and exalt principles, seeking only the best good for woman's enfranchisement, and that surely will come through the union of all the friends of woman suffrage into one great and grand national

[1] To these afterwards were added from the executive committee, Isabella Beecher Hooker, *Chairman*, Matilda Joslyn Gage, Mary B. Clay, Sarah M. Perkins, Lillie Devereux Blake, Mary F. Eastman, Clara Neymann, Elizabeth Boynton Harbert.

association which shall enable them to present a solid front to the enemy. This must be based on the principle of a genuine democracy, which shall give to each of its members a voice in all its deliberations, either in person or through representatives chosen by them, and to a constitution thus based I am sure each of my seven chosen ones will contribute her aid. Hoping that a consolidation of all our forces will be the result of this overture from Lucy Stone and her society, I am, very sincerely,   Susan B. Anthony.

On January 18, Miss Foster received from Miss Blackwell the list of the conference committee appointed by Mrs. Stone : Julia Ward Howe, *Chairman*, Wm. Dudley Foulke, Margaret W. Campbell, Anna H. Shaw, Mary F. Thomas, H. M. Tracy Cutler, Henry B. Blackwell, *Secretary*.

Miss Anthony again wrote Miss Foster : '' I can not think of any stipulation I wish to make the basis of union save that we *unite*, and after that discuss all measures and ways and means, officers and newspapers, and cheerfully accept and abide by the rule of the majority. I do not wish to exact any pledges from Lucy Stone and her adherents, nor can I give any for Mrs. Stanton and her followers. When united we must trust to the good sense of each, just as we have trusted during the existence of the division. As Greeley said about resuming specie payment, ' *the way to unite is to unite* ' and trust the consequences.''

It is not essential for the completeness of this work to reproduce in detail the official proceedings, which extended through two years and caused Miss Anthony often to write, '' I shall be glad when this frittering away of time on mere forms is past.'' A basis of agreement finally was reached, and the union was practically completed at the National Convention which met in Washington, January 21, 1889. A committee of thirteen was selected to confer with the committee from the American. This consisted of Miss Anthony and Mesdames Hooker, Minor, Duniway, Johns, Sewall, Perkins, Colby, Spofford, Brown, Blake, Gougar and Foster Avery. The Woman's Tribune thus described the result :

At the business session, January 24, 1889, they reported in substance as follows:

Name, etc.—The association to be called the National-American W. S. A. The annual convention to be held at Washington.

Chronology.—The next annual meeting of the joint society to be—as it would be for the National—the twenty-second annual Washington convention.

Work.—To be for National and State legislation protecting women in the exercise of their right to vote.

Representation.—As provided in the new National constitution.

Where two associations exist in one State and will not unite, both are to be accepted as auxiliary societies.

An earnest debate followed. Miss Anthony threw her influence strongly in favor of union and carried many with her, even those who openly expressed themselves that their judgment would be to continue the two societies. The vote was then taken on union, thirty voting for, eleven against.

Miss Alice Stone Blackwell and Rev. Anna H. Shaw were present on behalf of the American Association, accepted the deviations from the propositions as presented by that association, and felt reasonably certain that it would endorse their action.

Yours for equal rights,

Alice Stone Blackwell.

No one person contributed so much toward effecting the union of these two societies as Alice Stone Blackwell. On February 17, 1890, both bodies met in Washington and it was decided that the official boards of the two should form the voting force until the joint temporary organization was completed. Councils were held in the great parlor and dining-room of the Riggs House. Both Miss Anthony and Mrs. Stanton had been willing, from the beginning of negotiations, to accept the proposition of the Americans that neither one of them, nor Lucy Stone, should take the presidency of the united association, but from the Nationals in every part of the country came a cry of dissent. Letters poured in declaring that Miss Anthony and Mrs. Stanton had borne the brunt of the battle for forty years, that they had not once lowered the flag or made the question of woman suffrage subservient to any other, that they were the head and heart of the movement, and that for them to be deposed was out of the question.[1] It soon became evident that unless this point were conceded all hope of union would have to be banished. While most of the delegates agreed that, in respect to seniority in years and work and also in consideration of her commanding ability, Mrs. Stanton should be president, there were many who thought that, because of her advanced age and the fact that she spent most of her time abroad, it would be better to elect Miss Anthony. The latter was distracted by such a thought and at the final meeting of National delegates preliminary to the joint convention, with all the earnestness of her strong nature and in a voice vibrating with emotion, she said :

I appeal to every woman who has any affection for the old National or for me not to vote for Susan B. Anthony for president. I stand in a delicate position. I have letters which accuse me of having favored the union solely for personal and selfish considerations, and of trying to put Mrs. Stanton out, Now what I have to say is, don't vote for any human being but Mrs. Stanton There are other reasons why I wish her elected, but I have these personal ones: When the division was made twenty years ago, it was because our platform was too broad, because Mrs. Stanton was too radical; a more conservative organization was wanted. If we Nationals divide now and Mrs. Stanton is deposed from the presidency, we virtually degrade her If you have any love for our old association, which, from the beginning, has stood like a rock in regard to creeds and politics, demanding that every woman should be allowed to come upon our platform to plead for her freedom—if you have any faith in that grand principle—vote for Mrs. Stanton. . . .

The National always has allowed the utmost liberty. Anything and everything which stood in the way of progress was likely to get knocked off our platform. I want every one who claims to be a National to continue to stand for this principle. We have come now to another turning-point and, if it is necessary, I will fight forty years more to make our platform free for the Christian to stand upon whether she be a Catholic and counts her beads, or a Protestant of the straitest orthodox creed, just as I have fought for the rights of the infidels the last forty years. These are the principles I want you to maintain, that our platform may be kept as broad as the universe, that upon it may stand the representatives of all creeds and no creeds—Jew or Christian, Protestant or Catholic, Gentile or Mormon, pagan or atheist.

[1] Many letters are on file making these declarations. It is not practicable to quote them here, but a place may be made for an extract from that of Zerelda G. Wallace to Miss Anthony: "While they do not under-estimate the work of any of the pioneers, the hearts of the women all over the country are turning to you. They feel that they are yours, and you are theirs. The suffrage women look to you with as much loyalty and affection as the temperance women to Miss Willard. There are thousands of them who would rally around you with an enthusiasm which no one else can inspire. You will do me the credit to believe that I speak solely for the good of the work to which you have given your life."

At the joint executive session after the union was formally declared to be consummated, the vote was: For president, Mrs. Stanton, 131; Miss Anthony, 90; for vice-president-at-large, Miss Anthony, 213. Lucy Stone was unanimously elected chairman of the executive committee; Rachel Foster Avery, corresponding secretary; Alice Stone Blackwell, recording secretary;[1] Jane H. Spofford, treasurer; Eliza T. Ward and Rev. Frederick W. Hinckley, auditors. This uniting of the two associations was begun in 1887 and finished in 1890, in the most thoroughly official manner, according to the most highly approved parliamentary methods, and the final result was satisfactory to a large majority of the members of both societies, who since that time have worked together in unbroken harmony.

The action of the American Association was almost unanimous, but the members of the National were widely divided. Letters of protest were received from many States, and several of its members attempted to form new organizations. The executive sessions in Washington were the most stormy in the history of the association, and only the unsurpassed parliamentary knowledge of the chairman, May Wright Sewall, aided by the firm co-operation of Miss Anthony, could have harmonized the opposing elements and secured a majority vote in favor of the union. There had been no time during the twenty years' division when Miss Anthony was not ready to sink all personal feeling and unite the two societies for the sake of promoting the cause which she placed before all else in the world; and from the first prospect of combining the forces, she used every effort toward its accomplishment. It was a source of especial gratification that this was practically assured by the winter of 1888, when the International Council of Women met in Washington, as it enabled the American Association to accept the invitation and send representatives to this great convocation—which will now be considered.

It had long been the dream of Miss Anthony and Mrs.

[1] Mrs. Avery and Miss Blackwell have continued ever since to fill these positions most acceptably to the association.

To my
Dear friend
Susan B. Anthony
with love & reverence
Zerelda G. Wallace

Stanton to form an International Suffrage Association for purposes of mutual helpfulness and the strength of co-operation. During 1883, when in Great Britain, they discussed this subject with the women there and, as a result, a large committee of correspondence had been established to promote the forming of such an association. After a time it was judged expedient to enlarge its scope and make it an International Council, which should represent every department of woman's work. This was called to meet at Washington in 1888, the fortieth anniversary of the first organized demand for the rights of women, the convention at Seneca Falls, and active preparations had been in progress for more than a year. It was decided at the suffrage convention held the previous winter that the National Association should assume the entire responsibility for this International Council and should invite the participation of all organizations of women in the trades, professions, reforms, etc.

Mrs. Stanton and Mrs. Spofford were in Europe and this herculean task was borne principally by Miss Anthony, May Wright Sewall and Rachel Foster.[1] Miss Anthony stayed in Washington for two months preceding the council, perfecting the last arrangements. The amount of labor, time, thought and anxiety involved in this year of preparation can not be estimated. Nothing to compare with it ever had been attempted by women. Not the least part of the undertaking was the raising of the $13,000 which were needed to defray expenses, all secured by personal letters of appeal and admission fees, and disbursed with careful economy and judgment. The

[1] The magnitude of the work of the council may be better appreciated by the mention of a few figures in this connection. There were printed and distributed by mail 10,000 calls and 10,000 appeals; sketches were prepared of the lives and work of speakers and delegates and circulated by a press committee of over ninety persons in many States; March 10, the first edition (5,000) of the sixteen-page program was issued; this was followed by five other editions of 5,000 each and a final seventh edition of 7,000. About 4,000 letters were written. Including those concerning railroad rates, not less than 10,000 more circulars of various kinds were printed and distributed. A low estimate of the number of pages thus issued gives 672,000. During the week of the council and the week of the convention of the National W. S. A. the Woman's Tribune was published by Mrs. Colby eight times (four days sixteen pages, four days twelve pages), the daily edition averaging 12,500.

An international convention of men, held in Washington the same year, cost in round numbers $50,000.—Official Report.

intention was to give the suffrage association the same prominence as other organizations and no more. An entry in Miss Anthony's diary says: "I have just received proof of the 'call' for the council and struck out the paragraph saying, 'no one would be committed to suffrage who should attend.' I can't allow any such apologetic invitation as that! There is no need to say anything about it." To her old friend Antoinette Brown Blackwell, who asked if only those women ministers who had been regularly ordained were to be heard, Miss Anthony wrote:

I have felt all along that we ought to give a chance for the expression of the highest and deepest religious thought of those not ordained of men. Your wish to give the result of your research opens the way for us to make the last day—Easter Sunday—voice the new, the purer, the better worship of the living God. We'll have a real symposium of woman's gospel. It is not fair to give only the church-ordained women an opportunity to present their religious thoughts, and now it shall be fixed so that the laity may have the same. I don't want a controversy or a lot of negations, but shall tell each one to give her strongest affirmation. This forever saying a thing is false and failing to present the truth, is to me a foolish waste of time, when almost everybody feels the old forms, creeds and rituals to be only the mint, anise and cumin.

So, my dear, I am very, very glad that you and Lucy are both to be on our platform, and we are to stand together again after these twenty years. But none of the past! Let us rejoice in the good of the present, and hope for more and more in the future.

In response to her letter asking him to take part on Pioneer Day, Frederick Douglass wrote:

I certainly shall, if I live and am well. The cause of woman suffrage has under it a truth as eternal as the universe of thought, and must triumph if this planet endures. I have been calling up to my mind's eye that first convention in the small Wesleyan Methodist church at Seneca Falls, where Mrs. Stanton, Mrs. Mott and those other brave souls began a systematic and determined agitation for a larger measure of liberty for woman, and how great that little meeting now appears! It seems only yesterday since it took place, and yet forty years have passed away and what a revolution on this subject have we seen in the sentiment of the American people and, in fact, of the civilized world! Who could have thought that humble, modest, maiden convention, holding its little white apron up to its face and wiping away the tear of sympathy with woman in her hardships and the sigh of her soul for a larger measure of freedom, would have become the mother of an International Council of Women, right here in the capital of this nation?

Maria Mitchell, who was in feeble health (and died the next year) in expressing her regrets said : "I am taking a rest. I have worked more than a half-century and, like stronger people, have become tired.   I am meaning to build my small observatory and keep up a sort of apology for study—because I am too old to dare do nothing.   I wish I felt able to take the journey and hear what others have to say and are ready to do.   The world moves, and I have full faith it will continue to move and to move, for better and better, even when we have put aside the armor."

*The world moves and I
have full faith it will continue to move and to move, for
better and better, even when
we have put aside the
armor.*

Sincerely yours

Maria Mitchell.

During the winter, Mrs. Stanton had written Miss Anthony: "We have jogged along pretty well for forty years or more. Perhaps mid the wreck of thrones and the undoing of so many friendships, sects, parties and families, you and I deserve some credit for sticking together through all adverse winds, with so few ripples on the surface.   When I get back to America I intend to cling to you closer than ever.   I am thoroughly rested now and full of fight and fire, ready to travel and speak from Maine to Florida.   Tell our suffrage daughters to brace up and get ready for a long pull, a strong pull, and a pull all together when I come back."

What then were her amazement, anger and grief to receive another letter from Mrs. Stanton a short time before the council, saying that a voyage across the Atlantic so filled her with dread that she had about decided not to undertake it! A fortieth anniversary of the Seneca Falls convention without the woman who called it! And this when she had counted on Mrs. Stanton to make the greatest speech of the whole meeting and cover the National Association with immortal glory! She says in her journal: "I am ablaze and dare not write tonight." The next entry: "I wrote the most terrific letter to Mrs. Stanton; it will start every white hair on her head." And then the following day the little book records: "Well, I made my own heart ache all night, awake or asleep, by my terrible arraignment, whether it touches her feelings or not." Ten days later she writes: "Received a cablegram from Mrs. Stanton, 'I am coming,' so she has my letter. My mind is so relieved, I feel as if I were treading on air."

On Mrs. Stanton's arrival a few days before the convention, Miss Anthony learned, to her consternation, that she had prepared no speech for the occasion! She shut her up in a room at the Riggs House with pen and paper, kept a guard at the door, permitted no one to see her, and when the time arrived she was ready with her usual magnificent address.

The council opened Sunday, March 25, in Albaugh's new opera house, with religious services conducted entirely by women, Revs. Phebe A. Hanaford, Ada C. Bowles, Antoinette Blackwell, Amanda Deyo, and a matchless sermon by Rev. Anna H. Shaw, "The Heavenly Vision." It would be wholly impossible to enter into a detailed account of this council, the greatest woman's convention ever held.[1] Although twenty-five cents admission was charged, and fifty cents for reserved seats, the opera house was crowded during the eight days and evenings, and seats were at a premium. Miss Anthony presided over eight of the sixteen sessions. While every speaker was allowed the widest latitude, there was not at any time the slightest friction. Letters were read from celebrated people in

---

[1] One session each was given to Education, Philanthropy, Temperance, Industries, Professions, Organizations, Legal Conditions, Social Purity, Political Conditions, etc., which were discussed by the women most prominent in the several departments. Fifty-three different national organizations of women were represented by eighty speakers and forty-nine delegates from England, France, Norway, Denmark, Finland, India, Canada and the United States.

most of the countries of Europe and all parts of America. At the pioneer's meeting were eight men and thirty-six women who had been connected with the movement for woman suffrage forty years.[1]

Among the social courtesies extended to this distinguished body of women, were a reception at the White House by President and Mrs. Cleveland; handsome entertainments by Senator and Mrs. Leland Stanford, and Senator and Mrs. T. W. Palmer; a reception at the Riggs House ; many smaller parties, dinners and luncheons ; and numerous social gatherings of women doctors, lawyers, etc.   At all of the large functions Miss Anthony, Mrs. Stanton and Lucy Stone stood at the left hand of the hostess, while the other officials and the foreign delegates were also in the "receiving line."   At the White House Miss Anthony made the presentations to the President. As every newspaper in the country had complimentary notices of this council and the prominent ladies connected with it, it is scarcely possible to discriminate.   The Baltimore Sun said :

The council began its deliberations in the finest humor with everybody, particularly with that prime favorite, Susan B. Anthony. This lady daily grows upon all present; the woman suffragists love her for her good works, the audience for her brightness and wit, and the multitude of press representatives for her frank, plain, open, business-like way of doing everything connected with the council. Miss Anthony when in repose looks worn with the conflict she has waged, though when she goes into action her angular face loses its tired look and becomes all animation. Her word is the parliamentary law of the meeting.   Whatever she says is done without murmur or dissent. The women of the council are saved any parliamentary discussions such as arise in the meetings of men ; they acknowledge that she is an autocrat.   All are agreed that no better system than the absolute control of Susan B. Anthony can be devised.

The New York World commented :

If ever there was a gay-hearted, good-natured woman it is certainly Miss Anthony. From the beginning of this council it is she who has kept the fun barometer away up. The gray-headed friends of her youth are all "girls" to her, and she is a girl among them. Parliamentary rules have been by no

[1] The fine stenographic reports of this council were made by Mary F. Seymour and a corps of women assistants. The official proceedings, with speeches in full, may be obtained of the corresponding secretary of the National-American W. S. A.

means so severe as to keep even the regular proceedings free from her lively interpolation and comment. When Miss Anthony has felt the public pulse or looked at her watch and seen that a speech has gone far enough, she says under her breath, "Your time's about up, my dear." If the speaker continues, the next thing is, " I guess you'll have to stop now ; it's more than ten minutes." When this fails, she usually begins to hang gently on the orator's skirt, and if pluckings and pullings fail, she then subsides with a quizzical smile, or stands erect and uncompromising by the speaker's side. There is none of the rude beating of the gavel, nor any paraphrase of "The gentleman's time is up," which marks the stiff proceedings of men "in congress assembled." To an unprejudiced eye this free-and-easy method of procedure might lack symmetry and dignity, but there is not the slightest doubt that Miss Anthony has been as wise as a serpent while being as gentle as a dove.

When Frances E. Willard rose to address the council, she laid her hand tenderly on Miss Anthony's shoulder and said : " I remember when I was dreadfully afraid of Susan, and Lucy too; but now I love and honor them, and I can not put into words my sense of what it means to me to have the blessing of these women who have made it possible for more timid ones like myself to come forward and take our part in the world's work. If they had not blazed the trees and pioneered the way, we should not have dared to come. If there is one single drop of chivalric blood in woman's veins, it ought to bring a tinge of pride to the face that Susan B. Anthony, Lucy Stone, Elizabeth Cady Stanton, Julia Ward Howe and these other grand women, our leaders and our foremothers, are here for us to greet ; that they, who heard so much that was not agreeable, may hear an occasional pleasant word while they are alive." Very few of the speakers failed to express their deep feeling of personal obligation and the indebtedness of all women to the early labors of Miss Anthony and the other pioneers.

In her letter to the Union Signal, Miss Willard gave this bit of description : " The central figure of the council was Susan B. Anthony, in her black dress and pretty red silk shawl, with her gray-brown hair smoothly combed over a regal head, worthy of any statesman. Her mingled good-nature and firmness, her unselfish purpose and keen perception of the right thing to do, endeared her alike to those whom she admonished and those whom she praised. In her sixty-ninth year, dear ' Susan B.' seems not over fifty-five. She has a wonderful constitution, and the prodigies of work she has accomplished have forever put to rout the ignorant notion that women lack physical endurance.''

In the year of preliminary work for this great council, the thought came many times to May Wright Sewall that it ought to result in something more than one brief convention, and she conceived the idea of a permanent International and also a permanent National Council of Women. During the week in Washington she presented her plan to a large number of the leaders who regarded it with approval. Miss Anthony, chairman of the meeting, by request, appointed a committee of fifteen who reported in favor of permanent councils, and Miss Willard presented an outline of constitutions. After a number of meetings of the delegates the councils were officially formed, March 31, 1888, '' to include the organized working forces of the world's womanhood,'' in the belief that '' such a federation will increase the world's sum total of womanly courage, efficiency and esprit de corps, widen the horizon, correct the tendency of an exaggerated impression of one's own work as compared with that of others, and put the wisdom and experience of each at the service of all.'' A simple form of constitution was adopted, and it was decided that the National Council should meet once in three years and the International once in five.[1]

Immediately upon the close of the council, the National Suffrage Association held its twentieth annual convention and, as many of the delegates remained, the meetings were nearly as crowded as those of the council had been. A local paper remarked '' that it seemed as if the Washington people could never hear enough about woman suffrage.'' A fine address by Caroline E. Merrick was an especial feature, as it presented

[1]National Council: *President*, Frances E. Willard; *vice-president-at-large*, Susan B. Anthony; *corresponding secretary*, May Wright Sewall; *recording secretary*, Mary F. Eastman; *treasurer*, M. Louise Thomas.

the question from the standpoint of a southern woman. The Senate committee granted a hearing, the speakers being presented by Miss Anthony. Mrs. Stanton made the principal address, a grand plea for human equality, and the grave and dignified committee gave her a round of applause. She was followed by Frances E. Willard and Julia Ward Howe; Laura Ormiston Chant and Alice Scatcherd, England; Isabelle Bogelot, France; Sophia Magelsson Groth, Norway; Alli Trygg, Finland; Bessie Starr Keefer, Canada.

Miss Anthony received many pleasant letters after the council; among them one from her friend Mrs. Samuel E. Sewall, of Boston, in which she said: "We want to congratulate you upon the very satisfactory and gratifying result of the council. I hear from the delegates on all sides most enthusiastic accounts of the whole affair, and of your wonderful powers and energy. Mr. Blackwell is loud in your praise. All this might be expected from the delegates, but what pleases me still more is the respectful tone of nearly all the newspapers. Even the sneering Nation has admitted an article in praise of the council." In all Miss Anthony's own letters there was not the slightest reference to any feeling of fatigue or desire for rest, but she seemed only to be stimulated to greater energy. It was impossible for her to respond to half the invitations which came from all parts of the country, but usually she selected the places where she felt herself most needed, without any regard to her own pleasure or comfort. She did, however, accept a cordial invitation to attend the annual Boston Suffrage Festival, and was royally entertained for several days.

On the afternoon of June 9, Central Music Hall, Chicago, was packed with an audience of representative men and women. Frances E. Willard presided,[1] prayer was offered by Rev. Florence Kollock, and Mrs. Ormiston Chant gave a wonderfully electric address on the "Moral Relations of Men and Women to Each Other." She was followed by Dr. Kate Bushnell in a thrilling talk on "Legislation as it Deals with Social

[1] This meeting was arranged by Dr. Frances Dickinson, who had persuaded Miss Anthony to make the journey to Chicago in order to preside over it. On the way to the hall she was detained at a drawbridge and Miss Willard kindly took her place.

Purity.'' Miss Anthony closed the program with a ringing speech showing the need of the ballot in the hands of women to remedy such evils as had been depicted by the other speakers. No abstract can give an idea of her magnetic force when profoundly stirred by such recitals as had been made at this meeting.

A few days afterwards a largely-attended reception was given by the Woman's Club of Chicago to Miss Anthony, Isabella Beecher Hooker and Baroness Gripenberg, of Finland.

In the summer of 1888, the National Association as usual sent delegates to each of the presidential conventions, asking for a suffrage plank, and as usual they were ignored by Republicans and Democrats. Miss Anthony and Mrs. Hooker had headquarters in the parlors of Mrs. Celia Whipple Wallace, at the Sherman House, Chicago, during the Republican convention in June. They issued an open letter citing the record of the party in regard to women, and asking for recognition, but received no consideration. In the Woman's Tribune, Miss Anthony made this forcible statement:

Had the best representative suffrage women of every State in the Union been in Chicago, established in national headquarters, working with the men of their State delegations, as well as with the resolution committee, I have not a doubt that the Republican platform would have contained a splendid plank, pledging the party to this broad and true interpretation of the Constitution. Every other reform had its scores and hundreds of representatives here, pleading for the incorporation of its principles in the platform and working for the nomination of the men who would best voice their plans. Women never will be heard and heeded until they make themselves a power, irresistible in numbers and strength, moral, intellectual and financial, in all the formative gatherings of the parties they would influence. Therefore, I now beg of our women not to lose another opportunity to be present at every political convention during this summer, to urge the adoption of woman suffrage resolutions and the nomination of men pledged to support them. "Eternal vigilance is the price of liberty" for women as well as for men.

From Chicago Miss Anthony went directly to Indianapolis and, with Mrs. Sewall, called at the Harrison residence. She says: '' We met a most cordial reception and while the general did not declare himself in favor of woman's enfranchise-

ment, he expressed great respect for those who are seeking it.''
The two ladies then addressed an open letter to General Harrison, urging that in accepting the nomination he would interpret as including women that plank in the Republican platform
which declared: "We recognize the supreme and sovereign
right of every lawful citizen to cast one free ballot in all public elections and to have that ballot duly counted ; "[1] but this
reasonable request was politely ignored.

Sarah Knox Goodrich and Ellen Clark Sargent, of California, sent the following telegram to their fellow-citizen, Morris
M. Estee, chairman of the National Republican Convention :
"Please ascertain, for many interested women, if the clause
in the platform concerning the sovereign right of every lawful citizen to a free ballot, includes the women of the
United States." To this Mr. Estee telegraphed reply, "I do
not think the platform is so construed here." This ended the
battle of 1888, as far as women were concerned, and those who
might have been the ablest advocates which any political party
could put upon its platform were relegated to silence during the campaign.

On August 7, Miss Anthony and Mrs. Stanton spoke at
Byron Center, and were entertained by Mrs. Newton Green.
Miss Anthony addressed a large audience at Jamestown on the
10th and was the guest of Mrs. Reuben E. Fenton. During
part of the summer, for a little recreation, she took hold of the
great heterogeneous mass of bills and receipts of the National
W. S. A. for the past four years and compiled them into a neat,
accurate financial report of seventeen pages, in which every
dollar received and disbursed during that time was acknowledged and accounted for, without any "sundries" or other
makeshifts for the sake of accuracy. As the total amount
reached nearly $18,000, a large part of which had been re-
ceived in sums of one or two dollars, the labor involved may
be appreciated. Miss Anthony did this, as she did many other
disagreeable things, not because they were officially her duty,
but because they ought to be done and there was no one else

---

[1] See Appendix for full text of letter.

ready to undertake them. She always was restive under red tape regulations. For many years she was forced to take the lead in all departments of the suffrage work and when they finally became systematized, with a head at each, she sometimes grew impatient at delay and usurped the functions of others without intending any breach of official etiquette. And so when this financial statement was completed, she published it without waiting for money or authority, and wrote to the national treasurer, Mrs. Spofford, who had recently returned from Europe :

Andrew Jackson-like, I decided to assume the responsibility of sending to each member of the association a copy of the Council Report with one of the National's financial statement. I am writing a personal letter to all, explaining our double keeping of our pledge and asking them to return contributions, if they are able, for this permanent and nice report. I do not know what results in cash will come of it to the National, but I do know that the poorest and hardest-working women who pinched out their dollars to send, think that we promised them therefor this book-report of the council. So all in all I decided, against Miss Foster, Mrs. Stanton and your own dear self, to give each the report, leaving her to do as she feels most comfortable about sending to the treasurer payment in return.

A few days later she writes : " I mailed 800 letters yesterday, and we have sent over 1,500 Reports, with 800 more promised." Could any pen give an adequate idea of the amount of work accomplished by that tireless brain and those never-resting hands ?

Miss Anthony spoke on Woman's Day, October 12, at the Centennial Celebration in Columbus, O. A newspaper correspondent drew this contrast between her address and those of the women of the W. C. T. U.:

Each prayer started heavenward was weighted with politics—political prohibition. When the eloquent speakers of the afternoon dealt a stinging blow under the belt to one of the leading political parties, the applause was tremendous, cheers and " amens " mingling in a sacrilegious chorus of approval. On the other hand, when Miss Anthony made her calm, strong and really logical argument in favor of woman suffrage, giving each party, so far as related to action of States, just praise or censure, she was received coldly. It did not seem to count for anything that she had been a pioneer in the cause of temperance. That white record was stained because she cast their idol down—she showed that prohibition had failed in Kansas in the large cities, whether under a Democratic or a Republican governor, or under St. John, the Prohibition governor; in every administration it was a failure, because even there women had only a restricted vote, and public sentiment without the ballot counted for naught. There were no little graves in her speech, no weeping willows by winding streams where lay broken hearts in tombs unmarked. It was a simple statement of the cause a brave woman had at heart.

She attended the State conventions at Ames, Ia., and at Emporia, Kan., where she was the guest of Senator and Mrs. Kellogg. From there she went to Leavenworth, and later to Omaha for the Nebraska convention. She then engaged for the fall and winter with the Slayton Lecture Bureau at $60 a night, and began again the tiresome round throughout the Western States.

In this autumn of 1888, Miss Anthony received a severe shock in the announcement of the approaching marriage of Rachel Foster to Cyrus Miller Avery, of Chicago. He had attended the International Council the preceding spring with his mother, Rosa Miller Avery, known prominently in suffrage and other public work in Illinois. Here he had seen Miss Foster in her youth and beauty, carrying a large part of the responsibility connected with that important gathering, and had fallen in love with her at first sight. During her long life Miss Anthony had seen one young girl after another take up the work of woman's regeneration, fit herself for it, grow into a power, then marry, give it all up and drop out of sight. " I would not object to marriage," she wrote, " if it were not that women throw away every plan and purpose of their own life, to conform to the plans and purposes of the man's life. I wonder if it is woman's real, true nature always to abnegate self." Miss Foster had developed unusual ability and for a number of years had been Miss Anthony's mainstay in the suffrage work, and had grown very close into her heart; it is not surprising, therefore, that she learned of the coming marriage with dismay. She accepted the situation as gracefully as possible, however, and, although too far away to attend the wedding, sent most cordial wishes for the happiness of the newly-married.[1]

The year 1888 brought to Miss Anthony many honors, but it brought also the usual quota of the bereavements which come with every passing year when one nears threescore and ten.   Her cherished friend, Dr. Clemence Lozier, had passed away; Edward M. Davis, whose faithful friendship never had failed, was no more; A. Bronson Alcott and his daughter Louisa had gone to test the truth of the new philosophy; and other dear ones had dropped out of the narrowing circle.   But as a partial compensation, there had come into her life some new friends who were destined, if not to fill the place of those who were gone, to make another for themselves in her affections and her labors quite as helpful and important.   Chief among these was Rev. Anna Howard Shaw, who, from the time of the International Council, gave her deepest love and truest allegiance.   Until then she had not been near enough Miss Anthony to realize the nobility and grandeur of her character, but thenceforth she accorded to her all the devotion and reverence of her own strong and beautiful nature.   In a letter written after she had returned to her home in Boston, she said: "From my heart I pray that I may always be worthy your love and confidence. To know you is a blessing; to be trusted by you is worth far more than my efforts for our work have cost me."

[1] Mrs. Foster Avery has proved an exception to the rule and, during the ten years since her marriage, has performed as much work, to say the least, as any of the younger generation of women, besides contributing thousands of dollars.

CHAPTER XXXVI.

1889.

THE eleventh of January, 1889, found Miss Anthony in her usual pleasant suite of rooms at the Riggs House. She plunged at once into preparations for the approaching convention, interviewing congressmen, calling at the newspaper offices and conferring with local committees. The Twenty-first National Convention opened January 21, in the Congregational church, with the speakers as bright and full of hope as they had been through all the score of years. The opening address was given by Hon. A. G. Riddle and, during the sessions, excellent speeches were made by Hon. William D. Kelley, Senator Blair, Rev. Alexander Kent and State Senator Blue, of Kansas. Rev. Anna H. Shaw made her first appearance on the National platform and delivered her splendid oration, "The Fate of Republics." Laura M. Johns gave a practical and pleasing talk on "Municipal Suffrage in Kansas;" and there was the usual array of talent. Miss Anthony presided, putting every speaker to the front and making a substantial background of her own felicitous little speeches, each containing an argument in a nutshell.

While in Washington she was entertained at dinner by the "Six O'clock Club," and seated at the right hand of its presi-

(647)

dent, Dr. Wm. A. Hammond. The subject for the evening was "Robert Elsmere" and, in giving her opinion, she said she had found nothing new in the book; all those theological questions had been discussed and settled by the Quakers long ago. What distressed her most was the marriage of Robert and Catherine, who, any outsider could have seen, were utterly unfitted for one another, and she wondered if there could be any way by which young people might be able to know each other better before marrying.

On February 11, Miss Anthony spoke in Cincinnati to an audience of 2,000, under the management of A. W. Whelpley, city librarian.[1] The Commercial Gazette commented: "Miss Susan B. Anthony had every reason for congratulation on the audience, both as to quality and quantity, which greeted her Sunday afternoon at the Grand Opera House. Her discourse proved to be one of the most entertaining of the Unity Club lectures this season, and if she did not succeed in gaining many proselytes to her well-known views regarding woman's emancipation, she certainly reaped the reward of presenting the arguments in an interesting and logical manner. Every neatly turned point was received with applause and that good-natured laughter that carries with it not a little of the element of conviction. As of old, this pioneer of the woman's cause is abundantly able to return sarcasm for sarcasm, as well as to present an array of facts in a manner which would do credit to the most astute of our politicians."

Miss Anthony was much gratified at the cordial reception given her in Cincinnati and the evident success of her speech, and Tuesday morning, with a happy heart, took the train for her western lecture tour. She settled herself comfortably, glanced over her paper and was about to lay it aside when her eye caught the word "Leavenworth." A hasty glance told her of the drowning the day before of Susie B. Anthony, while out skating with a party of schoolmates! Susie B., her name-

[1] In response to a letter of introduction from Mr. Spofford, of the Riggs, Miss Anthony was the guest of the Burnet House with a fine suite of apartments. In a letter home she writes: "The chambermaid said, 'Why, you have had more calls than Mrs. Hayes had when she occupied these rooms.'"

sake, her beloved niece, as dear as a daughter, and with many of her own strong characteristics—she was almost stunned. Telegraphing at once to cancel her engagements, she hastened to Leavenworth. Just six months before, Colonel and Mrs. Anthony had lost a little daughter, five years old, and now the sudden taking away of this beautiful girl in her seventeenth year was a blow of crushing force. She found a stricken household to whom she could offer but small consolation out of her own sorrowing heart. After the last services she attempted to fill her engagements in Arkansas, speaking in Helena, Fort Smith and Little Rock ; at the last place being introduced to the audience by Governor James B. Eagle. She was so filled with sympathy for her brother and his wife that she gave up her other lectures and returned to Leavenworth, where she remained for two months, going away only for two or three meetings.

She lectured in Memorial Hall, St. Louis, March 5,[1] and a brilliant reception was given her at the Lindell Hotel. On March 9, she spoke at Jefferson City, where the Daily Tribune contained a full synopsis of her address, beginning as follows: "The hall of the House of Representatives was crowded last night as never before, with ladies and gentlemen—State officials, members of the general assembly, clerks of the departments and of the legislature, and all the students from Lincoln Institute. . . . Miss Anthony was received with applause, and plunged at once into the subject which for many years has made her name a household word in every English-speaking country on the globe."

Leavenworth was in the midst of an exciting municipal campaign and Colonel Anthony had been nominated for mayor by the Republicans. Miss Anthony made a number of speeches, at Chickering Hall, the Conservatory of Music, the different churches, meetings of colored people, etc. The night of the last great rally she writes in her diary: "It does seem as if the cause of law and order and temperance ought to win, but

[1] Mrs. Minor managed this meeting and also tried to arrange for Miss Anthony to address a large Catholic gathering but was unsuccessful. She writes: "The vicar-general was on the side of your lecture and spoke in complimentary terms of you and your work."

the saloon element resorts to such tricks that honest people can not match them." So it seemed in this case, and Colonel Anthony was defeated. The Republicans, both men and women, were divided amongst themselves with the usual results.

Her grief over the untimely death of Susie B. was still fresh, and in a letter to a friend who had just suffered a great bereavement, she said : "It is a part of the inevitable and the living can not do otherwise than submit, however rebellious they may feel ; but we will clutch after the loved ones in spite of all faith and all philosophy. By and by, when one gets far enough away from the hurt of breaking the branch from its tree, there does, there must, come a sweet presence of the spirit of the loved and gone that soothes the ache of the earlier days. That every one has to suffer from the loss of loving and loved ones, does not make our anguish any the less."

To the sorrowing father she wrote after she returned home : "Can you not feel when you look at those lonely mounds, that the spirits, the part of them that made life, are not there but in your own home, in your own heart, ever present ? It surely is more blessed to have loved and lost than never to have loved. . . . Which of us shall follow them first we can not tell, but if it should be I, lay my body away without the heartbreak, the agony that must come when the young go. Try to believe that all is well, that however misunderstood or misunderstanding, all there is clear to the enlarged vision. Whenever I have suffered from the memory of hasty or unkind words to those who have gone, my one comfort always has been in the feeling that their spirits still live and are so much finer that they understand and forgive."

Miss Anthony went from Leavenworth to Indianapolis for a few days' conference with Mrs. Sewall on matters connected with the National Suffrage Association and National Council of Women. She writes in her diary : "Mrs. Sewall introduced me to the girls of her Classical School as one who had dared live up to her highest dream. I did not say a word for fear it might not be the right one." From here she journeyed to Philadelphia, stopping, she says, "with dear Adeline

Thomson, whose door is always open to those who are working for women;"[1] thence to New York for the State convention April 26.

The preceding evening a reception was tendered Miss Anthony at the Park Hotel, where she notes, "I wore my garnet velvet and point lace." This did not suit the correspondent of the Chicago Herald, who said: "Her futile efforts to adjust her train with the toe of her number seven boot, instead of the approved backward sweep of heel, demonstrated that she certainly was not 'to the manner born.'" He then continued to sneer at the suffrage women for "adopting the social elegancies of life inaugurated by Mrs. Ashton Dilke, at the council last winter;" evidently unaware that Miss Anthony had been wearing her velvet gown since 1883. But the same day the New York Sun had a long and serious editorial to the effect that "equal suffrage never would be successful until it was made fashionable." This illustrates how hard it is to please everybody, and also how prone men are to make a woman's work inseparable from her garments, always giving more prominence to what she wears than to what she says and does, and then censuring her because she "gives so much time and thought to her clothes." Even from far-off Memphis the Avalanche tumbled down on Miss Anthony for wearing point lace "when the women who wore their lives out making it were no better than slaves." Doubtless the editor abjured linen shirt-bosoms because the poor Irishwomen who bleach the flax are paid starvation wages. The Brooklyn Times also jumped into the breach and, in a column editorial, attempted to prove that "the ballot for woman is as superfluous as a corset for a man." Thus does the male mind illustrate its superiority!

On May 17, Miss Anthony addressed the Woman's Political Equality Club of Rochester, in the Unitarian church, which was crowded to its capacity. She spoke in Warren, O., May 21, the guest of Hon. Ezra B. Taylor and his daughter, Mrs.

[1]In a letter Miss Thomson wrote: "I want you to know that my heart is warmer for you than for any other mortal, my thoughts follow you wheresoever you go, and I am always glad when your footsteps turn toward me."

Upton. The next day the two ladies went to the Ohio State Convention at Akron and were entertained at the palatial home of Mr. and Mrs. Lewis Miller. A dinner was given to Miss Anthony, Mrs. Zerelda G. Wallace and Rev. Anna Shaw by Mr. and Mrs. Adolph Schumacher.

A report went the rounds of the newspapers at this time saying that "Miss Anthony had renounced woman suffrage." It was started doubtless by some one who supposed her to be so narrow as to abandon a great principle because her brother had been defeated in a city where women had the suffrage. The Portland Oregonian having used this alleged renunciation as the basis for a leading editorial, the ladies of Tacoma, Wash., where women had been arbitrarily disfranchised by the supreme court, sent a telegram to Miss Anthony asking if the rumor were true. She telegraphed in reply: "Report false; am stronger than ever and bid Washington restore woman suffrage."

She went to Philadelphia to attend the wedding, June 21, of one of her family of nieces, who filled the place in her great heart which would have been given to her daughters, had she chosen marriage instead of the world's work for all woman-kind. When her sister Hannah had died years before, Miss Anthony had brought the little orphan, Helen Louise Mosher, to her own home, where she had remained until grown. For some time she had been a successful supervisor of kinder-garten work in Philadelphia and today she was the happy bride of Alvan James, a prominent business man of that city.[1] Miss Anthony was pleased with the marriage and the young couple started on their wedding tour with her blessing.

In July a charming letter was received from Madame Maria Deraismes, president of the French Woman's Congress, convey-ing "the greetings of the women of France to the leader of women in America." On the Fourth Miss Anthony addressed a Grangers' picnic, at Lyons, held under the great trees in the dooryard of Mr. and Mrs. Benjamin Bradley, who were

[1] A little incident showed the family spirit. When her lover was about to present her with a handsome diamond engagement ring, she requested that instead the money should be given to the National Suffrage Association, which was done.

her hosts. One hot week this month was spent with Dr. Sarah A. Dolley, a prominent physician of Rochester, in her summer home at Long Pond. Early in August, with her niece Maud, she took a very delightful trip through the lake and mountain regions of New York. After a visit at Saratoga they went up Mount McGregor, and Miss Anthony writes in her diary: "Here we saw the room where General Grant died, the invalid chair, the clothes he wore, medicine bottles, etc.— very repulsive. If the grand mementoes of his life's work were on exhibition it would be inspiring, but these ghastly reminders of his disease and death are too horrible."

They spent a few days at the Fort William Henry Hotel on beautiful Lake George, and she says: "Several of the colored waiters formerly at the Riggs House recognized me the moment I entered the dining-room, and one of them brought me a lovely bouquet." They sailed through Lake Champlain to Montreal, stopping at the Windsor, visiting the grand cathedrals and enjoying the glorious view from the summit of the Royal mountain. Then they journeyed to the Berkshire hills and enjoyed many visits with the numerous relatives scattered throughout that region. At Brooklyn they were the guests of the cousins Lucien and Ellen Hoxie Squier.

Early in July Miss Anthony had accepted an invitation to address the Seidl Club, who were to give a luncheon at Brighton Beach, the fashionable resort on Coney Island. The invitation had been extended through Mrs. Laura C. Holloway, one of the editorial staff of the Brooklyn Eagle and a valued friend of many years' standing, who wrote: "Not nearly all our members are suffragists, but all of them honor you as a great and noble representative of the sex. You can do more good by meeting this body of musical and literary women than by addressing a dozen out-and-out suffrage meetings. You will find many old friends to greet you, and a loving and proud welcome from yours devotedly." She addressed the club August 30, after an elegant luncheon served to 300 members and guests. She selected for her subject, "Woman's Need of Pecuniary Independence," and her remarks were received with much enthusiasm. "Broadbrim's" New York letter thus describes the occasion :

> The Seidl Club had an elegant time down at Coney Island this week, and dear old Susan B. Anthony addressed the members, many of whom are among the representative women of the land. It was the custom in years gone by for a lot of paper-headed ninnies, who write cheap jokes about mothers-in-law, to fire their paper bullets at Susan B. She has lived to see about one-half of them go down to drunkard's graves, and the other half are either dead or forgotten, while she today stands as one of the brightest, cheeriest women, young or old, to be found in our own or any other land. What a tremendous battle she has fought, what a blameless life she has led, rejoicing in the strength which enabled her to mingle with the weak and erring of her sex when necessary without even the smell of smoke on her garments. She made an address, and what an address it was, with more good, sound, hard sense in it than you would find in fifty congressional speeches, and how the women applauded her till they made the roof ring! Susan B. Anthony was by all odds the lioness of the day.

A few days were given to Mrs. Stanton, who was spending the summer with her son Gerrit and his wife at Hempstead, L. I., and they prepared the call for the next national convention. She reached home in time to speak on September 9 at Wyoming, where she was a guest at the delightful summer home of Mrs. Susan Look Avery for several days, as long as she could be persuaded to stay. She then hastened back to New York to visit Mrs. M. Louise Thomas, president of Sorosis, for a day or two, and arrange National Council affairs, and down to Philadelphia to plan suffrage work with Rachel Foster Avery.[1] Just as she was leaving she received a letter from Margaret V. Hamilton, of Ft. Wayne, announcing that her mother, Emerine J. Hamilton, had bequeathed to Miss Anthony for her personal use $500 in bank stock, a testimonial of her twenty years of unwavering friendship. While grieved at the loss of one whose love and hospitality she had so long enjoyed, she rejoiced in the thought that from the daughters she still would receive both in the same unstinted degree.

September 27 saw her en route for the West once more and

---

[1] In a letter to Mrs. Avery relative to some pressing work, Miss Anthony wrote: "I would not for anything have you drudge on this during your husband's vacation. No, no, there is none too much of life and happiness for any of us, so plan to go and be and do whatever seemeth best unto the twain made so beautifully one."

by October 1 she was at Wichita, ready for the Kansas State Convention. The Woman's Tribune had said: "It is the greatest boon to the president of a State convention to have the presence and counsel of Miss Anthony." At this meeting the committee reported a set of resolutions beginning, "We believe in God," etc., when she at once protested on the ground that "the woman suffrage platform must be kept free from all theological bias, so that unbelievers as well as evangelical Christians can stand upon it."

The 10th of October Miss Anthony, fresh, bright and cheery, reported for duty at the Indiana State Convention held at Rushville. On October 14, strong and vigorous as ever, she announced herself at Milwaukee, ready for the Wisconsin State Convention, where she spoke at each of the three days' sessions. In one of her addresses here she said that she did not ask suffrage for women in order that they might vote against the liquor traffic—she did not know how they would vote on this question—she simply demanded that they should have the same right as men to express their opinions at the ballot-box. Immediately the report was sent broadcast that Miss Anthony had said "as many women would vote for beer as against it."

Then down to Chicago she journeyed to talk over the "Isabella Memorial" with her cousin, Dr. Frances Dickinson, who was a prime factor of this movement. While there she had a charming visit with Harriet Hosmer, the great sculptor, who afterwards wrote her:

It was a real treat to see you once more. . . . How well do I remember our first meeting in the office of The Revolution. I do not know of anything that would give me so much pleasure as being present at the Washington convention, and if I am in America next January you may rest assured I shall be there. . . . Yes, you are quite right; there ought to be a National Art Association of women who are real artists, and it would be a good thing all round. There is nothing which has impressed me so much and so favorably since my return here as the number of helpful clubs and associations which are of modern growth, and one of the best fruits of the work that has been done among women. Not only are they full of pleasantness but where unity is there is strength.

Now that we have come together, don't let us permit a vacuum of twenty years to intervene again; we have a great deal to say to each other.

Keep me in your heart as I keep you in mine and hold me ever affy

Miss Anthony went from Milwaukee to the Minnesota State Convention at Minneapolis, and addressed the students of the university. She also visited the Bethany Home for the Friendless and writes in her journal: "I saw there over forty fatherless babes, and twenty or thirty girls who must henceforth wear the scarlet letter over their hearts, while the men who caused their ruin go forth to seek new recruits for the Bethany homes!" At Duluth she was the guest of her faithful friends, Judge J. B. and Sarah Burger Stearns, speaking here in the Masonic Temple. The judge introduced Miss Anthony in these words: "The first quality we look for in men is courage; the next, ability; the third, benevolence. It is my pleasure to present to you tonight a woman who has exhibited, in a marked degree, all three."

On November 11, 1889, at the beginning of the northern winter, she went from here to South Dakota. A woman suffrage amendment had been submitted to be voted on in 1890, and Miss Anthony had been receiving urgent letters from the members of the State Suffrage Association to assist them in a preliminary canvass and advise as to methods of organization, etc. "Every true woman will welcome you to South Dakota," wrote Philena Johnson, one of the district presidents. "My wife looks upon you as a dependent child upon an indulgent parent; your words will inspire her," wrote the husband of Emma Smith DeVoe, the State lecturer. "We are very grateful that you will come to us," wrote Alonzo Wardall, the vice-president.

Miss Anthony began the canvass at Redfield, November 12, introduced by Judge Isaac Howe. The Supreme Court decision allowing "original packages" of liquor to come into the State had just been announced, and the old minister who opened this meeting devoted all of his prayer to explaining to the Almighty the evils which would follow in the wake of these "original packages!" She held meetings throughout the State, had fine audiences and found strong friends at each place. There was much public interest and the comments of the press were favorable in the highest degree.[1]

She addressed the Farmers' Alliance at their State convention in Aberdeen; they were very cordial and officially endorsed the suffrage amendment. In a letter at this time she said: "I have learned just what I feared—the Prohibitionists in their late campaign studiously held woman suffrage in the background. The W. C. T. U. woman who introduced me last night publicly proclaimed she had not yet reached woman suffrage. Isn't it discouraging? When I get to Washington, I shall see all of the South Dakota congressmen and senators and learn what they intend to do. The Republican party here stood for prohibition, and if it will stand for woman suffrage we can carry it, and not otherwise." Her fine optimism did not desert her, however, and to the Woman's Tribune she wrote:

I want to help our friends throughout this State to hold the canvass for woman suffrage entirely outside all political, religious or reform questions—that is, keep it absolutely by itself. I advise every man and woman who wishes this amendment carried at the ballot-box next November to wear only the badge of yellow ribbon—that and none other. This morning I cut and tied a whole bolt of ribbon, and every woman went out of the court-house adorned with a little sunflower-colored knot.

[1] She spoke at Huron, Mitchell, Yankton, Sioux Falls, Madison, Brookings, DeSmet, Watertown, Parker, Pierre, St. Lawrence and Aberdeen, and presented a full set of the History of Woman Suffrage to libraries in each of these towns.

The one work for the winter before our good friends in South Dakota, should be that of visiting every farmhouse of every school district of every county in the State; talking and reading over the question at every fireside these long evenings; enrolling the names of all who believe in woman suffrage; leaving papers and tracts to be read and circulated, and organizing equal suffrage committees in every district and village. With this done, the entire State will be in splendid trim for the opening of the regular campaign in the spring of 1890.

She started eastward the very day her canvass ended, reaching Chicago on Thanksgiving evening, and went directly to Detroit where she spoke November 29, and was the guest of her old friends of anti-slavery days, Giles and Catharine F. Stebbins. Her nephew, Daniel R. Jr., came over from Michigan University to hear her and accompanied her back to Ann Arbor, where she was entertained by Mrs. Olivia B. Hall. He thus gives his impressions to his parents :

Aunt Susan spoke here for the benefit of the Ladies, Library Association, and had an excellent audience; and Sunday night she spoke at the Unitarian church. It was jammed full and people were in line for half a block around, trying to get inside. At the beginning of her lecture Aunt Susan does not do so well; but when she is in the midst of her argument and all her energies brought into play, I think she is a very powerful speaker.

Dr. Sunderland, the Unitarian minister, invited her to dinner and, as I was her nephew, of course I had to be included. The Halls are very fine people and as I took nearly every meal at their house while she was here, I can also testify that they have good things to eat. I brought Aunt Susan down to see where I lived. It being vacation time of course the house was closed and hadn't been aired for a week, and some of the boys having smoked a good deal she thought the odor was dreadful, but that otherwise we were very comfortably fixed.

Miss Anthony spoke at Toronto December 2, introduced by the mayor and entertained by Dr. Augusta S. Gullen, daughter of Dr. Emily H. Stowe. She addressed the Political Equality Club of Rochester in the Universalist church, December 5. During the past three months she had travelled several thousand miles and spoken every night when not on board the cars. Three days later she started for Washington to arrange for the National convention, and from there wrote Rachel Foster Avery :

I have done it, and to my dismay Mrs. Colby has announced my high-handedness in this week's Tribune, when I intended to keep my assumption of Andrew Jackson-like responsibility a secret. One night last week the new Lincoln Hall was opened and when I saw what a splendid audience-room it is, I just rushed the next day to the agent and found our convention days not positively engaged; then rushed to Mr. Kent and from him to Mr. Jordan and got released from the little church, and then back I went and had the convention booked for Lincoln Hall. I did not mean to have any notice of the change of place go out over the country, because it makes no differ-ence to friends outside of Washington. Well, no matter. I couldn't think of taking our convention into any church when we had a chance to go back to our old home, and that in a new and elegant house reared upon the ashes of the old. So if killed I am for this high-handed piece of work, why killed I shall be!

A letter will illustrate her efforts for South Dakota: "I have 50,000 copies of Senator Palmer's speech ready to go to the Senate folding-room, and thence to the South Dakota sen-ators and representatives to be franked, and then back to me to be addressed to the 25,000 men of the Farmers' Alliance, etc. If suffrage literature does not penetrate into every single family in every town of every county of South Dakota before another month rolls round, it will be because I can not get the names of every one. I am securing also the subscription lists of every county newspaper. If reading matter in every home and lectures in every school house of the State will convert the men, we shall carry South Dakota next November with a whoop! I do hope we can galvanize our friends in every State to concentrate all their money and forces upon South Dakota the coming year. We must have no scattering fire now, but all directed to one point, and get everybody to think-ing, reading and talking on the subject."

And again she writes: "With my $400 which I have con-tributed to the National this year, I have made life members of myself, nieces Lucy E. and Louise, and Mrs. Stanton. Now I intend to make Mrs. Minor, Olympia Brown, Phœbe Couzins and Matilda Joslyn Gage life members. I had thought of others, but these last four are of longer standing, were identi-fied with the old National and have suffered odium and perse-cution because of adherence to it."

In the diary's mention of busy days is one item: "Went to the Capitol to the celebration of the centennial of the First Congress. Justice Fuller made a beautiful oration on the progress of the century but failed to have discovered a woman all the way down;" and another: "This morning called on Mrs. Harrison, Mrs. Stanford and Mrs. Manderson to talk about having women represented in the Columbian Exposition of 1892. All are in favor of it."

Every hour was filled with business, and with social duties undertaken solely because of the influence they might have on the great and only question. The last day of 1889 she went to pay the final honors to the wife of her faithful ally, Hon. A. G. Riddle. Death had robbed her of many friends during the past year. On February 1 her old co-worker Amy Post, of Rochester, was laid to rest, one of the veteran Abolitionists who commenced the work in 1833 with Garrison, and who had stood by the cause of woman as faithfully as by that of the slave. In March passed away in the prime of womanhood, Mary L. Booth, editor of Harper's Bazar from its beginning in 1867. In June died Maria Mitchell, the great astronomer, in the fullness of years, having completed threescore and ten. In November was finished the work of Dinah Mendenhall, the venerable Quaker and philanthropist, wife of Isaac Mendenhall, whose home near Philadelphia had been for sixty years the refuge of the poor and oppressed, without regard to sex, color or creed.[1]

At the close of the old year, the Washington Star in a long interview, headed "A Leader of Women," said.

Miss Anthony is now at the capital, ready for the regular annual agitation before Congress of the proposed Sixteenth Amendment to the Constitution. She is one of the remarkable women of the world. In appearance she has not grown a day older in the past ten years. Her manner has none of the excitement of an enthusiast; never discouraged by disappointment, she keeps calmly at work, and she could give points in political organization and man-

[1] The year previous Mrs. Mendenhall had given Miss Anthony and Frances Willard each her note for $1,000 payable after her death, to be used for the cause of woman suffrage and temperance, but the heirs refused to honor the notes.

agement to some of the best male politicians in the land. Her face is strong and intellectual, but full of womanly gentleness. Her gold spectacles give her a motherly rather than a severe expression, and a stranger would see nothing incongruous in her doing knitting or fancy-work. In no sense does she correspond with the distorted idea of a woman's rights agitator. In conversation her manner is that of perfect repose. She is always entertaining, and the most romantic idealizer of women would not expect frivolity in one of her age and would not charge it to strong-mindedness that she is sedate. . . . Speaking of the Columbus celebration, she said she understood it was probable that the board of promotion at the capital would decide to permit women a part in the organization and management of the enterprise.

CHAPTER XXXVII.

AT THE END OF SEVENTY YEARS.

1890.

ISS ANTHONY received New Year's calls in the Red Parlor of the Riggs House, January 1, 1890, entertained a party of friends at dinner in the evening, and had the usual number of pleasant gifts and loving letters. While busy with preparations for the national convention, she learned of the project to celebrate her seventieth birthday on February 15. Supposing it to be simply a tribute from her friends, like the observance of her fiftieth anniversary twenty years before in New York, she was pleased at the compliment, but after the arrangements were commenced she learned that it was to take the form of an elegant banquet at the Riggs and tickets were to be sold at $4 each. Her feelings were expressed in a letter to May Wright Sewall and Rachel Foster Avery, who had the matter in charge :

I write in utter consternation, hoping it is not too late to recall every notice sent for publication. I never dreamed of your doing other than issuing pretty little private invitations signed by Mrs. Stanton and yourselves as officers of the National Association. If its official board is too far dissolved for this, please let the whole matter drop, and I will invite a few special friends to sup with me on my birthday. I know Mr. and Mrs. Spofford would love to unite with you in a personal entertainment of this kind. I may be wrong as to the bad taste of issuing a notice, just like a public meeting, and letting those purchase tickets who wish; but it seems to me the very persons least desired by us may be the first to buy them. I should be proud of a banquet with invited guests who would make it an honor, but with such persons as will pay $5, more or less, it resolves itself into a mere matter of cash. I would vastly prefer to ask those we wanted and foot the entire bill myself.

(663)

Mrs. Sewall wrote at once to Mrs. Avery, "This letter strikes dismay to my soul. I will share with you the expense of the banquet." In a day or two Miss Anthony's heart smote her and she wrote again: "I have blown my bugle blast and I know I have wounded your dear souls, but I can not see the plan a bit prettier than I did at first. I may be very stupid or supersensitive. If it were to honor Mrs. Stanton, I would be willing to charge for tickets." And then a few days later: "Have I killed you outright? I can not tell you how much I have suffered because I can not see this as you do, but I would rather never have a mention of my birthday than to have it in that way. I know you meant it all lovely for me, but you did not look at it outside your own dear hearts. Do tell me that I have not alienated the two best-beloved of all my girls."

They finally effected a compromise on the money feature by sending out handsomely engraved invitations to those whom they wished as guests and letting them pay $4 a plate if they came. Although they proved to Miss Anthony that this always was done in such cases, she assented very unwillingly, and begged that they would ask the friends to contribute $4 apiece to the fund for South Dakota instead of the birthday banquet. Finally, when all her scruples had been overcome, she made out so long a list of people whom she wished to have complimentary invitations that they would have filled every seat in the dining hall. She also was so anxious that no one should be slighted in a chance to speak that Mrs. Avery wrote: "The banquet would have to last through eternity to hear all those Miss Anthony thinks ought to be heard."

On the evening of the birthday over 200 of her distinguished friends were seated in the great dining-room of the Riggs House, including a delegation from Rochester and a number of relatives from Leavenworth, Chicago, New York and Philadelphia. Miss Anthony occupied the place of honor, on her right hand were Senator Blair and Mrs. Stanton; on her left, Robert Purvis, Isabella Beecher Hooker and May Wright Sewall. (Mrs. Foster Avery was detained at home.) The room was beautifully decorated and the repast elaborate, but with such an array of intellect, the after-dinner speeches were the distinguishing feature of the occasion. The Washington Star, in a long account, said:

A company of the most remarkable women in the world were assembled. As she sat there, surrounded by the skirted knights of her long crusade, Miss Anthony looked no older than fifty, but she had got a good start into her seventy-first year before the dinner ended. May Wright Sewall presided. Elizabeth Cady Stanton, that venerable and beautiful old stateswoman, sat at the right of Senator Blair, looking as if she should be the Lord Chief-Justice, with her white hair puffed all over her head, and her amiable and intellectual face marked with the lines of wisdom. Isabella Beecher Hooker, who reminds one of her great brother, with the stamp of genius on her brow and an energy of intellect expressed upon her face, sat at the left of Miss Anthony. Old John Hutchinson, the last of the famous singing family, his white hair and beard forming a fringe about his shoulders; Clara Barton, her breast sparkling with Red Cross medals; and many other women of wide fame were present. Before the banquet the guests assembled in the Red Parlor of the Riggs, where a levee was held and congratulations were offered. It was after 10 o'clock when the line was formed and the guests marched down to the dining-room, Miss Anthony, on the arm of Senator Blair, leading the way.

The correspondent of the New York Sun said in a brilliant description: "The dining-room was a splendid scene, long to be remembered. The American flag was everywhere and, with tropical flowers and foliage, made bright decorations. . . . It was a notable gathering of women world-wide in fame, and of distinguished men. The lady with a birthday—seventy of them indeed—was of course the star on which all others gazed. She never looked better, never happier, and never so much like breaking down before her feelings. No wonder, with such a birthday party! Friends of her youth calling her 'Susan,' affectionate deference from everybody, and all saying she deserved a thousand just such birthdays—young in heart, beautiful in spirit."

Phœbe Couzins replied to the toast "St. Susan," making a witty contrast between the austere St. Anthony of old and the St. Anthony of today, representing self-abnegation for the good, the beautiful, the true. Rev. Anna Shaw made a delightfully humorous response to "The Modern Peripatetic," referring to the ancient philospher who had founded the school of men, and Miss Anthony who had founded the modern school of women peripatetics, ready to grab their grips and start around the world at a moment's notice.   Matilda Joslyn Gage responded to " Miss Anthony as a Fellow-worker ; " Clara Bewick Colby to " Miss Anthony as a Journalist ; " Laura Ormiston Chant, of England, to " American Woman-hood ; " Mrs. Jane Marsh Parker, sent by the Ignorance Club of Rochester, to " Miss Anthony at Home," beginning : " To have brought to Miss Anthony all the testimonials which Rochester would have laid at her feet tonight would have made me appear at the banquet like the modern Santa Claus—the postman at Christmastide."   Rev. Frederick W. Hinckley, of Providence, began his graceful address by saying :

King Arthur, sword in hand, is not at the head of the table, but Queen Susan is, the silver crown of seventy honorable years upon her brow ; and we gather here from every quarter of the Union, little knights and great knights, without distinction of sex, to take anew at her hands the oath of loyal serv-ice to the cause of universal liberty.   Those of us who have followed her through all these years know that she has been a knight without reproach, that her head has been level and her heart true.   Faithful to the cause of her sex, she has been broad enough to grasp great general principles.   She has been not only an advocate of equal rights, but the prophet of humanity ; and a better advocate of equal rights because a prophet of humanity.   There never has been a time when Whittier's lines concerning Sumner would not have been applicable to her :

> " Wherever wrong doth right deny,
>   Or suffering spirits urge their plea,
> Here is a voice to smite the lie,
>   A hand to set the captive free."

Nineteenth century chivalry renders all honor to that type of womanhood of which she is an illustrious example.

Robert Purvis eloquently referred to Miss Anthony's grand work for the abolition of slavery, which, he said, was still continued in the vaster and more complicated work for the freedom of women.   Mrs. Stanton's two daughters, Mrs. Law-rence and Mrs. Blatch, made sparkling responses.   Represen-tative J. A. Pickler said in part :

Five years since, when a member of the Dakota legislature and in charge of the bill giving full suffrage to women, I was characterized in the public press as "Susan B. Pickler." I look upon this as one of the greatest honors ever bestowed upon me. I have never learned how Miss Anthony regarded it. . . .

Unswerved by the shafts of ridicule, without love of gain, she has sublimely borne through all these years ridicule and reproach for principle, for humanity, for womanhood. The soldier battles amid the plaudits of his countrymen, the statesman supported by his party, the clergyman sanctioned by his church, but alone, this great woman has stood for half a century, contending for the rights of women. Says Professor Swing: "Mark any life pervaded by a worthy plan, and how beautiful it is! Webster, Gladstone, Sumner, Disraeli; fifty years were these temples in the building!" How aptly these words describe our great advocate of woman. Gratifying it must be to Susan B. Anthony; gratifying, we bear witness, it is to her friends, that in her maturer years we see this cause, long hated by others but by her always loved, now respected by all; and herself, its representative and exponent, revered, loved and honored by a whole nation.

The main address was made by Mrs. Stanton, who responded to the sentiment "The Friendships of Women," in an oration full of humor, and closed:

If there is one part of my life which gives me more intense satisfaction than another, it is my friendship of more than forty years' standing with Susan B. Anthony. Ours has been a friendship of hard work and self-denial. . . . Emerson says, "It is better to be a thorn in the side of your friend than his echo." If this add weight and stability to friendship, then ours will endure forever, for we have indeed been thorns in the side of each other. Sub rosa, dear friends, I have had no peace for forty years, since the day we started together on the suffrage expedition in search of woman's place in the National Constitution. She has kept me on the war-path at the point of the bayonet so long that I have often wished my untiring coadjutor might, like Elijah, be translated a few years before I was summoned, that I might spend the sunset of my life in some quiet chimney-corner and lag superfluous on the stage no longer.

After giving up all hope of her sweet repose in Abraham's bosom, I sailed some years ago for Europe. With an ocean between us I said, now I shall enjoy a course of light reading, I shall visit all the wonders of the old world, and write no more calls, resolutions or speeches for conventions—when lo! one day I met Susan face to face in the streets of London with a new light in her eyes. Behold there were more worlds to conquer. She had decided on an international council in Washington, so I had to return with her to the scenes of our conflict. . . . Well, I prefer a tyrant of my own sex, so I shall not deny the patent fact of my subjection; for I do believe that I have developed into much more of a woman under her jurisdiction, fed on statute laws and constitutional amendments, than if left to myself reading novels in an easy-chair, lost in sweet reveries of the golden age to come without any effort of my own.

As Mrs. Stanton concluded, "The Guest of the Evening" was announced and, amidst long continued applause and waving of handkerchiefs, Miss Anthony arose and made one of those little speeches that never can be reported, in which she said:

I have been half inclined while listening here to believe that I had passed on to the beyond. If there is one thing I hope for more than another, it is that, should I stay on this planet thirty years longer, I still may be worthy of the wonderful respect you have manifested for me tonight. The one thought I wish to express is how little my friend or I could have accomplished alone. What she said is true; I have been a thorn in her side and in that of her family too, I fear. I never expect to know any joy in this world equal to that of going up and down the land, getting good editorials written, engaging halls, and circulating Mrs. Stanton's speeches. If I ever have had any inspiration she has given it to me, for I never could have done my work if I had not had this woman at my right hand. If I had had a husband and children, or opposition in my own home, I never could have done it. My father and mother, my brothers and sisters, those who are gone and those who are left, all have been a help to me. How much depends on the sympathy and co-operation of those about us! It is not necessary for all to go to the front. Every woman presiding over her table in the homes where I have been, has helped sustain me, I wish they could know how much.

Poems were read or sent by Harriet Hosmer, Elizabeth Boynton Harbert, Alice Williams Brotherton and a number of others. At the close of Mrs. Hooker's verses entitled "Should Auld Acquaintance be Forgot?" the entire company arose and sang two stanzas of "Auld Lang Syne," led by the venerable John Hutchinson. From the many letters received only a few extracts can be given:

Allow me to congratulate you on your safe arrival at the age of threescore and ten. How much we may congratulate ourselves on the great gains that have come to woman during these years; gains for which you have worked so hard and so long! Hoping that you may still be on this planet when the ballot is the sure possession of our sex, I am very truly your co-worker,

LUCY STONE.

None can more heartily congratulate thee on thy threescore and ten years nobly devoted to the welfare of humanity, to unremitting labor for temperance, for the abolition of slavery and for equal rights of citizenship, irrespect-

ive of sex or color. We have
lived to see the end of slavery,
and I hope thou wilt live to see
prohibition enforced in every
State in the Union, and sex no

longer the condition of citizenship. God bless thee and give thee many more
years made happy by works of love and duty. I am truly thy friend,

JOHN G. WHITTIER.

My heart honors, loves and blesses you. Every woman's would if she only
knew you. You'll have a statue some day in the Capitol at Washington, but
your best monument is built already in your countrywomen's hearts. God
bless you, brave and steadfast elder sister! Accept this as the only valentine
I ever wrote. May you live a hundred years and vote the last twenty-five, is
the wish and prediction of your loyal sister, FRANCES E. WILLARD.

Miss Anthony's sole and effective fidelity to the cause of the equal rights of
her sex is worthy of the highest honor, and I know that it will be eloquently
and fitly acknowledged at the dinner, which I trust will be in every way successful. Very respectfully yours, GEORGE WILLIAM CURTIS.

It is a grief to me that I can not be present to honor the birthday of our
dear Susan B. Anthony; long life to her! I should have been delighted to
respond to the toast proposed, and to bear my heartfelt tribute of respect and
love for the true and unselfish reformer, to whom women are no more indebted than are men. "Time shall embalm and magnify her name." Very
sincerely yours, WM. LLOYD GARRISON.

I know her great earnestness in every righteous cause, especially that most
righteous of all, woman suffrage, which I hope may receive a new impulse
from your gathering. As I grow older I feel assured, year by year, that the
granting of suffrage to women will remedy many evils which now are attendant on popular government; and if we are to despair of that cause we must
despair of the final establishment of justice as the controlling power in the
political affairs of mankind. I am faithfully yours, GEORGE F. HOAR.

I can not venture to promise to be present at the dinner to be given to Miss
Anthony, but I should be sorry to lose an opportunity to express my admiration of her life and character. In themselves they are ample refutation of the
charges made by the unthinking that participation in public affairs would
make women unwomanly. If any system of subjection has enabled any

woman to preserve more thoroughly the respect and affectionate regard of all
her friends than has Miss Anthony amid the struggles of an active and stren-

uous life I have yet to learn of it. With sincere hope that she may have many years still left to her, I am yours sincerely,   THOMAS B. REED.

I think I express the feeling of most if not all the workers in our cause when I say that the women of America owe more to Susan B. Anthony than to any other woman living. While Mrs. Stanton has been the standard bearer of liberty, announcing great principles, Miss Anthony has been the power which has carried those principles on toward victory and impressed them upon the hearts of the people. Yours truly,   OLYMPIA BROWN.

May you live many years longer to enjoy the results of your herculean work, and score as many triumphs in the future as you have in the past. On the morning of the 15th some flowers will be sent you with my love. I wish they were as imperishable as your name and fame. Affectionately,
MRS. JOHN A. LOGAN.

How good to have lived through the laugh of the world into its smiles of welcome and honor—how much better to have reached these with a heart gentle and humble like hers—how best of all to care, as she must, scarce a rush for the personal honor and accept it only as an honor to the cause for which she has given so many of the seventy years. Truly yours,
W. C. AND MARY LEWIS GANNETT.

With the hope that you may live to one hundred or until, like ancient Simeon, you behold what you hope for, I am yours very truly,
T. W. PALMER.

My wife and I send you our hearty congratulations on your birthday. May you have many happy returns of the day, with increasing honor and affection from your numerous friends, amongst whom we hope you will let us count ourselves. Yours very truly,   CHARLES NORDHOFF.

I congratulate you with all my heart upon your health and happiness on this your seventieth birthday, and wish to say that I believe no woman lives in the United States who has done more for her sex, and for ours as well, than yourself. The great advancement of women, not alone in the direction of suffrage, but in every field of labor and every department of the better and nobler life of manhood and womanhood, during the past generation, has sprung from the work which you inaugurated years ago. Mrs. Carpenter joins me in congratulations and good wishes. Very truly yours,
FRANK G. CARPENTER.

Cordial greetings were received from Neal Dow and Senator

Dawes, and letters and telegrams came from distinguished individuals and societies in every State and from many foreign countries. Over 200 of these are preserved among other mementoes of this occasion. Among the telegrams were these, representing the great labor organization of the country:

We congratulate you on the seventieth anniversary of a useful and successful life. May you enjoy many years of health and happiness.

HANNAH POWDERLY, T. V. POWDERLY.

May your noble, self-sacrificing life be spared to participate in your heart's dearest wish—woman's full emancipation.

LEONORA M. BARRY, *Grand Organizer K. of L.*

Mrs. Colby issued a birthday edition of the Woman's Tribune containing a history of Miss Anthony's trial, a fine biographical sketch written by herself and many beautiful tributes from other friends, among them this *Faithfully yours—Clara Bewick Colby.* from Laura M. Johns: "Always to efface herself and her own interests and to put the cause to the fore; to be striving to place a crown upon some other brow; to be receiving and giving, but never retaining; ever enriching the work but never herself; to be busy through weariness and difficulty and resting only in a change of labor; to bear the stinging hail of ridicule which fell on this movement, and to receive with surprised tears the flowers that bloomed in her thorny path; to be in the heat of the noonday harvest field at seventy, with years of activity and usefulness still remaining to add to her glorious life and crown it with such dignity as belongs to few—this is the story of Susan B. Anthony."

Miss Anthony carried in her arms seventy pink carnations with the card, "For she's the pink o' womankind and blooms without a peer," from Miss Cummings, of Washington. Flowers were sent in profusion, and there was no end of lovely little remembrances of jewelry, water colors, books, portfolios, card cases, handkerchiefs, fans, satin souvenirs, fancy-work, the gifts of loving women in all parts of the country.[1] The evening was one of the proudest and happiest of a life which, although filled with toil and hardship, had been brightened, as had that of few other women, with the bountiful tributes and testimonials not only of personal friends but of people in all parts of the world who knew of her only through her work for humanity. The next day she sat down to Sunday dinner at a table which, thanks to Mrs. Spofford's thoughtfulness, had been arranged especially for the occasion, surrounded by twenty-five of her own relatives who had come to Washington to celebrate her birthday.

Among many newspaper editorials upon this celebration, an extract from the Boston Traveller, which bears the impress of the gifted Lilian Whiting, may be taken as an example of the general sentiment:

Without any special relay of theories on the subject, Miss Susan B. Anthony discovered early in life the secret of imperishable youth and constantly increasing happiness—a secret that may be translated as personal devotion to a noble purpose. To devote one's self to something higher than self—this is the answer of the ages to those who would find the source of immortal energy and enjoyment. It is a statement very simply and easily made but involving all the philosophy of life. Miss Anthony recognized it intuitively. She translated it into action with little consciousness of its value as a theory; but it is the one deepest truth in existence, and one which every human soul must sometime or somewhere learn.

On February 15, 1820, when Susan B. Anthony was born, Emerson was a youth of seventeen; Henry Ward Beecher was a child of seven and Harriet Beecher Stowe a year his junior; Wendell Phillips was nine, Whittier thirteen, and Wm. Lloyd Garrison fifteen years of age. Elizabeth Cady Stanton was four years old, and Lucy Stone, Julia Ward Howe and James Russell Lowell were Miss Anthony's predecessors in this world only by one or two years. Margaret Fuller was ten, Abraham Lincoln was eleven, and thus, between 1803-20, inclusive, were born a remarkable group of people—a galaxy whose influence on their century has been unequalled in any age or in any country, since that of Pericles and his associates in the golden age of Greece. It is only now, as the work of these immortals begins to

---

[1] There were also more substantial tokens, an Irish wool shawl from Mrs. Chant; a Webster's Unabridged Dictionary from Mrs. Colby, with the inscription, "The words in this volume can not express what women owe you;" a silk dress pattern from brother Daniel R.; a $50 check from sister Mary; $200 from Sarah Willis of Rochester, and $100 from the Woman's Political Equality Club of that city; seventy golden dollars from the Toledo Suffrage Club; $50 from Mrs. Arthur A. Mosher of St. Louis, and enough $5 bills in friendly letters to bring the amount to over $500. The very next day Miss Anthony gave a part of this to friends who were ill or needy, including $50 to Phœbe Couzins.

assume something of the definite outline of completeness; as some results of the determining forces for which this great galaxy has stood, begin to be discerned, that we can adequately recognize how important to the century their lives have been. There are undoubtedly high spirits sent to earth with a definite service to render to their age and generation; a service that prepares the way for the next ascending round on the great cycle of progress, and it is no exaggeration to say that Susan B. Anthony is one of these. . . .

I am Always faithfully yours Lilian Whiting.

Even brief quotations must be omitted for want of space, but this from the Rochester Democrat and Chronicle, Charles E. Fitch, editor, is entitled to a place as the sentiment in the city where Miss Anthony had made her home for nearly half a century:

The occasion is a notable one. It is in honor of one of the noblest women of her time. The day is past when Susan B. Anthony is met with ridicule. She is honored everywhere. Consistent earnestness will, at the last if not at the first, command respect. Slowly but surely, Miss Anthony has won that respect from her countrymen. The cause of the emancipation of women, for which she has labored so long and so zealously, is not yet triumphant, nor is it probable that she will live to see woman suffrage the rule of the land; but at threescore years and ten, she may freely cherish the faith that it is a conquering cause, destined some day to be vindicated in the organic law of the separate American commonwealths and the Federal union.

But it is not alone for the service which Miss Anthony has rendered to the cause of woman suffrage that she is highly honored. She is honored because of her womanhood, because she has ever been brave without conceit and earnest without pretense, because she has the heart to sympathize with suffering humanity in its various phases, and the will to redress human wrongs. She has revealed a true nobility of soul, and has ever been patient under abuse and misrepresentation. She has allied herself with all good causes, and has been the friend of those struggling against the dominion of appetite as well as of those who have sought to free themselves from political thralldom. She has earned the esteem even of those who were diametrically opposed to her views. Within the movements which she has urged, she has been an administrator rather than an orator, although on occasions her speech has been

Ant.—43

informed with the eloquence of conviction. In private life she has constrained affection by a gentleness with which the world would hardly credit her; but those who best know her, best know also the gracious womanhood which illustrates itself in acts of unselfishness and beneficence.

The birthday was celebrated by individuals and clubs in many states with luncheons, teas, receptions and literary entertainments. After all these pleasant happenings, Miss Anthony felt new courage and hope to enter upon the Twenty-second National Suffrage Convention, February 18, at Lincoln Music Hall. This was to be an important meeting, as it was to consummate the union of the National and American organizations, and she was anxious for a large attendance. "Do come," she wrote to the most influential friends, "if you stay away forever afterwards. This will be the crucial test whether our platform shall continue broad and free as it has been for forty years. Some now propose secession because it is to be narrow and bigoted; others left us twenty years ago because it was too liberal. Some of the prominent women are writing me that the union means we shall be no more than an annex to the W. C. T. U. hereafter; others declare we are going to sink our identity and become sectarian and conservative. There is not the slightest ground for any of these fears, but come and be our stay and support."

She also had the annual struggle to secure the presence of Mrs. Stanton, who was about to sail with her daughter for England, but, after the usual stormy correspondence, the day of departure was postponed and she wrote: "You will have me under your thumb the first of February." As her time was limited, Miss Anthony arranged for the hearing before the Senate committee on February 8, which was held in the new room assigned to the committee on woman suffrage. A few days later the ladies spoke before the House Judiciary Committee.

The union of the two organizations was effected before the opening of the convention and Mrs. Stanton elected president.[1] She faced a brilliant assemblage at the opening of the National-American Convention and made one of the ablest speeches

---

[1] Described in detail in Chapter XXXV.

of her life, stating in the first sentence that she considered it a greater honor to go to England as the president of this association than to be sent as minister plenipotentiary to any court in Europe. She closed by introducing her daughter, Mrs. Stanton Blatch, who captivated the audience.[1] Hon. Wm. Dudley Foulke, ex-president of the American Association, then delivered an eloquent and scholarly address. At its close Mrs. Stanton was obliged to leave, as she sailed for Europe the next morning. When she arose to say farewell the entire audience joined in the waving of handkerchiefs, the clapping of hands, and the men in three rousing cheers.

The usual corps of National speakers received a notable addition in Wm. Lloyd Garrison, Julia Ward Howe, Henry B. Blackwell, Carrie Chapman Catt, Hon. J. A. Pickler and Alice Stone Blackwell. Lucy Stone, being detained at home by illness, sent a letter of greeting. When Miss Anthony, as vice-president-at-large, took the chair after Mrs. Stanton's departure, a great bouquet of white lilies was presented to her.

A woman suffrage amendment was pending in South Dakota, and the claims of the new State were presented by Representative and Mrs. Pickler and Alonzo Wardall, secretary of the Farmer's Alliance and vice-president of the suffrage association, all of whom felt confident that with financial help the amendment could be carried but, as the State was poor, most of this would have to come from outside. The convention became very enthusiastic and a South Dakota campaign committee was formed; Susan B. Anthony, chairman, Clara B. Colby, Alice Stone Blackwell. Rev. Anna H. Shaw made a stirring appeal for money. Miss Anthony pledged all that she could raise between then and the November election. Mrs. Clara L. McAdow, of Montana, headed the list with $250. A number of ladies followed with pledges for their respective States. In

---

[1] Miss Anthony wrote in her journal that night: "Harriot said but a few words, yet showed herself worthy her mother and her mother's life-long friend and co-worker. It was a proud moment for me."

a short time it seemed evident that a large sum could be raised and, at Miss Anthony's request, the association directed all contributions to be sent to its treasurer, Mrs. Spofford, at Washington, and she herself agreed to devote a year's work to Dakota.[1]

Miss Anthony remained in Washington several weeks, looking after various matters: first of all, a representation of women in the management of the Columbian Exposition; then there were the reports of the Senate and the House committees, upon which she always brought to bear as much as possible of that " indirect influence " which women are said to possess. Just now the admission of Wyoming as a State with woman suffrage in its constitution was hanging in the balance, but on March 26 she had the inexpressible pleasure of witnessing, from her seat in the gallery of the House, the final discussion and passage of the bill.[2] She also was arranging for the incorporation of the National-American Association, the old National, which had been a corporate body for a number of years, having added American to its name. The bills of the convention were to be settled,[3] and there were still other subjects claiming her attention before she started for the far West to inaugurate the South Dakota campaign.

Miss Anthony was a welcome guest at dinners and receptions

[1] Among those who contributed largely to this fund were Senator Stanford, $300; Rachel Foster Avery, $300; George C. Lemon, Washington City; Hon. Ezra V. Meeker, Puyallup; Rev. Anna H. Shaw; Isabella Hedenberg, Chicago; Alice Stone Blackwell; Emily Howland, Sherwood, N. Y.; O. G. and Alice Peters, Columbus, O.; John L. Whiting, Boston; Senator R. F. Pettigrew, Sioux Falls; Albert O. Willcox, New York, $100 each; Mary H. Johnson, Louisville, $115, which she earned by knitting wool shawls and fascinators; May Wright Sewall sent nearly $200, collected from Indiana friends; James and Martha Callanan, Des Moines, $150; Mary Grew, $143 for the Pennsylvania society. Other women sent their jewelry to be sold, and one offered a gift of western land. The rest of the $5,500 was sent in smaller amounts, and all receipts and expenditures were carefully entered on the national treasurer's books for 1890. When later some carping individuals complained at so much money passing through Miss Anthony's hands, Mrs. Livermore silenced them by saying: "Susan would use every dollar for suffrage if millions were given to her."

[2] Mary Grew wrote her immediately: "All hail and congratulations! I read in this morning's paper that you were in the House yesterday; and I have no doubt that today you are doing something to promote the passage of the bill through the Senate. . . . One object of this letter is to urge you to take more care of your health. Emily Howland reports that you are very much overworked and exhausted. Pray stop awhile and rest yourself, for the sake of the cause as well as for your own and your friends'."

[3] I will authorize you to add my signature to yours in approving any bills relating to the expenses of the National-American convention just past. It will save time and trouble. You are on the spot and know all about the bills. Yours sincerely,   LUCY STONE.

in the homes of many of the dignitaries in Washington, but accepted these invitations only when she saw an opportunity thereby to further the cause of woman suffrage. She realized fully that one important step in the work was to interest women of influence, socially and financially, and the high plane of respectability which this question had now attained was at least partly due to her winters in Washington, where, at the Riggs House and in society, she met and made friends with prominent men and women from all parts of the country and converted them to her doctrines, which they disseminated in their various localities upon returning home.

She writes her sister, in describing social events, of a dinner at the handsome home of John R. McLean, owner of the Cincinnati Enquirer, who in person brought the invitation, while his wife, the daughter of General Beale, looked after her "as if she had been the Queen of Sheba." Here she met Senator and Mrs. Payne of Ohio, Senator and Mrs. Cockrell of Missouri, Senator and Mrs. Butler of South Carolina, Speaker and Mrs. Reed of Maine, Justice and Mrs. Field and other notables. Then she speaks of a meeting of the Cobweb Club, composed of women in official life, where, at the close of her informal talk, they crowded around her and exclaimed: "Why, Miss Anthony, we never understood this question before; of course we believe in it." Mrs. Hearst, wife of the Senator, said: "Had any one ever presented this subject to me as you have done today, you should have had my help long ago." "And so you see," she writes, "that at this juncture of our movement much could be accomplished by accepting such invitations, but it costs me more courage than to face an audience of a thousand people."

While Miss Anthony was still in Washington she sat for her bust by a young sculptor, Adelaide Johnson. "So marble and canvas both are to tell the story," she wrote, "for I have sat also for a painting. The time draws near when I must start out campaigning and O, how I dread it!" During this winter she received an invitation from a State W. C. T. U. to bring a suffrage convention to their city and they would bear the expenses, stipulating only that she herself should be present, and that "no speaker should say anything which would seem like an attack on Christianity." She wrote Miss Shaw: "Won't that prevent your going, Rev. Anna? I wonder if they'll be as particular to warn all other speakers not to say anything which shall sound like an attack on liberal religion. They never seem to think we have any feelings to be hurt when we have to sit under their reiteration of orthodox cant and dogma. The boot is all on one foot with the dear religious bigots—but if they will all pull together with us for suffrage we'll continue to bear and forbear, as we have done for the past forty years."

In this winter of 1890 many loving letters passed between Miss Anthony and Rachel Foster Avery, almost too sacred to be quoted, and yet a few sentences may be used to show the maternal tenderness in the nature of the great reformer:

Of course I miss you from my side, but do not feel for a moment that any doubt of your love and loyalty ever crosses my mind. No, my dear, you and all of us must consider only the best interests of the loved though not yet seen. Banish anxiety and let the rest of us take all the work and care. Be happy in the new life you are molding; avoid all but lovely thoughts; let your first and nearest and dearest feelings be for the precious little one whose temperament and nature you are now stamping. Your every heartbeat, not only of love and peace and beauty, but of the reverse as well, is making its mark on the unborn. . . . I feel much better satisfied to know Sister Mary is with you for a few days. If her presence is comforting, why don't you ask her to stay with you till the wee one arrives?

And so the serene and helpful sister Mary remains until a telegram is sent to the anxious one, by that time in far-off Dakota, announcing the birth of a daughter. "My heart bounded with joy," wrote Miss Anthony, "to hear the ordeal was passed and the little, sassie Rose Foster Avery safely launched upon the big ocean of time." And in a little while the mother replied: "Darling Aunt Susan, when I lie with baby Rose in my arms, I think so often of what she and I and all women, born and to be born, owe to you, and my heart overflows with love and gratitude."

CHAPTER XXXVIII.

THE SOUTH DAKOTA CAMPAIGN.

1890.

ISS ANTHONY left Washington to attend the wedding of her nephew, Wendell Phillips Mosher, and Carolyn Louise Mixer, at Cleveland, O., April 17; stopped in Chicago for a day, and reached Huron, S. Dak., April 23, 1890.[1] During the early winter she had had the most urgent letters from this State, begging her to hasten her coming, that all depended upon her. " If you will come we will throw off our coats and go to work," wrote the men. " Woe to the man or woman who is not loyal to you ! If ever you were needed anywhere, you are needed here now," wrote the women. When she had been in South Dakota the previous autumn, all had united in urging her to take charge of the campaign, and for months she had been receiving appeals for help. " We have not enough money to organize one county," came from a member of the executive committee. In January, from Alonzo Wardall, vice-president of the State Association, " We are very grateful for your earnest efforts in our behalf and trust you will be able to spend the coming summer with us." His wife, the superintendent of press, wrote in February : " We shall give you the credit, dear Miss Anthony, if we succeed next November."

On March 5, the president of the association, S. A. Ramsey, said in the course of a long letter : " I had begun to feel misgivings relative to our success, because we were so poorly pre-

[1] "I am homesick already," she wrote Mrs. Spofford, "and have been every minute since I left Washington. My choice would be to live there most of the year, but no ! Duty first, ease and comfort afterwards, even if they never come."

(679)

pared for the great conflict which is pending; but the appointment by the national convention of a special committee to aid us in our work has inspired me with great hope, especially as you were placed at the head of that committee." Mrs. H. M. Barker, State organizer, wrote March 10: "Organizing must have stopped in the third district, had it not been for the money you sent. It is utterly impossible for us to pay even $10 a week to organizers. I have been disappointed in my home workers, so many incapacitated for various reasons. We shall make suffrage a specialty in all our W. C. T. U. county and district conventions." And April 11, the State secretary, Rev. M. Barker, supplemented this with: "It is absolutely impossible to raise money in the State to pay speakers and furnish literature. This you understand. The election must go by default if it is expected."

At the Washington convention it had been ordered that all contributions should be forwarded to the national treasurer and disbursed by order of the committee. Notwithstanding this, a large proportion was sent directly to Miss Anthony with the express stipulation that it should be expended under her personal supervision. There never was a woman connected with the suffrage movement who could collect as much money as she; people would give to her who refused all others, with the injunction that she should use according to her own judgment. That which was sent her for Dakota she turned over at once to the treasurer, Mrs. Spofford, and paid all the campaign bills by checks.

The Dakota people had made the mistake of electing a suffrage board entirely of men, except the treasurer and State organizer, and, although they had not a dollar in their treasury and no prospects, they agreed to pay the secretary $100 a month for his services! When money from all parts of the country had been sent to the national treasurer, until the Dakota fund reached $5,500, the executive committee of that State suddenly discovered that they could manage their own campaign, and made a demand upon the national committee to turn the funds over to them. Miss Anthony, as chairman, already had sent them $300 for preliminary work; had written and telegraphed that the services of Miss Shaw could be had for only one month, at that time, and asked if they would arrange her routes; and had twice written them to send her their "plan of campaign," but had received no answer to any of these communications. At the last moment she was obliged herself to make out Miss Shaw's route and send her into the field with practically no advertisement. On March 29 she wrote to the State president:

Immediately on the receipt of your answer to my first letter to your executive committee, instead of sending you a personal reply I wrote again to the entire committee, answering the various points presented by you, Mr. and Mrs. Barker and others. This I did to save writing the same thing to half a dozen different people, as well as to make sure that I should get your official action upon what seemed to me most important matters; but to this date I have received not only no official answer, but no information which shows my letter to have been acted upon. Nor have I heard from any member of the committee that you have mapped out any plan of campaign, or have accepted and proposed to work on the one which I outlined last November at the Aberdeen meeting, and twice over have stated in my letters.

You, personally, say to me that you must have the national funds put into your treasury before you can plan work. Now, my dear sir, as a business man you never would give your money to any person or committee until they had presented to you a plan for using it which met your approval. Then I have had no indication of any intention on the part of your executive committee or State organizer to hold any series of suffrage meetings or conventions. The only ones written of are W. C. T. U. county and district conventions. California's suffrage lecturer, I am informed, is to be introduced to the State at the First District W. C. T. U. Convention.

Now, I want to say to you individually, and to the executive committee generally, that the National-American South Dakota committee will pay the money entrusted to them only to *suffrage* lecturers and *suffrage* conventions. We shall not pay it to any individual or association for any other purpose, or in any other name, than suffrage for women, pure and simple. We talked this over fully in your executive committee meeting at Aberdeen last fall, and all agreed that, while the temperance societies worked for suffrage in their way, the suffrage campaign should be carried forward on the basis of the one principle. Our national money will not go to aid Prohibition leagues, Grand Army encampments, Woman's Relief Corps, W. C. T. U. societies or any others, though all, we hope, will declare and work for the suffrage amendment. We can not ally ourselves with the Prohibition or Anti-Prohibition party—the Democrats or the Republicans. Each may do splendid work for suffrage within its own organization, and we shall rejoice in all that do so; but the South Dakota and the National-American Associations must stand on their own ground.

Co-operation is what our committee desire, and we stand ready to aid in holding three series of county conventions with three sets of speakers, at least one of each set a national speaker, beginning on May 1 and continuing until the school election, June 24. I am feeling sadly disappointed that every voting precinct of every county has not been visited, and will not have been by the 1st of May, as was agreed upon at Aberdeen. Still, I want to begin now and henceforth push the work; but the entire fund would not pay every single man and woman in the State who helps, hence every one who can must work without cost either to the State or national committee.

On the 7th of April Miss Anthony wrote to the State secretary:

Yours mailed April 3 is received. The National-American committee have only about $1,300 yet in hand, and we have arranged a trip through your State for Rev. Anna Shaw. When your committee did not answer my telegram, I could not wait longer for fear of losing Miss Shaw's good work before the students of your various educational institutions, and having had urgent importunities from Mrs. D. W. Mayer to send some of our very best speakers to Vermillion so that the 600 students there might be roused to thought before separating for the summer, I felt the cause could not afford to lose Miss Shaw's effective services and so mapped out her route, and telegraphed and wrote asking that she be advertised.

Now, my dear friends, once for all, I want to say on behalf of our South Dakota committee, the National-American Association, and the friends who have placed money in our hands—that we shall no more turn it over to you to appropriate as your executive committee please, without our voice or vote, than you would turn over the money entrusted to your care to our committee to spend as we choose, without your voice or vote. But while we shall retain our right to expend the national fund in accordance with our best judgment, we shall in future, as I have several times written your committee, hold ourselves ready to help defray the cost of whatever work you present to us. I have once verbally, and twice or oftener by letter, presented a plan of campaign asking your adoption of it, or of one which suited you better, telling you that we would co-operate with you in executing the plan and paying therefor; and to all of my propositions to help, the one reply has been: "The wheels are blocked until you turn the money over to us. You in Washington can not run the South Dakota campaign." Now nearly five months have elapsed, and, so far as reported, the resident committee have adopted no plan and had no organizers at work in the different counties.

Rev. Anna Shaw made her lecture tour throughout the State, and wrote Miss Anthony that the people everywhere were most anxious for her to come and there was not the slightest disaffection except on the part of two or three persons who wished to handle the funds. To these Miss Shaw said:

What our committee object to, and what they have no right to do by the vote of our convention, is to put a dollar of our money into your treasury to be spent without our consent or for any purpose of which we do not approve. For example, not one of us, myself least of all, will consent to take out of the contributions from friends of suffrage one dollar to pay towards a salary of $100 a month to any man as secretary. We do not pay our national secretary a cent, and we have no doubt there are plenty of women in the State of Dakota who would be glad to do the secretary's work for love of the cause. I understand it has been planned, and the statement has gone out, that your committee propose to cut loose from Miss Anthony. Now if you do, you cut loose from the goose that lays the golden egg for the South Dakota work; you cut loose from all the national speakers and workers and all the money given.

Miss Anthony wrote Alice Stone Blackwell:

I fully agree with you and dear Mrs. Wallace about not antagonizing the prohibition and W. C. T. U. people who made the 6,000 majority last fall in South Dakota; but I also feel that we must not antagonize the license people, for they are one-half of the voters, lacking only 6,000, and fully 6,000 of the Prohibition men are anti-suffragists and can not be converted. Hence it is also vastly important that the license men shall not have just cause to feel that our national suffrage lecturers are W. C. T. U. agents. That is my one point—that we shall not at the outset repel every man who is not a Prohibitionist.

But we shall see. I surely am as earnest a prohibitionist and total abstainer as any woman or man in South Dakota or anywhere else. But they have prohibition, and now are after suffrage; therefore it should not be the old prohibition and W. C. T. U. yardstick in this campaign, but instead it must be the woman suffrage yardstick alone by which every man and every woman shall be measured. Rest assured I shall try not to offend a single voter, of whatever persuasion, for it is votes we are after now. I hope to make such a good showing of work done in this spring campaign, that our friends will feel like giving another and larger contribution to help on the fall canvass.

The editors of the two suffrage papers, the officers of the National-American Association, the largest contributors to the fund and the other members of the committee, all sustained Miss Anthony in her position. Zerelda G. Wallace published the following notice: " Having pledged to the committee on work in South Dakota one month's services in the projected suffrage campaign in that State, I wish to announce publicly that all I do there will be done under the direction of the South Dakota committee of which Susan B. Anthony is chairman."

Finally, on April 15, the executive committee of South Dakota forwarded their plan, which included a provision that "every dollar expended should pass through the State treasury, and that the State executive committee should have control of all plans of work and decide what lecturers should be engaged;" but by the time it reached Washington Miss Anthony was well on her way to South Dakota. When she arrived she found that it was just as she had been informed, the disaffection was confined to a few persons, but the body of workers made her welcome and she was cordially received throughout the State. Mrs. Emma Smith DeVoe, State lecturer and one of the ablest women, at once placed her services at Miss Anthony's disposal, and in a short time nearly all were working in harmony with the national plan.

The autumn previous, when Miss Anthony was attending a convention in Minneapolis, H. L. Loucks and Alonzo Wardall, president and secretary of the South Dakota Farmers' Alliance, had made a journey expressly to ask her to come into the State to conduct this canvass. She had replied that she never again would go into an amendment campaign unless it was endorsed and advocated by at least one of the two great political parties. They assured her that the Farmers' Alliance dominated politics in South Dakota, that it held the balance of power, and the year previous had compelled the Republicans to put a prohibition plank in their platform and, through the influence of the Alliance, that amendment had been carried by 6,000 majority. They were ready now to do the same for woman suffrage. It was wholly because of the assurance of this support that Miss Anthony took the responsibility of raising the funds and conducting the campaign in South Dakota.

When she arrived in the State, April 23, none of the political conventions had been held. In co-operation with the State executive board, she at once planned the suffrage mass meetings, arranged work for the corps of speakers, pushed the district organization and made speeches herself almost every night. The National-American Association sent into the State and paid the expenses of Rev. Anna Shaw, Rev. Olympia Brown, Laura

M. Johns, Mary Seymour Howell, Carrie Chapman Catt, Julia B. Nelson and Clara B. Colby.[1] It also contributed over $1,000 to the office expenses of the State committee, paid $400 to the Woman's Journal and Woman's Tribune for thousands of copies to be sent to residents of South Dakota during the campaign, and flooded the State with suffrage literature. The speakers collected altogether $1,400 in South Dakota, which went toward their expenses. California, as her contribution to the national fund, raised $1,000 through a committee consisting of Hon. George C. Perkins, Mrs. Ellen Clark Sargent, Mrs. Knox Goodrich, Hon. W. H. Mills, Miss Sarah C. Severance and Dr. Alida C. Avery. This was used to pay the expenses of Matilda Hindman for eight months, as one of the campaign organizers and speakers.

As Miss Anthony was on her way to a meeting June 3, she received a telegram which sent her at once to Huron, where the annual convention of the Farmers' Alliance was in session. Upon arriving she found her information had been correct, that the Alliance and the Knights of Labor had combined forces and were about to form an independent party. She was permitted to address the convention and in the most impassioned language she begged them not to take this step, as it would be death to the woman suffrage amendment. She appealed to them in the name of their wives and daughters at home, doing double duty in order that the men might attend this convention; she reminded them of their pledges to herself and the other women to stand by the amendment, and showed them that, of themselves, they would not be strong enough to carry it, and that the Republican party, unless sustained by the Alliance, would not and could not support it. Her appeals fell upon deaf ears, and the old story was repeated—the women sacrificed to party expediency.

The Alliance of 478 delegates, at its State convention the previous year, November, 1889, after Miss Anthony's speech

[1] Mrs. Wallace was kept at home by serious illness in her family. In a letter to Miss Anthony, August 18, expressing her deep regret, she said: "Money would be no object with me if I could overcome the other difficulties in the way, but as I can not, I fear I shall have to let you think I am unreliable. I regret this, as there is no woman (except Miss Willard) whose good opinion I value so highly as yours."

and after she had met with its business committee, had passed this resolution:

Resolved, That we will do all in our power to aid in woman's enfranchisement in South Dakota at the next general election, by bringing it before the local Alliances for agitation and discussion, thereby educating the masses upon the subject.

The Knights of Labor, at their annual convention in Aberdeen, January, 1890, had adopted the following:

Resolved, That the Knights of Labor, in assembly convened, do hereby declare that we will support with all our strength the amendment to the State Constitution of South Dakota, to be voted on at the next general election, giving to our wives, mothers and sisters the ballot. . . . We believe that giving to the women of our country the ballot is the first step towards securing those reforms for which all true Knights of Labor are striving.

This action was taken by both conventions after the amendment had been submitted, and it was intended as a pledge of support. And yet the following June these two bodies formed a new political party and refused to put a woman suffrage plank in their platform! H. L. Loucks was himself a candidate for governor on this Independent ticket, and in his annual address at this time never mentioned woman suffrage. Before adjourning, the convention passed a long resolution making seven or eight declarations, among them one that "no citizen should be disfranchised on account of sex," but, during the entire campaign, as far as their party advocacy was concerned, this question was a dead issue.[1]

The State Democratic Convention met at Aberdeen the following week, and a committee of representative Dakota women was sent to present the claims of the amendment. They were invited to seats on the platform and there listened to an address by Hon. E. W. Miller, of Parker county, land receiver of the Huron district, in which, according to the press reports, "he declared that no decent, respectable woman asked for the ballot; that the women who did so were a disgrace to their homes;

[1] In order to keep her next engagement, Miss Anthony was obliged to leave Huron at 7:30 A. M., drive sixteen miles in the face of a heavy northwest wind and rain, travel all day and speak that evening. "I did the best I could," she wrote in her journal.

that when women voted men would have to suckle the babies,"
and used other expressions of an indecent nature, "which
were received with prolonged and vigorous cheers." (Argus-
Leader, June 16, 1890.)[1] Judge Bangs, of Rapid City, who
had brought in a minority report in favor of a suffrage plank,
supported it in an able and dignified speech, but it was overwhelmingly voted down amidst great disorder. A large delegation of Russians came to this convention wearing great
yellow badges (the brewers' color in South Dakota) lettered
" Against woman suffrage and Susan B. Anthony."

The Republican State Convention met in Mitchell, August
27. A suffrage mass meeting was held the two days preceding,
and every possible effort made to secure a plank in the platform. Most of the national speakers and a large body of
earnest and influential South Dakota men and women were
present. Rev. Anna Shaw graphically relates an incident
which deserves a place in history :

When the Republicans had their State convention some of the leading men
promised that we should have a plank in the platform, so we went down to
see it through. We requested seats in the body of the house for our delegation, which was composed of most of the national speakers and the brainiest
women in South Dakota, but we were informed there was absolutely no room
for us. Finally a friend secured admission for ten on the very back of the
platform, where we could neither see nor hear unless we stood on our chairs.
We begged a good seat for Miss Anthony but no place could be made for her.
Soon after the convention opened, an announcement was made that a delegation was waiting outside and that back of this delegation would probably be
5,000 votes. It was at once moved and seconded that they be invited in, and
a committee was sent to escort them to seats on the floor of the house. In a
moment it returned, followed by three big, dirty Indians in blankets and
moccasins. Plenty of room for Indian men, but not a seat for American
women !

We asked for a chance to address the delegates, but the chairman adjourned
the convention, and then announced that we might speak during the recess.
That night we went back again to the hall, and the resolution committee not
being ready to report, the audience called for leading speakers, but none of
them dared say a word because they did not yet know what would be in the
platform. Finally when no man would respond they called for me, and I

[1] Then E. W. Miller took the floor, and in a disgusting manner and vile language berated the women present and all woman suffragists. . . . Miller disgraced the name of
Democracy, disgraced his constituents, disgraced South Dakota, disgraced the name of man
by his brutal and low remarks in the presence of ladies and gentlemen.—Aberdeen Pioneer.

went forward and said: "Gentlemen, I am not afraid to speak, for I know what is in *our* platform and I know also what I want you to introduce into yours."

She then made her plea. It was cordially received, but the platform entirely ignored the question of woman suffrage. This was true also of the press and party speakers during the campaign, with one exception. Hon. J. A. Pickler was renominated for Congress, and in his speech of acceptance declared his belief in woman suffrage and his regret that the Republicans did not adopt it in their platform. He was warned by the party leaders, but replied that he would advocate it even if he imperilled his chances for election. He spoke in favor of the amendment throughout his campaign and was elected without difficulty. His wife, Alice M. Pickler, was one of the most effective speakers and workers among the Dakota women and, although Mr. Pickler was a candidate, she did not once speak upon Republican issues but confined herself wholly to the question of woman suffrage. She was as true and courageous as her husband. Although fair reports of the suffrage meetings were published, scarcely a newspaper in the State gave editorial endorsement to the amendment.

The adverse action of the party conventions virtually destroyed all chance for success, but the suffrage speakers usually found enthusiastic audiences, and the friends still hoped against hope that they might secure a popular vote. Miss Anthony never lost courage, and her letters were full of good cheer. "Tell everybody," she wrote, "that I am perfectly well in body and mind, never better, and never doing more work. . . . Anna Shaw and I are on our way to the Black Hills, and shall rush into Sioux City for a pay lecture and turn the proceeds over to the Dakota fund. . . . O, the lack of the modern comforts and conveniences! But I can put up with it better than any of the young folks. . . . All of us must strain every nerve to move the hearts of men as they never before were moved. I shall push ahead and do my level best to carry this State, come weal or woe to me personally. . . . I never felt so buoyed up with the love and sympathy and confi-

With affectionate reverence
for women's truest friend.
    Anna Howard Shaw.

dence of the good people everywhere. . . . The friends here are very sanguine and if I had not had my hopes dashed to the earth in seven State campaigns before this, I, too, would dare believe. But I shall not be cast down, even if voted down.''

The eastern friends sent appreciative letters. ''The thought of you and your fellow-workers in South Dakota in this hot weather and with insufficient funds, has lain like lead upon my heart,'' wrote John Hooker. ''How I wish I could accept your invitation to come to you and talk to the old soldiers,'' said Clara Barton; ''but alas, I have not the strength. My heart, my hopes, are with you and if there is a spoke I can get hold of, I will help turn that wheel before the campaign is over. My love is always with you and your glorious cause, my dear, dear Susan Anthony.''

Hoping once more to see you I am my dear friend

Yours faithfully

Clara Barton

Anna Shaw wrote from Ohio in August: ''I am trying to follow your magnificent example, in quietly passing over every personal matter for the sake of the greatest good for the work. Whenever I find myself giving way, I think of you and all you have borne and get fresh courage to try once more. Dear Aunt Susan, my heart is reaching out with such a great longing for my mother, now eighty years old, that I must go to her for a few days before I enter upon that long canvass, but I will come to you soon.''

It was a hard campaign, the summer the hottest ever known, the distances long, the entertainment the best which could be offered, good in the towns but in the rural districts sometimes very poor, and the speakers slept more than once in sod houses where the only fuel for preparing the meals consisted of ''buf-

ANT.—44

falo chips." The people were in severe financial straits. A two years' drouth had destroyed the crops, and prairie fires had swept away the little which was left. "Starvation stares them in the face," Miss Anthony wrote. "Why could not Congress have appropriated the money for artesian wells and helped these earnest, honest people, instead of voting $40,000 for a commission to come out here and investigate ?"

Frequently the speakers had to drive twenty miles between the afternoon and evening meetings, in the heat of summer and the chill of late autumn ; at one time forty miles on a wagon seat without a back. On the Fourth of July, a roasting day, Miss Anthony spoke in the morning, drove fifteen miles to speak again in the afternoon, and then left at night in a pouring rain for a long ride in a freight-car. At one town the school house was the only place for speaking purposes, but the Russian trustees announced that "they did not want to hear any women preach," so after the long trip, the meeting had to be given up. Several times in the midst of their speeches, the audience was stampeded by cyclones, not a soul left in the house.[1] The people came twenty and thirty miles to these meetings, bringing their dinners. Miss Anthony speaks always in the highest terms of the fine character of the Dakota men and women, and of their large families of bright, healthy children.

The speakers never tire of telling their experiences during that campaign. Mary Seymour Howell relates in her own interesting way that once she and Miss Anthony had been riding for hours in a stage which creaked and groaned at every turn of the wheels, the poor, dilapidated horses not able to travel out of a walk, the driver a prematurely-old little boy whose feet did not touch the floor, and a cold Dakota wind blowing straight into their faces. After an unbroken, homesick silence of an hour, Miss Anthony said in a subdued and

[1] At one place where this happened, the Russian sheriff had locked the court house doors, but the women compelled him to open them. He was entirely converted by the addresses of the afternoon, and in the evening when the storm was approaching, he rushed to Miss Anthony and exclaimed, "Come, quick, and let me take you to the cellar, where you will be perfectly safe." "O, no, thank you," she replied, "a little thing like a cyclone does not frighten me."

solemn voice, "Mrs. Howell, humanity is at a very low ebb!" The tone, the look, the words, so in harmony with the surroundings, produced a reaction which sent her off into a fit of laughter, in which Miss Anthony soon joined.

They had been warned to keep away from a certain hotel, at one place, as it was the very worst in the whole State. At the close of the afternoon meeting there, a man came up and said he would be pleased to entertain the speakers and could make them very comfortable. This seemed to be a sure escape, so they thankfully accepted his invitation, but when they reached his home, they discovered that he was the landlord of the poor hotel! Miss Anthony charged Mrs. Howell to make the best of it without a word of complaint. They went to supper, amidst heat and flies, and found sour bread, muddy coffee and stewed green grapes. Miss Anthony ate and drank and talked and smiled, and every little while touched Mrs. Howell's foot with her own in a reassuring manner. After supper Mrs. Howell went to her little, bare room, which she soon learned by the clatter of the dishes was next to the kitchen, and through the thin partition she heard the landlady say: "Well, I never supposed I could entertain big-bugs, and I thought I couldn't live through having Susan B. Anthony here, but I'm getting along all right. You ought to hear her laugh; why, she laughs just like other people!" Mrs. Howell gives this graphic description of the meetings at Madison, July 10:

In the afternoon we drove some distance to a beautiful lake where Miss Anthony spoke to 1,000 men, a Farmers' Alliance picnic. When she asked how many would vote for the suffrage amendment, all was one mighty "aye," like the deep voice of the sea. That evening we spoke in the opera house in the city. While Miss Anthony was speaking a telegram for her was handed to me, and as I arose to make the closing address I gave it to her. I had just begun when she came quickly forward, put her hand on my arm and said, "Stop a moment, I want to read this telegram." It was from Washington, saying that President Harrison had signed the bill admitting Wyoming into the Union with woman suffrage in its constitution. Before she could finish reading the great audience was on its feet, cheering and waving handkerchiefs and fans. After the enthusiasm had subsided Miss Anthony made a short but wonderful speech. The very tones of her voice changed; there were ringing notes of gladness and tender ones of thankfulness. It was the first great victory of her forty years of work. She spoke as one inspired, while the audience listened for every word, some cheering, others weeping.

When Miss Anthony was starting for South Dakota she was urged not to go, through fear of the effect of such a campaign on her health. Her reply was, "Better lose me than lose a State." A grand answer from a grander woman. And this night in South Dakota we had won a State and still had Miss Anthony with us, the central figure of the suffrage movement as she was the central figure in that never-to-be-forgotten night of great rejoicing.

Ever affectionately and faithfully yours

Mary Seymour Howell.

As very few women were able to hire help, many were obliged to bring their babies to the meetings and, before the speaking was over, the heat and confusion generally set them all to crying. Miss Anthony was very patient and always expressed much sympathy for the overworked and tired mothers. One occasion, however, was too much for her, and Anna Shaw thus describes it:

One intensely hot Sunday afternoon, a meeting was held by the side of a sod church, which had been extended by canvas coverings from the wagons. The audience crowded up as close as they could be packed to where Miss Anthony stood on a barn door laid across some boxes. A woman with a baby sat very near the edge of this improvised platform. The child grew tired and uneasy and finally began to pinch Miss Anthony's ankles. She stepped back and he immediately commenced to scream, so she stepped forward again and he resumed his pinching. She endured it as long as she could, but at last stooped down and whispered to the mother, "I think your baby is too warm in here; take him out and give him a drink and he will feel better." The woman jerked it up and started out, exclaiming, "Well, this is the first time I have ever been insulted on account of my motherhood!" A number of men gathered around her, saying, "That is just what to expect from these old maid suffragists." Some one told Miss Anthony she had lost twenty votes by this. "Well," she replied, "if they could see the welts on my ankles where they were pinched to keep that child still, they would bring their twenty votes back."

She said to me the next day: "Now, Anna, no matter how many babies cry you must not say one word or it will be taken as an insult to mother-hood." That afternoon I gave a little talk. The church was crowded and there were so many children it seemed as if every family had twins. There were at least six of them crying at the top of their lungs. The louder they cried, the louder I yelled; and the louder I yelled, the louder they cried, for they were scared. Finally a gentleman asked, " Don't you want those chil-dren taken out?" "O, no," said I, " there is nothing that inspires me so much as the music of children's voices," and although a number of men pro-tested, I would not allow one of them taken from the room. I was bound I wouldn't lose any votes.

Among the racy anecdotes which Miss Shaw relates of that memorable campaign, is one which shows Miss Anthony's ready retort:

Many of the halls were merely rough boards and most of them had no seats. I never saw so many intemperate men as at ———, in front of the stores, on the street corners, and in the saloons, and yet they had a prohi-bition law! We could not get any hall to speak in—they were all in use for variety shows—and there was no church finished, but the Presbyterian was the furthest along and they let us have that, putting boards across nail kegs for seats. It was filled to overflowing and people crowded up close to the platform. One man came in so drunk he could not stand, so he sat down on the edge and leaned against the table. Miss Anthony gave her argument to prove what the ballot had done for laboring men in England and was work-ing up to show what it would do for women in the United States, when sud-denly the man roused and said: " Now look 'ere, old gal, we've heard 'nuf about Victoria; can't you tell's somethin' 'bout George Washington?'' The people tried to hush him, but soon he broke out again with, "We've had 'nuf of England; can't you tell's somethin' 'bout our grand republic?'' The men cried, " Put him out, put him out!'' but Miss Anthony said: " No, gentle-men, he is a product of man's government, and I want you to see what sort you make.''

In September Carrie Chapman Catt, one of the coolest, most logical and level-headed women who ever went into a cam-paign, at the request of the State executive committee gave her opinion of the situation as follows:

We have not a ghost of a show for success. Our cause can be compared with the work of prohibition, always remembering ours is the more unpopular. Last year the Methodist church led off in State conference and declared for prohibition. It was followed by every other church, except the German Lutheran and Catholic, even the Scandinavian Lutherans voting largely for it. Next the Republican, the strongest party, stood for it, because if they did not it meant a party break. The Farmers' Alliance were solid for it. The leaders were put to work, a large amount of money was collected and representative men went out in local campaigns. It was debated on the street, and men of influence converted those of weaker minds.

Now what have we? 1st.—The Lutherans, both German and Scandinavian, and the Catholics are bitterly opposed. The Methodists, our strongest friends everywhere else, are not so here. 2d.—We have one party openly and two others secretly against us. 3d.—While this county, for instance, gave $700 to prohibition, it gives $2.50 to suffrage and claims that for hall rent, the amount then not being sufficient. 4th.—When I suggested to the committee to start a vigorous county campaign and get men of influence to go out and speak, they did not know of one man willing to face the political animosities it would engender.

With the exception of the work of a few women, nothing is being done. We have opposed to us the most powerful elements in the politics of the State. Continuing as we are, we can't poll 20,000 votes. We are converting women to "want to vote" by the hundreds, but we are not having any appreciable effect upon the men. This is because men have been accustomed to take new ideas only when accompanied by party leadership with brass bands and huzzahs. We have a total lack of all. Ours is a cold, lonesome little movement, which will make our hearts ache about November 5. We must get Dakota *men* in the work. They are not talking woman suffrage on the street. There is an absolute indifference concerning it. We need some kind of a political mustard plaster to make things lively. We are appealing to justice for success, when it is selfishness that governs mankind. . . .

The campaign was continued, however, with all the zeal and ability which both State and national workers could command. There were between fifteen and twenty thousand Scandinavians in the State and a woman was sent to address them in their own language—one woman! A German woman was sent among the men of that nationality. The last night before election, mass meetings were held in all the large towns, Miss Anthony and Miss Shaw being at Deadwood. In her excellent summing-up of the campaign, Elizabeth M. Wardall, State superintendent of press, gives: "Number of addresses by the national speakers, 789; by the State speakers, 707; under the auspices of the W. C. T. U., 104; total, 1,600; local and county clubs of women organized, 400. Literature sent to every voter in the State."

What was the result of all this expenditure of time, labor and money? There were 68,604 ballots cast; 22,972 for woman suffrage; 45,632 opposed; majority against, 22,660. Eight months of hard work by a large corps of the ablest women in the United States, 1,600 speeches, $8,000 in money, for less than 23,000 votes! There were 30,000 foreigners in South Dakota, Russians, Scandinavians, Poles and other nationalities. It is claimed they voted almost solidly against woman suffrage, but even if this were true they must have had the assistance of 15,000 American men. If only those men who believed in prohibition had voted for woman suffrage it would have carried, as had that measure, by 6,000 majority. The opponents of prohibition, of course, massed themselves against putting the ballot in the hands of women.

The main interest of this election was centered in the fight between Huron and Pierre for the location of the capital. There never in any State was a more shameless and corrupt buying and selling of votes, and the woman suffrage amendment was one of the chief articles of barter. The bribers, the liquor dealers and gamblers, were reinforced here, as had been the case in other State campaigns, by their faithful allies, "the Remonstrants of Boston," who circulated their anonymous sheet through every nook and corner of the State.

All of the speakers who took any prominent part in the campaign were paid except Miss Anthony.[1] She contributed her services for over six months and refused during that time an offer of $500 from the State of Washington for ten lectures and a contract from one of the largest lecture bureaus in the country at $60 per night.[2] At the close of the canvass she gave from the national fund $100 each to Mrs. Wardall and Philena E. Johnson, who had worked so faithfully without pay Then, lacking $300 of enough to settle all the bills, she drew that amount from her own small bank account and put it in as a contribution to the campaign.

At the annual meeting of the State W. C. T. U., September 26, a strong resolution was adopted endorsing Miss Anthony's

[1] Henry B. Blackwell made a speaking tour of six weeks through the State at his own expense.

[2] A letter from Mrs. Catt said: "I think you are the most unselfish woman in all the world. You are determined to see that all the rest of us are paid and comfortable, but think it entirely proper to work yourself for nothing. If some of your self-sacrificing spirit could be injected into the great body of suffragists, we would win a hundred years sooner."

work in South Dakota and she was made an honorary member. After the election the State suffrage committee unanimously passed the following resolution: "The earnest and heartfelt gratitude of all the suffragists of South Dakota is hereby extended to Susan B. Anthony, who has devoted her entire time, energy and experience for six months to the cause of liberty and justice."

Anna Shaw said that in all her years of preaching and lecturing she had never been so exhausted as at the close of that canvass. Mrs. Catt was prostrated with typhoid fever immediately upon reaching home, and hovered between life and death for many months, in her delirium constantly making speeches and talking of the campaign. Mary Anthony said, "When my sister returned from South Dakota I realized for the first time that she was indeed threescore and ten."

CHAPTER XXXIX.

WYOMING—MISS ANTHONY GOES TO HOUSEKEEPING.

1890—1891.

ISS ANTHONY accepted the defeat in South Dakota as philosophically as she had those of the past forty years, bidding the women of the State be of good cheer and continue the work of education until at last the men should be ready to grant them freedom. With Mrs. Colby and Mrs. Julia B. Nelson she went directly to the Nebraska convention at Fremont, November 12.[1] The 18th found her in Atchison with Mrs. Catt and Mrs. Colby, at the Kansas convention," where," the Tribune says, " she took part in all the deliberations and methods of work as critically and earnestly as if she herself would have to carry them out."

Two weeks were pleasantly spent visiting at Leavenworth and Fort Scott. Thanksgiving was passed at the latter place and the next day the suffrage friends, under the leadership of Dr. Sarah C. Hall, whom Miss Anthony called " the backbone of Bourbon county," gave her a very pretty reception at the home of Mrs. H. B. Brown. Saturday she spoke, morning, afternoon and evening, at the county suffrage convention. Her time for rest and recreation was very brief, and by December 4 she and Mrs. Catt were in the midst of the Iowa convention at

[1] While here Miss Anthony received a letter from Rev. N. M. Mann, formerly pastor of the Unitarian church in Rochester but now residing in Omaha, which said: "Are you not coming to the metropolis of the State, when some of us here are just perishing for the sight of your face? I speak for myself and Mrs. Mann firstly, though judging from the number of parlors I go into where your picture is the first thing one sees, I fancy there are a good many others who would be hardly less glad than we to greet you. Come and spend a Sunday, and hear a good old sermon, and lecture in my church."

Des Moines.   As usual when flying from one side of the continent to the other, she stopped at Indianapolis for a few days' work with Mrs. Sewall, and they sat up into the wee, sma' hours, planning and arranging for the Washington convention, the National Council and the World's Fair Congress of Women.

She arrived in Rochester Saturday morning; that evening Anna Shaw came in from her tour of lectures all along the way from South Dakota, and it would not be surprising to know that a business meeting of two was held the next day after church services.   Monday evening the Political Equality Club tendered them a reception at the Chamber of Commerce, which was largely attended.   On December 16 and 17 they addressed the State Suffrage Convention in this city, and soon afterwards Miss Anthony started for Washington by way of New York and Philadelphia.

The year 1890 had been eventful for the cause of woman suffrage, in spite of the defeat in Dakota.   The bill for the admission of Wyoming as a State had been presented in the House of Representatives December 18, 1889.   Its constitution, which had been adopted by more than a two-thirds vote of the people, provided that "the right of its citizens to vote and hold office should not be denied or abridged on account of sex."   The House Committee on Territories, through Charles S. Baker, of Rochester, reported in favor of admission. The minority report presented by William M. Springer, of Illinois, covered twenty-three pages; two devoted to various other reasons for non-admission and twenty-one to objections because of the woman suffrage clause, "which provides that not only males may vote but their wives also."   Incorporated in this report were the overworked articles of Mrs. Leonard and Mrs. Whitney, supplemented by a ponderous manifesto of Goldwin Smith, and it ended with the same list of "distinguished citizens of Boston opposed to female suffrage," which had several times before been brought out from its pigeonhole and dusted off to terrify those citizens of the United States who did not reside in Boston.

As it was supposed Wyoming would be Republican its admission was bitterly fought by the Democrats, who used its suffrage clause as a club to frighten the Republicans, but even those of the latter who were opposed were willing to swallow woman suffrage for the sake of bringing in another State for their party.   The changes were rung on the old objections with the usual interspersing of those equivocal innuendoes and insinuations which always make a self-respecting woman's blood boil.   The debate continued many days and it looked for a time as if the woman suffrage clause would have to be abandoned if the State were to be admitted.   When this was announced to the Wyoming Legislature, then in session, the answer came back over the wire: "We will remain out of the Union a hundred years rather than come in without woman suffrage."[1] After every possible effort had been made to strike out the objectionable clause, the final vote was taken March 26, 1890; for admission 139; against, 127.

The bill was presented in the Senate by Orville H. Platt, of Connecticut, from the Committee on Territories, and discussed for three days.   After a repetition of the contest in the House, the vote was taken June 27; in favor of admission 29; opposed 18.   Woman suffrage clubs in all parts of the country, in response to an official request by Miss Anthony and Lucy Stone, celebrated the Fourth of July with great rejoicing over the admission of Wyoming, the first State to enfranchise women.

Another event of importance during 1890, was the first majority report from the judiciary committee of the House of Representatives in favor of the Sixteenth Amendment to the United States Constitution, which should confer suffrage upon women.   Hon. Ezra B. Taylor, of Warren, O., was chairman of the committee and had exerted all his influence to secure this report, which was presented May 29 by L. B. Caswell, of

---

[1] As women had been voting in the Territory over twenty years and this answer was sent by a legislature composed entirely of men, it would seem to show that the evils predicted of woman suffrage were wholly disproved by actual experience.

Wisconsin.[1] On August 12, the Senate committee on woman suffrage again presented a majority report for a Sixteenth Amendment.

Our country needs the votes of her best citizens - women -

E. B. Taylor.

It had long been Miss Anthony's earnest desire to have suffrage headquarters in Washington, pleasant parlors where local meetings could be held and friends gather in a social way. In the midst of her great work and responsibility she exchanged many letters during 1890 with ladies in that city regarding this project, but it was finally decided that it would not be judicious to incur the expense. Out of this agitation, however, was evolved a stock company, incorporated under the name of Wimodaughsis, organized for the education of women in art, science, literature and political and domestic economy by means of classes and lectures. As Miss Anthony never gave herself to any work except that which tended directly to secure suffrage for women, she took no part in the new enterprise except to bestow upon it her blessing and $100. Rev. Anna Shaw was elected its first president. The National-American Association took two large rooms in the new club house for headquarters.

Two deaths in 1890 affected Miss Anthony most deeply. Ellen H. Sheldon, of Washington, for a number of years had served as national recording secretary and had endeared herself to all. She was a clerk in the War Department and her entire time outside business hours was devoted to gratuitous work for the association. Her reports were accurate and dis-

[1] Mr. Taylor wrote Miss Anthony: "The delay, which seemed long to you, was absolutely necessary and I am sure you will understand that I have been faithful to the cause. My daughter Harriet, the most wonderful of all women to me, is largely influential in the result. . . ."

Faithfully Yours
Harriet Taylor Upton

criminating and Miss Anthony felt in her death the loss of a valued friend and helper. Julia T. Foster, of Philadelphia, who passed away November 16, was as dear to her as one of her own nieces. A sweet and beautiful woman, wealthy and accomplished, she was so modest and retiring that her work for suffrage and the large sums of money she contributed were known only to her most intimate friends. In remembrance Rachel Foster Avery sent Miss Anthony all the handsome furnishings of her sister's room.

Miss Anthony arrived in Washington January 3, 1891, and received the usual welcome by Mr. and Mrs. Spofford. On the 24th she went to Boston in response to an invitation to attend the Massachusetts Suffrage Convention.[1] She reached the Parker House Sunday morning, but Wm. Lloyd Garrison came at once and took her to his hospitable home in Brookline, and a most fortunate thing it was. Since leaving South Dakota she had been fighting off what seemed to be a persistent form of la grippe and the next morning she collapsed utterly, pneumonia threatened and she was obliged to keep her room for a week. She received the most loving attention from her hostess, Ellen Wright Garrison, and had many calls and numerous pleasant letters, among them the following:

What a mercy it was that you fell into the shelter and care of the Garrisons when so serious an illness came upon you. Of course everybody was disappointed that you could not be at the meeting so that they might at least see you. Now that you are convalescing and we trust on the high road to recovery we want to arrange an informal reception at our office, so that those or some of those who were sorry not to see you at the meeting, may have a chance to do so. I was too tired today to go with my two, and maybe you would have been too tired to see us if we had gone. It is not quite the same when we are seventy-two as when we are twenty-seven; still I am glad of what is left, and wish we might both hold out till the victory we have sought is won, but all the same the victory is coming. In the aftertime the world will be the better for it.

Trusting you may soon be well again, I am your fellow-worker,

LUCY STONE.

[1] DEAR SUSAN ANTHONY: We are to celebrate the fortieth anniversary of the First National Woman's Rights Convention in this State and want to make the meeting as useful to the cause as we can. You ought to be here. Will you come? The sheaves gathered in these forty years are to be presented, and of course there will be some reminiscences of pioneer times. We shall be glad to announce you as one of the speakers. I hope you are a little rested since the hard campaign in Dakota.   Yours truly,   LUCY STONE.

Her old comrade, Parker Pillsbury, urged her to come for a while to his home in Concord, N. H., saying: "Should you come you may be sure of a most cordial greeting in this household, and by others; but by none more heartily and cordially than by your old friend and coadjutor in the temperance, anti-slavery and suffrage enterprises." Mrs. Pillsbury supplemented this with a pressing invitation; and another came from the loved and faithful friend, Armenia S. White. Miss Anthony appreciated the kindness but there was too much work awaiting her in Washington to allow of visiting, and thither she hastened even before she was fully able to travel.

The first triennial meeting of the National Woman's Council, Frances E. Willard, president, Susan B. Anthony, vice-president, began in Albaugh's Opera House, February 22, 1891, and continued four days. It was as notable a gathering as the great International Council of 1888. Forty organizations of women were represented; "one," said Miss Willard in her opening address, "for every year during which this noble woman at my right and her colleagues have been at work." The meeting was preceded by a reception tendered by Mrs. Spofford at the Riggs to 500 guests. The services for two Sundays were conducted entirely by women, Revs. Anna Shaw, Anna Garlin Spencer, Ida C. Hultin, Caroline J. Bartlett, Amanda Deyo, Olympia Brown, Mila Tupper and, among the laity, Margaret Bottome, president of the King's Daughters, and Miss Willard. The most famous women of the United States took part in this council. Especial interest was centered in the beautiful Mrs. Bertha Honoré Palmer, president of the Board of Lady Managers of the Columbian Exposition, who occupied a seat on the stage. This board was represented also by its vice-president, Mrs. Ellen M. Henrotin and by Mrs. Virginia C. Meredith. Each great national organization sent its most representative women to present its objects and its work.

As Mrs. Stanton was still in Europe, her paper, "The Matriarchate," was read by Miss Anthony. Miss Willard introduced the reader in her own graceful way, saying: "I will not call her Mrs. Stanton's faithful Achates, for that would fail to express it, but will say that the paper written by one of the double stars of first magnitude will be read by the other star." Miss Anthony was so happy over this great assemblage, the direct result of all her long years' work for the evolution of woman into a larger life and a catholicity of spirit which would enable those of all creeds, all political beliefs and all lines of work to come together in fraternal council, that she herself scarcely could be persuaded to make even the briefest address. Her one anxiety was that all the noted speakers present should be seen and heard.[1] The council was received by Mrs. Harrison at the White House.

The Twenty-third Annual Convention of the National-American W. S. A. commenced the morning after the council closed, and the vast audiences which filled the opera house at every session hardly knew when one ended and the other began. The interest was sufficient to sell the boxes for the latter at $10, and single seats at 50 cents. Miss Anthony presided and read Mrs. Stanton's fine address, "The Degradation of Disfranchisement," saying as she commenced that "they might imagine how every moment she was wishing they could see, instead of her own, the sunny face and grand white head of the writer." At its close she introduced Lucy Stone, who came forward amid great applause, and said that "while this was the first time she had stood beside Miss Anthony at a suffrage convention in Washington, she had stood beside her on many a hard-fought battlefield before most of those present were born." She then gave a graphic picture of the work accomplished by the suffrage advocates from 1850 to 1890.

All sections of the United States were represented at this convention; delegates were present from Canada, and Miss

---

[1] In her letter describing the council Mrs. Margaret Bottome wrote of Miss Anthony: "I have met, since I have been in Washington, a woman whom I have heard of since I can remember anything. We are not of the same faith—she has devoted her life to what during the past I have shrunk from—and I met her here for the first time; but I shall carry with me always the impression of her spirit upon my own, of the Christ-life, the Christ-spirit. I got it before she had said five words to me, and I could have sat down at her feet and drank in the spirit of Jesus Christ that is in her, though she does not see him just as I do."

Florence Balgarnie, of London, spoke for the women of England.[1] Mrs. Henrotin presented an official invitation from the Board of Lady Managers for the association to take part in the Woman's Congress to be held during the World's Fair. The newspapers of Washington, and those of other cities through their correspondents, gave columns of reports, indisputable evidence of the important and stable position now secured by the question of woman suffrage. The board of officers was re-elected, Mrs. Stanton receiving for president 144 of the 175 votes; Miss Anthony's election unanimous.

The Women's Suffrage Society of England had sent official congratulations on the admission of Wyoming with enfranchisement for women, and Miss Anthony was determined they should be read in the United States Senate. This letter from Senator Blair will show how it was accomplished: "The memorial of congratulation which you sent me is not one which I could press for presentation as a matter of right, but fortunately, by a pious fraud, I succeeded in reading it without interruption, so that it will appear word for word in the Record, and it is referred to the noble army of martyrs known as the committee on woman suffrage."

At a delightful breakfast given by Sorosis at Delmonico's on its twenty-third birthday, Miss Anthony was the guest of honor, seated at the right of the president, Mrs. Ella Dietz Clymer, and in her short address recalled the fact that she had known Mrs. Clymer and their incoming president, Dr. Jennie de la M. Lozier, when they were no taller than the table.

She gave a Sunday afternoon reception at the Riggs to Mrs. Annie Besant, of London, and in his letter regretting that absence from the city would prevent his attendance, ex-Secretary of the Treasury Hugh McCulloch said: "I am sorry I can not see you often. I have been for many years a 'looker on' and I appreciate the work which you have done for the benefit of the race. You have not labored in vain and you have the

---

[1] After the convention Miss Balgarnie wrote: "It has been one of the most genuine pleasures of my life to meet you, my dear Miss Anthony. I felt 'strength go out of you,' as it were, directly you took my hand."

satisfaction of knowing that your good work will follow you." She accepted a cordial invitation to dine at his home and received assurance of his thorough belief in suffrage for women.

Sincerely Yours

Hugh McCulloch

Easter Sunday she went to Philadelphia to witness the christening, or consecration, of the Foster-Avery baby, by Rev. Anna Shaw, who had married the father and mother. On Monday Mrs. Avery gave a reception for her in the parlors of the New Century Club, and on the following day she addressed the 1,600 girls of the Normal School.

She made this entry in her diary May 1: "Left Washington and the dear old Riggs House today. For twelve winters this has been my home, where I have had every comfort it was possible for Mr. and Mrs. Spofford to give. For as many winters it has been the National Association's headquarters, but now both will have to find a new place, for the hotel is to pass under another management." Miss Anthony reached home the next day, and by the 12th was on hand for the State convention at Warren, O., the guest as usual of Mr. and Mrs. Upton at the home of Hon. Ezra B. Taylor. From here she went to Painesville, where she was entertained at the handsome residence of General J. S. and Mrs. Frances M. Casement, whose hospitality she had enjoyed for many years whenever her journeyings took her to that city.

After a few days at home Miss Anthony started for Meriden, to attend the Connecticut convention on May 22, and when this was over went home with Mrs. Hooker. A letter to the Woman's Tribune said:

I wish I could tell you of my journeyings. I had a pleasant visit with Mrs. Hooker at her charming home in Hartford. En route from Boston I spent a few days with Hon. and Mrs. William Whiting in their beautiful home at Holyoke. One day was devoted to a luncheon party of a hundred or more in their picturesque log cabin three miles down the river, through the lovely Connecticut valley. This cabin, with fireplace worthy the grandest old backlog and fore-stick, polished floors, and lunch served by a Springfield caterer, is

ANT.—45

not like those of our dear old grandmothers. After the tables were cleared, Mrs. Whiting called on me for a talk. Another day we visited Mount Holyoke Seminary, going through the various buildings and, in the great old kitchen, looking upon neat plateaus of light, sweet-smelling bread, biscuits and cake, all made by the girls during the morning. Each must do a certain amount of work, and all is done in memory of the sainted Mary Lyon, whose monument stands under the grand old trees which surround the buildings.

Then on Sunday I went to Cheshire, to dine with my mother's dear cousin, ninety-five years of age, bright and cheerful in her on-look. Next I hied me to the house of my Grandfather Anthony, who lived in it from the day of his marriage in 1792, to his death at the age of ninety-six. . . . From here I went to Saratoga and took a drink from the old Congress Spring, and Wednesday reached home. The paper tells you what happened on Thursday evening, and now I am enjoying to the fullest all the good-will of my dear friends.

"What happened" was that Miss Anthony went to housekeeping! After the mother's death, Miss Mary rented the lower part of the house, which now belonged to her, reserved the upper rooms for herself and sister, and took her meals with her tenants. This plan was followed for a number of years. Now, however, Miss Anthony had passed one year beyond the threescore and ten which are supposed to mark the limit of activity if not of life, and her friends urged that she should give up her long journeys from one end of the continent to the other, her hard State campaigns, her constant lectures and conventions. She felt as vigorous as ever but had long wished for the comforts and conveniences of her own home, and she concluded that perhaps her friends were right and she should settle down in one place and direct the work, rather than try to do so much of it herself. She thought this might be safely done now, as so many new and efficient workers had been developed and the cause had acquired a standing which made its advocacy an easy task compared to what it had been in the past, when only a few women had the courage and strength to take the blows and bear the contumely. So Miss Mary took possession of the house; masons, carpenters, painters and paper-hangers were put to work, and by June all was in in beautiful readiness.

The friends in various parts of the country were deeply interested in the new move. Letters of approval came from all directions, among them this from Mrs. Stanton in England:

" I rejoice that you are going to housekeeping. The mistake of my life was selling Tenafly. My advice to you, Susan, is to keep some spot you can call your own ; where you can live and die in peace and be cremated in your own oven if you desire."

When Miss Anthony returned from her eastern trip on June 11, a pleasant surprise awaited her. The Political Equality Club had taken part in the housekeeping program. Handsome rugs had been laid on the floor, lace curtains hung at the windows, easy chairs placed in the rooms, a large desk in Miss Mary's study, a fine oak table in the dining-room, all the gift of the club. Mrs. Avery had sent a big, roomy desk and Mrs. Sewall an office chair for Miss Anthony's study ; Miss Shaw and Lucy Anthony, a set of china ; Mr. Avery, the needed cutlery; the brother Daniel R., a great box of sheeting, spreads, bolts of muslin, table linen and towels, enough to last a lifetime. From other friends came pictures, silver and bric-a-brac without limit. The events of the evening after Miss Anthony arrived at home are thus described by the Rochester Herald :

The truth of the matter is that for a long time the Woman's Political Club has been in love with Miss Anthony, a feeling which she has not been slow to reciprocate. The affair culminated last evening, the nuptial ceremony being a housewarming tendered by the club. The reception was a complete success, and the rooms were crowded for several hours, the number of visitors being estimated at no less than 300. The house was brilliantly lighted and everywhere was a profusion of cut flowers and potted ferns. At the entrance the visitors were greeted by Mrs. Greenleaf, president of the club, who presented them to Miss Anthony. In greeting each new-comer the hostess displayed her remarkable power of memory and brilliance as a conversationalist, having a reminiscent word for every one. In the parlor before the fireplace stood the old spinning-wheel which in 1817 had been a wedding gift to her mother. It was decked with marguerites and received no small degree of attention. . . .

A short time after the housewarming, her cousin, Charles Dickinson, of Chicago, stopped over night and, after he had gone, Miss Anthony found this note : " It makes me blush for the wealthy people of the country, that they forget their duty to others. Here art thou, with thy moderate income, spending all of it for humanity's cause, thinking, speaking, doing a work that will last forever. Please take rest enough for good health to be with thee, and to make this easier I enclose a check for $300. Call it a loan without interest, already repaid by the good done to our fellow-beings."

In June she made a long-promised visit to her friend Henrietta M. Banker at her home in the Adirondacks, which she thus describes :

Rev. Anna Shaw and I have had a lovely week. Almost every day we drove out among the mountains; one day to the Ausable lakes, through beautiful woods, up ravines a thousand feet; another to Professor Davidson's summer school, high up on the mountainside. But the day of days was when we drove to the farm-home of old Captain John Brown at North Elba. We found a broad plateau, surrounded with mountain peaks on every side. We ate our dinner in the same dining-room in which the old hero and his family partook of their scanty fare in the days when he devoted his energies to teaching the colored men, who accepted Gerrit Smith's generous offer of a bit of real estate, which should entitle the possessor to a right to vote. Of all who settled on those lands, called the " John Brown opening," only one grayheaded negro still lives, though many of their old houses and barns yet stand, crumbling away on their deserted farms.

In front of the house is a small yard and occupying one-half of it is a grand old boulder with steps leading to the top, where one sees chiseled in large letters, " John Brown, December 2, 1859." At the foot is the grave of the martyr, marked by an old granite headstone which once stood at his grandfather's grave, and on it are inscribed the names of three generations of John Browns. The vandals visiting that sacred spot chipped off bits of the granite until it became necessary to make a cover and padlock it down, so that the farmer unlocks the cap and lifts it off for visitors now. Thus is commemorated that fatal day which marks the only hanging for treason against the United States Government. John Brown was crucified for doing what he believed God commanded him to do, "to break the yoke and let the oppressed go free," precisely as were the saints of old for following what they believed to be God's commands. The barbarism of our government was by so much the greater as our light and knowledge are greater than those of two thousand years ago. . . .

July 25 is to be Suffrage Day at Chautauqua, and dear Mrs. Wallace and Anna Shaw are to preach the gospel of equal rights. I do hope Bishop Vincent will be present and there learn from those two, who are surely " God's women," the law of love to thy neighbor—woman, as to thyself—man. I am hoping the gate receipts on that day will be greater than those of any other during the summer. Wouldn't that tell the story of the interest in this question ?

In June she accepted the urgent invitation of the Ignorance Club to honor them by being their guest at their annual frolic on Manitou beach and respond to a toast which should allow her to say anything she liked. Three most enjoyable weeks were spent at home and during this time Miss Anthony addressed the W. C. T. U. She expressed herself in no uncertain tones as to the futility of third parties, declaring that the Prohibition party already had taken some of the best temperance men out of Congress, and made a speech so forcible that it lifted the bonnets of some of the timid sisters. The evening paper reported:

. . . . Rev. C. B. Gardner said Miss Anthony had given the company some excellent political advice, but he inclined to the belief that the temperance reform could be brought about without woman suffrage. "The women would bring the men around in time; they could accomplish much by their moral influence; in this they resembled ministers." Miss Anthony wished to know if it would not be a good thing then, to disfranchise the ministers and let them depend entirely on their moral influence. She explained that in what she had said about prayer she meant prayer by action. She would not have it understood that she did not believe in prayer; she thought, however, that an emotion never could be equal to an action.

She went to Chautauqua July 25, when, for the first time in its history, woman suffrage was presented. Zerelda G. Wallace delivered a grand address and Rev. Anna Shaw gave "The Fate of Republics." Miss Anthony followed in a short speech, and the Jamestown Sunday News said: "Woman's Day was fully justified by the reception given to that intrepid Arnold Winkelreid of women." Frances Willard wrote a few days later from the assembly grounds: "Dearest Susan, I could sing hallelujah over you and our Anna Shaw and 'Deborah' Wallace! It was the best and biggest day Chautauqua ever saw. Do urge your suffragists to go in for this on next year's program."

Miss Anthony attended the golden wedding of John and Isabella Beecher Hooker, in Hartford, August 5; "a most beautiful occasion," she writes in her diary, "but to the surprise of all there was no speaking." An affair without speeches was to her what a feast without wine would have been to the ancients.   On the 15th suffrage had a great day at Lily Dale, the famous Spiritualist camp meeting grounds, Miss Shaw and herself making the principal addresses.   Miss Anthony thus speaks of the meeting in a letter :

 . . . . To Brother Buckley's assertion, made a short time before, that women should not be allowed to vote because the majority of Spiritualists, Christian Scientists and all false religions were women, Miss Shaw replied that there was a larger ratio of men in the audience before her than she had seen in any Methodist or temperance camp meeting or Chautauqua assembly this summer.   When Mr. Buckley charged that women were too numerous in the false religions to vote, she would remind him that there were three women to one man in the Methodist church also; and she was quite willing to match the vast majorities of women in the various religions, false and true, with the vast majorities of men at the horse races, variety theaters, police stations, jails and penitentiaries throughout the country.   She brought the house down with, "Too much religion unfits women to vote!   Too much vice and crime qualifies men to vote!"

People came from far and near.   Fully 3,000 were assembled in that beautiful amphitheater decorated with the yellow and the red, white and blue. . . There hanging by itself was our national suffrage flag, ten by fourteen feet, with its regulation red and white stripes, and in the center of its blue corner just one great golden star, Wyoming, blazing out all alone.   Every cottage in the camp was festooned with yellow, and when at night the Chinese lanterns on the piazzas were lighted, Lily Dale was as gorgeous as any Fourth of July, all in honor of Woman's Day and her coming freedom and equality.

Our hosts, Mr. and Mrs. Thomas Skidmore, are the center of things at Lily Dale, and right royal are they in their hospitality as well as their love of liberty for all.   This camp has been in existence twelve summers, there has been no police force, and no disturbance ever has occurred.   Every one is left to his own sense of propriety of behavior and every one behaves properly.

Miss Anthony still intended, however, to remain at home and in the intervals when she was not coaxed away no bride ever enjoyed more fully her first experiment at housekeeping. All the forty years of travelling up and down the face of the earth had not eradicated from her nature the domestic tastes, and she loved every nook and corner of the old home made new, going from room to room, putting the finishing touches here and there, and fairly revelling in the sense of possession.   Hospitality was her strongest instinct, and during all these years she had accepted so much from her friends in Rochester and elsewhere without being able to return it, that now she wanted to entertain everybody and all at once.   The diary speaks often of ten and twelve at the table for dinner or tea, and Miss Mary, who constituted the committee of ways and means, was quite overwhelmed with the new regime.   The story in the journal runs like this:

Our dear old friends, Sarah Willis and Mary Hallowell, shared our first Sunday dinner with us. . . . Our old Abolition friends, Giles B. and Catharine F. Stebbins and three or four others took tea with us tonight. . . My old friend Adeline Thomson has come to stay several weeks with us. How nice to have my own home to entertain my friends. . . . Anna Shaw and niece Lucy came today and we had five others to dinner. A very pleasant thing to be able to ask people to stop and dine. . . . Brother D. R., sister Anna and niece Maud came today for a week. It is so good to receive them in our own home. D. R. enjoys the fire on the hearth. . . . Had Maria Porter, Mr. and Mrs. Greenleaf and eleven altogether to tea this evening. How I do enjoy it! . . , Who came this day? O, yes, Mrs. Lydia Avery Coonley, of Chicago, her son and her mother, Mrs. Susan Look Avery, of Louisville, Ky. It makes me so happy to return some of the courtesies I have had in their beautiful home. . . . Just before noon Mrs. Greenleaf popped into the woodshed with a great sixteen-quart pail full of pound balls of the most delicious butter, and we made her stay to dinner. The girl was washing and I got the dinner alone: broiled steak, potatoes, sweet corn, tomatoes and peach pudding, with a cup of tea. All said it was good and I enjoyed it hugely. How I love to receive in my own home and at my own table!

She went to Warsaw September 17 to help the Wyoming county women hold their convention.   The 23d had been set apart as Woman's Day at the Western New York Fair, held at the Rochester driving park.   Mrs. Greenleaf presided; Miss Anthony and Rev. Anna Shaw were the speakers.   The former spoke briefly, insisting with her usual generosity that the honors of the occasion should belong to Miss Shaw.[1]   In the course of her few remarks she said: "We who represent the suffrage movement ask not that women be like men, but that they may be greater women by having their opinions respected at the ballot-box.   Only men's opinions have prevailed in this government since it was founded.   Enfranchisement

[1] Miss Anthony was equally generous in regard to speakers of less renown. She wrote to Mrs. Blake during this year: "I felt so happy to give half of my hour at Syracuse to Mrs. C., so that splendid audience might see and hear her. And I am always glad to surrender my time to any unknown speakers whom we find promising; but first they ought to have tried their powers at their home meetings and in rural districts."

says to every man outside of the State prisons, the insane and idiot asylums : 'Your judgment is sound ; your opinions are worthy of being crystallized in the laws of the land.' Disfranchisement says to all women : 'Your judgment is not sound ; your opinions are not worthy of being counted.' Man is the superior, woman the subject, under the present condition of political affairs, and until this great wrong is righted, ignorant men and small boys will continue to look with disdain on the opinion of women."

From the time that Mrs. Stanton had decided to return to America for the remainder of her days, Miss Anthony had hoped they might have a home together and finish their life-work of history and reminiscence. When she learned that her friend, with a widowed daughter and a bachelor son, contemplated taking a house in New York, she was greatly distressed, as she felt that this would be the end of all her plans. She wrote her immediately :

We have just returned from the Unitarian church where we listened to Mr. Gannett's rare dissertation on the religion of Lowell; but all the time there was an inner wail in my soul, that by your fastening yourself in New York City I couldn't help you carry out the dream of my life—which is that you should take all of your speeches and articles, carefully dissect them, and put your best utterances on each point into one essay or lecture; first deliver them in the Unitarian church on Sunday afternoon, and then publish in a nice volume, just as Phillips culled out his best. Your Reminiscences give only light and incidental bits of your life—all good but not the greatest of yourself. This is the first time since 1850 that I have anchored myself to any particular spot, and in doing it my constant thought was that you would come here, where are the documents necessary to our work, and stay for as long, at least, as we must be together to put your writings into systematic shape to go down to posterity. I have no writings to go down, so my ambition is not for myself, but it is for one by the side of whom I have wrought these forty years, and to get whose speeches before audiences and committees has been the delight of my life.

Well, I hope you will do and be as seemeth best unto yourself, still I can not help sending you this inner groan of my soul, lest you are not going to make it possible that the thing shall be done first which seems most important to me. Then, too, I have never ceased to hope that we would finish the History of Woman Suffrage, at least to the end of the life of the dear old National.

Mrs. Stanton's children would not consent to this plan, but she came to Rochester for a month's visit in September.   It was desired by many friends that to the very satisfactory busts of Miss Anthony and Lucretia Mott, which had been made by Adelaide Johnson, should be added one of Mrs. Stanton, and all be placed in the Woman's Building at the World's Fair. To accomplish this Miss Anthony rented a large room in the adjoining house for a studio and invited the sculptor to her home for a number of weeks, until the sittings were finished.

During Mrs. Stanton's visit Miss Anthony entertained the Political Equality Club and a large company of guests, the evening being devoted to the subject of the admission of women to Rochester University.   A number of the faculty, Congressmen Greenleaf and Baker, several ministers, the principal of the free academy—about 200 altogether were present and the discussion was very animated.   Practically all of them believed in opening the doors and a letter of approval was read from David J. Hill, president of the university.   The trustees were represented by Dr. E. M. Moore, who was in favor of admitting women but declared that it would be impossible unless an additional fund of $200,000 was provided beforehand. Miss Anthony insisted that the girls should first be admitted and then, when a necessity for more money was apparent, it would be much easier to raise it.   In the course of his remarks Dr. Moore said it was more important to educate boys than girls because they were the breadwinners.

The Utica Sunday paper came out a few days later with a half-page cartoon representing the university campus ; on the outside of the fence were Miss Anthony and Mrs. Stanton heading a long procession of girls, books in hand ; standing guard over the fence, labeled " prejudice and old fogyism," was Dr. Moore pointing proudly to the " breadwinners," who consisted of two confused and struggling masses, one engaged in a " cane rush " and the other in a fight over a football.   This little incident merely proved the oft-repeated assertion that these two women never were three days together without stirring up a controversy, in which the opposing forces invariably were worsted and public sentiment was moved up a notch in the direction of larger liberty for woman.

Together they visited the palatial home, at Auburn, of Eliza Wright Osborne, daughter of Martha C. Wright, where they were joined by Elizabeth Smith Miller, daughter of Gerrit Smith ; and there were delightful hours of reminiscence and chat of mutual friends, past and present. The diary shows that Miss Anthony purchased a full set of books to join the Emerson and Browning classes this year, but there is no record of attendance save at one meeting. One entry says : "Dancing to the dentist's these days." Another tells of forgetting to go to a luncheon after the invitation had been accepted ; and still another of inviting a number of friends to tea and forgetting all about it.

In November she went again to Auburn to the State convention, remaining four days. The Daily Advertiser said : "Miss Susan B. Anthony, the grand old woman of the equal rights cause, was then introduced and spoke at length upon the objects for which she had labored so faithfully all her life. Except for her gray hair and a few wrinkles, no one would suppose the speaker to be in her seventy-second year. The full, firm voice, the active manner and clear logic, all belonged to a young woman." At the close of the convention Mrs. Osborne gave a reception in her honor, attended by nearly one hundred ladies.

By invitation of the Unitarian minister, Rev. W. C. Gannett, Miss Anthony participated with himself and Rabbi Max Lansberg in Thanksgiving services at the Unitarian church. The topic was "The Unrest of the Times a Cause for Thankfulness," as indicated by "The Woman, the Social and the Religious Movements." Miss Anthony responded to the first in a concise address, considered under twelve heads and not occupying more than that number of minutes in delivery, beginning with Ralph Waldo Emerson's declaration, "A wholesome discontent is the first step toward progress," and giving a resume of women's advancement during the past forty years, due chiefly to dissatisfaction with their lot.

It had not been an easy matter for Miss Anthony to have even this fragment of a year at home. From many places she had received letters begging her to come to the assistance of societies and conventions, and she was just as anxious to go as they were to have her. The most urgent of these appeals came from Mrs. Johns, of Kansas, where a constitutional convention was threatened and the women wanted a suffrage amendment. When Miss Anthony did not go to the spring convention, Mrs. Johns wrote, April 18: "I can never tell you how I missed you, and the people—they seemed to think they must have you. Letter after letter came asking, 'Is there no way by which we can get Miss Anthony?'" When she declined to go to the fall convention, Mrs. Johns wrote, November 26: "I declare it seemed as if I did not know how to go on without you, and our women felt just as I did. We have had you with us so often that we depended on your presence more than we knew." In another long letter she said :

I hope the national association will not leave Kansas to work out her own salvation. Surely you, to whom we owe municipal suffrage, are not going to fail to come to us at this awful juncture! Dear Aunt Susan, you won't get any wounds here. I will take charge of the office and make the routes, which I am able to do well; I will speak; I will organize; I will do anything you think best, and there will be nobody inquiring what you do with funds, and there will be no disgraceful charges and counter-charges, unless I am greatly mistaken in Kansas women and in myself. We all love you here and we want the cause to succeed more than we want personal aggrandizement.

Mrs. Johns persuaded Mrs. Avery to join in her plea and finally Miss Anthony could hold out no longer, but December 11 wrote to the latter : " I have been fully resolved all along not to go to Kansas during this first campaign, because I felt that my threescore and ten and two years added ought to excuse me from the fearful exposure ; still, since you and dear Laura are left so deserted and will be so heartbroken if I stick to my resolve, I will say yes, tuck on my coat and mittens and start. But alas! how soon must that be ? I am thoroughly in the dark as to when and where I shall be wanted to begin, but I will do my level best.''

The closing days of 1891 were devoted to the voluminous correspondence which preceded every national convention. The large number of letters on file from prominent senators and representatives show that Miss Anthony was keeping an eye on the committees and pulling the wires to have known friends placed on those which would report on woman suffrage. '' I am in full sympathy with you upon the question of woman's enfranchisement,'' wrote Senator Dolph, of Oregon, ''and also with your effort to secure a chairman of the committee who favors the movement and is able to present it with intelligence and ability.'' Speaker Reed closed his letter by saying, '' When the eleventh hour comes, we all shall flock in, clamorous for pennies.'' Words of encouragement were received from many others, and Senator and ex-Governor Francis E. Warren, of Wyoming, wrote: '' I am always in harness for woman suffrage wherever I may be. My spoken and written testimony for a score of years has been in its praise and of its perfect working and results in Wyoming.''

CHAPTER XL.

1892.

N her way to the convention of 1892, Miss Anthony stopped in New York in response to an urgent letter from Mrs. Stanton, now comfortably ensconced in a pleasant flat overlooking Central Park, saying that unless she came and took her bodily to Washington she should not be able to go. "All the influences about me urge to rest rather than action," she wrote—exactly what Miss Anthony had feared. She was now in her seventy-seventh year and naturally her children desired that she should give up public work; but Miss Anthony knew that inaction meant rust and decay and, as her fellow-worker was in the prime of mental vigor, she was determined that the world should continue to profit by it. Her address this year was entitled "The Solitude of Self," considered by many one of her finest papers.

Mrs. Stanton received a great ovation at the opening session, January 16, but this proved to be her last appearance at a national convention. For more than forty years she had presided with a grace and dignity which never had been surpassed, and now she begged that the scepter, or more properly speaking the gavel, might be transferred to Miss Anthony, whose experience had been quite as extended as her own. The delegates yielded to her wishes and Miss Anthony was elected national president. The office of chairman of the executive committee was abolished; Mrs. Stanton and Lucy Stone were made honorary presidents, and Rev. Anna H. Shaw vice-president-at-large.

Miss Anthony presided over the ten sessions of the convention and they required a firm hand, for the discussions were spirited, as the questions considered were important. Among them were the work to be done at the World's Fair; the opening of the fair on Sunday; the proposition to hold every alternate convention in some other city than Washington; the plan to carry suffrage work into the southern States; the advisability of making another campaign in Kansas; and other matters on which there was a wide difference of opinion.

John B. Allen, of Washington, had introduced in the Senate, and Halbert S. Greenleaf in the House, a joint resolution proposing an amendment to the Constitution extending the right to women to vote at all federal elections. The House Judiciary Committee, January 18, granted a hearing to such speakers as should be selected by the national convention then in session. Miss Anthony, Mrs. Stanton, Lucy Stone and Mrs. Hooker were chosen. This was the first Democratic committee before whom an appeal had been made; they listened courteously, but brought in no report on the question.

The Senate committee granted a hearing January 20, and three-minute addresses were made by eighteen women representing as many States. Before they left the room, Senator Hoar moved that the committee make a favorable report and the motion was seconded by Senator Warren, Senator Blair also voting in favor. Senators Vance, of North Carolina, and George, of Mississippi, voted in the negative. Senators Quay and Carlisle were absent.

During the convention the district suffrage society gave a reception in the parlors of the Wimodaughsis club house. Later, Mrs. Noble, wife of the Secretary of the Interior, issued cards for a reception in honor of Miss Anthony, Mrs. Stanton and Lucy Stone. It was attended by members of the Cabinet, Senate, House, diplomatic corps and many others prominent in official and social life.

As Miss Anthony had no longer her comfortable quarters at the Riggs House free of all expense, she did not linger in Washington, but went to Philadelphia for a week with the

friends there and reached home February 6. " I send congratulations, I always wanted you to be president," wrote Mrs.
Johns. " Now can't you come to our Kansas City Inter-State
Convention? We do need you so and there wouldn't be standing room if you were there."   And later :   " Do any of my
wails reach you ? The Kansas City people plead for you to come
if only to be looked at.   Is there any hope ?"   Miss Anthony
was perfectly willing to make a winter campaign in Kansas,
but her friends insisted that there were plenty of younger
women to do this work and she should wait till spring.   So
Anna Shaw, Mary Seymour Howell and Florence Balgarnie,
of England, went to the assistance of the women there, and
Rachel Foster Avery gave $1,000 to this canvass.

Every day at home was precious to Miss Anthony.   Sometimes on Sunday afternoon she went to Mount Hope, on whose
sloping hillsides rest the beloved dead of her own family and
many of the friends of early days;[1] or she walked down to the
long bridge which spans the picturesque Genesee river and commands a fine view of the beautiful Lower Falls.   Occasionally a
friend called with a carriage and they took the charming seven-
mile drive to the shore of Lake Ontario.   Sunday mornings she
listened to Mr. Gannett's philosophical sermons ; and through
the week there were quiet little teas with old friends whom she
had known since girlhood, but had seen far too seldom in all the
busy years.   Instead of forever giving lectures she was able to
hear them from others ; and she could indulge to the fullest, on
the big new desk, her love of letter-writing, while the immense
work of the national association was always pressing.   She
had a number of applications for articles from various magazines and newspapers, but her invariable reply was, " I have
no literary ability; ask Mrs. Stanton ; " and no argument
could convince her that she could write well if she would give
the time to it.

She addressed the New York Legislature in April in reference to having women sit as delegates in the approaching Con-

---

[1] In the center of the Anthony lot, not far from the main gateway, is a square monument
of Medina granite, the four sides of its cap-stone inscribed Liberty, Justice, Fraternity,
Equality.

stitutional Convention. In response to a request from the Rochester Union and Advertiser, she wrote an earnest letter advocating the opening of the World's Fair on Sunday, and giving many strong reasons in favor. On April 22, she joined Miss Shaw, who was lecturing at Bradford, Penn., and Sunday afternoon addressed an audience which packed the opera house. The next day she organized a suffrage club of seventy members among the influential women of that city. After leaving there Rev. Anna Shaw, herself an ordained Protestant Methodist minister, wrote her that she had been shut out of several churches because she had addressed an audience at the Lily Dale Spiritualist camp meeting. She said: "I told them that I would speak to 5,000 people on woman suffrage anywhere this or the other side of Hades if they could be got together."

The first week in May, at the urgent invitation of her good friends, Smith G. and Emily B. Ketcham, of Grand Rapids, Miss Anthony attended their silver wedding. From this pleasant affair she went to the Michigan Suffrage Convention at Battle Creek, where she visited an old schoolmate, Mrs. Sarah Hyatt Nichols. She reached Chicago in time for the biennial meeting of the General Federation of Woman's Clubs. Special trains were run from New York and Boston, Central Music Hall was crowded and numerous elegant receptions were given for the 300 delegates from all parts of the country. Many eminent women sat upon the platform, among them the president of the federation, Mrs. Charlotte Emerson Brown, Frances E. Willard, Susan B. Anthony, Julia Ward Howe, May Wright Sewall, Jenny June Croly and Dr. Sarah Hackett Stevenson, all of whom were heard at different times during the convention. Miss Anthony was the guest of Lydia Avery Coonley, whose mother wrote to Mary Anthony:

I have been intending for several days to tell you that however your sister may have been regarded forty years ago, she is today the most popular woman in these United States. The federation closed, as you probably know, on Friday night. During the meetings she was several times asked to come forward on the platform, which she did to the manifest gratification of the people, saying something each time which "brought down the house." On the last night a note was sent to the president asking that "Susan B.," Julia Ward Howe and Ednah D. Cheney would please step forward. They came, but only your sister spoke and what she said was vociferously cheered over and over again.

The business committee of the National Council—Miss Willard, Mrs. Sewall, Mrs. Foster Avery, Miss Anthony and others—met in Chicago the same week, the principal subject of consideration being the Woman's Congress to be held the next year during the World's Fair. While in the city Miss Anthony gave a number of sittings to Lorado Taft, the sculptor. Miss Willard had asked that he might make the bust to be placed in the gallery of famous women at the World's Fair, she herself to be responsible for all expenses. "Come and spend a week with me in my home," she wrote, "while he prepares a model of that statesmanlike head, the greatest of them all." Desirous of pleasing her, Miss Anthony agreed, but at once many of the strong-minded protested that the bust must be made by a woman.

A number of amusing letters were exchanged. From Miss Willard: "Mr. Taft is the most progressive believer in woman and admirer of you, dear Susan, that I know. He is in full sympathy with all of our ideas. I am sure that as a friend of mine, appreciated by me as highly as you are by any woman living, you will not place me in the position of declining to have this work done. Please do not take counsel of women who are so prejudiced that, as I once heard said, they would not allow a male grasshopper to chirp on their lawn; but out of your own great heart, refuse to set an example to such folly."

Mr. Taft himself wrote Miss Anthony: "I can put myself in your place sufficiently to appreciate in part the objections which you or your friends may feel toward having the work done by a man. My only regret is that I am not to be allowed to pay this tribute to one whom I was early taught to honor and revere. . . . Come to think of it, I believe I am provoked after all. Sex is but an accident, and it seems to me that it has no more to do with art than has the artist's com-

ANT.—46

plexion or the political party he votes with.'' Again from Miss Willard: '' Do you not see, my friend and comrade, that having engaged a noble and large-minded young man, who believes as we do, to make that bust, engaged him in good faith and announced it to the public, it is a ' little rough on me,' as the boys say, for my dear sister to wish me to break my contract ? We can not have too many busts of you, so let Miss Johnson go on and make hers, and let me have mine, and let those other women make theirs, and we will yet have one of them in the House of Representatives at Washington, the other in the Senate, the third in the White House! . . . My dear mother and Anna wish to be remembered to you, knowing that you are one of our best and most trusted friends, only I must say that you are a naughty woman in this matter of the ' statoot.' '' Miss Anthony's common sense finally induced her to waive objections and she gave Mr. Taft as many sittings as he desired. When the work was finished Miss Willard wrote: '' My beloved Susan, your statue is perfect. Lady Henry and I think that *one* man has seen your great, benignant soul and shown it in permanent material.''

The 25th of May Miss Anthony attended a meeting of the Ohio association at Salem, where had been held in April, 1850, the second woman's rights convention in all history. There was present one of the pioneers who had called that convention, Emily, wife of Marius Robinson, editor of the Anti-Slavery Bugle. Miss Anthony read her paper for her, as she was over eighty years old, and added her own strong comments, of which the report of the secretary said: '' Her burning words can never be forgotten, and many a soul must have responded to her call for workers to carry to glorious completion what was begun in such difficulty.''

There was some talk at this time of holding a Southern Woman's Council and Miss Anthony wrote to the Arkansas Woman's Chronicle:

The New England States hold an annual suffrage convention and have done so for nearly thirty years, and I do not see any valid reason why the States of any section may not have a society or a convention. Larger numbers from the six New England States can meet and help each other in Boston, than could possibly go to Washington to get the soul-refreshing which comes through the gathering together of kindred spirits from the entire nation.

As I shall be glad to see the women of the South, of all possible aims and ends, meet in council, so I should rejoice to see them hold a southern States' suffrage convention. I say this because I want you to know that my heartiest sympathy goes with you in your effort to call together the women of your section of the Union; and I shall rejoice to see the women of the far-off northwestern States doing the same thing. Women should have their local societies and meetings, their county, State and section conventions, and then, for our great national gathering, each State should send its representatives to Washington, there to confer together and go before the committees of Congress to urge our claims. What a power women would be if all could but see eye to eye in their struggle for freedom!

She remained at home long enough to prepare the memorials to the national political conventions, and June 4 found her at Minneapolis ready for the Republican gathering. She was entertained by Mr. and Mrs. T. B. Walker, and found Mrs. J. Ellen Foster also a guest in that hospitable home. The memorial presented by the National-American W. S. A. contained the same unanswerable arguments for the enfranchisement of women which had been made for so many years, and asked for the following plank: "As a voice in the laws and the rulers under which we live is the inalienable right of every citizen of a republic, we pledge ourselves, when again in power, to place the ballot in the hand of every woman of legal age, as the only weapon with which she can protect her person and property and defend herself against all aggressive legislation."

Miss Anthony was notified that she could have a hearing before the platform committee on the evening of June 8. She was promptly on hand and was kept standing in the hall outside of the committee room until after 9 o'clock. Finally she was so tired she sent for one of the committee to ask how much longer she would have to wait. She learned that its chairman, J. B. Foraker, of Ohio, refused to preside or call the committee to order to hear any argument on woman suffrage. Senator Jones, of Nevada, then hunted him up and asked if he might preside in his place, and permission being given she was invited into the room. She spoke for thirty minutes as only a woman could speak who had suffered the persecution of an Abolitionist before the Republican party was born, who had been loyal to that party throughout all the dark days of the Civil War, who had not once repudiated its principles in all the years which had since elapsed. She pleaded that now she and the women she represented might have its support and recognition in their right to representation at the ballot-box. This committee was composed of twoscore of the most prominent men in the Republican party and, at the close of Miss Anthony's address, every one in the room arose and many crowded about her, giving her the most earnest assurance of their belief in the justice of her cause, but telling her frankly that they could not put a woman suffrage plank in their platform as the party was not able to carry the load ! The plank eventually adopted read as follows :

We demand that every citizen of the United States shall be allowed to cast one free and unrestricted ballot in all public elections, and that such ballot shall be counted as cast; that such laws shall be enacted and enforced as will secure to every citizen, be he rich or poor, native or foreign, white or black, this sovereign right guaranteed by the Constitution. The free and honest popular ballot, the just and equal representation of all the people, as well as their just and equal protection under the laws, are the foundation of our republican institutions, and the party will never relax its efforts until the integrity of the ballot and the purity of elections shall be guaranteed and protected in every State.

This was identical with the one adopted in 1888, at which time a number of women had telegraphed the chairman asking if the convention intended it to apply to women, and he had answered that he did not understand it to have any such intention. Therefore the women who went to the Republican convention of 1892 asking for bread, received instead " the water in which the eggs had been boiled."

There were present at this convention two regularly appointed women delegates from Wyoming, and the difference in the attention bestowed upon them and upon those who came to press the claims of the great class of the disfranchised, ought to have been an object lesson to all who assert that women will lose the respect of men when they enter politics.

Not a newspaper in the country had a slur to cast on these women delegates. The Boston Globe made this pertinent comment : "An elective queen in this country is no more out of place than one seated by hereditary consent abroad. It is no rash prediction to assert·that the child is now born who will see a woman in the presidential chair. Thomas Jefferson will not be fully vindicated until this government rests upon the consent of all the governed."

After just five days at home Miss Anthony left for Chicago to attend the Democratic National Convention, June 21, which was requested to adopt the following plank : " Whether we view the suffrage as a privilege or as a natural right, it belongs equally to every citizen of good character and legal age under government ; hence women as well as men should enjoy the dignity and protection of the ballot in their own hands."

Miss Anthony and Isabella Beecher Hooker took rooms at the Palmer House and the latter made arrangements for the hearing before the resolution committee, which was assembled in one of the parlors, Henry Watterson, of Louisville, chairman. The ladies made their speeches, were courteously heard, politely bowed out, and the platform was as densely silent on the question of woman suffrage as it had been during its whole history. Mrs. Hooker remained alone in the convention until 2 o'clock in the morning, hoping to get a chance to address that body. She had not been fooled as many times as Miss Anthony, who returned to the hotel and went to bed.

The Union Signal, Frances E. Willard, editor, spoke thus of the occasion :

That heroic figure, Susan B. Anthony, sure to stand out in history as plainly as any of our presidents, has given added significance to the two great political conventions of the year. Neither party has recognized her plea, but both have innumerable adherents who openly declare themselves in favor of her principles. She states that this year she felt for the first time that she had a pivot on which to hang her quadrennial plea, and that pivot was Wyoming, the men of that equal-minded State in both conventions holding up her hands. Miss Anthony's pathetic eyes reveal that she has attained to loneliness—the guerdon of great spirits who struggle from any direction toward the mountain tops of human liberty. But on the heights such souls meet God, and one day all women shall call her blessed.

The National Prohibition Convention at Cincinnati, June 30, was not visited by Miss Anthony, as she felt that the women of this party needed no assistance in looking after the interests of suffrage. The third plank in the platform there adopted read : '' No citizen should be denied the right to vote on account of sex.''

From Chicago she went directly to Kansas to look after the fences in that State. Mrs. Johns and Anna Shaw joined her and they spoke before the Chautauqua Assembly at Ottawa, June 27, going thence to Topeka, as Miss Anthony expressed it, '' to watch the State Republican Convention.'' They received a hearty greeting and she was invited to address the convention June 30. The Capital said : '' There were loud calls for Susan B. Anthony and as she advanced to the platform she was greeted with the most cordial applause.'' In the evening a reception was given in the Senate chamber to the ladies in attendance at the convention. Miss Anthony, Mrs. Johns and Mrs. May Belleville Brown addressed the resolution committee. The platform was reported with a plank favoring the submission to the voters of a woman suffrage amendment, which was enthusiastically adopted—455 to 267—in the largest Republican convention ever held in Kansas.[1]

Miss Anthony and Miss Shaw then hastened to Omaha for the first national convention of the People's party July 4. They arrived about 9 P. M., July 2, to find they were booked for speeches at the Unitarian church that evening and the audience had been waiting since 7:30, so they rushed thither, hot, dusty and tired, and made their addresses. Sunday afternoon they went to a workingwomen's meeting in the exposition building and heard Master Workman Powderly for the first time. At his invitation Miss Anthony also spoke.

---

[1] At the convention of Republican clubs a few days previous, Senator Ingalls, having been defeated for re-election to the Senate and feeling somewhat humbled, said in his speech: "I believe every man ought to be a politician; I might say every woman also. If a plank endorsing woman suffrage were inserted in the Republican platform, I would stand upon it." Ten years before, in this same city, he had declared it to be "that obscene dogma, whose advocates are long-haired men and short-haired women, the unsexed of both sexes, human capons and epicenes."

The People's party, from its inception, had recognized women as speakers and delegates and claimed to be the party of morality and reform, but after a day at the convention Miss Anthony writes in her diary: "They are quite as oblivious to the underlying principle of justice to women as either of the old parties and, as a convention, still more so." The resolution committee refused to grant the ladies even an opportunity to address them, which had been done willingly by the Republicans and Democrats. Their platform contained no reference to woman suffrage except that in the long preamble occurred the sentence: "We believe that the forces of reform this day organized will never cease to move forward until every wrong is righted, and equal rights and equal privileges securely established for all the men and women of this country." This sentiment, however, was universally accepted by the delegates as including the right of suffrage.

Miss Anthony spoke at the Beatrice Chautauqua Assembly, and then returned to Rochester. She had some time before received a letter from Chancellor John H. Vincent saying: "The subject of woman suffrage will be presented at Chautauqua on Saturday, July 30, 1892. A prominent speaker will be secured to present the question as forcibly as possible. In behalf of the Chautauqua management, I take pleasure in extending to you a hearty invitation to be present and take a place upon the platform on that occasion. Trusting that you will be able to accept this invitation, I am, faithfully yours."

She had had a long, hot and fatiguing trip and her cool, spacious home was so restful that she decided to defer her visit to Chautauqua until later in the season.[1] On August 8, Miss Shaw, Mrs. Foster Avery and Miss Anthony, who had been having a little visit together, started from Rochester for Chautauqua, where the Reverend Anna was to debate the question of woman suffrage with Rev. J. M. Buckley, editor New York Christian Advocate. She gave her address amidst a succession

[1] Henry B. Blackwell delivered the address at Chautauqua. At its close he asked all who were opposed to woman suffrage to rise, and about twenty persons stood up. He then asked all who were in favor to stand, and the great audience, filling the huge amphitheater, rose in a body.

of cheers and applause, Miss Anthony sitting on the platform with her, an honor rarely accorded at the assembly. In the evening a delightful reception was given to the three ladies in the Hall of Philosophy. Dr. Buckley made his reply the next day to an audience so cold that even his supreme self-satisfaction was disturbed. If any one thing ever has been demonstrated at Chautauqua, by those speeches and all preceding and following them on the same question, it is that the sentiment of the vast majority of the people who annually visit this great assembly is in favor of woman suffrage.

After speaking at the Cassadaga Lake camp meeting, August 24, Miss Anthony went in September to the Mississippi Valley Conference at Des Moines. It was thought that possibly by holding a great convention in the West, large numbers in that section of the country and the States along the Mississippi could attend who would find it inconvenient to go to Washington. She was glad to give her co-operation and spoke and worked valiantly through all the sessions. From Des Moines she went to Peru, Neb., at the urgent invitation of President George L. Farnham, to address the State Normal School.[1]

Early in October she began her tour of the State of Kansas under the auspices of the Republican central committee. She was accompanied one week by Mrs. Johns, and then each went with some of the men who were canvassing the State. Mrs. Johns made Republican speeches; Miss Anthony described the record of the party on human freedom and urged them to complete that roll of honor by enfranchising women. The campaign managers were very much dissatisfied because she talked suffrage instead of tariff and finance, but as she was paying her own travelling expenses and contributing her services, she reserved the right to speak on the only subject in which she felt a vital interest. If the Republicans had won the election, Miss Anthony and Mrs. Johns expected that of course they would take up the question of woman suffrage and carry it to

---

[1] When she spoke in the New York State Teachers' Convention in 1853, the first time a woman's voice had been heard in that body, Professor Farnham, then superintendent of the Syracuse public schools, was one of the three men who came up and congratulated her.

success ; but the State was carried by the newly formed People's party.

As soon as she was thoroughly rested and renovated in her own home, after this hard campaign, Miss Anthony left for the State convention at Syracuse, November 14.[1] The Standard, intending to compliment the ladies, said : "The loud-voiced, aggressive woman of other days was not here. In her place were low-voiced, quietly-dressed, womanly women, and those who expected to see the 'woman rioter' of the past failed to find one of the sort. The graceful, dignified and quiet woman of today bears no likeness to some who have gone before, who thought to break through and gain their desires."

A contemporary called the paper down as follows : "When it is remembered that Susan B. Anthony was one of the originators of the movement, that Lucy Stone and Mrs. Greenleaf and a host of others who have marched right along in the suffrage ranks from the beginning, were also the leaders in this 'low-voiced' assembly who came on tip-toe and acted in pantomime, the compliment, to say the least, has negative qualities." An interview on this statement contains the following paragraph :

"It simply shows," said Miss Anthony, smiling, "how differently the question is regarded now. Among the women who were pioneers in the movement were Elizabeth Cady Stanton and myself. I don't think it probable that we are any sweeter-faced or that our voices are any more melodious than they were thirty years ago. It is only that the whole matter was regarded with such horror and aversion then that any one connected with it was looked upon in a disagreeable light; it is very different now." Her pleasant face, with a suggestion of her Quaker descent in its soft bands of gray hair, took on a gently reminiscent expression, which her visitor could not help but contrast amusedly with the imaginary portrait of the redoubtable Amazon that in her early years was conjured up by the sound of Susan B. Anthony's name.

Thanksgiving Day she attended service at the Universalist church and comments in her diary : "Mr. Morrill, the asso-

---

[1] While here Miss Anthony received a telegram: "Greeting, gratitude and good-by to the noblest Roman of them all and her brave host, from Isabel Somerset and Frances E. Willard." They had expected to stop in Rochester and visit her before leaving for England, but had gone to New York by another route.

ciate pastor, spoke on 'The undiscovered Church without a Bishop;' Mr. Gannett, 'The undiscovered State without a King;' Mr. Lansberg, 'Many States in One;' all good, but all alike gave not the faintest hint of any undiscovered America, where the male head of the family should not be considered 'divinely appointed.' I had hard work to keep my peace."

The next day she went to Buffalo to address the alumnæ of the ladies' academy, and was entertained by Miss Charlotte Mulligan, founder of the missionary school for boys. During this time she was investigating the new law permitting women to vote for county school commissioners in New York, and found to her disgust that by the use of the words "county clerk" instead merely of "clerk who prints and distributes the ballots," all the women of the large towns and cities were still disfranchised; just as the law of 1880 had used the words "school meeting," which also cut off the women of the cities. This was another illustration of the manner in which every step of the way to suffrage for women has been made as difficult as possible.

In December Miss Anthony became an office-holder! It happened in this way: Her neighbor, Dr. Jonas Jones, who had been one of the trustees of the State Industrial School located at Rochester, died on the 4th. She immediately wrote to Governor Roswell P. Flower requesting that a woman be put on the board in his place, in addition to the one already serving (Mrs. Emil Kuichling), and suggested Mrs. Lansberg, wife of the rabbi; at the same time she asked Mary Seymour Howell, who resided in Albany, to see the governor and use her influence. She did so and found he was quite willing to appoint a woman but would not consider any but Miss Anthony. She, however, was away from home so much she thought that in justice to the institution she ought not take the position; but when she learned that her refusal might result in a man's being given the place, she telegraphed her willingness to accept. She was appointed at once to fill out the unexpired term of Dr. Jones, and May 4, 1893, was re-appointed by Governor Levi P. Morton for a full term. Of course numerous letters and telegrams of congratulation were received and the newspapers contained many kind notices, similar in tone to this from the Democrat and Chronicle:

It is a good appointment; a fitting recognition of one of the ablest and best women in the commonwealth. There has been a vast amount of cheap wit expended upon Miss Anthony during the past years, and although it has been almost entirely good-natured it has served to give a wrong impression to the unthinking of one of the clearest-headed and most unselfish women ever identified with a public movement. . . . Speaking of her appointment she said: "You see I have been regarded as a hoofed and horned creature for so long that even a little thing touches my heart, and when it comes to being recognized as an American citizen after fighting forty years to prove my citizenship, it begins to look as if we women have not fought in vain." . . . A braver-hearted woman than Susan B. Anthony never lived, but those who can read between the lines of her remark will not miss the little touch of pathos in her pride, and the hint of the disappointments which have hurt in the long struggle.

A new charter for the city of Rochester had been prepared and a mass meeting of citizens was announced for December 12, to hear an exposition of its points. The morning paper said: "By far the most largely attended meeting the Chamber of Commerce has ever held was that of last evening. The large attendance was due to the announcement that the new charter would be discussed by Miss Susan B. Anthony, and the interest of the meeting was largely due to the fact that, true to her colors, she kept her engagement. . . . ." Miss Anthony's commission had been received from the governor that day, which fact was announced by President Brickner as he introduced her, and she was greeted with cheers. In the course of her speech she said:

Since promising to address this body, I have tried in vain to find some word which would settle the question with every member present in favor of so amending the charter as to give our women equal voice in conducting the affairs of the city. It seems such a self-evident thing that the mother's opinion should be weighed and measured in the political scales as well as that of her son. It is so simple and just that the wife's judgment should be respected and counted as well as the husband's. And who can give the reason why the sister's opinion should be ignored and the brother's honored? . . . . Over 5,000 women of this city pay taxes on real estate, and who shall say they are not as much interested in every question of financial expenditure as any 5,000 men; in the public parks, street railways, grade crossings, pavements, bridges, etc.? And not only the 5,000 tax-paying women, but all the women of the city are equally interested in the sanitary condition of our streets, alleys, schools, police stations, jails and asylums. . . .

To repair the damages of society seems to be the mission assigned to women, and we ask that the necessary implements shall be placed in their hands. But, you say, women can be appointed to see to these matters without voting. Yes, but they are not; and if they were, without the ballot they would be powerless to effect the improvements they might find necessary. If the women of this city had the right to vote, those on the board of charities, for instance, would not be compelled year after year to beg each member of every new council for the appointment of some women as city physicians, as scores of them have done for the past six or eight years. Had we the right to vote, do you suppose we should have to plead in vain before the two parties to place women in nomination for the school board?

I want this amendment of the charter first, because it is right and just to women; second, that women may have a political fulcrum on which to plant their lever for everything they wish to secure through government; third, that the opinions of the women of this city may be respected, and there is no other way to secure respect but to have them counted with those of men in the ballot-box on every possible question which is carried to that tribunal; and fourth, to free the mothers from the cruel taunt of being responsible for the character of their grown-up sons while denied all power to control the conditions surrounding them after they pass beyond the dooryards of their homes.

She continued by showing the good effects of woman's municipal suffrage in England, Canada and also in Kansas, and full suffrage in Wyoming; and closed with an earnest appeal for an amendment to the new charter which should confer the municipal franchise upon women. A few days later the board of trustees took final action on the charter, of which the Democrat and Chronicle said: "The amendment proposed by Miss Susan B. Anthony extending the suffrage to women was defeated, although by a close vote. Had there been a full meeting of the board it is a question whether it would not have been adopted, as several of the members who were not present last evening had expressed themselves as favorable."[1]

[1] Jean Brooks Greenleaf, at this time in Washington with her husband, wrote Miss Anthony:
"I felt heart-sick when I learned the result of the charter business and I am not over it yet. I told Mr. Greenleaf I would dispose of every bit of taxable property I have in Rochester. I can not bear to think that, with so glorious an opportunity to be just, men prefer to be so unjust. They can help it if they will, those men who speak us so fair. If they would make one solid stand for our rights they could overrule the masses who are not half so un-

Miss Anthony addressed the Monroe County Teachers' Institute at Brighton, December 16.   The diary records many visits to the Industrial School, conferences with the other fourteen trustees and much correspondence with the boards of similar institutions elsewhere.   In her mail this year were letters from most of the civilized countries on the globe, among them several from the leaders of the movement in New Zealand, saying that her name was more familiar than all others there, and asking for advice and encouragement in their work of securing the ballot for women.[1]   The following was received from Mrs. Kate Beckwith Lee, Dowagiac, Mich. :   " Mr. Bonet, our sculptor, obtained your photograph, and we now have your grand face looking down in stone from the front of our theater, which was erected as an educator to our people and a memorial to my father, P. D. Beckwith, who was liberal toward all mankind and a believer in woman's equality, and I sincerely hope you may some time see the building."   The other women sculptured on this handsome edifice are George Eliot, George Sand, Rachel, Mary Anderson and Sarah Bernhardt.   Among the great mass of correspondence, this is selected :

An incident which is of no particular consequence to this inquiry, constrains me to write in the hope that you may find time to place upon paper your recollection of the connection that my father (the late George H. Thacher, then mayor of the city of Albany) had with your anti-slavery meeting in this city just before the war.   I was too young to have it make a vivid impression upon me, but it has sometimes been said that was the first opportunity your organization had to freely express its views within the State of New York.   I will be very grateful if you will permit your memory to go back some thirty years and recall that incident.[2]   Yours,   JOHN BOYD THACHER.

This illustrates the pride which the children of the future will have in showing that their parents or grandparents rendered some assistance to the cause of woman and of freedom. Yet Mr. Thacher, who, as a member of the New York Board

ready to do women justice as they are represented.   Good God! when I think of it I wonder how you have borne it all these years and not gone wild."

[1] Full suffrage was granted to the women of New Zealand in 1893.

[2] In February, 1861 ; see Chapter XIII.

of General Managers of the Columbian Exposition, had the selection of those who should compose the Woman's Board of the State, did not name one who had been identified with the great movement for equal rights during the past forty years, and had made it possible for women to participate in this celebration.

A case which had been commenced in the courts of New York in 1891 and had run along through several years, may as well be described here as elsewhere. Miss Anthony had but an indirect connection with it and it is mentioned more for its utter ridiculousness than for any other reason. A woman's art association in New York City, Mrs. Elizabeth Thompson, president, Miss Alice Donlevy, secretary, had the promise of a legacy to build an academy, and they decided to place a statue or bust at each side of the entrance, representing Reform and Philanthropy. Miss Anthony was selected for the one and Mrs. Mary Hamilton Schuyler for the other. The latter, in 1852, founded the New York School of Design for Women, had been the friend and patron of art, and for many years before her death had been noted for her philanthropic work.

A serious difficulty at once arose in the opposition of Mrs. Schuyler's nephew and stepson, Philip Schuyler, who objected to the "disagreeable notoriety." He carried the matter into the courts, which of course attracted the comment of all the newspapers of the country, pro and con, and caused more "disagreeable notoriety" than a dozen statues would have done. He obtained a preliminary injunction against the art association and then took the case to the supreme court for a permanent injunction, on the ground that the "right of privacy" had been violated. The real secret of his objections, however, was exposed in his complaint before the supreme court. Among the twenty-eight grievances alleged were the following:

Twenty-second.—The said Mary M. Hamilton Schuyler took no part whatever in any of the various so-called woman's rights agitations, with which the aforesaid Susan B. Anthony was, and is, prominently identified; and that she took no interest in such agitations or movements, and had no sympathy whatever with them; and that, as the plaintiff believes, she would have resented any attempt such as is made by the defendants to couple her name with that of the said Susan B. Anthony.

Twenty-third.—The acts of the defendants in attempting to raise money by public subscription for a statue of the said Mary M. Hamilton Schuyler; in associating her name with the name of Susan B. Anthony, and in announcing that the projected statue of her is to be placed on public exhibition at the Columbian Exposition as a companion piece to a statue of the said Susan B. Anthony, constitute, and are an unlawful interference with the right of privacy, and a gross and unwarranted outrage upon the memory of the said Mary M. Hamilton Schuyler, under the specious pretense of doing honor to her memory; and that the surviving members of her family have been, and are, greatly distressed and injured thereby.

The supreme court continued the injunction, and the art association then carried the case up to the court of appeals. Here the decision of the lower court was reversed. The opinion was rendered by Justice Rufus W. Peckham, afterwards appointed by President Cleveland to the Supreme Bench of the United States. It is not often that a judge of the highest court in the State incorporates in a legal decision a compliment to a woman, and for this reason the tribute of Justice Peckham is the more highly appreciated. After holding that "persons attempting to erect a statue or bust of a woman no longer living, if their motive is to do honor to her, and if the work is to be done in an appropriate manner, can not be restrained by her surviving relatives," he continued :

Many may, and probably do, totally disagree with the advanced views of Miss Anthony in regard to the proper sphere of women, and yet it is impossible to deny to her the possession of many of the ennobling qualities which tend to the making of great lives. She has given the most unselfish devotion of a long life to what she has considered would tend most for the benefit and practical improvement of her sex, and she has thus lived almost literally in the face of the whole world, and during that period there has never been a single shadow of any dark or ugly fact connected with her or her way of life to dim the lustre of her achievements and of her efforts.

CHAPTER XLI.

1893.

IT is not surprising that Miss Anthony writes in her journal at the beginning of the New Year, 1893: "The clouds do not lift from my spirit. I am simply overwhelmed with the feeling that I can not make my way through the work before me." Never a year in all her crowded life opened with such a mountain of things to be attended to—suffrage conventions, council meetings, the great Woman's Congress at the World's Fair, State campaigns, Industrial School matters, lecture engagements—the list seemed to stretch out into infinity, and it is no wonder that it appalled even her dauntless spirit.

The first necessity was to get the Washington annual convention out of the way. It had been set for an early date this winter, and she left home January 5. Headquarters were at Willard's Hotel and the convention opened in Metzerott's Music Hall, January 15, continuing the usual five days. At the opening session Miss Anthony read beautiful tributes by Mrs. Stanton to George William Curtis, John Greenleaf Whittier, Ernestine L. Rose and Abby Hutchinson Patton, who had died during the year, all earnest and consistent friends of woman's equality. Resolutions were adopted recognizing the splendid services of Francis Minor, Benjamin F. Butler, Abby Hopper Gibbons, Rev. Anna Oliver and a number of other active and efficient workers who also had passed away.

Miss Anthony, in her president's address, gave a strong, cheery account of the past year's work and an encouraging view of the future, and at both day and evening sessions there were the usual number of able and entertaining speeches. Reports were made by delegates from thirty-six States. At the business meeting the question again came up of holding the annual convention in Washington at the beginning of each new Congress and in some other part of the country in alternate years. This plan was vigorously opposed by Miss Anthony, who said in her protest:

The sole object, it seems to me, of this national organization is to bring the combined influence of all the States upon Congress to secure national legislation. The very moment you change the purpose of this great body from National to State work you have defeated its object. It is the business of the States to do the district work; to create public sentiment; to make a national organization possible, and then to bring their united power to the capital and focus it on Congress. Our younger women naturally can not appreciate the vast amount of work done here in Washington by the National Association in the last twenty-five years. The delegates do not come here as individuals but as representatives of their entire States. We have had these national conventions here for a quarter of a century, and every Congress has given hearings to the ablest women we could bring from every section. In the olden times the States were not fully organized—they had not money enough to pay their delegates' expenses. We begged and worked and saved the money, and the National Association paid the expenses of delegates from Oregon and California in order that they might come and bring the influence of their States to bear upon Congress.

Last winter we had twenty-three States represented by delegates. Think of those twenty-three women going before the Senate committee, each making her speech, and convincing those senators of the interest in all these States. We have educated at least a part of three or four hundred men and their wives and daughters every two years to return as missionaries to their respective localities. I shall feel it a grave mistake if you vote in favor of a movable convention. It will lessen our influence and our power; but come what may, I shall abide by the decision of the majority.

Miss Anthony was warmly supported by a number of delegates but the final vote resulted: in favor, 37; opposed, 28.

Among the notable letters received by the convention was the following from Lucy Stone: "Wherever woman suffragists are gathered together in the name of equal rights, there am I always in spirit with them. Although absent, my personal glad greeting goes to every one; to those who have borne the heat and burden of the day, and to the strong, brave, younger workers who have come to lighten the load and complete the victory. We may surely rejoice now when there are so many gains won and conceded, and when favorable indications are on every hand. The way before us is shorter than that behind; but the work still calls for patient perseverance and ceaseless endeavor. The end is not yet in sight, but it can not be far away.'' Those who listened little thought that this would be the last message ever received from that earnest worker of fifty long years. Letters of greeting were sent to her and to Mrs. Stanton. Miss Anthony was unanimously re-elected president.

She lingered for a few days' visit with Mrs. Greenleaf, who gave a reception for her, at which Grace Greenwood was one of the receiving party. She had a luncheon at Mrs. Waite's, wife of the Chief-Justice, and after several other pleasant social functions, left Washington February 1.[1] There was now a magnet in New York City and henceforth she always arranged her hurried eastern trips so that she might spend a few hours or days with Mrs. Stanton, when as in the old time, they wrote calls, resolutions and memorials and made plans to storm the strongholds.

On February 8, Miss Anthony spoke at Warsaw, the guest of Mrs. Maud Humphrey; and for the next week the journal says: ''Trying all these days to get to the bottom of my piles of accumulated letters.'' On her seventy-third birthday the Political Equality Club gave a reception at the pleasant home of Rev. and Mrs. W. C. Gannett, and presented her with a handsome silver teapot, spirit lamp and tray. Mrs. George Hollister gave her a set of point lace which had belonged to her mother, the daughter of Thurlow Weed; and there were numerous other gifts. She wrote to Mrs. Avery on the 23d: '' It is 'just ten years ago this morning, dear Rachel, since we two went gypsying into the old world. Well, it was a happy acquaintance we made then and it has been a blessed decade

---

[1] James G. Blaine died while she was in Washington and the diary says: '' He should have lived, and the Republicans should have honored him as their leader. He *was that*, though not chosen by them.''

which has intervened. Ten years of constant work and thought, but ten years nearer the golden day of jubilee ! ''

She arranged a meeting at the Rochester Chamber of Commerce, March 1, for May Wright Sewall, president National Council of Women, to speak on the approaching Woman's Congress at the World's Fair. On March 6 she began a brief lecture tour, speaking in Hillsdale, Detroit, Saginaw, Bay City, Grand Rapids, Lansing, Battle Creek, Charlotte and in Toledo. Nine evening addresses, several receptions, and over a thousand miles of travel in twelve days, was not a bad record for a woman past seventy-three.[1]

Among the pleasant letters received through the winter were several from the South. Miss Anthony was especially appreciative of the friendship of southern women, as her part in the '' abolition '' movement in early times had created a prejudice against her, and in later days the sentiment for suffrage had not been sufficient to call her into that part of the country, where she might form personal acquaintances and friendships. She had, during these months, earnest letters from the women of Italy asking for encouragement and co-operation in their struggles. Many letters came also from teachers, stenographers and other wage-earning women, full of grateful acknowledgment of their indebtedness to her. There were invitations enough for lectures to fill every month in the year, ranging from the Christian Association at Cornell to the Free-thinkers' Club in New York, and covering all the grades of belief or nonbelief between the two. She was asked to contribute to a symposium on ''The Ideal Man,'' to write an account of '' The Underground Railroad,'' and to give so many written opinions on current topics of discussion that to have complied would have kept her at her desk from early morning until the midnight hour.

[1] The newspapers, almost without exception, in all these places, spoke in unqualified praise of Miss Anthony and her work, of her "royal welcome," her "packed audiences," her "masterly address," etc. Several of them, notably the Bay City Tribune, contained strong editorial endorsement of woman suffrage. At Lansing she addressed the House of Representatives and the next day the bill conferring municipal suffrage on women was voted on; 38 ayes, 39 nays. It was reconsidered, received a good majority in both Houses and was signed by the governor, but afterwards declared unconstitutional by the supreme court of the State.

In a letter to a friend she said : "The other day a millionaire who wrote me, 'wondered why I didn't have my letters typewritten.' Why, bless him, I never, in all my fifty years of hard work with the pen, had a writing desk with pigeonholes and drawers until my seventieth birthday brought me the present of one, and never had I even a dream of money enough for a stenographer and typewriter. How little those who have realize the limitations of those who have not."

She wrote to Robert Purvis at this time : "What a magnificent opening speech Gladstone made, and how splendid his final remarks : 'It would be misery for me if I had foregone or omitted in these closing years of my life any measure it was possible for me to take towards upholding and promoting the cause—not of one party or one nation, but of all parties and all nations.' So can you and I say with Gladstone, we should be miserable but for the consciousness that we have done all in our power to help forward every measure for the freedom and equality of the races and the sexes."

In April she lectured at a number of places in New York to add to the limited fund which kept the pot boiling at home.[1] She also went to Buffalo to talk over Industrial School matters with Mrs. Harriet A. Townsend, president of the Women's Educational and Industrial Union, which had proved so great a success in that city. On the 28th she spoke before the Woman's Columbian Exposition Committee of Cincinnati, "to a very fashionable and representative audience," the Enquirer said. For this lecture she received $125. During the spring she wrote the Woman's Tribune :

How splendidly Kansas women voted, and now come suffrage amendments in Colorado, New York and Kansas! Well, we must buckle on our armor for a triple fight, and we must shout more loudly than ever to our friends all over the country for money to help these States. Although Kansas is the most certain to carry the question, nevertheless we must organize every school district of every county of each State in which the battle of the ballot for woman is to be fought. *Organize, agitate, educate,* must be our war cry from this to the day of the election.

[1] The diary shows a gift for this purpose, during the month, of $150 from Rachel Foster Avery and $50 from Adeline Thomson.

Today's mail brought $100 to our national treasury from Mrs. P. A. Moffett, of Fredonia. How my heart leaped for joy as I read her letter and again and again looked at her check, and how I ejaculated over and over, "O that a thousand of our good women who *wish* success to our cause would be moved thus to send in their checks!" Only a very few can go outside to work, but many can contribute money to help pay the expenses of those who do leave all their home-friends, comforts and luxuries. If the many who stay at home and wish, could only believe for a moment that we who go out not knowing where our heads will rest when night comes, really love our homes as they love theirs, they would vie with each other to throw in their mite to make the path smooth for the wayfarers. But we, every one of us who can speak acceptably, must do all in our power to persuade the men of these States to vote for the amendment. Do let us all take to ourselves new hope and courage for the herculean task before us. Who will send the next $100? O, that we had $10,000 to start with!

Miss Anthony and Mrs. Avery met at Mrs. Sewall's for a conference on Woman's Congress matters and then went to Chicago to attend, by invitation, the formal opening of the Columbian Exposition May 1, 1893. Miss Anthony wrote: "Mrs. Palmer's speech was very fine, covering full equality for woman." Her address the year before at the dedication ceremonies contained one of the noblest tributes ever paid to women, closing with these beautiful sentences: "Even more important than the discovery of Columbus, which we are gathered together to celebrate, is the fact that the general government has just discovered woman. It has sent out a flashlight from its heights, so inaccessible to us, which we shall answer by a return signal when the exposition is opened. What will be its next message to us?" Upon this occasion she was even more eloquent. Her keen expose of the absurd platitudes in regard to woman's sphere, and her fine defence of women in the industrial world, deserve a place among the classics.

Since Miss Anthony's part in this great world's exposition must necessarily be condensed into small space, it seems most satisfactory to place it all together. It has been related in the chapter of 1876 how women were denied practically all governmental recognition in the Centennial. They were determined that this should not be the case in 1893. As early as 1889 she began making plans to this effect and conferring with other prominent women. Several officials, who were in positions to influence action on this question, had declared that "those suffrage women should have nothing to do with the World's Fair;" and as some women whose social prestige might be needed were likely to be frightened off if suffrage were in any way connected with the matter, Miss Anthony felt the necessity of moving very discreetly. As "those suffrage women" had been behind every progressive movement that ever had been made in the United States for their own sex, it was hardly possible that they would not be the moving force in this. Miss Anthony was not seeking for laurels, however, either for herself or for her cause, but only to carry her point—that women should participate in this great national celebration and that they should do this with the sanction and assistance of the national government. In her plans she had the valuable backing of Mrs. Spofford, who made it possible for her to remain in Washington every winter, gave the use of the Riggs House parlors for meetings and aided in many other ways.

Miss Anthony went quietly about among the ladies in official life whom she could trust, and as a result various World's Fair meetings were held at the hotel, participated in by Washington's influential women, and a committee appointed to wait upon Congress and ask that women be placed on the commission. She did not appear at these gatherings, and only her few confidantes knew that she was behind them. Meanwhile it was announced early in January, 1890, that the World's Fair Bill had been brought before the House, and Miss Anthony at once prepared a petition asking for the appointment of women on the National Board of Management. This was placed in the hands of ladies of influence and in a few days one hundred and eleven names were obtained of the wives and daughters of the judges of the Supreme Court, the Cabinet, senators, representatives, army officials; as distinguished a list as could be secured in the national capital.

This petition was presented to the Senate January 12. It requested that women should be placed on the board with men, but instead, the bill was passed in March creating a commission of men and authorizing them to appoint a number of women to constitute a "Board of Lady Managers." These 115 appointments were intended to be practically of a complimentary nature, it was not expected that the women would take any prominent part, and no particular rule was observed in their selection. While perhaps in some States they were not the ablest who might have been found, they were, as a board, fairly representative. To bring this great body into harmonious action and guide it along important lines of work, required a leader possessed of a combination of qualities rarely existing in one person—not only the highest degree of executive ability but self-control, tact and the power of managing men and women. They were found, however, in the woman elected to preside over this board, Mrs. Bertha Honoré Palmer, of Chicago. At the close of the exposition it was universally conceded that she had proved herself pre-eminently the one woman in all the country for this place. Her record, during the several years that she held this very responsible position, is one of the most remarkable ever made by any woman.

At the time Miss Anthony prepared her petition to Congress for representation, no action had been taken by any organized body of women in the country, and if she had not been on the field of battle in Washington and acted at the very moment she did, the bill would have passed Congress without any provision for women. They would have had no recognition from the government, no appropriations for their work, no official power, and their splendid achievements at the Columbian Exposition, which did more to advance the cause of women than all that had been accomplished during the century, would have been lost to the world. Having secured this great object, she asked no office for herself or for any other woman. On several public occasions, in the early months of the fair, she refused to speak or to sit on the platform, lest she might embarrass the President of the Board of Lady Managers by committing her to woman suffrage. Mrs. Palmer, however, showed her the most distinguished courtesy, in both public and private affairs, inviting her to the platform and including her in the social functions at her own residence.

Miss Anthony soon felt that she was in full sympathy with herself in every measure which tended to secure for women absolute equality of rights, a point which Mrs. Palmer emphasized in the most unmistakable language in her eloquent address delivered in the Woman's Building, at the close of the exposition.

In these circumscribed limits it will be impossible to give any adequate account of that greatest of all accomplishments of women at the World's Fair—the Woman's Congress—whose proceedings fill two large volumes in the official report.   In order that intellectual as well as material progress should be presented, it had been decided to hold a series of congresses which should bring together a representation of the great minds of the world.   C. C. Bonney was made president of the Congress Auxiliary ; Mrs. Palmer, president, and Mrs. Ellen M. Henrotin, vice-president of the Woman's Branch.   Although women were to participate in all, Mr. Bonney desired to have one composed of them alone.   To assist Mrs. Henrotin, who had been made acting president, as well as to further insure the success of this congress, Mr. Bonney appointed May Wright Sewall chairman, and Rachel Foster Avery secretary, of the committee of organization, and they were assisted by an efficient local committee.

As president and secretary of the National Council of Women, and Mrs. Sewall vice-president of the International Council, no two could have been secured with so wide a knowledge of the organizations of women throughout the world and the best methods of securing their co-operation.   The magnitude of their labors can be appreciated only by an examination of the official report.   The fact of their merging into this congress the International Council of Women, which was to have been held in London that year, was one of the most potent elements of its success.   Miss Anthony wrote Mrs. Sewall : "The suffrage work has missed you, oh, so much, still I would not have had you do differently.   I glory in Rachel's and your work this year beyond words."

The World's Congress of Representative Women, which

opened May 15, 1893, was the largest and most brilliant of any of the series which extended through the six months of the fair, and was considered by many the most remarkable ever convened. Twenty-seven countries and 126 organizations were represented by 528 delegates. During the week eighty-one meetings were held in the different rooms of the Art Palace. There were from seven to eighteen in simultaneous progress each day and, according to official estimate, the total attendance exceeded 150,000 persons. The fifteen policemen stationed in the building stated that often hundreds of people were turned away before the hour of opening arrived, not only the audience-rooms but the halls and ante-rooms being so crowded that no more could enter the building, which held 10,000.

All who were in attendance at this congress, all who read the accounts in the Chicago daily papers, will testify that it is not the bias of a partial historian which prompts the statement that Susan B. Anthony was the central figure of this historic gathering. Every time she appeared on the stage the audience broke into applause ; when she rose to speak, they stood upon the seats and waved hats and handkerchiefs. People watched the daily program and when she was advertised for an address, there was a rush from other halls and an impenetrable jam in the corridors. Again and again she was obliged to call upon a stout policeman to make a way for her through the throngs which pressed about her, anxious to get even a sight of her face. No matter what department of the congress she visited, whether of education, religion, philanthropy or industries, the audience demanded a speech and would not be satisfied until it was made.[1] Large numbers of the women who gave addresses in these various meetings paid tribute to her work, and the mention of her name never failed to elicit a burst of applause. At the many public and private receptions given to the congress the post of honor was assigned to her,

[1] "More than once—indeed, I believe more than a score of times—I saw speakers of eloquence and renown interrupted in the midst of a discourse by audiences who simply would not listen, after Miss Anthony's entrance into the hall, until she had been formally introduced and an opportunity given them to express their reverence by prolonged applause."—From letter of Mrs. Sewall.

May Wright Sewall

and no guest ever was satisfied to leave without having touched her hand.

It is not too much to say that no woman in this country, or in any other, ever was so honored because of her own individual services to humanity. It was the universal recognition of her labors of nearly half a century, that had laid the foundation upon which had been reared all the great organizations represented by the women in this congress. Hers had been the pioneer work, the blazing of the pathway through the forests of custom and prejudice which for untold centuries had forbidden them to step beyond the narrow limits of domestic occupations. All of a sudden, it seemed, the women of the world had awakened to the knowledge that she had borne ridicule, abuse, misrepresentation, disgrace, that they might enter into the kingdom of woman's right to her highest development. Long-delayed though it had been, the women of her own and other countries came to lay their homage at her feet, to bow before her in loving gratitude, to rise up and call her blessed.

Letters of congratulation were received from far and wide ; one from Frances E. Willard in Switzerland said :

MY BELOVED SUSAN : You are a happy woman and we are all crowing to think the people love, honor and call for you so loud and long. It suits one's sense of poetic justice; it confirms one's faith in human nature and the Heavenly Power not ourselves "that makes for righteousness." Lady Henry, Anna Gordon and I have "hoorayed" over your laurels and said, "Bless her; she is not only *our* Susan but everybody's." Lady Henry says you have the true sign of greatness that you are absolutely without pretension. You do not take up all the time and luxuriate in the sound of your own voice, but are glad to give the other ones a bit of breath too. She says no woman of fame has ever so thoroughly made this impression of modesty and unselfishness upon her mind. And I say Selah.[1]

In her London letter the noted correspondent, Florence Fenwick Miller, of England, wrote :

Amidst all the attractive personalities and ideas presented, the most sought

---

[1] Lady Henry had just returned from Chicago where she had attended the World's Fair Temperance Congress and here had heard Miss Anthony for the first time. At the close of her speech declaring that there could be no effective temperance work among women until they had the ballot, Lady Henry came forward and gave it her most hearty endorsement.

of all—the one whose presence drew crowds everywhere, who was made to speak in whatever hall she entered, and who was surrounded in every corridor and every reception, just as the queen-bee is surrounded in the hive by her courtiers, was the veteran leader of the woman suffragists of America, Susan B. Anthony. At seventy-three she is as upright of form, as clear and powerful of mind, as strong of voice, as courageous and uncompromising as ever. Let our revered and beloved Miss Anthony have the last word.

The program for the Woman's Congress assigned but one session to the National-American Suffrage Association, and it was the honest intention to give no more time to the discussion of political equality than to each of the other departments. It made a place for itself, however, in practically every one of the meetings. Whether the subject were education, philanthropy, reform or some other, the speakers were sure to point out the disabilities of woman without the ballot. So strong was the desire to hear this question discussed that it became necessary to hold afternoon meetings in the large halls, aside from those on the regular morning and evening program, in order to give the eager crowds an opportunity to hear its distinguished advocates from all parts of the world. It is doubtful if the whole fifty years of agitation made as many converts to equal suffrage as did the great object lesson of the Woman's Congress.

Many pleasant letters passed between Miss Anthony and Mr. Bonney, Mrs. Palmer and Mrs. Henrotin. The last named asked her to take part in the Temperance, the Labor and the Social and Moral Reform Congresses and requested her advice and assistance. She was placed by Mr. Bonney on the advisory council of the Political, Social and Economic Congresses. Mrs. Palmer wrote: " I should like you to send us special suggestions for speakers and topics." Miss Anthony was much pleased at the selection of Mrs. Palmer for president of the Board of Lady Managers, heartily seconded all her efforts and lent no support to the dissensions made by several women who thought there should have been more recognition of those who had been pioneer workers. That this was appreciated is shown by a letter written as early as April, 1891:

I feel that I must express my thanks to you that you did not condemn us unheard, for I naturally supposed that as ———— ———— belonged to your organization you would take her view of any matter which interested her. I thank you very much for your fair-mindedness, and beg that you will read the statement which I shall send you and which will probably give you a better idea of this unpleasant matter than anything else you have seen.

I remember with great pleasure our meeting in Washington, and hope it was only the first of many such pleasant occasions for me. Thanking you again, I am most cordially yours,

Most Cordially yours,

Bertha M. H. Palmer

Miss Anthony spoke several times at the noon-hour meetings held in the Woman's Building.[1] Mrs. James P. Eagle, chairman, who edited the report of the noon-hour addresses, wrote her: "I would not take much pleasure in publishing our book if I could not have something from your addresses to go in it. You must not deny me. One of your talks was 'Woman's Influence vs. Political Power,' another 'The Benefits of Organization.' If it is your best and easiest way, make the speeches and employ a stenographer to take them and send me the bill. I can not afford to miss them. You have been so very kind and encouraging to me all along that I shall feel it a Brutus blow if you fail me now." As she never wrote a speech in these days and could not make the same one twice, she was unable to comply with this request.

Miss Anthony was invited to speak at the Press Congress May 27, the day when the religious press as a leader of reforms was under consideration. The managers became very uneasy and began trying to find out how she meant to handle the question. Her only reply was, "I shall speak the truth." The speech, delivered before an audience con-

[1] "As only the most gifted women will be invited to participate in these entertainments, we hope the invitation will be esteemed as an honor conferred by the Board of Lady Managers, and your acceptance will be gratefully appreciated."—Note of Invitation.

taining many ministers, caused a tremendous sensation. She took up the reforms, temperance, anti-slavery, woman's rights, labor; and showed conclusively that in every one the church and the religious press, instead of being leaders, were laggards. At the close the chairman remarked apologetically that of course the speaker did not expect people in general to agree with everything she had said. The Chicago Tribune thus finished its report: "As Miss Anthony had an engagement she was obliged to leave at this point, and most of the audience went with her."

The Congress on Government convened August 7 and, at Mr. Bonney's request, Miss Anthony was present at the opening ceremony and responded to an address of welcome in behalf of the civil service commission. Five sessions of this Government Congress were devoted to a discussion of equal suffrage, the speakers being women. The chairman, Hon. Wm. Dudley Foulke, said it was not the intention to give this subject such prominence, but women had shown so much more interest than men, half of them accepting the invitation to take part and only one man in twenty responding, that he was compelled thus to arrange the program.

Soon after the adjournment of the Woman's Congress Miss Anthony left the Palmer House, which had been its headquarters, and, accepting the invitation of Mrs. Lydia Avery Coonley, enjoyed the congenial atmosphere of her beautiful home for a month. At the conclusion of her visit with Mrs. Coonley she went for six weeks with Mr. and Mrs. Sewall, who had taken a large house for the season. This was a social center and the weekly receptions were a prominent feature, bringing together distinguished people from all countries, who were in Chicago, as officials or visitors, during this wonderful summer. While at Mrs. Coonley's Miss Anthony formed two acquaintances who from that date have been among her most valued friends—Mr. and Mrs. Samuel E. Gross. After leaving the Sewalls she spent a delightful month with them at their residence on the Lake Shore drive, where she was surrounded with every luxury which wealth and affection could bestow.

This added another to the homes in that city always open to her, and Mrs. Gross often wrote: "Your visits are a sweet benediction to our family."[1]

Among the most elegant of the many social affairs to which she was invited was the luncheon in the great banquet hall of the Hotel Richelieu, given by the officers of the National Council to those of the International, the foreign delegates and a few other guests, 150 in all. May Wright Sewall presided with great dignity and charm over the "after dinner speech-making" of this assemblage of the representative women from the most highly civilized nations of the world, and Miss Anthony sat at her right hand.

Once she went to Harvey and spoke at a camp meeting of 3,000 persons; and later to the Bloomington Chautauqua to give an address; then all the way to Kansas to speak at the State Fair in Topeka and fill a month's lecture engagements. Two weeks she spent in her own home visiting with relatives; then rushed down to Long Island to hurry Mrs. Stanton with her paper; and back again to Chicago to read it for her at the Educational Congress. Many days and evenings were passed among the wealth of attractions on the exposition grounds; and so the summer waxed and waned, one of the longest holidays she ever had known, and yet with not an idle hour through all the four months of delightful associations and cherished acquaintances. She writes in the diary October 30: "This was my last sight of the White City in its full glory by night."

Among the many graceful words of farewell spoken by the press of Chicago, may be quoted the following from the Inter-Ocean, which suggests the strong and graceful pen of Mary H. Krout:

It is pleasant in these reminiscent days when we talk over the glories and delights of the World's Fair, to recall the honors heaped upon Susan B. Anthony. Her personal friends vied with each other in arranging elaborate entertainments of which she was the central figure. There were dinners and luncheons, banquets and receptions, and at each and all the refined and deli-

---

[1] As a memento of these visits Mrs. Gross presented Miss Anthony with $100; and Mrs. Coonley gave her a rich brocaded silk dress and a travelling suit, both beautifully made by her own dressmaker, with bonnets to match.

cate face shone above the board with a beauty and tranquillity far exceeding the mere beauty of youth and faultlessness of feature. It was the beauty of experience, sweetened and purified by success and appreciation. . . .

It must seem a strange contrast to the woman who has worked so perseveringly in the face of untold difficulties—this change that a few years have wrought. It has not been so very long since she was the universal butt of ridicule, lampooned and caricatured, with all that malice, in its coarsest and most brutal form, could suggest. Her age was the favorite theme of the callow witling, her cause a never-failing subject for reproach and abuse. It is all over and done with, thanks to the new race of men which women themselves are training and educating. There are no words for her nowadays but those of praise and affection. She has lived to see truth survive and justice vindicated. Men no longer regard her as the arch-enemy to domestic peace, disseminating doctrines that mean the destruction of home and the disorganization of society. They perceive in her, rather, the advocate of that liberty which knows no limitations either of sex or of condition—a freedom which, achieved, means the incalculable advancement of the race.

In all the assemblages where Miss Anthony was present during those memorable months—the observed of all observers, holding a veritable court—her admirers were both men and women, and no belle at a ball was ever more unmistakably deferred to. It made her happy, as it should have done. But it made far happier those who have believed in her all these years, that she should have triumphed over ignorance and prejudice, and at threescore and ten have come into her kingdom at last. When it is asked what woman was most prominent, most honored, most in demand in all the public ceremonials and private functions held in Chicago during the Columbian Exposition, there can be but one answer—Susan B. Anthony.

Through all the summer and autumn of 1893 a campaign had been going forward in Colorado, where the legislature had submitted the question of woman suffrage to the voters. The national association was represented by Mrs. Carrie Chapman Catt, who rendered splendid service. Mrs. Leonora Barry Lake spoke under the auspices of the Knights of Labor. The rest of the work was done by the women of Colorado, who proved a host in themselves. Miss Anthony held herself in readiness to go at any time but the friends felt that, unless vitally necessary, she should be spared the hardships. Circumstances were favorable ; there had been a vast change in public sentiment since the defeat of 1877 ; the question was submitted at a time when only county elections were held and there was no political excitement; Populists and Republicans not only endorsed it but worked for it; Democrats offered no party opposition and many of them gave it cordial support ; more than half of the newspapers in the State advocated it. The campaign in Colorado differed from all those which had been conducted in other States in the fact that it was not left for women to carry on alone, but the most prominent men in all parties lent their assistance and made the victory possible.[1] The amendment was carried by nearly 6,000 majority, about three to one in favor. Miss Anthony received the telegram announcing the fact November 8, the day after election, and she was the happiest woman in America.

Immediately upon returning home from Chicago she went to the State suffrage convention which met in Historical Hall, Brooklyn, November 13. While in New York she was the guest of Mrs. Russell Sage at the dinner of the Emma Willard Alumnæ. Four days were given to the convention, one or two spent with Mrs. Catt, in her delightful home at Bensonhurst-by-the-Sea, and a few at the suburban residence of Mrs. Foster Avery. While here she addressed the New Century Club in Philadelphia, and for several days following was in attendance at the Pennsylvania convention. On December 18, she lectured at Jamaica ; the 19th at Riverhead ; the 20th at Richmond ; the 22d she attended the Foremothers' Day dinner in New York and made an address ; the 23d she spoke before the Women's Conference of the Ethical Society in that city.

When not lecturing she was struggling with her mass of correspondence, attending to her duties in connection with the Industrial School, and making preliminary arrangements for two big State campaigns which required the writing of hundreds of letters, all done with her own hand. Invitations came during these days to address the New York Social Purity League, the Women's Republican Association, the Pratt Institute and the National Convention of the Keeley Cure League ; and requests for articles on " Why Should Young Men Favor

---

[1] The " Remonstrants " flooded the State with their literature, but as this contained a conspicuous advertisement of a large liquor establishment, it defeated itself. The headquarters of the organized opposition were located in a Denver brewery.

Woman Suffrage?'' for the Y. M. C. A. paper of Chicago; "What Should the President's Message Say ? '' for the New York World ; " If you had $1,000,000 what would you do with it? '' for a symposium ; and at least a score of similar applications. The friendly letters included one from Judge Albion W. Tourgee, acknowledging receipt of the History of Woman Suffrage, "from one whose devotion to principle and brave advocacy of right have ever commanded my profound esteem.'' He also expressed his interest and belief in the principle of woman suffrage. The same mail brought a letter from Professor Helen L. Webster, asking for a copy of the History to place in the library of Wellesley College "so that it may be within reach of the students.''

The Kansas legislature again had submitted a suffrage amendment and many letters were coming from the women of that State, begging Miss Anthony's help. She filled reams of paper during December, telling them how to put everybody to work, to organize every election precinct in the State, to raise money, and above all else to create a public sentiment which would demand a woman suffrage plank in the platform of each of the political parties. " I am going to make a big raid to get a fund for Kansas,'' she wrote, " but nothing will avail without the support of the parties.'' The work in Kansas was not, however, by any means the most formidable undertaking which confronted her. The women of New York were about to enter upon the greatest suffrage campaign ever attempted, and toward its success she was bending every thought, energy and effort, earnestly coöperating with the strongest and best-equipped workers in the State.

CHAPTER XLII.

1894.

THE year 1894 is distinguished in the annals of woman suffrage for two great campaigns: one in New York to secure from the Constitutional Convention an amendment abolishing the word " male " from the new constitution which was to be submitted to the voters at the fall election; the other in Kansas to secure a majority vote on an amendment which had been submitted by the legislature of 1893, and was to be voted on in November. In order to make the story as clear as possible, each of these campaigns, both of which were in progress at the same time, will be considered separately. Before entering upon either, the leading features of the twenty-sixth of the series of Washington conventions, which have run like a thread through Miss Anthony's life for more than a quarter of a century, will be briefly noticed.

On January 13, she lectured before the University Association at Ann Arbor in the great University Hall—the second woman ever invited to address that body, Anna Dickinson having been thus honored during the war. Sunday morning she spoke for the University Christian Association, in Newbury Hall. Monday morning the State Suffrage Association commenced a three days' convention, during which she gave numerous short addresses. Wednesday evening a large reception was given by her hostess, Olivia B. Hall, whose home Miss Anthony always regarded as one of her most enjoyable resting-places in her many trips through Michigan. Mrs. Hall had

(755)

contributed hundreds of dollars to the cause of woman suffrage, and made a number of timely presents to Miss Anthony for her personal use.

From Michigan they went to the twenty-fifth anniversary of the suffrage association of Toledo. It is worthy of note that Miss Anthony had helped organize this society in the house of Mrs. Hall, who lived there at that time. She was here, as always when in this city, the guest of her friend, Anna C. Mott, whose father and uncle, Richard and James Mott, were her staunch supporters from the early days of the abolition movement. The papers contained long and flattering notices, which had now become so customary that to quote one is to give the substance of all.

Miss Anthony lectured in Baltimore February 13, going from there to Washington. The convention opened in Metzerott's Music Hall, February 15, welcomed by Commissioner John W. Ross, of the District. Among the speakers were Senator Carey and Representative Coffeen, of Wyoming; Senator Teller and Representatives Bell and Pence, of Colorado; Senator Peffer and Representatives Davis, Broderick, Curtis and Simpson, of Kansas; ex-Senator Bruce, of Mississippi; Hon. Simon Wolf, of the District; Catherine H. Spence, of New Zealand; Miss Windeyer, of Australia; Hannah K. Korany, of Syria; Kate Field; and Mary Lowe Dickinson, secretary King's Daughters.

Yours truly,
Kate Field

Appropriate memorial services were held for the distinguished dead of the past year who had rendered especial service to the cause of woman suffrage: Lucy Stone, George W. Childs, Leland Stanford, Elizabeth Peabody, Elizabeth Oakes Smith.

Eloquent tributes were offered by the various members of the convention, and Miss Anthony added one to Mary F. Seymour, founder of the Business Woman's Journal. The death of Myra Bradwell, editor Legal News, occurred too late for her honored name to be included in these services. Bishop Phillips Brooks and ex-President Rutherford B. Hayes, both of whom had unequivocally expressed themselves in favor of suffrage for women, also had died in 1893.

At the opening session, on Miss Anthony's birthday, she was presented by the enfranchised women of Wyoming and Colorado with a beautiful silk flag which bore two shining stars on its blue field. She accepted it with much emotion, saying: " I have heard of standard bearers in the army who carried the banners to the topmost ramparts of the enemy, and there I am going to try to carry this banner. You know without my telling how proud I am of this flag, and how my heart is touched by this manifestation." From the ladies of Georgia came a box of fresh flowers, and among other pleasant remembrances were seventy-four American Beauty roses from Mrs. S. E. Gross, of Chicago. A little later, when Virginia D. Young brought the greetings of South Carolina, Miss Anthony said :

I think the most beautiful part of our coming together in Washington for the last twenty-five years, has been that more friendships, more knowledge of each other have come through the hand-shakes here, than would have been possible through any other instrumentality. I shall never cease to be grateful for all the splendid women who have come up to this great center for these twenty-six conventions, and have learned that the North was not such a cold place as they had believed; I have been equally glad when we came down here and met the women from the sunny South and found they were just like ourselves, if not a little better. In this great association, we know no North, no South, no East, no West. This has been our pride for twenty-six years. We have no political party. We never have inquired what anybody's religion was. All we ever have asked is simply, " Do you believe in perfect equality for women ?" That is the one article in our creed.

There were many pleasant newspaper comments on Miss Anthony's re-election, among them the following from the Chicago Journal :

The national suffrage association honored itself yesterday by again electing to its presidency Susan B. Anthony. She has suffered long for a cause she believes to be right, and it is fitting that in these later years of her active life, when the cause has become popular, she should wear the honors her patient, persistent endeavor has won. Susan B. Anthony is one of the most remarkable products of this century. She is not a successful writer; she is not a great speaker, although a most effective one; but she has a better quality than genius. She is the soul of honesty; she possesses the gift of clear discrimination—of seeing the main point—and of never-wavering loyalty to the issue at hand. . . .

For more than forty years she has led the women of America through the wilderness of doubt, and now from Pisgah's heights looks over into the Canaan land of triumphant victory. Past the allotted time of threescore years and ten, Miss Anthony may never cross the Jordan of her hopes, but she has led her hosts safely through the gravest dangers and trained up others well fitted to wear the mantle of leadership. It is the hope of all who have learned to know and appreciate this heroic woman, that her wise counsel and earnest, faithful spirit may long continue to inspire and direct the affairs of this great association.

The office of national organizer was created and Carrie Chapman Catt elected to fill it. The association accepted an invitation to hold the next meeting in Atlanta, Ga. At the close of the convention a hearing was granted by the Senate and House committees. Miss Anthony introduced the various speakers, representing all sections of the country, and at the conclusion one of the new members came to her and said earnestly : "If you had but adopted this course earlier, your cause would have been won long ago." He was considerably surprised when she informed him that they had had just such hearings as this for the past twenty-six years.

The legislature of New York had ordered the necessary measures to be taken for a delegate convention to revise the constitution. Governor Hill in 1887 and Governor Flower in 1892 had recommended that women should have a representation in this convention. The bill, as it finally passed both branches of the legislature, provided that any male or female citizen above the age of twenty-one should be eligible to election as delegate. When the district conventions were called to choose these, both Democrats and Republicans refused to nominate any woman. As the delegates would draw $10 a day for five months, the political plums were entirely too valuable to give to a disfranchised class. The Republicans of Miss Anthony's district would not consider even her nomination, although she was recognized as the peer of any man in the State in a knowledge of constitutional law. The Democrats in that district, who were in a hopeless minority, made the one exception and, as a compliment, nominated Mrs. Jean Brooks Greenleaf, who ran several hundred votes ahead of the ticket.

The women then proceeded to inaugurate a great campaign in order to create a public sentiment which would demand from this convention an amendment conferring suffrage on women. To begin this, which would require a vast amount of money, they had not a dollar. No delegate owed his election to a woman, nor could any woman further his ambition for future honors to which his record in this body might prove a stepping-stone. So far as any political power was concerned, women were of less force than the proverbial fly on the wagon wheel, and the majority of men who go into a convention of this kind do so from that particular sort of lofty patriotism which sees an official position in the near or distant future. On the other hand, the element which is forever and unalterably opposed to any move in the direction of suffrage for women, represented the dominant financial and political power in the greatest metropolis in America, whose ramifications extend to every city, village and cross-roads in the State. With its money and its votes this element can make and unmake politicians at will, and under present conditions, with the ballot in the hands of men only, it is virtually an impossibility for a candidate to be elected if this organization exert its influence against him. How to persuade the parties and the individual men to risk defeat until they succeed in the enfranchisement of women, which alone will destroy the absolute domination of this oligarchy, is a problem yet to be solved. That the women of New York dared attempt it, showed courage and determination of the highest order.

This necessarily had to be a campaign of education, of forming new public sentiment and putting into definite shape

that which already existed.   This could be done in four ways :
by organization, by petitions, by literature and by speeches.
The petitions were put into circulation in 1893.[1]   As it would
be necessary to use every dollar to the very best advantage,
the Anthony home in Rochester was put at the service of the
committee in order to save rent.   Practically every room in
the house was called into requisition.   The parlors became
public offices ; the guest chamber was transformed into a mail-
ing department ; Miss Anthony's study was an office by day
and a bedroom by night ; and even the dining-room and
kitchen were invaded.   Here Mary S. Anthony, corresponding secretary, and Mrs. Martha R. Almy, vice-president-at-
large, with a force of clerks, worked day and night from
December, 1893, to July, 1894, sending out thousands of letters, petition blanks, leaflets, suffrage papers, etc.[2]   The letter
boxes were wholly inadequate, and the post-office daily sent
mail-sacks to the house, which were filled and set out on the
front porch to be collected.   Hither came every day the State
president, Mrs. Greenleaf, who toiled without ceasing from
daylight till dark ; and into this busy hive Miss Anthony
rushed from the lecture field every Saturday to get the report
of the work and consult as to the best methods for the coming
week.   It is not possible to describe in detail the vast amount
of labor performed at these headquarters, but it is thus summed
up in the report of the corresponding secretary :

.   .   .   Add to the correspondence incident to the circulation of our great
petition, the sending out of nearly 5,000 blank petition-books and instructions to insure the work's being properly done, literature for free distribution, the planning and arranging for sixty mass meetings in as many counties,
and we have a task before which Hercules himself might well stand aghast.
To accomplish this work has taken not only the entire time of your corre-

[1] In November of this year Miss Anthony called at the office of the New York Sun and had
an interview with Mr. Dana, who always had maintained that when any considerable number of women expressed a desire for the ballot, the men would grant it. She asked him
how many names would suffice and he replied: "If you can get a petition of 100,000 women
it will be amply sufficient to compel the convention to submit the amendment." Although
more than twice this number signed the petition, Mr. Dana's very first editorial after the convention had refused to submit the amendment, declared the reason was that not enough
women had asked for it !

[2] A salary was voted to Mary Anthony which she declined to accept; Mrs. Almy received
$50 a month; the clerks either donated their services or gave them for a mere trifle.

Your Sister
Mary S. Anthony

sponding secretary, but that of our president, Mrs. Greenleaf, for a full year. Hundreds of women over all the State worked as never before, petitions in hand, travelling from house to house in all sorts of weather to secure the names of people who believe in the right of women to a voice in the government under which they live.

It has so often been asserted by those in power that when any considerable number of women wanted to vote, there would be perfect freedom for them to do so, that it was now decided thoroughly to test the truth of such assertion. Over 332,000 individual names, more than half being those of women, were thus actually obtained, neatly put up in book form and presented to the Constitutional Convention with a feeling that such a showing could not, by any possible means, fail to make the men of that convention and of the State clearly understand that *women do want to vote*.[1]

The entire management of New York City was put in charge of Lillie Devereux Blake, and Brooklyn in that of Mariana W. Chapman. While the petition work was going forward a

Lillie Devereux Blake

great series of mass meetings was in progress, for which Miss Anthony, who knew every foot of New York State as well as her own dooryard, mapped out the routes. The management of these was placed in the hands of Harriet May Mills and Mary G. Hay, who proved remarkably efficient. Rev. Anna Shaw spoke at over forty of these meetings and Mary Seymour Howell at a large number. Several speakers from outside the State came in at different times and rendered excellent service. Carrie Chapman Catt made nearly forty speeches in New York, Brooklyn and vicinity. Miss Anthony herself, at the age of seventy-four, spoke in every one of the

---

[1] The president's report pays this tribute:

"The corresponding secretary, Miss Mary S. Anthony, ostensibly had charge of the department of distribution and State correspondence, but all this was only a small fraction of the labor performed by her. Being president of the local club of Rochester, she had charge of the canvass of that city; and it is enough to say that no city or town equalled hers in the work done or results obtained. As our chieftain was leading our hosts through the State, the housekeeping, too, fell to the said secretary's charge and, it being convenient for the speakers and managers to stay at headquarters when in town, her family was seldom a small one; and all this gratuitously, be it understood. I can not hope to tell the story in full, but I trust I have said enough to cause you all, when you say, "God bless Susan B. Anthony," to add "and her sister Mary, also.""

sixty counties of the State, beginning at Albion, January 22, and ending at Glens Falls, April 28.[1]

The campaign opened with a mass meeting at Rochester, of which the Democrat and Chronicle said in a leading editorial : " In pursuance of a call signed by over a hundred prominent citizens, a public meeting will be held January 8. . . . This should be largely attended, not only in honor of our distinguished townswoman, Miss Susan B. Anthony, but to declare in terms which can not be mistaken that the constitution should be revised. The negro and the Indian have been enfranchised; women alone remain under political disabilities. They demand justice. Let it be granted freely, and without any exhibition of that selfishness which has so long kept them waiting."

Judge George F. Danforth presided over this meeting and among the prominent citizens on the platform were Dr. E. M. Moore, Rev. Asa Saxe, Eugene T. Curtis, Mrs. Greenleaf, Mrs. Howell and Miss Anthony, all of whom made strong speeches in favor of the amendment. The list of vice-presidents comprised the leading men and women of the city. Forcible resolutions were presented by Henry C. Maine, and letters of approval read from Judge Thomas Raines, Rev. H. H. Stebbins, of the Central Presbyterian church, and others. The papers said, "Miss Anthony went home as happy as a young girl after her first ball."

On January 9 Miss Anthony addressed the Political Equality Club of Syracuse, and a handsome reception was given to Elizabeth Smith Miller and herself by its president, Mrs. E. S. Jenney. The next day, she went to a big rally at Buffalo, under the auspices of the city suffrage club, Dr. Sarah Morris, president, where speeches were made by Judge Stern, Rabbi Aaron, Rev. Joseph K. Mason and others. On the 22d, the great sweep of county mass meetings began.[2] The scrap-books con-

---

[1] During this time Miss Anthony gave ten days to the national convention in Washington; and the day after the last of the mass meetings she started for Kansas; stopped in Cincinnati for the Ohio convention, speaking each of the three days; opened the Kansas campaign May 4, spoke in that State every day for two weeks; and on May 21 presented herself, fresh and cheerful, at the Constitutional Convention in Albany, N. Y.

[2] As has been noted, Miss Anthony spoke at Ann Arbor, Mich., January 13, 14, 15, 16 and 17; at Toledo the 19th, and was ready to open the New York campaign the 22d.

taining the voluminous accounts show that usually the audiences were large and sympathetic ; that the newspapers, almost without exception, gave full and friendly reports, and although most of them were non-committal in the editorial columns, a number came out strongly in favor of having a suffrage amendment incorporated in the constitution. "Oh, if those who attend our meetings could do the voting," wrote Miss Anthony, "it would carry overwhelmingly, but alas, the riff-raff, the paupers, the drunkards, the very chain-gang that I see passing the house on their way to and from the jail, will make their influence felt on the members of the Constitutional Convention." In another letter she said : "I am in the midst of as severe a treadmill as I ever experienced, travelling from fifty to one hundred miles every day and speaking five or six nights a week. How little women know of the power of organization and how constantly we are confronted with the lack of it ! "[1]

Most of the other speakers were paid for their services but Miss Anthony would not accept a dollar for hers, and refused to take even her travelling expenses out of the campaign fund. That year she received the bequest of her friend, Mrs. Eliza J. Clapp, of Rochester, who had died in 1892, leaving her $1,000 to use as she pleased. The court costs were $55 and she received $945. Although she was drawing from her small principal for her current expenses, she gave $600 of this to the State of New York and $400 to the national association, paying the court fees out of her own pocket.

A new and gratifying feature of this campaign was the interest taken by the women of wealth and social position in New York and Brooklyn. Heretofore it had seemed impossible to arouse any enthusiasm on the question of woman's enfranchisement among this class. Surrounded by every luxury and carefully protected from contact with the hard side of life, they felt no special concern in the conditions which made the struggle for existence so difficult among the masses of

---

[1] In December Miss Anthony and Mrs. Stanton had issued an address calling upon the women of New York to unite in this grand effort for political freedom. During the entire campaign Mrs. Stanton contributed to the New York Sun masterly arguments for woman suffrage, which were widely copied by the press of the State.

women.   All of a sudden they seemed to awake to the importance of the great issue which was agitating the State.   This
possibly may have been because it met the approval of many
of the leading men of New York, for among those who signed
the petition were Chauncey M. Depew, Russell Sage, Frederick
Coudert, Rev. Heber Newton, Rev. W. S. Rainsford, Bishop
Potter, Rabbi Gottheil, John D. Rockefeller, Robert J. Ingersoll, William Dean Howells and others of the representative
men of the city.   The wives of these gentlemen opened their
elegant parlors for suffrage meetings, and in a short time the
following card was sent to a large number of people :

A committee of ladies invite you and all the adult members of your household, to call at Sherry's on any Saturday in March and April, between 9 and
6 o'clock, to sign a petition to strike out, in our State Constitution, the word
"male" as a qualification for voters.   Circulars explaining the reason for
this request may be obtained at the same time and place.—Mrs. Josephine
Shaw Lowell, Mrs. Joseph H. Choate, Mrs. Mary Putnam Jacobi, Mrs. J.
Warren Goddard, Mrs. Robert Abbe, Mrs. Henry M. Sanders, Miss Adele M.
Fielde.

Sherry, the famous restaurateur, placed one of his handsomest rooms at the disposal of the ladies and, for many weeks,
one or more of them might always be found there ready to receive signatures to the petitions.   The New York World expressed the situation in a strong article, saying in part :

Within the month there has been a sudden and altogether unexpected out-
break of the woman suffrage movement in New York. . . . Some one
gave a signal and from all parts of the State rose the cry for the enfranchisement of women.   It is not hard to discover the original cause which set on
foot the insurrection—for in a certain sense it is an insurrection.   It was an
appeal which appeared in the latter part of February and was signed by
many eminent men and women.   Here were nearly twoscore of names, as
widely known and honorable as any in this State—names of people of the
highest social standing, not because of extravagant display or fashionable
raiment, but because of distinction in intellect, in philanthropy and in the
history of the State.   The reason of the coming of the petition just at this
time was, of course, plain.   The meeting of the Constitutional Convention
would be the one chance of the woman suffragists in twenty years. . . .
It will be noticed that these women are in Mr. McAllister's Four Hundred,
but not of it.   They do not go in for frivolity.   They go in for charity, for
working among the masses, for elevating standards of living and morals in
the slums of the city.   They have awakened to the fact of the other half, and

of how that other half lives, and they have expressed their indignation over the small salaries paid women for doing men's work; over the dishonest men in political places, put there because they could vote and control the votes of a number of saloon loungers; over the wretched lot of the woman school teacher, ill-paid and neglected because useless on election day.

And to go back a little further, the most of these society women are the products of that higher education which the pioneer suffragists made possible. They are women of wide reading, of independent thought, of much self-reliance. They began to wonder why they could not vote, when the sloping-shouldered, sloping-skulled youths who proposed to marry them, or had married them, had that right and did not exercise it and showed no information and no concern as to the rottenness of the local government. . . . The upper class of women are enlisted. Woman suffrage is the one interesting subject of discussion in the whole fashionable quarter.

This campaign brought also another surprise. In all the forty years of suffrage work, one of the stumbling-blocks had been the utter apathy of women themselves, who took no interest either for or against, but now they seemed to be aroused all along the line. In Albany a small body of women calling themselves "Remonstrants" suddenly sprung into existence. For a number of years there had been a handful of women in Massachusetts under that title, but this was the first appearance of the species in New York. They seemed to be fathered by Bishop William Croswell Doane, and mothered by Mrs. John V. L. Pruyn. Seven men and a number of women were present at the first meeting in that lady's parlor, and they formed an organization to counteract the vicious efforts of those women who were asking for political freedom. Evidently under the direction of her spiritual adviser, Mrs. Pruyn submitted a set of resolutions, which were adopted, begging the Constitutional Convention "not to strike out the word 'male';" setting forth "that suffrage was not a natural right; that there was no reason why this privilege should be extended to women; that no taxation without representation did not mean that every citizen should vote; that universal suffrage was a mistake; that the possession of the suffrage would take women into conflicts for which they were wholly unfitted; and that it would rudely disturb the strong and growing spirit of chivalry." Another branch was formed in Brooklyn with Mrs. Lyman

Abbott at its head and the Outlook at its back, edited by Rev. Lyman Abbott. A society appeared in New York at about the same time and opened headquarters at the Waldorf. There was also an "Anti" club at Utica.[1]

The Democrat and Chronicle published a long interview with Miss Anthony in regard to these "Remonstrants," from which the following is an extract:

"This opposition movement is not the work of women," she said, "although it has that appearance. There was held in Albany yesterday afternoon a meeting at which resolutions condemning our work were adopted. Listen to the names of the women who were present. Do you see that they are all Mrs. John and Mrs. George and Mrs. William this and that? There is not a woman's first name in the whole list, and I do not see a Miss, either. This goes to show that the women are simply put forward by their husbands.

"Another point: These men who are stirring up the opposition would not only deny the right of women to vote but would qualify the word 'male' as it now stands in the constitution. They say in so many words in their resolutions that the right of suffrage is already extended to too many men; and they pay a doubtful compliment to the intelligence of their mothers, wives and sisters by adding that the class of undesirable voters would be swelled by giving the ballot to women. These are men of wealth who would confine the exercise of the right of suffrage to their own class—in fact would make this government an aristocracy."

These new organizations seemed to be abundantly supplied with money, but though they were able to pay for the work of circulating petitions, which with the suffrage advocates had to be a labor of love, they secured only 15,000 signatures. The petitions asking for a suffrage amendment received 332,148 individual signatures, including the 36,000 collected by the W. C. T. U. In addition to these the New York Federation of Labor sent in a memorial representing 140,000; the Labor Reform Conference, 70,000; several Trades Unions, 1,396;

[1] Mrs. Jane Marsh Parker, a newspaper woman of Rochester, attempted to organize a club there and secure a petition in opposition to the amendment. Her efforts evidently did not meet with marked success for, in a letter to the New York Evening Post, she says, "In offering the 'protest' for signatures, quality rather than quantity has been considered." That prince of editors, Joseph O'Connor, at that time in charge of the Rochester Post-Express, gave the lady a delicious dressing down in an editorial beginning: "What is 'quality'?" and ending: "Probably she means no more by the offensive words 'quality' and 'quantity' than this—that she has secured to the protest only the signatures of a few representative women, no better and no worse than many of their opponents. Such an interpretation saves the statement from being insulting; but unhappily very many women in Rochester give it a different interpretation."

Granges, 50,000 ; total, 593,544. Added to these were petitions from a number of societies, making in round numbers about 600,000. It had been impossible, for several reasons, to make a thorough canvass, and this was especially true of New York and Brooklyn, containing half the population of the State ; and yet there were over one-half as many signers as there were voters in the entire State.

The Constitutional Convention assembled in Albany, May 8, and elected Joseph H. Choate, of New York City, president. Although only a few months previous he had expressed himself favorable to woman suffrage, all his influence in the convention was used against it. Mr. Choate, according to universal opinion, accepted this office with the expectation that it would lead to his nomination as governor of the State, and he had no intention of offending the power behind the gubernatorial chair. The amendment was doomed from the moment of his election. His first move was to appoint a committee to have charge of all suffrage amendments, and on this committee of seventeen he placed twelve men, carefully selected, because they were known to be strongly opposed to woman suffrage. He appointed as chairman a man who could be depended on to hesitate at no means which would secure its defeat.[1] In all his efforts to kill the amendment beyond hope of resurrection, Mr. Choate was actively supported by his first lieutenant, Hon. Elihu Root, also of New York City.

Having ruined all the chances of the amendment, President Choate then announced that every courtesy and consideration would be extended to the ladies having it in charge. Miss Anthony was invited to address the suffrage committee May 24, and the hearing was held in the Assembly room of the Capitol. Not only the committee but most of the delegates were in their seats and a large audience was present. This was said to be one of her best efforts and she seemed to have almost the complete sympathy of her audience. She spoke

---

[1] Mr. Choate might claim that he did not know the position of these men on this question, but it was so well understood that Miss Anthony and her associates felt all hope depart when they read the names of the committee. John Bigelow and Gideon J. Tucker had favored a woman suffrage amendment when they were members of the Constitutional Convention in 1867, but, being now over eighty, were not able to make an aggressive fight for it.

for three-quarters of an hour, and then urged that those opposed should state their reasons and give her an opportunity to answer them. Although there were twelve men on the committee who even then intended to bring in an adverse report, and ninety-eight delegates who afterwards voted against it, not one could be persuaded to rise and present his objections. It was said by many that if the vote could have been taken at that moment, no power could have prevented a majority in favor.

The women of New York City were accorded a hearing May 31, and it was on this occasion, with the petitions of the 600,-000 stacked on a table in front of her, that Dr. Mary Putnam Jacobi made that masterly speech which ranks as a classic.

Very truly yours
Mary Putnam Jacobi

Miss Margaret Livingstone Chanler, in a beautiful address, also spoke in behalf of the "Sherry contingent." The regular New York City League was ably represented by Lillie Devereux Blake and Harriet A. Keyser. The platform was filled with the distinguished women of the State, Miss Anthony, Mrs. Greenleaf and Dr. Jacobi occupying the central position.

On June 7 a hearing was granted to the women from the senatorial districts, each presenting in a five-minute speech the claims of the thousands of petitioners from her district. Among these speakers were some of the best-known women in the State, socially and intellectually ; and a number of others, of equal standing, who never had taken part in public work and who now left their homes only to plead for the power which would enable women better to conserve the interests of home.[1] The State president, Mrs. Greenleaf, presided over all of these hearings, her commanding presence, great dignity and fine mental power giving especial prestige to these bodies of women, who in character and intellect could not be surpassed. The final hearing of those in favor of the amend-

---

[1] The addresses made on this occasion were issued in pamphlet form and presented to the suffrage association by Messrs. Lauterbach and Towns, of the committee.

ment was held June 28, when U. S. Senator Joseph M. Carey, who had come by urgent invitation, made a most convincing speech, describing the practical workings of woman suffrage in Wyoming and urging the men of New York to en-

cause has become the cause of states and nations, your success will form a theme for the generations to come.

Sincerely yours.

Joseph M. Carey

franchise the women of the State. He was followed by Mrs. Mary T. Burt, representing the W. C. T. U., and by Mary Seymour Howell.

One hearing was given to the "Remonstrants," or "Antis," as the press had dubbed them. Because of their extreme modesty, and for other more obvious reasons, they did not make their own appeals but were represented by the male of their species. Their petition was presented by Elihu Root. Hon. Francis M. Scott, whose wife was one of the leading "Antis" in New York, made the principal address. He described pathetically the timid and shrinking class of women for whom he pleaded, insisted that the legislature never had refused women anything they asked, declared the suffrage advocates represented only an "insignificant minority,"[1] and closed with the eloquent peroration: "I vote, not because I am intelligent. not because I am moral, but solely and simply because I am a man." Rev. Clarence A. Walworth, Hon. Matthew Hale and J. Newton Fiero were the other speakers. The first individual

[1] Although their petitions contained 600,000 names and those of the "Antis" 15,000.

ANT.—49

did not believe in universal manhood suffrage and could not favor anything which would double the vote. Mr. Hale devoted most of his argument to the so-called "bad women," declaring there were over 100,000 of them in the State who would sell their votes as they did their bodies—enough to overcome the votes of the virtuous women. Mr. Fiero said woman was unfitted for the ballot because she was influenced by pity, passion and prejudice rather than by judgment. A letter was read from Hon. Abram S. Hewitt, objecting to the amendment because the majority of women do not care to vote.

These insults to their sex seemed very acceptable to the fashionably dressed "Antis" who occupied the front rows of seats. How far their influence affected the adverse vote of the convention it is of course impossible to determine. While the liquor dealers were sending to wavering members their kegs of beer and jugs of whiskey, the "Antis" supplemented their efforts with champagne suppers, flowers, music and low-necked dresses. And the suffrage advocates hoped to offset these political methods by trudging through mud and snow with their petitions and using their scanty funds to send out literature! A mistaken policy, perhaps, but the only one possible to the class of women who are asking for enfranchisement.

The committee, as had been foreordained, brought in an adverse report. The evenings of August 8, 9, 14 and 15, were devoted to a discussion of this report. The Assembly chamber was crowded at each session. The women had known for weeks that they were defeated but had not abated their efforts in the slightest degree. Their work was now finished and they assembled in large numbers to hear the final debate. The amendment had, from first to last, an able and earnest champion in Edward Lauterbach, of New York, who opened the discussion in a speech of an hour and a quarter, said to have been the ablest made in the convention. Nineteen members spoke in favor and fourteen in opposition. The debate throughout was serious and respectful and as dignified as was possible with the frivolous objections made by the opponents. The delegates showed an evident appreciation of the importance of the question at issue, which was about to be sacrificed as usual to political exigency.

The opponents were led by Elihu Root, of New York, who begged pathetically that "we be not robbed of the women of our homes;" and declared that "he would hesitate to put into the hands of women the right to defend his wife and the women he loved and respected." William P. Goodelle, of Syracuse, chairman of the committee, closed the discussion with a long speech in which he asserted that "the question was not whether large numbers of male and female citizens asked for woman suffrage, or protested against it, or are taxed or not, but was it for the benefit of the State?" This being the case, why did Mr. Goodelle not favor its being submitted to the voters of the State in order that they might decide?

It required an hour and a half to take the vote, as most of the members found it necessary to explain why they voted as they did. While it was being taken President Choate left his chair and talked earnestly with many of the delegates—probably about the weather—stopping occasionally to receive the approving smiles of the "Antis." When his name was called for the last vote he recorded himself against the amendment, and the great battle was over![1] In favor of submission 58, opposed 98.

No question before the convention had attracted so much attention throughout the State. The New York Recorder led the newspapers which championed the submission of the amendment, and Harper's Weekly and the Evening Post were prominent among the opposition, a mighty descent from the days when they were under the editorial management of George William Curtis and William Cullen Bryant. The day after the vote was taken the suffrage committee closed its Albany headquarters in the Capitol and the ladies returned to their homes.

[1] Mrs. Choate was one of the women who signed the first call for the suffrage advocates to meet at Sherry's; just as, in 1867, Mrs. Greeley canvassed her whole county to secure signatures to the woman's petition. Horace Greeley, as chairman of the suffrage committee of that Constitutional Convention, threw the whole weight of his influence against the amendment, lest it might hurt the Republican party; just as Mr. Choate did in this one, lest it might hurt the party and himself. Significant answers to the threadbare assertion that the husband represents the wife!

They had raised $10,000 and expended it in the most economical manner ; they had given a year of the hardest and most conscientious work ; and they did not regret a dollar of the money or a day of the time.[1] In her president's report Mrs. Jean Brooks Greenleaf said :

These days will never be forgotten by the trio of the State committee who daily met to work and plan—to make the campaign "bricks" without financial "straw." No one with a heart will recall the pecuniary distress of last winter without a shudder, and to those who had, what was in their estimation, a cause at stake precious as life itself, the outlook was often well nigh disheartening. . . . Could the full history of the past winter's work be given, the doubts expressed of woman's desire for the ballot would be set at rest forever. No more pathetic stories are told of the struggle for liberty in the days of the Revolution than could be told of the women of New York in this campaign. . . .

In closing, we come to the name of one who, we all know, is the inspired leader of women up the heights of honor, purity and self-devotion—Susan B. Anthony. To her marvellous energy and resolution we owe both the conception and the success of this wonderful campaign. In her seventy-fifth year she started out as one of the principal speakers to be heard in the sixty counties of the State; never once did she fail to keep an appointment, never once did she cry a halt. . . . This noble woman, leaving a home of which she is as fond as any woman can be, travelled night or day, as the case required, not only speaking, but plying her busy pen—and all for what? Not for money, for she has stoutly refused to receive one penny of a salary, which, had it been paid, would have exceeded the sum of $3,000. She gave her services for love of liberty and justice, with the hope that New York would prove to be in truth the Empire State of the Union.

From the hour when she learned that a Constitutional Convention would be held, up to the opening of this convention, Miss Anthony had believed that it would incorporate a suffrage amendment which, in all probability, would be allowed by the voters to pass with the rest of the constitution. She found herself outwitted by the politicians, as she had been so many times before, but while this defeat was the bitterest disappoint-

[1]From official report: Emily Howland generously contributed $1,200. That staunch friend, Sarah L. Willis, of Rochester, gave $720. Abby L. Pettengill, of Chautauqua county, gave $220. General Christiansen, of Brooklyn, began the contributions of $100, of which there were, if I mistake not, seven others from our own State—Semantha V. Lapham, Ebenezer Butterick, of New York, Mrs. H. S. Holden, of Syracuse, Marian Skidmore, of Chautauqua county, Hannah L. Howland, of Sherwood, Mr. and Mrs. James Sargent and Colonel H. S. Greenleaf, of Rochester, completing the number.

ment of her life, it did not crush her dauntless spirit. It is related of her that as she came down the steps of the Capitol with the other ladies at midnight, after the vote had been taken, she began planning another campaign.

Among the many appreciative and sympathetic letters she received at this time was one from Isabella Charles Davis, secretary International King's Daughters, saying for herself and Mrs. Mary Lowe Dickinson: "I do not believe you know how tenderly we love you and in what high respect and honor we hold you. Mrs. Dickinson was present at one of those meetings at Sherry's, and she said the only thing lacking to make the occasion perfect was dear Miss Anthony's strong, brave face looking down upon the great multitude." Henry B. Blackwell wrote: "You are to be congratulated on having made a splendid fight in New York. To have secured 600,000 petitions is itself a victory."

In answer to a letter from Isabel Howland, the efficient State recording secretary, she expressed the welcome recognition which she always extended to young workers: "Well, I am truly glad for the discovery of our twin New York girls, Harriet May Mills and Isabel Howland, who promise to take up the laboring oar and pull us to the promised land. Give my warmest regards to your precious mother and aunt Emily; how I have learned to know and love the two!" She went as a guest of the Howlands for a few brief days in the Catskills, and they drove over to Eagle's Nest, in Twilight Park, where Miss Willard and Lady Henry Somerset were spending the summer.

Miss Anthony lectured at Keuka College, August 7, and on the 22d, gave the annual address on suffrage, at Cassadaga lake. The next day she found herself thus reported in the Buffalo Express:

If, instead of Spiritualists, this great body of people had been Baptists, Presbyterians, Methodists or Catholics, their praises for the firm stand they have taken for the enfranchisement of half the people of this country, would have been everywhere sung in song and told in story. But the suffrage women of America always have been afraid to give voice to the "thank you" in their hearts, for Spiritualism has been fully as unpopular as woman suffrage; and they feared if they displayed too much gratitude for this endorsement the public would at once pronounce them Spiritualists and they would thus be doubly damned. But there are a few of our members who are brave enough to rejoice in the damnation of orthodox religions and orthodox politics!

Her consternation at these closing words was intensified by the letters which began coming in upon her before forty-eight hours. She wrote at once to the paper: "This is all right until you come to the last sentence. I had illustrated also the danger of expressing kind words to unpopular political parties, and then I concluded—not as printed—but with: 'There are still a few of us brave enough to rejoice in every good word and work said and done for woman, and to publicly express our thanks therefor, notwithstanding the "denunciation" (not damnation) of orthodox religionists and orthodox politicians.'" The Express published her correction, but it is doubtful if it ever was able to overtake the original statement.

Miss Anthony was very anxious to influence the next legislature, through the public sentiment which had been created, to submit a suffrage amendment. For this purpose she laid out a plan of work to continue the organization and petitions, and herself held meetings in a number of counties. It was decided by the committee to go before the Republican and Democratic State Conventions, which were to be held at Saratoga. An address was prepared and a resolution asking for an endorsement of a woman suffrage amendment. Miss Anthony, Mrs. Greenleaf and Mr. Lauterbach went before the resolution committee, September 18, which allowed five minutes for the three to present their case, and never gave it one minute's attention afterwards.

Frances Willard and Lady Somerset came down from their mountain retreat to attend this convention, and after their return Miss Willard wrote: ". . . As for you, our leader of leaders, I wish I could transfer to your brain all the loving thoughts and words of our trio toward you. As you stood before that roomful of people, so straight and tall and masterful, with that fine senatorial head and face, on which the strength and heroism of your character are so plainly marked, I thought, ' There is one of the century's foremost figures ; there is the woman who has been faithful among the faithless and true among the false ! ' ''

I am with sisterly regard,

Frances Willard

Five minutes allowed such women! Had they represented an enfranchised class, the whole committee would have been at their feet.

Miss Anthony, Mrs. Blake and Mrs. Greenleaf went to the Democratic convention and met with about the same experience. They were permitted to address the resolution committee and bowed out as quickly as possible. There was no especial rudeness or discourtesy, but they had no constituency behind them, no political power, and in the hurry and worry of a State convention the men did not care to waste time with them, even had they been the most eminent women on the face of the earth.

Miss Anthony had a number of urgent invitations to spend the hot months of July, August and September at various charming summer homes in the mountains and at the seaside, but she declined all and resolutely continued at work. The hardest for her to resist had been a triumphant call from the women of Colorado to come and help them celebrate the Fourth of July. It was to be the jubilee of their political emancipation, the first since their enfranchisement. The State president, Mrs. Mary C. C. Bradford, wrote: '' The women of Colorado feel that their precious holiday will be less precious if the beloved suffrage leader and the suffrage flag are not present.'' At first she sent an acceptance, but later, affairs in

New York became so pressing that she was obliged, most reluctantly, to recall it. After filling an engagement to lecture before the alumnæ of the Girls' Normal School in Philadelphia, October 13, she started on the 16th for the final struggle in Kansas.

CHAPTER XLIII.

THE SECOND KANSAS CAMPAIGN.

1894.

THE Kansas legislature of 1893 had submitted an amendment conferring full suffrage on women, to be voted on in November, 1894. Mrs. Laura M. Johns, president of the State Suffrage Association, had written Miss Anthony in April, 1893: "Republicans and Populists are pledged to the support of the amendment. I consider both parties equally committed by their platforms this year, and by their votes in the legislature. We ought to have somebody present in each county convention of both, next year, to secure a suffrage resolution which would insure such a plank in each State platform. You see if one party leaves it out the other will take it up and use it against the first."

During all the voluminous correspondence of 1893, in which Mrs. Johns assured Miss Anthony again and again that her assistance in the campaign was absolutely necessary to success, the latter did not once fail to impress upon her that the endorsement of the political parties was the one essential without which they could hope for nothing. She mapped out and sent to Mrs. Johns a complete plan of work, covering many pages of foolscap, arranging for a thorough organization of every precinct in the State, for the specific purpose of bringing to bear a pressure upon the political conventions the next summer which would compel them to put a plank in their platforms endorsing the amendment. She made it perfectly clear that, if the conventions did not do this, she would not go into the State.

(777)

When the Kansas women came to the Washington convention in February, 1894, Miss Anthony for the first time had her suspicions aroused that the politicians of that State were getting in some shrewd work to prevent them from pressing the question of planks in the platforms. Mrs. Johns had made the serious mistake of accepting also the presidency of the State Republican Woman's Association, and had been actively organizing clubs and conferring with Republican leaders. She insisted that she was making woman suffrage the primary feature of her work, but Miss Anthony held that her strong Republican affiliations could not avoid weakening her influence with the Populists. She did, it is true, send out circulars urging the local organizations to work for planks in both State conventions; and she did advise the women to keep clear of partisan action, but this advice could hardly be effective coming from the State president of the Republican Woman's Association. Miss Anthony wrote her : "My dear Laura, you must choose whom you will serve—the Republican party or the cause of woman's enfranchisement ; " and she replied : "Please don't insult my loyalty with any such suggestion as this ; I have never served anything but the suffrage cause since I began the suffrage work ; " and continued to look after the welfare of her Republican clubs and arrange Republican meetings.

There is no question that a tremendous pressure was brought to bear upon the suffrage leaders by the Republican politicians. If space would permit the publication of their many letters now on file they would make interesting reading. That of Charles F. Scott, of the Iola Register, urging Mrs. Johns to call off her women and telling her the exact language in which to do it, is a masterpiece of political shrewdness. It concludes: "Try to get E. W. Hoch nominated for governor and we won't need any platform." As a specimen of pure humor might be quoted one from Case Broderick, M. C., in which he says :

I have thought a good deal about this question and have concluded we can recognize the movement by a resolution similar to this : "While the question of the amendment of the constitution, now pending, granting the right of suffrage to women, is wholly non-partisn and should not be made a test of

Republicanism, yet we can not view with apprehension the effort to fully confer upon the women of Kansas the elective franchise.''

He then closes : '' Some will contend that we ought to say one thing or the other . . . but such a resolution as this would not drive any from our party.'' One must admit that it would not scare them to death. Mr. Broderick, however, was an honest believer in woman suffrage and later did attempt to secure some recognition for it in the platform. The Republicans sent an agent of adroit address among the suffrage clubs to explain to them how '' an endorsement by the political parties would be really a hindrance to their success,'' and it was charged that this was done with the consent of some of the leading women.

Miss Anthony wrote to Mrs. Johns at this time : '' You know as well as I do that not one of those Republicans thinks party endorsement will damage the suffrage amendment, as they are trying to make the women believe, but every one of them does fear that it will hurt his chances for some position and lose the party the votes of the Germans and the whiskey dealers. The shame for them now is vastly greater than it was twenty-seven years ago, for then they feared to lose the enfranchisement of the negro. Their proposal to leave out the plank now, after they have carried the question thus far, is too wicked to be tolerated by any sane woman ![1] I marvel that you do not see and feel the insult and humiliation.''

On March 6, 1894, Mrs. Johns wrote: '' I find a stampede here on the plank question. *Women* of *both* parties are going against it. Judge Johnston of the supreme bench is opposed to it; so is Judge Horton. Do write them for their views; you know they are good friends of ours. I am worried. The Republicans will hold the first convention, and the general talk of candidates, managers and leaders is against a plank. I was yesterday about to go into print in regard to it, but am

[1] It was the Republicans who framed the original constitution of the State so as to give women liberal property rights, equal guardianship of their children, and school suffrage. In 1867 they gave to women an equal voice on the question of local option. In 1887 they granted to them municipal suffrage. In various State conventions they adopted an unequivocal endorsement of full suffrage for women.

afraid if I make strenuous efforts and am beaten that it will hurt us more than if I keep quiet. Prominent men are writing and besieging me to relieve the party of the embarrassment of this demand. I am not clear in my own mind what to do."

As the weeks went on it became more and more apparent that the women were yielding to the pressure. The officers of the National-American Association, which had pledged nearly $2,300 to help Kansas, insisted that the women should continue to demand the endorsement of the political parties and let the onus of failure rest upon the men and not upon themselves. It might not be worth while to quote from the official letters sent, the campaign having passed into history, but for the fact that they may serve as a guide to other States in the future.

Carrie Chapman Catt, the national organizer, wrote: "It is very plain that the chief fight is now. We must compel endorsement, and I believe we can do it. How any man in his sane senses could think non-endorsement would give votes and sympathy, I can not conceive; or how the women can have a hope of winning without it, after all the experience of our campaigns." Henry B. Blackwell, editor of the Woman's Journal and an experienced politician, wrote Miss Anthony:

At the request of Mrs. Johns I enclose a letter from Mr. Wagener, of Topeka. He gives the worst possible advice, and Mrs. Johns' letter seems to show that she is surrounded by bad advisers and in doubt as to her course. If there is anything which twenty-seven years' work has taught us, it is that a woman suffrage amendment can not be carried without at least one political party squarely behind it. In Colorado, for the first time, we have had a majority; and Mrs. Catt, and Mrs. Reynolds and Mrs. Stansbury of Denver, all say that the amendment could not have been carried if the Republican, Populist and many of the Democratic district conventions had not first endorsed it in their platforms. It thus became a live issue and the masses of voters became interested and enlightened.

On the other hand, our South Dakota experience is conclusive. . . . All three parties ignored it, and the press of the State joined in a conspiracy of silence. The campaign speakers were instructed not to name it. We had to rely for the discussions upon the efforts of suffragists as outsiders. Consequently . . . we were beaten two to one. The same will surely be true in Kansas in 1894. . . . If we do not capture the Republican and Populist State conventions we shall be beaten in advance. All hinges on that!

Yours Faithfully
Carrie Chapman Catt

I have just talked with Mrs. Lease, who fully agrees with me. The Republican convention will be the first to meet. If Mrs. Johns will go before the resolution committee and urge her plank, securing at least its presentation as a minority report offered in open session, it will stampede the convention and be carried. Then the Populists will put one in so as not to be behind the Republicans, and *then* we shall probably win. Do write Mrs. Johns to stand by her guns. No one but her can do this work, because she is personally dear to the Republicans. The fate of the amendment will be then and there decided.

Rev. Anna Shaw, vice-president-at-large, wrote Mrs. Johns in this vigorous language :

I must confess that while I can readily understand the abject cowardice and selfishness which prompt men and political tricksters to urge the abandonment of the plank, I can not understand how you or any other woman with a grain of sense can listen to such proposals for a moment. That endorsement is our only hope. If that fail us, our cause is lost in advance ; for it will show the body of the party what the leaders think and feel on the subject, and be a tacit command to kill it. The hypocrisy of the whole business should not receive from women even a show of belief. What wonder men despise us as a shallow lot of simpletons, if we are deceived by so thin a pretense as this ? I for one protest against it so strongly that if your committee agree to it and do not push party endorsement, I must decline to fool away my time in Kansas. If you give up that point I must refuse to go a single step or raise a dollar. I am sick of the weakness of women, forever dictated to by men. Experience has taught us what a campaign unendorsed means. Think of submitting our measure to the advice of politicians ! I would as soon submit the subject of the equality of a goose to a fox. No ; we must have party endorsement or we are dead.

If I am not to go to Kansas, I want to know it immediately. It is too late even now, for I refused twenty consecutive engagements for May in one State, thinking it was all given up to Kansas. The man or woman who urges surrender now is more a political partisan than a lover of freedom. I care nothing for all the political parties in the world except as they stand for justice. I can not tell you how even the suggestion of this surrender affects me. For the love of woman, do not be fooled by those men any longer.

Finally, as the case grew more hopeless, Miss Anthony, as president of the National-American Association, on March 11, sent the following :

To the Kansas Woman Suffrage Amendment Campaign Committee—Laura M. Johns, Bina M. Otis, Sarah A. Thurston, Annie L. Diggs and Others:

MY DEAR FRIENDS : I have the letter of your chairman, Mrs. Johns, together with one she forwards from a lawyer of Topeka, with the added assertion that Judges Horton, Johnston et al., and leading editors and politicians, are begging your committee to cease to demand of the two great political parties, the Republican and People's, that they put a suffrage plank in their platforms; but instead, simply allow the amendment to go before the electors on its merits—that is to say, repeat the experiment as it has been made and has failed eight times over. . . .

The one and only sure hope of carrying the amendment in Kansas is to have on its side all the aid of the political machinery of its two great parties. My one object in consenting to go into your campaign for May and June, was to create so strong a public demand as to make sure that every delegate elected to the State nominating conventions of the Republican and People's parties shall be instructed by his constituents, in county convention assembled, to vote for a woman suffrage plank in the platform. The moment your committee abandons this aim, I shall lose all interest in your work. You say: "Prominent Republicans are besieging us to relieve their party of the embarrassment of this demand." So did they besiege us twenty-seven years ago. No; not for a moment should you think of relieving the politicians from the duty of declaring for this amendment. If you do, you are unworthy the trust reposed in you. I surely never would have promised to go into your campaign, or begged the friends to contribute, had I dreamed of the possibility of your surrendering to the cowardice of political trimmers.

If the convention which meets first do not endorse the amendment, then the other will not; in which event, its discussion will not be germane in either party's fall campaign. On the other hand, if the first put a plank in its platform, the other will be sure to do so; and then the question will be a legitimate one to be advocated in the meetings of both parties and this will ensure the presentation of our cause to all the voters of the State.

By this means the two parties will run your amendment campaign, and you will not be compelled to make a separate suffrage campaign. That you can not do in any event, because (1st) you can not get either the speakers or the money necessary; and (2d) if you could get both, you would have only women in your meetings, and defeat would be just as certain as in the eight States which have had such separate woman's campaigns. Therefore, if you decide to abandon the demand for political endorsement and active help, as the first and chief object of this spring's work, you may count me out of it; for I will not be a party, even though a protesting one, to such a surrender of our only hope of success.

I came home for a rest over Sunday, after speaking five successive nights in five different counties, in our New York campaign, and these letters with the weak—the wicked—thought of not demanding of the political leaders to make their parties help carry the amendment, raged through my brain all night long. How to put the shame of surrender strongly enough was my constant study, sleeping and waking alike. No, a thousand times no, I say; and if you do yield to this demand at the behest of men claiming to be your friends, you make yourselves a party with those men to ensure your defeat. The speakers will advocate no measure, and the vast majority of men will vote for none, which is not approvingly mentioned in the platform. If you give

up trying for political endorsement, or fail after trying, all hope of carrying
the amendment will be gone. So, over and over I say, demand party help!

Lovingly but protestingly,   SUSAN B. ANTHONY.

Mrs. Johns, of course, indignantly rejected the imputation
that she was not working night and day to secure a plank
from the Republican convention. She was a most efficient
manager, but the cause of her weakness and that of the other
women, was that they were trying to serve two masters. The
very fact that the Republican men were begging them not to
ask for a plank, shows the power which the women already
possessed in their municipal suffrage, and they should have
had the courage to stand firm in their demands for recognition
in the platform, for the dignity of their cause and their womanhood, whether there were hope of getting it or not. There is
no doubt that Mrs. Johns did make an earnest effort to this
end, but there is also no doubt that every Republican leader
understood that even if the party did not endorse the suffrage
amendment, she and her associates still would be no less Republicans and would work no less vigorously for the party's success.
Miss Anthony's Kansas correspondence during 1894 comprises
300 letters and all confirm the statements thus briefly outlined.

The Republican politicians made the women believe if they
would not insist on the party's placing itself on record and
thus losing the support of the elements opposed to woman suffrage, all of them would vote for the amendment. Should the
women of Kansas ever become politically free, the publication
of these letters would be fatal to some aspiring male candidates,
but so long as the men still have it in their power to grant to
women or to withhold the full franchise, it is the part of wisdom to leave them on their files. There were many Kansas
women, however, who refused to be deceived and sustained
Miss Anthony's position. In April she wrote to one of the
Republican leaders :

If the Republicans had two grains of political sense, they would see that
for them to espouse the amendment and gain the glory, as they surely would,
of lifting the women of the State into full suffrage, would give them new life,
prestige and power greater and grander than they ever possessed; and they

would not be halting and belittling themselves with such idiotic stuff and nonsense as their advice to let the amendment go to the electors of the State
"on its own merits." But however politicians may waver, our suffrage
women must not have a doubt, but must persist in the demand for full recognition in both platforms. We must exact justice and if they do not give it,
the curse be on their heads, not ours.

The same month she wrote Mrs. Johns:

I can not tell you how more and more it is borne in upon me that our one
chance lies in securing the Republican pledge to carry us to victory, for that
will mean a Populist pledge, and both planks will mean a clean-cut battle between the different elements of the grand old party combined as one on this
question—and the Democracy of the State. Even with so solid an alliance of
the two branches, we shall have a hard enough fight of it. Every woman who
listens to the siren tongues of political wire-pullers and office-seekers not to
demand a plank, will thereby help to sell Kansas back into the hands of the
whiskey power. Behind every anti-plank man's word, written or spoken, is
his willingness to let Kansas return to saloon rule. Sugar coat it as they
may, that is the unsavory pill in the motive of every one of them.

Sincerely and hopefully yours, trusting in good and keeping our powder
dry.

Enough has been quoted to show the situation. Miss Anthony, Mrs. Catt and Miss Shaw went to Kansas to open the
spring canvass, May 4, to influence the State conventions.
Miss Anthony had been advertised for forty-three speeches.
The women of New York, where a great campaign was in progress, were highly indignant that she should leave her own
State, but she had put her heart into this Kansas campaign as
never into any other, and she fully believed that, if properly
managed, the result could not fail to be victory for the amendment. The three ladies held the first meeting in Kansas City,
May 4. Miss Anthony made a speech which fairly raised the
hair of her audience, demanding in unqualified terms the
endorsement of the amendment by the Republican and People's
parties. She closed by offering the following resolution, which
was unanimously adopted:

WHEREAS, From the standpoint of justice, political expediency and grateful
appreciation of their wise and practical use of school suffrage from the organization of the State, and of municipal suffrage for the past eight years, we, of
the Republican and People's parties, descendants of that grand old party of

splendid majorities which extended these rights to the women of Kansas, in mass meeting assembled do hereby

Resolve, That we urgently request our delegates in their approaching State conventions to endorse the woman suffrage amendment in their respective platforms.

That night she wrote in her journal: "Never did I speak under such a fearful pressure of opposition. Mrs. Johns, presiding, never smiled, and other women on the platform whispered angrily and said audibly, 'She is losing us thousands of votes by this speech.'" Miss Anthony repeated it in the county mass conventions at Leavenworth and Topeka, to the dismay of the Republican women and the wrath of the men.[1] While at the latter place she received an urgent summons to return immediately to New York, as fresh dangers threatened; and so she hastened eastward, leaving the others to fill her engagements. On her way, she stopped by invitation at Kansas City, Mo., and with Miss Shaw held a Sunday afternoon meeting at which $133 were raised for the Kansas campaign.

In three weeks Miss Anthony returned to Kansas, arriving June 5. She found the Republican Woman's State Convention in session, Mrs. Johns presiding. The committee reported a weak resolution declaring that they would not make the adoption of a suffrage plank by the Republican State Convention "a test of party fealty," etc. Miss Anthony and Miss Shaw condemned this in the strongest English they could command. Mrs. Johns also severely criticised the committee, but Mrs. J. Ellen Foster, who had come for both conventions, said: "I care more for the dominant principles of the Republican party than I do for woman suffrage." The committee finally were compelled to report a stronger resolution asking for recognition.

The Republican convention met June 6. C. V. Eskridge, of Emporia, the oldest and bitterest opponent of woman suffrage in the State of Kansas, was made chairman of the committee

[1] See Appendix for full speech.

ANT.—50

on resolutions. The proposal to hear the women speak, during an interim in the proceedings, was met by a storm of noes. Finally Mrs. Foster and Mrs. Johns were permitted to present the claims of women, but neither Miss Anthony nor Miss Shaw was given an opportunity to address the convention. They did, however, plead the women's cause most eloquently before the resolution committee of thirty-five members, but the platform was entirely silent on the subject, not even containing the usual complimentary allusions, recognition of their services, etc.[1] Not the slightest attempt was made to deny the fact that agents of the party had been at work for weeks among the various county conventions to see that delegates were appointed who were opposed to a suffrage plank, and that the resolution committee had been carefully "packed" to prevent any danger of one. In conversations which Miss Anthony held with several of the leading candidates who in times past had advocated woman suffrage, they did not hesitate to admit that the party had formed an alliance with the whiskey ring to defeat the Populists. "We must redeem the State," was their only cry. "Redeem it from what?" she asked. "From financial heresies," was the answer. "Yes," she retorted, "even if you sink it to the depths of hell on moral issues."

It is not probable that any earthly power could have secured Republican endorsement at this time, although heretofore the party always had posed as the champion of this cause. There never was a more pitiable exhibition of abject subserviency to party domination. Men who had stood boldly for woman suffrage in the legislature, men who had spoken for it on the platform in every county in the State, sat dumb as slaves in this convention, sacrificing without scruple a lifelong principle for the sake of a paltry political reward.

Your Brother

D R Anthony

While many of the papers had spoken earnestly in favor of

[1] The women of the Topeka Equal Suffrage Club, at their next meeting, adopted a resolution thanking the Republican convention *for not declaring against the amendment!*

the amendment, the Leavenworth Times, owned and edited by D. R. Anthony, was the only one of size and influence which demanded party endorsement.[1] The Republican managers had but one idea—to overthrow Populist rule and get back the reins of government—and they were ready to take on or pitch overboard whatever would contribute to this end.

A suffrage mass meeting was held in Topeka the Saturday following the convention and, in spite of a heavy thunderstorm, there was an audience of over one thousand. Annie L. Diggs presided and Miss Anthony and Miss Shaw spoke, the former on "Reasons why the dominant parties do not put a plank in their platforms;" the latter on, "Woman first, Republican or Populist afterwards."

The great question now was whether it were wise to ask for a suffrage plank in the Populist platform, and here again was great diversity of opinion. Some thought that endorsement by this party would make it appear like a Populist measure, and the Republicans would vote against it rather than allow them to have the credit of carrying it. Others held that the Populists carried the State at the last election and were likely to do so again, and with their party vote, the Prohibition and such Republican votes as certainly could be counted on, the amendment would go through without fail. Miss Anthony belonged to the latter class and directed every energy towards securing an endorsement in their State convention, June 12. Although woman suffrage had been one of the tenets of this party from its beginning, there was by no means a unanimous sentiment in favor of a plank of endorsement. This was especially true in regard to the leaders. Governor Lewelling, who was a candidate for re-election, was openly opposed, and

[1] It will be cowardice for the Republicans to fail to endorse woman suffrage in their State platform. In past years, when no amendment was pending, the Republican party of Kansas has encouraged the presentation of such an amendment. Will it now attempt to sneak out of the responsibility and go back on its past record? The women of our State have shown themselves intelligent voters, in every way worthy of being entrusted with full suffrage. None of the evils have come upon us which were predicted by the opponents of the reform, and they never will come. To place a plank in the platform will save many votes to the party. It is the right, the brave thing to do. What is brave and right has, in the past, been the thing that the Republican party has done. Let it not now begin to do the cowardly thing.—Leavenworth Times, May 17, 1894.

P. P. Elder, chairman of the resolution committee, made a determined fight against it.

While the resolution committee was out Miss Anthony addressed the convention, saying in the course of her remarks : " I belong to but one party under the shadow of the flag, and that is the party of idiots and criminals. I don't like my company. Are you going to leave your mothers, wives and sisters in that category? I ask you to say that every woman by your side shall have the same rights as you have." When she concluded one of the delegates said : " Miss Anthony, with all due respect, I wish to ask, in the event of the Populists putting a woman suffrage plank in their platform, will you work for the success of this party?" The newspapers thus report her reply and what followed :

" For forty years I have labored for woman's enfranchisement, and I have always said that for the party which endorsed it, whether Republican, Democratic or Populist, I would wave my handkerchief. I will go before the people at your meetings, and though I know very little about the other principles of your party and never discuss finance and tariff, I will try to persuade every man in those meetings to vote for woman suffrage."

" Miss Anthony," said Mr. Carpenter, " we want more than the waving of your handkerchief, and if the People's party put a woman suffrage plank in its platform, will you go before the voters of this State and tell them that because the People's party has espoused the cause of woman suffrage it deserves the vote of every one who is a supporter of that cause ? "

Miss Anthony answered: " I most certainly will ! "

Immediately upon hearing this, the convention went wild—yelled and cheered and applauded to its very utmost—hundreds rose to their feet—the cheering lasted five minutes without intermission.

In the confusion Miss Anthony thus finished her interrupted sentence :

" For I would surely choose to ask votes for the party which stood for the principle of justice to women, though wrong on financial theories, rather than for the party which was sound on the questions of money and tariff, and silent on the pending amendment to secure political equality to half the people."

None of the reporters caught this and, as a result, the simple statement, " I certainly will," appeared in all the Kansas papers and went the rounds of the press of the entire country.

The suffrage question had its opponents and advocates among leaders and delegates. It occupied the resolution committee until late at night, and finally went down to defeat, 8 to 13. When the resolutions were reported they considered finance, labor, taxes, banks, bonds, arbitration, pensions, irrigation, freight rates, transportation, initiative and referendum —everything under the sun but the suffrage amendment. In regard to that much agitated point they were painfully silent. On this committee was one woman delegate, Mrs. Eliza Hudson, who could not be coaxed or bullied. She gave notice at once that she would make a minority report and carry it to the floor of the convention. The following was signed by herself and seven other members of the committee: " *Whereas,* The People's party came into existence and won its glorious victories on the fundamental principles of equal rights to all and special privileges to none ; therefore be it resolved that we favor the pending constitutional amendment."

Meanwhile Miss Anthony, Mrs. Catt and Miss Shaw addressed the convention and were enthusiastically received. When the minority report was presented and every possible parliamentary tactic had failed to prevent its consideration, it was vehemently discussed for four hours, in five-minute speeches, Judge Frank Doster leading the affirmative. The debate was closed by Mrs. Diggs, and the resolution was adopted, ayes 337, noes 269 ; carried by 68 majority in a delegate body of 606. During the fray a tail in some way tacked itself on to the resolution, which said, *"but we do not regard this as a test of party fealty."* So the party adopted a plank declaring that it did not regard a belief in one of its own fundamental principles as a test of fealty ; but in the wild excitement which ensued, a little thing like this was not noticed. The State Journal thus describes the scene :

When it became evident the resolution had carried, and before the vote could be announced, the convention jumped up and yelled. Canes were waved, hats thrown high in the air, men stood on chairs and shouted frantically. The whole convention was one deep, all-prevailing impersonated voice.

How they howled and stamped, as though every one loved suffrage and suffragists with all their hearts!

" I want Miss Shaw to come forward and give that Populist whoop that she promised she would last night," said a delegate. Miss Shaw came to the front of the platform and said: " I do not know any better whoop than that good old tune, ' Praise God From Whom All Blessings Flow.' " " Sing," said Chairman Dunsmore. The vast audience shook every particle of air in the big hall with the full round notes of the long meter doxology. " Let all the people cry amen," said Alonzo Wardall, who was on the platform. Hundreds of voices which had not pronounced the word for years joined in the great, resounding, unanimous " amen " that filled the hall.

Susan B. Anthony, Annie L. Diggs and Anna Shaw leaned over the front of the stage and shook every man's hand as he passed along, and hundreds of brown, calloused hands were thrust up to give a grasp of congratulation. Miss Anthony warmed to her work and had to push up her sleeves, but she didn't mind that for suffrage, for which she had just won a glorious victory. Many said, as they grasped her hand: " You're going to be a Populist now, ain't you?"

During the confusion an old soldier came up and pinned a Populist badge on her dress, and this was magnified by the newspapers into the thrilling description: " Miss Anthony seized a Populist badge and, pinning it on her breast, declared: ' Henceforth and forever I belong to the People's party ! ' "

The State Prohibition convention was in progress at Emporia at the same time, and the women had been notified that a suffrage plank would be adopted without any effort on their part. On June 13 the following telegram was sent by the secretary of the convention to Miss Anthony and Miss Shaw : " Recognizing the right of suffrage as inherent in citizenship, the Prohibition party stands unequivocally pledged to use its utmost efforts to secure the adoption of the pending constitutional amendment for the enfranchisement of women." This was their response from the Populist convention hall : " The National-American Woman Suffrage Association sends greeting, and is gratified that there is one political party which does not need to be urged to declare for justice to women." The Capitol said : " There was a wild demonstration as their names were read."

It is hardly possible to give an adequate idea of the storm which followed the announcement of Miss Anthony's declaration in regard to the People's party. There was scarcely a newspaper in the country which did not have its fling. Kate Field's Washington led off with a full first page entitled, "The Unholy Alliance." Editors opposed to woman suffrage made it a text for double leaders. Republican papers berated her without mercy. Letters poured in upon her from personal friends, judges, mayors, ministers, members of Congress, accepting the published reports and condemning her in unmeasured terms. Others wrote begging her to set herself right in the eyes of the public, as they knew she had been misrepresented. It seemed impossible, however, for her to make herself clearly understood. She writes in her journal: "One would think I had committed the unpardonable sin against the Holy Ghost in thanking the Populists for their good promise and saying I preferred them with justice to women, no matter what their financial folly, to the Republicans without justice to women, no matter what their financial wisdom."

She returned home June 20 and all the Rochester reporters were on hand for an interview. The following from the Democrat and Chronicle is practically what appeared in all :

Miss Anthony was perfectly willing to talk, and this is a resume of what the reporter learned: 1. Miss Anthony is not a Populist. 2. Miss Anthony is not a Democrat. 3. Miss Anthony is not a Republican. 4. Miss Anthony can not say what party she will join when the right to vote is given her.

"I didn't go over to the Populists by doing what I did in Kansas," she said. "I have been like a drowning man for a long time, waiting for some one to throw a plank to me. The Republicans refused, but the Populists threw an excellent plank in my direction. I didn't step on the whole platform, but just on the woman suffrage plank. I went forward at the close of the convention and told the men how glad I was to see one of the dominant parties take up woman suffrage. I said that we had been besieging the big political parties for twenty-five years. Here is a party in power which is likely to remain in power, and if it will give its endorsement to our movement, we want it.

"I do not claim to know anything of the merits of the issues which brought the Populist party into existence. All I know is that it is chiefly made up from the rank and file of the old Republican party of that State, and that the men who compose it think they have better methods for the correction of existing evils. They are protesting against the present order of things, and certainly no one will deny there is ground for it. I do not endorse their platform, but I would be one of the last to condemn an honest protest."

"But," said the reporter, "it always has been understood that you are a strong Republican."

"Why has it been so understood? Simply because a majority of the national legislators who have favored us have been Republicans. Suppose the Republican party of New York, at its coming convention, refuses to endorse woman suffrage; suppose the Democratic does endorse it. My action with the Democrats would be just what it was with the Populists of Kansas. I am for woman suffrage and will work with any party which will help us. Remember I say ' with,' not ' for.' "

Miss Shaw finished her two months' engagement in Kansas and did not return to that State. Mrs. Catt wrote Miss Anthony a few weeks after the conventions :

It is remarkable the difference of opinion that is floating about. We hear of Populists who are so mad about the plank they declare they will go back to the Democratic party. Others, even those who are suffragists, are so mad at the women for putting the plank forward they say they will vote against the amendment. Democrats say there can be no fusion and that will mean death to the Populist party. Some Republicans say they will not vote for the amendment because it is now a Populist question. Again some Republicans and some Democrats say they will vote the Populist ticket because of the plank. From all these varied ideas it is impossible to find out whether we are better or worse off. . . . At any rate, the question now has a political standing, and it will depend upon party developments where we find ourselves. My own hope is that it may bring the Republicans to time, but if the Populists say too much, it may drive them to secret opposition, and then we are done for.

Miss Anthony took a much more cheerful view and replied to the various letters :

At last one of the dominant parties in a State, and that one the party in power, has adopted a woman suffrage amendment, and upon that one plank I have planted my feet. The Republicans by ignoring us give party sanction to every anti-suffrage man among them ; while the Populists' endorsement makes every anti-suffrage man among them feel that he will be the better Populist if he vote "yes." . . .

Meantime, every Farmers' Alliance picnic, every school-house meeting, will be on fire with the enthusiasm born of their party's heroic action ; for such it was, in defiance of their leaders' command to imitate the Republicans and ignore the amendment. The 900 Republicans in the State convention obeyed their masters ; while 68 more than one-half of the 606 Populists rebelled against theirs. Surely there is more to hope from the party, a majority of whose men dare vote opinions against their bosses, than for the one in which not a single man dares even raise a protest. What would our friends have had us do? Bless the Republicans for slapping us in the face, and blast the Populists for giving us a helping hand?

Among the comforting letters which came during these troublous times was one from Wm. Lloyd Garrison, with whose father she had fought the battle of Abolitionism, in which he said: "I saw Mrs. Isabel Barrows yesterday and heard from her of your weary journey together from Chicago, your discouragement regarding Kansas, and the personal pain occasioned you by untrue newspaper reports and the harsh criticism of friends. I write to express my word of sympathy and cheer. Send me a brief statement of the Populist matter and let me break a lance in your behalf. A reformer's life is full of misrepresentations. How little they signify in the long run and, if they did not wound the spirit, would not be worth the mention. To be misjudged by one's own friends hurts more than all the bitterness of the rest of the world."

In a public address made this summer, Miss Anthony referred to the matter in the following beautiful words:

Had the Republicans of Kansas adopted a woman suffrage plank, and Miss Shaw and Miss Anthony declared that, because of such endorsement, they would prefer the success of that party, nobody would have thought it meant that they had endorsed the whole Republican platform, and made themselves responsible for the right conduct of every officer and nominee of that party.

I was born and reared a Quaker, and am one still; I was trained by my father, a cotton manufacturer, in the Henry Clay school of protection to American products; but today all sectarian creeds and all political policies sink into utter insignificance compared with the essence of religion and the fundamental principle of government—equal rights. Wherever, religiously, socially, educationally, politically, justice to woman is preached and practiced, I find a bond of sympathy, and I hope and trust that henceforth I shall be brave enough to express my thanks to every individual and every organization, popular or unpopular, that gives aid and comfort to our great work for the emancipation of woman, and through her the redemption of the world.

To a letter from Henry B. Blackwell, urging her to be nonpartisan if she could not be Republican, she replied, July 9:

The difference between yourself and me, and Mrs. Johns and me, is precisely this—that you two are and have been Republicans *per se*, while I have been a Republican only in so far as the party and its members were more friendly to the principle of woman suffrage. I agree with you that it will be in line with Mrs. Johns' ideas for her to work for the Republican party, false though its platform and its managers are to the pending amendment; but I could not do so. The rank and file of the Populist men of Kansas may not possess equal book or brain power with the Republicans, but they are more honest and earnest to establish justice, and 337 of their delegates had manhood enough to break out of the whiskey-Democratic bargain which their leaders, like the Republican fixers, had made. No, I shall not praise the Republicans of Kansas, or wish or work for their success, when I know by their own confessions to me that the rights of the women of their State have been traded by them in cold blood for the votes of the lager beer foreigners and whiskey Democrats. . . .

I have not allied and shall not ally myself to any party or any measure save the one of justice and equality for woman; but the time has come when I strike, and proclaim my contempt for the tricksters who put their political heel on the rights of women at the very moment when their help is most needed. I never, in my whole forty years' work, so utterly repudiated any set of politicians as I do those Republicans of Kansas. When it is a mere matter of theory, a thousand miles from a practical question, they can resolve pretty words, but when the crucial moment comes they sacrifice us without conscience or honor. The hubbub with the Republicans shows they have been struck in the right place. I never was surer of my position that no self-respecting woman should wish or work for the success of a party which ignores her political rights.

These few extracts from scores of similar letters, speeches and interviews, show the position consistently and unflinchingly maintained by Miss Anthony, and justified by many years of experience in such campaigns. During the summer of 1894, while she was being thus harassed, she kept steadily on, speaking and working in the New York campaign and preparing to return to Kansas in the fall. She wrote to the Republican and the Populist central committees, offering to speak on the suffrage question upon their platforms. The former, through its chairman, Cyrus Leland, declined her offer.

To John W. Breidenthal, of the People's party, she wrote: "Do you not think it will be a great deal better, both for the suffrage amendment and the Populist party, if in all the announcements it shall be distinctly stated that Miss Anthony speaks only on the subject of woman's enfranchisement?" To this he replied, August 6: "I leave the matter entirely with you whether you confine yourself only to the suffrage amendment, or whether you add to that the discussion of the other questions now attracting public attention." Meanwhile she had been receiving cheerful messages from the Populist women of Kansas, among them a long and cordial letter from Annie L. Diggs, written August 16:

Nearly everything along the line of my experience and observation would make you glad. I have large audiences, say the best and strongest things I know for suffrage and always find the heartiest response. I see more and more the wisdom of your insistence on platform mention. Oh, I am so thankful that I, too, saw straight before it was too late to get the Populist endorsement. I have been speaking almost constantly, sometimes twice a day, and at every meeting other speakers and *candidates* say the best kind of words for the amendment. Governor Lewelling speaks in warm endorsement, reports to the contrary notwithstanding. I can not say that he does so always, but he did at the three meetings which we held together. The Populists who wanted to shake my head off at the convention, give me, if possible, warmer greetings than the others. They are truly glad they took that righteous step. . . .

We Populists wish so much for you and Miss Shaw to come to Kansas. People constantly ask me if you will talk for the Populists when you come. I answer that you will talk suffrage at Populist meetings and will also say that, inasmuch as in Kansas the Populists endorse suffrage, therefore the party ought to win. Is not that your intention? How I wish I could describe to you some of the success I have had in talking to German audiences. But I have not another minute only to thank you for your kind words about me, and to say again, as I have said so many years, "I love and revere you."

Faithfully yours

Annie L. Diggs.

Mrs. Johns wrote, August 27: "I think the Republicans are conscious dimly of the increasing strength of the Populists. It looks as if they will win, and it is generally believed the amendment will go through." As late as October 12, Mrs. Catt, who had been speaking at suffrage meetings for the past six weeks and whose judgment was generally sound, said in a letter from Hutchinson :

After all the vicissitudes, hard feelings and distresses of the campaign, it begins to look as if we were going to come in " on the home stretch." The last two weeks have wrought wonderful changes. The tide has set in our favor. I think the chief cause is the published fact that we are going to count the votes to see how many out of each party are cast for the amendment, and Republicans understand they will be in a bad way if they don't make a good showing. Since this came out, Morrill has spoken for the amendment. Judge Peters, at the big McKinley meeting here, advocated it and they tell me it created more enthusiasm than anything else during the meeting. Cyrus Leland admits that it will carry. The Republicans are coming over splendidly and, if the Populists stand firm, we will surely come in with a fine majority. It seems as if nothing can defeat us now.

Two weeks before the election, October 21, Mr. Breidenthal wrote her : " I am confident the amendment will have 30,000 majority." Miss Anthony reached the State October 20 and began her two weeks' tour the 22d, speaking at Populist meetings in the largest cities up to election day, November 6.[1] From the hour of her arrival she realized there was not a shadow of hope for the amendment, and it was marvellous to her how the others could have been so deceived.

At the previous election when the Populists came into power it had been through a fusion with the Democrats. This year the Democrats had their own ticket, and not only had ignored the pleading of the Democratic women for a suffrage plank, but had adopted a resolution denouncing it.[2] The great railroad strike and its attendant evils, during that summer, were attributed by many to Populistic sentiment and created a strong prejudice against the party. The argument was made that if the amendment carried, the women would feel so grateful to the Populists that it would result in securing to them the woman's

[1]Miss Anthony did not receive a dollar for her services during the year in Kansas, and was enabled to make the three trips there solely through the kindness of her brother Daniel R., who furnished transportation. It was also by his assistance that she had made her long railroad journeys from east to west during the past thirty years.

[2]Fifteenth.—We oppose woman suffrage as tending to destroy the home and family, the true basis of political safety, and express the hope that the helpmeet and guardian of the family sanctuary may not be dragged from the modest purity of self-imposed seclusion to be thrown unwillingly into the unfeminine places of political strife.

vote, thus keeping them in power. This induced many to vote against it who disliked Populism, and it decided a number of even those Republicans who believed in woman suffrage to reject the amendment this year rather than allow the Populists to have the credit of carrying it. To destroy the last hope, word came from Colorado that the People's party was about to be defeated there. It was the first time for the women of that State to vote and, while there was no evidence to prove that they were responsible, the bare possibility was enough to stampede the Kansas Populists and prevent their giving the ballot to the women of that State.

The amendment was lost by 34,827 votes; 95,302 for; 130,139 against. The total vote cast for governor was 299,231; total vote on suffrage amendment, 225,441; not voting on amendment, 73,790. There was an attempt to keep count of the ballots according to parties, but it was not successful and there was no way of correctly estimating the political complexion of the vote. The vote for Governor Morrill lacked only 1,800 of that for the other three candidates combined, which shows how easily the Republican party might have carried the amendment. Subtracting the 5,000 Prohibition votes which it was conceded were cast for the amendment, it lacked 28,000 of receiving as many votes as were cast for the Populist candidate for governor. Since some Republicans must have voted for it, the figures prove that a vast number of Populists did not do so. In Miss Anthony's journal on the night of the election she wrote: "Our friends remembered to forget to vote for the suffrage amendment, while not an enemy forgot to remember to stamp his ticket against it."

Though she had expected defeat, her regret was none the less keen. In all the past years she had given more time and work to Kansas than to any other State, even her own. Her hopes had been centered there. It having been the first State to grant school suffrage and the first to grant municipal suffrage to women, she had confidently expected that when the amendment for full suffrage was again submitted it would be carried. The events of the campaign confirmed her belief that the granting of municipal suffrage is a hindrance rather than a help toward securing full enfranchisement. By its exercise women naturally become partisan, show the influence they can wield through the ballot, and thereby create enmities and arouse antagonisms which bitterly oppose any further extension of this power. She resolved henceforth to advise women not to attempt to secure fragmentary suffrage, but to demand the whole right and work for nothing less.

CHAPTER XLIV.

THE SOUTHERN TRIP—THE ATLANTA CONVENTION.

1895.

THE day following the Kansas election, November 7, 1894, Miss Anthony started at 10 o'clock in the morning for Beatrice, Neb., to make the opening speech at the State Suffrage Convention ; arrived at 6 P. M., took a cup of tea, dressed and, without having had one moment's rest, found herself at the opera house in the presence of a splendid audience. After she was seated on the platform a telegram was handed her saying the suffrage amendment had been lost in Kansas by an immense majority. Yet, in spite of the terrible physical strain of the past weeks and in the face of this stunning news, it is said she never made a stronger, more logical and comprehensive speech than on this occasion. She reviewed the amendment campaigns of the last twenty-five years, describing the causes of defeat or success, and pointing out the necessity of educational effort beginning with the primaries and continuing through all the conventions and political meetings up to the very day of election.

Although she received urgent invitations to speak at various points in the State, she declined all and left the next morning early for Leavenworth ; and the day following, November 9, was on her way eastward. After a day in Chicago she went directly to Philadelphia, where she attended a reception given by the New Century Club to Mary Mapes Dodge ; had several business meetings regarding the affairs of the national association ; then hastened by night train to the New York convention at

Ithaca. Here again, without a day's rest, she made a stirring address to an audience which packed the opera house to the top row of the upper gallery, sat on the steps and filled the aisles. The convention was welcomed by the mayor of Ithaca and President Schurmann, of Cornell. The latter invited the officers and delegates to visit the university and accompanied them on their tour of inspection. Miss Anthony spoke to the girls of Sage College after dinner, gave them many new ideas long to be remembered, and was received with enthusiasm and affection.

The next evening, November 15, she returned to Rochester. She had just concluded two of the hardest campaigns ever made for woman suffrage ; for almost one year she had found no rest for the sole of her foot, not an hour's respite for the tired brain, and yet the letters and the entries in the journal show her to be as cheerful, as philosophical, as full of hopeful plans, as ever she had been in all her long and busy life. After just one day at home she started for Cleveland. The W. C. T. U. were holding a national convention in that city and were to have a great " gospel suffrage " meeting in Music Hall, Sunday afternoon, which she was invited to address. The Cleveland Leader, in describing the occasion, said :

Miss Willard, the chieftain of the white ribbon army, introduced Miss Anthony, the chieftain of the yellow ribbon army, saying: "Once we would not have allowed the yellow ribbon to be so generously displayed here. Had its wearers asked us to admit it with the white we might have voted it down ; but the yellow badge of the suffragists looks natural now. The golden rule has done it. Well do I remember that in the hard struggle mother and I had in paying the taxes on our little home, no man appeared to pay them for us. Had I been condemned to death I would not have expected a man to start up and take my place. Susan B. Anthony—she of the senatorial mind—will be remembered when the politicians of today have long been doomed to 'innocuous desuetude.' " Miss Willard then quoted a few familiar lines ending with the sentence, "And Susan B. Anthony has been ordained of God to lead us on."

Miss Anthony was greeted with a rousing Chautauqua salute. "I am delighted beyond measure," she said, "that at last the women of this great national body have found there is only one way by which they can reach their desired end, and that is by the ballot. What is 'gospel suffrage ?' It is a system by which truth and justice might be made the uppermost principles of government. Every election is the solution of a mathematical problem, the figuring out of what the majority desire. We have in this country mercantile, mining, manufacturing and all kinds of business by which money can be made. The interests of every one of these are put into the political scale, but when the moral issues are put in the other side the material pull them down. Why? Because the moral issues are not weighted with votes. The men who are associated with women in movements of reform get no more in the way of legislation than do women themselves, because when they go to the legislatures or to Congress they have back of them only a disfranchised class.

"If you would have your requests granted your legislators must know that you are a part of a body of constituents who stand with ballots in their hands. Women, we might as well be dogs baying the moon as petitioners without the power to vote! If you have no care for yourselves, you should at least take pity on the men associated with you in your good works. So long as State constitutions say that all may vote when twenty-one, save idiots, lunatics, convicts and women, you are brought down politically to the level of those others disfranchised. This discrimination is a relic of the dark ages. The most ignorant and degraded man who walks to the polls feels himself superior to the most intelligent woman. We should demand the wiping out of all legislation which keeps us disfranchised.

Almost every sentence of this brief address was punctuated with applause from the immense audience.

Always when in Cleveland Miss Anthony was a guest at the palatial home of Mrs. Louisa Southworth. At this time, with her hostess' permission, she had summoned the entire National-American Board to a business meeting, and all were entertained under this hospitable roof. For thirty years Mrs. Southworth had been among the leading representatives of the suffrage movement in northern Ohio, and during all that time had been Miss Anthony's staunch and unfailing friend. She had given thousands of dollars to the suffrage cause, and hundreds to Miss Anthony for her personal use. On this occasion she presented her with $1,000 to open the much desired national headquarters. One such supporter in every State would win many battles which are lost because of insufficient funds to do the necessary work.

Miss Anthony soon afterwards went to New York to prepare with Mrs. Stanton the call and resolutions for the approaching national convention, and to revise the article on "Woman's

ANT.—51

Rights " for Johnson's new edition of the Encyclopedia. She was the guest of her cousin, Mrs. Semantha Vail Lapham, whose home overlooked Central Park. Mrs. Stanton's cosy flat was on the other side, and through this lovely pleasure ground each bright day Miss Anthony took her morning walk. When the weather was inclement she was sent in the carriage, and the two old friends talked and worked together as they had done so many times in days gone by.

The evenings were spent with her cousin and various friends and relatives. Once they dined with a kinsman in his elegant Tiffany apartments. She and Mrs. Stanton, Mrs. Josephine Shaw Lowell, Mrs. Henry M. Sanders and Mrs. George Putnam, had a delightful luncheon with Dr. Mary Putnam Jacobi. She was invited by Mr. and Mrs. Edward Lauterbach to hear the opera of Faust, which was followed by a supper at the Waldorf. With a relative she attended the "Authors' Uncut Leaves Club," at Sherry's. One Sunday she went to hear Robert Collyer and the diary says : " His grand face, his rich voice, his white hair, were all as attractive as ever ; he was a beautiful picture in the pulpit. He gave me a cordial greeting at the close of the sermon." She ran over to Orange for a few days with a loved cousin, Ellen Hoxie Squier ; and then on down to Philadelphia and Somerton for a little visit with the friends there, of which she writes: "Rachel and I had a soul-to-soul talk all the day long and until after midnight." She was a guest at the Foremothers' Dinner, December 22, given at Jaeger's by the New York City Woman Suffrage League, Lillie Devereux Blake, president, with nearly 300 prominent women at the table.[1] The dinner and the speeches lasted until after 5 o'clock, Miss Anthony responding to the toast, " Our Future Policy."

Thus a month slipped pleasantly by, and then, with the work all finished, the body rested and the mind refreshed, she returned home to spend Christmas. The two sisters dined with Dr. and Mrs. F. H. Sanford and a few old-time friends,

---

[1] At these annual feasts gentlemen are permitted to sit in the gallery, listen to the toasts and watch the ladies enjoy the dinner.

and passed a happy day. Among the numerous Christmas remembrances were several pieces of fine china and an elegant velvet cloak from Mrs. Gross.[1]

On December 30, Miss Anthony received word of the death of her old co-worker, Amelia Bloomer, at Council Bluffs, Ia., aged seventy-seven, and sent a telegram of sympathy to the husband. A death felt most keenly in 1894 was that of Virginia L. Minor, of St. Louis, August 14, which closed a beautiful and unbroken friendship of thirty years. She left Miss Anthony a testimonial of her love and confidence in a legacy of $1,000.

The year ended amidst the usual pressure of requests, invitations and engagements. Would she lecture for the Art League, for the Musical Society, for the Church Guild and for a dozen other organizations of whose purposes she knew practically nothing? Would she accept a "reception" from the Scribblers' Club of Buffalo? Would she send a package of documents to the girls of Vassar College, who were going to debate woman suffrage? Would she please reply to the following questions, from various newspapers: "Have not women as many rights now as men have? What is woman's ideal existence and what woman has most nearly attained it? Have you formed any resolutions for the coming year, and what has been the fate of former New Year's resolutions?" and so on, ad infinitum.

The "woman's edition" fever raged with great violence at this time, and it is not an exaggeration to say that the editors of ninety-nine hundredths of them wrote to Miss Anthony for an article. Of course it was an impossibility to comply, but occasionally some request struck her so forcibly that she made time for an answer. For instance, the woman's edition of the Elmira Daily Advertiser was for the purpose of helping the Young Men's Christian Association, and to its editor, Mrs. J. Sloat Fassett, she wrote:

---

[1] During this year Mrs. Gross had presented Miss Anthony with $1,000 to complete the education of a nephew and niece.

I should feel vastly more interested in, and earnest to aid the Y. M. C. A., if the men composing it were, as a body, helping to educate the people into the recognition of the right of their mothers and sisters to an equal voice with themselves in the government of the city, State and nation. Nevertheless, I avail myself of your kindly request, and urge all to study the intricate problem of bettering the world; not merely the individual sufferings in it, but the general conditions. Such study will show the great need of a new balance of power in the body politic; and the conscientious student must arrive at the conclusion that this will have to be obtained by enfranchising a new class—women. If the Y. M. C. A. really desire to make better moral and social conditions possible, they should hasten to obey the injunction of St. Paul, and "help those women" who are working to secure enfranchisement.

Miss Anthony received soon after this a consignment of pamphlets, etc., that she had ordered printed, on the outside of which the manager of the printing house, a man entirely unknown to her, had written:

"A wreath, twine a wreath for the brave and the true,
Who, for love of the many, dared stand with the few."

Among the pleasant letters was one from Mrs. Mary B. Willard, who was then abroad, in which she said: "I am so glad that you live on to know how much you are loved and to enjoy the fruit of your blessed labors." One invitation which Miss Anthony especially appreciated came from Rev. Jenkin Lloyd Jones, of Chicago, editor of Unity and pastor of All Souls church: "I am sure your heart goes out with us in our dreams as represented by the enclosed printed matter.[1] One number of the program is, 'What is woman's part in this larger synthesis,' or 'What can woman do for liberal religion?' I enclose Dr. Thomas' letter that it may reinforce my own pleading that you should come and speak on this topic. Phrase it yourself. Pour your whole heart into it. Make it the speech of your life. Give your large religious nature freedom. We will pay all your expenses and I do hope you will make an effort to come. We will give you from thirty to forty minutes, then we would want to ask one or two women to follow in the discussion, perhaps a Jewess and may be some

[1] A plan for a great Liberal Religious Congress, the outgrowth of the Parliament of Religions in 1893.

woman who represents the independent church, like Dr. Thomas' and Prof. Swing's. . . ."

Dr. H. W. Thomas' letter said in part : " Your suggestion is wise ; no other can perhaps so fittingly and ably represent the larger place and work of woman as Susan B. Anthony. It will honor her and help the cause to have her speak at the congress. Bless her dear soul, how I would like to see her— to hear her—to have her one with us—her counsel, her spirit, her great heart of love and hope so much like the Christ."

After the receipt of Miss Anthony's reply Dr. Jones wrote again : " I received your modest protest against being made, as you are, one of the vice-presidents of the Liberal Congress organization ; but the very reason you urged against it is the very reason for putting you on. We want you not for what you can do but for what you are. We can not take the congress into the polemics of the woman question, but George Washington went into the first Continental Congress with his uniform on, said nothing, yet that was his speech. So we organize with Susan B. Anthony's name among our vice-presidents, and this is our war speech on that question. Do let your name stay there. . . . Ever rejoicing in your work and its slowly approaching triumph, I am, brotherly yours."

The New Year of 1895 promised less in the way of work and anxiety than the one which had just closed. There were to be no State amendment campaigns with their annoying complexities, their arduous labors, their usual defeats. So many capable and energetic women had come into the national organization that Miss Anthony was relieved of much of the burden which used to rest upon her in the olden times, when she had to attend personally to details of arrangement and assume the financial responsibility. She found it difficult at first to adapt herself to the new regime, but soon learned to have confidence in the judgment and ability of her much-loved "body guard," as she liked to call the official board. It was not so easy for others of the old workers to accept the new order of things, and they rebelled occasionally against the " red tape " requirements of this executive body. To one of these Miss Anthony wrote : " My dear, what we older ones all have to learn is that these young and active women now doing the drudgery in each of the forty-five States, must be consulted and must have a vote on all questions pertaining to the association, and we must abide by the decision of the majority. This is what I am trying to learn. No one or two can manage now, but all must have a voice."

The voluminous correspondence shows, however, that the new workers were very glad to feel the touch of her firm and experienced hand on the helm, and that usually she was consulted on every point. She especially impressed upon them the necessity of keeping the financial accounts with the strictest care and accuracy, and for a number of years would not allow a report to be published until she herself had examined every detail. At one time when two contributions had been accidentally omitted from the statement sent for her inspection, she wrote : " Not finding those two in your copy congealed the blood to the very ends of my fingers and toes, lest the givers should think I had not sent their money to you."

New Year's Day twelve friends were gathered around the Anthony table, the Gannetts, the Greenleafs, the Sanfords, Mrs. Hallowell and Mrs. Willis, and the occasion was a pleasant one. A week later Miss Anthony started on an extended southern trip. There had been practically no suffrage work done in the South, with the exception of Kentucky, Tennessee, Missouri and Louisiana. As the national convention was to meet in Atlanta, Miss Anthony thought it advisable to make a lecture tour through the South to arouse a sentiment which might be felt there a month later. She invited Mrs. Chapman Catt to accompany her, guaranteeing her expenses although she had no assurance she would be able to make even her own.

At Lexington they were guests in the fine old home of Mrs. Mary J. Warfield Clay and daughter Laura, and spoke in the Christian church to a sympathetic audience. They held meetings at Wilmore, Louisville, Owensboro, Paducah and Milan, receiving many social courtesies at each place visited, and they reached Memphis January 17. The management here was in the capable hands of the Woman's Council and a fine audience greeted them at the Young Men's Hebrew Association Hall. They were introduced by their hostess, Mrs. Lide Meriwether, president of the Equal Suffrage Club, and cordially received. The Appeal, Avalanche and Scimitar gave long and interesting reports. The next morning Miss Anthony and Mrs. Catt were handsomely entertained by the ladies of the Nineteenth Century Club. In the afternoon Mrs. Mary Jameson Judah, president of the Woman's Club, gave a reception in their honor. Saturday morning they were guests of the Colored Women's Club; in the afternoon the Woman's Counsel, com-

For your lifelong work for Truth and Liberty I am Gratefully yours,

Laura Clay.

posed of forty-six local clubs, tendered a large reception, and in the evening they lectured again. Sunday morning they spoke in the Tabernacle to the colored people; and they left at 5 :30 P.M. feeling they had not wasted much time at Memphis.

They reached New Orleans Monday morning; were met at the train by the president and several members of the Portia Club, and escorted to the residence of Judge Merrick. Each of the daily papers contained lengthy and excellent mention of the lectures. The Picayune said at the beginning of a four-column report.

If any one doubted the interest that southern women feel in the all-absorbing question of the day, "Woman and her Rights," that idea would have forever been dispelled by a glance at the splendid audience assembled last night to hear Miss Susan B. Anthony, the world-famed apostle of woman suffrage, and Mrs. Carrie Chapman Catt, the distinguished western leader. The hall was literally packed to overflowing, not only with women but with men, prominent representatives in every walk of life. Standing room was at a premium, corridors and windows were filled with a sea of earnest, interested faces, the name of Miss Anthony was on every lip, and all eyes were directed to the platform, which was beautifully decorated with palms and potted plants, the suffrage color, yellow, predominating among the verdant foliage.

Seated upon the platform were the four ladies who have successively filled the position of president of the Portia Club, Mrs. Elizabeth Lyle Saxon, Mrs. Caroline E. Merrick, Mrs. Evelyn B. Ordway and Miss Florence Huberwald. The entrance of Miss Anthony and Mrs. Catt was the signal for a burst of applause, which rose into an ovation when Miss Huberwald, in a few graceful words, presented Mrs. Merrick, who in turn introduced Miss Anthony as the most famous woman in America. When the applause subsided, Miss Anthony, whose voice is singularly sweet and clear, began to speak.

She was presented with a basket of flowers and a bouquet from Mrs. J. M. Ferguson, president of the Arena club. At the close hundreds pressed forward to take the hands of the speakers.

They left this charming and hospitable city Wednesday evening, Mrs. Catt going to Greenville, Miss Anthony to Shreveport. Here she was entertained by Mrs. M. F. Smith and Professor C. E. Byrd, principal of the high school. The Hypatia Club sent her two lovely floral offerings. Of her lecture the Times said editorially:

This veteran apostle of woman's rights addressed a magnificent audience last evening at the court-house, a representative assemblage comprising all the best elements of all the best classes of Shreveport's citizens, and one which was equally divided between men and women. Miss Anthony is certainly a remarkable woman in every respect, and one whose genius will leave its mark not only on the recorded history of the nineteenth century, but in the advanced position of woman now and for all time to come. She was one of the first women in America to raise her voice in advocacy of woman's rights, and she has lived to see herself and her sisters gradually released from legalized bondage and, in everything but suffrage, made the full equal of man. No one can deny that her claims are founded on justice; and in the light of cold and clear reason, divested of all sentiment and cleansed of all prejudice, her arguments can not be successfully controverted.

By failure of the train to connect with the ferry she was unable to join Mrs. Catt and keep her appointment at Jackson. When, after waiting two hours, she finally reached that station at half-past nine, she found a message from Mrs. Catt that she was holding a magnificent audience for her. According to her journal she "was too oozed-out even to be looked at, much less to try to speak in the House of Representatives packed with the flower of southern chivalry;" so she went on to Birmingham. Here she found inadequate arrangements had been made and a northern blizzard interfered with her meetings. The News, however, gave an excellent two-column account beginning:

Only a moderate audience greeted Susan B. Anthony, the chief suffrage leader in the United States, but that audience was cultured and able to appreciate the very energetic, clear-minded and vigorous woman, whose name is as well-known as that of any man in the Union, and who has done more than any other woman to prove, by her strong and unique personality, the mental equality of woman with man and her fitness for the things sought to be entrusted to her care, share and share alike with the sterner sex. After a graceful introduction by Colonel J. W. Bush, the lecturer plunged at once with ease and distinction into her subject and line of argument. . . . She is a very able and incisive speaker, talks fluently and distinctly, and makes easy and graceful gestures. In a word, she is as good a lecturer as a good man-lecturer.

They spoke in the opera house at New Decatur, and were the guests of Mrs. E. S. Hildreth. At Huntsville they were entertained by Mrs. Milton Hume, and introduced to the audience by Mrs. Clay-Klopton. The Evening Tribune headed its report, "Grand and Enthusiastic Meeting; Eloquent Addresses Presented by Noble and Gifted Women;" and said:

Much to the surprise of a great many, the city hall was filled last night with a very large and intelligent audience of ladies and gentlemen. . . . Miss Anthony spoke for an hour in a plain, unassuming manner, but ably and learnedly. She has been an active worker for more than forty years in this cause and now, at life's closing hours, sees the right accorded woman in the States of Wyoming and Colorado, and the cause gaining momentum as intelligence spreads and the blessings become known which follow in the pathway of woman's ballot. No one can look upon the face of that venerated, noble woman, who has grown gray in her life-work, and not be impressed that there has been something more than sentiment, more than a cranky idea, impelling her in all these long, sacrificing years.

Mrs. Chapman Catt as completely charmed as she surprised the large audience. She is a young woman of winning personality, as beautiful as she is brilliant, with a command of language and convincing eloquence that would do credit to the matchless Prentiss. . . .

The next day, with Mrs. Alberta Chapman Taylor, they started for Atlanta, joining the Kentucky delegation at Knoxville and reaching their destination at noon. The headquarters were at the Aragon, where they found a large number of delegates, warm rooms and everything bright and comfortable, with the promise of a fine meeting.

The Twenty-seventh Annual Convention opened at De Give's opera house, January 31, continuing six days. Ninety-three delegates were present from twenty-eight states, numbers were in attendance from southern cities, and the people of Atlanta turned out en masse. An evidence of the interest taken in this convention is the fact that a number of the New York papers had daily reports of several thousand words telegraphed, and the large newspapers throughout the country had extended accounts. The Atlanta Constitution had had columns of matter pertaining to it, pictures and personal descriptions of the prominent women, which, added to its extended daily reports, contributed largely to the success of the meeting; but it was as careful to avoid editorial endorsement as its contemporaries in the North. The other city papers were generous with space and complimentary mention, but the Sunny South, edited by Colonel Henry Clay Fairman, was the only one which advocated the principle of woman suffrage.

Many beautiful homes were opened to the visitors, and all the officers and speakers were entertained at the Aragon at the expense of the newly formed Georgia State Association. The most of it was borne, in fact, by three sisters residing at Columbus, H. Augusta Howard, Miriam Howard Du Bose and Claudia Howard Maxwell. With the genuine southern hospitality, they declined the offer of several societies and of the association to reimburse them. A handsome reception at the hotel was attended by hundreds of Atlanta's representative citizens. Mrs. W. A. Hemphill, one of the board of the Atlanta Exposition, received the visitors in her lovely home, assisted by the wife of the recently-elected Governor Atkinson.

A Baptist preacher, Rev. J. B. Hawthorne, built on the antiquated plan, delivered a sermon not only denouncing suffrage but abusing its advocates. The result was to make the other ministers in the city offer their pulpits to the convention speakers, and on Sunday lectures were given in various churches by Emily Howland, Elizabeth Upham Yates, Mrs. Colby and Mrs. Meriwether. Rev. Anna Shaw preached in the opera house and the Constitution prefaced its report as follows: "When the opening hour arrived there was not an empty chair in the house. So dense became the crowd that the doors were ordered closed before the services began. The vast congregation was made up of all classes of citizens. Every chair that could be found had been utilized and then boxes and benches were pressed into service. Many prominent professional and business men were standing on the stage and in different parts of the house."

Miss Anthony, besides her president's address, made many brief speeches and also read Mrs. Stanton's fine paper on "Educated Suffrage," which was especially acceptable to a southern audience.[1] One of the most eloquent speakers was General Robert R. Hemphill, member of the South Carolina legislature. Among the able and interesting southern delegates Laura Clay and Josephine K. Henry, of Kentucky, and A. Viola Neblett and Helen Lewis Morris, of North Carolina, were especial favorites. After the convention a mass meeting was held in the courthouse, which was crowded with an enthusiastic audience. Mrs. M. L. McLendon, president of the Atlanta Club, requested Miss Anthony to take charge. The Constitution said:

Miss Anthony was received with such a warmth of demonstration on the part of the large audience as to thoroughly convince her that she was addressing those who were in sympathy with the suffrage movement. As she stood up in the presence of the vast congregation of faces a profound silence filled the hall and every one seemed to be intently waiting for her opening words.

[1] After 1892 Miss Anthony had to read most of Mrs. Stanton's addresses, and the latter wrote her: "If you pronounce what I write 'good,' I know it is up to the mark. Many thanks for reading all my papers so well as everybody says you do. I am sure of your rich voice and deep sympathy with the subject, and I much prefer to have you read my speeches rather than any other person, as I am always told that your reading makes a deep impression. Our thoughts have the same trend on the woman suffrage question, and we have written and talked over every phase of the subject so much together that what I write is essentially yours as well as mine."

Within the railing a large number of men, who preferred to stand near the speaker rather than secure seats in the rear of the hall, were grouped in a solid mass, and appeared to be equally as much concerned as the ladies.

There were many distinguished women present at the convention, from the South and the North, and all separated with the feeling that fraternal bonds had been strengthened and many converts made to the belief in equal suffrage.

Miss Anthony was much revered by the colored race and while here she addressed the students of the Atlanta University, and spoke with Bishop Turner to an immense audience at Bethel church. She was invited also to address the alumnæ of the girls' high school. At the close of the convention she went, with her sister Mary, niece Lucy, Anna Shaw and Mrs. Upton, for a three days' visit at the spacious old-time mansion of the Howards, in Columbus. She left for Aiken, S. C., February 9, where she spoke in the courthouse and was introduced by the Baptist minister. Here she was the guest of Miss Martha Schofield, and was much interested in the very successful industrial school for colored children, founded by her during the war. On February 12, she lectured at Columbia for the Practical Progress Club, introduced by Colonel V. P. Clayton. The Pine Tree State contained an excellent editorial in favor of woman suffrage, but thought "it could be more successfully advocated in that locality by some one of less pronounced abolitionism." Her hostess, Mrs. Helen Brayton, gave a reception for her, and she met a large number of the representative people of Columbia. Her last lecture was given at Culpepper, Va. The six weeks' southern trip had been very pleasant; she had made many friends and found much sentiment in favor of suffrage. The only drawback had been the severity of the weather, the coldest ever known in that locality, which will long be remembered because of the destruction of the orange groves.

Miss Anthony reached Washington on the morning of her seventy-fifth birthday, February 15. The National Woman's Council was to open its second triennial meeting on the 18th, and its official board and many delegates were already in the city. When she arrived she found that "her girls," as she was fond of designating the younger workers, had arranged for a banquet in her honor at the Ebbitt House that evening. Covers were laid for fifty and it was a beautiful affair. After a number of speeches had been made, Rachel Foster Avery arose and stated that the friends of Miss Anthony from ocean to ocean and the lakes to the gulf, had placed in her hands sums of money amounting to $5,000. This she had put into a trust fund, purchasing therewith an "annuity" of $800, which she now took great pleasure in presenting. There were 202 contributors and although Mrs. Avery had been for several months collecting the money, incredible as it may seem, the whole matter was a complete surprise to Miss Anthony. Realizing that during the last forty-five years she had spent practically all she had earned and all that had been given her, to advance the cause to which she had devoted her life, they determined to put this testimonial into such shape as would make it impossible thus to expend it. She was greatly overcome and for once could not command the words to voice her feelings.

As each three months have rolled around since that occasion, and the $200 check has been sent with a pleasant greeting from the Penn Mutual insurance company, hoping that she might live to use the entire principal, her heart has thrilled anew with gratitude and affection to Mrs. Avery and the friends who put their love and appreciation into this material shape. It suffices to pay the monthly expenses of the modest household and, with the income from the few thousands that have been laid away, an occasional paid lecture and the gifts from generous friends, Miss Anthony is freed from financial anxiety, although obliged to exercise careful economy.

It is impossible in this limited space to attempt a description of that great council extending through the days and evenings of two weeks, attended by delegates from twenty national organizations, representing the highest intellects and activities among women and covering a wide range of vital questions. Miss Anthony stood for the department of Government Reform.   Although at this council she desired to be simply one of the many representatives of different organizations, the public would make her the central figure of all occasions.   On February 28, Mrs. John R. McLean, assisted by Mrs. Calvin Brice, gave a reception in her honor, attended by many of the official, literary, artistic and musical people of the capital.

Frederick Douglass came into the council the afternoon of the 20th and was invited by the president, Mrs. Sewall, to a seat on the platform. He accepted, but declined to speak, acknowledging the applause only by a bow.   Upon entering his home in Anacostia, a few hours later, he dropped to the floor and expired instantly.   Funeral services were held in the African Metropolitan church, Washington, February 25, in which, at the request of the family, Miss Anthony took part, paid a brief tribute and read Mrs. Stanton's touching memorial of the only man who sustained her demand for the enfranchisement of women in that famous first convention of 1848.

At the close of the council Miss Anthony lectured at Lincoln, Va., in the ancient Quaker meeting house.   Returning to Washington she was entertained by Mrs. Mary S. Lockwood at a dinner party on the evening of the Travel Club, at which she was one of the speakers.   Reaching Philadelphia March 9, she turned her steps, as was always her custom, directly towards her old friend Adeline Thomson, and her surprise and grief may be imagined when she found that she had died a month previous.   Her relations with Adeline and Annie Thomson, who had passed away nearly ten years before, had been those of affectionate sisters, and for nearly forty years their home had been as her own.   She had received many contributions from them, and Adeline had made her a personal gift of $1,000. She often had said to her and written in her letters, that she had $5,000 more laid away for her after she herself should have no further use for it, but as is so often the case she neglected to make provision for this, and all her property went to a nephew.

From Mrs. Avery's suburban home at Somerton, Miss Anthony sent grateful letters to every one of the 202 contributors

Always lovingly yours
Rachel Foster Avery

to her annuity. She addressed the 500 students at Drexel Institute, and left for New York March 12. Here she had an important business meeting with Mary Lowe Dickinson, the newly elected president of the National Council, and then went to tell all about the Atlanta convention, the Woman's Council and various other events to Mrs. Stanton, who still felt the liveliest interest although not physically able to take an active part.

The day after Miss Anthony reached home she read in the morning paper that two of the State Industrial School girls and two of the free academy boys had been seen the night before coming out of a questionable place; the girls were arrested and locked up in the station house, the boys were told to go home. It was an everyday injustice but she determined to protest, so she went straightway to the police court, where she insisted that the boys should not go free while the girls were punished. She pleaded in vain; the girls were sent to the reformatory, the boys being used as witnesses against them and then dismissed without so much as a reprimand.

A short time afterwards Miss Anthony went to the Baptist church one Sunday evening to hear a young colored woman, Miss Ida Wells, lecture on the lynching of negroes in the South. The speaker was rudely interrupted several times by a fellow from Texas who was in Rochester attending the theological school. She answered him politely but at length he asked: "If the negroes don't like it in the South, why don't they leave and go North?" At this Miss Anthony, who had been growing more indignant every moment, sprung to her feet and, with flashing eyes and ringing voice, said: "I will tell you why; it is because they are treated no better in the North than they are in the South." She then related a number of instances, which had come to her own knowledge, of the cruel discrimination made against colored people, to the utter amazement of the audience who did not believe such things possible.[1]

She took Miss Wells home with her for the rest of her stay.

[1] The Rochester dailies came out next morning with full reports of this episode and editorial remarks; citizens of both sexes wrote to the papers, pro and con; other newspapers took up the question, and a wave of comment swept over the country.

She had employed a young woman stenographer for a few weeks to clear up her accumulated correspondence and, having to go away the next day, she told Miss Wells the girl might help her with her pile of letters. When she returned in the evening she found her scribbling away industriously and the stenographer at leisure. In answer to her inquiry the latter replied: "I don't choose to write for a colored person." "If you can not oblige me by assisting a guest in my house," said Miss Anthony, "you can not remain in my employ." The girl, although in destitute circumstances, gave up her situation.

Miss Anthony had been feeling for a long time that, in justice to herself and to the State Industrial School, she should resign her position on the board of managers. When she accepted it she had intended to give up the greater part of her travelling and direct her forces from the seat of government in her own home, but she had found this practically impossible. The demands for her actual presence and personal work were too strong to be resisted. There were very few women in the country who could draw so large an audience as herself, or who knew so well how to manage a convention or carry on a campaign, and the women of the different States, who had one or the other of these in hand, were unwilling to accept a substitute. She was as well and vigorous as at fifty, and there seemed to be no adequate reason why she should refuse the many opportunities to advance the cause for which she had given the active service of nearly half a century. The several years since she began housekeeping, therefore, had found her at home no more of the time than those which had preceded.

When she first visited the school she found the boys' departments fitted up with all the appliances of a steam laundry, while a large number of the girls were bending their backs over washtubs and ironing-boards the whole of every week. She soon succeeded in having the washing sent over to the laundry, where a few girls were able to do it all in two or three days; she also made many valuable suggestions in the sewing department.   When in the city she went to the school on Sunday, helped with the services and talked to the 700 boys and 150 girls. Some of the latter came to her one Sunday and said pathetically that it was the first time a speaker ever had seemed to know there were any girls there! She wrote in her journal, with quiet humor, that the men on the board were going the next day to select a cooking stove. She realized even more strongly than ever that, though the best and wisest men may be on the boards of public institutions, there is need also of women, but she felt that, with so vast an amount of other work on hand, she could not do her duty by the school. As she was about to go away again for a number of months she decided to delay her resignation no longer and forwarded it to Governor Morton April 15, after having served about two and a half years. She then finished her lecture engagements and completed arrangements for what proved to be one of the pleasantest journeys of her life.

ANT.—52

CHAPTER XLV.

1895.

IT has been said in another chapter that Miss Anthony established herself firmly and forever in the hearts of the people at the Columbian Exposition of 1893. Men and women were there from every State in the Union, many of whom never had seen or heard her and had been deeply prejudiced against her, but she conquered all and they returned home henceforth to sing her praises. Naturally they wanted their friends and neighbors to be converted like themselves, and invitations to lecture came from all quarters. One of the most urgent was from the Woman's Congress Auxiliary of the great California Midwinter Exposition, which followed the World's Fair, but as she had two campaigns on hand in 1894 she could not accept it. Out of this auxiliary had grown a permanent Woman's Congress Association, with Sarah B. Cooper at its head. When a pressing request came to attend their first anniversary in San Francisco, in 1895, she accepted with pleasure. The corresponding secretary, Mrs. Minna V. Gaden, wrote in reply:

I can not attempt to express to you the joy and gratification of the executive board over your consent to be with us and take part in the congress in May. I wish I could have phonographed the exclamations of delight and photographed the beaming countenances of the members when I read them your letter. In answer to your question as to whether we desired to have you speak upon some special point of the subject for which you stand, I would say we want Susan B. Anthony and all that she is; and we are sure that the right word will be said, the great facts made plain and the true inspiration given. We want *you* and all that your presence means and all that your life's work has brought.

Miss Anthony had another reason for wishing to go to California in addition to the desire of meeting and helping the women of that beautiful State in their congress. Its legislature, the previous winter, had submitted a woman suffrage amendment which was to be voted on in 1896. This visit would enable her to look over the field, talk with the men and women, and render any assistance they might desire towards planning their campaign. She wrote Mrs. Cooper stating that she did not wish to make the journey alone, that she liked to have one of her "lieutenants" to relieve her of the burden of much speaking, and would be glad of the privilege of bringing with her Rev. Anna Shaw. Mrs. Cooper responded with a check of $450, for travelling expenses, saying: "We rejoice to know that Miss Shaw will come with you, as another grand helper for us. I send you the money and want you to have every possible comfort on the journey."

From that time until Miss Anthony reached California not over three days ever passed without a letter from Mrs. Cooper, rejoicing over the promised visit. "Everybody is full of expectancy looking for your advent. I have engaged the First Congregational church of San Francisco for Miss Shaw's sermon. Hattie and I send you a heart full of love. May God hold you safe in His keeping." "San Francisco and the whole Pacific coast have a warm welcome for you both; every one is looking forward to meeting you, great and noble champion of all that is good." So the letters ran, and they were supplemented by long and loving ones from the daughter Harriet, who lived but to second her mother's work and wishes.

When the papers heralded abroad the news that Miss Anthony was going to California, the large western towns along the route sent earnest requests for lectures and visits, and the journey assumed the aspect of a triumphal tour. She started April 27, full of health and spirit and with happy anticipations; spent one day with Mrs. Upton, at Warren, O., one with Mrs. Sewall, at Indianapolis, going thence to Chicago, where she was entertained by Mr. and Mrs. Gross. Here she found Harriet Hosmer, who had been with them seven months, while she worked on her statue of Lincoln. In the evening half a dozen reporters called and the papers bristled with interviews. The next day she went with her hostess to the famous Woman's Club. Miss Shaw joined Miss Anthony in Chicago, and May 1 they left for St. Louis, where they remained four days at the New Planters' Hotel, the guests of Mrs. Gross, who had accompanied them.

Their mission at St. Louis was to address the Mississippi Valley Woman's Congress, under the auspices of the W. C. T. U., Mrs. E. B. Ingalls, presiding. Miss Anthony spoke on "The Present Outlook," and the papers described enthusiastically "the splendid ovation" she received, the many floral offerings, and the hundreds of personal greetings at the close of the evening. Just before her address, seventy-five little boys and girls, several colored ones among them, marched past her on the platform, each laying a rose in her lap. The day after the congress the State Suffrage Association held its convention, and on the evening of May 4 a handsome banquet, with covers laid for 200, was given for her at the Mercantile Club rooms.

She reached Denver May 8, at 4 A. M., remained in the sleeper till six and then could stand it no longer but took a carriage and sallied forth. When the reception committee came to the station at seven to escort her to the elaborate breakfast which had been prepared at the Brown Palace Hotel, where a large number of friends were waiting, the guest had flown and could not be found. While in the city she was entertained at the home of Hon. Thomas M. Patterson, of the Rocky Mountain News, whose progressive and cultured wife was her warm personal friend and had been an advocate of suffrage long before it was granted to the women of Colorado. Reverend Anna was the guest of ex-Governor and Mrs. Routt. That afternoon Miss Anthony went to Boulder, where she was engaged to lecture.

The next day the Woman's Club gave a large reception in their honor at the Brown Palace Hotel, attended by over 1,200 women. The News, in its account, said : "The scene marked, to the retrospective mind, the enormous change that has taken place in the status of the sex within the lifetime of one woman. It hardly seemed possible, as the spectator beheld Miss Anthony surrounded by the richest and most conservative women of Denver, to believe that in her youth the great lecturer was hissed from the stage in the most cultured and liberal cities of the United States, and cast out from polite society like a pariah. It is not often either that one who has been a pioneer in an unpopular cause lives to see it become fashionable and herself the center of attention from a younger generation which has profited by her labors of earlier years." The same paper commented editorially : "To accomplish the political enfranchisement of her sex and open a broader field of work and influence for women everywhere, Miss Anthony has devoted her life. . . . Among all the noble women who have stood boldly to champion the cause of their sisters, she is easily chief, and is worthy of all the honors that have been bestowed upon her. It must have been a proud satisfaction for her yesterday to meet the women of Colorado, who are now endowed with equal political rights because of the crusade she has been instrumental in starting and maintaining. Well may these newly enfranchised women do her reverence. Not more loyal should the silver men of Colorado be to Dick Bland, than the women of Colorado to the apostle of equal suffrage—Susan B. Anthony."

The Denver Times said in a leading editorial : "To Miss Anthony the women of today owe a great debt, for through her life's work they enjoy a hundred privileges denied them fifty years ago. From her devotion to a cause which for decades made her a martyr to the derision of an unsympathetic public, has grown a new order of things. Her hand has most helped to open every profession and every line of business to women. While all the women of the United States are under many obligations to her, those of Colorado, who are now equal citizens, owe her the greatest allegiance.'' The Times also quotes in an interview with Miss Anthony : ''When asked what subject she would take for her speeches to the people of Colorado, she shook her head with a kindly smile and said : 'My usual lectures will not do. What can I say to the women who have the franchise ? I can only encourage them to use their new power wisely, to stand bravely for the right, and to help the equal suffrage cause in other States.'''

The ladies lectured that evening to an immense audience in the Broadway Theater. The papers reported with great headlines : ''Enthusiastic Greeting by Colorado's Enfranchised Citizens. Miss Anthony Overcome with Hearty Congratulations. America's Joan of Arc Shakes Hands with an Army of Women Voters.'' One searches in vain in these newspapers for evidences of the terrible loss of respect which women were to experience when they were endowed with the ballot. The News, in over a column report, said :

Miss Anthony's voice was clear and powerful, filling the big theater without any apparent effort. She began by saying that she believed the thing she had always claimed had come true; that the women had learned a new and higher self-respect with their added rights and responsibilities. . . . She paid the men of Colorado the compliment of declaring them the best in the world. The men of Wyoming had occupied this proud position up to 1893, but those of Colorado had granted the ballot to a disfranchised class not through the legislature, but by a popular vote. This act stands alone in the history of the world; no class of men has ever done as much for even another class of men. . . .

She said she had heard that some of the women had voted with sagacity and some had not. This was not strange, since men continued to do this after more than one hundred years of voting. If women made mistakes this year, they would remedy them next year, and in time she believed they would become the balance of power between the two parties in all social, moral and educational questions.

At Cheyenne Senator and Mrs. Carey gave an elegant dinner party in their honor, attended by Governor and Mrs. Rich, Senator and Mrs. Warren, Mrs. Esther Morris, the first woman judge, Mrs. Therese Jenkins, State president, Mrs. Amalia Post, a suffrage pioneer, and other distinguished guests. They went immediately from dinner to the new Baptist church, which was filled to overflowing, and were introduced by the governor. At the close of the lectures, Mrs. Jenkins said, "Now I desire to introduce the audience to the speakers." She then called the names of the governor and all his staff, the attorney-general, the United States judges, the senators and congressmen, the mayor and members of the city council. Each rose as his name was mentioned, and before she was through, it seemed as if half the audience were on their feet, and the applause was most enthusiastic. Here again one could not discern an indication of the dreadful loss of respect which was to be the portion of enfranchised women.

It was long after midnight before the travellers were quietly in bed in the delightful home of the Careys, but at half-past seven they had finished breakfast and were on board train en route for Salt Lake City. Learning from the conductor that Mrs. Leland Stanford's private car was attached, Miss Anthony sent her card and soon was invited to a seat in that luxurious conveyance, where she enjoyed a visit of several hours. Mrs. Stanford told her of the government suit against the estate, and Miss Anthony's parting words were a warning not to leave her lawyers to go before the Supreme Court alone, but to be present herself in Washington to protect her own interests and those of the great university.

At Salt Lake, on Sunday morning, a large delegation of women, representing the different religious sects and political organizations, met the travellers and drove to the Templeton, where seventy-five sat down to breakfast, and they were then taken for a drive over the city. Miss Anthony was the guest of Mrs. Beatie, daughter of Brigham and Zina D. H. Young, and Miss Shaw of Mrs. McVicker. At 3 P. M., the Reverend Anna preached in the great Tabernacle, Bishops Whitney and Richards assisting. At the close they congratulated her on having preached a Mormon sermon; afterwards a Methodist minister who was in the audience thanked her for her good Methodist sermon; and a little later a Presbyterian minister shook her hand heartily and expressed his pleasure at hearing her Presbyterian doctrine; so she concluded she had made a politic address. Sunday evening she preached in the theater at what was intended to be a union service. All of the Gentile ministers had been invited to take part and all declined but the pastor of the Unitarian church. He and the principal of the public schools, formerly a Unitarian minister, were the only men on the stage.

The Inter-Mountain Woman Suffrage Association of Utah, Montana and Idaho opened the next morning, May 13. The first day's sessions were held in the new city building, but it was so crowded that an overflow meeting was necessary and the next day the convention was transferred to the big assembly hall. The seat of honor was given to Miss Anthony ; on her right Mrs. Emmeline B. Wells, president of the Utah association, on her left, Rev. Anna Shaw. They were surrounded by a semicircle of the illustrious women of the Territory who, for many years, had been active in the work for suffrage. The hall was draped with the national colors and above the stage were portraits of Lincoln, Miss Anthony and Mrs. Stanton. The introductory address war made by Governor West, who, after paying an earnest tribute to Miss Anthony, predicted that the new State constitution, which was to go to the voters containing a woman suffrage clause, would be overwhelmingly ratified.

During their stay in Salt Lake Miss Anthony and Miss Shaw received the highest consideration. Monday afternoon Mr. and Mrs. F. S. Richards gave a reception in their honor, and were assisted in receiving by Governor West, President Woodruff, Hon. George Q. Cannon, and many ladies. The next afternoon a reception was tendered by the W. C. T. U. In the evening, a large party went to Ogden, where a banquet was given, a great meeting held in the city hall, and an overflow meeting in one of the churches.

The 16th of May found the travellers at Reno, Nev., where they were the guests of Mrs. Elda A. Orr, president of the State association. In the morning Miss Anthony talked to the 800 men and women students of the State University. In the evening they spoke in the opera house, which was crowded to its limits, while on the stage were the representative men and women of the city and neighboring towns. The house was beautifully decorated with flowers and banners, a brass band played on the balcony and an orchestra within. They were introduced by Miss Hannah H. Clapp, who had presented Miss Anthony to a Nevada audience at Carson, in 1871. Saturday afternoon they enjoyed a charming reception in the parlors of the women's clubhouse.

Late that day they resumed their journey, took supper at Truckee on the summit of the Sierras, and had a delicious glimpse of Lake Donner just as they plunged into the forty miles of snow-sheds. They were glad of a long night's rest after the strain of the last three weeks and, when they awoke the next morning, were rolling through the fertile Sacramento valley. California in May! Never was there a pen inspired with the power to describe its beauties. Not the brush of the most gifted artist could picture the mountains with their green foot-hills and snow-capped summits; the valleys, nature's own lovely and fragrant conservatories of brilliant blossoms and luxuriant, riotous vines, and the great oaks with their glossy foliage, all enveloped in a warm and shimmering atmosphere and, bending above, the soft blue sky scarcely dimmed by a fleeting cloud. They can not be put into words, they must be lived.

The travellers had been up and dressed and enjoying the sweet air and lovely landscape for a long time when the train stopped at the Oakland station at half-past seven Sunday morning, May 19. Early as was the hour, with the mists still hovering over the bay, they found awaiting them, laden with flowers, Mrs. Cooper and her daughter Harriet, from San Francisco, Mrs. Isabel A. Baldwin, Mrs. Ada Van Pelt and several other Oakland ladies, and Rev. John K. McLean, the Congregational minister, whose eldest brother was the husband of Miss Anthony's sister. He conveyed her at once to his own home, while the others took charge of Miss Shaw. At 11 o'clock the reverend lady was in Dr. McLean's pulpit, fresh and smiling, in her soft, black ministerial robes, with dainty white lawn at neck and wrists. Every seat was filled, chairs were placed in the aisles, people sitting on the steps, and the happiest woman in all the throng was Susan B. Anthony as she sat beside her friend. That evening the scene was repeated in the Congregational church of San Francisco, where the chancel was adorned with lilies and the revered Sarah B. Cooper made the opening prayer.

The Woman's Congress opened at Golden Gate Hall, on the morning of May 20. The newspapers of San Francisco had decreed that this congress should be a success, and to this end they had been as generous with space and as complimentary in tone as the most exacting could have desired. The result was that at not a session during the week was the great hall large enough to hold the audience which sought admission. It presented a beautiful sight on the opening morning, festooned from end to end with banners ; the stage a veritable conservatory, with a background of palms, bamboo and other tropical plants, and in front a bewildering array of lilies, roses, carnations, sweet peas and other fragrant blossoms. Grouped upon the platform, on chairs and divans, under tall, shaded lamps, were the speakers and guests. At the right of the president's desk was a large arm-chair artistically draped with flowers beneath a canopy of La France roses. At half-past ten Mrs. Cooper stepped out from the wings escorting Miss Anthony, followed by Mayor Adolph Sutro and Rev. Anna Shaw. The audience burst into a storm of applause and, amid cheers and the waving of handkerchiefs, Miss Anthony was conducted to her floral throne. As soon as she was seated, one woman after another came up with arms full of flowers until she was literally buried under an avalanche of the choicest blossoms. No one who was present ever will forget the lovely scene.

Mayor Sutro made the address of welcome, in which he emphasized his belief that "the ballot should be placed in the hands of woman as the most powerful agent for the uplifting of humanity." At the preceding congress the general topic had been, " The Relation of Women to the Affairs of the World," and the criticism had been made that it was too much of a woman suffrage meeting.   For this one the subject selected was "The Home," but the results were the same.   Whatever the paper—"Hereditary Influence, " "The Parents' Power," "The Family and the State "—all led to suffrage ; and the more suffrage, the greater the applause from the audience. Mrs. Cooper had written Miss Anthony, "I told the committee to put you and Miss Shaw anywhere on the program, that you could speak on one subject as well as another ; " so they found themselves down for "Educational Influences of Home Life ; " "Which Counts More, Father's or Mother's Influence ? " "Does Wifehood Preclude Citizenship ? " "The Evolution of the Home ; " "The Family and the State ; " "Shall We Co-operate ? " "The Rights of Motherhood ; " and numerous other topics. Both spoke every day during the Congress and the people seemed never to tire of hearing them.

Mrs. Cooper presided in her dignified and beautiful manner, and in her presentation said :   "I have the very great honor and pleasure of introducing to this assembly one who has done more towards lifting up women than any other one person— Miss Susan B. Anthony."   The Chronicle reported :   "Then the audience made still further demonstrations.   They clapped and cheered and waved, and some of the gray-haired women wiped their eyes because it is so seldom that people live to be appreciated.   But Susan B. stood like a princess of the blood royal.   Very erect of head and clear of voice she began her little speech.   It was full of reminiscences, but some few people have the privilege of telling recollections without the fear of ever boring any one.   Miss Anthony is one of these. . . ."

Miss Shaw also received a hearty welcome ; and all through that wonderful week the bright, appreciative, warmhearted California audiences crowded the hall and listened and applauded and brought their offerings of flowers and fruit to lay at the feet of these two women, who had come from the far East to clasp their hands and unite with them in one great cause—the uplifting of womanhood.   The Chronicle said :

Twelve hundred women went to Golden Gate Hall on Monday ; fourteen hundred went Tuesday ; two thousand Wednesday ; twenty-five hundred

Always Affectionately Yours

Sarah B. Cooper

Thursday.   Golden Gate Hall could not hold one-fourth of the crowds, so all three of yesterday's sessions were held at the First Congregational church. Even there a stream of humanity blocked every aisle clear to the platform. Nobody ever supposed that the women of San Francisco cared for aught except their gowns, their teas and their babies. But they do. They like brains, even in their own sex. And they can applaud good speeches even if made by women, and they have all fallen madly, desperately in love with a very short, very plump little woman whose name is Anna Shaw. A year ago there were not more than a hundred women in San Francisco who could have been dragged to a suffrage meeting, but yesterday twenty-five times that number struggled and tore their clothing in their determination to hear Miss Anthony and Miss Shaw.

Again it commented :   " There has been some talk that the Woman's Congress which expired last night attracted its crowds under false pretenses—that it promised to talk about the home and then preached suffrage.   That is usually the case when Miss Anthony is about, but it was always suffrage in its relation to the home.   Who, knowing Miss Anthony's reputation, could suppose that she would cross the continent in the evening of her life to discuss the draping of a lace curtain or the best colors for a parlor carpet ? . . .   Five thousand people waiting on the steps of the Temple Emanu-El for the purpose of hearing the woman preacher's last address does not look as if her position were uncertain.   Mere curiosity does not take the same people to nineteen consecutive sessions."

"Apotheosis of Woman," the Examiner headed its fine reports ; and the Call, the Bulletin, the Post, the Report, and the newspapers around the bay all gave columns of space to this great meeting which had discovered to the State of California its own remarkable women.

Miss Anthony had been the guest of her old friend, Mrs. A. A. Sargent, whose hospitality she had enjoyed so many years in Washington City.   As the suffrage amendment was to come up the next year, Miss Anthony and Miss Shaw met with a large number of ladies at the Congregational church and helped them organize a campaign committee, with Mrs. Cooper as its chairman.   In accepting the office she said :   " I intend to put all there is of me into current coin and use it to forward this Heaven-ordained work.   If ever a woman was thoroughly converted to this idea I have been, and in this spirit I accept the charge.''

In the afternoon of this same day Mrs. Cooper escorted them to the Y. M. C. A. Hall to address the Congregational ministers at their regular Monday meeting, to which they had been officially invited. That evening they were the guests of honor at the Unitarian Club dinner at the Palace Hotel, Miss Anthony responding to the toast, ''The Rights and Privileges of Man ; '' Miss Shaw to '' The Manly Man ; '' Rev. A. C. Hirst and Dr. Horatio Stebbins to '' The Rights and Privileges of Woman '' and ''The Womanly Woman ; '' and the evening was a lively one. They addressed the girls' high school, and accepted also an invitation to speak to the 900 teachers at the institute in session at Golden Gate Hall. They were the guests of the Century Club, Sorosis and other San Francisco societies of women.

A friend, Mrs. Mary Grafton Campbell, wrote from Palo Alto that she heard President Jordan say every remaining day and evening of the semester were filled, and when she exclaimed, '' But Miss Anthony is coming ; what about her ? '' he replied, ''There will be room for Miss Anthony if we have to give up classes.'' Immediately he wrote her a cordial invitation to visit the university, offering to pay her travelling expenses and expressing a wish to entertain her in his home. She accepted for herself and Miss Shaw, and they spoke to as many students as could crowd into the chapel. Mrs. Stanford sent a personal invitation for them to attend the reception which she was to give the first graduating class in her San Francisco residence.[1]

Yours, with friendly greetings

Jane L. Stanford

---

[1] As soon as they arrived in California they were presented by Mrs. Stanford with railroad passes throughout the State.

They were invited to the beautiful Water Carnival at Santa Cruz, and to the Flower Festival at Santa Barbara. It would be impossible, indeed, to mention all the delightful invitations of both a public and private nature, and there was not a day that did not bring a remembrance in the shape of flowers and the delicious fruit in which Miss Anthony revelled.

On May 29 the Ebell Club of Oakland gave them a breakfast at 11:30; at 2 P. M. they addressed the Alameda County Auxiliary of the Woman's Congress, Rev. Eliza Tupper Wilkes, president. The audience filled every inch of space in the Unitarian church, the most prominent ladies of Oakland occupied seats on the platform, and a large reception in the parlors followed the speaking. The evening session was held in the Congregational church, an enthusiastic crowd in attendance. The next afternoon they started for the Yosemite Valley, having for companions Dr. Elizabeth Sargent and Dr. Henry A. Baker, Miss Anthony's grand-nephew. There Miss Anthony, at the age of seventy-five, made the usual trips on the back of a mule. She relates that the name of her steed was Moses and Anna Shaw's Ephraim, and they had great sport over them. They enjoyed to the full all the beauties of that wonderful region, which never pall, no matter how often one visits them or how long one remains among them. During this trip Miss Shaw went with one of the Yosemite commissioners, George B. Sperry, to the Mariposa Big Trees. Two, in a group of the largest three, were christened George Washington and Abraham Lincoln, and he offered her the privilege of naming the third. She gave it the title of Susan B. Anthony, it was appropriately marked, and thus it will be known to future generations.

At San Jose they were the guests of Mrs. Sarah Knox Goodrich, who gave a dinner for them, and over a hundred called during the evening. Sunday afternoon Miss Anthony spoke in the Unitarian church, and Monday morning addressed the students of the Normal School. At noon Mrs. Elizabeth Lowe Watson gave a luncheon party under the great trees at her lovely home, Sunny Brae, where the ladies spoke in the afternoon to several hundred people from neighboring ranches.

In the evening they lectured at San Jose and, although fifty cents admission was charged, not nearly all who had bought tickets could get into the building. When they left for Los Angeles Mrs. Goodrich slipped into the hand of each $50 in gold, as a present; just as Mrs. Sargent had done when they left San Francisco.

Long before Miss Anthony had started for California, cordial invitations had been received from the southern part of the State, from old friends and new. It was of course impossible to accept more than a small fraction of these, but from the time the twain reached Los Angeles, there was one continuous ovation. On the evening of their arrival, June 12, they addressed an audience of over 2,000 in Simpson tabernacle, which had been transformed into a bower of choicest blossoms. While in the city they were the guests of Mrs. Caroline M. Severance, with whom Miss Anthony had worked for suffrage in Ohio forty years before.

In Riverside a reception was given them at the Glenwood by Mr. and Mrs. F. M. Richardson, relatives of Miss Anthony. The beautiful drives for which that place is famous were greatly enjoyed, and they went into raptures over the oranges, which they never before had seen in such quantities. They spoke to a large audience in the handsomely decorated Methodist tabernacle at Pasadena. While here they were the guests of Mrs. P. C. Baker, on Orange Avenue, and received many social attentions from the people of this lovely little city. Thence they went to Pomona, where they were met at the station by a delegation of ladies, escorted to the Palomares Hotel, and found the committee had adorned their rooms with flowers in a profusion which would be impossible outside of California. They spoke here also in the Methodist church. The next day Miss Shaw preached in Los Angeles and Miss Anthony spent the Sunday at Whittier with Mrs. Harriet R. Strong at her ranche, so widely noted for its walnut groves and pampas fields.

Monday morning they journeyed to San Diego where they were the guests of Miss Anthony's niece, Mrs. George L. Baker. Elaborate preparations had been made to receive them and they addressed a large audience in the evening. The next afternoon a reception was given at the Hotel Florence by all the woman's clubs of the city. The Union said : " The two guests of honor were simply loaded and garlanded with flowers. They were presented with baskets of sweet peas by the Y. W. C. A., yellow blossoms by the suffrage club, red, white and blue by the Datus Coon corps ; bouquets of white roses by the W. C. T. U., of red and white carnations in a holder of blue satin by Heintzelman W. R. C., of red roses by the Woman's League, of pink roses by the Jewish women. There was music by an orchestra as an accompaniment to the sociability of the occasion, in which some 700 women participated during the afternoon."

The following day a picnic was given by the Woman's Club at "Olivewood," the home of Mrs. Flora M. Kimball, near National City, where tables were spread on the lawn for the 200 guests who came by train and carriage. That same evening, by request of many who could not be present at the first meeting, the two ladies lectured again in San Diego. The next day they returned to Los Angeles, laden with souvenirs of their delightful visit ; and that evening, without an hour's rest, addressed a mass meeting there.

The following day the Los Angeles Herald gave an excursion to Santa Monica in their honor. The ladies of that pretty seaside resort, under the leadership of Mrs. C. H. Ivens, met them with carriages and conducted them to the Hotel Arcadia. After luncheon, as they started for the hall where they were to speak, twelve little girls strewed flowers in their pathway, and after the addresses twelve large bouquets of choice blossoms were laid at their feet. They were taken for a long drive by Mrs. E. J. Gorham, then to the residence of her brother, Senator John P. Jones ; and at the close of a lovely day, returned to Los Angeles. That evening a reception was given them by Mrs. Mark Sibley Severance, which Miss Anthony always remembered as one of the handsomest in her long experience. The next morning they met a committee from the suffrage club and had a conference on the broad piazza of their hostess in regard to the work of the coming campaign ; and in the afternoon took the train for San Francisco, after two of the most delightful weeks in all their recollection. An especially gratifying feature was the attitude of the press of Southern California. There had been scarcely a discordant note in the extended reports of the public meetings and social entertainments, and the editorial comments on the two ladies and the cause of which they were leading representatives, were dignified, fair and friendly.[1]

They reached San Francisco June 24 and were welcomed at the ferry by a number of friends from the two cities. The next day they were entertained at an elaborate dinner-party of ladies and gentlemen in the artistic home of Mrs. Emma Shafter Howard, of Oakland. From the table they went at once to the evening meeting. The Enquirer said : "It needed no preliminary brass band or blare of trumpets to pack the Congregational church with a live Oakland audience. The simple announcement that Susan B. Anthony and Rev. Anna H. Shaw were to speak was sufficient, and the chairman, Colonel John P. Irish, looked out over an animated sea of faces."

The following evening the San Francisco farewell meeting was held in Metropolitan Temple. Friday and Saturday were filled with social engagements, sight-seeing and shopping. On Sunday Miss Shaw preached in the California street Methodist church in the morning and the Second Congregational in the evening, while Miss Anthony addressed a union meeting of all the colored congregations in the city at the M. E. Zion church, the historic building in which Starr King preached before the war. Monday they spoke again at the Ministers' Meeting. The fact that they would be present had been announced in the papers, and ministers of all denominations were there from most of the towns within a radius of forty miles. Miss Anthony told them in vigorous language : "The reason why they, as a class, had so little influence with men of business

---

[1] The Los Angeles Times, Harrison Gray Otis, editor, furnished the only exception of any importance to this rule.

and political affairs was because the vast majority of the people they represented had neither money nor votes ; that if four or five hundred ministers of the State should go up to Sacramento to ask for any legislation, they would be treated politely and bowed out precisely as would so many of their women church members. Whereas, on the other hand, one manufacturer, one railroad official, one brewer or distiller, could go before the same body and get whatever he asked, because every member would know that behind this request were not only thousands of dollars but thousands of votes.'' The ministers seemed to realize fully the force of this statement and many expressed themselves thoroughly in favor of the enfranchisement of women.

The State Suffrage Association, with a good delegate representation, met in Golden Gate Hall, July 3, for their annual convention. There had been heretofore some dissensions in this organization and, at this critical time, co-operation was so vitally necessary that the friendly offices of Miss Anthony and Miss Shaw were requested in the interests of harmony. In view of the arduous campaign approaching, all desired that Mrs. A. A. Sargent should accept the presidency, and the close of the convention found the forces united and ready for work.

The Fourth of July witnessed the last public appearance of the two eminent visitors, and thereby hangs a tale. The last of May Miss Anthony had received from the chairman of the Fourth of July Executive Committee, William H. Davis, the following : '' Fully realizing the great importance of your lifework, and rejoicing with you in the certainty that the fruition of your labors and hopes is now no longer problematic, but merely a question of days, we take much pleasure in extending to you the right hand of American fellowship. . . . . We cordially invite you to an honorary position on our committee, and hope that you will do us the honor of allowing us to select for you an appropriate and prominent place in the celebration of our national independence.''

When it had been decided to celebrate the Fourth on a more elaborate scale than usual, an auxiliary board was appointed, composed of the leading women of the city, with Sarah B. Cooper, chairman. Thinking to add an interesting feature to the occasion, she requested of the literary committee that Rev. Anna Shaw be placed on the program as one of the orators of the day. To her amazement she was refused in discourteous manner and language. The executive committee, learning of this action, requested that it should be reconsidered and Miss Shaw invited to speak. This being refused, the executive committee notified them that unless it was done, their committee would be discharged and a new one appointed. They then yielded to the inevitable, placing Miss Shaw's name upon the list of orators, and the announcement was received with cheers by all the other committees. The reverend lady had not the slightest desire to make a Fourth of July speech, but she did wish to see Mrs. Cooper win her battle with the little sub-committee. Meanwhile the committee in Oakland, P. M. Fisher, chairman, did not wait to be asked, but invited her to deliver an oration in that city as soon as she had finished in San Francisco, and she accepted.

In the great Fourth of July procession, the very next carriage to that of the mayor contained Mrs. Cooper, Miss Anthony and Miss Shaw, and the rousing cheers of the people along the whole line of march showed their appreciation of the victory gained for woman. At 2 o'clock in the afternoon the ladies took seats on the platform at Woodward's Pavilion, facing an audience of 5,000 people. San Francisco never heard such an oration as was delivered that day by the little Methodist preacher, her natural eloquence fired by the efforts to prevent her making it. After she had finished and the cheers upon cheers had died away, there was a great shout from the immense crowd, "Miss Anthony, Miss Anthony!" Finally she was obliged to come forward and, when a stillness had settled upon the audience, she said in strong, ringing tones: "You have heard today a great deal of what George Washington, the father of his country, said a hundred years ago. I will repeat to you just one sentence which Abraham Lincoln, the savior of his country, uttered within the present generation:

'No man is good enough to govern another man without his consent.' Now I say unto you, 'No man is good enough to govern any woman without her consent;'" and sat down amidst roars of applause.

Miss Shaw had been placed at the very end of the program and when she got out into the street it was 5 o'clock. It would require an hour to reach Oakland, and she supposed of course some one had telegraphed the situation and the people there had long since gone home; but this had not been done, and a great audience on that side of the bay had assembled in the Tabernacle, many going as early as 1 o'clock, and had waited until 6. Knowing there was some mistake they separated with the understanding that if Miss Shaw could be secured for the evening the church bells would be rung. That lady had just seated herself at the dinner table when a telegram was received explaining the situation. She replied at once: "I will be with you at half-past eight." Miss Anthony would not let her go alone and so, exhausted as they both were by the hard demands of the day, they crossed the bay, reaching Oakland at 8 o'clock. No one was at the station to meet them, so they took a carriage and drove to the Tabernacle but found it dark and deserted. They then went the rounds of the churches, but all were closed. Finally they gave up in despair and made the long journey back to San Francisco, reaching the Sargent home at 11 o'clock. Why the telegram was not received was never satisfactorily determined.

After a meeting with the amendment campaign committee the next morning and a long discussion of their plan of work, the travellers started eastward at 6 P. M. They were met at the Oakland ferry by a crowd of friends from both cities with flowers, fruit and lunch baskets, and left amidst a shower of affectionate farewells. They carried away the sweetest memories of a lifetime and could find no words to express their love and admiration for the people of California.

Miss Anthony preserves, as a memento of this visit, a large scrap-book of over 200 pages entirely filled with personal notices from the newspapers of that State during the six weeks of her stay, all, with a few exceptions, of such a character as to make their reading a pleasure. A source of even greater satisfaction was the wide discussion of woman suffrage which her visit had inspired and the favorable consideration accorded it by the press. In the months which followed she received scores of letters from California women, many of them unknown to her, expressing the sentiments of one from a teacher, which may be quoted: "Many of us who could attend but few of the meetings and had not even time to meet you personally, have caught something of their spirit and have been with you in heart. We bless the day which brought you to us; for your kindly words to women, and to men for women, have lifted the fog, and the veiling mists are drifting away, leaving us a clearer view of our duty not only to humanity but to ourselves. You have left a trail of light."

CHAPTER XLVI.

1895—1896.

ON the way homeward they were met at every large station by friends with something to add to the pleasure of their trip. Miss Shaw went through to Chicago, but Miss Anthony journeyed towards Leavenworth. She dined with friends at Topeka, and while waiting in the station, one of them remarked, "We are to have our suffrage meeting tomorrow, what shall we tell them from you?" In a spirit of fun she dashed off a resolution saying that "since 130,000 Kansas men declared themselves against woman suffrage at the late election and 74,-000 showed their opposition by not voting; therefore it is the duty of every self-respecting woman in the State to fold her hands and refuse to help any religious, charitable or moral reform or any political association, until the men shall strike the adjective 'male' from the suffrage clause of the constitution."

She was in Topeka only five hours, but during that time attended a dinner party, gave a two-column interview to a reporter from each of the city papers, and furnished a resolution which set all the newspapers in the country by the ears. "Talk about hysterics," she said, laughingly, as she read the clippings, "it takes the editors to have 'em, if they are opposed to woman suffrage and can get hold of something to help them out." Any one who could have the patience to read the fearful morals which were deduced, the frightful sermons which were preached, from what was intended as a joking resolution, would quite agree with her. Even had it been meant seriously, it would have been only such retaliation as men would have visited upon women had the latter been possessed of the power and voted three to one to take the ballot away from them.

She visited a week in Leavenworth and Fort Scott, arrived at Chicago July 15, and was thus described by a Herald reporter :

Miss Anthony has grown slightly thinner since she was in Chicago attending the World's Fair Congresses, thinner and more spiritual-looking. As she sat last night with her transparent hands grasping the arms of her chair, her thin, hatchet face and white hair, with only her keen eyes flashing light and fire, she looked like Pope Leo XIII. The whole physical being is as nearly submerged as possible in a great mentality. She recalls facts, figures, names and dates with unerring accuracy. It was no Argus-eyed autocrat who told with pardonable pride last night of how her chair at every great function in San Francisco was hung with floral wreaths, how bouquets were piled at her feet until she could scarcely step for them. It was a pleasing story, told by a sweet old woman, of honors which she accepted for the sake of a beloved cause.

The next day she resumed her journey with Mr. and Mrs. Gross and Harriet Hosmer, who were going to Bar Harbor. She reached her own home at daybreak, and here, the diary shows, she sat down on the steps of the front porch and read the paper for an hour or two rather than disturb her sister's morning nap. The first word received from Miss Shaw was that she had arrived at her summer home on Cape Cod with a raging fever, the result of the great strain of constant speaking and travelling so many weeks without rest, and she continued alarmingly ill the remainder of the summer. She was much distressed because of an engagement she had to lecture to the Chautauqua Assembly at Lakeside, O., and to relieve her mind Miss Anthony telegraphed her that she would go in her place. She herself felt not the slightest ill effect from her journey, and the long interviews published in all the Rochester papers during the week she was at home, displayed the keenest and strongest mental power. She reached Lakeside on the 25th of July and the next day spoke to a large audience. Towards the close of her address, she ended abruptly, dropped into her chair and sank into a dead faint.

She was taken at once to Mrs. Southworth's summer home,

at which she was a guest, and telegrams were sent out by the press reporters announcing that she could not live till morning. She learned afterwards that long obituary notices were put in type in many of the newspaper offices. One Chicago paper telegraphed its correspondent: "5,000 words if still living; no limit, if dead." She was very much vexed at this momentary weakness and, using her will-power, by the next day had rallied sufficiently to return home. The national suffrage business committee, by previous arrangement, met at her house, and she forced herself to keep up for two days, but felt very dull and tired, and on the morning of July 30 she did not rise. A physician was summoned and a trained nurse, and for a month she lay helpless with nervous prostration; her first serious illness in seventy-five years.

She is quoted as saying that if she "had pinched herself right hard she would not have fainted." One of the papers remarked that "then she never would have known how much the American people thought of her." Every newspaper had something pleasant to say,[1] many friends wrote letters of sympathy, and scores whom she had not known personally sent their words of admiration. Only her body was weak, her mind was abnormally alert; she appreciated all that was said and done for her, and remarked often that this was the only real *rest* of her lifetime. A number of relatives came to visit her, and a little later Mrs. Coonley and Mrs. Sewall. Mr. and Mrs. Gross also stopped on their way home, the latter leaving $50 for "the very prettiest wrapper that could be had." From her old anti-slavery co-worker, Samuel May, now eighty-five, came the words:

I suppose there is hardly another person in the United States, man or

---

[1] The following from the Wichita Eagle is noteworthy because in the Kansas campaign the year before, and in all previous years, it had been abusive beyond description and had at all times put every possible stumbling-block in the way of woman suffrage and berated all who advocated it:

"What an experience Miss Anthony has had! None but a remarkable woman could have accepted such a life-work at a time when prejudice and education ran all in the opposite direction. Finely-balanced and self-educated as to her special cause, she has not only won a name and fame world-wide, but turned perceptibly the entire current of human conviction. And she has been, through it all, the modest woman, truly womanly. The men and women of this country—of the world—who believe that the ballot for woman means better government and the elevation of society to a higher plane, must ever recognize Susan B. Anthony as the real pioneer prophetess of the cause, for so will history record her."

woman, who has been engaged in actual hard public labor so long as yourself; and is it not a part of your business and a part of your duty—in view of the unattained results—to allow yourself larger spaces of rest and to put upon yourself more moderate and less exhausting tasks ? We would not willingly see you retire from the field altogether; therefore we want you to do less of the common soldier's work and take charge of the reserves, keeping watch from your tower of experience, and personally appearing only when and where the enemy rallies in unusual numbers or with unusual craftiness. This does not imply a lessening of your usefulness but an increase, being a wiser application of your strength and resources.

From Parker Pillsbury, the old comrade, aged eighty-six: "We have heard of your late illness, a warning to constant prudence and care for your health as you come down to ' life's latest stage.' Hold on, my dear—*our* dear—Susan, hold on to the last hour possible. You have seen great and glorious changes, almost revolutions, but yet how much remains to be encountered and accomplished. . . . We shall hope you may live to see the one grand achievement—the equal civil and political rights of all women before the law. Then you may well say : ' Lord, now lettest Thou Thy servant depart in peace; for mine eyes have seen Thy salvation.' "

Mrs. Stanton wrote : "I never realized how desolate the world would be to me without you until I heard of your sudden illness. Let me urge you with all the strength I have, and all the love I bear you, to stay at home and rest and save your precious self." From Mrs. Cooper this urgent message : "You are too far along in years to work as hard as you do. Take it easy, my beloved friend, and let your young lieutenants bear the heat and burden of the day, while you give directions from the hill-top of survey. Age has the right to be peaceful, as childhood has the right to be playful. You are the youngest of us all, nevertheless nature cries a halt and you must obey her call in order to be with us as our leader for a score of years to come."

There is a long hiatus in the diary, and then for many days the brief entry, " On the mend." In September she began to walk out a little and then to call on the nearest friends, and by the last of the month she attended a few committee meetings. The rumor had been persistently circulated that she was to resign the presidency of the National-American Association and retire to private life. In fact, she never had the slightest intention of giving up active work. She realized that inactivity meant stagnation and hastened both physical and mental decay, and she was determined to keep on and "drop in the harness" when the time came to stop.[1] It was evident, however, that she must have relief in her immense correspondence. This she recognized, and so secured an efficient stenographer and typewriter in Mrs. Emma B. Sweet, who assumed her duties October 1, 1895. The five large files packed with copies of letters sent out during the remaining months of the year show how pressing was the need of her services. Miss Anthony relates in her diary with much satisfaction, that she "managed to have a letter at every State suffrage convention held that fall."

She thought possibly she might have to work a little more moderately for a while, and one of her first letters was written to the head of the Slayton Lecture Bureau: "I should love dearly to say 'yes' to your proposition for a series of lectures at $100 a night. Nothing short of that would tempt me to go on the lyceum platform again, and even to that, for the present, I must say 'nay.' I am resolved to be a home-body the coming year, with the exception of attending the celebration of Mrs. Stanton's eightieth birthday and our regular Washington convention." Among the characteristic short letters is this to Dr. Sarah Hackett Stevenson, of Chicago, who had asked for a word of encouragement in regard to a hospital she was founding for mothers whose children were born out of wedlock:

I hope your beneficent enterprise may succeed. I trust the day will come

---

[1] Miss Anthony was many times besought to tell the secret of her wonderful vitality and power for work, and on one occasion wrote the following:

"As machinery in motion lasts longer than when lying idle, so a body and soul in active exercise escape the corroding rust of physical and mental laziness, which prematurely cuts off the life of so many women. I believe I am able to endure the strain of daily travelling and lecturing at over threescore years and ten, mainly because I have always worked and loved work. As to my habits of life, it has been impossible for me to have fixed rules for eating, resting, sleeping, etc. The only advice I could give a young person on this point would be: 'Live as simply as you can. Eat what you find agrees with your constitution—when you can get it; sleep whenever you are sleepy, and think as little of these details as possible.'"

when there will be no such unfortunate mothers, but until then, it certainly is the duty of society to provide for them. The first step towards bringing that day is to make women not only self-supporting but able to win positions of honor and emolument. Since no disfranchished class of men ever had equal chances in the world, it is fair to conclude that the first requisite to bring them to women is enfranchisement. It is not that all when enfranchised will be capable, honest and chaste, but it is that they will possess the power to control their own conditions and those of society equally with men. Therefore my panacea for the ills which your hospital would fain mitigate is the ballot in the hands of women.

The editor of the Voice wrote for her opinion as to the cause of the prevailing "hard times," and she answered:

The work of my life has been less to find out the causes of men's failure to successfully manage affairs, than to try to show them their one great failure in attempting to make a successful government without the help of women. It used to be said in anti-slavery days that a people who would tacitly consent to the enslavement of 4,000,000 human beings, were incapable of being just to each other, and I believe the same rule holds with regard to the injustice practiced by men towards women. So long as all men conspire to rob women of their citizen's right to perfect equality in all the privileges and immunities of our so-called "free" government, we can not expect these same men to be capable of perfect justice to each other. On the contrary, the inevitable result must be trusts, monopolies and all sorts of schemes to get an undue share of the proceeds of labor. There is money enough in this country today in the hands of the few, if justly distributed, to make "good times" for all.

Reporters were constantly besieging her for her views on "bloomers," which had been re-introduced by the bicycle, and she usually replied in effect:

My opinion about "bloomers" and dress generally for both men and women is that people should dress to accommodate whatever business or pastime they pursue. It would be quite out of good taste as well as good sense, for a woman to go to her daily work with trailing skirts, flowing sleeves, fringes and laces; and certainly, if women ride the bicycle or climb mountains, they should don a costume which will permit them the use of their legs. It is very funny that it is ever and always the men who are troubled about the propriety of the women's costume. My one word about the "bloomers" or any other sort of dress, is that every woman, like every man, should be permitted to wear exactly what she chooses.

When women have equal chances in the world they will cease to live merely to please the conventional fancy of men. As long as there was no alternative for women but to marry, it was about as much as any woman's

life was worth to be an old maid, and her one idea was to dress and behave
so as to escape this fate. She now has other objects in life, and her new liberty has brought with it a freedom in matters of dress which is cause for
rejoicing.

These opinions might be multiplied almost to infinity and
all would emphasize two points : 1st, the broad views entertained by Miss Anthony on all questions, based on her idea of
individual freedom, the same for both sexes ; 2d, her funda-
méntal belief that, until women cease to be a subject class, and
until they stand upon the plane of perfect equality of rights
and privileges, there can be no such thing as a fair solution or
adjustment of the issues of the day, either great or small; in other
words, that these can not be satisfactorily and permanently settled through the judgment and decision of only one-half the
people.

On October 18 she celebrated her complete recovery by accepting an invitation to " come and take a cup of tea with
Aunt Maria Porter," in honor of her ninetieth birthday. She
was obliged to cancel her engagement to speak at the Atlanta
Exposition, but during this month made a trial of her strength
by an hour's speech at the annual meeting of the Monroe
County Suffrage Club at Brockport, " attempting it," she says,
" with fear and trembling, but going through as if I never had
had a scare." Assured by this that she had herself well in
hand once more, she went to Ashtabula, Ohio, for a three
days' convention of the State association, attending every business meeting and public session. This fact being duly heralded in the newspapers, they put the obituary notices back
into their pigeonholes.

She started for New York November 6 to be present at an
event to which she had looked forward with more pleasure than
to anything of that nature in all her life—the celebration of the
eightieth birthday of Mrs. Stanton. At the convention in
February it had been unanimously decided that the National-
American Association should have charge of this, but at the
Woman's Council in Washington it was agreed that it would

have greater significance if held under the auspices of that body, which cheerfully accepted the charge. Its new president, Mary Lowe Dickinson, urged Miss Anthony to take the chairmanship of the committee of arrangements, insisting that no one else could make so great a success of it, but Miss Anthony assured her of what afterwards proved to be true, that no one could manage the affair more perfectly than Mrs. Dickinson herself.

Naturally many of the suffrage women resented having any one outside their own association as the leader on this great occasion, and Lillie Devereux Blake wrote: "Mrs. Stanton stands for suffrage above all else and she should be honored by our societies. To have the celebration under the charge of the secretary of the King's Daughters, an orthodox organization, seems very much out of taste, greatly as I honor Mrs. Dickinson. I do not think any one else will make the celebration such a success as you would; you, the long-time companion and co-worker with our dear leader, are the person who should be at the head and, with your admirable manner as a presiding officer, you would give a tone to it that no one else could." To this Miss Anthony replied:

All of you fail to see the higher honor to Mrs. Stanton in having the celebration mothered by a great body composed of twenty national societies, instead of by only our one. Surely, for all classes of women—liberal, orthodox, Jewish, Mormon, suffrage and anti-suffrage, native and foreign, black and white—to unite in paying a tribute of respect to the greatest woman reformer, philosopher and statesman of the century, will be the realization of Mrs. Stanton's most optimistic dream. I am surprised and delighted at the action of the council. It shows a breadth and comprehensiveness on the part of the leaders of its twenty-in-one organization of which I am very proud. Of course Mrs. Stanton stands for suffrage first, last and all the time, and the conservative women who join in this celebration do so knowing that she stands thus for a free and enfranchised womanhood.

Don't you see that for Anthony to head the fray, preside and be general master of ceremonies, would reduce it to a mere mutual admiration affair? The celebration is not taken away from us. We, the suffrage women, will have our modicum of time to set forth what Mrs. Stanton has done for our specific cause, and the other women will have theirs. O, no, my dear, it is not possible that the greater can be less than one of the parts which compose it.

Her own "girls," Mrs. Sewall and Mrs. Avery, could not help being a little jealous for their general, and insisted that her name should head the invitations, but to them she wrote :

Do you not see that for Susan B. Anthony's name to stand at the top, will frighten the conservatives? Everybody will conclude that the big suffrage elephant has possessed the council, body and soul—all thrust into the suffrage hopper and the wheel turned by S. B. A. To make me chairman will wholly spoil the intention of the council, which is and should be to bring the fruits of Mrs. Stanton's first demand, fifty years ago, and lay them at her feet; not only the suffrage children, but those of education, literature, science, reform, religion, all as one. If Mrs. Dickinson single out the hoofed and horned head of suffrage as the commander-in-chief, not only the nineteen other societies but all the world outside will say it is suffrage after all; which it will be, because the others won't train under our leadership. No, no; Mrs. Dickinson herself must be the chief cook of this broth and appoint her own lieutenants, one of whom, with name far down in the middle of the list, I shall be most happy to be, and do all I possibly can to help, but always in the name of the president of the council.

She was true to her word, and in every way assisted Mrs. Dickinson in the immense amount of preparation necessary for what was the largest and most perfect affair of this nature ever given in America. At her request Miss Anthony wrote over a hundred letters to collect funds, secure the presence of the pioneer workers among women, etc., but still insisted on keeping herself so much in the background as even to refuse to make one of the principal speeches of the occasion. When she reached New York, she went for the night to her cousin, Mrs. Lapham, and early the next morning to Mrs. Stanton's to read over the birthday speech, of which she writes : "My only criticism was that she did not rest her case after describing the wonderful advance made in state, church, society and home, instead of going on to single out the church and declare it to be especially slow in accepting the doctrine of equality to women. I tried to make her see that it had advanced as rapidly as the other departments but I did not succeed, and it is right that she should express her own ideas, not mine."

The next day she went to Newburgh to address the State convention, returning to New York on the 9th. Friends had come from all parts of the country to attend the celebration, and the three days following were pleasantly spent in visiting with them at the different hotels. On the evening of the 12th occurred the birthday fête. There is not room in these pages to describe in full that magnificent gathering, the great Metropolitan Opera House crowded from pit to dome, each of the boxes brilliantly and appropriately decorated and occupied by the representatives of some organization of women. On the stage was a throne of flowers and above it an arch with the name "Stanton" wrought in red carnations on a white ground. When Mrs. Stanton entered, the entire audience of 3,000 rose to salute her with waving handkerchiefs. At the right and left of the floral throne sat Miss Anthony and Mrs. Dickinson. Instead of responding with a set speech, when called upon, Miss Anthony paid an eloquent tribute to the "pioneers," and then read the most important of the one hundred telegrams of congratulation which had been received from noted societies and eminent men and women in the United States and Europe.[1] The New York Sun said: "In ordinary hands this task would have been dull enough, but Miss Anthony enlivened it with her wit and cleverness and made a success of it." It may be truly said that not one woman in that audience, not even Mrs. Stanton herself, was prouder or happier than Miss Anthony over this splendid ovation.

[1] Among others was a beautiful testimonial from Theodore Tilton, who had been for many years a resident of Paris, in which he said:

"At the present day, every woman who seeks the legal custody of her children, or the legal control of her property; every woman who finds the doors of a college or a university opening to her; every woman who administers a post-office or a public library; every woman who enters upon a career of medicine, law or theology; every woman who teaches a school, or tills a farm, or keeps a shop; every one who drives a horse, rides a bicycle, skates at a rink, swims at a summer resort, plays golf or tennis in a public park, or even snaps a kodak; every such woman, I say, owes her liberty largely to yourself and to your earliest and bravest co-workers in the cause of woman's emancipation. So I send my greetings not to you alone, but also to the small remainder now living of your original bevy of noble assistants, among whom—first, last and always—has been and still continues to be your fit mate, chief counselor and executive right hand, Susan B. Anthony; a heroine of hard work who, when her own eightieth birthday shall roll round, will likewise deserve a national ovation, at which she should not inappropriately receive the old Roman crown of oak."

This was accompanied by a personal letter to Miss Anthony, saying, besides other pleasant things: "I heard lately that you were dying! I did not believe the canard. Dying? No! You are to live forever. Give my love to the heroine of the hour—and prepare yourself for an equal picnic when your own time shall come. Ever yours as of old."

The next day a large reception was given at the Savoy by Mrs. Henry Villard, the only daughter of Wm. Lloyd Garrison; and after various luncheons and dinners and good-by calls, Miss Anthony returned to Rochester. She plunged into the mountain of correspondence and, expecting to spend most of the next year at home, gave every spare moment to the arranging and classifying of her mass of documents, preparatory to some contemplated literary work. On November 21, the Political Equality Club celebrated Mrs. Stanton's birthday in a beautiful manner at the Anthony home, over 200 guests attending. Several unkind newspaper attacks being made upon Miss Anthony by disgruntled women, she wrote Mrs. Stanton, who was much distressed: "This fresh onslaught reminds me of the old adage, 'When one is overpraised by the many, the few will try to pull down and destroy.' Certainly I know that in my head and heart there never has been any but the strongest desire that all the other workers should have their full meed of opportunity and reward."

A telegram came November 25 announcing the sudden death, in Boston, of Mrs. Ellen Battelle Dietrick. She had been actively in the suffrage work for only a few years, but in that time Miss Anthony had learned her splendid powers and had said of her: "I feel that into her hands can safely fall the work of the future, both as to principle and policy." She had been made chairman of the national press work, and had shown an unsurpassed beauty and strength of style and thought. "She was a philosopher, a student," Miss Anthony wrote, "possessed of the conscience and the courage to stand by the truth as she saw it. Can it be that she is gone in the very prime of her womanhood? Why can not we keep with us the brave and beautiful souls; why can not the weak and wicked go? The world seems darker to me now, a light has gone out."

On December 2 she gathered about her a group of the very oldest and dearest friends in memory of what would have been

ANT.—54

her mother's one hundred and second birthday. She records attending a lecture by President Andrew D. White, at the close of which he presented his wife to her, saying: "I want you to know her; she is of your kind." The day before Christmas came another telegram, this one from May Wright Sewall, containing simply the words: "Dear General, my Theodore is taken." It meant the desolation of one of the happiest, most perfect homes ever made by two mortals. It told the breaking of as strong and sweet a tie as ever united husband and wife. What could she write? Only, "Be brave in this inevitable hour; take unto yourself the 'joy of sorrow' that you did all in mortal power for his restoration, that his happiness was the desire of your life; find comfort in the blessed memories of his tender and never-failing love and care for you in all these beautiful years." But the poverty, the powerlessness of words in times like this!

And so the old year rolled into the past and the record was finished. Among the letters which came to cheer its close, was one from Mary Lowe Dickinson, which ended:

In every way, in all this work, how grandly you stood by and helped me! Some day you will understand how grateful I am, and how thoroughly I appreciate the support, moral and other, that you have given me. I know this holiday season will bring you a great many loving souvenirs from all over the world, and I haven't sent you anything at all; but I have a gift for you, notwithstanding, a gift of loyal reverence for the grand outspoken bravery of your life and service, a gift of genuine gratitude for what you have been and what you have done, and an affection that has been growing ever since my first talk with you in Chicago. This is quite a declaration for a reserved woman, but it is as sincere as it is unusual, and I wish you all sorts of blessings for the New Year, and most of all that it may show great progress in the work which lies so close to your heart.

And this from her beloved friend, Mrs. Leland Stanford:

It is needless for me to express all I feel in regard to your tender and long-continued friendship. I always prized it when I had my dear husband by my side to help me bear the burdens and sorrows of life, but now, standing as I do alone with the weighty cares and sacred duties depending upon me, I cherish your sympathy, your friendship and your tender words as an evidence of God's love. He can instigate and guide hearts to reach out sustaining helpfulness to His children, who need just such support as you have given me. Long years past and gone, you and Mrs. Stanton were appreciated and extolled by my husband more than you ever realized. He predicted twenty years ago what has now come, and mainly through the instrumentality of yourself and her—the advancement and elevation of womanhood—and we are only on the eve of what is to follow in the twentieth century.

Leland Stanford

Miss Anthony was very glad to go back to Washington with the annual convention, which was held January 23 to 28, 1896. She went on a week beforehand to satisfy herself that all was in readiness. Although the details of the work were assumed by the younger members of the board, she was always on the scene of action early enough to look over the ground before the battle opened. This year the papers said: "A notable feature of the suffrage movement is the large number of college alumnæ and professional women who are coming into the ranks." The committee reported organizations in every State and Territory except Alaska. Delegates were present from almost every one, among them Mrs. Hughes, wife of the governor of Arizona, Mrs. Teller, wife of the senator from Colorado, Mrs. Sanders, wife of the ex-senator from Montana, the wives of Representatives Arnold, Allen, Shafroth and Pickler, Mrs. Ella Knowles Haskell, assistant attorney-general of Montana. Most of them addressed the committees of the Senate and House, who gave long and respectful hearings.

The principal cause of rejoicing at this convention was the admission of Utah as a State with the full enfranchisement of women. A clause to this effect had been put into the State constitution, endorsed by all political parties, voted on by the men of the Territory and carried. This constitution had been accepted, the new State admitted by Congress, and the bill was signed by President Cleveland January 4, 1896. A noteworthy circumstance in this case was that, while the admission of Wyoming with a woman suffrage clause in its constitution was fought for many days in both Senate and House in 1890, that

of Utah was accepted with scarcely a protest against its enfranchisement of women.   There was also rejoicing over the
fact that, during the autumn of 1895, the full franchise had
been conferred upon the women of South Australia.

The occurrence of the convention which forever made its
memory a sad one to Miss Anthony was the so-called "Bible
resolution."   It had this effect not only because of the resolution itself but because those who were responsible for it were
especially near and dear to her.   Elizabeth Cady Stanton, assisted by a committee of women, had been for several years
preparing a work called the "Woman's Bible."   It contained
no discussion of doctrinal questions but was simply a commentary upon those texts and chapters directly referring to women,
and a few others from which they were conspicuously excluded.
Naturally, however, this pamphlet caused a great outcry,
especially from those who had not read a word of it.   That
women should dare analyze even the passages referring to
themselves in a book which heretofore, neither in the original writing nor in all the revisions of the centuries, had
felt the impress of a woman's brain or the touch of a woman's
hand, stirred the orthodox to their greater or less depths.
Mrs. Stanton was honorary president of the National-American Suffrage Association, but had not attended its meetings or
actively participated in its work for a number of years.

Several members of the board, who were children when she
and Miss Anthony founded that organization, and unborn when
Mrs. Stanton called the first woman's rights convention, decided that her Woman's Bible was injuring the association,
although only the chapters on the Pentateuch thus far had
been published.   They determined that this body should take
official action on the question, but they understood perfectly
that it would have to be brought before the convention without any previous knowledge on the part of Miss Anthony.
Therefore it was planned to have a paragraph of condemnation
and renunciation of the Woman's Bible incorporated in the
report of the corresponding secretary.   When it was read in
open meeting she was struck dumb.   Mrs. Colby sprung to

her feet and moved that the report be accepted, all but the paragraph relating to the Woman's Bible.   After an animated discussion the secretary's report was laid on the table and later was adopted with the offending clause stricken out.   Miss Anthony supposed this was the end of the matter but, to her amazement, the committee on resolutions reported the following: "This association is non-sectarian, being composed of persons of all shades of religious opinions, and has no official connection with the so-called Woman's Bible, or any theological publication."

This resolution was wholly gratuitous.   While true that the association was composed of persons of all shades of religious opinion, it comprised also among some of its oldest and ablest members those who entertained no so-called religious beliefs. Mrs. Stanton invariably had announced that this revision of the Scriptures was the individual work of herself and her committee, and there was no ground for holding the whole association responsible.   The resolution, however, was debated for an hour.   Miss Anthony was moved as never before.   Not only was she fired with indignation at this insult to the woman whom she loved and revered above all others, but she was outraged at this deliberate attempt to deny personal liberty of thought and speech.   Leaving the chair she said in an impassioned appeal :

The one distinct feature of our association has been the right of individual opinion for every member. We have been beset at each step with the cry that somebody was injuring the cause by the expression of sentiments which differed from those held by the majority. The religious persecution of the ages has been carried on under what was claimed to be the command of God. I distrust those people who know so well what God wants them to do, because I notice it always coincides with their own desires. All the way along the history of our movement there has been this same contest on account of religious theories. Forty years ago one of our noblest men said to me, "You would better never hold another convention than allow Ernestine L. Rose on your platform;" because that eloquent woman, who ever stood for justice and freedom, did not believe in the plenary inspiration of the Bible. Did we banish Mrs. Rose? No, indeed!

Every new generation of converts threshes over the same old straw. The point is whether you will sit in judgment on one who questions the divine inspiration of certain passages in the Bible derogatory to women. If Mrs. Stanton had written approvingly of these passages you would not have brought in this resolution for fear the cause might be injured among the *liberals* in religion. In other words, if she had written *your* views, you would not have considered a resolution necessary. To pass this one is to set back the hands on the dial of reform.

What you should say to outsiders is that a Christian has neither more nor less rights in our association than an atheist. When our platform becomes too narrow for people of all creeds and of no creeds, I myself can not stand upon it. Many things have been said and done by our *orthodox* friends which I have felt to be extremely harmful to our cause; but I should no more consent to a resolution denouncing them than I shall consent to this. Who is to draw the line? Who can tell now whether these commentaries may not prove a great help to woman's emancipation from old superstitions which have barred its way? Lucretia Mott at first thought Mrs. Stanton had injured the cause of all woman's other rights by insisting upon the demand for suffrage, but she had sense enough not to bring in a resolution against it. In 1860 when Mrs. Stanton made a speech before the New York Legislature in favor of a bill making drunkenness a ground for divorce, there was a general cry among the friends that she had killed the woman's cause. I shall be pained beyond expression if the delegates here are so narrow and illiberal as to adopt this resolution. You would better not begin resolving against individual action or you will find no limit. This year it is Mrs. Stanton; next year it may be I or one of yourselves, who will be the victim.

If we do not inspire in women a broad and catholic spirit, they will fail, when enfranchised, to constitute that power for better government which we have always claimed for them. Ten women educated into the practice of liberal principles would be a stronger force than 10,000 organized on a platform of intolerance and bigotry. I pray you vote for religious liberty, without censorship or inquisition. This resolution adopted will be a vote of censure upon a woman who is without a peer in intellectual and statesmanlike ability; one who has stood for half a century the acknowledged leader of progressive thought and demand in regard to all matters pertaining to the absolute freedom of women.

Rev. Anna Shaw, Carrie Chapman Catt, Henry B. and Alice Stone Blackwell, Laura M. Johns, Annie L. Diggs, Rachel Foster Avery, Laura Clay, Mariana W. Chapman, Elizabeth Upham Yates, and others spoke in favor of the resolution; Lillie Devereux Blake, Clara B. Colby, Mary S Anthony, Emily Howland, Charlotte Perkins Stetson and Caroline Hallowell Miller were among those who opposed it. The vote resulted, 53 ayes, 41 nays; and the resolution was adopted. The situation was felicitously expressed in a single sentence by Mrs. Caroline McCullough Everhard, president of the Ohio Suffrage Association: "If women were governed more by principle and less by prejudice, how strong they would be!"

Miss Anthony's feelings could not be put into words. At first she seriously contemplated resigning her office, but from all parts of the country came letters from the pioneer workers— the women who had stood by her for more than twoscore years—pointing out that this action of the convention was a striking illustration of the necessity for her remaining at the helm. Mrs. Stanton urged that they both resign, but Miss Anthony replied :

During three weeks of agony of soul, with scarcely a night of sleep, I have felt I must resign my presidency, but then the rights of the minority are to be respected and protected by me quite as much as the action of the majority is to be resented ; and it is even more my duty to stand firmly with the minority because principle is with them. I feel very sure that after a year's reflection upon the matter, the same women, and perhaps the one man, who voted for this interference with personal rights, will be ready to declare that their duty as individuals does not require them to disclaim freedom of speech in their co-workers. Sister Mary says the action of the convention convinces her that the time has not yet come for me to resign ; whereas she had felt most strongly that I ought to do it for my own sake. No, my dear, instead of my resigning and leaving those half-fledged chickens without any mother, I think it my duty and the duty of yourself and all the liberals to be at the next convention and try to reverse this miserable, narrow action.

In letters to the different members of her "cabinet," who had voted in favor of the resolution, she thus expressed herself :

In this action I see nothing but the beginning of a petty espionage, a revival of the Spanish inquisition, subjecting to spiritual torture every one who speaks or writes what the other members consider not good for the association. Such disclaimers bring quite as much of martyrdom for our civilization as did the rack and fire in the barbarous ages of the past.

That a majority of the delegates could see no wrong personally to Mrs. Stanton and no violation of the right of individual judgment, makes me sick at heart ; and still, I don't know what better one could expect when our ranks are now so filled with young women not yet out of bondage to the idea of the infallibility of that book. To every person who really believes in religious freedom, it is no worse to criticise those pages in the Bible which degrade woman than it is to criticise the laws on our statute books which degrade her. Everything spoken or written by Jew or Greek, Gentile or Christian, or by any human being whomsoever, is not too sacred to be criticised by any other human being.

She was far too magnanimous, however, and loved the cause too well to relax her efforts for the welfare of the association.

Before the year closed she received from Mrs. Avery and Mrs. Upton most tender and beautiful letters, acknowledging their mistake, expressing their sorrow and begging to be reinstated in her confidence and affection.[1]

In order that Miss Anthony's position may be clearly understood and that she may not appear biased and one-sided, and in order also to consider this question all at one time, her point of view will be a little further illustrated. In an interview in the Rochester Democrat and Chronicle she is thus reported:

"Did you have anything to do with the new Bible, Miss Anthony?" was asked.

"No, I did not contribute to it, though I knew of its preparation. My own relations to or ideas of the Bible always have been peculiar, owing to my Quaker training. The Friends consider the book as historical, made up of traditions, but not as a plenary inspiration. Of course people say these women are impious and presumptuous for daring to interpret the Scriptures as they understand them, but I think women have just as good a right to interpret and twist the Bible to their own advantage as men always have twisted and turned it to theirs. . . . It was written by men, and therefore its reference to women reflects the light in which they were regarded in those days. In the same way the history of our Revolutionary War was written, in which very little is said of the noble deeds of women, though we know how they stood by and helped the great work; and it is the same with history all through."

Although she stood so firm for individual rights she nevertheless regretted that Mrs. Stanton should give the few remaining years of her precious life to this commentary, and frequently wrote in the following strain, when importuned to assist in it:

I can not help but feel that in this you are talking down to the most ignorant masses, whereas your rule always has been to speak to the highest, knowing there would be a few who would comprehend, and would in turn give of their best to those on the next lower round of the ladder. The cultivated men and women of today are above the need of your book. Even the liberalized orthodox ministers are coming to our aid and their conventions are

[1] In a letter to the Woman's Tribune Mrs. Jean Brooks Greenleaf said: "I was absent from the convention and could not vote against that resolution. The 'Woman's Bible' a hindrance to organization? Of course it is. What of it? The belief in the old theories about women, which had their basis in doctrines taught from King James' version of the Bible, was a much more monumental hindrance to the work of the pioneers, in not only the woman suffrage movement but in all movements for the advancement of women."

passing resolutions in favor of woman's equality, and I feel that these men and women who are just born into the kingdom of liberty can better reach the minds of their followers than can any of us out-and-out radicals. But while I do not consider it my duty to tear to tatters the lingering skeletons of the old superstitions and bigotries, yet I rejoice to see them crumbling on every side.

Months after this Washington convention, when Miss Anthony was in the midst of a great political campaign in California, she sent Mrs. Stanton this self-explanatory letter:

You say "women must be emancipated from their superstitions before enfranchisement will be of any benefit," and I say just the reverse, that women must be enfranchised before they can be emancipated from their superstitions. Women would be no more superstitious today than men, if they had been men's political and business equals and gone outside the four walls of home and the other four of the church into the great world, and come in contact with and discussed men and measures on the plane of this mundane sphere, instead of living in the air with Jesus and the angels. So you will have to keep pegging away, saying, " Get rid of religious bigotry and then get political rights; " while I shall keep pegging away, saying, " Get political rights first and religious bigotry will melt like dew before the morning sun; " and each will continue still to believe in and defend the other.

Now, especially in this California campaign, I shall no more thrust into the discussions the question of the Bible than the manufacture of wine. What I want is for the men to vote " yes " on the suffrage amendment, and I don't ask whether they make wine on the ranches in California or believe Christ made it at the wedding feast. I have your grand addresses before Congress and enclose one in nearly every letter I write. I have scattered all your "celebration" speeches that I had, but I shall not circulate your "Bible" literature a particle more than Frances Willard's prohibition literature. So don't tell Mrs. Colby or anybody else to load me down with Bible, social purity, temperance, or any other arguments under the sun but just those for woman's right to have her opinion counted at the ballot-box.

I have been pleading with Miss Willard for the last three months to withdraw her threatened W. C. T. U. invasion of California this year, and at last she has done it; now, for heaven's sake, don't you propose a "Bible invasion." It is not because I hate religious bigotry less than you do, or because I love prohibition less than Frances Willard does, but because I consider suffrage more important just now.

It seems that Miss Anthony's attitude ought to be perfectly understood by the testimony here presented. It is one from which she never has swerved and on which she is willing to stand in the pages of history—entire freedom for herself from religious superstition—the most absolute religious liberty for every other human being.

To return to the Washington convention: Among many pleasant social features Miss Anthony was invited to an elegant luncheon given by Mrs. John R. McLean in honor of the seventieth birthday of Mrs. Ulysses S. Grant and, at the reception which followed, received the guests with Mrs. Grant and Mrs. McLean.

I am yours with great respect and sincere admiration

Julia D. Grant

At the close of the convention the principal speakers and many of the delegates went to Philadelphia to a national conference, which was largely attended. It was here that " Nelly Bly " had the famous interview published in the New York World of February 2, 1896. She had tried to secure this in Washington, but Miss Anthony could not spare time for it, so she followed her to Philadelphia. It filled a page of the Sunday edition and contained Miss Anthony's opinions on most of the leading topics of the day, in the main correctly reported, although not a note was taken. It began thus:

Susan B. Anthony! She was waiting for me. I stood for an instant in the doorway and looked at her. She made a picture to remember and to cherish. She sat in a low rocking-chair, an image of repose and restfulness. Her well-shaped head, with its silken snowy hair combed smoothly over her ears, rested against the back of the chair. Her shawl had half fallen from her shoulders and her soft black silk gown lay in gentle folds about her. Her slender hands were folded idly in her lap, and her feet, crossed, just peeped from beneath the edge of her skirt. If she had been posed for a picture, it could not have been done more artistically.

"Do you know the world is a blank to me?" she said after we had exchanged greetings. "I haven't read a newspaper in ten days and I feel lost to everything. Tell me about Cuba! I almost would be willing to postpone the enfranchisement of women to see Cuba free. . . ."

"Do you believe in immortality?"

"I don't know anything about heaven or hell," she answered, "or whether I will meet my friends again or not, but as no particle of matter is ever destroyed, I have a feeling that no particle of mind is ever lost. I am sure that the same wise power which manages the present may be trusted with the hereafter."

"Then you don't find life tiresome?"

"O, mercy, no! I don't want to die as long as I can work; the minute I can not, I want to go. I dread the thought of being enfeebled. The older I get, the greater power I seem to have to help the world; I am like a snow-ball—the further I am rolled the more I gain. But," she added, significantly, "I'll have to take it as it comes. I'm just as much in eternity now as after the breath goes out of my body."

"Do you pray?"

"I pray every single second of my life; not on my knees, but with my work. My prayer is to lift woman to equality with man. Work and worship are one with me. I can not imagine a God of the universe made happy by my getting down on my knees and calling him 'great.'   . . .

"What do I think of marriage? True marriage, the real marriage of soul, when two people take each other on terms of perfect equality, without the desire of one to control the other, is a beautiful thing; it is the highest condition of life; but for a woman to marry for support is demoralizing; and for a man to marry a woman merely because she has a beautiful figure or face is degradation.   . . ."

"Do you like flowers?" I asked, leading her into another channel.

"I like roses first and pinks second, and nothing else after," Miss Anthony laughed. "I don't call anything a flower that hasn't a sweet perfume."

"What is your favorite hymn or ballad?"

"The dickens!" she exclaimed merrily. "I don't know! I can't tell one tune from another. I know there are such hymns as 'Sweet By and By' and 'Old Hundred,' but I can not tell them apart. All music sounds alike to me, but still if there is the slightest discord it hurts me. Neither do I know anything about art," she continued, "yet when I go into a room filled with pictures my friends say I invariably pick out the best. I have good company, I always think, in my musical ignorance. Wendell Phillips couldn't recognize tunes; neither could Anna Dickinson."

"What's your favorite motto, or have you one?"

"For the last thirty years I have written in all albums, 'Perfect equality of rights for women, civil and political;' or, 'I know only woman and her disfranchised.' There is another, one of Charles Sumner's, 'Equal rights for all.' I never write sentimental things.   . . .

"Yes, I'll tell you what I think of bicycling," she said, leaning forward and laying a hand on my arm. "I think it has done more to emancipate woman than any one thing in the world. I rejoice every time I see a woman ride by on a wheel. It gives her a feeling of self-reliance and independence the moment she takes her seat; and away she goes, the picture of untrammelled womanhood."

"What do you think the new woman will be?"

"She'll be free," said Miss Anthony. "Then she'll be whatever her best judgment dictates. We can no more imagine what the true woman will be than what the true man will be. We haven't him yet, and it will be generations after we gain freedom before we have the highest man and woman. They will constantly change for the better, as the world does. What is the best possible today will be outgrown tomorrow."

"What would you call woman's best attribute?"

"Good common sense; she has a great deal of uncommon sense now, but I want her to be an all-around woman, not gifted overly in one respect and lacking in others. . . ."

"And now," I said, approaching a very delicate subject on tip-toe, "tell me one thing more. Were you ever in love?"

"In love?" she laughed. "Bless you, Nelly, I've been in love a thousand times!"

"Really!" I gasped, taken back by this startling confession.

"Yes, really," nodding her snowy head; "but I never loved any one so much that I thought it would last. In fact, I never felt I could give up my life of freedom to become a man's housekeeper. When I was young, if a girl married poverty, she became a drudge; if she married wealth, she became a doll. Had I married at twenty-one, I would have been either a drudge or a doll for fifty-five years. Think of it!" and she laughed again. . . .

Miss Anthony's seventy-sixth birthday was celebrated by the Rochester Political Equality Club at the residence of Dr. and Mrs. S. A. Linn. The spacious and beautifully decorated rooms were crowded with guests, and interesting addresses were given by Mrs. Greenleaf, Mrs. Gannett, Mr. J. M. Thayer and Mary Seymour Howell, to which Miss Anthony made a happy response. On February 17 she spoke at a church fair given by the colored people of Bath, and then completed her preparations for a long journey and a great campaign. It will be remembered that Miss Anthony had decided to rest from "field work" during 1896, and to arrange her papers for the writing of the history of her life, which her friends felt was now the most important thing for her to do. To this end a roomy half-story had been built on the substantial Rochester home, and therein were placed all the big boxes and trunks of letters and documents which had been accumulating during the last fifty years and stored in woodshed, cellar and closets; a stenographer had been engaged and all was in readiness for the great work. Then came an appeal from 3,000 miles away which rent asunder all her resolutions.

When she had been in California the previous year and had

helped the women plan their approaching campaign, nothing had been further from her thoughts than returning to give her personal assistance. As the time for action drew near, those who had the matter in charge began to realize that the task before them was far greater than they had anticipated, and that they were lacking in the experience which would be needed. There were very few women who could be depended on to draw together and address great audiences of thousands of people, to speak thirty consecutive nights in each month, and to be equal to every emergency of a political campaign ; nor were there any considerable number who understood the best methods of organization. It was then both natural and sensible that the State society should appeal to the national association for assistance. It is an essential part of the business of the officers of that body to respond to such calls.

Miss Anthony had been home from California but a short time in 1895 when Ellen C. Sargent, president of the State association, wrote an earnest official request for the help of the national board. At the same time Sarah B. Cooper, president of the campaign committee, sent the strongest letter her eloquent pen could write, emphasizing Mrs. Sargent's invitation. These were followed by similar pleas from the other members of the board and from many prominent women of the State. Miss Anthony felt at first as if it would not be possible for her to make the long trip and endure the fatigue of a campaign, which she understood so well from having experienced it seven times over. On the other hand she realized what a tremendous impetus would be given to the cause of woman suffrage if the great State of California should carry this amendment, and she longed to render every assistance in her power. It was not, however, until early in February that she yielded to the appeals and decided to abandon all the plans she had cherished for the year. The moment her decision reached California, Harriet Cooper, secretary of the committee, telegraphed their delight and sent her a check of $120 for travelling expenses.

The question now arose with Miss Anthony what she should

do with her secretary, whom she had engaged for a year but did not feel able to take with her. This was settled in a few days through the action of Rev. and Mrs. W. C. Gannett, who went among the friends and in a short time raised the money to pay Mrs. Sweet's expenses to California and back, all agreeing that Miss Anthony must have some one to relieve her of the mechanical part of the burden she was about to assume. This seemed too good to be true, as she had had no such help in all her forty-five years of public work. The two started on the evening of February 27, a large party of friends assembling at the station to say good-by to the veteran of seventy-six years about to enter another battle. They stopped at Ann Arbor for the Michigan convention, the guests of Mrs. Hall, and then a few days in Chicago, where Miss Anthony and Mrs. Gross sat for a statuette by Miss Bessie Potter.

She reached San Diego March 10 and, after attending the Woman's Club, went to Los Angeles where she was beautifully received, sharing the honors with Robert J. Burdette at the Friday Morning Club. Mrs. Alice Moore McComas wrote to Mrs. Sargent and Mrs. Cooper the next day: " Dear Miss Anthony came, saw and conquered, and we are hers ! Letters and telegrams were dispatched in every direction as soon as we found she was coming and she has been able to reach women that I have almost despaired of. Dozens who have heretofore held aloof, have promised me today to stand by the amendment till all is over, and with these recruits we feel that we can undertake the convention work in this county. The women are aroused and we will see that they stay aroused. Miss Anthony's visit was opportune and just what was needed.''

She arrived at San Francisco a few days later, being joyfully greeted at the Oakland station by Mrs. Cooper and Harriet. She went directly to the Sargent residence, and from this delightful home, Miss Anthony, the National president, and Mrs. Sargent, the State president, directed the great campaign.

CHAPTER XLVII.

THE CALIFORNIA CAMPAIGN.

1896.

IN their State convention of 1894 the Republicans of California had adopted the strongest possible plank in favor of woman suffrage and, as the legislature the next year was Republican by a considerable majority, Clara Foltz and Laura de Force Gordon, attorneys, and Nellie Holbrook Blinn, at that time State president, Mrs. Peet, Madame Sorbier, Mrs. Bidwell, Mrs. Spencer, of Lassen county, and others made a determined effort to secure a bill enfranchising women. That failing, the legislature consented to submit an amendment to the constitution to be voted on in 1896. This bill was signed by Governor James H. Budd and the women then prepared to canvass the State to secure a favorable majority.

Out of the officers of the State suffrage association and the amendment committee, a joint campaign committee was formed and, in addition to this, a State central committee.[1] These two constituted the working force at State headquarters. There were also speakers and organizers, and a regularly officered society in each county, co-operating with the officials at headquarters.

At the request of the State committee Miss Anthony's niece, Lucy E., for seven years Miss Shaw's secretary and thoroughly experienced in planning and arranging meetings, went out

[1] Joint campaign committee: Ellen C. Sargent, chairman; Sarah B. Cooper, vice-chairman; Ida H. Harper, corresponding secretary; Harriet Cooper, recording secretary; Mary S. Sperry, treasurer; Mary Wood Swift and Sarah Knox Goodrich, auditors. State central committee: Mrs. Sargent, Miss Anthony, Mrs. Swift, Mrs. Sperry, Mrs. Blinn, with Mary G. Hay, chairman.

early in February to assist Dr. Elizabeth Sargent in the preparations for the first series of conventions. She carried with her a complete list, made by Miss Anthony herself with great labor and care, of every town of over two hundred inhabitants in every county in the State, with instructions to plan for a meeting there during the campaign. One scarcely can describe the perplexing work of these young women in arranging this great sweep of conventions, two days in every county seat, each convention overlapping the next, getting the speakers from one to the other on time, finding women in each town or city who would take charge of local arrangements, and rounding up the whole series in season for the Woman's Congress in May. In March the campaign committee invited Mary G. Hay, who had had twelve years' experience in organization work, and Harriet May Mills, the State organizer of New York, to manage the conventions; and Rev. Anna Shaw and Miss Elizabeth Upham Yates as speakers. It is impossible to follow these meetings in detail further than to say that, with but few exceptions, they were very successful, the audiences were large and cordial, clubs were formed, much suffrage sentiment was created, and the conventions considerably more than paid all expenses. The women of California possessed ability, energy, patriotism and desire for political freedom, but up to this time they had no conception of the immense amount of money and work which would be required for a campaign. As soon as they grasped the situation they were fully equal to its demands and never in all the history of the movement was so much splendid work done, or so large a fund raised, by the women of any State.

It was unanimously agreed that Miss Anthony should remain in San Francisco, answering the numerous calls for addresses in that city and the surrounding towns, and having general oversight of the campaign. Mrs. Sargent assigned to her the largest, sunniest room in her spacious home, but her hospitality and her services to the cause of the amendment did not end here. Another large apartment was appropriated to Rev. Anna Shaw and her secretary. The room formerly used

Ellen Clark Sargent

as the senator's office was dedicated to the work, the type-
writers ensconced there, and it soon was crowded with documents, newspapers and all the paraphernalia of a campaign.
In a little while they encroached on the library and it was
filled with the litter. Then a typewriter found its way into
one corner of the long dining-room. The committee meetings
were held in the drawing-room; and, during the whole
eight months, there was scarcely a meal at which there were
not from one to half a dozen speakers, members of committees, out-of-town workers and others besides her family at
the table. Every hour of Mrs. Sargent's and Dr. Elizabeth's
time was devoted to the campaign. The latter was placed at
the head of the literary committee and also took entire charge
of the petition work for the State, involving months of most
exacting labor. In addition to all this, both gave most liberally in money. How much was accomplished by Mrs. Sargent's quiet influence, her wise and judicial advice, her many
logical and dignified appeals in person and by letter, never can
be estimated.

The State board and committees were composed of women
of fine character and social standing, who commanded the
highest respect; and during the long campaign they put aside
every other duty and pleasure and devoted themselves, mind
and body, to the success of the amendment. Across the bay
in Oakland, Alameda and Berkeley were a large and active
county society, Mrs. Isabel A. Baldwin, president, and city
organizations of women of equal ability and prestige, who
were in daily communication with State headquarters and performed the most valuable and conscientious work. What was
true here was equally so of the women in all the counties from
San Diego to Del Norte. It seems invidious to mention a
single name where so many gave such excellent service. It
must be admitted, however, that while hundreds of women
worked for their political freedom, thousands contributed absolutely nothing in either money or service; and yet there were
many among them who believed fully in the principle of

ANT.—55

woman suffrage.   They simply allowed domestic duties or the demands of society or apathetic indifference to prevent their rendering any assistance, and they could not be prevailed upon even to give money to help those who performed the labor.   If all such had lent their influence, the women of California today would be enfranchised ; but they left the whole burden to be carried by the few, and these could not do the work necessary for success, because human nature has its limits.

The attitude of the press of California deserves especial mention because to it was largely due the marked consideration which the suffrage amendment received throughout the State.   Miss Anthony met in California an acquaintance, Mrs. Ida H. Harper, recently of the editorial staff of the Indianapolis News, and requested her to act as chairman of the press committee.   As the press of San Francisco could kill the amendment at the very start, if it chose to do so, they decided to call upon the editors of the daily papers in that city and ascertain their position.   They visited the managing editors of the Call, Examiner, Chronicle, Post, Report and Bulletin and, without a single exception, were received with the greatest courtesy and assured that the amendment and the ladies who were advocating it would be treated with respect, that there would be no ridiculing, no cartooning and no attempt to create a sentiment in opposition.

The Post came out editorially in favor of the amendment and established a half-page department, headed "The New Citizen," which was continued daily during the campaign, the largest amount of space ever given by any paper to woman suffrage.   Dr. Elizabeth Sargent assumed most of the responsibility for this department, assisted by members of the staff. The Report gave editorial endorsement and a double-column department entitled "The Woman Citizen," edited every Saturday by Winnifred Harper.   The Bulletin expressed itself as friendly and later in the campaign opened a suffrage department conducted by Eliza D. Keith; but the paper contained editorials from time to time, which the friends did not construe as favorable to the measure. The managing editor gave the ladies to understand that there would be no opposition from the Chronicle, and during the campaign it contained several strong editorials, not advocating the amendment, but decidedly favorable to woman suffrage. This paper also gave a prominent place to a number of articles from Mrs. Harper and others. Two days before election, however, it advised its readers to vote against the amendment.

The Examiner was friendly and offered a column on the editórial page of the Sunday edition, throughout the campaign, if Miss Anthony would fill it. She protested that she was not a writer, but it was only upon this condition that the space would be given. It was too valuable to be sacrificed and so she accepted it, and for seven months furnished Sunday articles of 1,600 words. These were widely copied, not only throughout the State, but in all parts of the country. Every possible influence was exerted to persuade William R. Hearst, the proprietor, who was residing in New York, to bring out the paper editorially in favor of the amendment. Miss Anthony wrote an earnest personal letter which closed: ''So, I pray you for the love of justice, for the love of your noble mother, and for the sake of California—lead the way for the Democratic party of your State to advocate the suffrage amendment. The Examiner has done splendidly thus far in publishing fair and full reports of our meetings and articles from our leading suffrage women. The one and only thing we do ask is that it will editorially champion the amendment as it will every other measure it believes in which is to be voted upon next November.'' All pleadings were in vain and the great paper remained silent. It did not, however, contain a line in opposition.

During Miss Anthony's visit to San Francisco the previous year, the Monitor, the official Catholic organ of California, had come out in two editions with full-page editorials in favor of woman suffrage, as strong as anything ever written on that subject. When the two ladies called on the editor, he assured them of his full sympathy and agreed to accept a series of

articles from the chairman of the press committee. These
were published regularly for a time and then suddenly were
refused, and every effort to ascertain the reason was unsuccessful. Miss Anthony called on him several times and waited for
half an hour in his anteroom, but he declined to see her and,
during the remainder of the campaign, the amendment received no recognition from the Monitor.

The response from the other papers of the State was most
remarkable. The Populist press, without exception, was for
woman suffrage. Every newspaper in Oakland, Alameda and
Berkeley spoke in favor of the amendment. The majority of
those in Los Angeles and San Diego counties endorsed it. All
but one in San Jose, and all but one in Sacramento, did likewise. Before the campaign closed, 250 newspapers declared
editorially for the suffrage amendment. Only two of prominence in the entire State came out boldly in opposition, the
Record-Union, of Sacramento, and the Times of Los Angeles.
The former ceased its opposition some time before election;
the latter continued to the end, ridiculing, misrepresenting,
denouncing, and even going to the extent of grossly caricatur-
ing Miss Anthony.

The Star, the Voice of Labor and other prominent journals
published in the interests of the wage-earning classes; those
conducted by the colored people; the Spanish, French and
Italian papers; the leading Jewish papers; the temperance,
the A. P. A. and the Socialist organs; and many published
for individual enterprises, agriculture, insurance, etc., spoke
strongly for the amendment. The firm which supplied plate
matter to hundreds of the smaller papers accepted a short
article every week. There were very few newspapers in the
State which did not grant space for woman suffrage departments, and these were ably edited by the women of the different localities. Matter on this question was furnished to the
chairman of the press committee by the San Francisco Clipping
Bureau, and these clippings were carefully tabulated and
filed. At the close of the eight months' campaign they numbered 9,000, taken from the press of California alone. Twenty-

seven papers came out in opposition; these included a number of San Francisco weeklies of a sensational character and a few published in small towns.

It must be remembered, in this connection, that the woman suffrage organization had not a dollar to pay for newspaper influence, had no advertising to bestow, and that even the notices for meetings were gratuitous. All this advocacy on the part of the papers was purely a free-will offering and represented the honest and courageous sentiments of the editors. It is deemed especially worthy of notice because there was never anything like it in previous suffrage campaigns. Toward the end, when the influence of the opposition began to do its fatal work, these papers were closely watched and in not one instance was there a defection.

Notwithstanding this splendid support of the press, Miss Anthony was firm in her decision that she would not remain through the campaign unless the amendment could secure the endorsement of the political parties, and every energy was directed toward this point. Several of the Republican county conventions declared for it, and a number of Republican leaders who were visited, announced themselves in favor of the plank. The State Convention was to be held May 5. On May 3, the Sunday edition of the San Francisco Call, the largest and most influential Republican paper in the State, came out with flaming headlines declaring boldly and unequivocally for woman suffrage! The sensation created was tremendous, and amendment stock went up above par. The Monday and Tuesday editions continued the editorial endorsement, declaring that the Republican party stood committed to woman suffrage, and that the Call constituted itself the champion and would carry it to victory.

Tuesday morning the Republican convention opened at Sacramento. The woman suffrage delegation, consisting of Mrs. Sargent, Mrs. John F. Swift, Mrs. Blinn, Mrs. Austin Sperry, Mrs. Knox Goodrich, Miss Anthony, Rev. Anna Shaw, Miss Hay, Miss Yates, Mrs. Harper, opened their headquarters at the Golden Eagle Hotel, decorated their parlor with flowers,

spread out their literature and badges and waited for the delegates. They had not long to wait. With the influence of the
Sunday Call, a copy of which had been laid on the seat of
every delegate in the convention hall, they had a prestige
which found favor in the eyes of the politicians. The visitors
came early and stayed late; they went away and returned
bringing their friends to be converted. The Call account said:
"They went in twos and threes, in large groups and in entire
delegations, to pay homage to their more modest workers and
apparently to beg the privilege of serving them." The rooms
were crowded until after midnight.

The delegates put on the badges, and when the convention
opened 250 of them were wearing the little flag with its three
stars. The ladies were given the best seats in the great building. The delegates were divided into two hostile camps, representing opposite wings of the party, and the women had to
move very carefully, as it was by no means certain which fac-
tion would secure control of the convention. They also had
to frame many non-committal answers to the question, "How
do you stand on the A. P. A.?" The headquarters were
thronged with reporters; every woman was interviewed at length
and her opinions telegraphed to the great San Francisco dailies.
Miss Anthony's interviews occupied a column in the Examiner, each day of the convention. Those alarmists who
fear women will lose the respect of men when they are invested
with political influence should have had this object lesson.

The chairman of the convention was considered not favorable to woman suffrage. Of the seven men appointed on the
resolution committee, five were said to be opposed to the plank.
The spirits of the ladies began to droop. In the evening permission was given them to address the platform committee.
Mrs. Harper wrote the San Francisco Call:

I wish I could picture that scene. In the small room, seated around the
table, were the seven men who held the fate of this question in their hands.
At one end stood Miss Anthony, the light from above shining upon her silver
hair until it seemed like a halo, and she spoke as no one ever heard her speak
before. On the face of every delegate was an expression of the deepest
seriousness, and before she had finished tears were in the eyes of more than

one. She was followed by Miss Shaw, who stood there the embodiment of all that is pure, sweet and womanly, and in a low, clear voice presented the subject as no one else could have done. As we were about to leave the room, the chairman said, "Ladies, we will take the vote now, if you desire." We thanked him, but said no, we would withdraw and leave them to consider the matter at their leisure.

Within a very few minutes we had their decision—six in favor of the resolution and one opposed. Here I want to call attention to one thing. Eight women knew of the favorable action of the committee by 9 o'clock, but although we were besieged by reporters and delegates until nearly midnight we gave no sign, and the Wednesday morning papers could only say that it was probable there would be a woman suffrage plank. It is charged that women can not keep a secret, but this is one of those many ancient myths which take a long time to die.

The plank was adopted next day in the big convention with only one dissenting voice. The Woman's Congress was in session at San Francisco and when Mrs. Cooper, its president, stepped forward on the platform and read the telegram announcing the result, the enthusiasm hardly can be described. The ladies went down from Sacramento to the Congress the next day and received a continuous ovation throughout the rest of the meetings.

Among the pleasant letters which came to Miss Anthony was one from Abigail Scott Duniway, of Portland, Ore., in which she said: "Your triumphs in California are marvellous. Hurrah, and again, hurrah! I believe now the women of the Golden State will win. All honor to you and your noble confreres!" And one from Lucy Underwood McCann, of Santa Cruz, saying: "It is to you, most honored and revered of women, we owe the fact, because of your long martyrdom in this great reform, that we stand now, as we hope and pray, upon the brink of realization of our rights. This has been made possible only through the patient toil of such heroic souls as your own. Your wisdom in planning this campaign, in which we confidently expect a glorious victory, is our mainstay, upon which all other hopes depend."

Miss Anthony's happiness over the action of the Republicans knew no bounds, and she began with renewed courage to prepare for the Populist convention May 12. The prominent

Populists who were visited assured the ladies that they need not waste time or money going to Sacramento to secure a plank in their platform, as woman suffrage was one of the fundamental principles of their party. The suffrage leaders felt, however, that this convention was entitled to the same courtesy as the others and they attended in a body, headed by Miss Anthony and Mrs. Sargent. When they entered the convention hall they were received with cheers and waving of hats, escorted to the front seats, invited to address the convention and surrounded by delegates during the recess. Without any solicitation the resolution committee reported and the convention adopted a strong woman suffrage plank, and then gave three cheers for the ladies. They were told that not half a dozen men in that body were opposed to the amendment.

From here they went to the Prohibition convention at Stockton, were met at the station by a delegation of ladies, and received with distinguished consideration by the convention. Miss Anthony was twice invited to address them, and the plank endorsing the amendment was adopted by a hearty and unanimous vote. A reception was then held at the hotel and over a hundred ladies called.

One convention yet remained, the Democratic. While a few of the leaders of this party were in favor of the amendment, most of them were opposed and gave no encouragement to the attempt to secure a plank. The ladies, however, carried out the program, and the same large delegation returned to Sacramento June 16, the number increased by Mrs. Cooper, Mrs. E. O. Smith, of San Jose, Mrs. Alice M. Stocker, of Pleasanton, and several others. A month had intervened and the opposition had had time to organize. Some of the county conventions had declared against the amendment and many of the delegates had been instructed to vote against it.

The suffrage representatives were disappointed in the hope that they might come to this convention with the editorial endorsement of the Examiner, but they were greatly pleased to receive from that paper, on the morning of the opening, a package of 2,000 woman suffrage leaflets. The Examiner had collected at its own expense a large amount of fresh and valuable testimony from the leading editors and officials of Colorado and Wyoming, as to its satisfactory practical working in those States, and had arranged it in large type on heavy cream-tinted paper, making the handsomest leaflet of the kind ever issued. These were placed in the hands of the delegates, and also distributed throughout the State.

The women's headquarters at the Golden Eagle were practically unvisited. A few lone delegates, and two or three delegations that had been instructed to vote for the amendment, strayed up to express their sympathy, but most of them were too well subjugated by the political bosses even to pay a visit of courtesy. A new element was introduced here in the person of a woman of somewhat unpleasant record who claimed to be the representative of the anti-suffrage organization. The platform committee consisted of thirty-five and met in a large room filled with spectators. The ladies presented a petition signed by 40,000 California men and women asking for woman suffrage. The entire delegation of speakers, with Miss Anthony and Miss Shaw at the head, was granted twenty minutes to present its claims, and the one woman above referred to was given the same amount of time. She did not occupy more than a minute of it, simply saying that her anti-suffrage league was going to organize all over the State and work for the Democratic party. The resolution was laid on the table, almost before they were out of the room.

A minority report was prepared by Charles Wesley Reed, of San Francisco, and signed by himself, Mr. Alford, chairman of the committee, and two others. In a letter to the Call, Mrs. Harper thus describes subsequent events:

Mr. Reed assured the ladies that he would bring this report before the convention and he kept his word, although he had other fights on hand and endangered them by standing for woman suffrage. This minority report, although properly drawn and signed by four members of the platform committee, including the chairman, was "smothered" by the secretary of the convention and its chairman, Mr. Frank Gould. Every other minority report was read and acted upon by the convention; that alone on woman suffrage was held back. In vain Mr. Reed protested; the chairman ignored him and called for a vote on the platform as a whole. It was adopted with a roar, and our fight was lost! It was near midnight. We had sat two long hot days in the convention, had slept but little, were worn out and very, very wrathy. At this juncture John P. Irish addressed the convention, stating that a distinguished lady was present, etc., and would they hear Miss Susan B. Anthony? Thinking it was too late for her to do any harm, she was received with loud applause.

It was impossible to say what the convention expected, but they got a rebuke for allowing such action on the part of their chairman and for treating the women of the State in this unjust and undemocratic manner, which caused a hush to fall upon the whole body. It was a dramatic and impressive scene, one not to be forgotten. At its conclusion there were loud cries for Anna Shaw. The little fighter was at the boiling point, but she stepped upon the platform with a smile, and with that sarcasm of which she is complete master supplemented Miss Anthony's remarks. As she stepped down, half the convention were on their feet demanding the minority report. The chairman stated that it was too late for that, but a resolution might be offered. The original resolution was at once presented, and then there was an attempt to take a viva-voce vote, but our friends demanded a roll-call. It resulted in 149 ayes and 420 noes. Mr. Gould's own county voted almost solidly in favor. Alameda county, led by W. W. Foote, gave 32 noes and 3 ayes, yet this county sent in the largest petition for woman suffrage of any in the State.

To secure more than a one-fourth vote of a convention which had been determined not to allow the question even to come before it, was not a total defeat.[1]

The battle was now fairly begun and it grew hotter with every passing week for the next five months. A few days after the last convention the women held a mass meeting in Metropolitan Temple to ratify the planks. The great hall was crowded to the doors and hundreds stood during all the long exercises. As the ladies who had been to the conventions came upon the stage, the building fairly rang with applause. The Republican, Populist, Prohibition, Democratic and Socialist-Labor parties were represented by prominent men who made strong suffrage speeches. Congressman James G. Maguire spoke for those individual Democrats who believed

[1] About 1 o'clock in the morning, after this eventful night, the ladies were awakened by loud laughter and women's voices. They arose and went to the window and there in the brilliantly lighted street in front of the hotel were two carriages containing several gaily dressed women. A number of the convention delegates came out and crowded around them, three or four climbed into the carriages, wine bottles were passed and finally, with much talk and laughter, they drove off down the street, the men with their arms about the women's waists. The ladies returned to their slumbers thoroughly convinced that they had not used the correct methods for capturing the delegates of a Democratic convention.

in woman suffrage, among whom he was always a staunch advocate. Miss Anthony was cheered to the echo and it seemed as if the audience could not get enough of her bright, pithy remarks, as she introduced the different speakers.

The suffrage advocates, elated with their victory in three conventions, opened headquarters in the large new Parrott building and swung their banner across the street.[1] Five rooms were filled with busy workers directed by Mary G. Hay, chairman of the State central committee, while the other members took turns in receiving the reporters, the people on business and the throngs of visitors from all parts of the State. To follow this campaign in detail, to name all of those most prominently connected with it, would be obviously impracticable. It would be utterly impossible to mention individually the hundreds of women who thoroughly canvassed their own precincts and deserve a full share of the credit for the large vote cast. A number of competent California women took up the organization of the different counties. Every woman in the State who could address an audience found her place and work. Mrs. Alice Moore McComas and Rev. Mila Tupper Maynard headed the list of Southern California speakers. Miss Sarah M. Severance spoke under the auspices of the W. C. T. U. Mrs. Naomi Anderson represented the colored women. Rev. Anna Shaw spoke every night during the campaign, except the one month when she returned East to fill engagements. She paid the salary of her secretary and donated her services to the headquarters for five months. Miss Elizabeth Upham Yates, of Maine, made about one hundred speeches. The last two months Mrs. Carrie Chapman Catt, national organizer, gave several addresses each day. There were very few men who worked as hard during that campaign as did scores of the women, each according to her ability.

[1] The use of these rooms was donated by the manager of the Emporium, the large department store in the building. All through the summer and autumn a number of most capable young women, who were employed as stenographers, teachers, etc., gave every waking moment outside business hours to the work at headquarters, carrying home with them great packages of leaflets and circulars to be folded and addressed, looking after their own precincts, and rendering services which could not have been paid for in money. Although all were breadwinners they labored from love of the cause and without a thought of thanks or remuneration.

No description could give an adequate idea of the amount of labor performed by Miss Anthony during those eight months. There was scarcely a day, including Sundays, that she did not make from one to three speeches, often having a long journey between them. She addressed great political rallies of thousands of people ; church conventions of every denomination ; Spiritualist and Freethinkers' gatherings ; Salvation Army meetings; African societies; Socialists; all kinds of labor organizations; granges ; Army and Navy Leagues ; Soldiers' Homes and military encampments ; women's clubs and men's clubs ; Y. M. C. A.'s and W. C. T. U.'s. She spoke at farmers' picnics on the mountaintops, and Bethel Missions in the cellars of San Francisco; at parlor meetings in the most elegant homes ; and in pool-rooms where there was printed on the blackboard, "Welcome to Susan B. Anthony."

She was in constant demand for social functions, where her presence gave an opportunity for a discussion of the all-absorbing question. One of the handsomest of these was a breakfast of two hundred covers, given by the Century Club in the "maple room" of the Palace Hotel, where were gathered the leading women of San Francisco and other cities in the State. Miss Anthony sat at the right hand of the president and responded to the toast, "Those who break bread with us." The club privileges were extended to her and, at the close of the campaign, she was made an honorary member. This club was composed largely of conservative women, but its president, Mrs. Mary Wood Swift, was one of the most prominent of the suffrage advocates. She addressed the Woman's Press Association, the Laurel Hall Club, the Forum, Sorosis, Association of Collegiate Alumnæ and most of the other women's organizations of San Francisco. An invitation to luncheon was received from Mrs. Stanford signed, "Your sincere friend and believer in woman suffrage," and a very pleasant day was spent in her lovely home at Menlo Park.

A breakfast was given in her honor by the Ebell Club of Oakland, Mrs. G. W. Bunnell, president. She rode in a beautifully decorated carriage at the great Fabiola Fête, or floral festival, held annually in this city. Many social courtesies were extended in the towns around the bay, among them being dinner parties by Senator and Mrs. Fred Stratton, Mr. and Mrs. A. A. Moore, Mrs. Henry Vrooman, Mr. and Mrs. F. M. Smith, Mrs. Emma Shafter Howard, Mr. and Mrs. F. C. Havens, Mrs. Alice H. Wellman, of Oakland; Judge and Mrs. J. A. Waymire, of Alameda; Mr. and Mrs. William A. Keith, of Berkeley. All this would have been very enjoyable but for the fact that most of these occasions included a speech, and she was usually obliged to come from just having spoken, or to rush away to keep another engagement. One unique experience was a complimentary trip tendered, through Mrs. Lovell White, by the proprietors of the new Mill Valley and Mount Tamalpais Scenic Railway, to Miss Anthony and a large number of guests. From the top of this high peak, which overlooks the Golden Gate, they enjoyed a view that for beauty and grandeur is not surpassed in the world.

Miss Anthony visited also various towns throughout the central part of the State and along the coast, speaking in wigwams, halls, churches, schoolhouses and the open air, taking trains at all hours, travelling through heat and dust, wind and cold; and there was never a word of complaint during all the long campaign. She was always ready to go, always on time, always full of cheer and hope.

The first week in June she went to Portland to attend the Woman's Congress, Abigail Scott Duniway, president. Its officers were among the prominent women of the city, and she was royally received. She spoke a number of times during the nine sessions and was handsomely treated by the press. Sarah B. Cooper joined her here, on her way home from the National Federation of Clubs at Louisville, Ky. A number of receptions were given in their honor, among them one by the Woman's Club. There was an elaborate luncheon at "the Curtis;" and a reception was tendered by the managers of the Woman's Union. No effort was spared to make their visit in every way delightful. Miss Anthony lectured in the opera house at Seattle under the auspices of the Woman's Century

Club, and a reception was given by her hostess, Mrs. Kate Turner Holmes. Many inducements were offered for her to extend the visit, but she was desirous of returning to the field of work in California at the earliest possible moment and was absent only nine days.

Miss Anthony was invited by both Republican and Populist managers to address their ratification meetings in San Francisco, and received an ovation from the great audiences representing the two parties. One wing of the Democrats held their ratification meeting after night in the open air and of course she was not invited to speak, but the other wing extended a cordial invitation and she addressed them in Metropolitan Temple, receiving an enthusiastic greeting. The suffrage women themselves held a second mass meeting September 10, according to the Call, " amid a mighty outburst of popular enthusiasm, the like of which has seldom if ever been seen at a political meeting held in this city." Here again the part taken by prominent men from all political parties demonstrated the non-partisan character of the woman's campaign. This was Mrs. Catt's first appearance before a California audience and the papers said : " As she and the other ladies delivered their clear-cut, logical speeches, cheers rent the air and handkerchiefs and hats were waved with overmastering enthusiasm."

And so the months went by, with their cares and pleasures, their hopes and fears, their elation and depression. In her letters to her sister, Miss Anthony wrote : " Sometimes I have a homesick hour and feel as if I must leave all and rush back to my own hearthstone, but then I pull myself together and resolve to go through to the end." A similar campaign was in progress in Idaho and Mrs. Catt was there in August at the request of that State board, to represent the national association. They were very anxious that Miss Anthony should come also, but to their many letters she replied :

I should love dearly to go to Boise at once, as you request, and I should have been in Idaho during the last two months had it been possible for one human being to be in two places at the same time. . . . I learn that the men who believe in suffrage in your State, object to an open demand for party endorsement, but prefer a "still hunt." I have seen this tried before, but our opponents always can make a stiller hunt. Our only hope of success lies in open, free and full discussions through the newspapers and political party speakers. . . . Won't it be a magnificent feather in our cap if we get both California and Idaho into the fold this year? How beautiful the blue field will look with two more stars—five little gold stars! Remember that the woman suffrage stars are gold, not silver. Not that I think gold is better than silver, but it is a different color from the forty-five on the regular flag.[1]

There were, of course, some misrepresentations, both intentional and unintentional, of Miss Anthony's attitude. The fact of her speaking on the platforms of all political parties was something which many people could not comprehend, and the party organs could not refrain from twisting her remarks a little bit in the direction of their doctrines ; then would come a storm of protests from the other side, and she would have to explain what she actually said. Thus, with the reporters constantly at her elbow, the public watching every utterance and the politicians on the alert to discover what party she and her fellow-workers really did favor, she lived indeed for many months in "the fierce light that beats upon a throne."

"O, that I had you by my side ; what a team we would make!" she often wrote to Mrs. Stanton, who answered : "I read all the papers you send and watch closely the progress of the campaign. I feel at times as if I should fly to your help. We are the only class in history that has been left to fight its battles alone, unaided by the ruling powers. White labor and the freed black men had their champions, but where are ours?"

In June the National Republican Convention was held at St. Louis. Miss Anthony could not make the long journey but she sent the following resolution and asked its adoption : "The Republican Party in national convention assembled hereby recommends that Congress shall submit an amendment to the

[1] In Idaho all political State conventions, Republican, Populist and Democratic, endorsed the amendment, it received a majority of the popular vote, and the women now have full suffrage.

Federal Constitution providing that the right of citizens of the United States to vote shall not be denied or abridged by the United States, or by any State, on account of sex."

The platform committee labored and this is what it brought forth: "The Republican party is mindful of the rights and interests of women. Protection of American industries includes equal opportunities, equal pay for equal work, and protection to the home. We favor the admission of women to wider spheres of usefulness, and welcome their co-operation in rescuing the country from Democratic mismanagement and Populist misrule."

Miss Anthony's indignation, anger and contempt when she read this resolution can not be put into words. It required the combined efforts of those who were nearest her to prevent the expression of her opinion in reply to the many reporters and letters wanting to know how she regarded this plank. "You must not offend the Republicans and injure our amendment," they argued, and she would acquiesce and subside. Then, after thinking it over, she would again burst forth and declare the women of the country should not be compelled to submit to this insult without a protest from her. "Women want the suffrage as a sword to smite down Democratic and Populist misrule. Infamous!" she exclaimed again and again. "That climaxes all the outrages ever offered to women in the history of political platforms." To Mrs. Stanton she wrote: "O, that you were young and strong and free, and could fire off of the planet such ineffable slush as is being slobbered over our cause!" But she held her peace, and all the brainy women who were conducting this great campaign kept silent, although there was not one of them who did not feel exactly like Miss Anthony in regard to this plank. Nor was there a woman in the country, who was able to comprehend the resolution, that did not regard it as an insult and feel that she would prefer never again to have women mentioned in a national platform if the men who should make it had no higher conception of justice than this.

On October 11, Miss Anthony started on a southern tour,

speaking first at San Luis Obispo to an audience which crowded the hall. From here to Santa Barbara, through the courtesy of Superintendent Johnson, of the narrow gauge railroad, the train was stopped at every station for a ten-minute address. At some places a stage had been extemporized, at others she spoke from the rear platform of the car. Her coming had been announced and, even in those rather thinly settled regions, there would be as many as a thousand people gathered at the station. When she concluded, quantities of flowers would be thrown in her pathway and the platform literally banked with them.[1] After a stage ride of forty miles she received an enthusiastic welcome at Santa Barbara, where she was the guest of Dr. Ida Stambach. The ovation was continued at all the towns visited in the southern part of the State.

A little flurry had been caused early in the campaign by the announcement that the National W. C. T. U. Convention would be held in San Francisco during the autumn of 1896. Miss Anthony had written Miss Willard that she thought this would be very injudicious. She then had agreed to postpone it until after the election, and Miss Anthony again had objected, saying:

I am glad you think it will be possible to postpone your convention to November; but, you see, even to do that all California will be full of your advertisements, and the papers all telling how the W. C. T. U. is going to bring its convention to San Francisco immediately after the women have the right to vote, so as to educate them to destroy the wine-growing and brandy-distilling business; in other words, that it is going to start in the first thing to ruin what today is the one means of livelihood for immense numbers of ranchmen throughout the State. So, I hope—nay, I beseech—that you will withdraw the convention altogether from California for this year. I have had letters from the amendment campaign committee, and every one of them deplores the coming of the convention. . . .

Now, my dear, hold your convention any place but in a State where we are trying to persuade every license man, every wine-grower, every drinker and

---

[1] To commemorate this journey Miss Selina Solomons, of San Francisco, wrote a tender poem, beginning:

"She walks on roses! she whose feet
Have trod so long the stony way,
They tread who lead mankind to greet
The coming of a brighter day."

ANT.—56

every one who does not believe in prohibition, as well as every one who does, to vote "yes" on the woman suffrage question. If you only will do this, I am sure you will do the most effective work in the power of any mortal to secure the end we all so much desire.

Miss Willard replied in a cordial letter that she had not the slightest wish to antagonize her or the suffrage movement and would use her influence to have the place of the convention changed. To Mrs. B. Sturtevant Peet, president of the California W. C. T. U., who was somewhat in doubt as to the necessity for such change, Miss Anthony wrote:

What you say of the good influence of your national convention in San Francisco is true so far as concerns the actual Prohibition men; but we must consider those who are making their daily bread out of the manufacture as well as the sale of liquors. There are many excellent men in California who are not total abstainers, but who believe in wine as the people of Italy and France believe in it; and I think that, in waging our campaign, we should be careful not to run against the prejudices or the pecuniary interests of that class. As I have said before, if it were a Prohibition amendment which was pending I should think it exceedingly unwise to run that campaign under the banner of woman suffrage. The average human mind is incapable of taking in more than one idea at a time. The one we want to get into the heads of the voters this year is woman's enfranchisement, and we must pull every string with every possible individual man and class of men to secure their votes for this amendment. We should be extremely careful to base all our arguments upon the right of every individual to have his or her opinion counted at the ballot-box, whether it is in accordance with ours or not. Therefore, the amendment must not be urged as a measure for temperance, social purity, or any other reform, but simply as a measure to give to women the right to vote yea or nay on each and all of them. I want every woman in California to work for the amendment, but I want her to work in the name of suffrage, not of prohibition.

The national convention was withdrawn entirely from California, and the W. C. T. U. women, in most places, worked under the one banner of the suffrage amendment during the campaign. In proof that there was no feeling on the part of the leaders against Miss Anthony, it may be stated that she received official invitations to be present at the birthday celebration of Mrs. Peet, in April; to address the State W. C. T. U. Convention at Petaluma, in October; to attend the National Convention at St. Louis in November; and to join in the farewell reception to Miss Willard in New York on the eve of her departure for Europe.

The managers of the woman's campaign supposed of course that the endorsement by the Populist and Republican State Conventions meant not only that the speakers of those parties would advocate the suffrage plank just as they did the others in their respective platforms, but that they also would permit the women themselves to speak for it in their political meetings. When they applied to Mr. Wardall and the other members of the Populist Central Committee, the schedule was promptly furnished and they were assured that their speakers would be welcomed. When they applied to the Republican Central Committee, to their amazement, they were put off with an evasive answer. Meanwhile they had Miss Anthony, Miss Shaw, Mrs. Catt and other speakers waiting for engagements and did not dare make dates ahead lest it might interfere with the big Republican rallies which they wished them to address. Again and again they went to the Republican Central Committee and asked for the schedule of their meetings and the privilege of sending their speakers to them. Finally, after weeks of anxious waiting, the chairman, Major Frank McLaughlin, sent a letter to the suffrage headquarters saying in effect : " The committee had decided not to grant this privilege ; in the language used at one time by Miss Anthony, it meant ' too many bonnets at their meetings,' and they wished to reach the voters."

He added that they were at liberty to make any arrangements they chose with the county chairmen. This meant, of course, that they must ascertain the name and address of every county chairman in the State, watch the papers for the announcements of meetings, hold their speakers in reserve, and beg the privilege of having them heard. All this, when the endorsement of the suffrage amendment was the first plank in the Republican platform unanimously adopted by the State convention ! There was nothing, however, except to make the best of it ; but when they attempted to arrange with the county chairmen, they found Major McLaughlin had written them not to allow the women speakers on their platforms! While many of them refused to obey his orders, he had practically destroyed the best opportunity for reaching the people.

The Republican State Convention had enthusiastically adopted a resolution declaring for " the free coinage of silver at a ratio of 16 to 1." When the National Convention met in St. Louis soon afterwards it adopted a gold standard plank, and there they were! The Populists and Democrats who agreed on a financial plank saw here an opportunity and, in many counties, effected a fusion and held their meetings together. This, of course, nullified the permission given the women to put speakers on the Populist platform, since the Democrats, as a party, were opposed to woman suffrage, and there they were! If they attempted to hold simply suffrage meetings, they could get only audiences of women, because all the men were in attendance at the political rallies. So the only thing left was for the women in every city and town in the State, whenever a political mass meeting was advertised, to go to the managers and humbly beg to have one of their speakers on the platform.

This was not often refused, and it was just as easy to get this permission from Democrats as from Republicans. The former felt that if the amendment should carry they would not object to a little of the credit, and they soon found also that the women were a drawing card. Whenever there was a purely Populist meeting, a conspicuous place and all the time desired were given to the women, but at Republican, Democratic or Fusion meetings, they always were placed at the end of the program and allowed only five or, at most, ten minutes. In order simply to get this little word, the women speakers would make long journeys and sit on the platform until every long-winded male orator had finished his speech, and until they were ready to drop from their chairs. But the audience waited for them, no matter how late, and never failed to receive them with the wildest enthusiasm. Many times when the managers would have been willing to sandwich them between other speakers, the latter would object, saying the people would go home as soon as the women had finished!

As the campaign wore on it became a fight for life with the political parties. The Call, which had come out so valiantly for woman suffrage, had been struck in a vital part, i. e., in the counting-room, by the opponents of this measure, who withdrew valuable advertising and in every possible way sought to injure the paper. Its support was used by the other wing of the Republican party to create a prejudice against the candidates it advocated ; the principal stockholders were not friendly to the amendment ; as the organ of the Central Committee it was deprived of independent action. So it was not surprising that, long before the close of the campaign, the great fight which the Call agreed to make had dwindled to an occasional skirmish when the pleading of the women grew too strong to be resisted.

Almost without exception the Republican orators were silent on the question of woman suffrage, even those who personally favored it. The women wrote them, interviewed them and begged them to advocate the first plank in their platform as they did all the rest, and occasionally when they would go in a body and sit on the front seats to watch the speaker, he would say a few mild words in favor of the amendment, but there were several of the Democrats who did as much. Some of the Populists advocated it, but the most prominent, who always before had spoken for it, went through the entire campaign without so much as a mention, in order to secure Democratic support. When Thomas B. Reed came into the State, at the very end of the campaign, the women felt sure of an ally, as he had long been a pronounced advocate, but he did not so much as refer to the question in his tour of the State, although they bombarded him with letters which would have impressed a heart of stone. At the last grand rally in Oakland, the day before election, with Miss Anthony on one side of him and Miss Shaw on the other, he did say that he "knew of no more reason why a woman should not vote than why a man should not"—but the battle then was already lost.

Up to within a few weeks of election, in spite of all the

drawbacks, it looked as if the amendment would win. The general sentiment throughout the State seemed to be in favor. The mere mention of the subject at any meeting was received with the greatest enthusiasm. Almost every delegate body which assembled in convention during that summer adopted a resolution of endorsement; this was true of most of the church conferences, the teachers' institutes, the State Grange and farmers' institutes, the Chautauqua assemblies and countless others. And still the women watched and waited! There was one element more powerful than all these combined, which had not yet shown its hand. It never had failed in any State to fight woman suffrage to the death, and there was no reason to believe it would not kill it in California.

Ten days before election the fatal blow came. The representatives of the Liquor Dealers' League met in San Francisco and resolved " to take such steps as were necessary to protect their interests." The political leaders, the candidates, the rank and file of the voters recognized the handwriting on the wall. From that moment the fate of the amendment was sealed. The women had determined, from the beginning of the campaign, that they would give the liquor business no excuse to say its interests were threatened, and therefore the temperance question had been kept out of the discussion as had the religious, the tariff and the financial questions. They took the sensible view that it had no more place than these in the demand for women's right to vote as they pleased on all subjects. Therefore the action of the liquor dealers had no justification in anything which the women had said or done. It simply showed that they considered woman suffrage a dangerous foe. The following letter, signed by the wholesale liquor firms of San Francisco, was sent to the saloon-keepers, hotel proprietors, druggists and grocers throughout the State:

At the election to be held on November 3, Constitutional Amendment No. Six, which gives the right to vote to women, will be voted on.

It is to your interest and ours to vote against this amendment. We request and urge you to vote and work against it and do all you can to defeat it.

See your neighbor in the same line of business as yourself, and have him be with you in this matter.

The men in the slums of San Francisco were taken in squads and, with sample ballots, were taught how to put the cross against the suffrage amendment and assured that if it carried there never would be another glass of beer sold in the city. When the chairman of the press committee went to a prominent editor, who was opposed to woman suffrage and knew that these things were being done, and asked if there were no way by which some suffrage literature could be given to those men so that they might see there was no ground for these threats, he said: "Most of them can not read and if they could the whiskey men would never allow a page of it to get into their hands." In what way the liquor dealers worked upon the political parties, it is not necessary to speculate. The methods were not new and are pretty well understood. They control tens of thousands of votes not only in California but in every State, which they can deliver to either of the great parties that does their bidding and regards their interests.

It is absurd, however, to attribute the defeat of the suffrage amendment wholly to the liquor dealers, or to the densely ignorant, or to the foreigners. In the wealthiest and most aristocratic wards of San Francisco and Oakland, where there were none of these, the proportion of votes against the amendment was just as great as it was in the slum wards of the two cities. Those respectable, law-abiding citizens who cast their ballots against the amendment, thereby voted to continue the power of the above mentioned classes.

For weeks before the election, the most frantic efforts were made by the politicians to register new voters and colonize them in the wards where they would be most needed.[1] Columns of appeals were issued in all the newspapers to get the vast numbers of lately arrived immigrants to come to the city hall and register. Men were sent around ringing big bells and calling upon them to do this, and interpreters were employed to explain that it would not cost them a cent. Finally the

[1] Some of the women going the rounds with suffrage petitions in San Francisco found a house consisting of one room with three cots, where were registered twenty-seven voters.

registry books were carried to the parks and other places where these men were employed, in order to secure their names.

Meanwhile the intelligent, order-loving, sober and industrious women of the State were making such efforts as never were made by any class of men, to secure this same privilege of placing in the ballot-box and having counted their opinions on questions relating to the public welfare;—opinions, one would think, that ought to be considered of as much value to the State as those which such strenuous attempts were being made to obtain. It seems, however, that intelligence, morality and thrift must wait the pleasure of ignorance, vice and idleness.

During the months of the early spring, through the efforts of a few women who worked without pay and used only their spare moments, the names of nearly 30,000 women were secured to a petition asking for the suffrage. This, of course, represented only a fraction of those which might have been obtained by continued effort, but a petition signed by even 30,000 men would have been considered worthy of attention. The vast majority of women have no money of their own and those who work for wages, as a rule, receive but a pittance, and yet there were raised in California for this amendment campaign almost $19,000, and the amount contributed by men was so small as not to be worth mentioning. The financial success was due very largely to the State treasurer, Mrs. Austin Sperry. She not only made a donation of $500, but borrowed from the bank on her personal note, when necessary, and signed blank checks to be used when the treasury was empty and repaid when outstanding pledges were collected. Mrs. Phœbe Hearst headed the list with $1,000. Mrs. Stanford gave almost as much in railroad transportation to the speakers and organizers. The next largest contributor was Mrs. Knox Goodrich, of San Jose, who for nearly thirty years had stood in California a faithful advocate of woman suffrage, giving time, money and influence. She added to her past donations nearly $500 for this campaign. Mrs. Sargent's munificence has been mentioned. A few women subscribed

Sarah L. Knox. Goodrich

$100 each, but all the rest was given in sums ranging down to a few cents.

The true record of these contributions would wring the heart of every man in the State. A large photograph of Miss Anthony and Miss Shaw was given for every $2 pledge, and many poor seamstresses and washerwomen fulfilled their pledges in twenty - five cent installments, coming eight times with their mite. Often when there was not enough money on hand at headquarters to buy a postage stamp, there would come a timid knock at the door and a poorly dressed woman would enter with a quarter or half-dollar, saying, "I have done without tea this week to bring you this money;" or a poor little clerk would say, "I made a piece of fancy work evenings and sold it for this dollar." Many a woman who worked hard ten hours a day to earn her bread, would come to headquarters and carry home a great armload of circulars to

regard with deep respect your heroic life and entire devotion to the cause you have consecrated it to.

Yours very sincerely,
Phebe A. Hearst.

fold and address after night. And there were teachers and stenographers and other workingwomen who went without a winter cloak in order to give the money to this movement for freedom. This pathetic story ought to be written in full and given to every man who eases his conscience by saying, "The majority of women do not want to vote;" and to every well-fed, well-clothed woman who declares in her selfish ease, "I have all the rights I want."

Knowing that if the suffrage amendment were placed first or last among the six which were to be voted on, it would be a target for those who could not read, the ladies wrote to the Secretary of State asking that it be placed in the middle of the list. He answered, June 26: "It shall be as you request and the suffrage amendment be third in order as certified by me to the various county clerks." When the tickets were printed, however, it was placed at the end of the list and thus necessarily at the end of the whole ticket, making it a conspicuous mark. The explanation given was that Governor Budd had directed the amendments to be placed on the ballot in the same order as they had appeared in his proclamation. As this had not been issued until July 20, a month after the official request of the ladies had been granted, one must conclude there was a mistake somewhere. The results were exactly what had been feared. In San Francisco alone hundreds of ballots were cast on which there was only one cross and that against the amendment; not even the presidential electors voted for.

There were 247,454 votes cast on the suffrage amendment; 110,355 for; 137,099 against; defeated by 26,734. The majority against in San Francisco was 23,772; in Alameda county, comprising Oakland, Alameda and Berkeley, 3,627; total, 27,-399—665 votes more than the whole majority cast against the amendment. Berkeley gave a majority in favor, so in reality it was defeated by the vote of San Francisco, Oakland and Alameda.[1] Alameda is the banner Republican county and gave a good majority for the Republican ticket. There never

_____

[1] Los Angeles gave a majority of 3,600 in favor of the amendment.

had been a hope of carrying San Francisco for the amendment, but the result in Alameda county was a most unpleasant surprise, as the voters were principally Republicans and Populists, both of whom were pledged in the strongest possible manner in their county conventions to support the amendment, and every newspaper in the county had declared in favor of it. The fact remains, however, that a change of 13,400 votes in the entire State would have carried the amendment; and proves beyond question that, if sufficient organization work had been done, this might have been accomplished in spite of the combined efforts of the liquor dealers and the political bosses.

Near midnight of election day, a touching sight might have been witnessed on a certain street in San Francisco: two women over seventy years of age, one the beloved wife of a man whom California had selected as its representative in the United States Senate and whom the government had sent as its minister to the court of Germany; the other a woman universally admitted to be the peer of any man in the country in statesmanship and knowledge of public affairs—Mrs. A. A. Sargent and Susan B. Anthony. In the darkness of night, arm in arm, they went down the street, peering into the windows of the rough little booths where the judges and clerks of the election were counting votes. The rooms were black with tobacco smoke and in one they saw a man fall off his chair too drunk to finish the count. They listened to the oaths and jeers as the votes were announced against the suffrage amendment, to which they had given almost their lives. Then in the darkness they crept silently home, mournfully realizing that women must wait for another and better generation of men to give them the longed-for freedom.

The next morning when Miss Anthony came down to breakfast she found a group in the Sargent library reading the news of the election, and all looked at her in sorrowing sympathy. She stood still in the center of the room for a moment and then said sadly: "I don't care for myself, I am used to defeat, but these dear California women who have worked so hard, how can they bear it?"

Miss Anthony not only had donated her own services but had paid her secretary's salary of $75 per month and permitted her to give her entire time to the State headquarters for seven months, while she herself attended to the drudgery of her immense correspondence whenever she could get a spare hour. Even at the small sum of $25 for a regular speech, she would have contributed over $3,000 to this campaign, in addition to the scores of little parlor and club addresses. She gave her services freely and willingly and did not regret them, but often said that the California campaign was the most harmonious and satisfactory of any in which she ever was engaged. There was not the slightest friction between herself and the State association or State headquarters, and most of those prominent in the work were of such refinement and nobility of character that it was a pleasure to be associated with them. Not a day passed that she did not receive some token of affection from the women of the State. The Sargent home was filled with the flowers and baskets and boxes of fresh and dried fruits, etc., which were sent to her.[1]

On November 5, two days after the election, a large body of California women met in Golden Gate Hall to hold the annual State Suffrage Convention. Miss Anthony and all the national officers remained to help. There was not a trace of defeat or disappointment; all were brave, cheerful and ready to go to work again. Twelve hundred dollars were raised to settle all outstanding bills and the campaign closed without a dollar of indebtedness. As Mrs. Sargent was going abroad, a worthy presidential successor was elected, Mrs. Mary Wood Swift, wife of John F. Swift, minister to Japan, a fine presiding officer, a lady of much culture, travel and social prestige, who

---

[1] In her president's report, at the next annual convention, Mrs. Sargent said:

"Susan B. Anthony! We can never forget her labor of love and devotion to the cause of woman suffrage in California. She counted not her life dear to her so that she could help to awaken the interest of men and women in the great principle to which she has devoted her life. She was not cold, nor hungry, nor tired, nor sleepy, while there was a chance to push forward the work. Throughout the campaign Miss Anthony gave her own services and those of her secretary without money and without price. She reminds one of the great Niagara, which would be wonderful if its waters rolled and dashed for only a short period; but when they roll and dash on ceaselessly, nor ever stop to rest, there the wonder of it all comes in, and we can only gaze, admire and acknowledge the great law or power behind it."

had rendered valuable service throughout the campaign. The next evening the suffrage forces held a grand rally in Metropolitan Temple. Every seat in that fine auditorium was occupied and the aisles were crowded. It was not a meeting of the adherents of a lost cause, but of one which had suffered only temporary defeat. Miss Anthony presided and **was given a**

Yours with love
Mary Wood Swift

true California ovation and, as her voice rang out with all its old-time vigor, there was not one in that vast audience but hoped she might return to lead her hosts to victory.

Saturday evening at 6 o'clock the seven eastern women started homewards, laden with tokens of affection, accompanied across the bay by a large number of loving friends, and moving off amidst smiles and tears and a shower of fragrant blossoms.

CHAPTER XLVIII.

N the way home from California Miss Anthony and Mrs. Catt stopped at Reno, Nev., lecturing there Sunday, while Miss Shaw hastened on to speak at Salt Lake City. Then all met at Kansas City to attend the Missouri convention, where they were the guests of Mrs. Sarah Chandler Coates. The papers refer to Miss Anthony's speeches at this convention as being the very strongest she ever had made, and of her perfect physical condition at the close of an eight months' campaign.

She went from here directly home, and on November 19 a brilliant banquet was given in honor of Miss Shaw and herself at the Hotel Livingston by the Political Equality Club. Mary Lewis Gannett was toast-mistress and about 250 guests were seated at the tables. This was followed by the State convention at Rochester. After a few days' rest Miss Anthony went to the home of Mrs. Catt, near New York, where a business meeting was held of the national executive board. With Mrs. Avery she then took one of the great Sound steamers for Boston to attend a meeting of the National Woman's Council. A reception was given by Mrs. Charles W. Bond, of Commonwealth Avenue, and one at the Hotel Vendome. She ran up to Concord, N. H., for a few days' visit with her aged friends, Mr. and Mrs. Parker Pillsbury and Mrs. Armenia S. White. Then back again to the Garrisons', and out to Medford for a day with Mrs. Edward M. Davis, the daughter of Lucretia Mott.

She left Boston December 9, to fulfill a promise made to

Elizabeth Buffum Chace, to spend her ninetieth birthday at her home in Valley Falls, R. I.   Mrs. Chace had written a number of letters with her own trembling hand to arrange for this visit.   It was only a family party, but the diary tells of the cake with ninety little candles, and other birthday features. Anna Shaw came in time for the supper, and the next day Mrs. Chace sent them in her carriage to Providence to attend the State convention.   Here they were guests in the handsome old Eddy homestead, and Miss Anthony addressed a large audience in the evening.   She stopped a day in New York to tell Mrs. Stanton about the California campaign, and Sunday morning reached her own dear home.   Her old and loved friend, Maria Porter, had died the preceding night, and she attended the funeral services next day.   On December 23 she went to Niagara Falls with her stenographer to secure reminiscences from her cousin, Sarah Anthony Burtis, aged eighty-six, who was a teacher in the home school at Battenville over sixty years before.

The year just closed had been busy but pleasant.   It had brought the usual number of tokens of appreciation, one of which was notice of election as honorary member of the Chicago Woman's Club.   Among the scores of invitations on file were one from Judge George F. Danforth to meet the justices of the appellate court at his home; and one to the golden wedding of her old fellow-laborers, Giles B. and Catharine F. Stebbins, at Detroit, the latter one of the secretaries of that famous first convention of 1848.   Major James B. Pond, the well-known lecture manager, wrote Miss Mary Anthony: "Thank you for your kind letter and the excellent photograph of your great sister, whom I have admired and hoped and prayed for since I was a poor boy out in Kansas.   I still believe she will be spared to witness a general triumph of her noble cause."   The letter contained an offer of $100 for a parlor lecture by Miss Anthony at Jersey City.

A few of Miss Anthony's own letters, taken almost at random from copies on her file, will illustrate the vast scope of her correspondence and her peculiarly trenchant mode of expression. To one who wanted a testimonial from her that she might show in vindication of certain accusations, she wrote:

I went through all the fire of charges of stealing, and of every other crime in the whole calendar, twenty-five years ago—charges made, too, by people of vastly more influence than any of the women who are talking and writing today about you. I never made a public denial of one of them, through all the years of the bitterest kind of persecution, and believe I was greatly the gainer by working right on and ignoring them. It will be the mistake of your life if you go into print in your own defence. Your denial will reach a new set of people and start them to talking, while the ones who read the original charges will never see the refutation of them.

To one of the newly-enfranchised women of Utah:

The one word I should have to say to the women throughout your State would be, not so much to try to get women elected to the offices as to get the best persons, whether men or women. Naturally there will be a far less number of women than of men capable of holding office, from the very fact of their long disfranchisement. I do hope your women therefore will set a good example not only for Utah, but also for the States where they are not enfranchised; namely, that of proving it is not the spoils of office they are after. I think the women of Wyoming always have been wonderfully judicious in not being anxious to hold offices themselves, but mightily anxious as to what men hold them. It will be considered a strong objection to woman suffrage if the vast majority of your women should prove themselves mere partisans.

To a New York cousin: "Your little birthday present, the Book of Proverbs, came duly. Solomon's wise sayings, however, don't help me very much in my work of trying to persuade men to do justice to women. These men and their progenitors for generations back have read Solomon over and over again, and learned nothing therefrom of fair play for woman, and I fear generations to come will continue to read to as little purpose. At any rate, I propose to peg away in accordance with my own sense of wisdom rather than Solomon's. All those old fellows were very good for their time, but their wisdom needs to be newly interpreted in order to apply to people of today."

In answer to a letter from Illinois asking the secret of her success in life:

If I may be said to have made a success of my life, the one great element
     ANT.—57

in it has been constancy of purpose—not allowing myself to be switched off the main road or tempted into bypaths of other movements. It always has been clear to me that woman suffrage is the one great principle underlying all reforms. With the ballot in her hand woman becomes a vital force—declaring her will for herself, instead of praying and beseeching men to declare it for her It has been a long, hard fight, a dark, discouraging road, but all along the way here and there a little bright spot to cheer us on. And now we have four true republics, whose women are full-fledged citizens, and the prospects are hopeful for others soon to follow in the wake of those blessed four. One of the most cheering things in these days is the large number of young women who are entering the work, bringing to it a new, strong enthusiasm which will push on to victory. The women over all the country are waking up to the fact that truly to possess themselves, to have their opinions respected, they must have this right of suffrage.

A letter from the secretary of a national conference which was seeking to bring about a union of reformers, Prohibitionists, Free Silver advocates, etc., asked her assistance and called forth the following response :

It is all very well for you men, who have the power to make and unmake political parties, to form a third, fourth or fiftieth party, as the case may be ; but as for myself and all who are of my class, disfranchised and helpless, we have nothing to do with any of them—old or new—except to ask each and all to put a woman suffrage plank in their platform and educate their members to place a ballot in the hands of women. I never have identified myself with any political party, but have stood outside of all, asking each to pledge itself to the enfranchisement of women. Whenever any one of them has asked me to speak in its meetings on the suffrage question, I have accepted the invitation, but I never have advocated the specific measures of any.

So, you see, I can be of no help to you, but I do know that no one of the reform political parties ever will amount to much standing alone, and that it would be a good thing for all of them to come together in one body. I might say, however, that least of all could I join yours, which makes "God the author of civil government." If such civil government as we have was made by God, what reason is there to expect any improvement in the future ?

From a letter to Isabella Beecher Hooker :

Fortune indeed does not smile any too favorably upon us who feel so longingly the need to use money. I am crippled all the time and prevented from doing what I might by lack of funds. The old faith would say, I suppose, that whom the Lord loveth he chasteneth financially, but seems to me I could better do His work and my own for the regeneration of the world, if I had the money to do it with. . . . What a fuss the men are making nowadays over "good government"—the idiots! Can't they see it is impossible to improve things until they get a new and better balance of power that will outweigh the one which now pulls down the political scales and makes decency kick the beam every time? It does try my soul that we can not make them see they are simply trying to lift themselves by their bootstraps. Well, they are born of disfranchised mothers, a subject class, and one can not expect different results.

If I could spare the time and money I would love to accept your invitation to sit with you and your dear John in your summer retreat, and chat over the world of work for our good cause. Of the before and the after I know absolutely nothing, and have very little desire and less time to question or to study. I know this seems very material to you, and yet to me it is wholly spiritual, for it is giving time and study rather to making things better in the *between*, which is really all that we can influence; but perhaps when I can no longer enter into active, practical work, I may lapse into speculations.

To a debating society asking her opinion on the question of " educated and property suffrage : "

I always have taken the negative; that is, have believed in universal suffrage without either property or educational qualification. I hold that every citizen has a right to a voice in the government under which he lives. While an education is highly desirable, yet a man may be unable to read but may attend political meetings, talk with his neighbors and form intelligent opinions. He may be honest and beyond bribery, and a more desirable voter than many wily and unscrupulous men who have a graduate's diploma. It is, however, the duty of the State to educate its citizens; and the Australian ballot, which has been largely adopted, is in itself an educational qualification.

As to a property qualification: while in the majority of cases, perhaps, the possession of property is evidence of ability and thrift, there are many who do not own property and yet are possessed of good sense and are more capable of casting an honest and intelligent ballot than some of the wealthy men of the country; then, too, those who have least are the ones who suffer most from the legislation of the rich, and need the ballot for self-protection. I am decidedly opposed to a property qualification.

To one who was in deep grief she said in an affectionate letter: " Do assure me that you are beginning to think of your dear one as he was when well and moving about in his always helpful and cheering manner. To get far enough from the sickness, the suffering and the death of our friends, so as to be able to have only the thought of them in their full vigor of life, is the greatest joy which possibly can come to those who have lost their beloved."

While Miss Anthony was thus constantly giving out from

the vast wealth of her heart and brain, she was receiving, also, from all parts of the country the strong and loving tributes of noble souls. A beautiful one which shines on the pages of 1896 was pronounced by the eloquent Dr. H. W. Thomas, of Chicago, in the course of a Sunday sermon entitled "Progressive Greatness," delivered to a large audience assembled in McVicker's Theater :

A Washington and a Lincoln have come in our great century, and between their birthdays was born a Susan B. Anthony, whose grand life has been given to a noble cause; once the target for the cruel and bitter shafts of ridicule; now deemed the noblest among women. The task of Washington and Lincoln could not be complete till the crown was placed on the brow of woman as well as man; and when the angels shall call Susan B. Anthony to the life immortal, her name, her memory on earth should and will take its place among the martyrs and saints of liberty, not for man alone, but for woman and child."

To watch the old year out and the New Year in, Miss Anthony went to Geneva, and here spent a few days very pleasantly with Elizabeth Smith Miller and her guest, Harriot Stanton Blatch. Among the New Year's remembrances were $50 from Mrs. Elda A. Orr, of Reno, Nev.; $150 from Mrs. Gross, of Chicago; and $300 from Mrs. Cornelia Collins Hussey, of Orange, N. J. The usual number of congratulatory letters were received from all classes of people, high and low, old and young, white and colored.

To show their wide range two or three may be given. From Mrs. Ellen M. Henrotin, president of the General Federation of Women's Clubs: "I send to you on the New Year a fraternal greeting and my best wishes that this may prove for you and the interests you represent, a year of fulfillment. We are all serving the same cause and we are surely among the happy ones of earth that we are enabled to assist, by even a slight impetus, the ' power which makes for righteousness.' . . . Therefore I send you today my heartfelt wishes for the continued success of your cause and the peace and prosperity of your life. "

Her friend of fifty years, John W. Hutchinson, the last of that never-equalled family of singers, sent his New Year's greetings and added: "I bless you and your work. Wonderful possibilities will be the result of this great movement, which you have led, for equal rights and the franchise for women." The president of the National Council of Women, Mary Lowe Dickinson, an earnest, efficient worker for humanity, said in the course of a long letter dated January 9:

I pray that all strength and blessing of every kind may crown this coming year of your life; and O, how earnestly I hope that in it you may see the fruition of some of the work that you have been struggling with these many, many years. When I run over in my mind the present situation of the cause you represent—which seems to me more and more the one cause which must succeed if we are going to have genuine success anywhere else—I see what ground you have for encouragement and what a vast advance has been made; but I see, too, how slow it must seem to you, and how weary of waiting you must become. I know no courage like yours, and I do that courage full honor.

She had received a telegram of greeting from Frances E. Willard as soon as she arrived home from California, and January 5 accepted her urgent invitation for a little visit with her at the sanitarium of Dr. Cordelia Green, Castile; and while there addressed a parlor gathering of the patients. On January 15 she was guest of honor at a luncheon given by the Educational and Industrial Union of Rochester, at the Genesee clubhouse, to the State executive committee of the Federation of Clubs. Mrs. Charlotte Perkins Stetson spent a few days with her, and she arranged for her to hold Sunday evening services in the Unitarian church. On January 20 the two ladies, with Miss Mary, started for the twenty-ninth annual convention of the national association, which was to be held this year at Des Moines, Ia. The thermometer was 15° below zero, the snow very deep, and Miss Anthony's friends saw her set forth on the journey to this cold western city with much anxiety. All their protests, however, were not sufficient to keep her at home; but she thought with much longing of the clean, beautiful streets of Washington, the mild climate, the Congressional committees, the crowds of visitors there from various parts of the country who always came to the convention, and she felt more strongly than ever that it was a serious mistake to take it away from the national capital.

She stopped at Chicago for a few days, and a characteristic little entry in her diary says: "I slept on a $6,000 bed last night; my! how much good suffrage work could have been done with that money." On the afternoon of January 23, Miss Anthony addressed a large meeting of the Woman's Club and in the course of her remarks paid a tribute to that organization, in which she said: "This is the banner club of the United States, not because it has such nice women for members, and not even because it is located in Chicago, but because it is a club which does a large amount of practical work."

Mrs. Foster Avery joined the party at Chicago and they reached Des Moines January 24, where they found the rest of the executive board, and all were entertained in the suburban mansion of James and Martha C. Callanan. The meetings were held in the Central Christian church, whose pastor, Rev. H. O. Breeden, extended a cordial greeting. Notwithstanding the extreme severity of the weather, 24° below zero, the audience-room was crowded to its capacity at every public session, and overflow meetings were held. The convention was officially welcomed by Governor Francis M. Drake and Mayor John McVicar; Mrs. Adelaide Ballard, State president, made the opening address, and Mrs. Macomber spoke in behalf of the women's clubs of the city. State Senator Rowan was one of the speakers. Among the letters of greeting was one from Miss Kitty Reed, daughter of Speaker Thomas B. Reed. The memorial services showed that never in any previous year had so long a list of friends to the cause passed away as in 1896. There were thirty-seven names mentioned in the resolutions.[1]

In Miss Anthony's address she spoke of the great victories in 1896, as shown by the full enfranchisement of the women of Utah and Idaho. Mrs. M. C. Woods, from the latter State, presented an interesting account of the late campaign and an outline of their work for the future. Her mother, Emmeline B. Wells, made the report for Utah. Delegates were present

[1] Among them were Harriet Beecher Stowe, Sarah B. Cooper, Drs. Hiram Corson and Caroline B. Winslow, Judges E. G. Merrick and O. P. Stearns, Mary Grew, J. Elizabeth Jones, Hannah Tracy Cutler, Sarah Southwick.

from twenty States, and most of them were entertained in the hospitable homes of the city. A reception, attended by 500 guests, was tendered by Mr. and Mrs. Hubbell, at their elegant residence on Terrace Hill. An imaginative reporter on this occasion transformed Miss Anthony's historic garnet velvet gown, worn for the past fourteen years, into a "magnificent royal purple," and her one simple little pin into "handsome diamonds." A pleasant reception also was given by the Woman's Club in their commodious parlors. The daily newspapers contained excellent reports of the convention, but not one gave editorial endorsement of the cause it represented.

Those who believed in holding the alternate national conventions away from Washington were satisfied with the result; those who thought differently continued to hold the same opinion, and among the latter was Miss Anthony, who soon afterwards wrote to one of the business committee:

The conventions at Atlanta and Des Moines have but confirmed me in my judgment that our delegated body always should meet in Washington. For local propaganda both were undoubtedly good, but for effect in securing Congressional action, absolutely nil. I believe in resuming our old plan of holding at least two conventions every year, one for the election of officers and for its influence upon Congress in Washington every winter; the other in whatsoever State we have constitutional amendments pending, where we need to do our greatest amount of work in that direction. The best way for the national association to help create local sentiment is to build up and make a success of the different State annual meetings, and to have at least two of its ablest and most popular speakers attend as many of them as possible every year; and I think by this means we can do a great deal more to make the States feel that the national is mother to them, than by once in a lifetime holding a delegate convention within their borders. I am more and more convinced that some of the national officers must be present at every State annual meeting, and if well advertised there would be as many representatives of the local clubs present as go to our national convention.

On the way home from Des Moines Miss Anthony spent a few days at Indianapolis. The evening of February 3, Mrs. Sewall gave a reception in her honor, to which were invited the governor, members of the legislature, State officials and their wives, members of the Woman's Council and their husbands. At one end of the large drawing-room, on a slightly raised platform covered with rugs, sat Miss Anthony and Indiana's most revered woman, Zerelda G. Wallace, to whom Mrs. Sewall presented the guests.   Later in the evening both of these ladies, from their "throne," as it was laughingly called, gave pleasant informal addresses, to which Senator Roots responded on behalf of the legislature.   The next day Mrs. Wallace and Miss Anthony's old friend, Hon. George W. Julian, were entertained at luncheon and had a long afternoon chat.   In the evening a reception was given for her by Mr. John C. and Mrs. Lillian Wright Dean at their pleasant home "The Pines."

The morning of February 5 Miss Anthony was invited to address a joint session of the Indiana legislature in the Assembly chamber.   The judges of the supreme and appellate courts and most of the State officials were present, and all the visitors' seats on the floor and in the galleries were filled with Indianapolis ladies.   Miss Anthony was introduced with words of praise by Representative Packard, and spoke for an hour, making her usual strong plea for a Sixteenth Amendment enfranchising women.

On February 6, at 9 A. M., in the midst of rain and sleet, she arrived in Rochester and, in less than an hour, reporters from every newspaper in the city were on hand for an interview.   They had learned long since that they always were sure of a cordial reception at her cozy home, and that the returned traveller would not fail to tell them something which would make interesting reading.   Miss Anthony was actuated by two motives in this: One was her desire to get as much suffrage news as possible into the papers, for no one could have a higher appreciation of the value of the press; the other was a strong sentiment of admiration and friendship for the faithful and industrious men and women who earn a living at newspaper work.

Sunday night, February 14, the birthday of Frederick Douglass was observed in the Plymouth Congregational Church. Miss Anthony presided over the large meeting and introduced the speakers.

THE ANTHONY RESIDENCE.

SINCE 1865, ROCHESTER, N. Y.

There had been something in the air of Rochester for several weeks, something of a social nature in which most of the people in the city seemed interested, and it promised to culminate on the approaching 15th of February, when Miss Anthony should be eleven times seven years old.   This famous birthday, which had been beautifully celebrated in New York, Washington and numbers of other cities and towns throughout the country, also had been often pleasantly observed in Rochester; but it was thought by many people here that it was time Miss Anthony's own city should hold a celebration which should eclipse all on record.   The first intimation she had was the receipt of this invitation:

The woman's clubs of this city are planning to give a reception in your honor at Powers Hall on the evening of your seventy-seventh birthday, February 15, 1897. They have chosen this means of publicly expressing the great esteem in which they hold you, and the pride they feel in reckoning among their number a woman of national reputation. They trust that this date will be satisfactory, and this manner of showing their respect not distasteful to you. Very sincerely,   OLIVE DAVIS,
Corresponding Secretary of the Committee on Arrangements.

The committee was composed of one member of each of the sixteen woman's clubs, and the admirable manner in which the affair was conducted certainly indicated that it was in the hands of representative women.[1]   Most of the Rochester papers

---

[1] The idea of giving the reception originated among the members of the Wednesday Club, some of whom conceived the thought that it was time for the women of Rochester in some way to recognize Miss Anthony's ability, energy and labors in behalf of her sex. . . . Reformers, as a rule, are not popular in their day, and Miss Anthony ran the gauntlet of derision and abuse years ago, but today the magnificent services she has rendered for woman are everywhere recognized.

The plans have been perfected upon a very elaborate scale. The following are represented in the movement: the Wednesday Club, the Ethical Society, the Women's Educational and Industrial Union, the Wellesley Association, the Cornell Association, the Coterie, the Woman's Saturday Club, the Holyoke Association, the Jewish Council, the Sisterhood of Berith Kodesh, the Ignorance Club, the Tuesday Reading Club, the Livingston Park Seminary Alumnæ, the Rochester Female Academy Alumnæ, the Ladies' Travellers' Club, and Mrs. Hall's Art Class.

The reception is not to women only, but it is expected that a large number of men will be present. [Then follows a list of names of many of the prominent ladies of Rochester, who acted as a reception committee, and of equally well-known young men, who served as ushers.]—Democrat and Chronicle.

contained editorials of congratulation. Among others the Post-Express said of the celebration:

Its purpose is to indicate the esteem in which she is held by the people of the city of which she has, for many years, been a resident. It is not intended as a demonstration in behalf of the cause with which she has been especially identified. Its meaning is deeper and its scope is broader than this. It is the woman, rather than the advocate, who is to be honored. . . .

Rochester is proud of Susan B. Anthony—proud that it can call her its citizen. It has come to appreciate her quality. It understands, not alone that she has stood in the front ranks of those who have done battle for the equality of woman with man at the ballot-box, but that she has also done much for the emancipation of woman from civil thralldom and social inferiority, and that in all good causes she has been distinguished—in philanthropies as in politics, in the reformation of moral abuses as in the righting of what seemed to her civic wrongs. As her work has proceeded, she has conquered prejudice and persuaded respect—respect for herself independent of and even superior to that for the causes in which she has enlisted. And so it occurs that the citizens of Rochester, without regard to the opinions they entertain upon woman suffrage and cognate movements, but wholly in admiration and affection for a noble woman, unite in the reception which awaits her, cordial and full of meaning. It will be a notable occasion, and one long to be remembered.

The daily papers gave long and elaborate reports of this great reception, headed, "Our beloved Susan; Two thousand hands grasped by the Grand Old Woman;" "Rochester Shows its Love for Her," etc., etc. A portion of the Herald account may be quoted as indicating the tone of all:

The reception accorded to Susan B. Anthony at Powers Hall by the woman's clubs of Rochester was one of the most brilliant events of the kind ever held in this city. All the prominent people of both sexes were there, and each vied with the others in doing honor to the woman whose splendid attributes of mind and heart have reflected so much credit on the city. But little preliminary work was needed, as it partook largely of the nature of a spontaneous tribute. Fully 2,000 people, representing the beauty, wealth and intelligence of the city, passed before this unostentatious, kindly woman during the evening and esteemed it an honor to press her hand.

The guests began to arrive at 8:30 o'clock and continued to come in a steady stream for two hours thereafter. Miss Anthony stood at the western end of the large room and around her were gathered the reception committee, composed of representatives from each of the woman's clubs in the city. The guests formed in line as they entered and each in succession took the hand of Miss Anthony. She greeted every one cordially and had a pleasant word for each. In one hand she held a beautiful bouquet of white and yellow roses sent by Miss Frances E. Willard.

There were more than Rochester's most distinguished citizens; hundreds of the poor and the humble, a number of colored people, men and women in all the walks of life, thronged the great hall surrounded with famous paintings and radiant with electric lights, flowers and beautiful costumes. They came to grasp the hand of one who had made no distinction of race or rank or belief in her fifty years' work of uplifting all humanity. If these had not been present, Miss Anthony would have felt that her own city had not offered its full tribute of recognition.

At the Anthony home the day was a happy one. Rev. Anna Shaw came to help celebrate. The house was filled with guests from out of town and many callers, and the bell was ringing all day for telegrams, letters and packages. There were potted plants and cut flowers, baskets of violets and hyacinths, and great bunches of roses and carnations. Letters and telegrams came from California and Massachusetts, and a number of States between. Clubs of many descriptions sent messages, and even Sunday-schools offered greetings. Mariana W. Chapman, president New York State Suffrage Association, expressed the congratulations of that body, and from all the National-American officers came words of appreciation. Among these were the following from the national organizer, Carrie Chapman Catt:

When a woman lives to be seventy-seven years old, having given a whole half-century and more to the cause of human liberty, her age becomes a crown of glory, before which every lover of progress bows in acknowledgment. Such a woman is she whom we know as "Saint Susan." Upon her birthday I have but one wish, and in this millions of grateful American women join with me; may she live in health and strength undiminished, until she witnesses the last woman in the United States blessed with all the political privileges of citizenship. If this wish might be fulfilled, I know it would bring the highest joy ever permitted a human being; therefore because I love her tenderly I make it, with gratitude for her years of service and with a reverence unspeakable for the woman whose courage, determination and adherence to principle made the service possible.

A few evenings later Miss Anthony attended a meeting held in Rochester by the Cuban League. As soon as she entered she was invited to a seat on the stage and then the audience insisted on a speech. Finally she came forward and said:

From the report of the first outrage in Cuba down to the present time, there has not been a moment but that its people have had my sympathy. Never since I began to know the meaning of the word "freedom" has anything taken a stronger hold on me than this struggle in Cuba. Even where all men are free, women are not, and I trust that when Cuban men achieve their independence and frame their constitution, they will not forget the women who have borne the struggle with them, as our Revolutionary fathers forgot the women who toiled by their side. The men of only four out of forty-five States of our republic have yet granted liberty to the women. I never can speak in a meeting like this without bearing testimony to the cowardice of the men of this nation in refusing to make the women free. I believe in liberty and equality for every human being under every flag, not for men alone but for women also.

The last of February a telegram announced the death of Maude, wife of Senator L. H. Humphrey, who but a few weeks before had visited the Anthony home, and stated that the husband desired Miss Anthony to speak at the funeral. She was a young and lovely wife and mother, treasurer of the State Federation of Clubs and an officer of the State and county suffrage associations. It was said that Miss Anthony spoke as one inspired of the woman in whose death everything good had lost a helpful hand, who had gone out of life with no fear for herself but only loving thoughtfulness for others. She told of her courage in following the truth wherever it might lead, of the freedom into which she had grown, and the beautiful faith and trust in which she had lived; she said that it was such who walked with God, and that her spiritual life could be comprehended only by those who lived on the same high plane. It was a deep regret to all who heard this exquisite eulogy that it was not preserved word for word.

Reference has been made in a preceding chapter to Miss Anthony's preparations for the writing of her biography, which were interrupted by the urgent call from California. All her letters from friends and many from strangers, for several years, had urged that it should not longer be deferred. But who should do it? That was the important question. There were a number of women who possessed the ability and the desire, but some were absorbed in family cares and others in breadwinning occupations; where was the one who could and would give a year or more of her life to this vast undertaking? The question was still unanswered when Miss Anthony laid everything else aside and plunged into the California campaign. Long before this had ended, she had exacted a promise from Mrs. Harper, who had charge of the State press during that long and trying period, to come to Rochester and write the biography. She herself agreed to remain at home till the work should be finished, and give every possible assistance from the storehouse of reminiscence and the wealth of material which had been so carefully garnered during all the years.

So the first of March, 1897, the work began. A little while before, Miss Anthony had written to a friend: "Some one soon will write the story of my life and will want everything she can get about me, but she will find there is precious little when she sits down to the task." What the biographer did find was two large rooms filled, from floor to ceiling, with material of a personal and historical nature. It seemed at first as if nothing less than a cyclopedia could contain what would have to be used. Ranged around the walls were trunks, boxes and bags of letters and other documents, dating back for a century and tied in bundles just as they had been put away from year to year. There were piles of legal papers, accounts, receipts and memoranda of every description, and the diaries and note-books of sixty years. The shelves were filled with congressional, convention and other reports; there were stacks of magazines and newspapers, large numbers of scrap-books and bushels of scraps waiting to be pasted. There was, in fact, everything of this nature which can be imagined, all carefully saved and put away, waiting for the leisure when they could be sorted and classified.

It was fortunate indeed that the two women, who went to work so cheerfully on that March morning, did not realize the task which was before them, or their courage might have wavered. With the assistance of their efficient secretary, Miss

Genevieve Lel Hawley, the work went steadily on from daylight till dark for many days, until at length the sheep all were separated from the goats; the matter likely to be used placed in one room, and the remainder arranged conveniently for reference in the other. Every scrap of writing was pressed out and each year's quota not only placed in a separate box, but arranged according to months and days. The printed matter was carefully classified and the scrap-books all finished, a complete set of nearly fifty years.

Then commenced the far more difficult labor of culling the most important and interesting points from this great mass of material, and condensing them into such space as would permit the reading of the biography during at least an average lifetime. And thus was the task continued, day after day, and far into the night, for much more than a year. The snows of winter melted away; the bare branches of the tall chestnut trees which towered above the windows put forth their buds and burst into a wilderness of snowy blossoms; the birds built their nests among the green leaves, reared their young and flew away with them to warmer climes before the chill winds of approaching autumn; the luxuriant foliage faded and dropped to the earth; again the naked branches stretched out to a stormy sky, and the snow lay deep on the frozen ground; while the story followed the life and work of this great historic character through the slow unfolding out of the depths of the past; the development from the springtime of youth into the fruitful summer of maturity; the mellowing into the richness and beauty of autumn; the coming at last into the snowy spotlessness of serene and beautiful old age.

The attic workrooms were an ideal place for this long and exacting task, secluded from all interruption and dedicated so entirely to the work that not a book or paper ever was disturbed. A pretty description written by Mrs. Minette Cheshire Hair, of the Rochester Democrat and Chronicle staff, and published in a number of papers, thus began:

Way up on the third floor of the cozy home at 17 Madison street, away from the dust and noise of the pavement, in a charming den admirably

ATTIC WORK-ROOMS WHERE THE BIOGRAPHY WAS WRITTEN.

arranged for the purpose, two women have for months been busily engaged getting together material and putting it in shape for the publishers, which will give to the world a story—the story of a career as remarkable as any ever written. Pausing on the threshold, a description of the sanctum is not out of place, for the pleasant atmosphere and surroundings at once impress the visitor, so unconsciously have the occupants stamped it with their own strong individuality. It consists of two large and airy rooms which appear to be literally perched in the tree-tops, so close are the swaying branches, which seem to nod approval and encouragement to the two busy workers seated before a large bow window. Patches of the blue sky glimmer above and through them, and the scene without is restful and inspiring. Within is a large, low table where the writing is done, and an easy couch piled with pillows invites repose when the brain grows too weary.

The rooms are plain and ceiled above in natural wood, and on shelves arranged along the sides are boxes containing years of correspondence and documents, dating back to 1797—just one century. In the room beyond, three stenographers do their part of the work, and here also are large chests filled with the accumulations of years of public life. It would seem as if the task before these two dauntless women were almost endless, for every letter must be read and carefully noted, every newspaper clipping gleaned—and these alone would make volumes—old diaries perused, and the whole digested and woven into the fabric of facts which not only go to make the story of one woman, but the history of the great progressive movement of women during the past fifty years.

CHAPTER XLIX.

CHARACTERISTIC VIEWS ON MANY QUESTIONS.

1897.

ISS ANTHONY was strong in her determination to remain at home and devote herself to the biographical task, but found it almost an impossibility to resist the calls for her services which came from all directions. Occasionally she would slip out for a lecture, but long journeys and convention work for the most part were given up, and never during fifty years had she remained at home a fraction of the time that she spent here in 1897. Monday evening of each week was set apart to receive callers and the pleasant parlors often were crowded, many of the Rochester people declaring that this was their first chance of getting acquainted with their illustrious townswoman. There were two rôles, however, which she never could fill with any pleasure to herself, that of the society or the literary woman. While no one loves her friends more faithfully or better enjoys receiving visits from them, she cares for social life, in general, only so far as it can advance her cause. Although letter-writing is a pleasure, she hates the use of the pen for so-called literary work. Standing on the platform, words and ideas rush upon her more rapidly than she can give them utterance, but with pen in hand the thoughts still come but refuse to be formulated.

In the chapters describing the preparation of the History of Woman Suffrage was set forth in detail her restiveness at such confinement. "I love to make history but hate to write it,"

was her oft-repeated assertion. The years had brought no change of feeling and her correspondence shows how she chafed under the search of old records, the reading of faded letters. Many times she wrote: "There is so much to be done, so much more money is needed and so many more women are wanted for the present work, that half the time I feel conscience-smitten to be dwelling among the scenes and people of the past. There are so very few of my early co-workers now on this side of the big river, that I am really living with the dead most of the time; but as there is no way out of this job except through it—through it I must go." In the journal she says: "O, how it tires me to think over and talk over those old days, not only of my own labors, but of the never-ceasing efforts to stir up others to work."

The 9th of March Miss Anthony lectured before the Men's Club of the Central Church at Auburn. On the 12th she spoke at a meeting addressed by Booker Washington in the interest of the Tuskeegee Colored Institute. The 24th she went to Albany with Dr. Mary Putnam Jacobi, Mrs. Catt, Elizabeth Burrill Curtis, daughter of George William Curtis, Mrs. Chapman, State president; and all addressed the senate judiciary committee in behalf of a woman suffrage amendment. Miss Anthony went to this hearing much against her will and, at its conclusion, declared she never again would stoop to plead her cause before one of these committees. She had made her appeals to their fathers and grandfathers, and she was tired of begging for her liberty from men not half her own age and with not a hundredth part of her knowledge of State and national affairs.

The seventieth birthday of the devoted sister Mary would occur on April 2, and Miss Anthony decided to have a home reception in her honor. When she broached the subject to a few intimate friends in the Unitarian church and the Political Equality Club, she found they already had such arrangements well under way and they insisted that she should leave the matter entirely in their hands. Anything which concerned the Anthony sisters interested Rochester, and the city papers

contained extended notices.   The Herald began a long interview as follows:

Seventy! It did not seem possible that the sprightly, energetic little
woman who answered the reporter's ring could have reached the allotted
threescore and ten. Old Father Time is certainly no more than a myth to
Miss Mary Anthony. "Yes," said she, laughing, "I am about to make my
debut. Just think of it, a real reception in my honor ! By the time I'm
eighty, my existence will probably have become one whirl of delicious excitement."

The reporter asked to see Miss Susan B. Anthony; five minutes would be
sufficient; the matter was urgent and important. . . . Turning to her the
reporter said: "The Herald would like you to give an account of your sister.
You know she would never admit that she ever did anything worth mention-
ing, so it is from you that the true story must come."

She laughed as she took off her glasses, leaned back in her chair and asked,
"Where shall I begin ?"

"At the beginning, please."

"Well then, my sister was born in Battenville, the youngest of four
daughters. One thing may surprise you. She, not I, is the suffrage pioneer
in our family. She attended the first woman's rights convention, and when
I came home from teaching school, I heard nothing but suffrage talk, and
how lovely Lucretia Mott was, and how sweet Elizabeth Cady Stanton was.
I didn't believe in it then, and made fun of it; but sister Mary was a firm
advocate. My brother-in-law used to tell me that I could preach woman's
rights, but it took Mary to practice them.

"For twenty-six consecutive years, from 1857 to 1883, she taught in our
public schools. Many of the best citizens of Rochester once went to school to
her; and it is perhaps her influence upon those minds and lives that my sister
considers the most important part of her life-work. She has always been identified with the suffrage cause in this city and State, as I have with the national.
For a number of years she was corresponding secretary of the State society,
and for five years has been president of the city Political Equality Club.

"I can not tell you how she has helped and sustained me. She has kept a
home where I might come to rest. From the very beginning, she has cheered
and comforted me. She has looked after the great mass of details, my wardrobe, my business, etc., leaving me free. She is the unseen worker who
ought to share equally in whatever of reward and praise I may have won."

The Democrat and Chronicle thus commenced a two-column
account of the reception :

. . . The occasion was the seventieth anniversary of Miss Mary Anthony's
birth and, in the afternoon and evening, crowds of her friends gathered to offer
their congratulations and do homage to one who has done so much for the
educational interests of the city and social and political equality for her sex.
Miss Mary, to be sure, has not gained the national reputation which her

famous sister enjoys, yet among the people of Rochester she is regarded as a sharer in the laurels won by Susan B. Whenever one is mentioned the personality of the other is immediately brought to mind. . . . It was with rare hospitality, interwoven with personal love and respect, that Dr. and Mrs. J. E. Sanford devoted their handsome home to the celebration of this birthday. Attired in black satin and duchesse lace, with a pretty bouquet of bride roses in her hand, Miss Mary presented a womanly and attractive appearance.

In the name of the club, Mrs. Sanford presented, with a felicitous little speech, a handsome, jetted broadcloth cape. She was followed by Mrs. Greenleaf, who tendered in affectionate words a purse containing $70, a golden tribute for each year from many friends.[1] John M. Thayer then made a witty and interesting address. He was followed by Rev. W. C. Gannett, who dwelt especially on the work done by Miss Mary in looking after the poor and needy for the past twenty years, not only as an officer of the city charitable association but in a private capacity, and closed by saying:

It takes two sorts of people to make a reform: One who become public speakers and bear the brunt of obloquy, and the other who in obscurity lend their assistance to the work. There are hundreds of this latter class that the world never hears about. It is the blessed silent side of life, and it seems to me that Mary is the very incarnation of the quiet majority of this great reform which is yet to celebrate its triumphs. In after years, when the story is written of this political equality movement, men will say that the battle was won by the two sisters, because there never could have been a Susan abroad if it had not been for a Mary at home.

If there ever was a time when Miss Anthony was speechless from supreme satisfaction it was on this occasion. All the honors ever bestowed upon herself had not afforded her the joy of this testimonial to her gentle, unassuming but strong and helpful sister, on whom she leaned far more than the world could ever know.

Miss Anthony assisted at the elegant golden wedding celebration of Mr. and Mrs. James Sargent, April 29 ; not one in the receiving line under seventy, and yet not one broken or en-

[1] Among other birthday remembrances were a diamond pin from Miss Shaw, Mrs. Avery, Mrs. Louise Mosher James and Lucy E. Anthony; $50 from Mrs. Grors; many smaller gifts and quantities of flowers.

MARY S. AND SUSAN B. ANTHONY, 1897.

feebled by age. The men erect and vigorous, the women beautifully dressed and full of animation, formed a striking illustration of the changed physical and social conditions of the last half-century.

Early in June Miss Anthony, Rev. Anna Shaw, Miss Emily Howland and Mrs. Harper went to Auburn to visit Eliza Wright Osborne, with whom Mrs. Stanton and her daughter, Mrs. Lawrence, were spending the summer. The days were delightfully passed, driving through the shaded streets of that "loveliest village of the plain" and walking about the spacious park and gardens surrounding the Osborne mansion; while in the evenings the party gathered in the large drawing-room and listened to chapters from the forthcoming biography, followed wit' delightful reminiscences by the two elder ladies and Mrs. Osborne, whose mother, Martha C. Wright, was one of their first and best-beloved friends and helpers. It was a rare and sacred occasion, and those who were present ever will cherish the memory of those two grand pioneers, sitting side by side— Elizabeth Cady Stanton, Susan B. Anthony—the one just beyond, the other nearing the eightieth milestone of life, both having given to the world fifty years of unremitting service, and yet both as strong in mind, as keen in satire, as brimming with cheerfulness, as in those early days when they set about to revolutionize the prejudices and customs of the ages.[1]

The correspondence this year seemed heavier than ever before, letters pouring in from all parts of the United States and Europe. Even from far-off Moscow, in conservative Russia, came the cry of women for help. Pages written by the pen of another could not give so accurate an idea of Miss Anthony's opinions on various topics as single paragraphs culled from copies of her own letters, preserved, alas, only during the past few years since she has employed a stenographer. One scarcely knows which to select. To a newspaper inquiry she answered : "The 'greatest compliment' ever paid me was, that by my life-work I had helped to make the conditions of

[1] During this month a fine medallion of Miss Anthony was made for the Political Equality Club of Rochester and put on sale to obtain money for the suffrage fund. Some time before, a handsome souvenir spoon was designed by Mrs. Millie Burtis Logan, of Rochester.

the world better for women." She wrote to an exasperated Ohio woman :

The plan you propose, of our getting all the members of suffrage clubs, and all individual women outside, in each State, to march to the polls every election day and attempt to deposit their ballots, sounds very well. But, my dear, it is impossible thus to persuade the women, after the Supreme Court of the United States has declared they have no right to vote under the National Constitution. Your suggestion means a revolution which women will not create against their own fathers, husbands, brothers and sons. A whole race of men under a foreign or tyrannical government, like the Cubans, may rise in rebellion, but for women thus to band themselves against the power enthroned in their own households is quite another matter. Hundreds have recommended your plan, so it is nothing new, but it is utterly impractical. There can be but one possible way for women to be freed from the degradation of disfranchisement, and that is through the slow processes of agitation and education, until the vast majority of women themselves desire freedom. So long as mothers teach their sons and daughters, by acquiescence at least, that present conditions need no improving, you can not expect men to change them. Therefore do not waste a single moment trying to devise any sort of insurrectionary movement on the part of the women.

In a letter to Mrs. Stanton she said :

Mrs. Besant lunched with us, and I heard her last evening for the second time. She is master of the English language, and whether or not one can believe she sees and hears from the world of the disembodied what she feels she does, one can not but realize that she is a great woman and has a wonderful theory of how human souls return to earth. But I tell her that it seems to me repellent that we have to come back here through Dame Nature's processes, after a period of such great freedom in the occult world, and again go through with teething, mumps, measles, and similar inflictions. The truth is, I can no more see through Theosophy than I can through Christian Science, Spiritualism, Calvinism or any other of the theories, so I shall have to go on knocking away to remove the obstructions in the road of us mortals while in these bodies and on this planet; and leave Madam Besant and you and all who have entered into the higher spheres, to revel in things unknown to me. . . . I will join you at Mrs. Miller's Saturday, and we'll chat over men, women and conditions—not theories, theosophies and theologies, they are all Greek to me.

There had been a question after the late election in Idaho whether the suffrage amendment required a majority of all the votes cast, or only a majority of those cast on the amendment. If the former, then it was defeated. The case was carried to the supreme court, which put the latter construction on the law. Miss Anthony wrote to the judges, Isaac N. Sullivan, Joseph W. Huston, Ralph P. Quarles, (John T. Morgan retired):

On behalf of the suffrage women of the United States, I thank you for the decision which you have rendered. I had studied over the clause a great deal and felt that if your judgments were biased by the precedents and prejudices which had controlled the decisions of the Supreme Courts of the United States, and of the different States, upon the extension of rights to women, you certainly would give the narrow interpretation. Instead of that, for the first time in the history of our judiciary, the broadest and most liberal interpretation possible has been given.

The Kentucky Daughters of the American Revolution, who were marking historic spots, she advised as follows:

I hope in your selections you will be exceedingly careful to distinguish those actions in which our Revolutionary mothers took part. Men have been faithful in noting every heroic act of their half of the race, and now it should be the duty, as well as the pleasure, of women to make for future generations a record of the heroic deeds of the other half. It is a splendid thing for your association to devote the Fourth of July to a commemoration of women. If I had the time, I too might be one of the "Daughters,"[1] for my Grandfather Read enlisted and fought on the heights of Quebec and at the battles of Bennington and Ticonderoga; but I have been, and must continue to be, so busy working to secure to the women of this day the paramount right for which the Revolutionary War was waged, that I can give neither time nor money to associations of women for any other purpose, however good it may be.

When the answer came that they were doing the very thing that she wished, she replied:

I am delighted; for however heroic our pioneer fathers may have been, our pioneer mothers, in the very nature of things, must have braved all the hardships of the men by their side with the added one of bearing and rearing children when deprived of even the vital necessities of maternity. Self-government is as necessary for the best development of women as of men. Sentiment never was and never can be a guarantee for justice, but with equal political power women will be able to secure justice for themselves. We have had chivalry and sentiment from the beginning of time, with some privileges granted as a favor. We now demand rights, guaranteed to us by codes and constitutions; and if their possession shall forfeit us gallantry, we will make the best of it. But I do not believe woman's utter dependence on man wins

[1] Later Miss Anthony was made honorary member of Irondequoit Chapter, D. A. R. (Rochester).

for her his respect; it may cause him to love and pet her as a child, but never to regard and treat her as a peer.

To Prof. C. Howard Young, of Hartford, Conn., for thirteen years an invalid and yet an ardent advocate of woman suffrage, she wrote: "I want you to feel that the dollar you have sent from year to year all this time for your membership in the national association has helped bring to us Idaho, for our organization committee's work in that State was a large factor in securing the victory. Every one who gives a dollar helps do the work where it is most needed to gain the practical result."

The following extracts are self-explanatory:

The vast majority of women easily can have their sympathies drawn upon to help personal and public charities, while very few are capable of seeing that the cause of nine-tenths of all the misfortunes which come to women, and to men also, lies in the subjection of woman, and therefore the important thing is to lay the axe at the root. Now, my dear, if you and all the women who are working for the different charities and reforms of your city, had the right to vote, how long do you suppose the brothels and gambling houses would be allowed to keep their doors open? Do you believe that if women could vote for every officer whose duty it is to enforce the laws, these dens would be licensed, or if not absolutely licensed, would be allowed to run year in and year out merely by the payment of fines from time to time? How long do you think our streets would be infested with men walking up and down seeking whom they might devour, and with women doing the same? While some of you must work, as you are doing, giving heart and soul to the mitigation of the horrors of our semi-barbaric conditions, I must strike at the cause which produces them.

To the women of Kansas:

I hope your State association won't do the foolish thing of wasting your time in asking the legislature to pass a law granting "presidential" suffrage to women. Our chances in your State have been postponed, if not absolutely killed, because of municipal suffrage, and now if you should induce your legislature to give "presidential" suffrage and the women should thwart the men's wishes in their votes for President, as they already have done with their limited franchise, you would be doomed never to get the right to vote for congressmen, governor and legislators. I wish women never would ask for any but full suffrage; and also that they would stop asking the legislatures to submit an amendment to the voters, until they have created public sentiment enough to get at least one of the leading parties to stand for it from year to year. We have been working at the top with the members of legislatures, delegates to conventions, etc., too long; it is now time to begin at the bottom with the voting precincts. Nothing short of this should be considered organization.

Miss Anthony received many poems every year from admiring friends of both sexes. This acknowledgment of one raises the suspicion that she was not so appreciative as she might have been: "I find in a very handsome lavender envelope a poem inscribed on lavender paper, addressed to Susan B. Anthony. Since I know nothing of the merits of poetry, I am not able to pass any opinion upon this, but I can see that ' reap ' and ' deep,' ' prayers ' and ' bears,' ' ark ' and ' dark,' ' true ' and ' grew ' do rhyme, and so I suppose it is a splendid effort, but if you had written it in plain prose, I could have understood it a great deal better and read it a great deal more easily. Nevertheless, I am thankful to you for poetizing over me—although the fact is that I am the most prosaic, matter-of-fact creature that ever drew the breath of life."

A relative in California wrote that " God would punish the people in that State who worked against the woman suffrage amendment," and Miss Anthony replied :

It is hardly worth while for you or anybody to talk about "God's punishing people." If He does, He has been a long time about it in a good many cases and not succeeded in doing it very thoroughly. He certainly didn't punish the liquor dealers of San Francisco; instead of that, He let them rejoice over us women because of their power to cheat us out of right and justice. I think it is quite time, at least for anybody who has Anthony blood in her, to see that God allows the wheat and the tares to grow up together, and that the tares frequently get the start of the wheat and kill it out. The only difference between the wheat and human beings is that the latter have intellect and ought to combine and pull out the tares, root and branch. Instead of that, good men stay away from the ballot-box or else form third, fourth and forty-'leventh parties, thus leaving the liquor men and vicious elements, who always know enough to stand together, a balance of power on the side of the candidate or the party that will do most for their interests. If the good men were as bright as the bad men, they would pull together instead of separately.

To the Jewish Woman's Council: "From day to day I read the press reports of your meetings, and was pleased to see how successful they were ; especially was I glad at the answer one of your women made to the criticism of your holding a meeting on Sunday. It is time to teach some of our Protestant women that it is just as worthy to do a good thing on Sunday as on Monday or any other day in the week, and no worse to do a bad one. They should learn also that they have no more right to ask you to hold their Sunday sacred than you have to demand that they shall observe your Jewish Sabbath."

Some California women wrote her that the politicians were advising them to ask for "educated and property suffrage," and she replied:

I should answer them that it is quite difficult enough for women to push their demand for enfranchisement on an *equal* basis with men. They all know there is not a man who has any political aspirations or a party which hopes for success, that would take a public stand in favor of such a measure as they wish us to adopt. I do not agree with them that we have too many voters now. Instead of that, I say we have just half enough, for a majority of the opinions of all the people combined is sure to be better than the opinions of any one class. They call it a "mistake" giving to poor and uneducated men the right to vote; whereas, the greatest wrongs in our government are perpetrated by rich men, the wire-pulling agents of the corporations and. monopolies, in which the poor and the ignorant have no part.

No, they can not persuade me that it would be a right or even a politic thing to ask that only educated, tax-paying women be enfranchised. It would antagonize not only every man who had neither property nor education but also every one whose wife had neither, and all such would vote against the enfranchisement of the rich and educated women. You can not start a demand for any sort of restrictive qualification for women which will not lose more votes for the measure in one direction than it can possibly gain in another.

The habit of many women of continually intruding their religious beliefs into their public work was a great annoyance to Miss Anthony. To a prominent speaker on the Prohibition platform with whom she was well acquainted, she wrote: "It seems to me that by your using constantly the words 'God' and 'Jesus' as if they were material beings, when to you they are no longer such, you impress upon your audience, grounded as the vast majority yet are in the old beliefs, that you still hold to the idea of their personality. The world, especially women, love to cling to a personal, material help— God a strong man, Jesus a loving man." And then a little further on, referring to the common habit of regarding physical misfortunes as the punishment of God, she said : "God is not responsible for our human ills and we should not believe or disbelieve in Him on account of our aches and pains. It surely is not the good people who escape bodily ailments. Certain fixed laws govern all, and those who come nearest to obeying these laws will suffer least; but even then we must suffer for the failures of our ancestors."

One of the leading women in a State where a suffrage amendment was pending, wrote her that she felt sure the Lord would interpose in its behalf and she should try to influence the voters by prayer. In response Miss Anthony said :

I think you do not fully realize that the vast majority of the men whom you have to convert to suffrage, neither know nor care whether you and the rest of the women who want to vote, are especially inspired by God to make the demand. Those who are good Methodists like yourself ought to believe in suffrage already, and therefore your appeals are to be made to the men who are not Methodists, possibly not even Christians, and would be repelled by your presenting any of the religious motives which are so powerful with you and other church members. To prevail with the rank and file of voters, you must appeal to their sense of justice. I am glad to have you tell me personally about your communings with the Lord, but for you to give that talk of "miraculous intervention" to the common run of voters would be, as the Good Book says, "casting pearls before swine."

To a nephew, D. R. Anthony, Jr., and his bride on the day of their wedding, she telegraphed the beautiful words of Lucretia Mott: "May your independence be equal, your dependence mutual, your obligations reciprocal."

In the winter of 1897 a great cry was raised about what was called "yellow" journalism, the mischievous sensationalism of certain metropolitan newspapers. The matter was taken up by the W. C. T. U. and Miss Willard sent out an address to prominent women asking that they should protest against this journalism and also against such spectacles as the recent Corbett-Fitzsimmons prize fight. When it reached Miss Anthony she answered :

Your circular letter came duly, proposing that women should refuse to patronize the so-called "yellow" newspapers, and also protest against prize fighting. It seems to me that for the women of the country to come out now with their little piping voices, after all the great daily papers of the nation have written the strongest kind of editorials against both these evils, would be very like the caricatures of the old Conkling-Platt fight in the United States Senate—the tall Conkling dealing his blow, and the little Platt peeping, " Me, too."

Instead of going around echoing one or another class of men, it is time for women to put their heads together and demand to have their opinions counted the same as those of the men who make possible "yellow journalism" and prize fighting. They who wish may waste their time trying to make bricks without straw—to change the conditions of society without votes—I shall go on clamoring for the ballot and trying not to antagonize any man or set of men. Don't you see, if women ever get the right to vote it must be through the consent of not only the moral and decent men of the nation, but also through that of the other kind? Is it not perfectly idiotic for us to be telling the latter class that the first thing we shall do with our ballots will be to knock them out of the enjoyment of their pet pleasures and vices? If you still think it wise to keep on sticking pins into the men whom we are trying to persuade to give women equal power with themselves, you will have to go on doing it. I certainly will not be one of your helpers in that particular line of work.

In reading these and scores of similar expressions of wisdom and philosophy, one can but echo the words of Rev. Anna Shaw, who wrote to Miss Anthony : " Your letters sound like a trumpet blast. They read like St. Paul's Epistles to the Romans, so strong, so clear, so full of courage." Miss Anthony and Miss Willard always continued the best of friends, each great enough to respect the other's individuality. In reply to the above, Miss Willard wrote : " Dearest Susan, two women as settled in their opinions as you and I, show their highest wisdom when they mildly agree to differ and go on their way rejoicing, with mutual good word, good will, good heart. Ever yours with warm affection." A little later Miss Willard added to the official invitations to the World's and the National W. C. T. U. Conventions, her warm personal request for Miss Anthony's presence.

There was no end to the invitations which came by every mail : a banquet given by the New York Woman's Press Club ; the twenty-fifth anniversary of the Woman's Club at Orange, N. J. ; an anniversary breakfast of Sorosis, at the Waldorf ; a reunion of the old Abolitionists in Boston ; the Pilgrim Mothers' Dinner in the Astor Gallery ; the dedication of the Mother Bickerdyke Hospital in Kansas ; the opening reception of the Tennessee Centennial—the very answering of them consumed hours of precious time.[1] Neither was there any limit to the newspaper requests for opinions, such as, " Do you favor the use of birds for personal adornment ?   Why, or why not ? " " Christ's message, ' Peace on earth, good will to men '—what, has it done and what does it mean after nineteen centuries ? " etc.   She seldom attempted to answer such queries, but her comments while looking them over in her daily mail, if preserved by stenographer and historian, would make piquant reading.

An amusing letter turns up among the almost nine hundred received in 1897, in which a county official, not seventy-five miles from Rochester, asks these questions :   " In how many cities have you spoken ?   How many lectures delivered ? Have you ever spoken in Washington before Congress ?   Have you ever spoken in Albany before the legislature ?   How many people would you think you had addressed in your lifetime ? "   Miss Anthony responded :   " It would be hard to find a city in the northern and western States in which I have not lectured, and I have spoken in many of the southern cities.   I have been on the platform over forty-five years and it would be impossible to tell how many lectures I have delivered ; they probably would average from seventy-five to one hundred every year.   I have addressed the committees of every Congress since 1869, and our New York legislature scores of times."

As has been stated, she never replied to personal attacks, but during 1897 one so unjust and so bitter was made by a disgruntled woman of New York City in the St. Louis Republic, that she yielded to the importunity of friends and answered briefly :

I have been an officer in the National Suffrage Association since 1852, and its president since 1892.   During that time I never have had one dollar of salary, nor have I ever received any money for my suffrage work from this associa-

[1] Miss Anthony was this year made honorary member of the Cuban League, the Rochester Historical Society, the Ladies of the Maccabees, and various other organizations.

tion. I usually am paid for lectures by any society which sends for me to come to a special place. In all of the laborious State campaigns I have given my services without money and without price. The various bequests which have been left to me, to use at my discretion, all have been appropriated directly to the suffrage cause. Not one officer of the national association is or ever has been paid for her services, and most of them have contributed many years of hard work and a large amount of their own money.

By the middle of July the biography was so well advanced that the two workers felt entitled to a vacation during mid-summer. The completed chapters were locked securely in the safety deposit vault and, with a fervent hope that the house would not catch fire and burn up the unwritten part of the book during their absence, they started, July 15, for a little tour, going first to the home of Mr. and Mrs. James Sargent on "Summerland," one of the loveliest of the Thousand Islands. Here Miss Anthony tried very hard for a whole week to do nothing. Even letter-writing was laid aside and she sat on the veranda and watched the great steamers and the pleasure boats go up and down the broad St. Lawrence; took long naps in the hammock swayed by the soft breezes; wandered through the picturesque ravine and along the water's edge; at evening watched the sun set in gorgeous splendor, leaving a trail of glory on the waters which slowly faded as the stars came out in the beauty of the night and were reflected in the still depths. Every day, with host and hostess and the other guests in the house, she boarded the little launch and sailed up the river, winding in and out among those wonderful islands with their diversity of hotels, clubhouses, elegant mansions and pretty cottages; but all surpassed by the adornments of nature, tall trees with luxuriant vines climbing to the very tops, and the great rocks of the ages, rent and cleft and covered with mosses and ferns.

It was a charming week but, although the stay might have been prolonged through the summer, Miss Anthony was far too busy a woman for much visiting, and on the 22d started for her old home at Adams, Mass., where a unique and long anticipated event took place, which will be described in the next chapter. A number of relatives, who had come from various parts of the country for this occasion, returned to Rochester with her. A little trip was made to Geneva to visit with Mrs. Stanton at Mrs. Miller's, and so the summer sped quickly and pleasantly away.

Miss Anthony attended the Ohio convention at Alliance, October 5, and was the guest of Mrs. Emma Cantine. While here, at the request of President Marsh, she addressed the students of Mount Union College on "The Progress of Women during my Lifetime." She had said again and again that she would not leave her work and go to this convention, but when at last a telegram was received, "For heaven's sake come; all depends on you"—she put on her bonnet and went, just as she had done a hundred times before.

She spoke, October 20, at the celebration of the hundredth birthday of Rev. Samuel J. May, in the beautiful church erected to his memory in Syracuse. She had known Mr. May intimately from 1850 to the time of his death, and those who have read the first chapters of this book and seen what he was to her in those early days of abolitionism and woman's rights when the enemies far outnumbered the friends, can imagine how eloquently she voiced the love and gratitude in her heart.

The next evening Miss Anthony left Rochester for ten days at Nashville, Tenn. The Woman's Board had invited a number of national organizations to hold conventions during the Exposition, and the last week was set apart for the Woman's Council. This was not a suffrage meeting; it was simply a national council where each one of the speakers asked for the suffrage to enable her association to do its work. Headquarters were at the Maxwell House, and the officers and many other notable women came from various parts of the country for the week. The public sessions were held in the Woman's Building, which was crowded to its capacity. Although suffrage was a comparatively new subject in this city, the announcement of Miss Anthony's address filled the assembly-room and she was received with enthusiasm.

They met with a hearty greeting from the people of Nashville. Among the elegant receptions given in their honor was one by Mr. and Mrs. W. W. Berry at Vauxhall Place. The president of the Exposition, Mr. John W. Thomas, and his wife gave a handsome entertainment, of which the American's account said : "By the hostess stood her honored guest, Miss Susan B. Anthony, in simple attire. Warm was the reception accorded this gray-haired woman, and her grand face impressed all with the noble part she had played in this century." At the close of the council the visitors, as the guests of the lady directors, were driven in tally-ho and carriages to the beautiful country-seat of the president of the board, Mrs. Van Leer Kirkman, where they were royally received.

Miss Anthony spoke also before the Liberal Congress of Religions in session at this time, and was introduced by the president, Dr. Thomas, as "one who had stood for the cause of liberty when it cost something to stand, and had borne the storm of calumny and abuse for fifty years." While she was in Nashville President Erastus M. Cravath, of Fiske University, called with his carriage and took her to that institution, where she addressed the faculty and 600 students, speaking, by request, on "The Early Days of Abolitionism."

After a day or two at home Miss Anthony attended the New York Suffrage Convention at Geneva, November 3. Here she made a speech criticising the women of New York City for having gone so actively into partisan politics during the recent campaign, although none of the parties advocated giving them the right of suffrage, and pointed out the absurdity of hoping for "good government" from any party until it was reinforced by the votes of women. The speech created something of a sensation, and when she reached home a reporter was waiting for her, to whom she gave an interview which intensified the original excitement. Not only did she review the political situation in New York, but she declared also that no movement could succeed unless it were managed by a so-called "ring." Leaders must be surrounded by those who are in sympathy with their ideas and willing to carry out their methods, or nothing can be accomplished. In commenting, the paper quoted the remark so often made, "When Susan B.

Anthony was born a woman, an adroit statesman was lost to the world."

On November 11 Miss Anthony started on a great swing of western conventions, or conferences, stopping on her way to the railroad station to attend the golden wedding reception of her friends of nearly fifty years, Dr. and Mrs. Edward M. Moore. These conferences—Miss Anthony, Mrs. Catt, Miss Shaw, speakers—were for the purpose of arousing interest and raising money for the suffrage celebration to be held in Washington in the winter of 1898. They began at Minneapolis and continued for two days each in Madison, Chicago, Grand Rapids, Kalamazoo and Toledo. At the first city Miss Anthony addressed the students of the State University, introduced by President Cyrus Northrop. A reception was given in the public library building by the local Woman's Council.

At each of the cities visited the ladies were entertained by prominent residents, the audiences were large and appreciative, and the newspapers contained long and favorable reports. There was not a discord in the chorus of pleasant welcome ; not a disrespectful word of either the speakers or the cause they advocated. The question was treated with the same consideration and dignity as others before the public for discussion, and it required no more courage to present it than to talk of any other reform of the day.

If one desire an illustration of the progress made by women during half a century, let him turn to the early chapters of this book and read the story of those first meetings where Miss Anthony, rising timidly in her seat and asking to make a remark, was literally howled down because no woman was allowed to speak in public ; and then let him read these closing chapters of her ovations extending from ocean to ocean. From a canvass of New York State in a sleigh, speaking to little handfuls of people in country schoolhouses, ridiculed by the newspapers and outlawed by society—to an endless series of conventions and congresses in all the great cities of the country, with no hall large enough to hold the audiences and with

almost the unanimous approval of press and people! Only a
short period of less than fifty years, scarcely a second in the
eons of history, and yet in that brief time a revolution in public sentiment, an overturning of the customs and prejudices of
the ages, the release of womanhood from unknown centuries
of bondage!

CHAPTER L.

1897.

HE unsurpassed powers of endurance, which have enabled Miss Anthony to work without ceasing for more than sixty years, are due to her perfect physical condition. She comes of a long-lived race, in which centenarians have been not unusual. Her paternal grandfather lived past the age of ninety-seven, able to oversee his farm to the very last; the grandmother lived beyond sixty-seven ; both the maternal grandparents died in their eighty-fourth year ; her father at sixty-nine, and her mother at eighty-six. She never has abused her inheritance of a fine, strong constitution. Travelling so much of the time, she has not been able to observe regular hours and, being usually entertained in private families, has not had a choice of food, but nevertheless, as far as possible, she has observed the laws of health which she made for herself in youth.

She never fails to take each morning, regardless of the weather, a cold sponge bath from head to foot, followed by a brisk rubbing, which puts the skin in excellent condition. She has a good appetite, drinks tea and coffee moderately and eats always the simplest food, cereals, bread and butter, vegetables, eggs, milk, a little meat once a day, plenty of fruit at every meal, whatever is in season, and never can be tempted by rich salads, desserts or fancy dishes. Whenever it is possible she rests a short time after each meal, and lies down for an hour during the afternoon, even if she can not sleep ; retires at nine or ten and rises at six or seven. She travels by night, when

(931)

convenient, as she thus can avoid much of the fatigue of the journey. When travelling in the daytime she reads very little, never writes or dictates letters on the train, as many busy people do, but makes herself comfortable and dozes and rests.

An invariable rule, with which nothing is allowed to interfere, is plenty of fresh air and exercise, and she regards these as the mainspring of her long years of health and activity. If she has been on the cars all day, she walks from the station to her stopping-place. After a speech, she walks home. When in Rochester she often writes until nearly 10 o'clock at night, then puts on a long cloak, ties a scarf over her head, goes out to the mail box, and walks eight or ten blocks, returning in a warm glow; gives herself a thorough rubbing, and is ready for a night's rest in a room where the window is open at all seasons. The policemen are accustomed to the late pedestrian and often speak a word of greeting as she passes. It is not an unusual thing for her to take up a broom, when it has been snowing all the evening, and sweep the walks around and in front of the house, just before going to bed. While not an adherent of any special " sciences " or "cures," she believes thoroughly in not dwelling upon either mental or bodily ills; giving disagreeable things and people only such attention as is absolutely necessary, and then putting them out of mind; observing the laws of hygiene with regard to the body and then banishing it also from the thoughts. Over and above all else is she an advocate of work, employment for mind and body, as a means of salvation.

In dress Miss Anthony is extremely particular. She considers it poor economy to wear cheap material, always buys the best fabrics, linings and trimmings, and employs a competent dressmaker. She has one gown a year and often this is a present from some loving friend. While she wears only black silk or satin in public, she loves color and her house dress is usually maroon or soft cardinal. Her laces and few pieces of jewelry are gifts from women. The slender little ring, worn on the "wedding finger," was placed there thirty years ago by her devoted friend, Dr. Clemence Lozier. She never in a lifetime has changed the style of wearing her hair, once dark brown, glossy and abundant, now thin and fine and shining like spun silver, which is always evenly parted, combed over the ears and coiled low at the back, thus showing the fine contour of her head. In all the details of the toilet she is most fastidious, and a rent, a missing button or a frayed edge is considered almost an unpardonable sin.

Miss Anthony attends Unitarian church but retains her membership in the Society of Quakers. On the rare occasions when she needs a physician, she consults some woman of the homeopathic school, but she is opposed to much medicine, believing that proper diet and exercise are the best cure for most maladies. Although pleased always to welcome callers, she makes few visits, except to the faithful friends of olden times whose names so often have been mentioned in these pages. She finds the days all too short and too few for the great work whose demands increase with every year. While Miss Anthony feels an abiding interest in household affairs, the details and management necessarily devolve upon her sister Mary, who also looks carefully after the finances, to see that the modest income is not all appropriated to the cause of woman suffrage. In matters of a material nature she is the needed complement to the life of her gifted sister. On all vital questions, suffrage, religion, the various reforms, the two are in perfect accord and, as they sit together in the quiet home for the usual twilight chat before the lamps are lighted, there is none of that dwelling in the past, to which old people are so prone, but all is of the present, the live topics of the day, and the plans and hopes which they share alike.

The Anthony home in Rochester stands in Madison street, one of the nicely paved, well-shaded avenues in the western part of that beautiful city. It is a plain, substantial two-and-a-half story brick house of thirteen rooms, with modern conveniences, and belongs to Miss Mary. It is furnished with Quakerlike simplicity but with everything necessary to make life comfortable. In the front parlor are piano, easy chairs and many pictures and pieces of bric-a-brac, given by friends.

Over the mantel hangs a fine, large painting of the Yosemite, presented to Miss Anthony in 1896 by William Keith, the noted artist of California. Beneath it stand three fine photographs, Mary Wollstonecraft, Lucretia Mott and Frederick Douglass. Between the windows is the very mahogany table upon which were written the call and resolutions for the first woman's rights convention ever held—the gift of Mrs. Stanton. In the back parlor the most conspicuous object is the library table strewn with the papers and magazines which come by every mail. This is surrounded with arm-chairs, tempting one to pause awhile and enjoy this luxury of literature. On one side are the bookcases, and on the walls large engravings of Elizabeth Cady Stanton, Susan B. Anthony, and a handsome copy of Murillo's Madonna, while in one corner stands the mother's spinning-wheel. Opening out of this room is Miss Mary's study, the big desk filled with work pertaining to the Political Equality Club of 200 members, whose efficient president she has been for a number of years; and here she spends several hours every day looking after her own work and relieving her sister of a part of hers. There is a sewing-machine here also, and a big, old-fashioned haircloth sofa, suggesting a nap and a dream of bygone days.

In the dining-room is a handsomely carved mahogany sideboard, a family heirloom, containing china and silver which belonged to mother and grandmother, and here hang very old steel engravings of Washington and Lincoln. The large, light kitchen, with its hard coal range, is a favorite apartment, and Miss Anthony especially enjoys sitting there in a low rocking-chair while she reads the morning paper. The front room upstairs, with little dressing-room attached, is the guest chamber. It contains a great chest of drawers, a dressing-table and mirror which were part of the mother's wedding outfit over eighty years ago, a mahogany bedstead and a modern writing-desk and rocking-chairs. On the walls are several paintings, the work of loved hands long since at rest, and two engravings, over one hundred years old, such as used to hang in every Abolitionist's parlor in early days. They are copies of paintings by G. Morland, engraved in 1794, by "J. R. Smith, King St., Covent Garden, engravers to H. R. H. the Prince of Wales." One is entitled "African Hospitality," and represents a ship wrecked off the coast of Africa with the white passengers rescued and tenderly cared for by the natives; the other is named "The Slave Trade," and shows these same negroes loaded with chains and driven aboard ship by the white men whom they had saved. These pictures have little meaning to the present generation, but one can imagine how they must have fired the hearts of those who were laboring to eradicate the curse of slavery from the nation.

Back of the guest chamber, in this interesting home, is Miss Mary's sleeping-room, with quaint old furniture and family pictures; then the maid's room, another guest chamber and, in the southwest corner, next the bathroom, the pleasant bedroom of Miss Anthony with the pictures of those she loves best, and the dresser littered with the little toilet articles of which she is very fond. The most attractive room in the house, naturally, is Miss Anthony's study in the south wing on the second floor. It is light and sunshiny and has an open gas fire. Looking down from the walls are Benjamin Lundy, Garrison, Phillips, Gerrit Smith, Frances Wright, Ernestine L. Rose, Abby Kelly Foster, Harriet Beecher Stowe, Lucy Stone, Lydia Maria Child and, either singly or in groups, many more of the great reformers of the past and present century. On one side are the book shelves, with cyclopedia, histories and other volumes of reference; on another an inviting couch, where the busy worker may drop down for a few moment's repose of mind and body. By one window is the typewriter, and by the other the great desk weighted with letters and documents.

Each morning, as soon as the postman arrives, Miss Anthony sits down at her desk and, going over the piles of letters, puts to one side those which can wait, dictates replies to those requiring the longest answers and, while they are being typewritten, plunges with her pen into the rest. Many hours every day and often into the night she writes steadily, but the pile never diminishes.   As president of the National-American Association not only must she direct the work for suffrage, which is being carried on in all parts of the country to a much greater extent than the public imagines, but she also must keep in touch with the hundreds of individuals each of whom is helping in a quiet but effective way.   There are few days that do not bring requests from libraries, associations, colleges, high schools or clubs for literature and other information concerning woman suffrage, which is now the subject of debate from the great universities down to the cross roads schoolhouse. In past years libraries have been very deficient in matter upon this question because there was no general call for it, but now the demand is so large that it scarcely can be supplied, and all instinctively turn to Miss Anthony for information.

Some idea has been given of the scope of her correspondence of a public nature, but it hardly would be possible to describe the private letters.   Standing for half a century as the friend and defender of women, and known so widely through her travels and newspaper notices, she is overwhelmed with appeals for advice and assistance.   From the number of wives, and husbands also, who pour the tale of their domestic grievances into her ears, she would be fully justified in believing marriage a failure.   She is daily requested to sign petitions for every conceivable purpose, and begged for letters of recommendation by people of whom she never heard.   Women entreat her to obtain positions for their husbands and children and to help themselves get pensions, or damages, or wages out of which they have been defrauded.   Girls and boys want advice about their plans for the future.   Women, and men too, without education or experience, insist upon being placed as speakers on the suffrage platform.   Authors send books asking for a review. People write of their business ventures, their lawsuits, their surgical operations, their diseases and those of all their family, and of every imaginable household matter.   Scores of letters ask for a " word of greeting " on all sorts of occasions.   Editors of papers and pamphlets, advocating every ology and ism under the sun, send them with the entreaty that she will examine and express an opinion, each insisting that "it will take only a few hours of her time." She is besieged to dress dolls and make aprons for fairs, to write her name upon pieces to be used for quilts and cushions, and to furnish scraps of her gowns for the same purpose. Babies are named for her and she is asked to send a letter of acknowledgment and a little keepsake. Requests for autographs outnumber the days of the year.

She is constantly importuned to examine MSS., and not only to do this but to secure a publisher. During the year 1897 one man sent an article of sixty-eight closely typewritten pages of legal cap, asking that she give it a careful reading, revise it, and send it where it would be published; and no postage stamps accompanied this nervy request. A woman whose grammar and rhetoric were most defective announced that she had written a book called "The Intemperate Life of my Father;" also two stories and a play. She would send all of them to Miss Anthony, to 'fix up just as if they were her own and help her sell them; she wanted the proceeds to assist her brothers who had failed in business.' It is a common occurrence for persons to ask, without so much as enclosing a stamp, that she prepare an address on woman suffrage and send for them to read as their own production. One enthusiastic poem begins:

> "When the grain is ripe we will gather the sheaves,
> And weave a crown for your brow of laurel leaves."

A man from the great Northwest sends a long article entitled, "Sun and Moon Bathed in Blood! Ring, Ring the Bells!" desiring that it be put in the "index of the biography," meaning the appendix. One writes: "You are said to be very good about assisting helpless girls; now you could not find one more helpless than I am;" and then requests that she select, have made and pay for a school outfit for her. Another has a great scheme for starting a "workingwoman's home" and wants Miss Anthony to furnish the money. The list might be extended almost indefinitely and, while one is amused and disgusted by turns, there are among this vast correspondence many letters which touch the heart. During the tariff debate in Congress in 1897 a paragraph was widely published that a tax was to be placed on tea, and this note, evidently written by a child, was received: "My mamma goes out to work while I go to school and she loves her cup of tea. Our groceryman tells us we will have to pay more for it now. I have heard how good you are to the poor, do please spare time to write to the President and ask him not to make our tea dearer. Tell him to put the tax on beer and whiskey."

Miss Anthony is very conscientious about answering letters, too much so, her friends think, for she is a slave to her correspondence. Sometimes, however, she reaches the point of exasperation, as when she opened eight pages of a faintly written scrawl beginning, "My heart goes out to you in sympathy." "Well, I wish it would go out in blacker ink," she exclaimed, and threw it into the waste-basket. Invitations to lecture and to attend all sorts of gatherings pour in, and she often says to the younger workers, "If I might but transfer them to you, how much good you could accomplish." Every mail brings also loving and appreciative letters which illuminate the whole day, take the sting out of the unkind ones and lighten the burdens never entirely lifted. The women who have come into the work in late years continually ask, "How have you borne it so long?" Sometimes when their own endurance ceases they write her that they will have to resign, and she makes answer: "If all the young women fail, then the octogenarian must work the harder till a new reserve comes to the rescue;" and of course they are ashamed and redouble their labors to show their loyalty.

With all her hours of toil she is never satisfied with what she has accomplished, but always feels that she might have done a little more, that something or somebody has been neglected. In looking over the mention made in these chapters of a few of the most valuable gifts and noteworthy letters, she said with sadness: "And no notice has been taken of the hundreds of little tokens of affection which cost far more of

THE ANTHONY FAMILY AT THE REUNION, ADAMS, MASS., JULY 30, 1897.

sacrifice on the part of the givers, and of the thousands of letters from obscure but faithful women, without which I never could have had the courage to do my work.''

While Miss Anthony has remained at home more days in 1897 than in any previous year for half a century it has been one of the busiest in regard to letter-writing. It is the dream of her life to raise a permanent fund to be placed in the hands of trustees, after the manner of the famous Peabody fund, the income to be used to further the cause of woman suffrage. To accomplish this she is exerting her strongest powers of appeal. During all these years of labor for humanity she has had to beg practically every dollar she has used, and she longs to relieve the workers of the future from this drudgery and humiliation, by providing an assured income, so they may not be obliged to expend half their time and strength in obtaining the money with which to do the work. In addition to this Standing Fund, she is endeavoring also to secure enough money for the early establishment of a Press Bureau for the purpose of taking up and answering, day by day, the false statements made in regard to woman suffrage, its ultimate aims and actual results; to furnish news and arguments where they are desired; and to enlist the support of the press for this question, which is now acknowledged to be one of the leading issues of the day.

The event of 1897 which gave Miss Anthony more pleasure than all others, in fact one of the happiest incidents of her life, was the Anthony Reunion at Adams, Mass., the last of July. The Historical and Scientific Society of Berkshire had for many years held an annual meeting at some one of the historic spots for which that county is especially noted. In 1895 this had been held in the dooryard of the old Anthony homestead, and she had been invited to be present, but was otherwise engaged. It had been the custom to eulogize her highly at these gatherings but it was determined that now she must come and speak for herself, therefore the invitation was repeated for 1896, but then she was in California. In 1897 the letter from the president, A. L. Perry, said: ''The present writing is to give you a formal and official invitation, in the name of the people of the entire county, whose representatives we are, to be present and participate in our next meeting. You may be sure of a warm welcome from your old neighbors who remain, and from the generation of Berkshire people, men and women, now on the stage.''

The meeting was to be held in Lee, and she wrote that if they would again hold it at the old Anthony homestead she would put aside everything else and come. She soon received this answer from Rev. A. B. Whipple: '' It gives me pleasure, as vice-president of the Berkshire Historical Society, to inform you that we have decided to gratify your ' bit of sentiment' as well as our own inclination to meet again ' in that old dooryard,' to do you honor as one of the natives of Berkshire whose historic lives are finding a deserved and permanent record in our society.''

Miss Anthony ever wanted her friends to share in her joys and was anxious that everybody should know her friends, so she wrote that she would like to have the Berkshire people hear Miss Shaw and others among the noted speakers. After some exchange of letters the officers of the society requested her to take charge of the program of the day, and promised to second all her arrangements. As she always combined business with pleasure she appointed a meeting of the national suffrage committee that week, and thus brought to Adams her '' body guard,'' Miss Shaw, Miss Blackwell, Mrs. Catt, Mrs. Avery, Mrs. Upton[1] and, by invitation, Mrs. Sewall, Mrs. Colby and Mrs. Harper. She had decided also to have at this time a family reunion, and for many weeks had been writing far and wide to the Anthonys, the Laphams, the Reads and the Richardsons, bidding all come to Adams on the 29th of July, and as a result the '' Old Hive '' swarmed as it never had done, even in the early days. She went on a week ahead and joined forces with her cousin, Mrs. Fannie Bates, who lived in the house. Albert Anthony, another cousin and near neighbor,

---

[1] Miss Laura Clay and Mrs. Catharine Waugh McCulloch, the national auditors, were unable to be present.

put himself, his horses and vehicles at their service; other relatives came to their assistance, beds were set up, provisions laid in; and for a week fifteen people picnicked in the old homestead. The overflow was received in the hospitable homes of other relatives in the neighborhood, and even Hotel Greylock, in the village, was pressed into service to entertain the guests, who came from Kansas, Illinois, New York, Pennsylvania, New Jersey, New Hampshire and other States.

The suffrage committee meetings were held during several days and evenings preceding the Historical Society celebration. It was a picture always to be remembered, that group of distinguished women, standing at the very head of the greatest progressive movement of the age, gathered in serious conclave in those old-fashioned, low-ceiled rooms built over a century ago, concocting schemes which would have filled their Quaker owners with holy horror. It seemed almost as if they would come back from the dim past to ask what it all meant. And yet, when one recalled that the Quakers never commanded their women to keep silence in the meeting house, but recognized their full equality there and elsewhere, and stood for liberty in a world given over to religious and political tyranny, it seemed indeed most fitting that the representatives of this great association for securing freedom to all, should come together under the roof of one of these old Friends. One felt as if the ancient door-latch should lift, and Aunt Hannah, the wise and gentle Quaker preacher, should glide in and take her seat among these other women whom the Spirit also had moved. But the most remarkable feature of this unique occasion was that the woman presiding over the deliberations of this body of reformers, should have carried on her childish games in this very room, seventy-five years before, and listened with awe to parents and grandparents as they discussed the burning questions of intemperance, slavery and religious intolerance.

An unseasonable storm of several days' duration had made it necessary to transfer the meeting of the Historical Society to the pavilion in Plunkett's Park. The ladies of Adams and vicinity, with Mrs. Susan Anthony Brown at their head, had prepared a bountiful luncheon for the officers of the society and the fifty invited guests, and here, at noon on July 29, Miss Anthony sat at the upper end of the long table with Rev. Anna Shaw on one hand and Rev. A. B. Whipple on the other. At the conclusion of the luncheon, the officers and speakers took seats on the stage in the large pavilion, which soon was filled with an audience that had come from Williamstown, North Adams, Pittsfield, Great Barrington, Lee and other surrounding towns. The Adams Freeman said : "If the group of women speakers were brilliant, the audience that honored them, while less so perhaps in renown, was equal in intellectual attainments. It was a cultured assembly, including the most progressive people of Berkshire."[1]

In a few words of welcome Rev. Louis Zahner, the Episcopal minister, spoke of the Anthony family as having laid the foundations of the schools, the industries and the prosperity of Adams, and of the community's indebtedness to them for the best it has today. Mr. Whipple, in a cordial address, then introduced Miss Anthony and placed the meeting in her charge. Can any pen describe her pride and happiness in returning thus to the loved home of her birth and childhood, to meet this warm and appreciative welcome and to introduce in turn her cabinet of eminent women ?

After relating some very interesting recollections of her ancestors and of early events, which were especially appreciated by the old residents, she introduced Mrs. Carrie Chapman Catt, who said in the course of a graceful address :

There is no citizen of this great nation who would not be delighted with the privilege of visiting these Berkshire hills, famed for their beauty, but it is not because of this that most of us have made this pilgrimage to Adams; rather have we come with much of that spirit which led the thousands upon thousands of Christians in the early centuries to Jerusalem, or which later prompted thousands of Mohammedans to make their pilgrimage to the city of Mecca. We have come to Adams because it is the birthplace of the greatest woman of our time.

[1] There were present also reporters from the New York Sun, New York World, Springfield Republican, Rochester Democrat and Chronicle, and other papers.

AT THE OLD HOMESTEAD, JULY 30, 1897.

Many centuries ago, on the 15th of February, there was born a man whose name is familiar to every school-child throughout the civilized world, and yet that man never knew a happy day. He was reviled, persecuted, martyred, tried, condemned, and died sorrowful and broken-hearted. And what was his offense? He declared that this earth turned upon its axis and that it moved around the sun. There were no newspapers in that day, but every pulpit thundered its denunciation against the great Galileo. When he was condemned to die he was compelled to renounce this belief, but under his breath he said, "The world does move!" A century after he had gone, not a pulpit in Christendom, not a scholar, was there but knew that he had told the truth.

It is a curious coincidence that upon the anniversary of the birthday of Galileo there was born Susan B. Anthony. She also perceived a great truth and the world did not agree with her. It reviled her for the belief she had propounded, but in this century she never renounced that belief, but thundered back to the pulpit and to the newspapers that the world does move and the time will come when women shall be free; the time will come when they shall have every right, every privilege, every liberty which any man enjoys. . . . We, today, are making the first pilgrimage to the birthplace of Susan B. Anthony, but I prophesy that in another quarter of a century there will be many pilgrimages hither, and no child will be so illiterate as not to know that in this county it was this greatest of American women was born.

Mrs. Rachel Foster Avery followed with an entertaining account of her trip abroad with Miss Anthony and the latter's utter indifference to the titles of the nobility. As she never could get them right she discarded all of them and insisted on calling everybody plain "Mr." and "Mrs." She then related this incident:

We had in our party for a few weeks a couple of English ladies. When driving in Rome, one of them, a great dame of noble lineage, was admiring an old palace belonging to some very ancient Roman family and made the statement that this same family owned five other famous palaces in Italy. Miss Anthony seemed to be making a mental calculation, and finally said with enthusiasm, "What a magnificent orphan asylum that would make."

"Why, Miss Anthony, do you mean that you would actually turn the home of this old family into an orphan asylum?"

"Yes," said she, "I think about 700 of these little ragamuffins could be put in there. Think of the streets just full of them, and all these big houses vacant! I don't see a better use to which these old palaces could be put."

Mrs. Upton in her bright, humorous way related some amusing stories which she had heard from her ancestors, who were born in Berkshire, and adroitly turned them into an argument for woman suffrage. A beautiful poem was read, entitled "Pioneers," dedicated to Miss Anthony by her old friend John M. Thayer, of Rochester. Col. D. R. Anthony created great mirth by telling among other stories that eighty years ago his father had a cotton mill of twenty-six looms; one day all of them suddenly stopped and, rushing out to ascertain the cause, he found that his wife, in rinsing her mop in the stream, had stopped the power which moved the machinery! He then referred to the Plunkett factories with 2,600 looms, and the other great mills of Adams, as illustrating the progress of the century. In an address which glowed with beauty and eloquence, Mrs. May Wright Sewall thus compared Miss Anthony's character with the scenes amidst which she was born:

We, who own and follow our general, know that she goes where Liberty leads, where Justice calls, where Love whispers his divine commands; and we have found in her the gravity of your stately mountains, the yearning for freedom of your lofty hills lifted toward the sky spaces. We have found in her the impetuosity of your mountain streams, which, fretting against narrow bounds, broke through them, widening and widening ever the channel of the life of American womanhood; and so we, who love appropriateness, gaze with delight upon this scenery, the environment of her infancy and the nurturing influence of her childhood, as a fine illustration of the eternal fitness of things.

One of the most exquisite addresses of the day was made by Mrs. Clara B. Colby, who said in part:

Miss Anthony's love of justice links her with the divine. This has been her impelling motive, and her patient endurance has been the secret of her success. No matter how keen might have been her sense of the injustice done to women, no matter how courageously she might have set out to right the wrong, had she lacked endurance, she had never been the one to lead us to victory. As justice is the root of the tree of character, and patience the stalk from which all growth proceeds, so tenderness is the outflowering of the divinity within. By her tenderness Miss Anthony has made herself loved where she might have only been honored.

It was perhaps the drop hardest to swallow from the cup of bitterness which was ever pressed to the lips of the early woman suffragists, that they were destroyers of the home. To Miss Anthony, the home and kindred-lover—homeless only for the sake of the homes of the mother-half of the race—this must have been especially hard to bear. There are such all over the land where she has been a tender and sympathetic friend and where she is enshrined in the hearts of the homekeepers. . . . Thus Miss Anthony, justice-loving, patient and tender, has erected for herself a lasting monument in the hearts of the women of this nation. May the time be long deferred when she shall pass from the leadership of her now triumphant host, but when that day comes, let there be, as she has enjoined upon us, no tears, but only glad thankfulness for a great life-work wrought in courage, fidelity and tenderness.

Mrs. Colby urged the Historical Society to purchase the old homestead, if possible, as a depository not only for relics of the Anthony family but for mementoes of suffrage work and workers. No report ever can give an adequate idea of the eloquence of Anna Shaw, so artistically diversified by delicious bits of humor and keen points of satire. A portion of her address was as follows :

Amidst all the eulogy which has surrounded Miss Anthony this afternoon, her brother said to me, " Don't you think they will turn Susan's head? " I answered, " No, she has had so many years of misrepresentation and abuse that if they keep on eulogizing her as long as she lives, it won't balance the other side." There is no danger in this world that the leader of an unpopular cause ever will die of overpraise, for, in America as in Jerusalem, the prophets of God have always been received with stones. We who know her best love her most, and to me the truest and deepest love of my existence, since my mother entered the life beyond, is that which I cherish for Susan B. Anthony.

The remonstrants today tell us that our movement will destroy the affectionate tenderness of the womanly nature and unsex woman until she becomes a weak man. I believe in men, and I do not believe that all the love, the tenderness, the power to sacrifice is feminine. I believe that the love of man is as true and deep and tender as the love of woman. I will not accept the theory that "man is the head" and "woman is the heart." I believe that when God created head and heart for the human race He divided them equally and gave man his part and woman hers, and both have kept their own all the way down the centuries.

The part of Miss Anthony's life which is dearest to us is that into which she has admitted the few who belong to the sacred inner circle, who have seen her toil, her suffering, her soul's anguish and travail for the freedom, the larger growth, the diviner possibilities of womanhood; and if there is any evidence that living in the world, working for its uplift, does not destroy this trait in human character, it is shown in the life of Miss Anthony. There is no human being whom I have ever known who had more tenderness for the erring and greater willingness to overlook the frailties of human life. In this she shows that contact with the most disagreeable side of the reformer's work, makes the real woman not less but more womanly. I believe that if the principles which she advocates, the ideals for which she stands, were

ANT.—60

embodied in all womankind, we would have a motherhood diviner than any this world has ever known, a motherhood such as God had in his thought when he created woman to be the mother of the race. . . .

It is not a name we love today, it is not a person we revere, but a great, an ideal life of a woman who has battled with the world, who has been misunderstood, who has borne its scorn, who has been ostracised, and who, in the midst of all, has kept her life sweet, her heart young, her love tender; and when the best thing shall be said of her which men and women can say, it will be—she was true, she was noble, she was woman.

The day after the meeting of the Historical Society, occurred the Anthony Reunion at the old homestead, when eighty of the clan sat down at the long tables spread in grandfather's room, the keeping-room and the weaving-room; and what a dinner the famous cooks of the Anthony-Lapham-Read-Richardson families had prepared for this great occasion! Not the least important features were the eighteen apple-pies eaten with the world-renowned Berkshire cheese; and then the sweet bread and butter, the fried chicken, the baked beans, the rich preserves and cream, the delicious cake—but why attempt to describe a New England dinner prepared by New England women? Those who have eaten know what it is; those who have not, can not be made to understand.

Where Susan B. Anthony sat was the head of the table; at her right hand, the brother Daniel R.; at her left, the brother Merritt; and close by, the quiet, smiling sister Mary; and then all along down the line, the cousins, the nephews, the nieces, three and four generations, who had joined so heartily with her for the success of this rare occasion. Before the dinner began, Miss Anthony asked that, in accordance with the custom of their ancestors, there might be a moment of silent thanks; and at the close of the meal, when the chatter and mirth were stilled, she arose and in touching words paid tribute to the loved and gone who once blessed these rooms by their presence. She then called upon the representatives of the different branches, old and young, who, in prose or poetry, with wit or pathos, made delightful response.

After all had finished they adjourned to the dooryard and a reception commenced which even the roomy old house could

THE QUAKER MEETING HOUSE, ADAMS, MASS.

150 YEARS OLD. SEVERAL MEMBERS OF THE ANTHONY FAMILY IN THE GROUP OF PIONEERS.

not have accommodated. For several hours a long line of
carriages wound up the hill—the people of Adams and vicinity
coming to pay respect to their illustrious townswoman and her
relatives and friends. The immediate members of the family
were photographed in a group on the old porch, as was also
the dinner party gathered in the historic dooryard. The mountain air was sweet and invigorating, and the view in every
direction most enchanting. A more picturesque spot scarcely
can be imagined : in front, the long range of Berkshire hills,
a spur of the Green mountains of Vermont whose faint out-
lines are visible in the distance ; at the back, glorious " Old
Greylock," the highest peak in the State ; at the right, the
steep, winding road leading down to the village a mile below,
through a ravine perfectly bewildering in its beauty of over-
hanging trees, moss-grown rocks and fern-bordered brook
tumbling over the massive boulders in its rapid descent to join
the Hoosac ; and then united they flow through the pretty
town of Adams, turning the countless wheels of the great mills
and factories.

The next day after the reunion a merry party of thirty, the
guests of a cousin, William Anthony, started in two great
coaches, each drawn by six horses, for the all-day trip to the
top of Mount Greylock. The gayest and happiest of them all
was Miss Anthony, with her red shawl over her shoulders, and
her heart as light as when she used to climb these mountain-
sides, a little, barefooted girl, more than seventy years ago.
Several days thereafter were spent visiting the pleasant homes
of the relatives, and going with her friends to point out the
various places of interest. Every spot connected with her early
life was as sacred to them as it was dear to her. Together they
went to the deserted Quaker meeting house, a century and a
half old, and were shown the very spot where sat the grandfather, the father, mother and little ones ; and the raised bench
occupied by the grandmother, who was a "high-seat Quaker,"
and Aunt Hannah Hoxie, the preacher. They strolled through
the little graveyard, with its lines of unmarked mounds. They
visited the site of the old mill, built by Daniel Anthony at the

very beginning of the manufacturing industry, where now only a few sunken stones mark the foundation. They rested beneath the great trees which stand like sentinels in front of the girlhood home of the mother, the house long since crumbled away. They gazed curiously at the ancient Bowen's Tavern, the favorite stopping-place of the mountaineers in early days.

And then they went with Miss Anthony into her own old home. They stepped reverently into the very room where she was born. They climbed to the garret and she pointed out the exact spot by the tiny window where she used to sit with her simple playthings. They stood with her by the little stream which still ran merrily through the dooryard, and listened with misty eyes as she recalled many touching incidents of days long past; but, however her own heart might have ached with tender recollections, there were no words of vain longing, no useless tears for those who had fulfilled their mission and passed away, leaving to her their legacy of hope and courage and determination. Strong, brave and cheerful, she honored the memory of the dead in showing herself by her works to be the worthy descendant of a noble race. And here, where the story of this pure, single-hearted, self-sacrificing life began, it shall be ended.

The usual fate of reformers is " praise when the ear has grown too dull to hear, fame when the heart it should have thrilled is numb." Seldom it is, indeed, that they live to see the fulfillment of the end for which they labored, and even recognition usually is deferred until it can be given only to a memory, but there are a few happy exceptions. While true reformers seek no personal reward, those who love them rejoice when they are spared to receive the honors they have earned. Susan B. Anthony's self-imposed task, for almost half a century, has been to secure equal rights for women— social, civil and political. When she began her crusade, woman in social life was " cabin'd, cribb'd, confined," to an extent which scarcely can be conceived by the present inde-

pendent and self-reliant generation ; in law she was but little
better than a slave ; in politics, a mere cipher.   Today in society she has practically unlimited freedom ; in the business
world most of the obstacles have been removed ; the laws,
although still unjust in many respects, have been revolution-
ized in her favor; in four States women have the full franchise,
in one the municipal ballot, in twenty-five a vote on school
questions, and in four others some form of suffrage ; while in
each campaign their recognition as a political factor grows
more marked.   Miss Anthony's part in securing these concessions may be judged from the record of these pages.   She is
the only woman who has given her whole time and effort to
this one end, with no division of interest in behalf of husband
and children, no diversion of other public questions.   Is there
an example in all history of either man or woman who devoted
half a century of the hardest, most persistent labor for one reform ?

   " Of the dead naught shall be spoken except good," is a rule
so universally observed that post mortem compliments have
little weight, but when beautiful things are said of those who
still live and toil, they are full of meaning.   Not only is it a
delight to her contemporaries, but it will be a pleasure to future
generations who shall read her history, that Miss Anthony
lived to receive her meed of appreciation.   While not all of
even the enlightened minds of today have progressed far
enough to accept her doctrine of perfect equality, which will
be universally admitted by the next generation, there are few
who do not recognize and honor the splendid character of the
woman and the service she has rendered.   Just as these closing words are being written, the State superintendent of public works, George W. Aldridge, announces that he has ordered
her face to be carved in the Capitol at Albany, one of the magnificent public buildings of the world.   Here, wrought in imperishable stone, amidst those of the country's greatest warriors
and statesmen, it will look down forever upon that grand stair-
case whose marble steps were so many times pressed by her

weary feet, as she made her annual pilgrimage to plead for liberty.

The sweetest strains in this great oratorio are the tributes of women voicing their love and gratitude. They come from those in all the walks of life, and a distinguishing feature is that they who have known her longest and best are most loyal and devoted. The secret of this is perfectly expressed by May Wright Sewall, when she says:

Mortals with all their consciousness of their own infirmities are exacting of one another. It is a proof of the infinite possibilities involved in the human soul, and a foundation for the infinite hope which sustains us, that we are satisfied with nothing less than perfection in other people. Is a woman great? To please us she must be also good. Is a woman both great and good? We are not satisfied unless she be likewise loving and lovable. No one can come near to the life of Miss Anthony without realizing how responsive she is to personal needs; how lively in her sympathies; how instinctive her out-reaching of the helping hand. The same fidelity and single-minded loyalty which have characterized her public career, distinguish her in all private relations. Others may forget us in our griefs, she never forgets. Others may forget us in our pleasures, she never forgets.

It is indeed true that Miss Anthony never forgets. In her letters to hundreds of people, she recollects always to send a message to the different members of the family, to refer to some agreeable incident of their acquaintance, and to express either pleasure or regret over personal affairs which any one else would have failed to remember amidst such a pressure of work and responsibility.

After an unbroken friendship of twenty-five years, Frances E. Willard, herself one of the grandest women of the century, paid this beautiful tribute in December, 1897:

Ever since I "came to myself" my love and loyalty have enveloped the name, Susan B. Anthony. I look upon her as that figure full of courage, re-source and dignity which will yet be enshrined in the admiring affection of the whole republic, even as it already has been for so long in that of thought-ful women. Others have done nobly and we count over their names with devout remembrance and gratitude, but Susan B. Anthony by reason of her heroic self-sacrifice, her lonely life, her changeless devotion, her disregard for money and position, her concentration of purpose and universal good will, has made for herself a place on the highest pedestal in America's pan-theon of women.

We do not forget "the slings and arrows" of the earlier time, now that she is justly honored in these years of greater intelligence and progress; we do not forget that high sense of personal integrity which led her to pay off the debts on The Revolution, although no legal obligation rested upon her to do so; we do not forget her testing of an unjust law in the great "case" in Rochester; we do not forget that (jointly with her great associate, Mrs. Stanton) she prepared for us that invaluable historic record of the suffrage movement from its earliest inception; we do not forget the untiring labors which have carried her, from youth to age, into every nook and corner of the Union; and many of us are cognizant of unnumbered acts of personal kindness toward women in need who cherish her as if she were their sister or their mother. Although the press once misrepresented her, it would hardly venture to do so now, for her standing with the public is such that not to know Miss Anthony argues one's self unknown, and to vilify her argues one's self a villain.

Blessed Sister Susan, accept the homage of one whom you have cheered and comforted, and who rejoices to believe that the loving friendship begun here shall grow and deepen in the bright light of that happier world where there is no injustice, and where we have abundant reason to believe that women will stand on a plane of perfect equality.

A number of years ago, Elizabeth Cady Stanton, in her own unsurpassed beauty of language, said:

I will attempt no analysis of one as dear to me as those of my own household. In an intimate friendship of many years, without a break or shadow; in daily consultation, sometimes for months together under the same roof, often in circumstances of great trial and perplexity, I can truly say that Susan B. Anthony is the most charitable, self-reliant, magnanimous human being that I ever knew.

As I recall the honesty and heroism of her public life; her tenderness and generous self-sacrifice to friends in private; her spontaneous good will towards her worst enemies, a new hope kindles within me for womankind—a hope that by giving some high purpose to their lives, all women may be lifted above the petty envy, jealousy, malice and discontent that now poison so many hearts which might, in healthy action, overflow with love and helpfulness to all humanity. Miss Anthony's grand life is a lesson to all unmarried women, showing that the love-element need not be wholly lost if it is not centered on husband and children. To live for a principle, for the triumph of some reform by which all mankind are to be lifted up—to be wedded to an idea— may be, after all, the holiest and happiest of marriages.

In the twilight of age, when Mrs. Stanton prepared for future generations the Reminiscences of her life and work of fourscore years, she wrote to her old friend: "The current of our lives has run in the same channel so long it can not be separated, and my book is as much your story as, I doubt not, yours is mine;" and when it was ended she placed upon it the inscription, "I dedicate this volume to Susan B. Anthony, my steadfast friend for half a century."

Steadfast! No other word so fitly defines the keystone of the arch of noble attributes upon which this heroic life is founded—as constant to a principle as to a friendship. There is nothing of the martyr in Miss Anthony's nature and she refuses to consider herself in the light of a vicarious sacrifice. "I do not look back upon a hard life," she says; "I have been continually at work because I enjoyed being busy. Had this never-ending toil made me wretched in mind or body, I have no doubt that in some way I should have gotten out of it." "What thanks did you receive for the stand you made?" once was asked her. "I had my own thanks for retaining my self-respect," was the reply. Again one inquired, "Did you not grow discouraged in those olden times?" "Never," she answered; "I knew that my cause was just, and I was always in good company." Her character, instead of growing embittered by the hard experiences of early days, has been sweetened and strengthened by the high moral purpose which has dominated her life. She is a philanthropist in her love of mankind and her work for humanity, but she is governed by philosophy rather than emotion, ever examining causes and effects by the pure light of reason and logic.

Susan B. Anthony has been called the Napoleon of the woman suffrage movement and, in the planning of campaigns and the boldness and daring of carrying them forward, there may be the qualities of that famous general, but in character and principles the comparison fails utterly. She has been termed the Gladstone among women, and in statesmanlike ability and long years of distinguished service, there may be points of resemblance, but she would repudiate the sacrifice of justice to party expediency, oftentimes charged against the noted English politician. It has been said that she has been the great Liberator of women, as Lincoln was of the negroes. There is indeed something in her countenance and manner which reminds one of Lincoln, the same unconscious dignity, the same rugged endurance, the same strong, resolute face, softened by lines of weariness and care and spiritualized by an expression of infinite patience and indescribable pathos. She has not, however, the conservatism, the forbearance, the reverence for existing laws and constitutions, which made Lincoln slow to act and tolerant almost to the point of criticism.

She has been described as being to the cause of woman's emancipation, what Garrison was to that of the slave. She has, perhaps, more of the characteristics of Garrison than of the other three conspicuous figures of the century. His motto, "No Compromise," has been her watchword. Like Garrison, she strikes a body-blow straight from the shoulder. She recognizes no such word as expediency and accepts no halfway measures. Theoretically a non-resistant, she fights to the last ditch and never accepts a defeat as final. She has the natural gift of selecting always the strongest word, and the power of carrying conviction to her audience. She is conventional in outward observances, but most radical in thought and speech. She detests all forms of cruelty and oppression, but it is the action, not the person, that she censures, and she is most charitable in excuses for the faults and failings of others. She bears the ills of life with cheerful fortitude, and accepts the blessings with fine humility. There is no need of comparison. She has her own strong individuality, which has made its indelible impress upon history and secured for her a place among the immortals. Now, in life's evening, her world is illumined with the beauty of a sunset undimmed by clouds—and as she contemplates the infinite, she takes no heed of the gathering darkness of night, but looking into a clear sky beholds only the ineffable glory of other spheres.

APPENDIX.

APPENDIX

ADDRESS TO PRESIDENT LINCOLN.

Adopted by the Women's National Loyal League, May 14, 1863.

. . . We ask not for ourselves or our friends redress of specific grievances or posts of honor or emolument. We speak from no considerations of
mere material gain; but, inspired by true patriotism, in this dark hour of our
nation's destiny, we come to pledge the loyal women of the Republic to freedom and our country. We come to strengthen you with earnest words of
sympathy and encouragement. We come to thank you for your proclamation, in which the nineteenth century seems to echo back the Declaration of
Seventy-six. Our fathers had a vision of the sublime idea of liberty, equality
and fraternity; but they failed to climb the heights which with anointed eyes
they saw. To us, their children, belongs the work to build up the living
reality of what they conceived and uttered. It is not our mission to criticise
the past. Nations, like individuals, must blunder and repent. It is not wise
to waste our energy in vain regret, but from each failure we should rise up with
renewed conscience and courage for nobler action. The follies and faults of
yesterday we cast aside as the old garments we have outgrown. Born anew to
freedom, slave creeds and codes and constitutions all now must pass away.
"For men do not put new wine into old bottles, else the bottles break and
the wine runneth out and the bottles perish; but they put new wine into
new bottles and both are preserved."

Our special thanks are due to you, that by your proclamation 2,000,000
women are freed from the foulest bondage humanity ever suffered. Slavery
for man is bad enough, but the refinements of cruelty ever must fall on the
mothers of the oppressed race, defrauded of all the rights of the family relation and violated in the most holy instincts of their nature. A mother's life
is bound up in that of her child. There center all her hopes and ambitions.
But the slave-mother in her degradation rejoices not in the future promise of
her daughter, for she knows by experience what her sad fate must be. No
pen can describe the unutterable agony of that mother whose past, present
and future all are wrapped in darkness; who knows the crown of thorns she
wears must press her daughter's brow; who knows the wine-press she treads
those tender feet must tread alone. For, by the law of slavery, "the child
follows the condition of the mother."

By your act, the family, that great conservator of national virtue and
strength, has been restored to millions of humble homes around whose altars
coming generations shall magnify and bless the name of Abraham Lincoln.
By a mere stroke of the pen you have emancipated millions from a condition

of wholesale concubinage. We now ask you to finish the work by declaring that nowhere under our national flag shall the motherhood of any race plead in vain for justice and protection. So long as one slave breathes in this republic, we drag the chain with him. God has so linked the race, man to man, that all must rise or fall together. Our history exemplifies this law. It was not enough that we at the North abolished slavery for ourselves, declared freedom of speech and press, built churches, colleges and free schools, studied the science of morals, government and economy, dignified labor, amassed wealth, whitened the sea with our commerce and commanded the respect and admiration of the nations of the earth—so long as the South, by the natural proclivities of slavery, was sapping the very foundations of our national life. . . .

You are the first President ever borne on the shoulders of freedom into the position you now fill. Your predecessors owed their elevation to the slave oligarchy, and in serving slavery they did but obey their masters. In your election, northern freemen threw off the yoke, and with you rests the responsibility that our necks never shall bow again. At no time in the annals of the nation has there been a more auspicious moment to retrieve the one false step of the fathers in their concessions to slavery. The Constitution has been repudiated and the compact broken by the southern traitors now in arms. The firing of the first gun on Sumter released the North from all constitutional obligations to slavery. It left the government, for the first time in our history, free to carry out the declaration of our Revolutionary fathers, and made us in fact what we ever have claimed to be, a nation of freemen.

"The Union as it was"—a compromise between barbarism and civilization—can never be restored, for the opposing principles of freedom and slavery can not exist together. Liberty is life, and every form of government yet tried proves that slavery is death. In obedience to this law, our republic, divided and distracted by the collisions of class and caste, is tottering to its base and can be reconstructed only on the sure foundation of impartial freedom to all. The war in which we are involved is not the result of party or accident, but a forward step in the progress of the race never to be retraced. Revolution is no time for temporizing or diplomacy. In a radical upheaving the people demand eternal principles on which to stand.

Northern power and loyalty never can be measured until the purpose of the war be liberty to man ; for a lasting enthusiasm ever is based on a grand idea, and unity of action demands a definite end. At this time our greatest need is not men or money, valiant generals or brilliant victories, but a *consistent policy*, based on the principle that "all governments derive their just powers from the consent of the governed." The nation waits for you to say that there is no power under our declaration of rights nor under any laws, human or divine, by which free men can be made slaves; and therefore that your pledge to the slaves is irrevocable, and shall be redeemed.

If it be true, as it is said, that northern women lack enthusiasm in this war, the fault rests with those who have confused and confounded its policy. The pages of history glow with instances of self-sacrifice by women in the hour of their country's danger. Fear not that the daughters of this republic will count any sacrifice too great to insure the triumph of freedom. Let the men who wield the nation's power be wise, brave and magnanimous, and its women will be prompt to meet the duties of the hour with devotion and heroism.

When Fremont on the western breeze proclaimed a day of jubilee to the bondmen within our gates, the women of the nation echoed back a loud amen. When Hunter freed a million men and gave them arms to fight our battles, justice and mercy crowned that act and tyrants stood appalled. When Butler, in the chief city of the southern despotism, hung a traitor we felt a glow of pride; for that one act proved that we had a government and one man brave enough to administer its laws. And when Burnside would banish Vallandigham to the Dry Tortugas, let the sentence be approved and the nation will ring with plaudits. Your proclamation gives you immortality. Be just, and share your glory with men like these who wait to execute your will.

On behalf of the Women's National Loyal League,

ELIZABETH CADY STANTON, *President.*
SUSAN B. ANTHONY, *Secretary.*

RECONSTRUCTION.

Address Delivered at Ottumwa, Kansas, July 4, 1865.

Mr. President, and Men and Women of Kansas:

It is a pleasure to me, beyond the reach of words, to be with you today. I accepted the invitation of your committee that I might feast my eyes on your grand prairies, ever fringed with the darker green of their timber-skirted creeks and rivers. I came here on this 89th anniversary of our National Independence, that I might look into the honest, earnest faces of the men and the women who, ten years ago, taught the nation anew, that "resistance to tyrants is obedience to God." Through all this glorious decade of heroic struggle, my interests, my sympathies, my affections have been bound up with yours; for, during and since the cruel outrages of the summer of 1856, my two and only brothers have stood shoulder to shoulder with the freedom-loving, freedom-voting, freedom-fighting men of Kansas. And, as I have waited the telegraphic word that trembled along the western wires, telling of your successes and your defeats, it has ever been with bated breath lest those of my own home circle, too, should be numbered among the slain. Therefore, though not here in person through all these trial years, in spirit I have been with you, in your privations and hardships, in your sufferings and sacrifices to make freedom and free institutions the sure inheritance of Kansas and the nation.

You have already listened to the grand old Declaration of the Fathers of 1776. You have heard the true words of your representative to the next Congress.[1] His manly utterances here today give you assurance that he will faithfully reflect the highest and truest sentiments of his constituency. Men and women of Kansas, I congratulate you, that you have in this chosen agent a man who will speak and vote on the vital questions to come before the next Congress from the standpoint of human equality.

It is my purpose to call your attention to the recent declarations of our President to our "erring sister States" of the South. I ask you specially to note his proclamation to Mississippi. After pointing out that the Constitution of the United States guarantees to every State in the Union a republican form of government, and that the late rebellion has deprived the people of Mississippi of all civil government, he continues:

Now, therefore, in obedience to the high and solemn duties imposed upon me by the Constitution of the United States, and for the purpose of enabling the loyal people of said State to organize a State government, whereby justice may be established, domestic tranquillity in-

[1] Sidney Clark, of Lawrence.

sured, and loyal citizens protected in all their rights of life, liberty, and property, I, Andrew Johnson, President of the United States, and Commander-in-Chief of the army and navy of the United States, do hereby appoint William L. Sharkey Provisional Governor of the State of Mississippi, whose duty it shall be, at the earliest practicable period, to prescribe such rules and regulations as may be necessary and proper for convening a convention, composed of delegates to be chosen by that portion of the people of said State who are loyal to the United States, and no others, for the purpose of altering or amending the constitution thereof; and with authority to exercise, within the limits of said State, all the powers necessary and proper to enable such loyal people of the State of Mississippi to restore said State to its constitutional relations to the Federal government, and to present such republican form of State government as will entitle the State to the guarantee of the United States therefor, and its people to protection by the United States against invasion, insurrection, and domestic violence: Provided, That in any election that may be hereafter held for choosing delegates to any State Convention as aforesaid, no person shall be qualified as an elector, or shall be eligible as a member of such convention, unless he shall have previously taken and subscribed the oath of amnesty, as set forth in the President's proclamation of May 29, A. D. 1865, *and is a voter qualified as prescribed by the Constitution and laws of the State of Mississippi, in force immediately before the ninth (9th) of January, A. D. 1861, the date of the so-called ordinance of secession;* and the said convention, when convened, or the Legislature that may be thereafter assembled, will prescribe the qualifications of electors, and the eligibility of persons to hold office under the Constitution and laws of the State, a power the people of the several States composing the Federal Union have rightfully exercised from the origin of the government to the present time.

The President says he finds the people of Mississippi "deprived of all civil government" by the revolutionary progress of the rebellion; therefore he appoints a provisional governor, to call an election of the loyal people for delegates to a convention to alter or amend the constitution that was in force prior to the rebellion. He does this "for the purpose of enabling the loyal people of said State to organize a State government whereby justice may be established, domestic tranquillity insured, and loyal citizens protected in all their rights of life, liberty and property." To this laudable end he instructs the governor, who is his military agent, to allow no man to vote or to be voted for, unless he shall have previously taken and subscribed to the oath of amnesty of May 29, 1865, *and is a voter by the old constitution and laws of the slaveholding State of Mississippi.* By this ordering, the President makes it impossible for the great mass of the loyal people to have a voice in organizing the new government. He re-establishes precisely the same basis of class representation that worked out the ruin of the old State government. Not to mention the loyal women, who make fully one-half of the loyal people, he shuts out all the loyal black men, with all the loyal poor white men, who were not allowed to vote under the old regime of slavery.

Thus, by this initiative step, the President makes it inevitable that the rebuilding of the government shall be controlled by the ex-rebels; the men who have fought desperately for four years to overthrow the federal government; the men who hate republicanism; the men who love and are determined to enjoy aristocracy. The loyal white men there, who have stood firmly and truly by the government through all the cruel persecutions of this bloody rebellion, are today a most powerless and pitiable minority; and yet the President tells this little handful that their only hope of organizing a genuine republican form of government lies in their ability to outvote the vast horde of disloyal civilians and pardoned, but not penitent, returned rebel soldiers. Such an offence against white loyalty is enough to make the very stones cry out.

But what shall we say of the other and deeper crime against the thousands of loyal black soldiers, who have fought bravely for us from the hour we permitted them to shoulder the musket; against the entire slave population, who have welcomed our Yankee soldiers, been faithful spies and guides to our armies, nursed our sick and wounded, relieved and rescued our starving prisoners, and in every conceivable way and manner given "aid and comfort" to our Union cause? I tell you, men and women of Kansas, no tongue can speak the ingratitude, the injustice, the shame and outrage of a proposition thus to leave those true and faithful freedmen to the cruel legislation of their old tyrants and oppressors, made tenfold more their enemies, because of their attachment and service to the government which they themselves have failed to destroy. Think of it, to thrust four million loyal people under the political heel of eight millions, almost to a man, disloyal!

I am sure you, who have given the best blood of Kansas to put down the slaveholders' rebellion against the rightful rule of the majority, will never by your silence give seeming consent to a reorganization of those rebel States on any basis save that of the ballot to all loyal citizens, black and white. You will never consent that loyal Union soldiers and friends, for no crime but the color of their skin, shall be made subjects, if not slaves, to disloyal rebel soldiers and enemies, with no virtue but that of belonging to the "governing race," as the President's North Carolina appointee calls the white faces. No, no, you will make these grand old prairies ring with your thunder-toned protests until they shall be felt and feared in the legislative halls at Washington. Then will your honorable and honored representative say for you on the floor of the next Congress, as he has said here today in the shadow of these mighty oaks of your Neosho, "no reconstruction except on the basis of the ballot in every loyal hand, black and white." Then will your senator[1] echo your voice from his seat in the Capitol, as he did the other day in old Faneuil Hall, when he said, "the price of our victories is lost unless we give the negro the homestead, the musket, and the ballot."

And then will your other senator,[2] who has not spoken since he, with his colleagues in the Senate, said, "colonize" the faithful, loyal blacks; since he said, admit Louisiana and Arkansas back into the Union on the vote of the merest minority of their freshly-oathed white men—then will he say "no reconstruction without negro suffrage." But, good people, I charge you, suffer not this man to return to his seat in the Senate, until he has not only repented and confessed, but given sure promise forever to forsake his old sins of "white suffrage" and "black colonization." You owe it to yourselves and your country to see that your entire representation in the next Congress is right on this one vital question of reunion. Tell your senator if he must advocate a class and caste government in the rebel States, it must be loyal blacks, not disloyal whites. If he must colonize somebody, it must be the cowed, unconverted rebels, the anti-negro-equality white faces. Tell him

[1] S. C. Pomeroy.
[2] James H. Lane.

henceforth to speak and vote to disfranchise, and drive out if need be, the persons who make war and oppress and outrage, and are resolved not to give "fair play" to peaceable, industrious citizens. You have but to speak and you will be obeyed, for it is the people's will, not that of their servants, which is law.

Now, a word on your State legislature: One of the first reports that met my ear on my arrival in your State last winter, was that the Republicans of Kansas, almost in a body, had voted against a bill for "negro suffrage," and that they voted thus for the reason that the question was introduced and urged by the opposition party of the State. My humble but earnest advice to you is that you permit those delegates who voted against right, against justice, against equality to all men, for so paltry a reason, henceforth to remain quietly at home. Teach them and all other aspirants for your suffrages that your representatives must speak and vote for the right, though the arch-demon from the pit below shall present the measure. That miserable political quibbling at Topeka last winter lost Kansas the place which of right belonged to her—that of being the first of the loyal States to give her freedmen their inalienable right to self-protection.

Our hope of salvation from the fatal errors that are now fastening themselves upon the plan and the policy of reorganization, lies in the prompt and right action of the coming Congress. The delegates from any and all of the rebel States, sent up to Washington by "free white loyal male" suffrages to knock for admission into the Union, must be sent home with instructions that no member will be admitted to Congress except he be elected by a majority of all the loyal men of the State, black as well as white. To the end that Congress may thus reject the amnestied white suffrage delegates, the people, all over the country, should unite in one mighty voice and demand that their representatives shall thus speak and thus vote. "The price of liberty is eternal vigilance." If we sleep now, all is lost; for on this one question of the negro hangs the future of our republic.

Since the firing of the first gun of the rebellion there has been no hour fraught with so much danger as is the present. To have been vanquished on the field of battle would have involved much of misery; but to be foiled now in gathering up the fruits of our blood-bought victories, and to re-enthrone slavery under the new guise of negro disfranchisement, negro serfdom, would be a defeat and disaster, a cruelty and crime, which would surely bequeath to coming generations a legacy of wars and rumors of wars, equalled only by that which the Revolutionary fathers entailed upon their descendants by their fatal compromises with slavery. It would leave the final triumph of the great principles of republicanism, universal freedom and equality, "taxation and representation inseparable," the "consent of the governed," to be worked out and established in each of those old slave States, through a fearful re-enactment of the early struggles which you of Kansas so well remember.

If Congress shall admit the rebel representatives on the basis of white suffrage, those States will have added to their old representation the other two-fifths of what used to be "all other persons," which will give them an increase of fourteen votes in the House as a reward for their four years of fire and sword against the government. With this added power on the floor of Congress united to their political aiders and abettors from the Northern States, there is scarcely any project they may not be able to carry through in their own time and way. Nor is there room for a doubt, that it is the spirit and purpose of the slave oligarchy, whipped and cowed as they say by force of might, not right, to make a most desperate political fight to regain their old supremacy in the legislation of the country.

I base my estimate of the nature and intentions of the to-be-restored representation of the South, on the results of the elections already held in several of the rebel States, and from the efforts everywhere among the old planters again to reduce the black freedmen, as nearly as possible, to the status of slavery. In Virginia, the elections gave a legislature largely secession and almost wholly anti-negro. The planters have solemnly leagued themselves together to pay only five dollars per month to able field hands, each laborer to furnish his own clothes and pay his own doctor bills. This, too, when these same planters used to pay or receive for the hire of these same laborers, the sum of fifteen dollars and upwards. In South Carolina, Gen. Rufus Saxton reports that the old planters are actually driving the freedmen to work in the fields in chain gangs, and that the woods are strewn with the bodies of negroes shot dead in their efforts to escape the cruel torture. In Murfreesboro, Tennessee, the city election resulted in a secession mayor and common council. The only Union success I have noticed is that of Fernandina, Florida, and there the negroes were allowed to vote. Even the loyal State of Missouri saved her free constitution by less than two thousand votes.

The result of white suffrage can not be other than the election of large majorities of anti-negro, if not absolutely secession State and National representatives. Tennessee, the President's own State, of the loyalty of whose people we have heard much, has adopted a free constitution, and under it framed a new code of anti-negro laws; and we can hardly expect any rebel State to do better, for these new free State law-makers are the persecuted loyal men of Tennessee who have been outraged in their homes, hunted to the caves and mountains, or for a time driven out of the State altogether by the secessionists. One of these new free State laws says, the testimony of no "free colored person shall be received in court against any white person." By this enactment, the meanest white man may enter the home of the bravest black soldier, or wealthiest colored citizen, may murder his sons, ravish his wife and daughters, pillage and burn his house, commit any and every possible crime against him and his, and yet, if no human eye but his own, or that of his family, or his colored friends, witness the barbarisms, that black man, the father, the husband, the land-holder, outraged beyond measure, has no possible legal redress in the courts of Tennessee.

Then again, in case a free colored person is imprisoned and unable to pay his jail fees, he may be apprenticed out to labor until the sum be paid. And yet again, the courts may apprentice colored children as they see proper. The law does not even say friendless or orphan children. Is not that slavery under a new form? Thus, to leave those devoted black men's lives, liberties and property to be protected by white men, whose loyalty to the government is because it is a means to secure power to themselves, not from any love of its republican principles, is to doom them to all the ignominies and cruelties of slavery itself.

Let us not be deceived by the wicked wiles of politicians who tell us that President Johnson can not give the right to the ballot to the black loyalists of the South; for it is but the new "refuge of lies" to which slavery resorts. The same men told us that Lincoln had not the power to emancipate the slaves; that the government had no right to arm the negro, etc. If President Johnson has constitutional authority, either civil or military, to take away a man's right to vote, as a punishment for disloyalty, he must have power to give a man the same right, as a reward for loyalty; if the President may disfranchise a rebel soldier in order to enable the loyal people of a State to organize a republican form of government, he may also enfranchise a Union soldier to accomplish the same purpose. If the President has not the right nor the power to give the ballot to any person not entitled to it under the old order of slavery, how will he organize South Carolina, by whose old constitution no person was allowed to vote unless he owned ten slaves or was worth ten thousand dollars? Of course nobody owns ten slaves, and how many men, think you, who remained loyal at home, or how many returned soldiers or amnestied civilians have the requisite ten thousand dollars? In South Carolina, therefore, the President will be compelled to create voters; and, if he shall enfranchise any of the white non-voters, can he not also enfranchise the loyal black non-voters?

Let us watch and pray without ceasing. Let us hope that the day will dawn, and that soon, when law shall be found on the side of justice to the black race. These objectors never questioned McClellan's military right to put down slave insurrections with an "iron hand," or Halleck's infamous Order No. 3 to drive all negroes outside the military lines. It was only when Generals Fremont, Hunter and others declared the slaves free, that they might cripple the rebel armies and add them to our Union forces, that the cry of no law, no power was raised. Thus it is clear that the blindness and inability to find rightful authority, civil or military, first to emancipate, then to arm, and now to enfranchise the negroes, have the one source. Slavery perpetrated the "sum of all villainies" on the negroes, and then, to justify its wickedness, filled the whole land with atrocious lies of their depraved and degraded nature. The American people consented to the outrage; and their continued prejudice against that oppressed race but proves the adage, " we hate those whom we have injured."

Last of all comes the objection that the old masters will influence the vote of the negroes, and that, therefore, to enfranchise them will but give increased power to the old lords of the lash. Do not believe such nonsense. Think you, men who for four years have withstood every possible temptation and torture to induce them to fight for the slave oligarchy, can now be wheedled into voting for it? No, no. Those loyal, brave, black men who have known enough to fight on the right side will know enough to vote on the right side; and it is because the aiders and abettors of the old slave power believe and know that the negroes will be an invincible host on the side of equality, that they thus fear them.

We never from the beginning have had a genuine republican form of government in any State in the Union; for in no State have "the people" ever been permitted to elect their representatives. Even in Massachusetts and Vermont, the States nearest republican, only one-half of the people, the "male inhabitants," are allowed to vote. In other States it is only all " free white male persons," and in others still, all "free white male inhabitants owning so many slaves or so much property." It is not true therefore that *the people* have ever exercised the right to prescribe the qualifications of voters or officers. From the beginning, Congress always has settled the question in its organic act. That of your own Territory read, "Every free, white, male inhabitant shall vote at the first election, and be eligible to any office within the Territory." Thus you see Congress, not you, the people, decided who should and who should not vote in Kansas. And when the delegates of the prescribed "free, white, male" order met in convention, they proved themselves nothing above human, very like the so-elected conventions of other States, and retained all legislative power within the limits of the original congressional permit. The same is true of the rebel States, in which the President now finds the people destitute of all civil government; when he specifies who may vote, when he excludes any class from the ballot-box, he makes it impossible for "the people" to form a republican government.

When the loyal black men are not allowed their right to vote in the first election of the rebel States, their governments are thrown into the hands of a very small minority, and that too of very doubtful loyalty. The President by adhering to the old slave definition of "the people," rules that all our brave black Union soldiers and our best friends and allies, without whose aid we should still be struggling with rebels in arms, shall be subjects, not citizens, of the government they have rescued from the Confederate usurpers. It is not in human nature that a people fanatically believing themselves a superior race, and thereby rightful legislators over another and inferior race, shall execute justice and equality toward those whom they decree shall be " hewers of wood and drawers of water." No, the black man's guarantee to the protection of his inalienable rights to "life, liberty and property," is bound up in his right to the ballot.

When I speak of the inalienable rights of the negro, I do not forget that these belong equally to woman. Though the government shall be reconstructed on the basis of universal manhood suffrage, it yet will not be a true republic. Still one-half of the people will be in subjection to the other half, and the time will surely come when the whole question will have to be reopened and an accounting made with this other subject class. There will have to be virtually another reconstruction, based on the duty of the national government to guarantee to every citizen the right of self-protection, and this right, for woman as for man, is vested in the ballot.

That this superior " white male " class may not be trusted even to legislate for their own mothers, sisters, wives and daughters, the cruel statutes in nearly all the States, both slave and free, give ample proof. In scarcely a State has a married woman the legal right to the control of her person, to the earnings of her hands or brain, to the guardianship of her children, to sue or be sued, or to testify in the courts, and by these laws women have suffered wrongs and outrages second only to those of chattel slavery itself. If this be true, that this so-called superior class can not legislate justice even to those nearest and dearest in their own hearts and homes, is it not a crime to place a separate race, one hated and despised, wholly at the will of that governing class?

It must not be; and the one great work for the people at this hour, and every hour, between this and next December, is to agitate this question until the entire nation shall speak in tones not to be mistaken, which shall compel the coming Congress to refuse admission to every representative from the rebel States, who is sent there by the so-called "loyal white male" people.

"*No reorganization without Negro Suffrage*" is the word to send back to every rebel State. Until Congress shall define and settle this question, it can not in the future, as it has not in the past, perform its duty—guarantee a republican form of government in each of the States. When Congress shall thus decide, there will be work to do in most of the loyal States. Let us all labor to that end.

Men and women of Kansas, what say you, shall new loyal States or old rebel States be admitted into the Union until they present constitutions and laws truly republican, until they send representatives to Washington elected by a majority of all the people—white and black, men and women? You say No; your blood-enriched prairies, your battle-fought ravines, your sacked and burned cities, say No; your martyred dead, your own immortal John Brown, their freed souls all gloriously marching on, say No!

My friends, there is one word more I must leave with you. There is yet another danger. The reverence, the almost idolatry of the American people for their martyred President, is being used and abused by the political managers at Washington, and over all the country. The people are lulled to sleep over the most startling propositions, by insidious whisperings that President Lincoln originated or approved them. Almost every reconstruction plan is sent over the wires "sugar-coated" with, "President Johnson, in this, is but carrying out the spirit and purpose of Mr. Lincoln!" And there is no disguising or denying the fact, that the people are today accepting, and that too without questioning, the anti-negro reorganization plans already inaugurated, because of these wily, insinuating appeals to their reverence for the memory of their sacred dead.

If the four years' administration of Abraham Lincoln taught the American people any one lesson above another, it was that they must think and speak and proclaim, and that he, as President, was bound to execute their will, not his own. And if Lincoln were alive today, he would say as he did four years ago, "I wait the voice of the people." The stern logic of the events of today would guide him, not those of yesterday. Therefore let us not be thrown off our watch by any of these appeals to our reverence for the opinions and plans of our departed President. If his freed spirit is permitted today to hover over each and all of the vast gatherings of the loyal people throughout the nation, it is beckoning every soul upward and onward in the path of equal justice to all; it is urging the great heart of the nation to plant our new Union on the everlasting rock of republicanism—universal freedom and universal suffrage.

ADDRESS TO CONGRESS.

Adopted by the Eleventh National Woman's Rights Convention, held in New York City, Thursday, May 10, 1866.

Prepared by Elizabeth Cady Stanton and Susan B. Anthony.

To the Senate and House of Representatives:

We already have presented to your honorable body during this session many petitions asking the enfranchisement of women; and now, from our national convention, we again make our appeal and urge you to lay no hand on that "pyramid of rights," the Constitution of the Fathers, unless to add glory to its height and strength to its foundation.

We will not rehearse the oft-repeated arguments on the natural rights of every citizen, pressed as they have been on the nation's conscience for the last thirty years in securing freedom for the black race, and so grandly echoed on the floor of Congress during the past winter. We can not add one line or precept to the comprehensive speech recently made by Charles Sumner in the Senate, to prove that "no just government can be formed without the consent of the governed;" to prove the dignity, the education, the power, the necessity, the salvation of the ballot in the hand of every man and woman; to prove that a just government and a true church rest alike on the sacred rights of the individual.

As you are familiar with Sumner's speech on "Equal Rights to All," so convincing in facts, so clear in philosophy, and so elaborate in quotations from the great minds of the past, without reproducing the chain of argument, permit us to call your attention to a few of its unanswerable assertions regarding the ballot:

I plead now for the ballot, as the great guarantee, and the only sufficient guarantee—being in itself peacemaker, reconciler, schoolmaster and protector—to which we are bound by every necessity and every reason; and I speak also for the good of the States lately in rebellion, as well as for the glory and safety of the republic, that it may be an example to mankind.

Ay, sir, the ballot is the Columbiad of our political life, and every citizen who has it is a full-armed Monitor.

The ballot is schoolmaster. Reading and writing are of inestimable value, but the ballot teaches what these can not teach.

Plutarch records that the wise man of Athens charmed the people by saying that equality causes no war, and "both the rich and the poor repeated it."

The ballot is like charity, which never faileth, and without which man is only as sounding brass or a tinkling cymbal. The ballot is the one thing needful, without which rights of testimony and all other rights will be no better than cobwebs which the master will break through with impunity. To him who has the ballot all other things shall be given—

protection, opportunity, education, a homestead. The ballot is like the horn of abundance, out of which overflow rights of every kind, with corn, cotton, rice and all the fruits of the earth. Or, better still, it is like the hand of the body, without which man, who is now only a little lower than the angels, must have continued only a little above the brutes. They are fearfully and wonderfully made; but as is the hand in the work of civilization, so is the ballot in the work of government. "Give me the ballot, and I can move the world."

Do you wish to see harmony truly prevail, so that industry, society, government, civilization, may all prosper, and the republic may wear a crown of true greatness? Then do not neglect the ballot.

Lamartine said, "Universal suffrage is the first truth and only basis of every national republic."

In regard to "taxation without representation," Mr. Sumner quotes from Lord Coke:

The supreme power can not take from any man any part of his property without consent in person or by representation.

Taxes are not to be laid on the people, but by their consent in person or by representation.

I can see no reason to doubt but that the imposition of taxes, whether on trade, or on land or houses or ships, or real or personal, fixed or floating property in the colonies, is absolutely irreconcilable with the rights of the colonies, as British subjects and as men. I say men, for in a state of nature no man can take any property from me without my consent. If he does, he deprives me of my liberty and makes me a slave. The very act of taxing, exercised over those who are not represented, appears to me to deprive them of one of their most essential rights as freemen, and if continued seems to be in effect an entire disfranchisement of every civil right. For what one civil right is worth a rush, after a man's property is subject to be taken from him at pleasure without his consent?

In demanding suffrage for the black man you recognize the fact that, as a freedman, he is no longer a "part of the family," and that therefore his master is no longer his representative; hence, as he will now be liable to taxation, he must also have representation. Woman, on the contrary, has never been such a "part of the family" as to escape taxation. Although there has been no formal proclamation giving her an individual existence, the single woman always has had the right to property and wages, the right to make contracts and do business in her own name. And even married women, by recent legislation, have been secured in these civil rights. Woman now holds a vast amount of the property in the country and pays her full proportion of taxes, revenue included. On what principle, then, do you deny her representation? By what process of reasoning was Charles Sumner able to stand up in the Senate, a few days after these sublime utterances, and rebuke 15,000,000 disfranchised tax-payers for the exercise of their mere right of petition? If he felt that this was not the time for woman even to mention her right to representation, why did he not, in some of his splendid sentences, propose to release the wage-earning and property-owning women from the tyranny of taxation?

We propose no new theories. We simply ask that you secure the practical application of the immutable principles of our government to all, without distinction of race, color or sex. And we urge our demand now, because you have now the opportunity and the power to take this onward step in legislation. The nations of the earth stand watching and waiting to see if our Revolutionary idea, "all men are created equal," can be realized in government. Crush not, we pray you, the myriad hopes which hang on our success.

Peril not this nation with another bloody war. Men and parties must pass away, but justice is eternal; and only they who work in harmony with its laws are immortal. All who have carefully contrasted the speeches of this Congress with those made under the old regime of slavery, must have seen the added power and eloquence which greater freedom gives. But still you propose no action on your grand ideas. Your joint resolutions, your reconstruction reports, do not reflect your highest thought.

The Constitution, as it stands, in basing representation on "respective numbers" covers a broader ground than any you have yet proposed. Is not the only amendment needed to Article 1, Section 3, to strike out the exceptions which follow "respective numbers?" And is it not your duty, by securing a republican form of government to every State, to see that these "respective numbers" are made up of enfranchised citizens, thus bringing your legislation up to the Constitution—not the Constitution down to your party possibilities? The only tenable ground of representation is universal suffrage, as it is only through universal suffrage that the principle of "equal rights to all" can be realized. All prohibitions based on race, color, sex, property or education are violations of the republican idea; and the various qualifications now proposed are but so many plausible pretexts to debar new classes from the ballot-box. The limitations of property and intelligence, though unfair, can be met; as with freedom must come the repeal of statute laws that deny schools and wages to the negro, and time will make him a voter. But color and sex! Neither time nor statutes can make black, white, or woman, man! You assume to be the representatives of 15,000,000 women— American citizens—who already possess every attainable qualification for the ballot. Women read and write, hold many offices under government, pay taxes and suffer the penalties of crime, and yet are denied individual representation.

For twenty years we have labored to bring the statute-laws of the several States into harmony with the broad principles of the Constitution, and have been so far successful that in many of them little remains to be done except to secure the right of suffrage. Hence, our prompt protest against the propositions before Congress to introduce the word "male" into the Federal Constitution, which, if successful, would sanction all State action in withholding the ballot from woman. As the only way in which disfranchised citizens can appear before you, we availed ourselves of the sacred right of petition; and, as our representatives, it was your duty to give those petitions a respectful reading and a serious consideration. How a Republican Senate failed in that duty, is already inscribed on the page of history. Some tell us it is not judicious to press the claims of women now; that this is not the time. Time? When you propose legislation so fatal to the best interests of woman and the nation, shall we be silent until after the deed is done? No! As we love justice, we must resist tyranny. As we honor the position of American senator, we must appeal from the politician to the man.

With man, woman shared the dangers of the Mayflower on a stormy sea, the dreary landing on Plymouth Rock, the rigors of New England winters and the privations of a seven years' war. With him she bravely threw off the British yoke, felt every pulsation of his heart for freedom, and inspired the glowing eloquence which maintained it through the century. With you, we have just passed through the agony and death, the resurrection and triumph of another revolution, doing all in our power to mitigate its horrors and gild its glories. And now, think you, we have no souls to fire, no brains to weigh your arguments; that, after education such as this, we can stand silent witnesses while you sell our birthright of liberty to save from a timely death an effete political organization ? No, as we respect womanhood, we must protest against this desecration of the magna charta of American liberties; and with an importunity not to be repelled, our demand must ever be, "No compromise of human rights"—"No admission to the Constitution of inequality of rights or disfranchisement on account of color or sex."

In the oft-repeated experiments of class and caste, who can number the nations that have risen but to fall ? Do not imagine you come one line nearer the demand of justice by enfranchising but another shade of manhood; for, in denying representation to woman, you still cling to the same false principle on which all the governments of the past have been wrecked. The right way, the safe way, is so clear, the path of duty is so straight and simple, that we who are equally interested with yourselves in the result, conjure you to act not for the passing hour, not with reference to transient benefits, but to do now the one grand deed which shall mark the zenith of the century—proclaim Equal Rights to All. We press our demand for the ballot at this time in no narrow, captious or selfish spirit; from no contempt of the black man's claims, nor antagonism to you who, in the progress of civilization, are now the privileged order; but from the purest patriotism, for the highest good of every citizen, for the safety of the republic, and as a glorious example to the nations of the earth.

MISS ANTHONY'S FIFTIETH BIRTHDAY.

February 15, 1870.

Careful readers of the Tribune have probably succeeded in discovering that we have not always been able to applaud the course of Miss Susan B. Anthony. Indeed, we have often felt, and sometimes said, that her methods were as unwise as we thought her aims undesirable. But through these years of disputation and struggling, she has thoroughly impressed friends and enemies alike with the sincerity and earnestness of her purposes. . . .

Fifty years ago the full moon of suffrage rose in the small, red and wrinkled countenance of the infant Susan B. Anthony. "Agitation is the word," says Miss Anthony, in these her later years. Agitation was probably the word then, as a happy family surrounded the cradle of the boisterous phenomenon. Miss Anthony has compressed into her half-century a deal of work, talk, hurry and resolution. Beginning with the women's temperance conventions in 1848, she has strewn the gliding years with organizations, societies, conventions innumerable, to the wonderment, if not always to the admiration, of an observant world. "Through all these years," remarks Mrs. Henry B. Stanton, "Miss Anthony was the connecting link between me and the outer world—the reform scout who went to see what was going on in the enemy's camp, and returned with maps and observations to plan the mode of attack." It has been intimated that Miss Anthony has not remained sweet Dian's votary, in maiden meditation fancy free, because nobody asked her to change her name and station. Many victims, we are told, are carrying crushed hearts and blighted hopes through life, and all because of the unrelenting cruelty exercised by this usually good-humored woman towards the whole male sex.—The Tribune.

Miss Anthony bears her fifty summers lightly. Whatever our sentiments may be as to the cause she advocates, we do full justice to her resistless energy and activity and unswerving fidelity to her principles. Charming and cordial in her manners, with kind words for all, she welcomed every guest last evening and made them at ease.—The Times.

It was regarded last night, and was a topic of conversation, that the public announcement that Miss Anthony was fifty years old was one more of the courageous things for which her life has been distinguished. Battling with the wrong and striving for the right has not left so rigid a mark of the progress of time upon her features as to prevent her keeping up a little fiction about being fair and forty. Miss Anthony prefers the truth, and she says that the register in the family Bible supports the assertion that a half-century of rolling years have passed before her.—The Herald.

Miss Anthony looked her very best last night, and let the truth be said, even should it be followed by persecuting proposals from the bachelors, she didn't look much more than five-and-twenty. The genial salutations and happy surroundings of the hour effaced for the time those lines which care and labor and fifty years will make, however pure the soul within. Miss Anthony was happy and she looked it. . . . She wears her years and honors well. May we live till the celebration of her centenary, and she read the report thereof next day in the columns of the Evening Mail.—The Mail.

In these latter days the aspirations and activities of woman are greatly quickened, and her day of pure and perfect freedom seems near at hand. When the year of jubilee shall at last ring in, no name will be more highly honored than that of Miss Susan B. Anthony; and her honors have been well deserved. Early and late, in season and out, in places high and low, all over this broad land, by voice and pen, has she labored with unflagging zeal for the exalted liberty of woman. . . . Men who have honored mothers, pure sisters, devoted wives and loving daughters, owe to Miss Anthony a heavy debt of gratitude for her life-work in behalf of women.—The Globe.

Miss Anthony's reception has been one of the events of the week. . . . Men who have expended about half of the time and half of the energy in the business of money-making which Miss Anthony has expended in benefiting the race, have become millionaires, and have been held up to the rising generation as examples of energy and industry worthy of imitation. Bronzes have been erected and numerous biographies written to do them honor. Had Miss Anthony labored for herself as devotedly as she has for others, she would no doubt have received the usual reward in greenbacks; and but for the fact of her being a woman, might have had a bronze erected in her honor. —The Courier.

It is not always true that "the good die young," for Miss Susan B. Anthony has lived to celebrate her fiftieth birthday. . . . Right glad are we that the anniversary was observed with due pomp and circumstance. No kindly tribute to great moral worth is too good for this good woman. As one of the chief heroines of our generation, she abundantly deserves all the honors which were paid her on that festal night. There are many public-spirited workers in our busy land; many noble souls who have devoted their life-long energies to the elevation of their fellow-beings; many moral pioneers, who, when they die, will leave the world better than they found it; and conspicuous among these is the staunch, unwearied and indomitable woman who, at the end of half a century of life, can remember but few idle or wasted days. If Miss Anthony's persevering efforts in behalf of her sex are not worthy of generous praise, then there is no just fame due to a brave career. If her methods have sometimes lacked soundness of judgment, they have never lacked nobility of purpose. There exists a peculiar, invaluable and time-honored class of plain and substantial women who are said to be "as honest as the day is long;" and Susan B. Anthony is the queen of this royal race. Dauntless and tireless as the sterner sex, sympathetic and tender as the gentler, we sometimes think that she is both man and woman in one. She is one of the sterling characters of our day. The whole people ought to rejoice that such a woman was born, has lived and still toils.—The Independent.

Out of scores of letters received space allows the reproduction of but a few:

I shall always be present in sympathy with any number of people who will express their admiration of the sterling traits which adorn the life and character of the lady who now passes the fiftieth anniversary of her most devoted and unselfish life. I am glad to tender the legal representative of a dollar for each of these years, with the confident assurance of the early triumph of that cause to which her life has been singularly devoted. This greenback is no surer of being redeemed in gold than is my confidence in the golden era of legal enfranchisement for woman ! . . . Long before Miss Anthony sees her "threescore and ten," the political equality of all American citizens will be fully established. With sentiments of the highest esteem, I am, very cordially and truly,   S. C. POMEROY.

. . . God bless her, and may she live many happy, joyous years ! That she and her noble co-workers are soon to see the complete triumph of the woman's cause I firmly believe. And when in after years the great benefactors of this century are sought for, Susan B. Anthony's name will be found occupying one of the highest niches in the temple of honest fame. Truly yours,   J. P. ROOT. [Lieutenant-Governor of Kansas.]

. . . Enclosed is a check for $50, one for each year of your life. Will agree to give you the same pro rata sum on your one hundredth birthday. With love, your brother,   D. R. ANTHONY.

There will be among those who sympathize with and rejoice in your labors, no lack of testimony tonight to their persistency and value; but from one who deplores both, you will perhaps be willing to hear a hearty, cordial, admiring expression of the regard he is nevertheless forced to cherish for the sincerity and the unmistakably disinterested devotion which has marked your long and hopeful work in the cause you hold so dear and serve so faithfully. I can not wish you the success you seek—let me give you this better wish, that the anniversary your friends celebrate tonight may never bring fewer tokens of regard than now, and never find you seeming less the faithful worker "of cheerful yesterdays and confident tomorrows." With renewed congratulations I am, very cordially yours,   WHITELAW REID.

I could not be where I longed to be last evening, where I could look upon the toilworn face of the true, tried and never found wanting—the one of all others who has borne the heat of the day, and that without wilting or complaining—ever hopeful and ever pursuing "the even tenor of her way." Absence shall not keep from thee my mite, and how I wish it were ten, yes, twenty times as much, but here it is with my love, respect and genuine friendship. Be of brave heart and believe that I am thy fast friend,
                                             ABBY HOPPER GIBBONS.

Yours is a "golden wedding" indeed—for the fiftieth anniversary of a life that has been wedded to a great cause is a far more glorious golden wedding than those which generally go by that name. Accept my heartiest wishes for your welfare and for the success of your novel celebration. Heretofore the privilege of growing old and possessing common sense has belonged exclusively to the other sex. Sincerely yours, FRANCES ELLEN BURR.

Please accept the enclosed check of $50, as a slight token of regard from our absent trio. As I hardly need tell you, the lion's share of this birthday gift is sent by my father, but neither mother nor I will admit that in the unsubstantial, and yet I hope not valueless part of the offering, the personal regard and appreciation of your noble work for woman which accompany it, our contribution is any less than his. I remain yours very truly, LAURA CURTIS BULLARD.

You have worked for the slave and for woman. Your fifty years shine about you and rest like a halo of glory around your head. . . . Fifty years to-day! When that half-century again rolls around, you and I will be in our graves and our names and work will stand back of us to all time. But into that future I look with prophetic eye to see woman no longer enslaved, and to find, not only on this continent, but over the world, as benefactor of the race, the name of Susan B. Anthony. Your affectionate friend, MATILDA JOSLYN GAGE.

My good husband in writing from Toledo says: "Tell Susan that all the newspaper accounts taken together could not increase the pride which I have long felt in her pertinacious, obstinate, fault-finding, raspish, strong-minded, dogmatic and grand career. God bless her!" To all of which I subscribe most affectionately, ELIZABETH R. TILTON.

. . . . If your Bible says you are fifty, I will try to be as reverential as possible when next we meet. I wish you similar health and strength when you are seventy-five—you'll find no change in me. I send you by express today Whittier's poems. Ever affectionately, ELLEN WRIGHT GARRISON.

All the people who know you and who don't know you were given opportunity to utter their good wishes, and poor me, wandering across these western spaces, quite left out in the cold! Please ma'am, why did I know nothing of your reception till it was all over? I should have sent you what I now send—a gray silk gown, wherein you are to make yourself fine and grand, and a draft for $200 as a little nest-egg.

If I only had a happy ease with my pen, how glad I would have been to put on paper in glowing words just what I think of the faithful, unselfish, earnest, single-minded, courageous years, which my dear old Susan has given to the service of humanity. How, through poverty and persecution, evil tongues and slanderous words, ridicule and reproach, she has said, "Nothing shall daunt me; 'tis God's service;" and so speaking, has held fast the profession of her faith without wavering. . . . God bless her! God bless her! The tears come to my eyes as I write that benediction, and think how gently and earnestly men and women alike in time to come will repeat it when her name is mentioned; when those same men and women shall see her life and her work, not as now "through a glass darkly," but as those who gaze through the sunshine of truth. Good-by, dear friend—many happy years for you, prays your loving   ANNA E. DICKINSON.

Accept the enclosed check for $50, not as a present, merely, but as a debt, honestly due, for "services rendered." Had there been no "agitation" for the last twenty years, resulting in so complete a "Revolution," we teachers might still be working for $1 per week and "boarding 'round." But thanks to your unfailing "persistency," and the faithfulness of your co-workers in speaking for a class, the majority of whom dare not speak for themselves through fear of losing the little already gained, the salaries of all working-women have been largely increased. . . . So, if need be, fight as valiantly, dear sister, for the next twenty years as for the last, or at least till woman's right to a voice in the laws by which she is governed shall be acknowledged in every State and Territory of our country. Affectionately your sister,   MARY S. ANTHONY.

On this, your fiftieth birthday, permit me to present you my check for $50, as a slight and very inadequate expression of admiring gratitude on my part for your twenty years of arduous and self-sacrificing labor in the cause of woman. What woman has gained already, and it is much, what I and others have been able to achieve in professional life, must be mainly ascribed to you, and such as you. . . . Your faithful friend and co-worker,
CLEMENCE S. LOZIER.

Although away here in Rome, I have kept track of your goings-on through The Revolution, which comes regularly. . . . I wish I could have been there to assist at the merrymaking. Miss Manning has kindly offered to take a little remembrance [an Etruscan gold and garnet pin] to you when she goes home, which you are to wear with that new silk dress. You see how selfish I am. I wish to compel you not only to think of me, but to associate me in your mind with our peerless Anna, God bless the dear child! Ever affectionately,   KATE N. DOGGETT.

The presents received were too numerous to mention. From Mr. and Mrs. Cheney, South Manchester, Conn., $50; Erie Co. (N. Y.) Suffrage Association, $50; Henry Ward Beecher, the Tiltons, Frank D. Moulton, Mrs. Hooker, Mrs. S. C. Pomeroy, $25 each; Mr. and Mrs. Samuel E. Sewall, $20; and from other friends, sums of ten, fifteen and twenty dollars, amounting in all to $1,000. In addition were a broché shawl from Mrs. Stanton, gold watch, chain and pin from Miss Sarah Johnston, pen-and-ink sketch from Eliza Greatorex, point and duchesse lace collars and handkerchiefs, sets of books, engravings, gold pens, pocket-books, travelling case, and floral offerings.

CONSTITUTIONAL ARGUMENT.

Delivered in twenty-nine of the post-office districts of Monroe, and twenty-one of Ontario, in Miss Anthony's canvass of those counties prior to her trial in June, 1873.

Friends and Fellow-Citizens:—I stand before you under indictment for the alleged crime of having voted at the last presidential election, without having a lawful right to vote. It shall be my work this evening to prove to you that in thus doing, I not only committed no crime, but instead simply exercised my citizen's right, guaranteed to me and all United States citizens by the National Constitution beyond the power of any State to deny.

Our democratic-republican government is based on the idea of the natural right of every individual member thereof to a voice and a vote in making and executing the laws. We assert the province of government to be to secure the people in the enjoyment of their inalienable rights. We throw to the winds the old dogma that government can give rights. No one denies that before governments were organized each individual possessed the right to protect his own life, liberty and property. When 100 or 1,000,000 people enter into a free government, they do not barter away their natural rights; they simply pledge themselves to protect each other in the enjoyment of them through prescribed judicial and legislative tribunals. They agree to abandon the methods of brute force in the adjustment of their differences and adopt those of civilization. Nor can you find a word in any of the grand documents left us by the fathers which assumes for government the power to create or to confer rights. The Declaration of Independence, the United States Constitution, the constitutions of the several States and the organic laws of the Territories, all alike propose to *protect* the people in the exercise of their God-given rights. Not one of them pretends to bestow rights.

All men are created equal, and endowed by their Creator with certain inalienable rights. Among these are life, liberty and the pursuit of happiness. To secure these, governments are instituted among men, deriving their just powers from the consent of the governed.

Here is no shadow of government authority over rights, or exclusion of any class from their full and equal enjoyment. Here is pronounced the right of all men, and "consequently," as the Quaker preacher said, "of all women," to a voice in the government. And here, in this first paragraph of the Declaration, is the assertion of the natural right of all to the ballot; for how can "the consent of the governed" be given, if the right to vote be denied? Again:

Whenever any form of government becomes destructive of these ends, it is the right of the people to alter or abolish it, and to institute a new government, laying its foundations on such principles, and organizing its powers in such form, as to them shall seem most likely to effect their safety and happiness.

Surely the right of the whole people to vote is here clearly implied; for however destructive to their happiness this government might become, a disfranchised class could neither alter nor abolish it, nor institute a new one, except by the old brute force method of insurrection and rebellion. One-half of the people of this nation today are utterly powerless to blot from the statute books an unjust law, or to write there a new and a just one. The women, dissatisfied as they are with this form of government, that enforces taxation without representation—that compels them to obey laws to which they never have given their consent—that imprisons and hangs them without a trial by a jury of their peers—that robs them, in marriage, of the custody of their own persons, wages and children—are this half of the people who are left wholly at the mercy of the other half, in direct violation of the spirit and letter of the declarations of the framers of this government, every one of which was based on the immutable principle of equal rights to all. By these declarations, kings, popes, priests, aristocrats, all were alike dethroned and placed on a common level, politically, with the lowliest born subject or serf. By them, too, men, as such, were deprived of their divine right to rule and placed on a political level with women. By the practice of these declarations all class and caste distinctions would be abolished, and slave, serf, plebeian, wife, woman, all alike rise from their subject position to the broader platform of equality.

The preamble of the Federal Constitution says:

We, the people of the United States, in order to form a more perfect union, establish justice, insure domestic tranquillity, provide for the common defence, promote the general welfare and secure the blessings of liberty to ourselves and our posterity, do ordain and establish this Constitution for the United States of America.

It was we, the people, not we, the white male citizens, nor we, the male citizens; but we, the whole people, who formed this Union. We formed it not to give the blessings of liberty but to secure them; not to the half of ourselves and the half of our posterity, but to the whole people—women as well as men. It is downright mockery to talk to women of their enjoyment of the blessings of liberty while they are denied the only means of securing them provided by this democratic-republican government—the ballot.

The early journals of Congress show that, when the committee reported to that body the original articles of confederation, the very first one which became the subject of discussion was that respecting equality of suffrage. Article IV said:

The better to secure and perpetuate mutual friendship and intercourse between the people of the different States of this Union, the free inhabitants of each of the States (paupers, vagabonds and fugitives from justice excepted) shall be entitled to all the privileges and immunities of the free citizens of the several States.

Thus, at the very beginning, did the fathers see the necessity of the universal application of the great principle of equal rights to all, in order to produce the desired result—a harmonious union and a homogeneous people.

Luther Martin, attorney-general of Maryland, in his report to the legislature of that State of the convention which framed the United States Constitution, said:

Those who advocated the equality of suffrage took the matter up on the original principles of government: that the reason why each individual man in forming a State government should have an equal vote, is because each individual, before he enters into government, is equally free and equally independent.

James Madison said:

Under every view of the subject, it seems indispensable that the mass of the citizens should not be without a voice in making the laws which they are to obey, and in choosing the magistrates who are to administer them. . . . Let it be remembered, finally, that it has ever been the pride and the boast of America that the rights for which she contended were the rights of human nature.

These assertions by the framers of the United States Constitution of the equal and natural right of all the people to a voice in the government, have been affirmed and reaffirmed by the leading statesmen of the nation throughout the entire history of our government. Thaddeus Stevens, of Pennsylvania, said in 1866: "I have made up my mind that the elective franchise is one of the inalienable rights meant to be secured by the Declaration of Independence." B. Gratz Brown, of Missouri, in the three days' discussion in the United States Senate in 1866, on Senator Cowan's motion to strike "male" from the District of Columbia suffrage bill, said:

Mr. President, I say here on the floor of the American Senate, I stand for universal suffrage; and as a matter of fundamental principle, do not recognize the right of society to limit it on any ground of race or sex. I will go farther and say that I recognize the right of franchise as being intrinsically a natural right. I do not believe that society is authorized to impose any limitations upon it that do not spring out of the necessities of the social state itself. Sir, I have been shocked, in the course of this debate, to hear senators declare this right only a conventional and political arrangement, a privilege yielded to you and me and others; not a right in any sense, only a concession! Mr. President, I do not hold my liberties by any such tenure. On the contrary, I believe that whenever you establish that doctrine, whenever you crystallize that idea in the public mind of this country, you ring the death-knell of American liberties.

Charles Sumner, in his brave protests against the Fourteenth and Fifteenth Amendments, insisted that so soon as by the Thirteenth Amendment the slaves became free men, the original powers of the United States Constitution guaranteed to them equal rights—the right to vote and to be voted for. In closing one of his great speeches he said:

I do not hesitate to say that when the slaves of our country became "citizens" they took their place in the body politic as a component part of the "people," entitled to equal rights and under the protection of these two guardian principles: First, that all just governments stand on the consent of the governed; and second, that taxation without representation is tyranny; and these rights it is the duty of Congress to guarantee as essential to the idea of a republic.

The preamble of the constitution of the State of New York declares the same purpose. It says: "We, the people of the State of New York, grateful to Almighty God for our freedom, in order to secure its blessings, do establish this constitution." Here is not the slightest intimation either of receiving freedom from the United States Constitution, or of the State's conferring the blessings of liberty upon the people; and the same is true of every other State constitution. Each and all declare rights God-given, and that to secure the people in the enjoyment of their inalienable rights is their one and only object in ordaining and establishing government. All of the State constitutions are equally emphatic in their recognition of the ballot as the means of securing the people in the enjoyment of these rights. Article I of the New York State constitution says:

No member of this State shall be disfranchised or deprived of the rights or privileges secured to any citizen thereof, unless by the law of the land, or the judgment of his peers.

So carefully guarded is the citizen's right to vote, that the constitution makes special mention of all who may be excluded. It says: "Laws may be passed excluding from the right of suffrage all persons who have been or may be convicted of bribery, larceny or any infamous crime."

In naming the various employments which shall not affect the residence of voters, Section 3, Article II, says "that neither being kept in any almshouse, or other asylum, at public expense, nor being confined in any public prison, shall deprive a person of his residence," and hence of his vote. Thus is the right of voting most sacredly hedged about. The only seeming permission in the New York State constitution for the disfranchisement of women is in Section 1, Article II, which says: "Every male citizen of the age of twenty-one years, etc., shall be entitled to vote."

But I submit that in view of the explicit assertions of the equal right of the whole people, both in the preamble and previous article of the constitution, this omission of the adjective "female" should not be construed into a denial; but instead should be considered as of no effect. Mark the direct prohibition, "No member of this State shall be disfranchised, unless by the law of the land, or the judgment of his peers." "The law of the land" is the United States Constitution; and there is no provision in that document which can be fairly construed into a permission to the States to deprive any class of citizens of their right to vote. Hence New York can get no power from that source to disfranchise one entire half of her members. Nor has "the judgment of their peers" been pronounced against women exercising their right to vote; no disfranchised person is allowed to be judge or juror—and none but disfranchised persons can be women's peers. Nor has the legislature passed laws excluding women as a class on account of idiocy or lunacy; nor have the courts convicted them of bribery, larceny or any infamous crime. Clearly, then, there is no constitutional ground for the exclusion of women from the ballot-box in the State of New York. No barriers whatever stand today between women and the exercise of their right to vote save those of precedent and prejudice, which refuse to expunge the word "male" from the constitution.

The clauses of the United States Constitution cited by our opponents as giving power to the States to disfranchise any classes of citizens they please, are contained in Sections 2 and 4, Article I. The second says:

The House of Representatives shall be composed of members chosen every second year by the people of the several States; and the electors in each State shall have the qualifications requisite for electors of the most numerous branch of the State legislature.

This can not be construed into a concession to the States of the power to destroy the right to become an elector, but simply to prescribe what shall be the qualifications, such as competency of intellect, maturity of age, length of residence, that shall be deemed necessary to enable them to make an intelligent choice of candidates. If, as our opponents assert, it is the duty of the United States to protect citizens in the several States against higher or different qualifications for electors for representatives in Congress than for members of the Assembly, then it must be equally imperative for the national government to interfere with the States, and forbid them from arbitrarily cutting off the right of one-half the people to become electors altogether. Section 4 says:

The times, places and manner of holding elections for senators and representatives shall be prescribed in each State by the legislature thereof; but Congress may at any time, by law, make or alter such regulations, except as to the places of choosing senators.

Here is conceded to the States only the power to prescribe times, places and manner of holding the elections; and even with these Congress may interfere in all excepting the mere place of choosing senators. Thus, you see, there is not the slightest permission for the States to discriminate against the right of any class of citizens to vote. Surely, to regulate can not be to annihilate; to qualify can not be wholly to deprive. To this principle every true Democrat and Republican said amen, when applied to black men by Senator Sumner in his great speeches from 1865 to 1869 for equal rights to all; and when, in 1871, I asked that senator to declare the power of the United States Constitution to protect women in their right to vote—as he had done for black men—he handed me a copy of all his speeches during that reconstruction period, and said:

Put "sex" where I have "race" or "color," and you have here the best and strongest argument I can make for woman. There is not a doubt but women have the constitutional right to vote, and I will never vote for a Sixteenth Amendment to guarantee it to them. I voted for both the Fourteenth and Fifteenth under protest; would never have done it but for the pressing emergency of that hour; would have insisted that the power of the original Constitution to protect all citizens in the equal enjoyment of their rights should have been vindicated through the courts. But the newly-made freedmen had neither the intelligence, wealth nor time to await that slow process. Women do possess all these in an eminent degree, and I insist that they shall appeal to the courts, and through them establish the powers of our American magna charta to protect every citizen of the republic.

But, friends, when in accordance with Senator Sumner's counsel I went to the ballot-box, last November, and exercised my citizen's right to vote, the courts did not wait for me to appeal to them—they appealed to me, and indicted me on the charge of having voted illegally. Putting sex where he did color, Senator Sumner would have said:

Qualifications can not be in their nature permanent or insurmountable. Sex can not be a qualification any more than size, race, color or previous condition of servitude. A permanent or insurmountable qualification is equivalent to a deprivation of the suffrage. In other words, it is the tyranny of taxation without representation, against which our Revolutionary mothers, as well as fathers, rebelled.

For any State to make sex a qualification, which must ever result in the disfranchisement of one entire half of the people, is to pass a bill of attainder, an ex post facto law, and is therefore a violation of the supreme law of the land. By it the blessings of liberty are forever withheld from women and their female posterity. For them, this government has no just powers derived from the consent of the governed. For them this government is not a democracy; it is not a republic. It is the most odious aristocracy ever established on the face of the globe. An oligarchy of wealth, where the rich govern the poor; an oligarchy of learning, where the educated govern the ignorant; or even an oligarchy of race, where the Saxon rules the African, might be endured; but this oligarchy of sex which makes father, brothers, husband, sons, the oligarchs over the mother and sisters, the wife and daughters of every household; which ordains all men sovereigns, all women subjects—carries discord and rebellion into every home of the nation. This most odious aristocracy exists, too, in the face of Section 4, Article IV, which says: "The United States shall guarantee to every State in the Union a republican form of government."

What, I ask you, is the distinctive difference between the inhabitants of a monarchical and those of a republican form of government, save that in the monarchical the people are subjects, helpless, powerless, bound to obey laws made by political superiors; while in the republican the people are citizens, individual sovereigns, all clothed with equal power to make and unmake both their laws and law-makers? The moment you deprive a person of his right to a voice in the government, you degrade him from the status of a citizen of the republic to that of a subject. It matters very little to him whether his monarch be an individual tyrant, as is the Czar of Russia, or a 15,000,000 headed monster, as here in the United States; he is a powerless subject, serf or slave; not in any sense a free and independent citizen.

It is urged that the use of the masculine pronouns *he, his* and *him* in all the constitutions and laws, is proof that only men were meant to be included in their provisions. If you insist on this version of the letter of the law, we shall insist that you be consistent and accept the other horn of the dilemma, which would compel you to exempt women from taxation for the support of the government and from penalties for the violation of laws. There is no *she* or *her* or *hers* in the tax laws, and this is equally true of all the criminal laws.

Take for example the civil rights law which I am charged with having violated; not only are all the pronouns in it masculine, but everybody knows that it was intended expressly to hinder the rebel men from voting. It reads, " If any person shall knowingly vote without *his* having a lawful right." It was precisely so with all the papers served on me—the United States marshal's warrant, the bail-bond, the petition for habeas corpus, the bill of indictment—not one of them had a feminine pronoun; but to make them applicable to me, the clerk of the court prefixed an " s " to the " he " and made " her " out of " his " and " him;" and I insist if government officials may thus manipulate the pronouns to tax, fine, imprison and hang women, it is their duty to thus change them in order to protect us in our right to vote.

So long as any classes of men were denied this right, the government made a show of consistency by exempting them from taxation. When a property qualification of $250 was required of black men in New York, they were not compelled to pay taxes so long as they were content to report themselves worth less than that sum; but the moment the black man died and his property fell to his widow or daughter, the black woman's name was put on the assessor's list and she was compelled to pay taxes on this same property. This also is true of ministers in New York. So long as the minister lives, he is exempted from taxation on $1,500 of property, but the moment the breath leaves his body, his widow's name goes on the assessor's list and she has to pay taxes on the $1,500. So much for special legislation in favor of women!

In all the penalties and burdens of government (except the military) women are reckoned as citizens, equally with men. Also, in all the privileges and immunities, save those of the jury and the ballot-box, the foundation on which rest all the others. The United States government not only taxes, fines, imprisons and hangs women, but it allows them to pre-empt lands, register ships and take out passports and naturalization papers. Not only does the law permit single women and widows the right of naturalization, but Section 2 says, "A married woman may be naturalized without the concurrence of her husband;" (I wonder the fathers were not afraid of creating discord in the families of foreigners;) and again:

When an alien, having complied with the law and declared his intention to become a citizen, dies before he is actually naturalized, his widow and children shall be considered citizens, entitled to all rights and privileges as such, on taking the required oath.

If a foreign born woman by becoming a naturalized citizen is entitled to all the rights and privileges of citizenship, do not these include the ballot which would have belonged to her husband? If this is true of a naturalized woman, is it not equally true of one who is native born?

The question of the masculine pronouns—yes, and nouns too—was settled by the United States Supreme Court, in the case of Silver *versus* Ladd, December, 1868. The court said:

In construing a benevolent statute of the government, made for the benefit of its own citizens, inviting and encouraging them to settle on its distant public lands, the words "single man" and "unmarried man" may, especially if aided by the context and other parts of the statute, be taken in a generic sense. Held, accordingly, that the Fourth Section of the Act of Congress, of September 27, 1850, granting by way of donation lands in Oregon Territory to every white settler or occupant, American half-breed Indians included, embraced within the term single man an unmarried woman.

Though the words persons, people, inhabitants, electors, citizens, are all used indiscriminately in the national and State constitutions, there was always a conflict of opinion, prior to the war, as to whether they were synonymous terms, but whatever room there was for doubt, under the old regime, the adoption of the Fourteenth Amendment settled that question forever in its first sentence:

All persons born or naturalized in the United States, and subject to the jurisdiction thereof, are citizens of the United States, and of the State wherein they reside.

The second settles the equal status of all citizens:

No State shall make or enforce any law which shall abridge the privileges or immunities of citizens of the United States; nor shall any State deprive any person of life, liberty or property without due process of law, or deny to any person within its jurisdiction the equal protection of the laws.

The only question left to be settled now is: Are women persons? I scarcely believe any of our opponents will have the hardihood to say they are not. Being persons, then, women are citizens, and no State has a right to make any new law, or to enforce any old law, which shall abridge their privileges or immunities. Hence, every discrimination against women in the constitutions and laws of the several States is today null and void, precisely as is every one against negroes.

Is the right to vote one of the privileges or immunities of citizens? I think the disfranchised ex-rebels and ex-State prisoners all will agree that it is not only one of them, but the one without which all the others are nothing. Seek first the kingdom of the ballot and all things else shall be added, is the political injunction.

Webster, Worcester and Bouvier all define citizen to be a person, in the United States, entitled to vote and hold office. Prior to the adoption of the Thirteenth Amendment, by which slavery was forever abolished and black men transformed from property to persons, the judicial opinions of the country had always been in harmony with this definition: In order to be a citizen one must be a voter. Associate-Justice Washington, in defining the privileges and immunities of the citizen, more than fifty years ago, said: "They include all such privileges as are fundamental in their nature; and among them is the right to exercise the elective franchise, and to hold office." Even the Dred Scott decision, pronounced by the Abolitionists and Republicans infamous because it virtually declared "black men had no rights white men were bound to respect," gave this true and logical conclusion, that to be one of the people was to be a citizen and a voter.

Chief-Justice Daniels said:

There is not, it is believed, to be found in the theories of writers on government, or in any actual experiment heretofore made, an exposition of the term citizen which has not been considered as conferring the actual possession and enjoyment of an entire equality of privileges, civil and political.

Associate-Justice Taney said:

The words "people of the United States" and "citizens" are synonymous terms, and mean the same thing. They both describe the political body, who, according to our republican institutions, form the sovereignty, and who hold the power and conduct the government through their representatives. They are what we familiarly call "the sovereign people," and every citizen is one of this people, and a constituent member of this sovereignty.

Thus does Judge Taney's decision, which was so terrible a ban to the black man while he was a slave, now that he is a person and no longer property, pronounce him a citizen, possessed of entire equality of privileges, civil and political; and not only the black man, but the black woman, and all women. It was not until after the abolition of slavery, by which the negroes became free men and hence citizens, that any contrary opinion was rendered. U. S. Attorney-General Bates then said:

The Constitution uses the word "citizen" only to express the political quality, [not equality, mark,] of the individual in his relation to the nation; to declare that he is a member of the body politic, and bound to it by the reciprocal obligations of allegiance on the one side and protection on the other. The phrase, "a citizen of the United States," without addition or qualification, means neither more nor less than a member of the nation.

Then, to be a citizen of this republic is no more than to be a subject of an empire. You and I, and all true and patriotic citizens, must repudiate this base conclusion. We all know that American citizenship, without addition or qualification, means the possession of equal rights, civil and political. We all know that the crowning glory of every citizen of the United States is that he can either give or withhold his vote from every law and every legislator under the government.

Did "I am a Roman citizen" mean nothing more than that I am a "member" of the body politic of the republic of Rome, bound to it by the reciprocal obligations of allegiance on the one side and protection on the other? When you, young man, shall travel abroad, among the monarchies of the old world, and there proudly boast yourself an "American citizen," will you thereby declare yourself neither more nor less than a "member" of the American nation?

This opinion of Attorney-General Bates, that a black citizen was not a voter, given merely to suit the political exigency of the Republican party in that transition hour between emancipation and enfranchisement, was no less infamous, in spirit or purpose, than was the decision of Judge Taney, that a black man was not one of the people, rendered in the interest and at the behest of the old Democratic party in its darkest hour of subjection to the slave power. Nevertheless, all of the adverse arguments, congressional reports and judicial opinions, thus far, have been based on this purely partisan, time-serving decision of General Bates, that the normal condition of the citizen of the United States is that of disfranchisement; that only such classes of citizens as have had special legislative guarantee have a legal right to vote.

If this decision of Attorney-General Bates was infamous, as against black men, but yesterday plantation slaves, what shall we pronounce upon Judge Bingham, in the House of Representatives, and Carpenter, in the Senate of the United States, for citing it against the women of the entire nation, vast numbers of whom are the peers of those honorable gentlemen themselves in morals, intellect, culture, wealth, family, paying taxes on large estates, and contributing equally with them and their sex, in every direction, to the growth, prosperity and well-being of the republic? And what shall be said of the judicial opinions of Judges Cartter, Jameson, McKay and Sharswood, all based upon this aristocratic, monarchial idea of the right of one class to govern another?

I am proud to mention the names of the two United States judges who have given opinions honorable to our republican idea, and honorable to themselves—Judge Howe, of Wyoming Territory, and Judge Underwood, of Virginia. The former gave it as his opinion a year ago, when the legislature seemed likely to revoke the law enfranchising the women of that Territory that, in case they succeeded, the women would still possess the right to vote under the Fourteenth Amendment. The latter, in noticing the recent decision of Judge Cartter, of the Supreme Court of the District of Columbia, denying to women the right to vote under the Fourteenth and Fifteenth Amendments, says:

If the people of the United States, by amendment of their Constitution, could expunge, without any explanatory or assisting legislation, an adjective of five letters from all State and local constitutions, and thereby raise millions of our most ignorant fellow-citizens to all of the rights and privileges of electors, why should not the same people, by the same amendment, expunge an adjective of four letters from the same State and local constitutions, and thereby raise other millions of more educated and better informed citizens to equal rights and privileges, without explanatory or assisting legislation ?

If the Fourteenth Amendment does not secure to all citizens the right to vote, for what purpose was that grand old charter of the fathers lumbered with its unwieldy proportions? The Republican party, and Judges Howard and Bingham, who drafted the document, pretended it was to do something for black men; and if that something were not to secure them in their right to vote and hold office, what could it have been? For by the Thirteenth Amendment black men had become people, and hence were entitled to all the privileges and immunities of the government, precisely as were the women of the country and foreign men not naturalized. According to Associate-Justice Washington, they already had:

Protection of the government, the enjoyment of life and liberty, with the right to acquire and possess property of every kind, and to pursue and obtain happiness and safety, subject to such restraints as the government may justly prescribe for the general welfare of the whole ; the right of a citizen of one State to pass through or to reside in any other State for the purpose of trade, agriculture, professional pursuit, or otherwise ; to claim the benefit of the writ of habeas corpus, to institute and maintain actions of any kind in the courts of the State ; to take, hold, and dispose of property, either real or personal, and an exemption from higher taxes or impositions than are paid by the other citizens of the State.

Thus, you see, those newly-freed men were in possession of every possible right, privilege and immunity of the government, except that of suffrage, and hence needed no constitutional amendment for any other purpose. What right in this country has the Irishman the day after he receives his naturalization papers that he did not possess the day before, save the right to vote and hold office? The Chinamen now crowding our Pacific coast are in precisely the same position. What privilege or immunity has California or Oregon the right to deny them, save that of the ballot? Clearly, then, if the Fourteenth Amendment was not to secure to black men their right to vote it did nothing for them, since they possessed everything else before. But if it was intended to prohibit the States from denying or abridging their right to vote, then it did the same for all persons, white women included, born or naturalized in the United States; for the amendment does not say that all male persons of African descent, but that all persons are citizens.

The second section is simply a threat to punish the States by reducing their representation on the floor of Congress, should they disfranchise any of their male citizens, and can not be construed into a sanction to disfranchise female citizens, nor does it in any wise weaken or invalidate the universal guarantee of the first section.

However much the doctors of the law may disagree as to whether people and citizens, in the original Constitution, were one and the same, or whether the privileges and immunities in the Fourteenth Amendment include the right of suffrage, the question of the citizen's right to vote is forever settled by the Fifteenth Amendment. "The right of citizens of the United States to vote shall not be denied or abridged by the United States, or by any State, on account of race, color or previous condition of servitude." How can the State deny or abridge the right of the citizen, if the citizen does not possess it? There is no escape from the conclusion that to vote is the citizen's right, and the specifications of race, color or previous condition of servitude can in no way impair the force of that emphatic assertion that the citizen's right to vote shall not be denied or abridged.

The political strategy of the second section of the Fourteenth Amendment failing to coerce the rebel States into enfranchising their negroes, and the necessities of the Republican party demanding their votes throughout the South to ensure the re-election of Grant in 1872, that party was compelled to place this positive prohibition of the Fifteenth Amendment upon the United States and all the States thereof.

If once we establish the false principle that United States citizenship does not carry with it the right to vote in every State in this Union, there is no end to the petty tricks and cunning devices which will be attempted to exclude one and another class of citizens from the right of suffrage. It will not always be the men combining to disfranchise all women; native born men combining to abridge the rights of all naturalized citizens, as in Rhode Island. It will not always be the rich and educated who may combine to cut off the poor and ignorant; but we may live to see the hard-working, uncultivated day laborers, foreign and native born, learning the power of the ballot and their vast majority of numbers, combine and amend State constitutions so as to disfranchise the Vanderbilts, the Stewarts, the Conklings and the Fentons. It is a poor rule that won't work more ways than one. Establish this precedent, admit the State's right to deny suffrage, and there is no limit to the confusion, discord and disruption that may await us. There is and can be but one safe principle of government—equal rights to all. Discrimination against any class on account of color, race, nativity, sex, property, culture, can but embitter and disaffect that class, and thereby endanger the safety of the whole people. Clearly, then, the national government not only must define the rights of citizens, but must stretch out its powerful hand and protect them in every State in this Union.

If, however, you will insist that the Fifteenth Amendment's emphatic interdiction against robbing United States citizens of their suffrage "on account of race, color or previous condition of servitude," is a recognition of the right of either the United States or any State to deprive them of the ballot for any or all other reasons, I will prove to you that the class of citizens for whom I now plead are, by all the principles of our government and many of the laws of the States, included under the term "previous condition of servitude."

Consider first married women and their legal status. What is servitude? "The condition of a slave." What is a slave? "A person who is robbed of the proceeds of his labor; a person who is subject to the will of another." By the laws of Georgia, South Carolina and all the States of the South, the negro had no right to the custody and control of his person. He belonged to his master. If he were disobedient, the master had the right to use correction. If the negro did not like the correction and ran away, the master had the right to use coercion to bring him back. By the laws of almost every State in this

Union today, North as well as South, the married woman has no right to the custody and control of her person. The wife belongs to the husband; and if she refuse obedience he may use moderate correction, and if she do not like his moderate correction and leave his "bed and board," the husband may use moderate coercion to bring her back. The little word "moderate," you see, is the saving clause for the wife, and would doubtless be overstepped should her offended husband administer his correction with the " cat-o'-nine-tails," or accomplish his coercion with blood-hounds.

Again the slave had no right to the earnings of his hands, they belonged to his master; no right to the custody of his children, they belonged to his master; no right to sue or be sued, or to testify in the courts. If he committed a crime, it was the master who must sue or be sued. In many of the States there has been special legislation, giving married women the right to property inherited or received by bequest, or earned by the pursuit of any avocation outside the home; also giving them the right to sue and be sued in matters pertaining to such separate property; but not a single State of this Union has ever secured the wife in the enjoyment of her right to equal ownership of the joint earnings of the marriage copartnership. And since, in the nature of things, the vast majority of married women never earn a dollar by work outside their families, or inherit a dollar from their fathers, it follows that from the day of their marriage to the day of the death of their husbands not one of them ever has a dollar, except it shall please her husband to let her have it.

In some of the States, also, laws have been passed giving to the mother a joint right with the father in the guardianship of the children. Twenty-five years ago, when our woman's rights movement commenced, by the laws of all the States the father had the sole custody and control of the children. No matter if he were a brutal, drunken libertine, he had the legal right, without the mother's consent, to apprentice her sons to rumsellers or her daughters to brothel-keepers. He even could will away an unborn child from the mother. In most of the States this law still prevails, and the mothers are utterly powerless.

I doubt if there is, today, a State in this Union where a married woman can sue or be sued for slander of character, and until recently there was not one where she could sue or be sued for injury of person. However damaging to the wife's reputation any slander may be, she is wholly powerless to institute legal proceedings against her accuser unless her husband shall join with her; and how often have we heard of the husband conspiring with some outside barbarian to blast the good name of his wife? A married woman can not testify in courts in cases of joint interest with her husband.

A good farmer's wife in Illinois, who had all the rights she wanted, had had made for herself a full set of false teeth. The dentist pronounced them an admirable fit, and the wife declared it gave her fits to wear them. The dentist sued the husband for his bill; his counsel brought the wife as witness; the judge ruled her off the stand, saying, " A married woman can not be a witness in matters of joint interest between herself and her husband." Think of it, ye good wives, the false teeth in your mouths are a joint interest with your husbands, about which you are legally incompetent to speak! If a married woman is injured by accident, in nearly all of the States it is her husband who must sue, and it is to him that the damages will be awarded. In Massachusetts a married woman was severely injured by a defective sidewalk. Her husband sued the corporation and recovered $13,000 damages, which belong to him absolutely, and whenever that unfortunate wife wishes a dollar of that money she must ask her husband for it; and if he be of a niggardly nature, she will hear him say, every time, " What have you done with the twenty-five cents I gave you yesterday?" Isn't such a position humiliating enough to be called "servitude?" That husband sued and obtained damages for the loss of the services of his wife, precisely as he would have done had it been his ox, cow or horse; and exactly as the master, under the old regime, would have recovered for the services of his slave.

I submit the question, if the deprivation by law of the ownership of one's own person, wages, property, children, the denial of the right as an individual to sue and be sued and testify in the courts, is not a condition of servitude most bitter and absolute, even though under the sacred name of marriage? Does any lawyer doubt my statement of the legal status of married women? I will remind him of the fact that the common law of England prevails in every State but two in this Union, except where the legislature has enacted special laws annulling it. I am ashamed that not one of the States yet has blotted from its statute books the old law of marriage, which, summed up in the fewest words possible, is in effect " husband and wife are one, and that one the husband."

Thus may all married women and widows, by the laws of the several States, be technically included in the Fifteenth Amendment's specification of " condition of servitude," present or previous. The facts also prove that, by all the great fundamental principles of our free government, not only married women but the entire womanhood of the nation are in a " condition of servitude" as surely as were our Revolutionary fathers when they rebelled against King George. Women are taxed without representation, governed without their consent, tried, convicted and punished without a jury of their peers. Is all this tyranny any less humiliating and degrading to women under our democratic-republican government today than it was to men under their aristocratic, monarchial government one hundred years ago? There is not an utterance of John Adams, John Hancock or Patrick Henry, but finds a living response in the soul of every intelligent, patriotic woman of the nation. Show me a justice-loving woman property-holder, and I will show you one whose soul is fired with all the indignation of 1776 every time the tax-collector presents himself at her door. You will not find one such but feels her condition of servitude as galling as did James Otis when he said:

The very act of taxing exercised over those who are not represented appears to me to be depriving them of one of their most essential rights, and if continued seems to be in effect an entire disfranchisement of every civil right. For what one civil right is worth a rush after a man's property is subject to be taken from him at pleasure without his consent? If a man is not his own assessor in person, or by deputy, his liberty is gone, for he is wholly at the mercy of others.

What was the three-penny tax on tea or the paltry tax on paper and sugar to which our Revolutionary fathers were subjected, when compared with the taxation of the women of this republic? And again, to show that disfranchisement was precisely the slavery of which the fathers complained, allow me to cite Benjamin Franklin, who in those olden times was admitted to be good authority, not merely in domestic but also in political economy:

Every man of the commonalty, except infants, insane persons and criminals, is, of common right and the law of God, a freeman and entitled to the free enjoyment of liberty. That liberty or freedom consists in having an actual share in the appointment of those who are to frame the laws, and who are to be the guardians of every man's life, property and peace. For the all of one man is as dear to him as the all of another; and the poor man has an equal right, but more need, to have representatives in the legislature than the rich one. They who have no voice or vote in the electing of representatives do not enjoy liberty, but are absolutely enslaved to those who have votes and to their representatives; for to be enslaved is to have governors whom other men have set over us, and to be subject to laws made by the representatives of others, without having had representatives of our own to give consent in our behalf.

Suppose I read it with the feminine gender:

Women who have no voice or vote in the electing of representatives do not enjoy liberty, but are absolutely enslaved to men who have votes and to their representatives; for to be enslaved is to have governors whom men have set over us, and to be subject to the laws made by the representatives of men, without having representatives of our own to give consent in our behalf.

And yet one more authority, that of Thomas Paine, than whom not one of the Revolutionary patriots more ably vindicated the principles upon which our government is founded:

The right of voting for representatives is the primary right by which other rights are protected. To take away this right is to reduce man to a state of slavery; for slavery consists in being subject to the will of another; and he that has not a vote in the election of representatives is in this case. The proposal, therefore, to disfranchise any class of men is as criminal as the proposal to take away property.

Is anything further needed to prove woman's condition of servitude sufficient to entitle her to the guarantees of the Fifteenth Amendment? Is there a man who will not agree with me that to talk of freedom without the ballot is mockery to the women of this republic, precisely as New England's orator, Wendell Phillips, at the close of the late war declared it to be to the newly emancipated black man? I admit that, prior to the rebellion, by common consent, the right to enslave, as well as to disfranchise both native and foreign born persons, was conceded to the States. But the one grand principle settled by the war and the reconstruction legislation, is the supremacy of the national government to protect the citizens of the United States in their right to freedom and the elective franchise, against any and every interference on the part of the several States; and again and again have the American people asserted the triumph of this principle by their overwhelming majorities for Lincoln and Grant.

The one issue of the last two presidential elections was whether the Fourteenth and Fifteenth Amendments should be considered the irrevocable will of the people; and the decision was that they should be, and that it is not only the right, but the duty of the national government to protect all United States citizens in the full enjoyment and free exercise of their privileges and immunities against the attempt of any State to deny or abridge. In this conclusion Republicans and Democrats alike agree. Senator Frelinghuysen said: "The heresy of State rights has been completely buried in these amendments, and as amended, the Constitution confers not only National but State citizenship upon all persons born or naturalized within our limits."

The call for the National Republican Convention of 1872 said: "Equal suffrage has been engrafted on the National Constitution; the privileges and immunities of American citizenship have become a part of the organic law." The National Republican platform said: "Complete liberty and exact equality in the enjoyment of all civil, political and public rights, should be established and maintained throughout the Union by efficient and appropriate State and Federal legislation."

If that means anything it is that Congress should pass a law to protect women in their equal political rights, and that the States should enact laws making it the duty of inspectors of elections to receive the votes of women on precisely the same conditions as they do those of men.

Judge Stanley Matthews, a substantial Ohio Democrat, in his preliminary speech at the Cincinnati Liberal Convention, said most emphatically: "The constitutional amendments have established the political equality of all citizens before the law."

President Grant, in his message to Congress, March 30, 1870, on the adoption of the Fifteenth Amendment, said, "A measure which makes at once four millions of people voters, is indeed a measure of greater importance than any act of the kind from the foundation of the government to the present time."

How could *four* million negroes be made voters if two million out of the four were women?

The California Republican platform of 1872 said:

Among the many practical and substantial triumphs of the principles achieved by the Republican party during the past twelve years, it enumerates with pride and pleasure the prohibiting of any State from abridging the privileges of any citizen of the republic, the declaring the civil and political equality of every citizen, and the establishing all these principles in the Federal Constitution, by amendments thereto, as the permanent law.

Benjamin F. Butler, in a recent letter to me, said: "I do not believe anybody in Congress doubts that the Constitution authorizes the right of women to vote, precisely as it authorizes trial by jury and many other like rights guaranteed to citizens."

It is upon this just interpretation of the United States Constitution that our National Woman Suffrage Association, which celebrates the twenty-fifth anniversary of the woman's rights movement next May in New York City, has based all its arguments and action since the passage of these amendments. We no longer petition legislature or Congress to give us the right to vote, but appeal to women everywhere to exercise their too long neglected "citizen's right." We appeal to the inspectors of election to receive the votes of all United States citizens, as it is their duty to do. We appeal to United States commissioners and marshals to arrest, as is their duty, the inspectors who reject the votes of United States citizens, and leave alone those who perform their duties and accept these votes. We ask the juries to return verdicts of "not guilty" in the cases of law-abiding United States citizens who cast their votes, and inspectors of election who receive and count them.

We ask the judges to render unprejudiced opinions of the law, and wherever there is room for doubt to give the benefit to the side of liberty and equal rights for women, remembering that, as Sumner says, "The true rule of interpretation under our National Constitution, especially since its amendments, is that anything *for* human rights is constitutional, everything *against* human rights unconstitutional." It is on this line that we propose to fight our battle for the ballot—peaceably but nevertheless persistently—until we achieve complete triumph and all United States citizens, men and women alike, are recognized as equals in the government.

NEWSPAPER COMMENT ON MISS ANTHONY'S TRIAL.

It is perhaps needless to say that whoever listens candidly to Susan B. Anthony, no matter how he previously regarded her and her sentiments, is certain to respect her and them afterwards.—Geneva Courier.

Miss Susan B. Anthony is sharp enough for a successful politician. She is under arrest in Rochester for voting illegally, and is conducting her case in a way which beats even lawyers. She stumped the county of Monroe and spoke in every post-office district so powerfully that she has actually converted nearly the entire male population to the woman suffrage doctrine. The sentiment is so universal that the United States district-attorney dare not trust his case to a jury drawn from that county, and has changed the venue to Ontario. Now Miss Anthony proposes to stump Ontario immediately, and has procured the services of Matilda Joslyn Gage, of Fayetteville, to assist her. By the time the case comes on, Miss Anthony will have Ontario county converted to her doctrine.—Syracuse Standard.

If Miss Anthony has converted every man in Monroe county to her views of the suffrage question, as the district-attorney intimates in his recent efforts to have her case adjourned, it is pretty good evidence—unless every man in Monroe county is a fool—that the lady has done no wrong. "Her case," remarks the Auburn Bulletin, "will probably be carried over to another term, and all she has to do is to canvass and convert another county. A shrewd woman that! Again we say she ought to vote."—Rochester Democrat and Chronicle.

There is perplexity in the northern district of New York. It was in that jurisdiction that Miss Susan B. Anthony and sundry "erring sisters" voted at the November election. For this they were arrested and indicted. The venue was laid in Monroe county and there the trial was to take place. Miss Anthony then proceeded to stump Monroe county and every town and village thereof, asking her bucolic hearers the solemn conundrum, "Is it a crime for a United States citizen to vote?" The answer is supposed generally to be in the negative, and so convincing is Sister Anthony's rhetoric regarded that it is supposed no jury can be found to convict her. Her case has gone to the jurymen of Monroe, in her own persuasive pleadings, before they are summoned. The district-attorney has, therefore, postponed the trial to another term of the court, and changed the place thereof to Ontario county; whereupon the brave Susan takes the stump in Ontario, and personally makes known her woes and wants. It is a regular St. Anthony's dance she leads the district-attorney; and, in spite of winter cold or summer heat, she will carry her case from county to county precisely as fast as the venue is changed. One must rise very early in the morning to get the start of this active apostle of the sisterhood.—New York Commercial Advertiser.

It seems likely that the decision of the court will be in Miss Anthony's favor. If such be the result the advocates of woman suffrage will change places with the public. They will no longer be forced to obtain hearings from congressional and legislative committees for their claims, but will exercise their right to vote by the authority of a legal precedent against which positive laws forbidding them from voting will be the only remedy. It is a question whether such laws can be passed in this country. A careful examination of the subject must precede any such legislation, and the inference from the result of Judge Selden's investigation is that the more the subject is studied the less likely will any legislative body be to forbid those women who want to vote from so doing.—New York Evening Post.

Miss Susan B. Anthony, whatever else she may be, is evidently of the right stuff for a reformer. Of all the woman suffragists she has the most courage and resource, and fights her own and her sisters' battle with the most wonderful energy, resolution and hopefulness. It is well known that she is now under indictment for voting illegally in Rochester last November. Voting illegally in her case means simply voting, for it is held that women can not lawfully vote at all. She is to be tried soon, but in the meantime, while at large on bail, she has devoted her time to missionary work on behalf of woman suffrage, and has spoken, it is said, in every post-office district in Monroe county, where her trial would have been held in the natural course of things. She has argued her cause so well that almost all the male population of the county have been converted to her views on this subject. The district-attorney is afraid to trust the case to a jury from that county, and has obtained a change of venue to Ontario on the ground that a fair trial can not be had in Monroe.

Miss Anthony, rather cheered than discouraged by this unwilling testimony to the strength of her cause and her powers of persuasion, has made arrangements to canvass Ontario county as thoroughly as Monroe. Some foolish and bigoted people who edit newspapers are complaining that Miss Anthony's proceedings are highly improper, inasmuch as they are intended to influence the decision of a cause pending in the courts. They even talk about contempt of court, and declare that Miss Anthony should be compelled to desist from making these invidious harangues. We suspect that the courts will not venture to interfere with this lady's speech-making tour, but will be of the opinion that she has the same right which other people, male or female, have to explain her political views and make converts to them if she can. We have never known it claimed before that a person accused of an offense was thereby deprived of the common right of free speech on political and other questions.—Worcester Spy.

The vapid efforts of a part of the newspaper press to entertain the public, of late, by descriptions, criticisms and comments, founded upon pretended interviews with Miss Anthony, reveal a standard of courtesy and truth discreditable to the American press, and a meagerness of interesting matter suggesting the propriety of the suspension of such sheets altogether. The Pittsburg Leader, among others, disgraces itself by a scurrilous report of what "the gay old girl said to a reporter;" and the New York World, of course, waxed very funny in its account of the late convention. These gibes at Miss Anthony's personal appearance, unwillingness to tell her age, "fishy eyes," etc., are read by her friends in Rochester with indignation and with contempt for the press which will publish such misrepresentations as truth.

All Rochester will assert—at least all of it worth heeding—that Miss Anthony holds here the position of a refined and estimable woman, thoroughly respected and beloved by the large circle of staunch friends who swear by her common sense and loyalty, if not by her peculiar views. As for her age, she tells it often enough unsolicited, whenever the famous silk dress is alluded to; the dear old dress that a New York reporter held up as such perfection of taste and fashion! Anna Dickinson gave that dress to Miss Anthony upon her fiftieth birthday a number of years ago, and the news was in all the papers. That dress is going into history with Commissioner Storrs, Judge Selden and the illustrious rest. It has always been worn by a lady—a genuine lady—no pretense nor sham—but good Quaker metal. She is no "sour old maid," our Miss Anthony, nor are the young men shy of her when she can find time to accept an invitation out; genial, cheery, warm-hearted, overflowing with stories and reminiscences, utterly fearless and regardless of mere public opinion, yet having a woman's delicate sensitiveness as to anything outre in dress or appearance.

Our Susan B. Anthony will work up into a charming bit of biography some day without a dull page within the covers, providing, of course, stupidity does not have the writing of it. Never mind what she has been fighting for, and will fight for till the victory is sure, we must all own hers a brave record, and she has already accomplished for her sex much that their scorn and contumely did not prevent her striving for. We heard a lady remark after attending the suffrage convention: "No, I am not converted to what these women advocate, I am too cowardly for that; but I am converted to Susan B. Anthony."—Rochester Evening Express.

WOMAN WANTS BREAD, NOT THE BALLOT!

Delivered in most of the large cities of the United States, between 1870 and 1880.
The speech never was written, and this abstract was prepared
from scattered notes and newspaper reports.

My purpose tonight is to demonstrate the great historical fact that disfranchisement is not only political degradation, but also moral, social, educational and industrial degradation; and that it does not matter whether the disfranchised class live under a monarchial or a republican form of government, or whether it be white workingmen of England, negroes on our southern plantations, serfs of Russia, Chinamen on our Pacific coast, or native born, tax-paying women of this republic. Wherever, on the face of the globe or on the page of history, you show me a disfranchised class, I will show you a degraded class of labor. Disfranchisement means inability to make, shape or control one's own circumstances. The disfranchised must always do the work, accept the wages, occupy the position the enfranchised assign to them. The disfranchised are in the position of the pauper. You remember the old adage, "Beggars must not be choosers;" they must take what they can get or nothing! That is exactly the position of women in the world of work today; they can not choose. If they could, do you for a moment believe they would take the subordinate places and the inferior pay? Nor is it a "new thing under the sun" for the disfranchised, the inferior classes weighed down with wrongs, to declare they "do not want to vote." The rank and file are not philosophers, they are not educated to think for themselves, but simply to accept, unquestioned, whatever comes.

Years ago in England when the workingmen, starving in the mines and factories, gathered in mobs and took bread wherever they could get it, their friends tried to educate them into a knowledge of the causes of their poverty and degradation. At one of these "monster bread meetings," held in Manchester, John Bright said to them, "Workingmen, what you need to bring to you cheap bread and plenty of it, is the franchise;" but those ignorant men shouted back to Mr. Bright, precisely as the women of America do to us today, "It is not the vote we want, it is bread;" and they broke up the meeting, refusing to allow him, their best friend, to explain to them the powers of the franchise. The condition of those workingmen was very little above that of slavery. Some of you may remember when George Thompson came over to this country and rebuked us for our crime and our curse of slavery, how the slaveholders and their abettors shouted back to Mr. Thompson, "Look at home, look into your mines and your factories, you have slavery in England."

You recollect a book published at that time entitled, "The Glory and Shame of England." Her glory was the emancipation of slaves in the British West Indies, and her shame the degraded and outraged condition of those very miners and factory men. In their desperation, they organized trades unions, went on strike, fought terrible battles, often destroying property and sometimes even killing their employers. Those who have read Charles Reade's novel, "Put Yourself in his Place," have not forgotten the terrible scenes depicted. While those starving men sometimes bettered their condition financially, they never made a ripple on the surface of political thought. No member ever championed their cause on the floor of Parliament. If spoken of at all, it was as our politicians used to speak of the negroes before the war, or as they speak of the Chinese today—as nuisances that ought to be suppressed.

But at length, through the persistent demands of a little handful of reformers, there was introduced into the British Parliament the "household suffrage" bill of 1867. John Stuart Mill not only championed that bill as it was presented, but moved an amendment to strike out the word "man" and substitute therefor the word "person," so that the bill should read, "every person who shall pay a seven-pound rental per annum shall be entitled to the franchise." You will see that Mr. Mill's motive was to extend the suffrage to women as well as men. But when the vote was taken, only seventy-four, out of the nearly seven hundred members of the British Parliament, voted in its favor.

During the discussion of the original bill, the opposition was championed by Robert Lowe, who presented all the stock objections to the extension of the franchise to "those ignorant, degraded workingmen," as he called them, that ever were presented in this country against giving the ballot to the negroes, and that are today being urged against the enfranchisement of women. Is it not a little remarkable that no matter who the class may be that it is proposed to enfranchise, the objections are always the same? "The ballot in the hands of this new class will make their condition worse than before, and the introduction of this new class into the political arena will degrade politics to a lower level." But notwithstanding Mr. Lowe's persistent opposition, the bill became a law; and before the session closed, that same individual moved that Parliament, having enfranchised these men, should now make an appropriation for the establishment and support of schools for the education of them and their sons. Now, mark you his reason why! "Unless they are educated," said he, "they will be the means of overturning the throne of England." So long as these poor men in the mines and factories had not the right to vote, the power to make and unmake the laws and law-makers, to help or hurt the government, no measure ever had been proposed for their benefit although they were ground under the heel of the capitalist to a condition of abject slavery. But the moment this power is placed in their hands, before they have used it even once, this bitterest enemy to their possessing it is the first man to spring to his feet and make this motion for the most beneficent measure possible in their behalf—public schools for the education of themselves and their children.

From that day to this, there never has been a session of the British Parliament that has not had before it some measure for the benefit of the working classes. Parliament has enacted laws compelling employers to cut down the number of hours for a day's work, to pay better wages, to build decent houses for their employes, and has prohibited the employment of very young children in the mines and factories. The history of those olden times records that not infrequently children were born in the mines and passed their lives there, scarcely seeing the sunlight from the day of their birth to the day of their death.

Sad as is the condition of the workingmen of England today, it is infinitely better than it was twenty years ago. At first the votes of the workingmen were given to the Liberal party, because it was the leaders of that party who secured their enfranchisement; but soon the leaders of the Conservative party, seeing the power the workingmen had, began to vie with the Liberals by going into their meetings and pledging that if they would vote the Tory ticket and bring that party into control, it would give them more and better laws even than the Liberals. In 1874 enough workingmen did go over to bring that party to the front, with Disraeli at its head, where it stood till 1880 when the rank and file of the workingmen of England, dissatisfied with Disraeli's policy, both domestic and foreign, turned and again voted the Liberal ticket, putting that party in power with Gladstone as its leader. This is the way in which the ballot in the hands of the masses of wage-earners, even under a monarchial form of government, makes of them a tremendous balance of power whose wants and wishes the instinct of self-interest compels the political leaders to study and obey.

The great distinctive advantage possessed by the workingmen of this republic is that the son of the humblest citizen, black or white, has equal chances with the son of the richest in the land if he take advantage of the public schools, the colleges and the many opportunities freely offered. It is this equality of rights which makes our nation a home for the oppressed of all the monarchies of the old world.

And yet, notwithstanding the declaration of our Revolutionary fathers, "all men created equal," "governments derive their just powers from the consent of the governed," "taxation and representation inseparable"—notwithstanding all these grand enunciations, our government was founded upon the blood and bones of half a million human beings, bought and sold as chattels in the market. Nearly all the original thirteen States had property qualifications which disfranchised poor white men as well as women and negroes. Thomas Jefferson, at the head of the old Democratic party, took the lead in advocating the removal of all property qualifications, as so many violations of the fundamental principle of our government—"the right of consent." In New York the qualification was $250. Martin Van Buren, the chief of the Democracy, was a member of the Constitutional Convention held in Buffalo in 1821, which wiped out that qualification so far as white men were concerned. He declared, "The poor man has as good a right to a voice in the government as the rich man, and a vastly greater need to possess it as a means of protection to himself and his family." It was because the Democrats enfranchised poor white men, both native and foreign, that that strong old party held absolute sway in this country for almost forty years, with only now and then a one-term Whig administration.

In those olden days Horace Greeley, at the head of the Whig party and his glorious New York Tribune, used to write long editorials showing the working-men that they had a mistaken idea about the Democratic party; that it was not so much the friend of the poor man as was the Whig, and if they would but vote the Whig ticket and put that party in power, they would find that it would give them better laws than the Democrats had done. At length, after many, many years of such education and persuasion, the workingmen's vote, native and foreign, was divided, and in 1860 there came to the front a new party which, though not called Whig, was largely made up of the old Whig ele-ments. In its turn this new party enfranchised another degraded class of labor. Because the Republicans gave the ballot to negroes, they have been allied to that party and have held it solid in power from the ratification of the Fifteenth Amendment, in 1870, to the present day. Until the Democrats convince them that they will do more and better for them than the Repub-licans are doing, there will be no appreciable division of the negro vote.

The vast numbers of wage-earning men coming from Europe to this coun-try, where manhood suffrage prevails with no limitations, find themselves invested at once with immense political power. They organize their trades unions, but not being able to use the franchise intelligently, they continue to strike and to fight their battles with the capitalists just as they did in the old countries. Neither press nor politicians dare to condemn these strikes or to demand their suppression because the workingmen hold the balance of power and can use it for the success or defeat of either party.

[Miss Anthony here related various timely instances of strikes where force was used to prevent non-union men from taking the places of the strikers, and neither the newspapers nor political leaders ventured to sustain the officials in the necessary steps to preserve law and order, or if they did they were defeated at the next election.]

It is said women do not need the ballot for their protection because they are supported by men. Statistics show that there are 3,000,000 women in this na-tion supporting themselves. In the crowded cities of the East they are com-pelled to work in shops, stores and factories for the merest pittance. In New York alone, there are over 50,000 of these women receiving less than fifty cents a day. Women wage-earners in different occupations have organized themselves into trades unions, from time to time, and made their strikes to get justice at the hands of their employers just as men have done, but I have yet to learn of a successful strike of any body of women. The best organized one I ever knew was that of the collar laundry women of the city of Troy, N. Y., the great emporium for the manufacture of shirts, collars and cuffs. They formed a trades union of several hundred members and demanded an increase of wages. It was refused. So one May morning in 1867, each woman threw down her scissors and her needle, her starch-pan and flat-iron, and for three long months not one returned to the factories. At the end of that time they were literally starved out, and the majority of them were compelled to go back, but not at their old wages, for their employers cut them down to even a lower figure.

In the winter following I met the president of this union, a bright young Irish girl, and asked her, " Do you not think if you had been 500 carpenters or

500 masons, you would have succeeded?" "Certainly," she said, and then she told me of 200 bricklayers who had the year before been on strike and gained every point with their employers. "What could have made the difference? Their 200 were but a fraction of that trade, while your 500 absolutely controlled yours." Finally she said, "It was because the editors ridiculed and denounced us." "Did they ridicule and denounce the bricklayers?" "No." "What did they say about you?" "Why, that our wages were good enough now, better than those of any other workingwomen except teachers; and if we weren't satisfied, we had better go and get married." "What then do you think made this difference?" After studying over the question awhile she concluded, "It must have been because our employers bribed the editors." "Couldn't the employers of the bricklayers have bribed the editors?" She had never thought of that. Most people never do think; they see one thing totally unlike another, but the person who stops to inquire into the cause that produces the one or the other is the exception. So this young Irish girl was simply not an exception, but followed the general rule of people, whether men or women; she hadn't thought. In the case of the bricklayers, no editor, either Democrat or Republican, would have accepted the proffer of a bribe, because he would have known that if he denounced or ridiculed those men, not only they but all the trades union men of the city at the next election would vote solidly against the nominees advocated by that editor. If those collar laundry women had been voters, they would have held, in that little city of Troy, the "balance of political power" and the editor or the politician who ignored or insulted them would have turned that balance over to the opposing party.

My friends, the condition of those collar laundry women but represents the utter helplessness of disfranchisement. The question with you, as men, is not whether you want your wives and daughters to vote, nor with you, as women, whether you yourselves want to vote; but whether you will help to put this power of the ballot into the hands of the 3,000,000 wage-earning women, so that they may be able to compel politicians to legislate in their favor and employers to grant them justice.

The law of capital is to extort the greatest amount of work for the least amount of money; the rule of labor is to do the smallest amount of work for the largest amount of money. Hence there is, and in the nature of things must continue to be, antagonism between the two classes; therefore, neither should be left wholly at the mercy of the other.

It was cruel, under the old regime, to give rich men the right to rule poor men. It was wicked to allow white men absolute power over black men. It is vastly more cruel, more wicked to give to all men—rich and poor, white and black, native and foreign, educated and ignorant, virtuous and vicious—this absolute control over women. Men talk of the injustice of monopolies. There never was, there never can be, a monopoly so fraught with injustice, tyranny and degradation as this monopoly of sex, of all men over all women. Therefore I not only agree with Abraham Lincoln that, "No man is good enough to govern another man without his consent;" but I say also that no man is good enough to govern a woman without her consent, and still further, that all men combined in government are not good enough to govern all women without their consent. There might have been some plausible excuse for the rich governing the poor, the educated governing the ignorant, the Saxon governing the African; but there can be none for making the husband the ruler of the wife, the brother of the sister, the man of the woman, his peer in birth, in education, in social position, in all that stands for the best and highest in humanity.

I believe that by nature men are no more unjust than women. If from the beginning women had maintained the right to rule not only themselves but men also, the latter today doubtless would be occupying the subordinate places with inferior pay in the world of work; women would be holding the higher positions with the big salaries; widowers would be doomed to a "life interest of one-third of the family estate;" husbands would "owe service" to their wives, so that every one of you men would be begging your good wives, "Please be so kind as to 'give me' ten cents for a cigar." The principle of self-government can not be violated with impunity. The individual's right to it is sacred—regardless of class, caste, race, color, sex or any other accident or incident of birth. What we ask is that you shall cease to imagine that women are outside this law, and that you shall come into the knowledge that disfranchisement means the same degradation to your daughters as to your sons.

Governments can not afford to ignore the rights of those holding the ballot, who make and unmake every law and law-maker. It is not because the members of Congress are tyrants that women receive only half pay and are admitted only to inferior positions in the departments. It is simply in obedience to a law of political economy which makes it impossible for a government to do as much for the disfranchised as for the enfranchised. Women are no exception to the general rule. As disfranchisement always has degraded men, socially, morally and industrially, so today it is disfranchisement that degrades women in the same spheres.

Again men say it is not votes, but the law of supply and demand which regulates wages. The law of gravity is that water shall run down hill, but when men build a dam across the stream, the force of gravity is stopped and the water held back. The law of supply and demand regulates free and enfranchised labor, but disfranchisement estops its operation. What we ask is the removal of the dam, that women, like men, may reap the benefit of the law. Did the law of supply and demand regulate work and wages in the olden days of slavery? This law can no more reach the disfranchised than it did the enslaved. There is scarcely a place where a woman can earn a single dollar without a man's consent.

There are many women equally well qualified with men for principals and superintendents of schools, and yet, while three-fourths of the teachers are women, nearly all of them are relegated to subordinate positions on half or at most two-thirds the salaries paid to men. The law of supply and demand is ignored, and that of sex alone settles the question. If a business man should advertise for a book-keeper and ten young men, equally well qualified, should present themselves and, after looking them over, he should say, "To you who have red hair, we will pay full wages, while to you with black hair we will pay half the regular price;" that would not be a more flagrant violation of the law of supply and demand than is that now perpetrated upon women because of their sex.

And then again you say, "Capital, not the vote, regulates labor." Granted, for the sake of the argument, that capital does control the labor of women, Chinamen and slaves; but no one with eyes to see and ears to hear, will concede for a moment that capital absolutely dominates the work and wages of the free and enfranchised men of this republic. It is in order to lift the millions of our wage-earning women into a position of as much power over their own labor as men possess that they should be invested with the franchise. This ought to be done not only for the sake of justice to the women, but to the men with whom they compete; for, just so long as there is a degraded class of labor in the market, it always will be used by the capitalists to checkmate and undermine the superior classes.

Now that as a result of the agitation for equality of chances, and through the invention of machinery, there has come a great revolution in the world of economics, so that wherever a man may go to earn an honest dollar a woman may go also, there is no escape from the conclusion that she must be clothed with equal power to protect herself. That power is the ballot, the symbol of freedom and equality, without which no citizen is sure of keeping even that which he hath, much less of getting that which he hath not. Women are today the peers of men in education, in the arts and sciences, in the industries and professions, and there is no escape from the conclusion that the next step must be to make them the peers of men in the government —city, State and national—to give them an equal voice in the framing, interpreting and administering of the codes and constitutions.

We recognize that the ballot is a two-edged, nay, a many-edged sword, which may be made to cut in every direction. If wily politicians and sordid capitalists may wield it for mere party and personal greed; if oppressed wage-earners may invoke it to wring justice from legislators and extort material advantages from employers; if the lowest and most degraded classes of men may use it to open wide the sluice-ways of vice and crime; if it may be the instrumentality by which the narrow, selfish, corrupt and corrupting men and measures rule—it is quite as true that noble-minded statesmen, philanthropists and reformers may make it the weapon with which to reverse the above order of things, as soon as they can have added to their now small numbers the immensely larger ratio of what men so love to call "the better half of the people." When women vote, they will make a new balance of power that must be weighed and measured and calculated in its effect upon every social and moral question which goes to the arbitrament of the ballot-box. Who can doubt that when the representative women of thought and culture, who are today the moral backbone of our nation, sit in counsel with the best men of the country, higher conditions will be the result?

Insurrectionary and revolutionary methods of righting wrongs, imaginary or real, are pardonable only in the enslaved and disfranchised. The moment any class of men possess the ballot, it is their weapon and their shield. Men with a vote have no valid excuse for resorting to the use of illegal means to fight their battles. When the masses of wage-earning men are educated into a knowledge of their own rights and of their duties to others, so that they are able to vote intelligently, they can carry their measures through the ballot-box and will have no need to resort to force. But so long as they remain in ignorance and are manipulated by the political bosses they will continue to vote against their own interests and turn again to violence to right their wrongs.

If men possessing the power of the ballot are driven to desperate means to gain their ends, what shall be done by disfranchised women? There are grave questions of moral, as well as of material interest in which women are most deeply concerned. Denied the ballot, the legitimate means with which to exert their influence, and, as a rule, being lovers of peace, they have recourse to prayers and tears, those potent weapons of women and children, and, when they fail, must tamely submit to wrong or rise in rebellion against the powers that be. Women's crusades against saloons, brothels and gambling-dens, emptying kegs and bottles into the streets, breaking doors and windows and burning houses, all go to prove that disfranchisement, the denial of lawful means to gain desired ends, may drive even women to violations of law and order. Hence to secure both national and "domestic tranquillity," to " establish justice," to carry out the spirit of our Constitution, put into the hands of all women, as you have into those of all men, the ballot, that symbol of perfect equality, that right protective of all other rights.

SOCIAL PURITY.

First delivered at Chicago in the Spring of 1875, in the Sunday afternoon Dime lecture course.

Though women, as a class, are much less addicted to drunkenness and licentiousness than men, it is universally conceded that they are by far the greater sufferers from these evils. Compelled by their position in society to depend on men for subsistence, for food, clothes, shelter, for every chance even to earn a dollar, they have no way of escape from the besotted victims of appetite and passion with whom their lot is cast. They must endure, if not endorse, these twin vices, embodied, as they so often are, in the person of father, brother, husband, son, employer. No one can doubt that the sufferings of the sober, virtuous woman, in legal subjection to the mastership of a drunken, immoral husband and father over herself and children, not only from physical abuse, but from spiritual shame and humiliation, must be such as the man himself can not possibly comprehend.

It is not my purpose to harrow your feelings by any attempt at depicting the horrible agonies of mind and body that grow out of these monster social evils. They are already but too well known. Scarce a family throughout our broad land but has had its peace and happiness marred by one or the other, or both. That these evils exist, we all know; that something must be done, we as well know; that the old methods have failed, that man, alone, has proved himself incompetent to eradicate, or even regulate them, is equally evident. It shall be my endeavor, therefore, to prove to you that we must now adopt new measures and bring to our aid new forces to accomplish the desired end.

Forty years' efforts by men alone to suppress the evil of intemperance give us the following appalling figures: 600,000 common drunkards! Which, reckoning our population to be 40,000,000, gives us one drunkard to every seventeen moderate drinking and total-abstinence men. Granting to each of these 600,000 drunkards a wife and four children, we have 3,000,000 of the women and children of this nation helplessly, hopelessly bound to this vast army of irresponsible victims of appetite.

[Reference was here made to woman's helplessness under the laws.]

The roots of the giant evil, intemperance, are not merely moral and social; they extend deep and wide into the financial and political structure of the government; and whenever women, or men, shall intelligently and seriously set themselves about the work of uprooting the liquor traffic, they will find something more than tears and prayers needful to the task. Financial and political power must be combined with moral and social influence, all bound together in one earnest, energetic, persistent force.

[Statistics given of pauperism, lunacy, idiocy and crime growing out of intemperance.]

The prosecutions in our courts for breach of promise, divorce, adultery, bigamy, seduction, rape; the newspaper reports every day of every year of scandals and outrages, of wife murders and paramour shootings, of abortions and infanticides, are perpetual reminders of men's incapacity to cope successfully with this monster evil of society.

The statistics of New York show the number of professional prostitutes in that city to be over twenty thousand. Add to these the thousands and tens of thousands of Boston, Philadelphia, Washington, New Orleans, St. Louis, Chicago, San Francisco, and all our cities, great and small, from ocean to ocean, and what a holocaust of the womanhood of this nation is sacrificed to the insatiate Moloch of lust. And yet more: those myriads of wretched women, publicly known as prostitutes, constitute but a small portion of the numbers who actually tread the paths of vice and crime. For, as the oft-broken ranks of the vast army of common drunkards are steadily filled by the boasted moderate drinkers, so are the ranks of professional prostitution continually replenished by discouraged, seduced, deserted unfortunates, who can no longer hide the terrible secret of their lives.

The Albany Law Journal, of December, 1876, says: "The laws of infanticide must be a dead letter in the District of Columbia. According to the reports of the local officials, the dead bodies of infants, still-born and murdered, which have been found during the past year, scattered over parks and vacant lots in the city of Washington, are to be numbered by hundreds."

In 1869 the Catholics established a Foundling Hospital in New York City. At the close of the first six months Sister Irene reported thirteen hundred little waifs laid in the basket at her door. That meant thirteen hundred of the daughters of New York, with trembling hands and breaking hearts, trying to bury their sorrow and their shame from the world's cruel gaze. That meant thirteen hundred mothers' hopes blighted and blasted. Thirteen hundred Rachels weeping for their children because they were not!

Nor is it womanhood alone that is thus fearfully sacrificed. For every betrayed woman, there is always the betrayer, man. For every abandoned woman, there is always *one* abandoned man and oftener many more. It is estimated that there are 50,000 professional prostitutes in London, and Dr. Ryan calculates that there are 400,000 men in that city directly or indirectly connected with them, and that this vice causes the city an annual expenditure of $40,000,000.

All attempts to describe the loathsome and contagious disease which it engenders defy human language. The Rev. Wm. G. Eliot, of St. Louis, says of it: "Few know of the terrible nature of the disease in question and its fearful ravages, not only among the guilty, but the innocent. Since its first recognized appearance in Europe in the fifteenth century, it has been a desolation and a scourge. In its worst forms it is so subtle, that its course can with difficulty be traced. It poisons the constitution, and may be imparted to others by those who have no outward or distinguishable marks of it themselves. It may be propagated months and years after it seems to have been cured. The purity of womanhood and the helplessness of infancy afford no certainty of escape."

[Medical testimony given from cities in Europe.]

Man's legislative attempts to set back this fearful tide of social corruption have proved even more futile and disastrous than have those for the suppression of intemperance—as witness the Contagious Diseases Acts of England and the St. Louis experiment. And yet efforts to establish similar laws are constantly made in our large cities, New York and Washington barely escaping last winter.

To license certain persons to keep brothels and saloons is but to throw around them and their traffic the shield of law, and thereby to blunt the edge of all moral and social efforts against them. Nevertheless, in every large city, brothels are virtually licensed. When "Maggie Smith" is made to appear before the police court at the close of each quarter, to pay her fine of $10, $25 or $100, as an inmate or a keeper of a brothel, and allowed to continue her vocation, so long as she pays her fine, *that is license.* When a grand jury fails to find cause for indictment against a well-known keeper of a house of ill-fame, that, too, is *permission* for her and all of her class to follow their trade, against the statute laws of the State, and that with impunity.

The work of woman is not to lessen the severity or the certainty of the penalty for the violation of the moral law, but to prevent this violation by the removal of the causes which lead to it. These causes are said to be wholly different with the sexes. The acknowledged incentive to this vice on the part of man is his own abnormal passion; while on the part of woman, in the great majority of cases, it is conceded to be destitution—absolute want of the necessaries of life. Lecky, the famous historian of European morals, says: "The statistics of prostitution show that a great proportion of those women who have fallen into it have been impelled by the most extreme poverty, in many instances verging on starvation." All other conscientious students of this terrible problem, on both continents, agree with Mr. Lecky. Hence, there is no escape from the conclusion that, while woman's want of bread induces her to pursue this vice, man's love of the vice itself leads him into it and holds him there. While statistics show no lessening of the passional demand on the part of man, they reveal a most frightful increase of the temptations, the necessities, on the part of woman.

In the olden times, when the daughters of the family, as well as the wife, were occupied with useful and profitable work in the household, getting the meals and washing the dishes three times in every day of every year, doing the baking, the brewing, the washing and the ironing, the whitewashing, the butter and cheese and soap making, the mending and the making of clothes for the entire family, the carding, spinning and weaving of the cloth—when everything to eat, to drink and to wear was manufactured in the home, almost no young women "went out to work." But now, when nearly all these handicrafts are turned over to men and to machinery, tens of thousands, nay, millions, of the women of both hemispheres are thrust into the world's outer market of work to earn their own subsistence. Society, ever slow to change its conditions, presents to these millions but few and meager chances. Only the barest necessaries, and oftentimes not even those, can be purchased with the proceeds of the most excessive and exhausting labor.

Hence, the reward of virtue for the homeless, friendless, penniless woman is ever a scanty larder, a pinched, patched, faded wardrobe, a dank basement or rickety garret, with the colder, shabbier scorn and neglect of the more fortunate of her sex. Nightly, as weary and worn from her day's toil she wends her way through the dark alleys toward her still darker abode, where only cold and hunger await her, she sees on every side and at every turn the gilded hand of vice and crime outstretched, beckoning her to food and clothes and shelter; hears the whisper in softest accents, "Come with me and I will give you all the comforts, pleasures and luxuries that love and wealth can bestow." Since the vast multitudes of human beings, women like men, are not born to the courage or conscience of the martyr, can we wonder that so many poor girls fall, that so many accept material ease and comfort at the expense of spiritual purity and peace? Should we not wonder, rather, that so many escape the sad fate?

Clearly, then, the first step toward solving this problem is to lift this vast army of poverty-stricken women who now crowd our cities, above the temptation, the necessity, to sell themselves, in marriage or out, for bread and shelter. To do that, girls, like boys, must be educated to some lucrative employment; women, like men, must have equal chances to earn a living. If the plea that poverty is the cause of woman's prostitution be not true, perfect equality of chances to earn honest bread will demonstrate the falsehood by removing that pretext and placing her on the same plane with man. Then, if she is found in the ranks of vice and crime, she will be there for the same reason that man is and, from an object of pity, she, like him, will become a fit subject of contempt. From being the party sinned against, she will become an equal sinner, if not the greater of the two. Women, like men, must not only have "fair play" in the world of work and self-support, but, like men, must be eligible to all the honors and emoluments of society and government. Marriage, to women as to men, must be a luxury, not a necessity; an incident of life, not all of it. And the only possible way to accomplish this great change is to accord to women equal power in the making, shaping and controlling of the circumstances of life. That equality of rights and privileges is vested in the ballot, the symbol of power in a republic. Hence, our first and most urgent demand—that women shall be protected in the exercise of their inherent, personal, citizen's right to a voice in the government, municipal, state, national.

Alexander Hamilton said one hundred years ago, "Give to a man the right over my subsistence, and he has power over my whole moral being." No one doubts the truth of this assertion as between man and man; while, as between man and woman, not only does almost no one believe it, but the masses of people deny it. And yet it is the fact of man's possession of this right over woman's subsistence which gives to him the power to dictate to her a moral code vastly higher and purer than the one he chooses for himself. Not less true is it, that the fact of woman's dependence on man for her subsistence renders her utterly powerless to exact from him the same high moral code she chooses for herself.

Of the 8,000,000 women over twenty-one years of age in the United States, 800,000, one out of every ten, are unmarried, and fully one-half of the entire number, or 4,000,000, support themselves wholly or in part by the industry of their own hands and brains. All of these, married or single, have to ask man, as an individual, a corporation, or a government, to grant to them even the privilege of hard work and small pay. The tens of thousands of poor but respectable young girls soliciting copying, clerkships, shop work, teaching, must ask of men, and not seldom receive in response, " Why work for a living? There are other ways!"

Whoever controls work and wages, controls morals. Therefore, we must have women employers, superintendents, committees, legislators; wherever girls go to seek the means of subsistence, there must be some woman. Nay, more; we must have women preachers, lawyers, doctors—that wherever women go to seek counsel—spiritual, legal, physical—there, too, they will be sure to find the best and noblest of their own sex to minister to them.

Independence is happiness. "No man should depend upon another; not even upon his own father. By depend I mean, obey without examination— yield to the will of any one whomsoever." This is the conclusion to which Pierre, the hero of Madame Sand's "Monsieur Sylvestre," arrives, after running away from the uncle who had determined to marry him to a woman he did not choose to wed. In freedom he discovers that, though deprived of all the luxuries to which he had been accustomed, he is happy, and writes his friend that "without having realized it, he had been unhappy all his life; had suffered from his dependent condition; that nothing in his life, his pleasures, his occupations, had been of his own choice." And is not this the precise condition of what men call the " better half " of the human family?

In one of our western cities I once met a beautiful young woman, a successful teacher in its public schools, an only daughter who had left her New England home and all its comforts and luxuries and culture. Her father was a member of Congress and could bring to her all the attractions of Washington society. That young girl said to me, "The happiest moment of my life was when I received into my hand my first month's salary for teaching." Not long after, I met her father in Washington, spoke to him of his noble daughter, and he said: "Yes, you woman's rights people have robbed me of my only child and left the home of my old age sad and desolate. Would to God that the notion of supporting herself had never entered her head!" Had that same lovely, cultured, energetic young girl left the love, the luxury, the protection of that New England home for marriage, instead of self-support; had she gone out to be the light and joy of a husband's life, instead of her own; had she but chosen another man, instead of her father, to decide for her all her pleasures and occupations; had she but taken another position of dependence, instead of one of independence, neither her father nor the world would have felt the change one to be condemned. . . .

Fathers should be most particular about the men who visit their daughters, and, to further this reform, pure women not only must refuse to meet intimately and to marry impure men, but, finding themselves deceived in their husbands, they must refuse to continue in the marriage relation with them. We have had quite enough of the sickly sentimentalism which counts the woman a heroine and a saint for remaining the wife of a drunken, immoral husband, incurring the risk of her own health and poisoning the life-blood of the young beings that result from this unholy alliance. Such company as ye keep, such ye are! must be the maxim of married, as well as unmarried, women. . .

[Numerous instances cited of the unjust discrimination against women where men were equally guilty.]

So long as the wife is held innocent in continuing to live with a libertine, and every girl whom he inveigles and betrays becomes an outcast whom no other wife will tolerate in her house, there is, there can be, no hope of solving the problem of prostitution. As long experience has shown, these poor, homeless girls of the world can not be relied on, as a police force, to hold all husbands true to their marriage vows. Here and there, they will fail and, where they do, wives must make not the girls alone, but their husbands also suffer for their infidelity, as husbands never fail to do when their wives weakly or wickedly yield to the blandishments of other men.

[Examples given to prove this point.]

In a western city the wives conspired to burn down a house of ill-fame in which their husbands had placed a half-dozen of the demi-monde. Would it not have shown much more womanly wisdom and virtue for those legal wives to have refused to recognize their husbands, instead of wreaking their vengeance on the heads of those wretched women? But how could they without finding themselves, as a result, penniless and homeless? The person, the services, the children, the subsistence, of each and every one of those women belonged by law, not to herself, but to her unfaithful husband.

Now, why is it that man can hold woman to this high code of morals, like Cæsar's wife—not only pure but above suspicion—and so surely and severely punish her for every departure, while she is so helpless, so powerless to check him in his license, or to extricate herself from his presence and control? His power grows out of his right over her subsistence. Her lack of power grows out of her dependence on him for her food, her clothes, her shelter.

Marriage never will cease to be a wholly unequal partnership until the law recognizes the equal ownership in the joint earnings and possessions. The true relation of the sexes never can be attained until woman is free and equal with man. Neither in the making nor executing of the laws regulating these relations has woman ever had the slightest voice. The statutes for marriage and divorce, for adultery, breach of promise, seduction, rape, bigamy, abortion, infanticide—all were made by men. They, alone, decide who are guilty of violating these laws and what shall be their punishment, with judge, jury and advocate all men, with no woman's voice heard in our courts, save as accused or witness, and in many cases the married woman is denied the poor privilege of testifying as to her own guilt or innocence of the crime charged against her.

Since the days of Moses and the prophets, men and ministers have preached

ANT.—64

the law of " visiting the iniquity of the fathers upon the children and the children's children, to the third and fourth generations." But with absolute power over woman and all the conditions of life for the whole 6,000 years, man has proved his utter inability either to put away his own iniquities, or to cease to hand them down from generation to generation; hence, the only hope of reform is in sharing this absolute power with some other than himself, and that other must be woman. When no longer a subject, but an equal—a free and independent sovereign, believing herself created primarily for her own individual happiness and development and secondarily for man's, precisely as man believes himself created first for his own enjoyment and second for that of woman—she will constitute herself sole umpire in the sacred domain of motherhood. Then, instead of feeling it her Christian duty to live with a drunken, profligate husband, handing down to her children his depraved appetites and passions, she will *know* that God's curse will be upon her and her children if she flee not from him as from a pestilence.

It is worse than folly, it is madness, for women to delude themselves with the idea that their children will escape the terrible penalty of the law. The taint of their birth will surely follow them. For pure women to continue to devote themselves to their man-appointed mission of visiting the dark purlieus of society and struggling to reclaim the myriads of badly-born human beings swarming there, is as hopeless as would be an attempt to ladle the ocean with a teaspoon; as unphilosophical as was the undertaking of the old American Colonization Society, which, with great labor and pains and money, redeemed from slavery and transported to Liberia annually 400 negroes; or the Fugitive Slave Societies, which succeeded in running off to Canada, on their "under-ground railroads," some 40,000 in a whole quarter of a century. While those good men were thus toiling to rescue the 400 or the 40,000 individual victims of slavery, each day saw hundreds and each year thousands of human beings born into the terrible condition of chattelism. All see and admit now what none but the Abolitionists saw then, that the only effectual work was the entire overthrow of the system of slavery; the abrogation of the law which sanctioned the right of property in man.

In answer to my proposal to speak in one of the cities of Iowa, an earnest woman replied, " It is impossible to get you an audience; all of our best women are at present engaged in an effort to establish a ' Home for the Friendless.' All the churches are calling for the entire time of their members to get up fairs, dinners, concerts, etc., to raise money. In fact, even our woman suffragists are losing themselves in devotion to some institution."

Thus, wherever you go, you find the best women, in and out of the churches, all absorbed in establishing or maintaining benevolent or reform institutions; charitable societies, soup-houses, ragged schools, industrial schools, mite societies, mission schools—at home and abroad—homes and hospitals for the sick, the aged, the friendless, the foundling, the fallen; asylums for the orphans, the blind, the deaf and dumb, the insane, the inebriate, the idiot. The women of this century are neither idle nor indifferent. They are working with might and main to mitigate the evils which stare them in the face on every side, but much of their work is without knowledge. It is aimed at the effects, not the cause; it is plucking the spoiled fruit; it is lopping off the poisonous branches of the deadly upas tree, which but makes the root more vigorous in sending out new shoots in every direction. A right understanding of physiological law teaches us that the cause must be removed; the tree must be girdled; the tap-root must be severed.

The tap-root of our social upas lies deep down at the very foundations of society. It is woman's dependence. It is woman's subjection. Hence, the first and only efficient work must be to emancipate woman from her enslavement. The wife must no longer echo the poet Milton's ideal Eve, when she adoringly said to Adam, "God, thy law; thou, mine!" She must feel herself accountable to God alone for every act, fearing and obeying no man, save where his will is in line with her own highest idea of divine law.

The president of the Howard Mission School, New York, said, "Miss Anthony, it is a marvel to me that, with so much brain and common sense, you should always devote yourself to mere abstractions. Why is it that you never set yourself about some practical work?"

"Like the Howard Mission?" said I. "How many less children have you now than ten years ago?"

"Oh, no less, but many, many more."

"Would it not be a practical work, then, to make it possible for every mother to support her own children? That is my aim and my work; while yours is simply to pick up the poor children, leaving every girl-child to the mother's heritage of helpless poverty and vice. My aim is to change the condition of women to self-help; yours, simply to ameliorate the ills that must inevitably grow out of dependence. My work is to lessen the numbers of the poor; yours, merely to lessen the sufferings of their tenfold increase."

If the divine law visits the sins of the fathers upon the children, equally so does it transmit to them their virtues. Therefore, if it is through woman's ignorant subjection to the tyranny of man's appetites and passions that the life-current of the race is corrupted, then must it be through her intelligent emancipation that the race shall be redeemed from the curse, and her children and children's children rise up to call her blessed. When the mother of Christ shall be made the true model of womanhood and motherhood, when the office of maternity shall be held sacred and the mother shall consecrate herself, as did Mary, to the one idea of bringing forth the Christ-child, then, and not till then, will this earth see a new order of men and women, prone to good rather than evil.

I am a full and firm believer in the revelation that it is through woman that the race is to be redeemed. And it is because of this faith that I ask for her immediate and unconditional emancipation from all political, industrial, social and religious subjection.

"What is most needed to ensure the future greatness of the empire?" inquired Madame Campan of the great Napoleon. "Mothers!" was the terse and suggestive reply. Ralph Waldo Emerson says, "Men are what their mothers made them." But I say, to hold mothers responsible for the character of their sons while you deny them any control over the surroundings of their lives, is worse than mockery, it is cruelty! Responsibilities grow out of rights and powers. Therefore, before mothers can be held responsible for the vices and crimes, the wholesale demoralization of men, they must possess all possible rights and powers to control the conditions and circumstances of their own and their children's lives.

A minister of Chicago sums up the infamies of that great metropolis of the West as follows: 3,000 licensed dram-shops and myriad patrons; 300 gambling houses and countless frequenters, many of them young men from the best families of the city; 79 obscene theatres, with their thousands of degraded men and boys nightly in attendance; 500 brothels, with their thousands of poor girls, bodies and souls sacrificed to the 20,000 or 30,000 depraved men—young and old, married and single—who visit them. While all the participants in all these forms of iniquity, victims and victimizers alike—the women excepted—may go to the polls on every election day and vote for the mayor and members of the common council, who will either continue to license these places, or fail to enforce the laws which would practically close them— not a single woman in that city may record her vote against those wretched blots on civilization. The profane, tobacco-chewing, whiskey-drinking, gambling libertines may vote, but not their virtuous, intelligent, sober, law-abiding wives and mothers!

You remember the petition of 18,000 of the best women of Chicago, a year ago, asking the common council not to repeal the Sunday Liquor Law? Why were they treated with ridicule and contempt? Why was their prayer unheeded? Was it because the honorable gentlemen had no respect for those women or their demand? No; on the contrary, many of them, doubtless, were men possessed of high regard for women, who would have been glad to aid them in their noble efforts; but the power that placed those men in office, the representatives of the saloons, brothels and obscene shows, crowded the council chamber and its corridors, threatening political death to the man who should dare give his voice or his vote for the maintenance of that law. Could those 18,000 women, with the tens of thousands whom they represented, have gone to the ballot-box at the next election and voted to re-elect the men who championed their petition, and defeat those who opposed it, does any one doubt that it would have been heeded by the common council?

As the fountain can rise no higher than the spring that feeds it, so a legislative body will enact or enforce no law above the average sentiment of the people who created it. Any and every reform work is sure to lead women to the ballot-box. It is idle for them to hope to battle successfully against the monster evils of society until they shall be armed with weapons equal to those of the enemy—votes and money. Archimedes said, "Give to me a fulcrum on which to plant my lever, and I will move the world." And I say, give to woman the ballot, the political fulcrum, on which to plant her moral lever, and she will lift the world into a nobler and purer atmosphere.

Two great necessities forced this nation to extend justice and equality to the negro:

First, Military necessity, which compelled the abolition of the crime and curse of slavery, before the rebellion could be overcome.

Second, Political necessity, which required the enfranchisement of the newly-freed men, before the work of reconstruction could begin.

The third is now pressing, Moral necessity—to emancipate woman, before Social Purity, the nation's safeguard, ever can be established.

OPEN LETTER TO BENJAMIN HARRISON,
Republican Nominee for President.

INDIANAPOLIS, IND., June 30, 1888.

DEAR SIR: We, representatives of the National Woman Suffrage Association, respectfully ask you to consider the following facts:

The first plank in the platform adopted by the Republican convention recently held in Chicago, entitled "The Purity of the Ballot," reaffirms the unswerving devotion of the Republican party to the personal rights and liberties of citizens in all the States and Territories of the Union, and especially to "the supreme and sovereign right of every lawful citizen, rich or poor, native or foreign, white or black, to cast one free ballot in public elections and to have that ballot duly counted." And again the platform says: "We hold the free and honest popular ballot, and the just and equal representation of all the people, to be the foundation of our republican government."

These declarations place the Republican party in its original attitude as the defender of the personal freedom and political liberties of all citizens of the United States. These sentiments, even the phraseology in which they are here expressed, may be found in every series of resolutions adopted by the National Woman Suffrage Association since its organization.

The advocates of woman suffrage would have been glad to see the phrase "male or female" inserted after the phrase "white or black" in the resolution above quoted, because this would be a fitting conclusion to the enumeration by antithesis of the classes into which citizens are divided. However, no enumeration of classes was necessary to explain or to enforce the declaration of the party's devotion to "the supreme and sovereign right of every lawful citizen to cast one free ballot in public elections and to have that ballot duly counted." It is the unimpeded exercise of this "supreme and sovereign right of every lawful citizen" which the women we represent demand.

That women are "lawful citizens" is undeniable, since the law recognizes them as such through the visits of the assessor and tax-gatherer; since it recognizes them as such in the police stations, the jails, the courts and the prisons. Only at the ballot-box is the lawful citizenship of women challenged! Only at the ballot-box, which is declared to be the sole safe-guard of the citizen's liberty—only there is the liberty of the female citizen denied.

But reverting to the first resolution in the Republican platform, so satisfactory in its sentiments, we beg to suggest that its value will depend solely upon its interpretation, and that its authoritative interpretation must be given by the leaders of the Republican party. Therefore to you, the chosen

(1013)

head of that party, we address ourselves, asking that your letter of acceptance of the nomination to the presidency of the United States be so framed as to indicate clearly your recognition of the fact that the Republican party has pledged itself to protect *every citizen* in the free exercise of "the supreme and sovereign right" to vote at public elections.

It appears to us that the application of Republican principles which we seek must be in harmony with your own inherited tendencies. One familiar with the history of the English-speaking people, during the last two and a half centuries, with their struggles for conscience, and freedom's sake, must deem it a matter of course that by this time the sense of individual responsibility has become strong even in the hearts of women; and the descendant of one who in the name of individual liberty stood with Cromwell against the "divine right of kings" and the tyranny consequent upon that obnoxious doctrine, can not be surprised to find himself appealed to by his countrywomen, in that same sacred name, to stand with the most enlightened portion of his party—with such men as Morton, Sumner and Lincoln—against the divine right of sex and the political tyranny involved in this doctrine, which in a republic presents such an anomaly.

Hoping that the question suggested by this appeal will command from you the attention which its importance merits, we subscribe ourselves,

Yours with high esteem,

SUSAN B. ANTHONY,

Vice-President-at-Large N. W. S. A.

MAY WRIGHT SEWALL,

Chairman Executive Committee N. W. S. A.

DEMAND FOR PARTY RECOGNITION.

Delivered in Kansas City at the opening of the campaign, May 4, 1894.

I come to you tonight not as a stranger, not as an outsider but, in spirit and in every sense, as one of you. I have been connected with you by the ties of relationship for nearly forty years. Twenty-seven years ago I canvassed this entire State of Kansas in your first woman suffrage campaign. During the last decade I have made a speaking tour of your congressional districts over and over again. Now I come once more to appeal to you for justice to the women of your State.

To preface, I want to say that when the rebellion broke out in this country, we of the woman suffrage movement postponed our meetings, and organized ourselves into a great National Women's Loyal League with headquarters in the city of New York. We sent out thousands of petitions praying Congress to abolish slavery, as a war measure, and to these petitions we obtained 365,000 signatures. They were presented by Charles Sumner, that noblest Republican of them all, and it took two stalwart negroes to carry them into the Senate chamber. We did our work faithfully all those years. Other women scraped lint, made jellies, ministered to sick and suffering soldiers and in every way worked for the help of the government in putting down that rebellion. No man, no Republican leader, worked more faithfully or loyally than did the women of this nation in every city and county of the North to aid the government.

In 1865 I made my first visit to Kansas and, on the 2d of July, went by stage from Leavenworth to Topeka. O, how I remember those first acres and miles of cornfields I ever had seen ; how I remember that ride to Topeka and from there in an open mail wagon to Ottumwa, where I was one of the speakers at the Fourth of July celebration. Those were the days, as you recollect, just after the murder of Lincoln and the accession to the presidential chair of Andrew Johnson, who had issued his proclamation for the reconstruction of Mississippi. So the question of the negro's enfranchisement was uppermost in the minds of leading Republicans, though no one save Charles Sumner had dared to speak it aloud. In that speech, I clearly stated that the government never would be reconstructed, that peace never would reign and justice never be uppermost until not only the black men were enfranchised but also the women of the entire nation. The men congratulated me upon my speech, the first part of it, every word I said about negro suffrage, but declared that I should not have mentioned woman suffrage at so critical an hour.

A little later the Associated Press dispatch came that motions had been made on the floor of the House of Representatives at Washington to insert

(1015)

the word "male" in the second clause of the Fourteenth Amendment. You remember the first clause, "All persons born or naturalized in the United States, and subject to the jurisdiction thereof, are citizens of the United States and of the State wherein they reside. No State shall make or enforce any law which shall abridge the privileges and immunities of citizens." That was magnificent. Every woman of us saw that it included the women of the nation as well as black men. The second section, as Thaddeus Stevens drew it, said, "If any State shall disfranchise any of its citizens on account of color, all that class shall be counted out of the basis of representation;" but at once the enemy asked, "Do you mean that if any State shall disfranchise its negro women, you are going to count all of the black race out of the basis of representation?" And weak-kneed Republicans, after having fought such a glorious battle, surrendered; they could not stand the taunt. Charles Sumner said he wrote over nineteen pages of foolscap in order to keep the word "male" out of the Constitution; but he could not do it so he with the rest subscribed to the amendment: "If any State shall disfranchise any of its MALE citizens all of that class shall be counted out of the basis of representation."

There was the first great surrender and, in all those years of reconstruction, Elizabeth Cady Stanton, the great leader of our woman suffrage movement, declared that because the Republicans were willing to sacrifice the enfranchisement of the women of the nation they would lose eventually the power to protect the black man in his right to vote. But the leaders of the Republican party shouted back to us, "Keep silence, this is the negro's hour." Even our glorious Wendell Phillips, who said, "To talk to a black man of freedom without the ballot is mockery," joined in the cry, "This is the negro's hour;" but we never yielded the point that, "To talk to women of freedom without the ballot is mockery also." But timidity, cowardice and want of principle carried forward the reconstruction of the government with the women left out.

Then came in 1867 the submission by your Kansas legislature of three amendments to your constitution: That all men who had served in the rebel army should be disfranchised; that all black men should be enfranchised; and that all women should be enfranchised. The Democrats held their State convention and resolved they would have nothing to do with that "modern fanaticism of woman's rights." The Germans held a meeting in Lawrence, and denounced this "new-fangled idea." The Republicans held their State convention and resolved to be "neutral." And they were neutral precisely as England was neutral in the rebellion. While England declared neutrality, she allowed the *Shenandoah*, the *Alabama* and other pirate ships to be fitted up in her ports to maraud the seas and capture American vessels. The fact was not a single stump speaker appointed by the Republican committee advocated the woman suffrage amendment and, more than this, all spoke against it.

Then, of course, we had to make a woman suffrage campaign through the months of September and October. We did our best. Everywhere we had splendid audiences and I think we had a larger ratio of men in those older times than we have nowadays. Election day came, that 5th day of

November, 1867, when 9,070 men voted yes, and over 18,000 voted no. On the negro suffrage amendment, 10,500 voted yes and the remainder voted no. Both amendments were lost. All the political power of the national and State Republican party was brought to bear to induce every man to vote for negro suffrage; on the other hand, all the enginery and power of the Republican, as well as of the Democratic party, were against us; and many were so ignorant they absolutely believed that to vote for woman suffrage was to vote against the negro. It was exactly like declaring here tonight that if every woman in this house should fill her lungs with oxygen, she would rob all you men of enough to fill yours. Nobody is robbed by letting everybody have equal rights.

Since 1867 seven other States have submitted the question. Let me run them over.

[Miss Anthony then gave a graphic description of the campaigns in Michigan, 1874; Colorado, 1877; Nebraska, 1882; Oregon, 1884; Rhode Island, 1886; Washington, 1889; South Dakota, 1890; all of which failed for lack of support from the political platforms, editors and speakers.]

But at last in Colorado, in the second campaign, we won by the popular vote, *gained through party endorsement,* the enfranchisement of women. During the summer of 1893 nearly every Republican and Populist and not a few Democratic county conventions put approving planks in their platforms. When the fall campaign opened every stump orator was authorized to speak favorably upon the subject; no man could oppose it unless he ran counter to the principles laid down in his party platform. That made it a truly educational campaign to all the voters of the State. A word to the wise is sufficient. Let every man who wants the suffrage amendment carried, demand a full and hearty endorsement of the measure by his political party, be it Democrat, Republican, Populist or Prohibition, so that Kansas shall win as did her neighbor State, Colorado.

The Republicans of Kansas made the Prohibition amendment a party measure in 1880. After they secured the law they had planks in their platform for its enforcement from year to year, until they were tired of fighting the liquor dealers, backed by the Democrats in the State and on the borders. They wearied of being taunted with the fact that they had not the power to enforce the law. Then in 1887 they gave municipal suffrage to women as a sheer party necessity. Just as much as it was a necessity of the Republicans in reconstruction days to enfranchise the negroes, so was it a political necessity in the State of Kansas to enfranchise the women, because they needed a new balance of power to help them elect and re-elect officers who would enforce the law. Where else could they go to get that balance? Every man in the State, native and foreign, drunk and sober, outside of the penitentiary, the idiot and lunatic asylums, already had the right to vote. They had nobody left but the women. As a last resort the Republicans, by a straight party vote, extended municipal suffrage to women.

This political power was put into the hands of the women of this State by the old Republican party with its magnificent majorities—82,000, you remember, the last time you bragged. It was before you had the quarrel and division in the family; it was by that grand old party, solid as it was in those bygone days!

Last year, and two years ago, after the People's party was organized, when their State convention was held, and also when the Republican convention was held, each put a plank in its platform declaring that the time had come for the submission of a proposition for full suffrage to women. What then could the women infer but that such action meant political help in carrying this amendment? If I had not believed this I never would have come to the State and given my voice in twenty-five or thirty political meetings, reminding the Republicans what a grand and glorious record they had made, not only in the enfranchisement of the black men but in furnishing all the votes on the floor of Congress ever given for women's enfranchisement there, and in extending municipal suffrage to the women of Kansas. I have vowed, from the time I began to see that woman suffrage could be carried only through party help, that I never would lend my influence to either of the two dominant parties that did not have a woman suffrage plank in its platform.

I consider, by every pledge of the past, by the passage of the resolution through the legislature when the representatives of the two parties, the People's and Republican, vied with each other to see who would give the largest majority, that both promised to make this a party measure and I speak tonight to the two parties as the old Republican party. You are not the same men altogether, but you are the descendants, the children, of that party; and I am here tonight, and have come all the way from my home, to beg you to stand by the principles which have made you great and strong, and to finish the work you have so nobly begun.

The Republicans are to have their State convention the 6th of June. I shall be ashamed if the telegraph wires flash the word over the country, "No pledge for the amendment," as was flashed from the Republican League the other day. Should this happen, as I have heard intimated, and there is a woman in the State of Kansas who has any affiliation with the Republican party, any sympathy with it, who will float its banner after it shall have thus failed to redeem its pledge, I will disown her; she is not one of my sort.

The Populist convention is to be held the 12th of June. If it should shirk its responsibility, and not put a strong suffrage plank in its platform, pledging itself to use all its educational powers and all its party machinery to carry the amendment, then I shall have no respect for any woman who will speak or work for its success.

The Democrats have declared their purpose. They are going to fight us. What does the good Book say? "He that is not for me is against me." We know where the Democratic party is, it is against us. If the Republican and People's parties say nothing for us, they say and do everything against us. No plank will be equivalent to saying to every woman suffrage Republican and Populist speaker, "You must not advocate this amendment, for to do so will lose us the whisky vote, it will lose us the foreign vote." Hence, no plank means no word for us, and no word for us means no vote for us. But while no word can be spoken in favor, every campaign orator, as in 1867, is free to speak in opposition.

Men of the Republican party, it comes your time first to choose whom you will have for your future constituents, to make up the bone and sinew of your party; whether you will have the most ignorant foreigners, just landed on our shores, who have not learned a single principle of free government—or the women of your own households; whether you will lose to-day a few votes of the high license or the low license Republicans, foreign or native, black or white, as the case may be, and gain to yourselves hereafter the votes of the women of the State. These are the alternatives. It has been stated that you can not have a suffrage plank in the Republican platform in Saline county because it would lose the votes of the Scandinavians. Will those 1,000 Scandinavian men be of more value to the Republicans than will be the votes of their own wives, mothers, daughters and sisters in all the years to come?

The crucial moment is upon you now, and I say unto you, men of both parties, you will have driven the last nail in the coffin of this amendment and banished all hope of carrying it at the ballot-box if you do not incorporate woman suffrage in your platforms. I know what the party managers will say, I have talked with and heard from many of them. I read Mr. Morrill's statement that "this question should go to the ballot-box on its merits and should not be spoken of in the political meetings or made a party measure."

The masses are rooted and grounded in the old beliefs in the inferiority and subjection of women, and consider them born merely to help man carry out his plans and not to have any of their own. Now, friends, because this is true, because no man believes in political equality for woman, except he is educated out of every bigotry, every prejudice and every usage that he was born into, in the family, in the church and in the state, so there can be no hope of the rank and file of men voting for this amendment, until they are taught the principles of justice and right; and there is no possibility that these men can be reached, can be educated, through any other instrumentality than that of the campaign meetings and campaign papers of the political parties. Therefore, when you say this is not to be a political question, not to be in your platform, not to be discussed in your meetings, not to be advocated in your papers, you make it impossible for its merits to be brought before the voters.

Who are the men that come to our women's meetings? We have just finished the tour of the sixty counties in the State of New York. We had magnificent gatherings, composed of people from the farthest townships in the county, and in many of them from every township, with the largest opera houses packed, hundreds going away who could not get in. Our audiences have been five-sixths women, and the one man out of the six, who was he? A man who already believed there was but one means of salvation for the race or the country, and that was through the political equality of women, making them the peers of men in every department of life. How are we going to reach the other five-sixths of the men who never come to women's meetings? There is no way except through the political rallies which are attended by all men. Now if you shut out of these the discussion of this question, then I say the fate of this amendment is sealed.

Even if it were possible to reach the men through separate meetings, the women of Kansas can not carry on a fall campaign. They can not get the money to do it unless you men furnish it. Our eastern friends have already contributed to the extent of their ability to hold these spring meetings, and you very well know that after the husbands shall have paid their party assessments there will be nothing left for them to "give to their wives" to defray the expenses of a woman suffrage campaign. Therefore, no discussion in the regular political meetings means no discussion anywhere. But suppose there were plenty of money, and there could be a most thorough fall campaign, what then? Why, the same old story of "women talking to women," not one of whom can vote on the question.

Again, with what decency can either of the parties ask women to come to their political meetings to expound Populist or Republican doctrines after they have set their heels on the amendment? Do you not see that if it will lose votes to the parties to have the plank, it will lose votes to allow women to advocate the amendment on their platforms? And what a spectacle it would be to see women pleading with men to vote for the one or the other party, while their tongues were tied on the question of their own right to vote! Heaven and the Republican and Populist State Conventions spare us such a dire humiliation!

But should the Republicans refuse to insert the plank on June 6 and the Populists put a good solid one in their platform on June 12, what then? Do you suppose all the women in the State would shout for the Republicans and against the Populists? Would they pack the Republican meetings, where no word could be spoken for their liberty, and leave the benches empty in the Populist meetings where at every one hearty appeals were made to vote for woman's enfranchisement? My dear friends, woman surely will be able to see that her highest interest, her liberty, her right to a voice in government, is the great issue of this campaign, and overtops, outweighs, all material questions which are now pending between the parties.

I know you think your Kansas men are going to vote on this amendment independently of party endorsement. You are no more sanguine today than were the men and women, myself included, in 1867, that those Free State men, who had given up every comfort which human beings prize for the sake of liberty, who had fought not only through the border ruffian warfare but through the four years of the rebellion, would vote freedom to the heroic women of Kansas. Where would you ever expect to find a majority more ready to grant to women equal rights than among those old Free State men? You have not as glorious a generation of men in Kansas today as you had in 1867. I do not wish to speak disparagingly, but in the nature of things there can not be another race of men as brave as those. If you had told me then that a majority of those men would have gone to the ballot-box and voted against equal rights for women, I should have defended them with all my power; but they did it, two to one.

Do you mean to repeat the experiment of 1867? If so, do not put a plank in your platform; just have a "still hunt." Think of a "still hunt" when it must be necessarily a work of education! My friends, I know enough of this State, to feel that it is worth saving. I have given more time and money and effort to Kansas than to any other State in the Union, because I wanted it to be the first to make its women free. Women of Kansas, all is lost if you sit down and supinely listen to politicians and candidates. Both reckon what they will lose or what they will gain. They study expediency rather than principle. I appeal to you, men and women, make the demand imperative: "The amendment must be endorsed by the parties and advocated on the platform and in the press." Let me propose a resolution:

WHEREAS, From the standpoint of justice, political expediency and grateful appreciation of their wise and practical use of school suffrage from the organization of the State, and of municipal suffrage for the past eight years, we, Republicans and Populists, descendants of that grand old party of splendid majorities which extended these rights to the women of Kansas, in mass meeting assembled do hereby

Resolve, That we urgently request our delegates in their approaching State conventions to endorse the woman suffrage amendment in their respective platforms.

[The resolution was adopted by a unanimous vote.]

That vote fills my soul with joy and hope. Now I want to say to you, my good friends, I never would have made a 1,500 mile journey hither to appeal to the thinking, justice-loving men of Kansas. They already are converted, but they are a minority. We have to consider those whose votes can be obtained only by that party influence and machinery which politicians alone know how to use. This hearty response is a pledge that you will demand of your State conventions that the full power of this political machinery shall be used to carry the woman suffrage amendment to victory.

INDEX.*

* Lists of names not included in index will be found in footnotes on pp. 284, 327, 353, 566, 590, 621, 772.

ANT.—65

economies in dress, sympathetic lets., no faith in own power as speaker, 151; describes Remond's speech, 152; abandons written addresses, notes of speeches, 153; spks. in Me., newspaper comment, 154; res. in favor of colored pupils and of co-education, State Teachers Con. in Bing-hamton, 155; defended by Republican 156; resumes A. S. meet., 157; on soul-communing, longing for sympathy, 158; raspberry experiment, 159; out-door life for women, " good old days," 160; " health food cranks," glad to reach home, 161; on com. to arrange A. S. Annivers. and W. R. Con., no one else for common work, on large families, 162; unterrified by mob, rebukes teachers at Lockport con., 163; demands equal pay for women, not frightened by fogies, 164; calls meet. to oppose capital punishment, hissed by mob, trustee of Jackson fund, 165; desire for Free church, 167; persists in lecture courses for Rochester, shrinks from active work, feels spiritual loneliness, 168; exhorts women to be discontented, no freedom without pecuniary independence, outrage of denying to woman right of self-govt., married woman sinks individuality, 169; true woman will have purpose, married women can not be relied on for public work, 170; distrusts own power to resist marriage, though it blots out freedom, would use Hovey fund for wom. suff. propaganda, 171; spicy extracts from diary, criticises Curtis' lecture, 172; at Albany working for Personal Liberty Bill, member of lobby, arranges lect. for Cheever, finishes lect. on True Woman, love of gardening, 173; presides over suff. con. in Mozart Hall, 174; prepares Memorial to legis., goes to picnic, escort lacks moral spine, opens canvass at Niagara Falls, 175; speaks at N. Y. watering places, lectures teachers en route to Poughkeepsie, waiter at hotel refuses to take order, 176; rebukes young Quaker preacher, drains millpond too low, need of souls baptized into work, women keep her in suspense, 177; disapproves women's neglecting households, makes canvass alone, carefully kept expenses, assists Mrs. Nichols and Mrs. Wattles to plan Kan. campn., 178; too busy to see humorous features, ignores complaints, incident at Gerrit Smith's when Mrs. Blackwell preached, 179; we dwell in solitude, arranges John Brown meet., 180; no one to assist, 181; urged to resume A. S. work, 182; speaks to southerners at Ft. Wm. Henry, meets Judge Ormond of Ala., sends memorial to him and urges his daughters to take up serious work in

life, his two replies, 183; right of suff. underlying principle, 185; urges Mrs. Stn. to address legis. at Albany, 186; distaste for writing, power as critic, joint work with Mrs. Stn., caring for children, 187; speeches in appendix her own work, 188; gives radical bill to legis. com., 189; carrying petit. in face of insult and ridicule, debt owed by women, arranges course of lectures for Rochester, 190; rec. vote of thanks at W. R. Con. in Cooper Instit., "better have been at home," 193; marriage one sided contract, favors divorce res., 194; regrets Phillips' action, rec. lets. of approval, no desire to dictate platform, 195; writes Phillips for money, he praises her, tilt with Rev. Mayo, 196; fights Mrs. Stn.'s battles, on the skirmish line, looks after "externals," domestic work, 197; extracts from journal, demands equal pay for women at State Teacher's Con., Syracuse, writes from birthplace of women's hard work there, 198; climbs "Greylock," describes visit to old home, receives invitation to give agricultural ad. at Dundee Fair, 199; describes fair, speech contains modern ideas on farming, takes up cause of wronged mother, 200; goes with mother and child to New York, refused admission to hotels, rejected by landlady at boarding-house, 201; declines to leave hotel, places charges with Mrs. Gibbons, welcomed home by Lydia Mott, persecuted by family of mother, 202; defies brothers, 203; refuses to yield to Garrison's and Phillips' requests, sustained by her father, 204; arranges Garrisonian meet., mobbed at Buffalo, 208; hissed at Rochester, will not give up meet., 209; encounter with mayor of Utica, mob at Rome, 210; declines to abandon meet. at Syracuse, mobbed and burned in effigy, goes to Albany, 211; agrees to adjourn meet. there, 212; begged to give up W. R. Annivers. because of war, refuses, rearing children a profession, offers to care for Mrs. Stn.'s, 213; attitude of Abolits. towards War, 214; takes charge of farm and does housework, 215; sharp points from diary, Douglass, negroes shd. be enlisted, slavery must be blotted out, loneliness, opinion of "Adam Bede," 216; A. S. meet. at Albany, sends Phillips money for lecture which he returns, sends Tilton check, he defines her "sphere," 217; compelled to give up W. R. Annivers., leaves "Abrahamic bosom of home" for A. S. lecture field, visits Adams and censures men for not furnishing kitchen properly, visits Hoosac Tunnel, speaks on summit of Green Mts., 218; let. on work of E. B. Browning, H. Hosmer, R. Bonheur,

corresponds with H. B. Blackwell relative
to women's working for Repub. party, 416;
at Dem. Natl. Con. in Baltimore, interview
with Jas. R. Doolittle, 417; no hope for
women here, urges women to work for
Repub. party, 418; her political position,
cares only for woman's interests, joy over
action of Repubs., rallying cry to Mrs.
Bloomer, 419; "Ft. Sumter gun of our war
fired," congratulat. note from Henry Wilson, 420; Natl. Com. invites her to Washington, gives her $500 and N. Y. Com.
gives $500 for campaign meet., 421; holds
rallies at Rochester and New York, insists
that women shall speak only on wom.
suff. plank, objects to hounding of Greeley,
422; advocates no party that does not stand
for wom. suff., is registered to vote, 423;
comments of press, tells Mrs. Stn. about it,
424; Judge Selden advises that she has
right to vote under Amend. XIV, 425; assures inspectors she will bear expenses if
they are arrested, is herself arrested, refuses to take herself to court, the warrant,
426; examination before U. S. officers, does
not want trial to interfere with lecture engagements, 427; sad anniversary, second
hearing, speaks in behalf of inspectors, refuses to give bail, trib. from Rochester
Express, her own defense, 428; at Wash.
con., opening speech on methods of securing wom. suff., 431; res. declare her
arrest a blow at liberty, speakers defend
her, appears with counsel before Judge
Hall at Albany, bail increased, 432; refuses
bail, overruled by Judge Selden, indictment of grand jury, delivers "Constitutional Argument" in western cities, 433;
becomes unconscious on platform at Ft.
Wayne, rallies and lectures at Marion,
votes again, issues call for May Anniversary in New York, tells of arrest, 434; res.
of endorsement, speaks in twenty-nine
postoffice districts of Monroe Co., Dist.-
Atty. threatens to move case to another
county, tells him she will canvass that,
speech a masterpiece, her appearance, 435;
speaks in twenty-one places in Ontario Co.
on "Is it a crime for a U. S. citizen to vote?"
Rochester Union and Advertiser calls her a
"corruptionist," newspaper comment, trial
opens, 436; refused permission to testify,
437; believed she had a right to vote, 438;
counsel demands jury be polled, refused
and new trial denied, encounter of words
with Judge Hunt, dramatic scene, 439;
fined $100, 440; declares she never will pay
it, believes Conkling influenced judge, trial
a farce, extended newspaper comment,
441; advised by Albany Law Journal to

emigrate, attends trial of inspectors, another tilt with Judge Hunt, 443; Mr. Van
Voorhis' opinion of her case after twenty-
four years, 444; heavy debts, 445; sympathy
and financial help, has Selden's speech and
report of trial printed, lect. in Rochester for benefit of inspectors, omitted as
charter member of Assn. for Advancement
of Women, 446; death of sister Guelma, let.
to mother, love of family, "shall we meet
the dead?" tries to vote but finds name
struck from register, 447; Anson Lapham
returns her notes for $4,000, 448; decides to
appeal to Cong., 449; takes appeal to Washington, asks remission of fine, case presented by Sargent and Loughridge, Tre-
maine reports adversely, 450; says president
has pardoned her, Butler presents minority
report in favor, Sen. Edmunds presents
insulting report, Sen. Carpenter reports
favorably, 451; writes Pres. Grant and Gen.
Butler in behalf of inspectors, urges them
not to pay fine, breakfasts with them in
jail, presented with purse at Dansville
Sanitarium, Sargent and Butler telegraph
inspectors are pardoned, 452; fine still
stands against A., 453; returns to work of
securing amends. to Federal and State
constit., invites Vice-Pres. Wilson speak on
suff. platform, Gen. Butler in favor of wom.
suff., 454; conversation with Pres. Grant,
455; tour of Conn. with Mrs. Hooker, Sumner's death, helps women organize temp.
crusade, 456; tells them they can not succeed without ballot, anecdote of Douglass,
writes to Leavenworth Times on this subject, tells Industrial Cong. women are a
millstone around their necks, criticises Dio
Lewis, 457; writes one hundred lets. for
May meet., telegram saying she smoked on
platform, etc., 458; slips home often to see
mother, writes fiftieth anniversary let. to
brother D. R., honesty best policy in home
and society, 459; canvassed Mich., larger
audiences than Sen. Chandler, small
profits, suff. first, money afterwards, 460;
efforts to compel disclosures in regard to
Beecher-Tilton trouble, 461; complimented
on silence by Chicago Tribune, J. Hooker,
N. Y. Sun, Rochester Democrat and Chronicle, refutes belief in "free love," 462; does
not believe in second marriage or platonic
friendship, love for Mr. and Mrs. Tilton,
463; in latter's praise for Beecher, A. saw
only friendship, 464; death of Gerrit Smith
and Martha Wright, struggle to hold Washington conv., 467; advances funds and works
without ceasing, Anson Lapham gives her
$1,000, lectures on Social Purity at Chicago,
468; eulogized by St. Louis Democrat, con-

demned by country papers, addresses Normal School at Carbondale on marrying for love, sixty lectures in Iowa, trying experiences, 469; telegram announcing brother shot, works all night on con. accounts, journey to Kan., 470; nine weeks by brother's bedside, skill and tenderness in sickroom, takes niece Susie B. home with her, 471; first hears F. E. Willard, refuses to compromise her by sitting on platform, lectures in Rochester on Social Purity, misses Washington con. for first time, lectures in Chicago, Bread and Ballot, pays last dollar of Revolution debt, 472; at New York Suff. Anniversary, chmn. Centennial Campn. Com., 474; offers Hist. of Wom. Suff. as premium and fulfills pledges, opens headquarters at Philadelphia and assumes financial responsibility, 475; besieges natl. polit. cons., "the golden hour," prepares Woman's Declaration of Independence, 476; obtains seat on platform as reporter, 477; presents Declaration at Centennial Celebration, reads it on Independence square, 478; and in con., Luc. Mott's tea-pot, 479; contibu. to Centennial Headqrs., Mrs. Mott sends tea, A. dees not work for financ. reward, begins Hist. Wom. Suff., 480; dislike of the work, spks. at Mrs. Davis' funeral, sorrow at her death and that of Anson Lapham, writes wom. suff. article for encyclop., 481; grief at absence from home, 482; appeal for Amend. XVI, 483; on floor of House of Repres., 485; circular of Slayton Bureau, 486; cancels engagements to be with sister Hannah, 487; her death, takes orphan daughter home, gift of Helen Potter, Mrs. Stn.'s let. on their friendship, misses May Annivers. first time, 488; friendship for Mrs. Stn., love of her children for A., trib. of Annie McDowell, offers services to Col., 489; accepted, hard campn. experiences, 65 mile stage-ride, 490; how husbands represent wives, spks. in saloons, no locks on doors, Gov. Routt stands by her, 491; insulting placards, receipts less than expenses, gifts of Mr. and Mrs. Hall, Mrs. Knox Goodrich, at Denver meets Miss Hindman, Mrs. Campbell, Abby S. Richardson, her memory of sister Hannah, 492; at Dr. Avery's writing "Homes of Single Women," spks. at Boulder and Denver, lect. tour of Neb., longs for sister Mary, fears mother may die, man wants credit for holding children, 493; sends $100 to Washington con.. friends urge not to miss another con., 494; compli. by Phillips, by P. Couzins, arranges 30th Annivers. at Rochester, 495; comment of Roch. Demo. and Chronicle,

remains with invalid mother, declines Kan. invitations, writes Hayford regarding wom. suff. in Wy., 496; let. to L. Stone on attitude of women toward polit. parties, 497; strong res. at Natl. Con., 499; address to Pres. Hayes, 500; lect. in New England, personal notices in scrap-books, change in attitude of press, 502; compli. by Ind. papers, 503; attack of Richmond, Ky., and Grand Rapids papers, 504; St. Paul lady acknowledges conversion, wom. needs ballot for temp. legis., 505; men fear wom. suff., trib. of Globe-Demo., 506; response to floral offering, "used to stones," made vice-pres.-at-large, friendship of Sargents, 507; death of Garrison, has now a bank account, generosity, 508; never fails to keep engagements, friends anxious she shd. save money, desirous of woman's paper, efforts for one, helps edit Ballot-Box, 509; need of woman's work and opinion in daily papers, press work shd. be feature of Natl. Assn., invited to Concord School of Philos., 510; new friends, at Washington con., compli. by Edmunds, 511; Mrs. Spofford's hospitality, sees Luc. Mott last time, death of mother, 512; starts out again, 513; carries point for series of cons., rallying cry for mass meet. in Chicago, 515; all send ideas to Mrs. Stn., watching legislators, on death of sister, doubts of future life, 516; apprecia. of sister Mary, presides at Indianapolis con., suff. women married and number of children, 517; ten minutes at Natl. Repub. Con., ad. Greenback-Labor Con., 518; trib. of Cin'ti Commercial, 519; calls on Gen. Garfield, 520; official let. to president. candidates, 521; let. to Garfield on Repub. party, 522; blames women for rushing into campn., defends Garfield, criticises Hancock, 523; hopes for help from Repubs., continues work on History, Eliz. Thomson gives $1,000, 524; hates the work, calls on Whittier, death of Luc. Mott, persuades Mrs. Stn. to vote, 525; suggests Natl. Con. be omitted, owns Mrs. Stn. persuaded her, 526; trib. to Luc. Mott, day at her home, her hosts in Philadelphia, ridiculous account of Skye terrier, 527; N. Y. Graphic on terrier, her disgust, 528; love for Mrs. Nichols, wd. not spare parents for children's sake, 529; did not carry out theory, pushing the history, bound to have Rose and Nichol's pictures, 530; valuable work done by Hist. Wom. Suff., 531; starts for Mass. taking Mrs. Stn., 532; tells Gov. Long women are weary, rec. gold medal from Phila. Suff. Assn., entertained by Bird Club, Boston Globe pays trib., 534; relief to roll burden on young shoulders, entertained by Pillsburys, compli. let. from Mrs. Pillsbury,

Mrs. Harbert, trib. of Mrs. Wallace, 535; death of Phebe Jones, no home in Albany, death of Garfield, no will, his religion, 536; Mrs. Stn.'s work for women kept her young, A. goes to Natl. W. C. T. U. Con. in Washington, introduced by Miss Willard, delegate declares she does not recognize God, sees wom. suff. adopted by con., 537; delegates announce A. did not influence con., souvenir from Childs, writes Phillips on his seventieth birthday, his reply, 538; attacks her work with courage, Phillips announces Eddy legacy, her joy and gratitude, 539; suit to break will, appeals from public for money, at Wash. con., 540; delight at appointment of cong. com. on rights of woman, presents each member with Hist. Wom. Suff., con. at Phila., luncheon with Hannah W. Smith, at N. Y. State Con., appeals to House Com. to abolish "male" from Constit. of Dak., 541; restive under history work, trib. of Elmira Free Press and Wash. Republic, 542; reads proof of Vol. II of Hist., influential friends in Cong., trib. of Harriot Stanton, 543; goes into Neb. campn., "not a white-haired woman on plat., not sure of younger ones, 544; gives time and $1,000, speaks in forty counties, debates with Edward Rosewater, students make effigy, 545; at St. Louis, ad. Lincoln Club in Rochester, confers with Cong. Com. in Wash., decides to go abroad, birthday recep. in Phila., dislike of "Aunt Susan," 546; Times account of recep., ad. of Purvis, A. gives credit to other workers, wd. have worked for man's freedom, Mrs. Sewall's description of farewell honors, testimonial from Rochester citizens and Natl. Assn., song dedicated, 547; point lace, India shawl, trib. of Chicago Tribune, A. has "no peer," 549; farewell from Kan. City Journal, N. Y. Times' description of departure, flag in stateroom, 550; own description of tour abroad, on shipboard, stuck in mud, recollect. of those left, 551; rough sea, three falls, thoughts of nieces, talks suff. with passengers, 552; invited to Sargent's at Berlin, Mrs. Stn.'s welcome, at Liverpool, Hist. of Wom. Suff. not in library, visit to Mrs. Rose, 554; sees Irving and Terry, objects to lovemaking, at Contag. Dis. Act. Meet., crossing channel, en route to Rome, no sleeper, bedrooms at Milan, 555; painting of Christ in railway station, Easter Sunday in Rome, at Naples, Herculaneum, John Bright's address, 556; invited to write for Italian Times, climbs Vesuvius, dishonest tradesmen, Palermo, the dead Christ, Lake Avernus, streets of Naples, interest in suff. work and friends at home, 557; Vati-

can, no hope for freedom in old world, mother's knowledge of history, too many languages, hears Ristori, at Milan, disadvantages of compartment travel, 558; at Zurich, at Munich, every girl shd. go abroad, at Sargents' in Berlin, at Worms, Luther's statue at Cologne, lets. sent back from post-office, 559; up the Rhine, Heidelberg, Potsdam, emperors' tombs and palaces, degradation of masses, at Strasburg, 560; Alsace and Lorraine, in Paris, guest of Mme. de Barron, breakfast in bed, calls on friends, Communists in Pere la Chaise, funeral of Laboulaye, Le Soir wishes interview, 561; calls on Hubertine Auclert and Leon Richer, disadvantage of not speaking French, longs to be fighting battle for women in America, Miss Foster's presentation at court, tomb of Napoleon, homesick, begs sister Mary to come to Europe, 562; shall we accept religious teaching of young, strong intellects or old, weakened ones? 563; Stopford Brooke on temp., talks to ladies under trees, visits Albemarle and Somerville Clubs, prepares speeches, nights all days, 564; goes to Poor Law Guardian meet., spks. at Prince's Hall, Conway delighted, 565; St. James' Hall, 4th of July recep. at Mrs. Mellen's, 566; at many dinners, recep., suff. meet., clubs, etc., calls from factory women, velvet dress and India shawl, hears Canon Wilberforce on temp., indignation, sees Bernhardt, 567; bound to get all possible good, refuses to interfere in suff. work in England, platonic friendship, goes to Edinburgh, at Mrs. Nichol's, 568; let. from Priscilla B. McLaren, celebrated places in Scotland, outside of stage, home of Queen Mary, 569; converts Prof. Blackie to wom. suff., he "seals it with a kiss," loses trunk, criticises English check system, drives among lakes, visits Dr. Jex-Blake, 570; at Ambleside, compares hills with those of America, home of H. Martineau, 571; class and caste ideas, urges discontent, in Belfast, men can not vote on temp. question, meets old abolits., rides in third-class car, at Cork, 472; drunken men and women, filth, visits convent, incident at Killarney, 573; woman with twins, sad spectacles, to Galway in rain, butter in tobacco smoke, 574; in Dublin, meets Davitt, Youghal, reads Children of Abbey, Belfast, buys linen, Rugby, Kenilworth Castle, "Americans never see leg of mutton," Stratford, Oxford, back in London, extracts from diary, London fog, 575; at Leeds, home of Brontë sisters, dreads trip home, 576; hears John Bright forget to mention wom. suff. at Bristol, at

Jacob Bright's, let. from Mrs. Bright on little son's admiration for A., 577; urges sister to continue work if she never reach home, especial interest in England on account of suff. movement, efforts to secure co-operation between Eng. and Amer. women, 578; recep. in Liverpool, com. formed to promote organizat., friends come from London to say good-bye, safe landing in New York, 579; welcome home, interview, did not see Queen, social idea more important, trib. of N. Y. Evening Telegram, 581; Cleveland Leader, woman of the future, Cin'ti Times-Star's criticism, 582; kindness to reporters, conferring with congressmen, agony of it, 583; begs Kelley to take up suff. question, Repubs. in favor, 584; writes to 112 congressmen, heads off injudicious women, 585; on Douglass' marriage, everybody's burden on her shoulders, 586; helpless women wear her out, always writes cheerful lets., death of Phillips, 587; goes to funeral, at Washington con., speech before Cong. Com. urging Amend. XVI, 588; goes to Conn., hastens back to watch congressmen, how she follows them up, 591; report of suff. con. fails, she and Mrs. Stn. get out report, wants everybody to have credit, begins Vol. III of Hist. Wom. Suff., anxiety over Ore. election, sends Mrs. Duniway $100, restive under historical work, 592; criticises Gladstone, 593; advises women to work for Repub. party, decides it was unwise, criticises Miss Willard for favoring State Rights, Prohib. party will repudiate wom. suff., prophecy fulfilled, 594; at Wash. con., death of Mrs. Nichols, opposes res. denouncing dogmas, answers St. Paul, 595; rebukes Rev. Patton for sermon, regrets it, Mrs. Stn. approves, 596; sends out Palmer's speech, goes to Mass., then to New Orleans Expo., guest of Mrs. Merrick, many addresses, trib. of Picayune, 597; cordial recep., at Bishop's University, at St. Louis, message of J. Ellen Foster, death of Grant, goes to Boston to rec. Eddy legacy, fright on sleeper, 598; appeals to share money, friends who repudiated come flocking back, determined to finish Hist. Wom. Suff., agreement with Fowler and Wells, 599; buys out their rights, begins work again at Tenafly, assumes all financ. responsibil., grief at not being a writer, good critic, keeps Mrs. Stn. keyed up, applies lash to own back, 600; meets Miss Eddy, they go to Mrs. Stn.'s, A. commends her, drudgery on Hist., women complain of Mrs. Stn.'s blue pencil, between two fires, 601; refuses appeals for speeches, dislike of literary work, Mrs. Stn.'s 70th birthday, trib. from

H. Stn. Blatch., 602; comforts Julia and Rachel Foster at death of mother, 603; starts to Wash. with light heart, taste in dress, holds members of Cong. to their word, 605; humorous note from Sen. Blair, A. directly connected with all cong. action on wom. suff., 606; at Wash. con., rec. $100 from Childs, looking after congressmen, extracts from diary, Stanford, Dolph, 607; Eustis, lets. from Mrs. Merrick, O. Brown, sends P. Couzins $100, Vol. III of Hist. completed, visits in Kan., 608; speaks at Salina for W. C. T. U., at Lake Bluff, Ill., camp meet., at Lake Geneva accompanied by Susie B., at Miss Willard's, at Racine, at St. Louis, at Leav., spks. in cong. dists. of Kan., 609; splendid audiences, mother brings baby for her to take in arms, Baptist minister refuses church and then blesses meet., 610; "spirit wd. not always soar," Municipal Suff. Bill signed on 67th birthday, Chief-Justice Horton congratulates her, at Racine, 611; canvassses Wis., eloquence in State House, lively let. to Mrs. Spofford, get orthodox church for con., 612; immense amount of money put into Hist. Wom. Suff., years of careful collecting and saving of material, resumé of the work, 613; world indebted to her for it, in over 1,000 libraries, commendatory lets., 614; from Mary L. Booth, 615; D. W. Wilder, Sarah B. Cooper, hopes to publish Vol. IV, goes to Neb., 616; at Chicago, Lansing, Wash. con., yellow dog, 617; denounces Sen. Ingalls, he asks interview, 621; proposes truce, she declines, refuses to go to Conn., "feels guilty," visits Maria Mitchell at Vassar, ad. Constit. Con. at Albany, back to Wash. "year after year," lying reports from Leavenworth, corres. with Miss Willard regarding suff. plank in Prohib. plat., 622; opposes Third Party, will not fight Repubs., dreads starting out, State Cons. at Indpls. and Cleveland, "only sister Mary left," rebukes conserv. women, faith in Repub. party, 623; seminary graduates' essays, at Cape May, at childhood home, at Magnolia, advises O. Brown and A. Gray not to bring suit under school suff. law, 624; tries to arrange old lets., etc., Mrs. Stn. advises to burn, in Wis., campn. in Kan., scores Ingalls, 625; at Mrs. Ingalls' luncheon, senator "will not argue with woman," Ind. campn. in Wash., Blair's little joke, 626; on com. for union of two assns., 627; meets L. Stone and A. S. Blackwell in Boston, receives plan of union from Mrs. Stone, advised not to take pres. of united assns., approves and urges union, 628; "the way to unite is to unite," impatient of "red tape," exacts and makes no pledges, chmn. com. on conference, 629; carries meet. in favor of union, willing to decline pres., lets. declare she must take it, 630; sp. in favor of Mrs. Stn., Natl. suff. platform means individ. freedom, 631; elected vice-pres.-at-large, co-operates with Mrs. Sewall in securing union, always ready to sink personal feeling, 632; dream of internatl. suff. assn., results in Internatl. Council, her part in arranging it, 633; "can't allow apologetic invitat.," women not ordained shall preach, wants affirmations, not negations, glad L. Stone and A. Blackwell are to be on plat., 634; Mrs. Stn. expresses friendship and is coming back to Amer. to do best work, later writes can not cross ocean, 635; A. cables, she comes, A. shuts her up to write sp., presides over Council, 636; at receptions, pres. delegates to Pres. Cleveland, compli. from Baltimore Sun and N. Y. World, her way of presiding, 637; sp. and let. of Miss Willard, 638; speakers acknowledge pers. indebtedness to A., chmn. of meet. to form permanent councils, made Vice-Pres. Natl. Council, 639; ad. Senate Com., praise from Mrs. S. E. Sewall, Mr. Blackwell, no desire for rest, at Boston festival, 640; in Central Music Hall at Chicago, recep. by Woman's Club, at Natl. Repub. Con., Chicago, urges women to go to these cons., calls on Gen. Harrison, 641; open letter to him on "free ballot" plank, makes four years' financ. rep. of Natl. Assn., 642; publishes without authority of assn., restive under "red tape," "Andrew Jackson responsibility," poorest women want report, vast amount of work, at W. C. T. U., Centennial, Columbus O., not well recd., no little graves in speech, 643; begins again with Slayton Bureau, Rachel Foster's marriage, young workers throw away all plans when they marry, A.'s disappoint., 644; forms friendship with Rev. A. H. Shaw, old friends pass away, new ones come, 645; in Wash. preparing for con., little speeches, Six O'clock Club, 647; on "Rbt. Elsmere," spks. in Cin'ti, Commercial-Gazette compli., guest of Burnet House, "more calls than Mrs. Hayes," namesake Susie B. drowned, 648; hastens to Leav., spks. in Ark., Jefferson City, recep. in St. Louis, not able to ad. Catholics, vicar-gen. favors, spks. in Leav. municipal campn., 649; brother defeated for mayor, grief over death of Susie B., hurt of breaking branch from tree, urges no heartbreak when she dies, spirits of loved ones will forgive, at Indpls. Classical School, 650; at Adaline Thomson's, recep. at Park Hotel, New York, newspapers criticise velvet dress and point

lace, spks. in Rochester and Warren, 651, and Akron, O., denies report that she had renounced wom. suff., attends wedding of niece Helen Louise Mosher, rec. let. from Maria Deraismes, 652; at Mt. McGregor, Grant relics condemned, waiter at Ft. Wm. Henry, trip with niece Maude, ad. Seidl Club, Coney Island, 653; "Broadbrim" pays trib., visits Mrs. Stn. at Hempstead, M. Louise Thomas, legacy of $500 from Mrs. Hamilton, Ft. Wayne, tells Mrs. Avery not to work during husband's vacation, 654; at Wichita con., objects to God in suff. plat., at Ind. Suff. Con. uncertain how women wd. vote on liquor question, visit with H. Hosmer, 655; "Bethany Homes," at Duluth, goes to S. Dak., lets. of invitat., 656; minister explains to Almighty evils of orig. packages, A. canvasses State, ad. Farmers' Alliance, Prohibs. keep wom. suff. in background, presents Hist. Wom. Suff. to every town, 657; plans winter's work in S. Dak., nephew describes her lecture in Ann Arbor, at Toronto, spks. every night for three months, 658; "Andrew Jackson-like" action in engaging hall at Wash., immense work for S. Dak., makes eight women life members of Natl. Assn., 659; Justice Fuller fails to discover women, work for Columbian Expo., death of friends, Mrs. Mendenhall leaves her $1,000, Washington Star compli., 660; at Riggs House, objects to having tickets sold for birthday banquet, 663; wd. use money for S. Dak., wants everybody to have compli. ticket and be invited to speak, description of banquet, 664; accts. Wash. Star and N. Y. Sun, toasts by Couzins, Shaw, 665; Gage, Colby, Chant, Parker, Hinckley, Rbt. Purvis, Mrs. Lawrence, Mrs. Blatch, J. A. Pickler, 666, Mrs. Stn., 667; poems by H. Hosmer, A. W. Brotherton, E. B. Harbert, I. B. Hooker, her response, cd. have accomplished little alone, obligations to Mrs. Stn., to family and friends, lets., etc., from L. Stone, 668; Whittier, F. E. Willard, Curtis, Garrison, Hoar, Reed, 669; O. Brown, Logan, Gannett, Palmer, Nordhoff, Carpenter, Dow, 670; Dawes, Mr. and Mrs. Powderly, Barry, Colby, Johns, Cummings, 671; dinner to relatives at Riggs House, presents, trib. of Boston Traveller, A.'s theory of life, distinguished contemporaries, gift to P. Couzins, 672; trib. of Roch. Dem. and Chronicle, allied with all good causes, 673; urges friends to come to union of assns., keep platform broad, not annex to W. C. T. U., struggle to secure Mrs. Stn.'s presence, arranges hearing before Cong. Coms., 674; presides at Natl.-Am. Con., pride in H. Stanton Blatch, pledges

of God," 800; material outweigh moral interests, men in reforms handicapped by disfranchis. women, might as well be dogs baying moon, Natl. Amer. Bus. Com. entertained by Mrs. Southworth, her friendship and generosity, goes to New York to prepare call with Mrs. Stn., 801; and revise article for cycloped., guest of Mrs. Lapham, walk thro. Central Park, lunch with Dr. Jacobi, opera with Lauterbachs, Uncut Leaves Club, hears Robt. Collyer, visits Orange, Philadelphia, Somerton, guest Foremother's Dinner, home for Christmas, 802; Mrs. Minor leaves legacy $1,000, Mrs. Gross makes present $1,000, velvet cloak, many invitations, requests for lectures, articles, woman's edition fever, 803; wd. have more interest in Y. M. C. A. if they stood for wom. suff., manager of printing house writes verse, let. Mary B. Willard, invited by Revs. Jenkyn Lloyd Jones, H. W. Thomas to take part in Lib. Relig. Cong., 804; Dr. Thomas compares to Christ, urged to come as Geo. Washington went into first Continent. Cong., relieved of part of work by younger women, confidence in "body guard," 805; urges old workers to consult with young ones, strictness in financ. accts., alarm lest contribs. be omitted, entertains friends New Year's, starts on south. tour taking Mrs. Catt, at the Clays in Lexington, 806; entertained at Memphis, spks. to col'd people in Tabernacle, at New Orleans, Picayune's descrip. of lect., 807; at Shreveport, floral offerings, trib. of Times, misses connect. for Jackson, 808; too "oozedout" to speak, goes to Birmingham, trib. of News, at New Decatur, Huntsville, compli. of Tribune, 809; in Atlanta, 810; presides over con., reads Mrs. Stn.'s paper, takes charge mass meet., compli. of Constitution, Mrs. Stn.'s thanks for reading her papers, 811; ad. Atlanta Univers., etc., visits Howards in Columbus, spks. in Aiken, guest Martha Schofield, in Columbia, Pine Tree State obj. to Abolitionism, in Culpepper, in Wash., 812; 75th birthday banquet, Mrs. Avery presents annuity from friends, A.'s surprise, freed from financ. anxiety, at Wom. Council, 813; represents Govt. Reform, recep. by Mrs. McLean, spks. at funeral F. Douglass, at Travel Club, lect. Lincoln, Va., death Adaline Thomson, gave A. $1,000, sends thanks to contribs. to annuity fund, 814; at Drexel Instit., visits Mrs. Stn., goes to Police Court in Rochester to have boys punished same as girls, at lect. on lynching, tells audience col'd people treated no better in north than south, takes Miss Wells home with her, 815; discharges her

stenog. because she refuses to write Miss Wells' lets., impossible to refuse calls for help in suff. work, resigns from Board St. Indus. Sch., her work for School, 816; gratitude of girls, arrang. for long journey, 817; invitations follow World's Fair, declines one but later accepts from Calif. Wom. Cong., delight of exec. board, 819; A. asks permis. to bring Anna Shaw, Mrs. Cooper sends money for both, writes A. many loving lets., western towns want lect., starts for Calif., 820; at Chicago, meets H. Hosmer, many interviews, at St. Louis, Missis. Valley Cong., ovation, "75 roses," banquet, at Denver, misses recep. com., at Boulder, 821; recep. by Wom. Club, tribute Rocky Mountain News, Col. women owe suffrage to her, trib. Times, all women under obligat. to her, 822; knows not what to say to enfranchised women, lect. in Broadway Theatre, ovation, compliments men, at Sen. Carey's, Cheyenne, 823; distinguished aud. in Mrs. Stanford's private car, advises her to watch case before Sup. Court, breakfast at Templeton, Salt Lake, 824; guest of honor at Inter-Mountain Suff. Con., trib. Gov. West, receps., banquet at Ogden, State Univers., Reno, 825; spks. in opera house, Wom. Club recep., in lovely Calif., friends at Oakland ferry, entertained by Rev. McLean, 826; with Miss Shaw in pulpit, happiness at cordial recep., beautiful scene at Wom. Cong., great ovation, 827; spks. every day of Cong., "princess blood royal," 828; immense audiences, guest of Mrs. Sargent, helps women organize suff. campn., 829; ad. Congregat. ministers' meet., spks. at Unit. Club dinner, teach. institute, societies, Pres. Jordan invites to Stanford Univers., Mrs. Stanford sends passes and invites graduates' recep., 830; social courtesies, Ebell Club, Alameda Co. Wom. Cong., in Yosemite, big tree named for her, 831; lect. in San Jose, guest Mrs. Knox Goodrich, ovation in Los Angeles, at Riverside, Pasadena, Pomona, Whittiers, San Diego, 832; recep. Hotel Florence, floral offerings. picnic at Olivewood, day at Santa Monica, recep. Mrs. Severance, suff. meet., 833; attitude of press, entertained by Emma Shafter Howard, spks. in Oakland, in San Fr. Zion's Church to col'd people, at ministers' meet., 834; tells why they shd. favor wom. suff., at Calif. Suff. Assn., invited to take part in 4th of July celebra., 835; rides in procession, makes short speech, 836; goes with Miss Shaw to Oakland, can not find audience, beautiful farewell, 200 pages newspaper notices, 837; apprecia. lets. from Calif. women, 838; suff. res. at Topeka,

dom of speech; trib. to A., 828; chmn. campn. com., consecrates herself to suff., 829; takes A. to minister's meet., 830; chmn. 4th July wom. com., refused permission for A. Shaw to speak, gains her point, rides in procession, 836; sympathy for A., 842; appeals to A. for help in Calif. campn., 861; meets at ferry, 862; 863; suff. plank in Repub. platform, 871; at Demo. St. Con., 872; at Portland Wom. Cong., 877.

CORLISS, DR. HIRAM, 45; 902.

COUDERT, FREDERICK, for wom. suff., 764.

COUZINS, PHOEBE, 322; 327; 349; 360; urges A. and Mrs. Stn. to resume head of Natl. Assn., 382; presents Wom. Dec. of Ind. at Centennial, 478; 479; compli. A.'s management of Wash. cons., 495; welcomes suff. con. to St. Louis, recep. to A., 506; ad. Cong. Com., 511; 517; dele. to Natl. Prohib. Con., 520; at Mott memorial serv., 527; in Neb. campn., 545; A. sends $100, 608; meets A. at station, 609; A. makes her life memb. of Natl. Assn., 659; at A.'s birthday banq., 665; A. gives money, 672.

COWAN, SEN. EDGAR, moves to strike "male' from D. C. Suff. Bill, 266; 422.

CRAMER, MRS., 381.

CRAMPTON, REV. R. C., 87.

CRAVATH, PRES. ERASTUS M., invites A. to ad. students Mt. Union Coll., 928.

CRAWFORD, S. G., endorses wom. suff., 284.

CRITTENDEN, A. P., 390.

CROLY, "JENNY JUNE," 353; 720.

CROMWELL, OLIVER, 1014.

CROSBY, ABBY BURTON, 327.

CROWELL, EX-MAYOR, 248.

CROWLEY, RICHARD, U. S. Dist. Atty., examines A. for having voted, 427; threatens to move trial into another county, 435; does so, 436; two hrs. speech in prosecut. A., 438; says A. had fair trial by jury, 450.

CULVER, PRES. & MRS., 598.

CULVER, JUDGE E. D., 330.

CULVER, MARY, registers and votes, 424.

CUMMINGS, —— —— MISS, A.'s birthday, 671.

CUNNINGHAM, STEPHEN M., 393.

CURTIS, ELIZ. BURRILL, ad. N. Y. legis., 914.

CURTIS, EUGENE T., spks. for suff., 762.

CURTIS FAMILY, 395.

CURTIS, GEO. WM., hissed at W. R. con., 163; lect. on Fair Play for Women, dislikes term, "woman's rights," 167; objects to Ernestine L. Rose, replies to A.'s criticism, 172; 233; 270; stands by women, presents Mrs. Greeley's petit., 279; argu. for wom. suff. bef. N. Y. Constit. Con., real support comes from Repubs., 280; endorses suff., 284; 373; let. on A.'s birthday, 669; death, 737; ed. Harper's Weekly fav. wom. suff., 771; daught. Eliz. Burrill ad. N. Y. legis., 914.

CURTIS, MARY B. F., votes, 447.

CURTIS, NEWTON M., ad. suff. con., 756.

CUTLER, HANNAH M. TRACY, lectures with A.,178; 629; 902.

DAHLGREN, MRS. ADMIRAL, 372; petit. agnst. wom. suff., 377.

DALL, CAROLINE H., 131; conservative con., 196; 253.

DALLAS, MARY KYLE, 316.

DANA, CHAS. A., not enough women ask for suff., 760.

DANA, RICHARD H., lect. against women, 59.

DANFORTH, JUDGE GEO. F., presides suff. meet., 762; invites A. to meet Justices Appellate Court, 896.

DANIELS, ASSO. JUSTICE, P. V. citizenship means entire equality, 984.

DANIELS, HATTIE, 553.

DARLING, ANNA B., 341.

DAVIES, CHARLES, LL. D., Pres. State Teach. Con., 98; agnst. woman's right to speak, 99; agnst. co-educa., 155; reads first cable, 163.

DAVIS, EDWARD M., wants woman to wait till negro is enfranchised, 314; pres. Cit. Suff. Assn. tenders A. recep., 546; 550; death, 645.

DAVIS, MRS. EDWARD M., A. visits, 895.

DAVIS, ISABELLA CHARLES, letter to A., 773.

DAVIS, JOHN, M. C., ad. suff. con., 756.

DAVIS, OLIVE, 905.

DAVIS, PAULINA WRIGHT, at Syracuse W. R. Con., 72; pres. cons., 1850-1851, 75; work in 1840-48, 82; discouraged with women, 130; 253; 327; entertains A., Mrs. Stan. and Mrs. Hooker, 332; 349; gives $500 to Rev., 356; 358; arranges 20th suff. annivers., 367; ill and sends for A., 368; 20 yrs. Hist. of W. R. movement, her early work, 369; 372; 375; 376; at N. Y. con., 384; death, 481.

DAVIS, WILLIAM H., invites A. to 4th of July celebration, rejoices in her work, 835.

DAVITT, MICHAEL, asks all for wom., 575; 775.

DAWES, H. L., SENATOR, for suff., 621; on A.'s birthday, 671.

DEAN, JOHN C. AND LILLIAN WRIGHT, 904.

DEBS, EUGENE V., invites A. to lecture, 503.

DE GARMO, RHODA, votes, 424; death, 447.

DELAVAN, MRS. E. C., Wom. Temp. Con., 67.

DELIVERGE, DORIS AND HULDAH, employ A. as teacher, 24.

DE LONG, JAS. C., A. S. assn. formed at house, 210.

DEMOREST (MME.), LOUISE, 282.

DEPEW, CHAUNCEY M., for wom. suff., 764.

DEPUY, MARIA WILDER, 615.

DERAISMES, MARIA, 652.

D'ESTRIA, DORA (see Koltzoff Massalsky).

DETCHON, ADELAIDE, 566.

OSCAR, PRINCE OF SWEDEN, 477.
OSGOOD, JULIA, travels with A., 569; 570; 573.
OTIS, BINA M., on Kan. wom. suff. com., 781.
OTIS, HARRISON G., disrespectful to A. and Miss Shaw, 834.
OTIS, JAMES, man without representation is without liberty, 989.
OWEN, J. J., ed. San Jose Mercury, compli. A., 394.
OWEN, RBT. DALE, supports Wom. Loyal League, chmn. Freedmen's Inquiry Com., 235; 529.
OWEN, MRS. RBT. DALE, 349; 353.
OWEN, ROSAMOND DALE, 529.

PACKARD, HON. JASPER A., presents A. to Ind. Legis., 904.
PAINE, THOMAS, right of voting is primary right, 990.
PALMER, GEN. (Colorado), 564.
PALMER, GOV. (Ill.), 315.
PALMER, BERTHA HONORE, at Wom. Council, 702; ad. at opening World's Fair, 742; fine qualif. for pres. board lady manag., remark. record, courtesy to A., 744; in sympathy with wom. suff., pres. Wom. Cong. Auxil., 745; asks A. for suggestions, 748; thanks her for fair mindedness, 749.
PALMER, SENATOR T. W., rep. in favor wom. suff., 590; 591; urges A. to keep up suff. agitation, 593; masterly sp. on 16th Amend., 596; 637; let. on A.'s birthday, 670.
PALMER, SENATOR AND MRS., recep. for Wom. Council, 637.
PARKER, JANE MARSH, at A.'s birthday banq., 666; organizes club agnst. suff., 766.
PARKER, JULIA SMITH, ad. Cong. Com., 446; 511; at Lucretia Mott's, 512.
PARKER, MARGARET E., at Phila. Centennial, 479; 565; A. visits, 577; com. for internatl. organization, 579.
PARKER, THEO., A. visits him in study, 131; "only noise and dust of wagon," 195.
PATTERSON, MR. AND MRS. THOMAS M., entertain A. friends of wom. suff., 821.
PATTON, ABBY HUTCHINSON (see Htchis'n.).
PATTON, LUDLOW, 260.
PATTON, REV. W. W., preaches agnst. wom. suff., 596.
PAYNE, SENATOR AND MRS., 677.
PEABODY, ELIZ., 131; 756.
PEASE, DR. R. W. AND HANNAH F., 211.
PECKHAM, LILIE, 327.
PECKHAM, JUSTICE, RUFUS W., pays fine trib. to charac. of A., 735.
PEDRO, DOM, 477.
PEFFER, SENATOR WILLIAM A., ad. suff. con., 756.
PEET, MRS. B. STURTEVANT, tries to sec.

suff. amend. from Calif. Legis., 863; A. writes obj. to Natl. W. C. T. U. Con. in San Fr., 882.
PELLET, SARAH, at Saratoga con., 121.
PENCE, LAF., M. C., addresses suff. con., 756.
PENNOCK, DEBORAH, 601.
PERKINS, GEO. C., 685.
PERKINS, MARY (see Randall).
PERKINS, SARAH M., 628; 629.
PERRY, A. L., invites A. to Berkshire Hist. Soc. meet, 939.
PETERS, JUDGE, advoc. suff. amend., 796.
PETERS, O. G. AND ALICE, 676.
PETTINGELL, ABBY L., 772.
PETTIGREW, SENATOR R. F., 676.
PHELPS, ELIZ. B., establishes Wom. Bureau, 320; 327; 341; 349; gives up Wom. Bureau, 360; 480.
PHILLEO HELEN (see Jenkins).
PHILLIPS, WENDELL, visits Anthony home, 60; goes with Antoinette Brown to World's Temp. Con., 101; 102; opp. Bloomer dress, 115; gives A. $50 for first canvass of N. Y., 122; refuses to let her pay it back, 128; 131; 132; spks. at N. Y. wom. rights con., 147; 162; on gift of Jackson to wom. rights cause, 165; approves A.'s N. Y. canvass, 171; lashes the mob, 174; prepares suff. memorial to legis., 175; 182; 185; 192; 193; opp. divorce resolutions, 194; attitude grieves A. and Mrs. Stn., 195; praises A., 196; 197; urges A. to restore child to father, 203; can not feel for woman, 204; declares for war, 214; refuses check for lect., 217; A. hoped wd. redeem pledge to woman, 225; A. "salt of earth," 226; 233; lively let. on A.'s getting Mrs. Stn. to invite him to speak, 237; urges A. to return East, 244; on disbanding Anti. Slav. Soc., 245; elected pres. A. S. Soc., 246; no freedom without ballot, objects to union of A. S. and W. R. Soc., 256; prevents the union, 259; argues against trying to strike "male" from N. Y. consti., 261; declines to sustain demands of women, 270; refuses to give money from Jackson fund, 275; endorses wom. suff., 284; 290; bids woman stand aside, 300; and wait for negro, 304; gives preference to negro suff., 317; wom. suff. intellectual theory, 323; first meet. with A. since dif. of opinion on Amend. XIV, 370; 373; will help toward Amend. XVI; A. stands at head of suff. movement, 495; replies to A.'s 70th birthday greet., faith in her, 538; announces Eddy legacy to A., 539; tells of suit to break will, 540; 548; 549; Harvard ad., 557; 568; 577; death, 587; 593; 859; 935; freedom without ballot is mockery, 990.
PHILLIPS, MRS. WENDELL, 219.
PICKLER, ALICE M., presents claims S. Dak.,

Supreme Court, 502; returns to Calif., friend of wom. suff., 507; U. S. Minister to Berlin, 553; genuine Repub., 559.

SARGENT, ELLA, 560.

SARGENT, ELLEN CLARK, entertains A. as guest, 405; while snow bound on eastward journey, 406; 407; 480; urges A. not to be troubled, 494; 495; returns to Calif., personal characteris., 507; 509; 512; 553; genuine Repub., 559; asks Estee Chairman Natl. Repub. Con. if "free ballot" plank includes women, 642; work for S. Dak.,685; entertains A. during Wom. Cong., 829; gift to A. and Miss Shaw, 832; made pres. Calif. Suff. Assn., 835; asks A. to help in campn., 861; directs it with A., 862; on committees, 863; entertains A. and Miss Shaw during campn., 864; gives up entire home to work, her services and money, 865; at Repub. St. Con., 869; at Popu., Prohib. and Demo. Cons., 872; 888; scenes in election booths, 891; trib. to A.'s services in Calif., 892.

SARGENT, DR. ELIZ., A. visits in Zurich, 559; in Yosemite with A., 831; arrang. county cons. in Calif. campn., successful results, 864; head of literary com. and petit. work, contributes money, 865; suff. work on San Fr. Post, 866.

SARGENT, GEORGE, 408.

SARGENT, MR. AND MRS. JAMES, 772; A. assists at golden wedding, 916; entertain A. at Thous. Is., 926.

SAUNDERS, ALVIN, SENATOR, ad. suff. con., 541.

SAXE, REV. ASA, spks. for wom. suff., 762.

SAXON, ELIZABETH LYLE, ad. Cong. Com., 511; in Neb. campn., 545; in Kan. campn., 609; 808.

SAXTON, GEN. RUFUS, approves equal rights for women, 272; negroes still enslaved, 964.

SCATCHERD, ALICE, secures admission wom. dele. to Lib. Con., 576; com. for internatl. organizat., 579; ad. Senate Com., 640.

SCHENCK, ELIZ. B., 327.

SCHIEFFELIN BROTHERS, 234.

SCHOFIELD, MARTHA, A. visits industrial school, 812.

SCHUMACHER, MR. AND MRS. ADOLPH, entertain A., 652.

SCHURMAN, PRES. JACOB GOULD, welcomes suff. con., invites to visit Cornell, 800.

SCHURZ, CARL, opponent wom. suff., 415.

SCHUYLER, MARY M. HAMILTON, Art. Assn. desire to make statue rep. Philanthropy,734; stepson obj. to having name coupled with A.'s, 735.

SCHUYLER, PHILIP, obj. to stepmother's statue by side of A., 734; enjoins Art Assn., she wd. resent attempt to couple name with A.'s, defeat in court of appeals, 735.

SCOTT, CHARLES F., urg. Mrs. Johns to call off women, 778.

SCOTT, FRANCIS M., ad. N. Y. Consti. Con. in opp. wom. suff., 769.

SEARS, JUDGE T. C., assails wom. suff., 281; res. agnst. it, 283.

SEDGWICK, CATHARINE MARIA, born in Berkshire, 1.

SELDEN, HENRY R., women have valid claim to vote, 425; assures A. of this, 424; tells her she has committed no crime, 426; 427; appears for A. before U. S. Commiss., 428; argues for writ of habeas corpus, gives bail for A., 432; wishes he had heard her argument first, 433; defends her at trial, 436; argument before jury, 437; demands jury be polled and moves for new trial, 439; Judge Hunt's action indefensible, 441; Van Voorhis' trib., 445; A. has argument printed, 446; prepares appeal to Cong. in A.'s case; Hunt's action judicial outrage, 449; 994.

SENEY, GEO. E., M. C., opp. wom. suff., 590.

SEVERANCE, CAROLINE M., 131; 252; 260; signs call for Am. Suff. Assn., 328; entertains A., 832.

SEVERANCE, MRS. MARK SIBLEY, recep. for A., 833.

SEVERANCE, SARAH M., work for S. Dak., 685; spks. for wom. suff. in Calif. campn., 875.

SEWALL, MAY WRIGHT, first app. on natl. suff. plat., 495; presents flowers to A. at St. Louis, 507; 511; arranges suff. con. Indpls., 517; 527; presentation speech to A., 534; chmn. natl. ex. com., 535; appears bef. House Com., 541; 545; description of honors paid A. on departure for Europe, 547.; A. at New Orleans Expo., 597; applies lash to own back, 600; entertains A., 623; 626; chmn. com. on union of two assns., 628; 629; skill as pres. offic., 632; arranges internat. council, 633; originates idea of permanent Councils, 639; made cor. sec., 641; open let. to Gen. Harrison, 642; introduces A. to Classical School, 650; arranges birthday banq. for A., 664; presides, 665; 676; A. visits, 698; present to A., 707; at Fed. of Clubs, 720; 721; spks. at Rochester, 740; at opening World's Fair, 742; ch. com. org. Wom. Cong., A. glories in her work, 745; A.'s popularity at World's Fair, 746; entertains A. during World's Fair, 750; presides at lunch to Internat. Council, 751; 821; 841; wants A. to manage Stn.'s birthday, 847; death of husband, A.'s sympathy, 850; receives State officials in honor of A.,903; at Anthony homestead, 940; at Berk. Hist. meet., 944; A.'s character, 950; open let. to Gen. Harrison on "free ballot" pl. in Repub. plat., 1013.

SEWALL, SAMUEL E., endorses wom. suff.,284; 373; birthday gift to A., 976.

SEWALL, MRS. SAMUEL E., congratulat. let. to A., 640; birthday gift to A., 976.

SEWALL, THEODORE L., at World's Fair, 750; death, 850.

SEWARD, MRS. W. H., favors divorce, 195.

SEYMOUR, GOV. HORATIO, heads opposit. to A. S. meet., 210; ad. Demo. mass meet. N. Y., 305; pres. Natl. Demo. Con., 306.

SEYMOUR, HORATIO, JR., leads disturbance at A. S. meet., 208.

SEYMOUR, MARY F., reports wom. council, 637; death, 757.

SHAFROTH, MRS. JOHN F., at Wash. con., 851.

SHARKEY, WM. L., Provis. Gov. Miss., 961.

SHARSWOOD, JUDGE, agnst. wom. suff., 985.

SHATTUCK, HARRIETTE ROBINSON, spks. at suff. con. Boston, 533; 541; in Neb. campn., 545; 628.

SHAW, REV. ANNA HOWARD, in Kan., 625; 629; accepts proposals for union, 630; 636; beginning of friendship with A., 645; first appears on Natl. plat., 647; 652; at A.'s birthday banq., 665; appeal for S. Dak., 675; 676; must not attack Christian relig., 678; goes to S. Dak., 681; writes A. people anxious for her to come, 682; scores State com., better not cut loose from A., 683; 684; at Repub. con. seats for Indians, none for wom., 687; rebukes con., in Black Hills, 688; gets courage from A., longs for mother, 689; A.'s experience with crying baby, 692; her own experience, A.'s retort in case of drunken man, 693; at Deadwood, 694; hardest campn. ever known, 696; at Rochester, 698; first pres. Wimodaughsis, 700; at Wom. Council, 702; christens Avery baby, 705; present to A., 707; in Adirondacks, 708; at Chautauqua, 709; J. H. Buckley's obj. to wom. suff. from relig. standpoint, 710; at West. N. Y. Fair, 711; vice-pres.-at-large Natl. Am. Assn., 717; in Kan. campn., 719; shut out of churches bec. spoke at spiritual meet., will speak on suff. anywhere, 720; at Kan. Repub. con., at Omaha Popu. con., 726; deb. suff. with Dr. Buckley at Chau., 727; recep. at Hall of Philos., 728; spks. in N. Y. campn., 761; will not work for wom. suff. in Kan. unless politic. part. endorse it, weakness of wom., 781; opens campn. in Kan. City, 784; demands Repub. Wom. con., ask for suff. plank, 785; ad. res. com. at Repub. St. con., 786; ad. suff. mass. meet. in Topeka, 787; ad. Popu. St. con., 789; shakes hands with dele., telegram Kan. Prohib. con. adopts wom. suff. plank, 790; finishes Kan. engagements, 792; 793; Mrs. Diggs urges return to Kan., 795; in Atlanta, 811; in Columbus, 812; invit. to Calif. Wom. Cong., 820; at Chi. St. Louis, Denver, entertained by Gov. and Mrs. Routt, 821; enthusiastic greet. in

Broadway Thea., 823; preaches Tabernacle, Salt Lake, "politic. sermon," 824; preaches in theater; at Inter-Mount. Suff. Assn., receptions, banq. in Ogden, at Reno, Nev., 825; spks. in theat., in Calif., at Oakland ferry, in Dr. McLean's pulpit, 826; in Congreg. church San Fr., at Wom. Cong., 827; spks. every day, royal welcome, 828; all in love with, preaches in synagogue, helps org. suff. campn., 829; ad. Congreg. ministers' meet., Unit. Club dinner, Stanford Univers., 830; social courtesies, Yosemite, names big tree S. B. A., at San Jose, 831; Los Angeles, Riverside, Pasadena, Pomona, San Diego, 832; Olivewood, Santa Monica, Los Angeles, 833; spks. in Oakland, in Method. ch., San Fr., at ministers' meet., 834; meets with Calif. Suff. Assn., 835; 4th July com. refuse to let spk., reconsider, she rides in proces. and makes sp., 836; goes to Oakland, can not find audience, starts homeward, 837; goes to Chicago, 839; stricken with fever, 840; favors res. agnst. Wom. Bible, 854; spks. at county cons. in Calif., in Sargent residence, 864; at Repub. St. Con., 869; bef. res. com., 871; ad. Dem. res. com. for two min., 873; scores con. for action on wom. suff. pl., at ratificat. meet. in San Fr., 874; spks. every night dur. campn. and donates serv. of sec., 875; 883; at "Tom Reed" rally, Oakland, 885; photo. given for pledges, 889; at Salt Lake, Kan. City, banq. at Roch., 895; R. I. suff. con., 896; A's 77th birthday, 907; present to Mary Anthony, 916; visits Mrs. Osborne, 917; A.'s letters like Paul's Epistles, 924; spks. at western conferences, 929; at Anthony homestead, 940; at A.'s right hand, 942; at Berk. Hist. meet., trib. to A., her belief in men and women, great, ideal life, 945.

SHAW, FRANCIS G., gives A. $100 for Rev. 355.

SHAW, SARAH B., 282.

SHELDON, ELLEN H., serv. for Natl. Assn., 700.

SHIPPEN, REV. RUSH R., ad. suff. con., 607.

SHERMAN, GEN. WM. T., 249.

SHERMAN, MRS. GEN., agnst. wom. suff., 377.

SIMONTON, J. W., at press dinner, 316.

SIMPSON, JERRY, M. C., ad. suff. con. 756.

SIMPSON, BISHOP MATTHEW, 337; favors wom. suff., 588.

SIZER, NELSON, phrenolog. chart of A., 85.

SKIDMORE, MR. AND MRS. THOS. J., hospitality, love of liberty, 710.

SLAYTON (Lect. Bureau), tells A. she has ruined lect. prospects, 468; compli. circular of A.'s lect., 486.

SLOCUM, MRS., interviews Gen. Hancock, 520.

SMALLEY, GEO. W., 246.

SMITH, ABBY, 446.

SMITH, MRS. E. O., at Calif. Dem. Con., 872.

sells rights to A., fine ability, 613; adv. A. to burn old letters, 625; advised not to take presidency united assns., 628; 629; willing to decline, but lets. insist she shall take presidency, 630; A. spks. in her favor, 631; elect. pres., 632; 633; friendship for A., coming back to Amer. to do best work, 635; dreads ocean trip, can not come to Council, A. brings her and shuts her up to write sp., 636; at recep. for Wom. Council, 637; trib. of Fr. Willard, 638; ad. Sen. com., 640; 642; 654; 659; 664; looks like Lord Chief.Just., 665; response at A.'s birthday banq., thorn in side, meets A. in London, oblig. to her, 667; inspiration to A., 668; A. will have her under thumb, ad. Cong. Coms., presides Natl. Am. Assn., 674; honored to go abroad as its represent., farewell, 675; The Matriarchate, 702; 703; re-elect. pres. natl. assn., 704; keep home and be cremat. in own oven, 707; returns to Amer., A. urges to make home with her and prepare writings for posterity, 712; goes for month's visit to A., sits for bust by Ad. Johnson, sp. in favor opening Roch. Univers. to women, cartoon in Utica paper, 713; settled in N. Y., children urge to give up work, paper on Solitude of Self, ovation at con.; begs scepter be transfer. to A., elect. hon. pres. natl. assn., last app. at Wash. con., 717; ad. Cong. Coms., recep. in Wash., 718; 719; 729; trib. to disting. dead, 737; natl. com. sends greet. to, 739; paper for Educat. Cong. World's Fair, 751; ad. to N. Y. women contrib. to Sun, 763; prep. call for natl. con., 801; cosy home, 802; thanks A. for read. her papers, 811; memorial to Fred. Douglass, 814; A. visits to tell about cons., etc., 815; portrait at Utah Con., 825; let. sympathy to A., 842; 80th birthday, 845; all wom. shd. pay tribute, 846; birthday sp.. 847; magnific. fête, Tilton's testimonial, 848; recep. by Mrs. H. Villard, birthday celebrat. in Roch., 849; extolled by Sen. Stanford, 851; prepares Woman's Bible, res. agnst. introd. in natl. suff. con., 852; always announc. to be her individ. work, 853; always in advance of times, A. defends her, 854; urges that she and A. resign office, 855; A. tells her she is talking down to people in her Bible commentary, 856; and says suff. wd. take women out of relig. bigotry, urges not to send Bible literature to Calif., 857; women only class left to fight battles alone, 879; A. wishes she were young and strong, 880; 896; 915; at Mrs. Osborne's, 917; A. writes of Mrs. Besant and Theosophy, 918; at Geneva, 927; pict. in Anthony parlor, 934; A.'s magnanimity, honesty, heroism, tenderness. "to be wedded to an idea may be holiest and happiest of marriages," dedicates Reminiscences, 951; to "my steadfast friend.," 952; ad. to Pres.Lincoln, "free women as you have slaves," 957; ad. to Cong., eloquent demand for woman's enfranchisement, 968; birthday gift to A., 976; Repubs. will lose power to protect black men in right to vote, 1016.

STANTON, MR. AND MRS. GERRIT, 654.

STANTON, HARRIOT, (See Blatch).

STANTON, HENRY B., on condition of country, urges A. to gird on armor, 226.

STANTON, MRS. HENRY B., Greeley's revenge, 280; 972.

STANTON, THEODORE AND MARGUERITE, 532; take A. to Chamber of Deputies, to St. Cloud, to station, 561.

STARRETT, HELEN EKIN, compares A. and Mrs. S. when in Kan., 273; how A. won all hearts, 285; 287.

STARRETT, REV. WM., 287.

STEARNS, JUDGE J. B., introd. A., 656; 902.

STEARNS, SARAH BURGER, 656.

STEBBINS, GILES AND CATHARINE F., old friends of A., 658; visit A., 711; golden wed., 896.

STEBBINS, REV. H. H., for wom. suff., 762.

STEBBINS, DR. HORATIO, 830.

STEPHENS, PROF. KATE, in Germany, 560.

STETSON, CHARLOTTE PERKINS, opp. res. agnst. Wom. Bible, 854; visits A. and spks. in Rochester, 901.

STEEN, JUDGE, ad. wom. suff. con., 762.

STEVENS, THADDEUS, tries to have women included in Amend. XIV, 250; bids women stand aside for negro, 267; 318; elective franchise inalienable right, 979; Amendment XIV, 1016.

STEVENSON, DR. SARAH HACKETT, at Fed. Clubs, 720; let. from A. on maternity hospital, 843.

STILLMAN, JAS. W., 350.

STEWART, SEN. WM., favors wom. suff., 500.

STOCKER, ALICE M., Calif. Dem. Con., 872.

STONE, LUCINDA HINSDALE, 379.

STONE, LUCY, first meets A., 64; unjust laws for women, 73; does not favor Maine law, 81; 87; 90; on divorce, 93; assists Whole World Temp. Con., 96; commends A., praises Channing, 111; writes A. regarding Bloomers, 115; defends costume, but abandons it, 116; marries, 128; playful letter on marriage, 130; will retire from public work, 135; 139; encourages A. to speak in public, 145; shows legal posit. of women, has faith in A., 146; pres. N. Y. con., 147; sympathetic let., 151; care of children, 162; trustee of Jackson fund, 165; wd. use Hovey fund for test cases, 171; 185; opp. divorce res., 195; pres. Loyal League meet., 229; 234; petit. for Cong. action, 250; 253; favors union of A. S. and W. R. Soc., 256;

INDEX TO SUBJECTS.

ABOLITIONISTS, 39, 40, 44, 59; meetings, in Anthony home, 48, 60, 61; A.'s first meeting with, 60, 63; 78, 198; attitude in 1861, 207; canvass under A.'s management, 208; at beginning of War, 214; need of in 1863, 226; dissensions among, 244-247; one wing demands negro suff., 256; refuse to stand for woman suff., 265; almost all desert women, 268, 270; Lucy Stone on, 275; 311, 498; Robert Purvis on A.'s services to, 547; 567; in Scotland, 568, 570; in Ireland, 572, 575; 724; Southern prej. against A., 740; same, 812; 924; A. speaks on at Fiske Univers., 928; pictures in A.'s home, 934, 935; foresight of, 1010.

ADDRESSES, APPEALS, TESTIMONIALS, etc., A.'s for temp. and woman suff., 71; for better laws in N. Y., 110; memorial to all Legislatures in 1859, 175; first to Cong. for Woman Suff. in 1865, 250; Woman's Rights Soc. to Cong. in 1866, 259, 968; A. and Mrs. Stanton to Cong. for woman suff. in 1867, 277; to women on polit. parties in 1872, 418; A.'s to Cong. to remit her fine for voting, 450; Natl. Wom. Suff. Assn. at Centennial in 1876, 475; 483; Wom. Natl. Loyal League to President Lincoln, 957; Natl. Wom. Rights Conv. to Cong. in 1866, 968.

AMENDMENTS to U. S. Constitution, 13th, 238; dif. of opinion on, A.'s attitude, 245; 14th, "male" first used, protest of A., Mrs. Stanton and Lucy Stone, 250; *Independent* criticises, 252; Sumner would avoid "male," 256; women implore not to be excluded, 267; campaign for woman suff. in Kansas, 274; same, 281 et seq.; efforts for in N. Y., 278-280; Pomeroy, Julian and Wilson present resolutions for woman suff. in 1868, 310, 311, 317; first effort to secure

woman suff. in U. S. Constn., 313; 15th adopted, first suggested by Anna Dickinson, 317; dispute over in Equal Rights Assn., A. demands it shall include women, 323, 324; Francis Minor on woman's right to vote under 14th, 331; A. on same, 338; A. will never cease working for 16th, 343; Natl. Wom. Suff. Assn. on right of women to vote under 14th, 377; attempt to make 14th and 15th enfranch. women, 409-411; A. and other women vote in 1872, 423-453; women vote again, 434; woman's right to vote under 14th, 431, 432; Mrs. Minor attempts to vote under 14th, 453; it does not confer suffrage, 454; for woman suff. submitted in Mich., 459; defeated, 461; beginning of systematic efforts for 16th, 483; war amends. will fail to protect black men, 500; Mrs. Stanton on same, 1016; for woman suff. submitted in Neb., 544, 545; in Ore., 592; A.'s argument for 16th before Congressl. Coms. in 1884, 588; defeat of woman suff. in Ore., 592; Palmer in U. S. Senate, on 16th, 596; first vote in Senate on, 617, 621; for woman suff. in S. Dak., A. canvasses for, 656; urged to assist, 679; Natl. Assn. contributes to, 675; campaign for, 679 et seq.; 16th in Cong. in 1891, 718; for woman suff. in charter of Rochester, 731; woman suff. carried in Col., 753; Kas. Legis. submits, 754; campaign for, 777; Calif. Legis. submits, 820; campaign for, 863; causes of its defeat, 886 et seq.; Secy. of State breaks his word, 890; Idaho Sup. Court decides only majority of votes cast on amend. necessary to carry, 918; war amends. and woman suff., 979-984; 16th not necessary, Sumner on, 981; Grant on 15th, 991; A. on efforts to keep "male" out of 14th,

of, 799; objects to Bible or Prohib. in Calif., 857; A. begged to assist in Calif., consents, 861; greeted by South. Calif., arrives in San Fr., 862; great campaign for woman suff. in 1896, 863 et seq.; in Kas. in 1867, 1016; in other States, 1017.

CANVASSES, A. and others in N. Y. for temp., 71; same, 103; for Woman's Rights, 105; unpleasant experience, 108; A.'s long work, 111; first of N. Y. for woman suff., 122 et seq.; for Woman's Rights in 1856, 138 et seq.; for Anti-Slavery, graphic pictures, 150 et seq.; for rights of women in 1860, 175, 178; for Anti-Slavery in 1861, 208 et seq.; for Equal Rights in 1866, 265; A. bore all the burdens, 273; of Conn. in 1874, 456; of Mich. for suff. amend. in 1874, 460; of Iowa in 1875, hard conditions, 470; of Kas. in 1886, 609-611; of Wis., 612; of Kas. in 1887, 625; of Ind., 626; of S. Dak. in 1890, 656; same, 679-696; of Kas. in 1892, 719; same, 728; of N. Y. in 1894, 759-763; of Kas. in 1894, 784, 785, 796; only women come to meetings, 1019 (see Campaigns).

CAPITAL PUNISHMENT, A. organizes meeting in protest, ends in mob, 164.

CASES (see Trials).

CHARACTERISTICS,* clear - sightedness, 141, 182, 185, 261, 519, 758, 929; courage, moral and physical, 43, 72, 111, 156, 158, 163, 164, 181, 190, 197, 202, 208-212, 272, 291, 292, 391, 396, 412, 428, 436, 468, 469, 534-542, 549, 583, 656, 689, 692, 773, 782, 783, 786, 799, 854, 855, 857, 901, 952, 974, 994; duty and principle, devotion to, 116, 117, 218, 222, 224, 482, 542, 679, 907; energy and perseverance, 36, 55, 105, 127, 148, 157, 179, 188, 190, 213, 221, 251, 288, 314, 414, 496, 581, 667, 772, 944, 973, 974, 994; executive ability, 62, 110, 154, 323, 473; expediency, disdain for, 95, 214, 262, 953; generosity, 20, 217, 329, 494, 508, 545, 592, 599, 608, 659, 695, 707, 711, 763, 796, 849, 892, 925; injustice, sense of, viii, 29, 30, 81, 107, 844; judgment, 150, 225, 293, 425, 638, 654, 857, 871, 882; justice, love of, 134, 169, 270, 592, 919, 944; kindness of manner, 285, 550, 597, 674, 838, 946, 972; optimism and cheerfulness, 587, 638, 660, 688, 773, 800, 877, 898, 938, 953; philosophy and logic, 185, 380, 511, 644, 648, 666, 672, 714; presiding,

*Superficial and inadequate grouping.

gift for, 163, 174, 637; self-sacrifice, viii, 127, 190, 273, 316, 323, 335, 396, 460, 480, 489, 504, 550, 615, 667, 671, 744, 772, 846, 891, 892, 944, 950; sense of humiliation and insult, 238, 268, 269, 584; sensitiveness, 28, 29, 30, 120, 168, 542, 583, 584; unselfishness, 384, 535, 695, 731, 735, 975 (see chart of head, 85; Domestic Traits, Love of Family, Newspapers, Tributes).

CHILDREN, hardships of A.'s mother, 12, 19; severity of early days, 31; 52; Mrs. Mott's and Mrs. Stanton's, 76; Mrs. Greeley's, 86, 97; A.'s answer to minister, 108; A. on "baby show," 132; mothers' trials, 139; Mrs. Stanton on, 142; maternity and conventions, 158, 162; Lucy Stone and Mrs. Stanton on, 162; A.'s care of Mrs. Stanton's, 142, 187, 213, 219; woman's immortal product, 193; mother no right to, sad story, 200; care of is a profession, 213; A.'s care of, 213; illegitimate, 216, 656, 844; A. would educate in public schools, 221; baby panacea for woman suff., 267; woman's right to have, 296; *The Revolution*, A.'s child, 362; Mrs. Stanton's belong to A., 489; Neb. man wants credit, 493; alleged effect of woman suff. in regard to, 504; A.'s care of nieces, 513; great number among suffragists, 517; impudent advice, 517; must suffer disgrace of parents' hostility to woman suff., 529; A.'s experience with woman and babies in Killarney, 573; God held responsible, 574; brought for A. to take in arms, 610; A. on pre-natal influence, 678; men suckle babies, 687; 690; trying experiences with in S. Dak. campaign, 692; Mrs. Stanton's, 713, 717; A. would turn palace into orphan asylum, 943 (see Guardianship).

CHINESE, A. compares status with women, 398; 986.

CHURCHES, St. Bartholomew the Great, 3; A.'s maternal grandparents members of Baptist, 5; later Universalist, 5; paternal, Quakers, 6; record Anthony and Read families, 5, 6, 7, 11, 21; father disciplined by Quakers, 10, 20, 36; A. on Lord's Supper, 36; 38; attitude toward colored people, 39; on a woman's preaching in 1839, 40; first knowledge of Unitarianism, 44; attends that church, 58; 65; Mrs. Stanton on in 1852, 67, 68; 70; bondage for women, relation to woman's

---

*In later years churches have been so freely opened for woman suffrage meetings that it would be impossible to tabulate them.

277; bills for Wom. Suff. in 1868, 310; appeal sent by women in 1869, 314; A. urges to enfranchise women of D. C., 338; Act under which A. was indicted, 437; A. appeals to remit her fine for voting, 449; majority and minority reports, 450-452; treatment by Senate of petits. for woman suff. in 1877, 485; Sen. Hoar hopes to see A. there, 485; condemned for treatment of women, 499-501; A. watches and distrusts, 516; members attend mem. serv. to Lucretia Mott, 526; opposed to Wom. Suff. Com., 540; attitude of members on woman suff., 250, 256, 266, 310, 317, 337, 375, 377, 405, 410, 411, 454, 455, 457, 477, 485, 500, 501, 502, 507, 543, 583, 584, 590, 596, 617-621, 688, 698, 699, 716, 718, 778, 969, 985; A. dislikes to interview members, 583; vote on Wom. Suff. Com. in 1884, 585; A. watches, 591, 603; persistence with, 605-608; same, 622; Sen. Blair's humor, 606, 626; action on admission of Wy. with woman suff., 698, 699; A.'s constant watchfulness, 716; efforts to secure recog. of women at Columb. Expos., 743, 744; admits Utah with woman suff., 851; A. demands no members be admitted unless elected by a maj. of all voters, black and white, 963, 967; power to create voters, 966; address of Natl. Wom. Rights Conv. in 1866, 968; fails in its highest duty, 970; as representatives of women, 970; right to control suff., 981; Repub. record on wom. suff., 1018.

CONGRESSES, Woman's, in Paris, 434, 496, 652; Woman's, Miss. Valley, 728, 821; Woman's at Columb. Expos., 745-748; 750, 751; Liberal Religious, 804, 805; Woman's Calif. in 1895, 819, 827-829, 831; in 1896, 871; in Ore., 877.

CONSTITUTION, U. S., protects slavery, 149, 184, 207; Sumner on, 235; 248; A. begins 30-years' war to amend, 249; "male" first introduced, protest of A., Mrs. Stanton and Lucy Stone, 250; *Independent* speaks, 253; 257; first effort to amend for woman suff., 313; B. F. Butler on its power over woman suff., 429; A. asks for broad interpret., 440; does not confer suffrage on any one, 453; arguments for right of women to vote under its provisions, 483; compact with slavery broken, 958; base use of it by President Johnson, 961; bring legislation

up to Constitu., 970; protest against introd. word "male," 970; A.'s sp. on woman's right to vote under its provisions, 977-992; distinguished testimony for, 979-991.

CONSTITUTIONS, STATE, Phillips, Tilton, A. and Mrs. Stanton on striking out "male" from N. Y., 261; woman suff. in Utah, 825, 851; while "male" remains women should not help men, 839; of N. Y. guarantees woman suff., 979 (see Amendments).

CONSTITUTIONAL ARGUMENT, on right of women to vote, delivered by A. previous to her trial for voting, 977-992; newspaper comment, 993.

CONVENTIONS, first Woman's Rights, 59; in Worcester, 61, 75; Men's Temp. silence women in 1852, 64; first Wom. St. Temp., 66; Greeley's advice, 66; Men's Temp. reject women delegates, 68; Teachers' at Elmira, 71; Woman's Rights at Syracuse, 72; Mrs. Mott and Mrs. Stanton had objected to woman pres., 72; lofty character of first Wom. Rights Convs., 80; World's Temperance in New York, 1853, 87; women rejected, hold own meeting, abuse, 88-92; second Woman's St. Temp., 92; men gain control, 94; Women's Whole World's, 96, 100; A.'s first address to St. Teachers', 98; not supported by women, 98, 99, 100; Davies' sp., 99; sustained by a few, 100; Men's Whole World's Temp., Antoinette Brown rejected, 101; Woman's Rights in 1853, 102; in Cleveland, 103; in Rochester, 105; before the War, 107; in Albany, 108; A. again goes to Teachers' for rights of women, 120; Wom. Rights in Phila., 121; Teachers' in Utica, 130; Wom. Rights in Boston, 131; Teachers' in Troy, 143; Wom. Rights in New York, 147; Teachers' in Binghamton, 155; Wom. Rights in New York in 1858, under mob rule, 162; A. stirs up Teachers' in Lockport, 163, 164; Anti-Slavery in Albany in 1859, 173; Wom. Rights in New York, the mob, 174; Wom. Rights in Albany in 1860, 186; Conservatives' in Boston, 196; A. and Pillsbury on, 197; Wom. Rights, last before War, 212; A.'s dislike of giving up, 213, 215, 218; results of A.'s labors in Teachers', 221. 222; Anti-Slavery in Phila., 234; first Wom. Rights after War, 256 et seq.; N. Y. Constitl., A. arranges to present petitions, tilt with Greeley, 278; latter checkmated, 279; his anger, 280; first for woman suff. held in Washtn., 313; woman suff. at Hartford, 333; second of Natl. Wom. Suff. Assn., 337; woman suff. in New York in 1870, 368; third of Natl. Wom. Suff. Assn. in Washtn., managed by Mrs. Hooker, 371 et seq.; appearance of Mrs. Woodhull, 375; woman suff. in New York in 1871, excitement over Mrs. Woodhull, 383; Natl. Wom. Suff. in 1872, struggle to secure woman suff. under 14th amend., 409-411; woman suff. in New York, A. thwarts scheme for alliance with Woodhull party, 414; women attend Natl. Liberal in 1872, 415; Natl. Repub. in 1872, woman's plank, 416; Natl. Wom. Suff. in Washtn. in 1873, 431; woman suff. in New York in 1873, 434; Natl. Woman Suff. of 1874, 453; in New York, adverse accounts, 458; Natl. Wom. Suff. of 1875, A. conquers all objections to, 467; A. misses Natl. Suff. for first time, 472; Natl. Wom. Suff. of 1876 arranges to celebrate Centennial, 474; Natl. Wom. Suff. Assn. in 1877, 484 et seq.; A. misses May Anniv. first time, 488; of Natl. Wom. Suff. Assn. in 1878, need of A.'s management and Mrs. Stanton's presence, prayer meet. in Capitol, 494; 30th annivers. celebr. in Rochester, 495; last attended by Lucretia Mott, 496; Natl. Wom. Suff. of 1879, 499-501; Natl. Suff. Assn. in 1880, 511; A. plans great series in 1880 and overcomes opposition, 515; begins at Indpls., 517; mass meet. in Chicago, 517; other cities, 519; Natl. polit. convs. appealed to by women in 1880, 518-520; A.'s amusing attempt to postpone Natl. Suff. of 1881, compels Mrs. Stanton's attendance, 526; same, 532; Natl. Assn. in New England, 533; W. C. T. U. in 1881 adopts franchise dept. but repudiates influence of A., 537, 538; Natl. Wom. Suff. of 1882, 540; in Phila., 541; in Nebraska in 1882, 544, 545; Natl. Wom. Suff. of 1883, 546; Liberal in Eng., 575, 576, 577; A.'s efforts for Intl. Wom. Suff., 578; Natl. Wom. Suff. in 1884, 588; holiday refused dept. women to attend, 588; Natl. polit. in 1884 appealed to by women, 594; Natl. Wom. Suff. in 1885, 595; Mrs.

Stanton's satire on esthetic convs., 605; Natl. Suff. in 1886, 607; in Kas. in 1886, 609-611; in Wis. and Ills., 611; in Mich., 617; Natl. Wom. Suff. in 1887, 617; in Indiana, 623; in Kansas in 1887, 625; in Indiana, 626; Fred. Douglass on first Woman's Rights, 634; Natl. Wom. Suff. of 1888, 639; Natl. polit. in 1888 appealed to by suffragists, 641, 642; in Iowa, Kas., Neb., 644; of 1889, 647; in New York, 651; Akron, O., 652; in Kas., Ind., Wis., 655; Minn., 656; of Natl. Amer. Wom. Suff. Assn. in 1890, 674; Farmers' Alliance and Knights of Labor in S. Dak., act. on woman suff., 685, 686; same of Democrats, 686; of Repubs. 687; in Neb., in Kas., in Iowa, 697; in N. Y., 698; in Mass., 701; Natl. Wom. Suff. of 1891, 703; in Ohio, Conn., 705; Natl. Suff. of 1892, Mrs. Stanton's last appear., A. made pres., 717; in Mich., 720; A. urges Southern women to hold, 722; Natl. polit. for 1892, 723-727; Kas. St. Repub. adopts woman suff. plank, 726; Miss. Valley, 728; N. Y. State in 1892, pioneers and modern workers contrasted, 729; Natl. Wom. Suff. of 1893, 737; the conv. taken from Washtn., A.'s opposition, 738; in N. Y., Penn., 753; in Mich., 755; in O., 756; Natl. Wom. Suff. of 1894, 756; Constitl. of N. Y. in 1894, treatment of woman suff. amend., 767-771; N. Y. St. Repub., A. and others ask woman suff. plank, Miss Willard describes scene, 774; Democratic, asked for same, 775; Kas. Repub. refuses woman suff. plank, 785-787; Popu. adopts, 787-790; Prohib., 790; Dem. anti-plank, 796; Neb. St. Suff., 799; N. Y. same, 800; Natl. Woman. Suff. of 1895 in Atlanta, 810-812; in St. Louis, 821; in Utah, 825; in Calif., 835; in O., 845; Natl. Wom. Suff. in 1896, 851; at beginning of Calif. suff. campaign, 864; Repub. St. in Calif. adopts woman suff. plank, 871; Popu. and Prohib., same, 872; Dem. refuses, 872; efforts of women with delegates, 869-874; Idaho polit. convs. on woman suff., 879; W. C. T. U. withdrawn from Calif. in 1896, 881, 882; Calif. St. Suff. of 1896, 892; Natl. Wom. Suff. of 1897, 901; A. opposed to holding outside of Washtn., 903; A. begged to come to O., 927; N. Y.

St. Suff., A. speaks on "rings" and
women in politics, 928; round of
convs. in Middle West, contrast between past and present, 929; Natl.
Wom. Rights in 1866 sends memorial
to Congress, 968; Natl. Repub. of 1872
on equal rights, Natl. Liberal, same,
Calif. Repub., same, 991.

COOPER INSTITUTE, Beecher's sp. in
1860, 192; meet. of Wom. Loyal
League, 229; headqrs. of same, 230;
264, 274, 303; meeting in Hester
Vaughan case, 309; Anna Dickinson
speaks for woman suff., 327; polit.
meet. of women in 1872, 422.

DEATHS, of Deborah Moulson, 31; ma-
ternal grandparents and baby sister,
35; cousin Margaret, 52; of father,
222; niece, 241; nephew, 369; Greeley,
428; sister Guelma, 447; Sumner, 456;
Gerrit Smith, Mrs. Wright, 467;
Lydia Mott, 471; Mrs. Davis, Anson
Lapham, 481; sister Hannah, 488;
Garrison, A.'s tribute, 508; of mother,
512; Lucretia Mott, A.'s great loss,
525; memorial service, 526; Phoebe
Jones, 536; Garfield, A.'s comment,
536; Wendell Phillips, 587; Wm.
Henry Channing, Sarah Pugh,
Frances D. Gage, Mrs. Nichols, 595;
General Grant, 598; Mrs. Julia
Foster, 603; Dr. Lozier, E. M. Davis,
A. Bronson and Louisa M. Alcott,
645; niece Susie B., 648; Emerine J.
Hamilton, 654; Mrs. Riddle, Amy
Post, Mary L. Booth, Maria Mitchell,
Dinah Mendenhall, 660; Ellen Shel-
don, 700; Julia T. Foster, 701; A.
on Blaine's, 739; distinguished suf-
fragists in 1893, 737; same in 1894, 756;
Mrs. Bloomer, Mrs. Minor, 803;
Frederick Douglass, Adeline Thomp-
son, 814; Mrs. Dietrick, 849; Mr.
Sewall, 850; Maria Porter, 896; how
to remember the dead, 899; in 1896,
902; Mrs. Humphrey's, 908.

DEBATES, on Divorce in Wom. Rights
Conv. of 1860, 194; on Wom. Suff. in
Cong., 1866, 266; in U. S. Senate on
creating Wom. Suff. Com., 540; same
on 16th amend., 617-621; Sen. Ingalls
refuses to debate with woman, 626;
in Cong. on admission of Wy. with
woman suff., 698, 699; Rev. Miss
Shaw and Dr. Buckley at Chautauqua, 727; on woman suff. in N. Y.
Constitl. Conv., 770; in Kas. St. Popu.

Conv. on woman suff., 789; on Woman's Bible in Natl. Suff. Conv., 853.

DECISIONS, of Judge Hunt on A.'s voting, 438; U. S. Sup. Ct. on women's
voting under 14th amend., 453; 735;
Mich. Sup. Ct. on Munic. Suff. for
women, 740; Idaho Sup. Court only
majority of votes cast on amend.
necessary to carry, 918; U. S. Sup.
Ct. on women's entering public lands,
983; Dred Scott, 454, 984; others, 985.

DECLARATION OF INDEPENDENCE, 253,
475; women's in 1876, 476-479; Sen.
Morton on, 500; compared to Eman-
cip. Proc., 957; 960; should protect
rights of women, 977; gives women
right to vote, 977, 978.

DEMOCRATS, 59, 149, 211; would not
fear to act, 216; 263, 264; embarrass
Repubs. by approving woman suff.,
265, 266, 267; in Kas. campaign for
woman suff., 284, 287, 291; press comment, 293; A. and Mrs. Stanton attend Natl. Conv. of 1868, 305; insulted
by it, 306; 311; nothing expected
from, 365; Mrs. Hooker on, 381, 382;
in Wyoming, 407, 411; women attend
Natl. Conv. in 1872, 417, 418; 419, 420;
A.'s attitude toward, 422; on A.'s reg-
istering to vote, 426; Natl. Conv. of
1876 on wom. suff., 476; Natl. Conv.
of 1880, 519; A. criticises women for
helping, 523; opposed to Wom. Suff.
Com. in Congress, 585; Natl. Conv.
of 1888, 641; disgraceful treatment of
woman suff. in S. Dak., 686; Natl.
Conv. of 1892 grants hearing to
women, Miss Willard describes, 725;
on woman suff. in Col., 753; in N. Y.
refuse to make women delegates,
758, one exception, 759; N. Y. St.
Conv. refuses woman suff. plank,
775; action in Kas. toward woman
suff., 796; scene on night of conv. in
Calif., 874; Maguire stands by wom-
en, 874; invite A. to address ratif.
meeting, 878; in Idaho, 879; attitude
toward woman suff. speakers, 884;
abolish property qualif. for voting,
998; Greeley on, 999; in Kas. in 1867,
oppose woman suff., 1016, 1017; in
Col. in 1893, 1017; on Prohibition,
1017; op. woman suff. in Kas., 1018.

DISFRANCHISEMENT, degradation of,
318, 382, 584; A. points out disadvantages of to Pres. Garfield, 523; Mrs.
Stanton's speech, 703; A.'s view, 711,
712; 801; way for women to be free

certificate, 136; men speakers break down, 161; effect of hard work on A., 168, 169; powers of endurance, 408; prostrated in Ft. Wayne in 1873, 433; physical condition in 1877, 486; Mrs. Stanton's illness not due to work for suff., 537; effects of S. Dak. campaign, 696; A.'s illness in Boston, 701; illness in 1895, 840; secret of health, 843; after Calif. campaign, 895; of A. and Mrs. Stanton after 50 yrs.' work, 917; dependent on natural, not supernatural laws, 923; laws observed by A., 931; does not think of bodily ills or disagreeable things, 932; medicine and physicians, 933.

HEARINGS, first granted to women by Congressl. Com., 314; second, 338; Sumner on, 339; Mary Clemmer on, 340; of Mrs. Woodhull and others, 375; in 1872, on right of women to vote under 14th and 15th Amends., 410; in 1880, 511; in 1882, 541; in 1884, A.'s address, 588; A. has speeches printed, 591; in 1886, 607; in 1888, 640; in 1890, 674; in 1892, 718; at Natl. Repub. Conv. of 1892, 723; at Dem., 725; Congressl. in 1894, member asks why never held before, 758; in 1896, 851.

HISTORY OF WOMAN SUFFRAGE, first move towards writing, 475; beginning, 480; financial help recd., 524; A.'s restiveness, 525; Mrs. Nichols' assistance, A. orders names of opponents to be published, 529; 1st Vol. published, cost of pictures, favorable comment of press and prominent people, imperfections, services of the three authors, Mrs. Stanton replies to critics, rest of material stored, 530-532; Mrs. Stanton's fears, may not live to finish, 537; presented to Senators, 541; A.'s longing to be through, 542; 2d Vol. finished, 543; A. looks for in Rome, 553; 565; work on 3d Vol., A.'s restiveness, 592; 595; financial status, 599; serious and amusing difficulties, 601; A.'s dislike of it all, 602; 3d Vol. finished, 603; 608; immense outlay, 612; tribute to authors, synopsis of work, extensive donations, 613, 614; commendation, 614-616; sales, desire for 4th Vol., 616; A. begs Mrs. Stanton to write, 712; 754; Miss Willard's estimate, 951.

HOME LIFE, in Adams, 5-15; in Battenville, 17-35; in Center Falls (Hardscrabble), 35-46; near Rochester, 47 et seq.; in Rochester, beginning, 231;

706; in 1897, 913, 931-939; A. on beautifying country homes, 200; Abrahamic bosom, 218 (see Domestic Traits, Love of Family).

HOMES FOR SINGLE WOMEN, A.'s lecture, visit to Alice Cary, 359; A. writes it in Denver, 493.

HONORARY MEMBERSHIP, Chicago Woman's Club, 896; Rochester D. A. R., 919; other organizations, 925.

HOUSE OF COMMONS, A. visits, 553, 563, 567.

HUMANITIES, CHARITIES, etc., A.'s interest in, 60; women fail to lay ax at root of difficulty, 920; 1004 et seq.

IMMIGRATION AND IMMIGRANTS, 59; in S. Dak., 687, 690, 694, 695; efforts to secure votes of, 887 (see Citizenship, Naturalization).

IMMORTALITY, A.'s ideas of, 119, 242, 508, 516, 650, 859, 899.

INDIANS, in Repub. conv. in S. Dak., 687; preferred to white women, 762.

INDIFFERENCE OF WOMEN, 73, 98, 130, 251; should be shocked into action, 366; Mrs. Stanton on, 382; 456; A.'s strong statement, 641; in Calif. suff. campaign, 866.

INDIRECT INFLUENCE, dangers of, 590.

INDUSTRIES, PROFESSIONS, etc., demand for woman's admission to, 73; to law, 74; 79; Greeley on woman's right to enter, 147; A. urges agriculture for women, 160; on status of workingwomen, 333; women may practice bef. Sup. Ct., 502; dentistry in Berlin, 559; law in Gr. Brit., 564; medicine in, 570; indebtedness to woman suff. advocates, 80, 740, 822, 848, 949, 973, 976 (see Labor).

INDUSTRIAL SCHOOL, N. Y. St., A. appointed trustee, 730; her work, 733, 737, 816; recognizes girls, need of women on boards, resigns, 817.

INFIDELITY, woman suff. advocates charged with, 77-79, 91; Mrs. Rose's, 118, 121; 147, 311; woman suff. leads to, 401; suff. advocates and Dr. Patton, 596; A. stands for infidel's rights, 631; same, 655, 854.

INSURANCE, N. Y. Life, father connected with, 49, 55; A. insures in, 136.

INTEMPERANCE, in early days, 15, 18, 19; A.'s tilt with uncle, 40; on Martin Van Buren, 41; Whig festivals, 42; no disgrace, 61; Mrs. Stanton demands shall be cause for divorce, 67; wives and drunken husbands, 74, 84; in London, 564; in Ireland, 573; A. on woman's vote, 655; specimen of man's govt. in S. Dak., 693; women greatest sufferers from, statistics, root of the evil, 1004; effects of, 1005; in Chicago, women's petition spurned, 1012 (see Laws, Liquor Dealers).

INTERNATIONAL COUNCIL OF WOMEN, its conception, carrying forward, first great meeting in Washtn., newspaper comment, speeches, permanent organization, 633-639; during Columb. Expos., 745.

INTERVIEWS, A. on Beecher - Tilton case, 461; effect of woman suff. on saloons, 505; source of the opposition, 506; Mrs. Blake with Gen. Hancock on woman suffrage, 520; requested of A. by editor of Le Soir in Paris, 561; impressions of Gr. Brit., 581; change in public men, and on woman of the future, 582; contrast between pioneer and modern suffragists, 729; on N. Y. anti-suffragists, 766; on her alliance with Popu. party, 791; in Chicago in 1895, 821; in Denver, 823; on the Bible and the Woman's Bible, 856; of "Nelly Bly" in N. Y. World, 858; in San Fr. Examiner, 870; on Sister Mary's 70th birthday and early life, 915; on "rings" and "bosses," 928.

INVITATIONS, specimens of, 740, 753, 803, 924.

JOURNALS, MISS ANTHONY'S, used in writing Biog., vii; in boarding school, 24 et seq.; in 1838, 34; in girlhood days, 35, 36, 38, 39; woman's financ. independ., 104; first St. canvass for Wom. Rights, 125 et seq.; in 1856, 138; almost discouraged, 151; daily doings in 1859, 172, 173; life at home and abroad in 1860, 197, 198; in 1862, 216; public work in 1865, 252; on Chas. Sumner, 269; on 50th birthday, 344; in 1870, 346; 362; work for woman suff. conv. in New York, 368; on treatment in San Francisco, 392; stage driver, 394; the "reform world," 395; trip by boat in 1871, 395; Calif. experiences, 404; snowed in in the Rocky Mts., 406-408; our ship nearly lost, 415; joy over Repub. action in 1872, 419; on death of Greeley, 428; on outrage of her trial, 441; on death of Sumner, 456; on degraded labor of women and "coaxing" women, 457; on Beecher-Tilton case, 463; on death of Martha C. Wright, 467; of Lydia Mott, 471; on

Frances Willard, 472; on writing the History, 480, 525, 542; on Anson Lapham, 481; 532, 535; on W. C. T. U., 537; 541; while in Europe, 560; in Scotland, 569; in Ireland, 575; in England, 577; shrinks from pleading with politicians, 583; on inefficient women, 586; no blame for any one, 587; on Miss Eddy, 601; on literary "style," 601; racy comments on writing the History, 602; work in Congress, 607, 608; on Phoebe Couzins, 608; in Chicago, St. Louis, Leavenworth, 609; 623; on Mrs. Stanton's refusal to come to Intl. Council, 636; tricks of saloon element, 649; Grant mementoes at Mt. McGregor, 653; unmarried mothers, 656; on Chief Just. Fuller, 660; on Harriot Stanton Blatch, 675; first housekeeping experiences, 711; amusing bits in 1891, 714; on Popu. party, 727; on divinely-appointed male head of family, 730; overwhelmed with work, 737, 739; on death of Blaine, 739; 785; "alliance" with Populists, 791; on Robt. Collyer, 802; 843; the $6,000 bed, 902; on thinking of past, 914.

JURIES, men judge women, 74; A. demands women have one of their peers, 309; Gov. Geary declares need of women on, 310; right to trial by under Constitu., 429; Judge refuses to have polled in A.'s trial, 439; A. pleads for jury of her peers, 440; opinions of press, 441-443; of John Van Voorhis, 444; same, 449; of Judge Selden, 449; A.'s appeal to Congress, 449; majority and minority reports, 450-453; mothers with infants, 618, 619; A. accused of trying to influence by speeches before her trial, 993-995.

LABOR, the wife's wages, 74, 108, 110; proceeds of wife's work, 139; A. demands vote for workingwomen, 263; rebuke to married ex-teacher, 272; workingmen's influence compared to women's, 306; The Revolution's efforts for wage-earning women, assn. formed, 307; Labor Congress for women's rights, but not for suff., 307; A. teaches workingwomen to organize, 307; A. to women typesetters, 308; on women wage-earners, 333; rejected as delegate to Labor Cong. in Phila., 366; gratitude of workingwomen, 405; women a millstone, 457; Greenback-Labor party on

like of "red tape," immense correspondence, 643; death and immortality, 650; best campaign methods, 657, 658, 659; Prohibition and woman suff., 657; "Andrew Jackson-like methods," 659; immense circulation of literature, 659; on selling tickets for her birthday banquet, 663, 664; union of two assns., 674; value of social functions, 677; disregard of orthodox Christians for feelings of liberals, 678; pre-natal influence, 678; love for Washtn. City, 679; on financial management of S. Dak. campaign, 681, 682; W. C. T. U. and suff. campaign in S. Dak., 683; hardships of, 688; criticises commission to S. Dak., 690; visits to Holyoke and Cheshire, 705; to John Brown's grave, 708; meeting at Lily Dale, Miss Shaw answers Dr. Buckley, 710; 711; begging Mrs. Stanton to end her days in Rochester, 712; agrees to help in Kas., 715; objects to male sculptor for her bust, 721; urges Southern women to organize, 722; first trip to Europe, 739; never dreamed of stenographer, 741; joy of having worked for liberty, 741; on situation in Kas., 741; women make burden heavy for others, 742; 745; Kas. campaign, 754; lack of organization, votes of drunkards, 763; corrects report of sp. on orthodoxy, 774; scores Repub. party in Kas., 779; to Kas. Woman's Campaign Com. on plank, 781; to Repub. leader, same, 783; to Mrs. Johns, 784; joy over Populist plank, 792; repudiates Kas. Repubs., 793, 794; on speaking in Kas., 794; Y. M. C. A. and wom. suff., 804; majority rule, financial mistake, 806; to contribs. to annuity, 814; first serv. of stenographer, 843; virtue and financial independence, 844; "trusts" and woman suff., dress, 844; all organizns. should celebrate Stanton birthday, 846; suff. elephant and horned head must stand back, 847; objects to Mrs. Stanton's attack on church, 847; desire to give all an opportunity, 849; tribute to Mrs. Dietrick, 849; to Mr. Sewall, 850; grief at action of Natl. Suff. Assn. on Woman's Bible, 855; Spanish inquisition methods, 855; Mrs. Stanton writes down instead of up in Woman's Bible, 856; religious superstition, refuses to mix relig. or temp. discuss. in Calif. suff. campaign, 857; begging W. R. Hearst to favor woman suff. in

Examiner, 867; longing for home, 878; to Idaho women, 878; to Mrs. Stanton, 879; woman plank of Natl. Repub. Conv. of 1896, 880; urging Miss Willard to withdraw Natl. W. C. T. U. Conv. from Calif. in 1896, 881; to Mrs. Sturtevant Peet on same, 882; opposed to public denial of charges, 897; urging women not to scramble for office, 897; prefers her own wisdom to Solomon's, 897; secret of her success, 897; declines alliance with political parties, 898; objects to making God author of Govt., 898; need of money for her work, 898; on educated and property suffrage, 899; same, 922; think of dead as in vigor of life, 899; holding Natl. Convs. in Washtn., 903; the writing of her Biog., 909; dislike of groping in past, 914; greatest compliment, 917; impossibility of "insurrection" of women, 918; Theosophy, Christian Science, etc., 918; to Sup. Court of Idaho thanking for broad decision, 919; to D. A. R. on Revolutionary mothers, 919; every dollar given helps woman suff., 920; suffrage great need of women working in charities and reforms, 920; objects to asking for partial suff., 920; on poetry, 921; God's special interference, 921; Sunday no more sacred than other days, 922; personal God, 922; miraculous intervention, 923; compared to St. Paul's, 924; foolishness of women's attacking public evils until they get suff., 924; number of cities visited, 925; giving her services, 925; to man asking how many times she had lectured, 925; toil of correspondence, 935; endless requests, 936; amusing instances, 937; loving messages, 938.

LETTERS OF OTHERS, number used in writing Biog., vii; Anthony family life in 1836, 22; father on daughter's teaching, 24; to A. in boarding school, 27; panic of 1838, 33, 34; Washtn. City, 33; Aaron McLean on negroes, 39; Uncle Albert scores A., 40; Van Buren, drinking and dancing, 42; to woman's temp. meet. in 1852, 65; Greeley on Wom. Temp. Conv., 66; Mrs. Stanton, Mrs. Nichols encourage A.'s temp. work, 66; Mayo and Geo. W. Johnson on woman's rights, 73; Gerrit Smith, same, 75; Lucy Stone on Maine Law, 81;

A.'s lectures in Ore., 399; indignant husbands and wives in Victoria, B. C., 402; Blackwell urges women to support Repub. party, 416; Cochran to Mrs. Stanton, 418; Henry Wilson to A., 420; Mrs. Stanton's bitterness against polit. parties, 420; B. F. Butler on woman's right to vote under U. S. Constn., 429; same, favoring woman suff., Senator Lapham, same, 455; A. G. Riddle on great strength and little working power of woman suff. cause, 455; lets. of faith in A., 458; Lucretia Mott, 480; Garrison opposed to 16th amend., Phillips in favor, 484; Mary Clemmer on treatment of woman suff. petits. by U. S. Senate, 485; Mrs. Stanton on friendship for A., 488; Annie McDowell tribute to A. in Phila. *Press*, 489; Mrs. Stanton, Mrs. Sargent, Mrs. Minor and Miss Couzins on prayer meet. in Capitol, need of A.'s management of natl. convs., 494; to 30th annivers. in Rochester, 495; Mary Clemmer on woman suffrage, 501; lady asking forgiveness, 505; Sens. and Reps. ask seats for women, 518; Garfield to A. on woman suffrage, 521; Mrs. Stanton on A.'s "dragooning," 526; on Hist. of Wom. Suff., 532; Mrs. Pillsbury to A., 535; Mrs. Harbert on her love and Zerelda G. Wallace's, 535; Phillips' cordial letter, 538; Mrs. Eddy's legacy, 539; lawsuit, 540; Mrs. Blatch on writing Biog., 544; Sen. Ingalls, 547; Rochester people to A. when starting abroad, 548; Mrs. Stanton and Mrs. Sargent welcome her, 553; editors of *Italian Times* ask A. to write, 557; to A. from editor of *Le Soir*, 561; Mrs. McLaren on A.'s visit, 569; Mrs. Bright on A.'s impression on son, 577; Bishop Simpson on woman suff., 588; eminent foreigners, 588; Sen. Palmer urges agitation for woman suff., 593; J. Ellen Foster, 598; Mrs. Sewall on A.'s energy, 600; Mrs. Blatch on friendship of mother and A., 602; Mrs. Stanton on esthetic convs., 605; Sen. Blair on A.'s persistence, 606; G. W. Childs, 607; Mrs. Merrick, 608; Olympia Brown, 608; Sen. Anthony, Mary L. Booth, D. W. Wilder, Sarah B. Cooper on Hist. of Wom. Suff., 614-616; Miss Booth on woman suff., 615; Mary Rogers Kimball, 616; Sen. Ingalls, 622; Mrs.

Stanton advises A. to destroy letters, 625; Lucy Stone on union of two suff. assns., 628; Alice Stone Blackwell on same, 628; Zerelda G. Wallace and others on A. or Mrs. Stanton for pres., 630, 631; Fred. Douglass on first Woman's Rights Conv., 634; Maria Mitchell on work, 635; Mrs. Stanton's friendship for A. but she won't come to Intl. Council, 635; Miss Willard on A. at Council, 638; tribute from Mrs. S. E. Sewall, 640; Miss Shaw's first let. to A., 645; Adeline Thompson's love for A., 651; Marie Deraismes, 652; Laura C. Holloway, 653; Harriet Hosmer, 655; from S. Dak., 656; nephew D. R. on his aunt Susan, 658; Mrs. Sewall, Mrs. Avery on A.'s 70th birthday banquet, 664; on 70th birthday from Lucy Stone, Whittier, Miss Willard, Curtis, Garrison, Hoar, Reed, Olympia Brown, Mrs. Logan, Mr. and Mrs. Gannet, T. W. Palmer, Nordhoff, F. G. Carpenter, Mrs. Johns, etc., 668-671; Lillian Whiting on A.'s contemporaries, 672; Mrs. Livermore, Mary Grew, Lucy Stone, 676; Mrs. Avery on woman's gratitude to A., 678; to A. regarding S. Dak. campaign in 1890, 679, 680; Miss Shaw on financial management of, 683; Mrs. Wallace on A.'s leadership, 683, 685; Miss Shaw's account of treatment by S. Dak. Repub. Conv., 687; John Hooker, Clara Barton, Anna Shaw on campaign, 689; Mrs. Howell's account of A.'s and her experiences, 690, 691; same by Miss Shaw, 692, 693; Mrs. Catt's summing up, 693; her tribute to A., 695; N. M. Mann, 697; E. B. Taylor, 700; Lucy Stone inviting A. to Mass. Conv., on A.'s illness, 701; from the Pillsburys, 702; Mrs. Bottome, on A.'s "Christ-like spirit," 703; Sen. Blair's "pious fraud," 704; Secy. McCulloch, Miss Balgarnie, 704; Charles Dickinson, 707; Mrs. Stanton on home of one's own, 707; Miss Willard on Chautauqua, 709; Mrs. Johns begs A.'s help for Kas., 715, 719; members of Cong. on woman suff., 716; Mrs. Stanton, 717; Mrs. Susan Look Avery on A.'s popularity, 720; A. objects to male sculptor for her bust, Miss Willard protests, Mr. Taft's apology, Lady Somerset's approval, 721, 722; Miss Willard on loneliness of great spirits, 725; Bish-

pared to man's, 169; wife's loss of name, 170, 183; A. protests against wife's loss of individuality and self-annihilation, 170; true woman not dwarfed by, 170, 171; Lydia Mott disagrees, 171; good effect on suff., 176; moments of solitude, 180; wife's name on tombstone, 183; why women marry, 186; wife should be supreme, 193; Mrs. Stanton on, 193; one-sided contract, 194; A.'s tilt with Mayo, 196; A. the picket, married women the army, 197; rights of husbands, 204; in Adam Bede, 216; married life of A.'s parents, 223; A. scores wife for advocating low wages for women, 272; how husbands represent wives, 279, 491, 771; A. on women's proposing, 316; wives object to A.'s statements, 331; Catharine Beecher and Mrs. Woodhull on, 378; A. on love in, 388; in Victoria, B. C., 402; incidents in Washtn. Ty., 403; A. on mistake of outside confidences, 459; opposed to second, wives should not live with unfaithful husbands, 463, 1009; should be only for love, 469; women should travel first, 559; Platonic friendship, 568; of Frederick Douglass, A.'s view, 586; objects to crucifying wives according to St. Paul, 595; U. S. Sens. on effect of woman suff., 618-620; Rachel Foster's, A.'s feelings, 644, 645; of "Robert Elsmere," 648; of niece Helen Louise Mosher, 652; A. on mutual love, 654; of nephew Wendell Mosher, 679; Hooker golden wedding, "no speeches," 709; anti-suffragists put forward by husbands, 766; A. on Mrs. Sewall's, 850; idea of true marriage, 859; woman a doll or a drudge, 860; golden wedding of Sargents, 916; sentiment for nephew's, 923; golden wedding of Dr. and Mrs. E. M. Moore, 929; woes confided to A., 936; wedded to a principle holiest of marriages, 951; A.'s golden wedding, 975; legal slavery in, 987; must be luxury not necessity for women, 1007; statistics, 1008; parents rather daughters marry than work, 1008; laws must be same for husbands and wives, 1009; God will curse mothers for endowing children with father's sins, 1010; God thy law, thou mine, 1011.

MEDALLION, A.'s made in 1897, 917.

MEDICAL PRACTICE in early times, 30,

39, 40, 49; "water cure," 91, 112, 126; 129; at Worcester Institute, 131; its methods, 134.

MINISTERS, Murray (Univ.), 5; Quaker preachers, 6, 15, 19; A. on women in 1838, 40; first ordained, 74; women educate, 68, 76; S. J. May, 65, 69, 151, 270, 927; Luther Lee, 70; Channing, 73, 102, 104, 110, 112; Higginson, 88; treatment of women speakers in early days, 69-80, 87-92, 101, 102, 119, 121, 125;* 133; 165; Quaker preacher at Easton, 177; 181; Beecher's power, 464; Stopford Brooke, 564; Dr. Patton in Washtn., 596; Baptist in Kas., 610; sign anti-suff. petition, 620; A. on ordained and non-ordained women, 634; conduct Intl. Council services, 636; in S. Dak. on "original packages," 657; N. M. Mann, 697; women at Natl. Council, 702; A. asks one if willing to be disfranchised, 709; Miss Shaw answers Dr. Buckley, 710; W. C. Gannett, 712, 714, 719, 916; Dr. J. M. Buckley deb. woman suff., 727; A. comments on Thanksgiving sermons, 729; Robert Collyer, 802; Jenkyn Lloyd Jones, 804, 805; H. W. Thomas, 805, 900; J. B. Hawthorne attacks woman suff., 810; in Salt Lake City on Rev. Anna Shaw's address, 824; A. addresses in San Francisco, 830, 834; why they have no polit. influence, 834; coming to aid of woman suff., 856; Louis Zahner (Adams), 942 (see Church).

MISSOURI COMPROMISE, 121, 149.

MOBS, in New York in 1853, 101-103, 163; against Bloomer costume, 113; in Rochester, 165; Phillips' power over, 174; throughout N. Y., 208, et seq.; A.'s account, 210; 217; N. Y. draft riots, 230.

MT. HOPE CEMETERY, Anthony burial place, 218, 241, 445, 719.

MUSIC, mother's voice, 10; Quaker ideas, 11; in Anthony family, 23; the Hutchinson's in 1867, 286, 291; Ristori's, 558; A.'s feeling towards, 859.

NATIONAL COUNCIL OF WOMEN, organized in 1888, 639; first triennial, 702; work for Columb. Expos., 745; second triennial, 812-814; manage celebr. of Mrs. Stanton's 80th birthday, 845-848; in Boston, 895; 901; at Nashville

---

*In later years this attitude changed, and it would be impossible to list the instances of their helpfulness.

include women in platform adopted by Natl. Conv. of 1888, 1013; approve of negro but not of woman suff., 1015; action on 14th Amend., 1016; Mrs. Stanton tells cannot protect black men, 1016; opp. woman suff. in Kas. in 1867, 1016, 1017; approve in Col. in 1893, 1017; give prohib. in Kas., 1017; also munic. suff. for women, 1017; for full suff., 1018; in Congress, 1018; Kas. League of Rep. Clubs refuses to endorse, 1018; must .choose between women and low constituents, 1019; would drive women to Populists, 1020; adopt res. for woman suff., 1021.

RESOLUTIONS, on Bible, 76; equal pay for women teachers in 1853, 100; color question in schools, 155; coeducation in 1857, 155; Mrs. Stanton on Divorce, 193; National Loyal League in 1863, 227; women's as well as negroes' rights, 229; for an Equal Rights Assn., 259, 260; A. on proposed 14th Amend. in 1867, 276; Kas. Repubs. to defeat woman suff. amend. in 1867, 283; Equal Rights Assn. censuring A. and Mrs. Stanton, 300; same advising them to go to Democrats, 305; of Labor Congress in 1868, 307; in Hester Vaughan's case, for jury of women, 309; in Cong. in 1868 for woman suff., 310, 311; 15th Amend. dispute in Equal Rights Assn., 323, 324; Mrs. Livermore on "free love," 324; on woman's right to vote under 14th Amend., 331; Ingersoll on equal laws for women, 345; in 1871 on right of women to vote under 14th Amend., 377; indirectly on "free love," 384; declaring 14th and 15th Amends. enfranchise women, 410; attempt to secure res. from Natl. Liberal Conv. of 1872, 415; personal rights and criminal prosecution of A. for voting, 431; trial of A., 434; exclusion of women from Centennial, 474; treatment of woman's petitions by Cong., ignoring of women in Pres. Hayes' message, tyranny of Fed. Govt. over women, etc., 499; res. for woman suff. by Greenback party, 519; A.'s departure for Europe, 548; disfranch. of Utah women, 607; Blair's on 16th Amend., 617; Am. Wom. Suff. Assn. on union with Natl., 627; Farmers' Alliance and Knights of Labor in S. Dak. on woman suff., 686; Natl. Popu. Conv. adopts woman suff., 727; of N. Y.

Anti-Suff. Society in 1894, 765; on woman suff. proposed by Kas. politician, 778; wom. suff. endorsed by Repub. and Popu. parties in Kas., 784; of Kas. Wom. Repub. Assn., 785; woman suff. res. refused by Kas. Repub. St. Conv., 786; res. against in Dem. St. Conv., 796; A. on women's refusing to help men while "male" is in Constitu., 839; on Woman's Bible by Natl. Suff. Assn., 853; on woman suff. at Dem. St. Conv. in Calif. in 1896, 874; Repubs. and Populists in Kas. adopt res. for woman suff., 1021.

REUNION OF ANTHONY FAMILY in Adams, Mass., in 1897, 939-947.

REVOLUTION, woman suff. will cause, 620; impossible for women, 918; excusable only in enslaved, 1002; women driven to it in temp. work, 1003.

REVOLUTION, THE, first notice of, 290; A.'s delight, 294; paper started, editors and editorials, financial struggle, etc., 295-311; petitions for woman suff., 313; Train withdraws from, 319; offices moved, 320; end of paper, 354-364; prospectus, Alice Cary's story, its contributors, 359; A. will pay immense debt, 362; efforts to do so, 441, 459, 460, 468; last dollar paid, 472; comments of press, 473; 509, 655, 951.

RIGGS HOUSE, home of A. for 12 winters, 512; loses home there, 705.

SCHOOL LIFE, of father at "Nine Partners'," 8; of mother, 9; in Anthony home, 9, 19, 22, 23, 35; A. in boarding school, 24-34.

SCRAP BOOKS, used in writing Biog., vii, 910; begun in 1855, 125; of N. Y. campaign, 762; visit to Calif., 837.

SCULPTURE, A. will have statue in Washtn., 669; bust of A. by Adelaide Johnson, 677; Mrs. Stanton by same, 713; of A. by Lorado Taft, amusing corres., 721, 722; A.'s face carved on theater, 738; proposed statue of Mrs. Schuyler, 734; Harriet Hosmer's Lincoln, 821; A.'s statuette by Bessie Potter, 862; in N. Y. Capitol, 949; would have bronze if not a woman, 973.

SEASICKNESS, 395, 552, 555.

SEX DISTINCTIONS, 69, 74, 76; woman inferior by nature, 78; 79, 84, 89, 90, 93, 109; let man compare woman's position with his, 169; 306, 324; Kentucky editor's view, 504; God intended none, 945.

---

*Only a reference to principal points is possible. Its various phases are listed under their respective heads.

228, 230; **woman's services,** 239; lesson **for women,** 239; woman's position after, 256, 280; ravages in Europe, 562; A.'s effort to secure results of Revolution for women, 919; Civil, a step toward progress, 958; work of women in, 1015.

WEDDINGS (see Marriage).

WIVES (see Divorce, Guardianship, Laws, Marriage, Property Rights).

WOMAN'S BUREAU, estab. in N. Y., 320; Natl. Wom. Suff. Assn. formed there, 326; weekly meetings, 330; celebr. of A.'s 50th birthday, 341; clubs object to *The Revolution* office, Anna Dickinson's gift, 360.

WOMAN'S CHRISTIAN TEMPERANCE UNION, 96; A. addresses in Rochester, 457; needs votes, 505; A. attends conv. in Washtn., Miss Willard introduces, delegates disapprove, society adopts woman suff., 537; delegates repudiate A.'s influence, 538; A. addresses in Kas., in Ills., 609; petitions for woman suff. in 1887, 620; A.'s addresses too practical for, 643; 674; in S. Dak., 681, 683; to A. on religious matters, 677; A. addresses in Rochester against third party, 709; petitions in N. Y. for woman suff., 766; speeches in constitl. conv., 769; Miss Willard introd. A. in Cleveland, might as well be dogs as without a vote, 800, 801; Cong. in St. Louis, 821; recep. to A. in Utah, 825; A. asks Miss Willard to withdraw conv. from Calif., 857; request granted, its women work for suff., 882; attitude toward A., 882, 901; A. declines to join protest against "yellow" journalism and prize-fighting, 923, 924.

WOMAN OF FUTURE, A. urges outdoor life, 160; the true woman, 170; physical culture, 198; her ideal of, 582; same, 860.

WOMEN'S NATIONAL LOYAL LEAGUE, great work in 1863, 225-240; address to Pres. Lincoln, 957.

WOMAN'S RIGHTS, first conv., 59; N. Y. *Tribune,* 61; in Worcester, 61, 75; A. demands, 71; her first conv., 72; Mayo, Geo. W. Johnson, Lucy Stone on, 73; Antoinette Brown, Mrs. Nichols, 74; Gerrit Smith, Mrs. Rose, 75; opposition of young minister and teacher, 76; abuse of advocates, 76-80; gains made, 80; 84, 90, 91, 92; Mrs. Stanton on right to speak, 92; Gerrit Smith on, 93; N. Y. conv. of 1853, A.'s vow, 102; mob rules, 103; conv. in Rochester, 105; courage required for early meetings, 119; Greeley on, 126; conv. of 1856, in New York, 147; conv. of 1858 under mob rule, 162; Geo. Wm. Curtis on, 167; A.'s tilt with, 172; conv. in New York in 1859, the mob rules, 174; from Southern standpoint, 183, 184; gradual merging into Suffrage, 185; in Albany in 1860, 186; Henry Ward Beecher on, 192; conv. of 1860 in New York and Divorce question, 193, 194; retarded by War, 225; foundation of democracy, 229; first conv. after War, 256 et seq.; Anna Dickinson's first speech for, 262; sacrificed to negro, woman avenges herself, 301; 304; divisions among workers for not recorded, 336; earliest advocates, 369; 25th annivers. first conv., 434; 30th anniv., 495; Fred. Douglass recalls first conv., 634; annivers. of first conv. in Salem, O., 722; conv. of 1866 sends address to Congress, 968 (see Suffrage, Woman).

YOUNG MEN'S CHRISTIAN ASSOCIATION, 754; A. tells should work for woman suff., 804.

INDEX TO PLACES.

ALABAMA, Birmingham, 809; New Decatur, 809; Tuscaloosa, 183.

ARKANSAS, Ft. Smith, 649; Helena, 649; Little Rock, 649.

CALIFORNIA, 52, 59, 341; A.'s first visit, 1871, 390; help in S. D. campaign, 685; 738; Woman's Cong., A. visits, 819, 826; urged to help woman suff. campaign, 861; the campaign, 863; results, 890; 922; Alameda, 865; Berkeley, 865; Chico, 404; Geysers, 394; Los Angeles, first visit, 832; second, 862; Marysville, 404; Mayfield, 405; Mt. Shasta, 404; Oakland, A.'s first visit, 394; second, 826; 831, 834; fails to find hall, 837; 865, 876, 885; Palo Alto, 830; Pasadena, 832; Pomona, 832; Red Bluff, 404; Sacramento, 869-872; San Diego, A.'s first visit, 832; second, 862; San Francisco, A.'s first visit, 390; 396; 405; 493; Woman's Congress, 819, 827; a suff. meet., 829; 834; St. Conv., 835; 4th of July, 835; 862; woman suff. headqrs., 864; same, 875; liquor dealers, 886; St. Suff. Conv., 892; San Jose, 394, 405, 831; San Luis Obispo, 881; Santa Barbara, 881; Santa Cruz, 831; Santa Monica, 833; Truckee, 826; Whittier, 832; Yosemite Valley, A. visits, 392; trees named, 831; Yreka, 403.

COLORADO, A. canvasses for woman suff., 489; granted, 752; 757; invites A. to celebr., 775; 780; party records, 1017; Boulder, 493; Del Norte, 490; Denver, A.'s first visit, 387; 492; writes lecture, 493; visit in 1895, 821; Lake City, 490; Leadville, "free love" placards, 491; Oro City, 491; Ouray, 491; Wagon Wheel Gap, 490.

CONNECTICUT, canvass for woman suff., 456; 622; Bridgeport, 89; Glastonbury, 511; Hartford, 293; first Wom. Suff. Conv., 332; 387, 535; Hooker golden wed., 709; Meriden, 705; New Haven, 535.

DAKOTA, 541, 666.

SOUTH DAKOTA, canvass for woman suff., 656; A.'s great work, 659; help of Natl. Assn., 675, 684; campaign of 1890, 679; action of polit. convs., 686, 687; results, 694, 696; 780; Aberdeen, 657, 686; Brookings, 657; De Smet, 657; Huron, Farmers' Alliance, 657, 685; 695; Madison, 657; A.'s sp., 691; Mitchell, 657, 687; Parker, 657; Pierre, 657, 695; Redfield, 657; Sioux Falls, 657; St. Lawrence, 657; Watertown, 657; Yankton, 657.

DISTRICT OF COLUMBIA, bill for woman suff., 266, 311; A. argues for, 338; Anacostia, 814; Washington, father visits in 1838, 33; A.'s first visit in 1854, 117; goes for *The Revolution*, 297; first woman suff. conv. held, 313; in 1870, 337; 370; conv. of 1871, 371; suff. headqrs. in Capitol, 381; A. comes from Calif., 408; conv. of 1872, 410; A. meets Natl. Rep. Com., 421; conv. of 1873, 431; A. takes her case for voting, 450; conv. 1874, 453; of 1875, 467; of 1876, 472; of 1877, 484; of 1878, prayer meet. conv., 494; of 1879, 499; of 1880, 511; of 1881, 526; W. C. T. U. Conv., 537; Natl. Suff. of 1882, 540; of 1883, 546; 549; of 1884, 588; of 1885, 595; A.'s Congressl. work, 605, 607; conv. of 1886, 607; A.'s amusing start for, 612; conv. of 1887, 617; union of suff. assns., 630; first Intl. Council of Wom., 636; Natl. Suff. Conv. of 1888, 639; of 1889, 647; 660; 70th birthday, 664; conv. of 1890, 674; A.'s social life, 677; love for, 679; Wimodaughsis, 700; Natl. Council, 702; Natl. Suff. Conv. of 1891, 702; A. leaves Riggs House, 705; Mrs. Stanton's last appearance, 1892, 717; conv. of 1893, 737; of 1894, 756; 778; Natl. Council, 812; 75th birthday, 813; conv. of 1896, 851; A. longs for, 901; 903, 1005.